Sex Offenders

Sex Offenders

A Criminal Career Approach

Edited by

Arjan Blokland and Patrick Lussier

WILEY Blackwell

This edition first published 2015

Registered Office
John Wiley & Sons, Ltd, The Atrium, Southern Gate, Chichester, West Sussex, PO19 8SQ, UK

Editorial Offices
350 Main Street, Malden, MA 02148-5020, USA
9600 Garsington Road, Oxford, OX4 2DQ, UK
The Atrium, Southern Gate, Chichester, West Sussex, PO19 8SQ, UK

For details of our global editorial offices, for customer services, and for information about how to apply for permission to reuse the copyright material in this book please see our website at www.wiley.com/wiley-blackwell.

Library of Congress Cataloging-in-Publication Data

Sex offenders (John Wiley & Sons)
Sex offenders : a criminal career approach / edited by Arjan Blokland and Patrick Lussier.
pages cm
Includes bibliographical references and index.
ISBN 978-0-470-97545-9 (cloth) – ISBN 978-0-470-97546-6 (pbk.) 1. Sex offenders.
2. Sex offenders–Rehabilitation. 3. Sex crimes. I. Blokland, Arie Aart Jan, 1973–
II. Lussier, Patrick. III. Title.
HV6556.S4257 2015
364.15′3–dc23

2015008528

A catalogue record for this book is available from the British Library.

Cover image: Brushstrokes © Stella Levi/iStockphoto

Set in 10.5/13pt Minion by SPi Global, Pondicherry, India
Printed and bound in Malaysia by Vivar Printing Sdn Bhd

1 2015

For my loving wife and daughters, Lucile, Dagmar, and Jytte.
Arjan Blokland

To my three loves, Nadine, Émile, and Lily Madeleine.
Patrick Lussier

Contents

Notes on Contributors

Sytske Besemer, University of California, Berkeley, USA Sytske Besemer works at the Institute of Human Development and School of Social Welfare at UC Berkeley. She has a background in developmental psychology as well as criminology and was educated at Leiden University, VU University Amsterdam and the University of Cambridge, where she was a Gates Scholar. She is interested in intergenerational transmission of behavior, life-course and developmental criminology, mental health and crime, the impact of criminal policies, and prevention of criminal behavior.

Catrien Bijleveld, NSCR and VU University, Amsterdam, the Netherlands Catrien Bijleveld was trained as a psychologist and criminal lawyer. She is Professor of Research Methods in Criminology as well as Director of the Netherlands Institute for the Study of Crime and Law Enforcement (NSCR). Her research interests are (sexual) violence, the intergenerational transmission of delinquency, and international crimes.

Arjan Blokland, NSCR and Leiden University, Amsterdam/Leiden, the Netherlands Arjan Blokland is Professor of Criminology and Criminal Justice at Leiden University and Senior Researcher at the Netherlands Institute for the Study of Crime and Law Enforcement (NSCR). His research interests include developmental and life-course criminology, interpersonal violence, and the effects of formal interventions on criminal career development.

Alfred Blumstein, Carnegie Mellon University, Pittsburgh, USA Alfred Blumstein is J. Erik Jonsson University Professor of Urban Systems and Operations Research and former Dean of the Heinz School at Carnegie Mellon University. He was also director of the National Consortium on Violence Research (NCOVR), a multi-university initiative funded by the National Science Foundation. His research over the past 20 years has covered many aspects of criminal justice phenomena and policy, including crime measurement, criminal careers, sentencing, deterrence and incapacitation, prison populations, flow through the system, demographic trends, juvenile violence, and drug-enforcement policy.

Martin Bouchard, Simon Fraser University, Burnaby, Canada Martin Bouchard is an Associate Professor at the School of Criminology, Simon Fraser University. Prior to this appointment, he received his PhD in Criminology from University of Montreal, and completed postdoctoral work at the University of Maryland. Dr Bouchard's work specializes in the organization of illegal drug markets, and in research on criminal careers.

Jesse Cale, University of New South Wales, Sydney, Australia Jesse Cale is currently a lecturer at the School of Social Sciences at the University of New South Wales. He completed his PhD in Criminology at Simon Fraser University in 2010. He has authored and co-authored numerous research studies for the Canadian government, journal articles, and book chapters in the field of criminology on topics including sexual offenders and offenses, homicide, serious and violent youth, Aboriginal victimization in Canada, and public safety issues.

Garth Davies, Simon Fraser University, Burnaby, Canada Garth Davies is an Associate Professor at Simon Fraser University. His research interests include terrorism, communities and crime, housing and crime, policing, criminological theory, statistical analyses, and research methods.

Matt DeLisi, Iowa State University, Ames, USA Matt DeLisi is Coordinator of Criminal Justice Studies, Professor in the Department of Sociology, and Faculty Affiliate of the Center for the Study of Violence at Iowa State University. His primary research interests include criminal careers/career criminals, self-control theory, corrections, psychopathy, and the molecular/behavioral genetics of antisocial behavior.

Nadine Deslauriers-Varin, Laval University, Quebec, Canada Nadine Deslauriers-Varin is an Assistant Professor of Criminology at the Faculty of Social Sciences at Laval University. She completed her PhD at the School of Criminology at Simon Fraser University. She has published numerous scientific articles on police investigation and interrogation, criminal profiling and crime linkage, and environmental criminology, as well as on sex offending.

Brian Francis, Lancaster University, UK Brian Francis is a Professor of Social Statistics at the Centre for Applied Statistics, Department of Maths and Statistics, Fylde College, Lancaster University. He has over 30 years of experience of statistical consultancy and applied statistical research with over 200 research papers and seven co-authored books. His statistical interests are in statistical modeling, the analysis of ranked data, data visualization, case-control studies, and statistical computing, with applications in the social sciences, medicine, and local government finance. He has worked extensively in criminology, developing analytic approaches for research problems, particularly in the areas of criminal careers and crime seriousness and escalation.

Claire Hargreaves, Lancaster University, UK Claire Hargreaves is a Research Associate at the University of Manchester and a PhD student at the Centre for Applied Statistics, Department of Maths and Statistics, Fylde College, Lancaster University. Her principal research interests lie in the field of crime policy, with focus on offenders' criminal careers. Her doctoral research quantitatively investigates the risk of sexual offenders' recidivism over time, when a sexual offender can be considered low risk, and whether criminal history and demographic factors affect sexual offenders' risk of recidivism.

Jan Hendriks, VU University, Amsterdam, the Netherlands Jan Hendriks is a forensic and clinical psychologist. He is Professor of Forensic Psychiatry and Psychology at the VU University, Amsterdam, and professor of Forensic Orthopedagogics at the University of Amsterdam. His research interests are juvenile and adult sex offenders, female offenders, and interventions for delinquent youth.

Wesley G. Jennings, University of South Florida, Tampa, USA Wesley G. Jennings, PhD, is Associate Professor, Associate Chair, and Undergraduate Director in the Department of Criminology, has a Courtesy Appointment in the Department of Mental Health Law and Policy, and is a Faculty Affiliate of the Florida Mental Health Institute in the College of Behavioral and Community Sciences at the University of South Florida. In addition, he also has a Courtesy Appointment in the Department of Health Outcomes & Policy and is a Faculty Affiliate of the Institute for Child Health Policy in the College of Medicine at the University of Florida. He received his doctorate degree in criminology from the University of Florida. He has over 175 publications, his *h*-index is 26 (*i*-index of 61), and he has over 2,200 citations to his published work. He was recently recognized as the #1 criminologist in the world (at his previous rank of Assistant Professor: Copes et al., *JCJE*, 2013) and the #3 criminologist in the world *across all ranks* in terms of his peer-reviewed scholarly publication productivity in the top criminology and criminal justice journals (Cohn & Farrington, *JCJE*, 2014). He is also the author (with David Farrington & Alex Piquero) of a recently published, academic press book with Springer, *Offending from childhood to late middle age: Recent results from the Cambridge Study in Delinquent Development*, and is the author (with Jennifer Reingle) of a recently published textbook with Wolters Kluwer, *Criminological and Criminal Justice Research Methods*. His major research interests include longitudinal data analysis, police body-worn cameras, sex offending, gender, race/ethnicity, the victim-offender overlap, and early childhood prevention. In addition, he is a member of the American Society of Criminology, a Lifetime Member of the Academy of Criminal Justice Sciences, and a member of both the Midwestern and the Southern Criminal Justice Associations.

Benoit Leclerc, Griffith University, Brisbane, Australia Benoit Leclerc is a Senior Lecturer in the School of Criminology and Criminal Justice at Griffith University, Brisbane, Australia. His research interests focus on the application and development of crime script analysis for purposes of situational prevention, crime event analysis as well as sexual offending. He is currently leading a project on the effectiveness of situational prevention to prevent sexual offenses. Key publications include articles in *Criminology, British Journal of Criminology, Journal of Research in Crime and Delinquency* and *Sexual Abuse: A Journal of Research and Treatment* as well as books entitled *Cognition and Crime: Offender Decision-Making and Script Analyses* (co-edited with Wortley) and *Pathways to Sexual Aggression* (co-edited with Proulx, Beauregard and Lussier).

Rolf Loeber, University of Pittsburgh, Pittburgh, USA Rolf Loeber is Distinguished University Professor of Psychiatry and a Professor of Psychology and Epidemiology at the University of Pittsburgh. He is co-director of the Life History Program and principle investigator of the Pittsburgh Youth Study and the Pittsburgh Girls Study. He has published widely in the fields of juvenile antisocial behavior and delinquency, substance use, and mental health problems.

Patrick Lussier, Laval University, Quebec, Canada Patrick Lussier is a full Professor of Criminology at the Faculty of Social Sciences at Laval University, in Quebec, Canada. He is the principal investigator of the Vancouver Longitudinal Study on the Psychosocial Development of Children as well as the principal investigator of the Longitudinal Cohort Study on the Community Re-entry of Adult Sex Offenders. His research interests include developmental criminology, criminal careers and trajectories, risk assessment, and risk management, and his work has been published in journals such as *Criminology, Criminal Justice and Behavior, Justice Quarterly,* and *Psychology, Public Policy and Law.*

Jeff Mathesius, Simon Fraser University, Burnaby, Canada Jeff Mathesius is a third-year PhD student in the School of Criminology at Simon Fraser University. His current research interests include the development of violence and sexual aggression, as well as the risk assessment and management of serious violent juvenile offenders.

Kiminori Nakamura, University of Maryland, College Park, USA Kiminori Nakamura is an Assistant Professor of Criminology and Criminal Justice at the University of Maryland. He received his PhD in Public Policy and Management from Carnegie Mellon University's Heinz College in 2010. His research interests include corrections and re-entry, criminal career, life-course criminology, collateral consequences of criminal justice interventions, and quantitative methods including social network analysis. His current research focuses on the issue of redemption for those with stale criminal-history records, which is when risk of recidivism declines to a level of appropriate benchmarks so that it is no longer necessary for an employer to be concerned about a criminal offense in a prospective employee's past.

Dustin Pardini, University of Pittsburgh, Pittburgh, USA Dustin Pardini is currently an Assistant Professor of Psychiatry at the University of Pittsburgh and co-principle investigator of the Pittsburgh Youth Study. His research interests include the development of antisocial behavior across the life span, especially among boys who exhibit a callous and unemotional interpersonal style. He is also interested in the application of innovative statistical methods to address developmental questions related to antisocial behavior.

Alex R. Piquero, University of Texas at Dallas, Tallahassee, USA Alex R. Piquero is Ashbel Smith Professor in the Program in Criminology in the School of Economic, Political, and Policy Sciences at the University of Texas at Dallas, Adjunct Professor Key Centre for Ethics, Law, Justice, and Governance, Griffith University, and co-editor of the *Journal of Quantitative Criminology*. He has published over two-hundred peer-reviewed articles in the areas of criminal careers, criminological theory, and quantitative research methods, and has collaborated on several books including Key Issues in Criminal Careers Research: New Analyses from the Cambridge Study in Delinquent Development (Cambridge University Press, co-authored with David P. Farrington and Alfred Blumstein) and Handbook of Quantitative Criminology (Springer, co-edited by David Weisburd).

In addition to his membership on over a dozen editorial boards of journals in criminology and sociology, he has also served as Executive Counselor with the American Society of Criminology, Member of the National Academy of Sciences Panel Evaluating the National Institute of Justice, Member of the Racial Democracy, Crime and Justice Network at Ohio State University, and Member of the MacArthur Foundation's Research Network on Adolescent Development & Juvenile Justice.

Professor Piquero has given congressional testimony on evidence-based crime prevention practices in the area of early-family/parent training programs, and has provided counsel and support to several local, state, national, and international criminal justice agencies.

Professor Piquero is past recipient of the American Society of Criminology's Young Scholar and E-Mail Mentor of the Year Awards, Fellow of both the American Society of Criminology and the Academy of Criminal Justice Sciences, and has also received numerous teaching awards including the University of Florida's College of Arts & Sciences Teacher of the Year Award and the University of Maryland's Top Terp Teaching Award.

Jennifer M. Reingle, University of Texas Health Science Center, Dallas, USA Jennifer M. Reingle is an Assistant Professor in the Department of Epidemiology, Human Genetics, and Environmental Sciences at the University of Texas School of Public Health in Dallas. She earned her doctoral degree in epidemiology from the University of Florida in 2011. She has published more than 60 peer-reviewed articles, and her major research interests include correctional health, epidemiological criminology, Health, delinquency prevention, and health disparities in crime and substance use.

Stephen Smallbone, Griffith University, Brisbane, Australia Stephen Smallbone is the clinical and research Program Leader of Griffith Youth Forensic Service (GYFS), a team of practitioners and researchers concerned with understanding and preventing youth sexual violence and abuse. He is also the project leader of the Griffith Longitudinal (adult child-sex offender) Study, which was originally funded in 1999 by the Criminology Research Council and the Queensland Crime Commission, and is currently funded by the Australian Research Council and Queensland Corrective Services. Other work includes the design, implementation, and evaluation of offender rehabilitation programs.

Keith Soothill, Lancaster University, UK Keith Soothill was Emeritus Professor in the Department of Sociology of Lancaster University. His research career was wide ranging, covering both health and social policy, but his consuming interest was criminology. He has published over 300 articles on the topics of sexual crime, arson, serious offending and homicide. Keith Soothill died in February 2014.

Jo Thakker, University of Waikato, Hamilton, New Zealand Jo Thakker is a lecturer in Clinical Psychology at the University of Waikato in Hamilton, New Zealand. She received her PhD from the University of Canterbury and has worked as a clinical psychologist in a variety of therapeutic contexts. Along with work in the substance abuse area, her research interests include cultural psychology and mental health issues in relation to migrants and refugees.

Steve van de Weijer, NSCR and VU University, Amsterdam, the Netherlands Steve van de Weijer studied sociology and received his PhD from the Department of Criminal Law and Criminology at the VU University, Amsterdam. He is currently employed as researcher at the NSCR and as teacher at the VU University. His research interests include the intergenerational transmission of crime, criminal careers and life-course criminology.

Chantal van den Berg, Leiden University, Leiden, the Netherlands Chantal van den Berg is currently employed as an Assistant Professor in Criminology at Leiden University, the Netherlands. She did her PhD at the VU University, Amsterdam, which entailed the study of long-term criminal careers of juvenile sex offenders and their transitions into adulthood, in terms of labor market outcomes, romantic relationships, and parenthood.

Victor van der Geest, VU University, Amsterdam, the Netherlands Victor van der Geest studied developmental psychology. He is an Assistant Professor of Criminology at the VU University, Amsterdam, and Researcher at the Netherlands Institute for the Study of Crime and Law Enforcement (NSCR). His research interests include criminal careers, and more specifically, mutual influences between employment, intimate relationships, and crime, and the role of substance abuse.

Tony Ward, Victoria University of Wellington, Wellington, New Zealand Tony Ward is a clinical psychologist by training and has been working in the clinical and forensic field since 1987. He was formerly Director of the Kia Marama Sexual Offenders' Unit at Rolleston Prison in New Zealand, and has taught both clinical and forensic psychology at Victoria, Deakin, Canterbury, and Melbourne Universities. He is currently the Director of Clinical Training at Victoria University of Wellington. His research interests fall into four main areas: correctional and clinical rehabilitation models and issues; cognition and sex offenders; ethical issues in clinical and forensic psychology; and evolutionary explanations of crime and mental disorders.

Miriam Wijkman, VU University, Amsterdam, the Netherlands Miriam Wijkman studied Law as well as Psychology. She is an Assistant Professor in Criminology at the VU University Amsterdam. Her research interests focus on (juvenile) sexual offending, female offending, and organized crime. For her PhD she studied offender characteristics, criminal careers and co-offending patterns of adult and juvenile female sexual offenders.

Franklin E. Zimring, University of California, Berkeley, USA Franklin E. Zimring is Simon Professor of Law and Wolfen Distinguished Scholar at the University of California at Berkeley. His recent writing includes *An American Travesty: Legal Responses to Adolescent Sexual Offending*, a paperback version of which was published by the University of Chicago Press in 2009.

Forewords

This is a brilliant, path-breaking book that should be of great interest to all criminologists and psychologists. As the title indicates, the book details the many different ways in which findings from criminal career research can contribute to knowledge and policies on sex offenders. As the editors point out, sex offending has generally been studied as a clinical or medical problem, with a focus on individual pathology and an emphasis on retrospective case-control studies and risk assessment. Criminologists have generally studied versatile offenders who commit many different types of crimes. There have been no major prospective longitudinal studies that have focused primarily on sex offenders, largely because of the belief that they are too rare to study in community samples. The major developmental and life-course theories have rarely been applied to explain sex offending, although Stephen Smallbone and Jesse Cale propose a very interesting theory and usefully compare and contrast features of general and sex offending.

There is much to admire in this book. Different types of sex offenders are investigated and compared, especially "hands-on" versus "hands-off" sex offenders. There are praiseworthy efforts to study sex offending in major longitudinal studies such as the Cambridge Study in Delinquent Development, the Pittsburgh Youth Study, and the Philadelphia and Racine cohort studies, as well as in longitudinal studies of offender samples. All the major dimensions of criminal careers are studied, including prevalence, frequency, ages of onset and desistance, continuity, specialization, life-course transitions, escalation, and de-escalation. Other important topics are investigated, including criminal career trajectories and age-period-cohort effects. Research results are described from several different countries, including Canada, the United States, the United Kingdom, Australia, and the Netherlands. There is a chapter on the neglected topic of female sex offenders.

This book has important implications for public policy regarding sex offenders. Generally, they have a low probability of persistence and specialization in sex offenses, calling into doubt compulsory registration policies. Kiminori Nakamura and Alfred Blumstein document how their risk of offending can decline to zero or to a rate similar to that of nonoffenders. Knowledge from criminal career research should be provided to criminal justice personnel who have to deal with sex offenders, including judges, probation officers, and parole board members.

Despite the great advances in knowledge described in this book, it is clear that sex offending needs to be studied in large-scale prospective longitudinal surveys, extending from childhood into adulthood, with frequent face-to-face interviews as well as criminal record data. The yield of sex offenders could be increased by choosing high-risk male samples in large cities. In addition, more efforts should be made to link up knowledge about individual development with situational and environmental factors that encourage sex offending. Also, more attempts should be made to formulate developmental and life-course theories of sex offending. The editors and contributors should be warmly congratulated for their Herculean – and successful – efforts to push forward the frontiers of knowledge about sex offending.

David P. Farrington,
Institute of Criminology,
Cambridge University

For a majority of people, sex offenders nurture deviant sexual fantasies and plan sexual assaults all day long. Furthermore, these criminals are considered recidivists who specialize in sexual crimes. In this view, there is only one way to deal with these incurable perverts – long-term incarceration. Are these beliefs about sex offenders confirmed by scientific studies on these offenders' motivations and criminal careers? Do all sex offenders have the same motivation to commit their crimes? Are all sex offenders sexual recidivists and specialists in sexual crime? In sum, are sexual offenders a unique and distinct type of criminal who deserve their own theoretical framework distinct from that of other forms of crime?

In the 1960s, Kurt Freund developed a methodology, known as phallometric assessment, to determine whether sex offenders have a sexual preference for sexual aggression (i.e., sexual abuse of children, rape of women). After 50 years of research on this topic, there is clear evidence that approximately half of sexual aggressors of children prefer to have sex with children rather than with adults. However, the other half do not present this sexually deviant preference. On the other hand, only 20% of sexual aggressors against women (i.e., those characterized as sadistic rapists) prefer sexual coercive activities to consensual sex. In sum, a deviant sexual preference is absent in the majority of sex offenders. These results highlight the heterogeneity of motivations for sexual offenses – which include, apart from deviant sexual preference, a proclivity to use sex as coping strategy, antisociality, opportunism, and anger (see Chapter 3 by Smallbone & Cale).

Over the past 20 years, Karl Hanson has conducted an ambitious research program on recidivism by sexual aggressors. This program has produced two meta-analyses that indicate that the sexual recidivism rate in sexual offenders is only 17%. Clearly, a majority of sex offenders do not recidivate. Those who do recidivate are characterized by sexual problems (deviant sexual preference, sexual coping) and by antisociality (e.g., psychopathy). Finally, sex offenders have a higher rate of recidivism for nonsexual crimes than for sexual ones. This last result seriously calls into question the belief that sexual aggressors specialize in sexual crimes. In addition, the results of Proulx and Lussier's large-scale empirical study (600 participants) indicate sexual crimes represent two thirds of crimes committed by child sexual abusers but only one third of crimes committed by sexual aggressors of women. Thus, beliefs about sexual aggressors' recidivism rates and specialization in sexual crime are largely unsupported by empirical evidence. Furthermore, in sexual aggressors, criminal career heterogeneity appears to be the rule rather than the exception.

Apart from recidivism, the criminal career characteristics of sexual aggressors have received little attention. However, Blokland and Lussier's contribution here is an exception to this rule. In fact, this book is a landmark, since it presents state-of-the-art empirical results and theoretical discussions related to the criminal career of sexual aggressors. Furthermore, it suggests new avenues of research. The first part of the book includes three chapters that establish links between, on the one hand, developmental and life-course criminology, and on the other, the literature on sex offenders. Thus, Thakker and Ward (Chapter 2) speculate about the influence that factors suggested by leading theories of sexual aggression have on different parameters of sexual aggressors' criminal careers. In Chapter 3, Smallbone and Cale present similarities (e.g., versatility, the fact that a small proportion of offenders commit a large proportion of crimes) and differences (e.g., age of onset, desistance patterns) between the criminal careers of general offenders and sexual aggressors. In addition, they present an original theory of sexual aggression that integrates concepts from both developmental criminology and research on sexual aggression. Such a new theory is necessary because developmental dimensions of sexual offending may not be simply reduced to those of nonsexual crimes.

In the second part of this book, we find original empirical studies on the criminal career of different types of sexual aggressors, such as adolescent offenders, adult offenders, female sexual offenders, and sexual murderers. Furthermore, in this second part, the authors analyze a large variety of criminal career parameters (e.g., age of onset, specialization, escalation, and desistance), as well as the factors associated with them. The 11 chapters of this section constitute the most ambitious research program ever conducted on the criminal career of sexual aggressors, and provide a unique perspective on the longitudinal patterning of sexual and nonsexual crimes committed by sexual aggressors.

The third part of this book concerns policy issues. If a majority of sex offenders are not recidivists specialized in sexual crimes, then several of the current measures to deal with these criminals are not appropriate (e.g., long-term incarceration, public notification). The authors in this part of the book discuss alternative ways of dealing with sex offenders. Their proposals are based on empirical evidence about the criminal career of different types of sex offenders, rather than on the general population's fear and desire for retaliation. Their proposals offer promising avenues for the reduction of the frequency and the severity of sexual aggression in our society.

I find this book to be of very high quality on both theoretical and empirical grounds. Furthermore, I consider this book to be the cornerstone of a line of research on the criminal career of sexual aggressors – a heterogeneous group of offenders who present both specific criminogenic factors (e.g., deviant sexual preference) and general criminogenic factors (e.g., antisociality and psychopathy). Blokland and Lussier are two outstanding researchers, and they are to be congratulated for so successfully merging contributions from some of the most prominent researchers in the fields of sexual aggression and developmental criminology. In each of the chapters of this book, the authors successfully integrate these two traditions of research, which have rarely intersected in the past.

Jean Proulx,
School of Criminology,
University of Montreal

Preface

The idea for this book came about following discussions during the annual meeting of the American Society of Criminology in Los Angeles in 2010. At the time, there were growing concerns of a widening gap between scientific knowledge on sex offenders on the one side and recent trends in policy development on the other. In fact, in several countries, scholars were coming forward to criticize emerging repressive policies on the grounds that not only they were not effective, they were detrimental to the prevention of sexual violence and abuse. There was also a widening gap occurring between general knowledge about the criminal career and emerging policies. For example, in Canada, about 90% of individuals legally defined as dangerous offenders and serving indeterminate prison sentences are sex offenders.

Sex offenders are typically in their forties when given a dangerous offender status, a period where criminal careers are usually fading even for the most chronic offenders. In the United States, juvenile sex offenders are increasingly subject to sex offender registration, and public notification to deter them from future offending and to minimize continuity in adulthood. Similar policies are being adopted in several European countries as well. Yet, the idea of continuity in sex offending is in sharp contrast to the observation that most juvenile offenders do not become adult criminals. Our discussion led us to two important conclusions that became driving forces behind the conception and elaboration of this book. The first observation had to do with the relative absence of criminologists from the arena of research on sexual violence and abuse.

Traditionally, the individual committing sex crimes had not been the subject of much empirical work by criminologists. Yet, in our opinion, recent criminological research in the areas of criminal career and life-course perspective had much to offer to the field of sexual violence and abuse. Driven by several longitudinal cohort studies in different countries, criminologists had made several important findings in the past three decades with respect to the understanding of the onset of criminal activity, its persistence and aggravation, and more recently on desistance from offending. Unfortunately, there had been, at the time, limited attempts to translate these findings and their implications to the field of sex offending. Understandably, researchers, practitioners, and treatment providers in the field of sexual violence and abuse were not, for the most part, aware of these developments. In fact, it wasn't even clear whether these findings could be translated and generalized to offenders committing sex crimes.

The book aims to address these limitations and these assumptions. The second observation had to do with the concept of sex offender. It is easy to forget that research on sexual violence is relatively recent. The first detailed description of a large sample of sex offenders was conducted in the early 1960s by Paul Gebhard and colleagues at the Institute of Sex Research founded by Alfred Kinsey. Much of the empirical research to date has been largely focused on sex offenders' sexual arousal, sexual fantasies, cognitions, cognitive processes, personality, and psychopathology. The focus of past research is understandable given the objectives put forward by clinical researchers to inform treatment providers and therapists about the factors in need of intervention to reduce the risk of recidivism. Limited research, however, had focused on the very behavior that the treatment aimed to change, that is, sex offending. Further, past research, having focused on sex offenders' criminal behavior, has been limited to sexual recidivism, a concept that has been virtually abandoned by criminologists with the advent of the criminal career approach in the 1980s due to conceptual and methodological shortcomings of the concept of recidivism. To move forward, it is important to disaggregate the concept of sex offender by differentiating the individual committing a sex crime and the individual's offending behavior.

The idea of disaggregating the individual from his or her offending is not too distant from the suggestion made by John Monahan and Harry Steadman more than two decades ago in the field of risk assessment of violence. They argued that the concept of dangerousness confounded three interrelated components, that is, the risk factors on which a prediction is based, the type of event being predicted, and the likelihood of the event occurring in the future. Similarly, the concept of sex offender encompasses the individual having committed a sex crime as well as his or her criminal activity. The importance of disaggregating the individual and his or her offending can be illustrated by the assumption of crime specialization characterizing this group. Until recently, it has been assumed that sex offenders, as their label suggests, were sex crime specialists. It is easy to forget that sex offenders are involved in other crime types as well. It is also easy to forget that a sex crime tends to occur in a sequence of nonsex crimes.

Furthermore, it is easy to forget that if sex offenders do reoffend after their prison release, it will most likely be a nonsex crime. By disaggregating the concept of sex offender into its two main parts, that is, the individual and the criminal activity, we are forced to think about the broader picture: the offender's entire criminal activity over time. Why are sex offenders involved in other crime types? What other crime types are they involved in? What is the meaning of their involvement in other crime types? What about sex offenders who tend to restrict their offending to sex crimes? Are factors responsible for their nonsex offending also contributing to their sex offending, and vice versa? The label of sex offender is also suggestive of persistence in sex offending and the same type of questions can be raised. The book provides a framework to guide empirical research and policy development by thinking more clearly about offending in a manner that can provide policy-relevant information. We also believe that the book will challenge preconceived ideas about the sex offender in a way that will stimulate ideas and research for years to come.

We would like to express our gratitude to everyone at Wiley Blackwell for their professionalism and the way the publication of this book was handled. Special thanks to Karen Shield, project editor at Wiley Blackwell, for her enthusiasm and advice at the beginning of this project. Her assistance and patience during the realization of this book were invaluable. As editors, we also want to express our appreciation to all contributors to this book. The response to the idea of introducing the criminal career approach to the field of sexual violence and abuse was extremely positive among contributors who were solicited for this book. Their enthusiasm gave us more leverage as to how to approach this book, its content, and its format. Given the innovative aspect of the ideas proposed here, a review book would have been unsatisfactory to us, given the scarcity of research on the criminal career of individuals committing sex crimes. The enthusiasm of the contributors allowed us to think about this book as a series of theoretical and empirical pieces.

This book contains new theoretical ideas, new empirical studies never published before. All contributors accepted our challenge to put forward ideas on the criminal career approach and to apply those to the issue of sexual violence and abuse. We are also indebted to several scholars who shared their expertise with us by reviewing all chapters included in this book. For the review process, we approached criminologists with an expertise in criminal career research as well as researchers from the field of sexual abuse and violence. Criminologists were helpful in reminding us of the complexities and the intricacies of the criminal career dimensions discussed, while researchers from the field of sexual violence assisted us in further linking the criminal career concepts to the existing scientific literature on sex offenders. We are grateful to all reviewers for their insightful and constructive comments. Their work allowed us to mirror, if not to surpass, the level and quality that would be expected from scientific articles published in a special issue of an academic journal. We hope that the process will also help to strengthen the ties between criminologists and researchers from the field of sexual violence and abuse.

Patrick Lussier
Arjan Blokland

Acknowledgements

All chapters in this book were reviewed by external reviewers. We, the editors, are indebted to them for their constructive criticism and thoughtful comments. All reviewers are mentioned below in alphabetical order.

Eric Beauregard, Centre for Research on Sexual Violence, School of Criminology, Simon Fraser University, Burnaby, Canada

Emily Blake, School of Psychology, Keynes College, University of Kent, Canterbury, United Kingdom

Shawn Bushway, School of Criminal Justice, University of Albany, Albany, USA

Michael F. Caldwell, Department of Psychology, University of Wisconsin-Madison, Madison, USA

Jesse Cale, Faculty of Social Sciences, University of New South Wales, Australia

Maarten Cruyff, Department of Methodology and Statistics, Utrecht University, Utrecht, the Netherlands

Douglas L. Eckberg, Department of Sociology and Anthropology, Winthrop University

Gabriel Escarela, Department of Mathematics, Autonomous Metropolitan University, Iztapalapa, Mexico

Alasdair M. Goodwill, Department of Psychology, Ryerson University, Toronto, Canada

Karl Hanson, Public Safety Canada, Ottawa, Canada

Danielle Harris, Justice Studies, San Jose State University, San Jose, California, USA

Lila Kazemian, Department of Sociology, John Jay College of Criminal Justice, New York, USA

Martin Killias, Department of Law, Zurich University, Switzerland

Michael H. Miner, Program in Human Sexuality, Department of Family Medicine and Community Health, University of Minnesota, USA

Joseph Murray, Department of Psychiatry, School of Clinical Medicine, Cambridge University, UK

Jean Proulx, University of Montreal, Quebec, Canada

Lisa L. Sample, School of Criminology and Criminal Justice, University of Nebraska at Omaha, Omaha, USA

Michael Seto, Royal Ottawa Health Care Group, University of Toronto, Canada

G. Matthew Snodgrass, H. John Heinz III College of Public Policy and Management, Carnegie Mellon University, Pittsburgh, USA

Pierre Tremblay, School of Criminology, University of Montreal, Quebec, Canada

Part I

Theoretical and Conceptual Issues in the Study of Sex Offending

1

The Criminal Career Paradigm and Its Relevance to Studying Sex Offenders

Arjan Blokland
NSCR and Leiden University, the Netherlands

Patrick Lussier
Laval University, Canada

Introduction

In the early 1980s the U.S. crime rate was on the rise, the nation's prison population experienced an unprecedented growth – over 200% over a period of only 10 years – and crime control policies were largely perceived to be ineffective. Against this background, the National Institute of Justice, via the National Academy of Sciences, organized the Panel on Research on Criminal Careers that was asked to review extant scientific knowledge on criminal careers and to explore alternatives to mass incarceration as the conventional – but increasingly costly – way of crime control. Informed by the findings from the Philadelphia birth cohort study (Wolfgang, Figlio, & Sellin, 1972), which showed that a relatively small portion of the cohort members was responsible for a disproportionate share of all serious crime in this cohort, and the results from interviews with imprisoned offenders conducted by the Rand Corporation (Peterson & Braiker, 1980; Chaiken & Chaiken, 1982) showing considerable variety in the frequency of offending reported by these inmates, the Panel's attention was drawn to ways of distinguishing the most persistent, most frequent, and most serious offenders and the potential benefits of selectively incarcerating these "career criminals."

To accomplish their mission the Panel devised a novel way of organizing knowledge on key aspects of individual offending patterns that was motivated by its theoretical stance that different causal processes drive development in these different dimensions (Blumstein, Cohen, Roth, & Visher, 1986). By doing so, the Panel's report laid the fundaments of the criminal career approach to studying crime and

Sex Offenders: A Criminal Career Approach, First Edition. Edited by Arjan Blokland and Patrick Lussier.

deviance, providing criminologists not only with a new set of empirical and theoretical challenges, but also with a shared vocabulary in which to address these issues. Since its publication a vast amount of empirical, theoretical, and policy-orientated research has been published making use of the tools laid out in the Panel's report, greatly increasing our knowledge on the longitudinal patterning of offending, the factors contributing to this development, and the ways in which formal interventions may impact the course of criminal careers (Piquero, Farrington, & Blumstein, 2003).

In many ways, the current situation with regard to sexual offending is similar to that leading to the commissioning of the Panel's report. Public outrage and fear concerning sexual offenders in the United States and elsewhere is unprecedentedly high (Quinn, Forsyth, & Mullen-Quinn, 2004). Policies aimed at sexual offenders, as well as the number of individuals subjected to these policies, are rapidly increasing and with them public expenditures to monitor and enforce sex offenders' compliance to these policies are skyrocketing (Zimring, 2004). In part this is due to the fact that policymakers, as do the general public, tend to treat all sex offenders alike and view them as highly repetitive, extremely dangerous, and incorrigible offenders – the worst of the worst – this in spite of the fact that available empirical evidence consistently points to considerable variety in sex offenders' criminal behavior (Levenson, Brannon, Fortney, & Baker, 2007). Furthermore, as with sex offenders, sex crimes also vary greatly along various dimensions, including seriousness (degree of violence) and sexual intrusiveness (nature of sexual behavior). The most serious forms of sexual offenses are among the most hideous violations of individual rights, and utmost efforts should be made to prevent harm to future victims. This is precisely why these efforts should be guided, not by moral panic but by detailed knowledge of the way criminal careers of sexual offenders develop over time. Breaking up sex offenders' criminal careers into different dimensions and gaining insight into the causal processes that underlie these dimensions will allow us to develop strategies to deal with sexual offending more effectively and more efficiently.

The current volume champions a criminal career approach to studying sexual offending. Its central aim is to bridge the criminal career literature and the sex offender literature that thus far have developed largely separately. These scientific literatures have emerged from two relatively distinct research traditions, theoretical perspectives, and methodological traditions. For example, coming from a clinical perspective, the field of sexual offending has described and detailed underlying motivations and associated cognitive processes of sex offenders. Sociologically orientated criminologists studying criminal development, on the other hand, have applied sophisticated statistical techniques to large data sets in efforts to establish which outside factors causally impact the course of criminal careers. We believe these fields of research can benefit from each other in various ways. Bringing these two fields of research together is beneficial to researchers in the sexual offending field as the criminal career literature provides them with a set of tools currently underutilized in studies on sexual offending. Applying these tools will yield insight into the way sexual offending develops over the individual's life span, both quantitatively and qualitatively. Taking a criminal career perspective will also shed light on the way patterns of sexual offending interrelate with developmental patterns in other types of crime and deviance. Further, applying the criminal career approach to sexual offending will inform both treatment and policy as it yields valuable information on the behavioral antecedents of sexual (re)offending, as well as the way sexual offending is most likely to progress if left unaddressed. In turn, the study of sex offenders' criminal careers advances the criminal career literature by providing insight into the extent to which conclusions based on current criminal career research also apply to this specific subgroup of offenders. In consequence, studying the criminal development of sex offenders speaks on the generalizability of the theoretical explanations that are being offered to understand the development of crime over the life course.

The current chapter will lay the foundations for the subsequent chapters in the volume by providing a definition of the criminal career and explicating the various criminal career dimensions. The chapter continues with a brief synopsis of the current knowledge base on criminal career development of general, nonsexual offenders and an overview of the currently dominant theoretical perspectives on criminal career development. Against the background of these empirical results, possibilities and pitfalls for policy and interventions are discussed. The latter part of this chapter will apply the criminal career approach to sexual offending, sketching its applications and potential ramifications for the study, prevention, and treatment of sexual offending over the life span.

What Is a Criminal Career?

The Panel defined the criminal career as the longitudinal sequence of crimes committed by an individual offender (Blumstein et al., 1986). By no means does the term "career" imply that offenders derive their livelihood from offending, that offenders are or aim to become professionals of sex offending, or that they commit a certain number of offenses. The career concept is merely proposed to systematically structure the chain of criminal behaviors associated with an individual. In the criminological literature criminal careers are sometimes also referred to as developmental pathways or criminal trajectories (Loeber & Leblanc, 1990; Leblanc & Loeber, 1998). The Panel distinguished four key dimensions that characterize criminal careers:

1. Participation – the distinction between those who engage in crime and those who do not
2. Frequency – the rate of criminal activity of those who are active
3. Seriousness of offenses committed, or crime mix
4. Career length – the length of time an offender is active.

Participation refers to the portion of a population that engages in crime. Participation depends on the scope of the criminal acts considered and the length of the observational period, and is conditional on factors such as sex and age. Age of onset is used to refer to the age of first participation in crime.

Frequency refers to the number of offenses per year per active offender. Frequency, which is often denoted by the Greek letter lambda (λ), varies between individuals, as well as for individuals over time, as in the course of their criminal career offenders go through periods in which they accelerate or decelerate their offending.

Seriousness deals with the kinds of crimes committed and is also referred to as crime mix. As with frequency, offenders may differ in the kinds of crimes they commit, with one offender committing more serious crimes than another. Again, as with offending frequency, criminal careers may be characterized by (periods of) increasing seriousness – escalation – or by (periods of) decreasing seriousness – de-escalation. In addition, if offenders commit many different types of crimes they are commonly referred to as generalists; if, on the other hand, their criminal behavior is more limited in scope and they engage in only one or a group of closely related offenses, they are said to be specialists. Adding a time dimension to this distinction, criminal careers may be characterized by (periods of) generalization or diversification in which offenders engage in increasingly different types of crime, or by (periods of) specialization in which one offense increasingly dominates the offending pattern.

Career length or duration refers to the time period between the first and the last offense. Like participation, career length depends heavily on the length of the observational period. Ideally, to determine the criminal career duration of an individual offender, this offender would have to be followed up from birth to death. In practice, however, observational periods are more limited than that and often data are right censored – the observational period ending before the death of the offender – which introduces uncertainty as to whether offending was actually terminated after the last offense observed. Residual career length refers to the number of future years that a currently active offender is expected to remain criminally active.

While seemingly clear cut, these dimensions are complexly linked, and when thinking about (or researching) criminal careers it is always important to be mindful of these complexities. A notorious example is the age/crime curve (Farrington, 1986). If, for a particular cohort, one were to plot the total number of offenses per age, a curve steeply accelerating to a peak around the end of adolescence, followed by a more gradual decline during adulthood, would be most likely to emerge. However, from this graph it would remain unclear to what extent the observed peak in offending was caused by increasing numbers of adolescents becoming criminally active – increased participation – and to what extent the group of already active criminals had increased their frequency of offending during this period. Similarly, specialization could result from an offender increasing his offending frequency for a particular offense type or from him ending his committing other offense types, or both. Even career length can be disputable: many offenders have criminal careers that are characterized be extensive periods of nonoffending or intermittency (Piquero, 2004); how long can a period of intermittency be for the offender to still be referred to as criminally active? And, provided the intermittent period is long enough, can a person be considered to be engaging in two criminal careers in different periods of his or her life? By itself the career approach does not provide answers to these questions as they link directly to theory. What the career approach does do is provide the language to address these issues and with it the opportunity to increase the explanatory value of our theories.

Studying Criminal Careers

The Current Knowledge Base on Criminal Careers

In his 2002 Sutherland address before the American Society of Criminology, David Farrington reviewed the current empirical knowledge base on criminal careers (Farrington, 2003). He summarized his findings in what he deemed 10 accepted conclusions on the development of criminal behavior over the life course.

First, the prevalence in offending reaches its zenith in the late teenage years; more young people than adults engage in crime (e.g., Stattin, Magnusson, & Reichel, 1989; Farrington, 1986).

Second, the onset of offending usually occurs in late childhood or early adolescence, while most offenders terminate their criminal careers somewhere during the third decade of life (Farrington, 1992).

Third, there is continuity of offending over the life course, meaning that those individuals who commit many offenses during one age period are at increased risk of committing offenses during the next (Tracy & Kempf-Leonard, 1996). This continuity is thought to primarily reflect stable individual differences, though dynamic processes may also lead to stability in behavior (Sampson & Laub, 1997). Continuity does not preclude within-individual development as offenders' criminal careers may show signs of acceleration or escalation, or changes in the mix of crimes that are committed.

Fourth, onset, frequency, and duration are linked such that an early onset predicts a relatively long criminal career duration and a relatively high offending frequency (Farrington, Lambert, & West, 1998). This does not necessarily mean that those with an early onset show a continuously high rate of offending across their entire criminal career (Piquero, 2007). It does mean that compared to those starting their criminal career at later ages, early onset offenders tend to have a higher offending frequency and a more prolonged criminal career.

This links to the fifth conclusion, which was already the focus of the Panel on Criminal Careers, that a relatively small group of offenders – namely those showing an early onset, high offending frequency, and prolonged criminal career duration – are responsible for a disproportionate share of all crime (Wolfgang et al., 1972). The extent of this overrepresentation depends on the time scale across which it is calculated and increases with the period under scrutiny (Blokland & Nieuwbeerta, 2007).

Sixth, offenders tend to show a very diverse set of offenses. While there is some evidence of specialization, either measured from one offense to the next (Paternoster, Brame, Piquero, Mazerolle, & Dean, 1998), or with age across the entire criminal career (Nieuwbeerta, Blokland, Piquero, & Sweeten, 2011), it always occurs against the background of much versatility in offending.

Seventh, notwithstanding versatility in offending, some offenses tend to be committed before others, and some types of offenses are more common in certain age groups compared to others (Leblanc & Fréchette, 1989).

Eight, versatility extends beyond judicial boundaries and offending is usually part of a larger, much broader behavioral repertoire consisting of potentially harmful behaviors like substance use, reckless driving, and unsafe sex (Gottfredson & Hirschi, 1990).

Ninth, with increasing age, offending changes from being a group activity to being a solo activity. During the teenage years offenses are usually committed with co-offenders, while during the adult years offenses are most times committed alone (McCord & Conway, 2002). This change does not stem from group-offenders terminating their criminal careers earlier, or solo-offenders showing a late onset of offending, rather individual offenders tend to shift from group- to solo-offending as they age.

Tenth, motivations for offending, in contrast to offending itself, do tend to become less diverse with age. While teenagers may attest to committing crimes out of boredom and need for excitement, or because of compelling emotional states, adults usually report more utilitarian motives (Leblanc, 1996).

While based upon a vast number of empirical studies, Farrington hastens to add that the generalization of these conclusions might be compromised by the relative lack of empirical research among samples other than white, lower-class, Anglo-Saxon boys and the fact that the available studies pertain mostly to run-of-the-mill street-crime type of offenses. Available research among women and organized crime offenders, for example, shows that these conclusions might not readily apply to these groups (Block, Blokland, Van der Werff, Van Os, & Nieuwbeerta, 2010; Van Koppen, De Poot, & Blokland, 2010).

Furthermore, Farrington's conclusions were based on observations and empirical findings from longitudinal research conducted with different cohorts of individuals followed over long periods of time and describing criminal careers in general offending, taking offenders' whole criminal activity into account. Whereas research on sexual offenders is typically based on individuals convicted for their crime and recruited to participate in research studies while they are in prison or taking part in a treatment program, criminal career research has typically been based on general samples of youth recruited in schools, at-risk neighborhoods, and so on, often before their first police contact or first conviction. While research with sex offenders is often based on retrospective data, criminal career research usually relies on prospective longitudinal data. The two methodological approaches espoused in the different fields of study can yield very different pictures of the same phenomenon. For example, research has shown that retrospective data, as opposed to prospective data, tend largely to overestimate persistence in offending. The lack of empirical research into the criminal careers of different subgroups of offenders thus far not only limits the ability to draw definitive conclusions about the development of criminal careers, but has also influenced the theoretical explanations that have been offered to account for these developments.

Explaining Empirical Findings on Criminal Careers

While itself rather devoid of theory, the criminal career approach has fueled many recent theoretical debates about the best way to conceptualize criminal development.

From the start, the criminal-career approach's basic theoretical stance – namely that, in principle, different causal mechanisms could govern each criminal career dimension (Blumstein, Cohen, & Farrington, 1988) – has been disputed. Flag bearers of the opposition to distinguishing criminal career dimensions have been Michael Gottfredson and Travis Hirschi, whose critique of the criminal career approach culminated into the development of their General Theory of crime (Gottfredson & Hirschi, 1990). These authors question the need for distinguishing criminal career dimensions by stating that these dimensions are all intrinsically linked in such a way that rank ordering offenders on these different dimensions will produce the same outcome across each dimension (Gottfredson & Hirschi, 1987). That is, those who begin participating in crime the earliest will also tend to be the most frequent and most persistent offenders, and, merely due to their total number of offenses, will show the largest variety in terms of crime mix. According to Gottfredson and Hirschi, the risk factors for participation are therefore similar to those predicting frequency or career length. They go on to argue that offending develops similarly across age for all offenders (Hirschi & Gottfredson, 1983; Gottfredson & Hirschi, 1990). They underpin their argument by showing that the age distribution of offenders is similarly shaped across geographical places and historical periods. Given that, to these authors, participation and frequency amount to the same thing, they argue that individual offending patterns show the same rise and decline with age as does the aggregate curve for all offenders. They propose a maturational take on desistance from crime, and argue that no variable other than age itself has been offered that can explain the decline in offending across the individual's life span.

Various authors have taken issue with Gottfredson and Hirschi's maturational stance, including Hirschi's former students Robert Sampson and John Laub. These criminologists proffer a less deterministic view of development, stating that human behavioral development is not to be interpreted as the unfolding of something that is already latently present in the individual, but rather as a dynamic process characterized by plasticity and receptivity to random outside influence (Sampson & Laub, 1993; Laub & Sampson, 2003).

Building on insights from social control theory, Sampson and Laub argue that changes in criminal behavior over the life course can be understood as resulting from changes in the level of social control that individuals experience (Sampson & Laub, 1990). During times in which social control is low, criminal behavior is more likely. Important life events and transitions in conventional life-course domains, such as school, work, and personal relationships, often are accompanied by changes in the level of control one experiences, therefore allowing these transitions to be potential turning points in the individual's criminal career. While decreasing levels of social control during adolescence are argued to explain the observed peak in offending during this period, increasing levels of social control resulting from individuals engaging progressively more in conventional adult social roles – for example, employee, husband, father – in turn are argued to underlie the decrease in offending during the adult period (Laub & Sampson, 2001). Unlike Gottfredson and Hirschi, who argue that the observed association between certain life circumstances and crime is spurious and merely based on some underlying variable making people both more likely to experience certain transitions and more likely to refrain from crime (Hirschi & Gottfredson, 1995), Sampson and Laub thus ascribe causal power to such transitions in rerouting individual criminal careers (Sampson & Laub, 1995).

Transitions, however, do not only explain change in criminal behavior, they can also explain continuity. While cognizant of the fact that stable individual differences may contribute to the observed stability of crime over the life course, Sampson and Laub argue that continuity can also result from the same dynamic processes that bring about change in offending (Sampson & Laub, 1997). To explain continuity or escalation of crime over the life course, these authors refer to the process known as cumulative disadvantage. While transitions in other life-course domains influence the likelihood of criminal behavior, criminal behavior itself may also impact development in these conventional domains. A conviction may lead an offender to experience a divorce or cause him or her to get fired. Similarly, a "bad reputation" may alter the offender's chances in the marriage market in much the same way that a criminal record complicates his or her transition into the labor market. In turn, the severance or continued absence of these social bonds makes future criminal behavior even more likely, giving rise to a perpetual process of accumulating risks and, in the end, continuity in deviant behavior.

While at odds with each other on the nature of the causal processes that govern criminal development, the above theories do agree that one theory is sufficient to explain criminal behavior in all offenders. That is, both maturational theories and dynamic theories are general theories as they assume that the behavior of all offenders is the product of the same causal forces. Typological theories, on the other hand, paint a more complex picture and seek to identify special subgroups of offenders whose criminal behavior is argued to be explained by different causal factors (Paternoster, Dean, Piquero, Mazerolle, & Brame, 1997).

One of the most popular typological theories in developmental criminology is the dual taxonomy put forth by Terrie Moffitt. Based on her research on the Dunedin cohort, she proposed that there are at least two types of offenders (Moffitt, 1993). The large majority of offenders become criminally active only during adolescence and have criminal careers of relatively short duration. A small minority, however, exhibits an early onset of problematic and antisocial behavior during childhood, and a continued pattern of crime and deviance far into adulthood. Together, according to Moffitt, these two groups can explain the shape of the age-crime curve, with the many adolescents participating in crime explaining the peak during the teenage years, and those starting early and persisting in crime causing the age-crime curve to flare at both the youngest and older ages (Moffitt, 1993; Moffitt, 2006).

Besides distinguishing these two different types of offenders based on their criminal career features, the dual taxonomy also offers different explanations for the criminal development of these two groups (Moffitt, 1997). According to Moffitt, those criminally active mainly during adolescence – the adolescence-limited type – commit crimes primarily as a way to express their need for personal autonomy. As in modern day Western society social maturity lags behind physical maturity, delinquency in this group is best seen as a temporal surrogate for achieving adult status, which is easily abandoned when, with age, conventional opportunities start to present themselves. For those with criminal careers showing an early onset, high frequency of offending, and a prolonged duration, however, the root cause of their problematic behavior is said to lie in neuropsychological deficits taxing early parent-child interactions. As these children are progressively deprived of opportunities to learn and practice prosocial behavior, their problematic behavior quickly escalates to delinquency and crime as they reach school-going age. As antisocial behavior increasingly becomes ingrained in the behavioral repertoire of these youths, by the time conventional opportunities start to present themselves, these children are both less equipped and less able to seize these opportunities and materialize these transitions into turning points in their criminal development (Moffitt, 1994).

Criminal Career Dimensions and Strategies for Crime Control

From the criminal career approach three general orientations to crime control follow: prevention, career modification, and incapacitation (Piquero, Farrington, & Blumstein, 2003). Prevention policies aim at inhibiting participation and diminishing the number of nonoffenders becoming offenders. Career modification strategies, on the other hand, focus on already active offenders and aim to achieve changes in different career dimensions that are associated with reducing the costs of crime. Career modification strategies can, for example, target offending frequency or career duration, but can also focus on preventing novice offenders from developing toward committing more serious offenses. Finally, incapacitation seeks to reduce the number of offenses committed by an offender by effectively taking out a slice of his criminal career.

To illustrate the usefulness of the career approach with regard to policy issues, let us consider, as did the Panel (Blumstein et al., 1986), selective incapacitation. General or collective incapacitation strategies aim at reducing crime by increasing the total level of incarceration, either by increasing the number of offenders sentenced to incarceration, or by increasing the length of the average incarceration period (Spelman, 2000). General incapacitation strategies are largely insensitive to the fact that the frequency of offending among active criminals is most times heavily skewed with relatively few very active offenders accounting for a disproportionate share of the total number of crimes committed. Selective incapacitation policies, on the other hand, try to selectively target this group of frequent offenders in an effort to achieve the greatest possible crime reduction for the lowest possible costs (Stemen, 2007). Offending frequency is the criminal career dimension of essence in deciding which offenders to target, and the degree to which the benefits of selective incapacitation can be realized depends heavily on the ability to identify frequent offenders ahead of time and not only in hindsight.

Assuming stability in offending frequency over the course of the criminal career, the selection criterion for selective policies is usually based on the total number of crimes committed or the rate of offending offenders have evidenced in the recent past. The benefits of selective incapacitation – the number of crimes prevented by incarcerating that particular offender – are usually estimated by extrapolating the offender's criminal history into the period of incarceration (Spelman, 1994). However, to the extent that offending frequency is more erratic and that criminal careers are riddled with periods of intermittency, the benefits of selective incapacitation based on the stability thesis may be overestimated.

Furthermore, once certain offenders have been identified as targets of selective policies, knowledge of their criminal career duration is necessary to determine the length of the incapacitation period. If too short, selectively incarcerated offenders might resume their criminal career upon release. If too long, offenders might end up being incarcerated in years in which they, if out on the street, would not have committed any new offenses, greatly reducing the efficiency of the selective policy. Finally, levels of specialization among the selectively targeted group will influence the outcome of selective incapacitation in terms of the types of crimes for which rates are most likely to be reduced (Blokland & Nieuwbeerta, 2007).

Despite the Panel's focus on incapacitation, the criminal career approach, given that it is largely devoid of theory, does not beforehand favor one crime control strategy over the other. In fact, many criminal-career researchers have been very critical toward selective incapacitation. Insights gained from systematically studying the different criminal career dimensions can, however, equally benefit prevention and career modification strategies. In fact, there is no watershed between these strategies as most crime control efforts combine elements from these different general strategies. Increased periods of incarceration can, for instance, also be used to actively modify the criminal careers of those selectively incapacitated by, for example, providing treatment or vocational training. In sum, policy decisions on whom to target, when to target them, and for how long to target them, as well as estimates of the potential benefits of these policies, may be greatly improved by considering different criminal career dimensions.

Applying the Criminal Career Approach to Sex Offending

Career Dimensions in Sexual Offenders' Criminal Careers

Ever since the heydays of the Chicago school, sociological explanations of crime have occupied mainstream criminologists. While biological and psychological explanations have never been completely abandoned, in most current biological or psychological theories crime and delinquency are not considered "pathological" in the strict sense of the word. At least three factors have contributed to the popularity of sociological explanations of general crime. First, the sheer commonality of rule breaking makes it hard to maintain that crime and delinquency result from individual pathology. In fact, self-report studies have shown that among adolescents, delinquency is the norm rather than the exception (Elliott, Ageton, Huizinga, Knowles, & Canter, 1983). Second, it has long been recognized that crime is unequally distributed across age, with delinquency being most common among the young (Farrington, 1986). Again, if large numbers of young people who engage in delinquency and crime grow up to be law-abiding adults, theoretical explanations referring to individual pathology become harder to reconcile with the empirics of crime. Third, many forms of crime and delinquency, while perhaps conceived as morally wrong at some level, do not have serious consequences, which, together with crime being common, tends to limit the psychological distance between "them," the wrongdoers, and "us," the conformists. More so than sociological theories, biological and psychological theories allow us to consider criminals as different from ourselves. In proffering sociological explanations, criminologists have made it easier to conceive of crime as resulting from circumstances in which, even if only in theory, we could imagine ourselves being. Finally, policymakers see themselves confronted with questions on how to deal with large groups of offenders and even larger groups of potential offenders. Therefore they tend to focus on changing structural variables that apply to many people at once, rather than on individual risk factors. Consequently, many criminological theories focus on the convergence of contextual factors that produces criminal behavior, but often remain opaque on the precise individual mechanisms that translate these broader contextual factors into individual behavior.

More so than mainstream criminology, the sex offender literature has remained close to its biological and psychological roots. While plagued by – possibly huge – dark figures in official registrations (Ahlmeyer, Heil, McKee, & English, 2000; Marshall & Barbaree, 1990), sexual transgressions are still relatively uncommon compared to other types of crime. Furthermore, the severity of many sex offenses and the moral outrage that follows make it harder to identify with the perpetrator, resulting in explanations for sexual offending in terms of individual pathology being more easily accepted. (Quinn, Forsyth, & Mullen-Quinn, 2004). Lastly, clinicians assigned to treat sex offenders need to make one-on-one decisions based on detailed personal information on the perpetrator involved, rather than devise a more general policy. As a result, the most common explanations for sexual offending have focused on individual pathologies and early trauma. While sociological criminology has been criticized for neglecting the individual-level mechanisms via which sociological variables influence behavior, sex offender researchers can be said to have focused on individual factors at the cost of a broader view of sexual offending. The field of sexual offending has typically promoted theoretical views describing sex offending as the result of trait-like features (e.g., cognitive distortions, low victim empathy, deviant sexual preferences, poor attachment style, sexual regulation) that are not well suited for a longitudinal perspective aiming to describe and explain the development of sexual offending (e.g., Lussier & Healy, 2009). This raises questions such as: if cognitive distortions are responsible for the onset and persistence of sex offending, how can we explain desistance from sex offending? If low victim empathy is a precursor to sex offending, how can we explain that for some persistent offenders, offending will escalate in seriousness over time, but for others, it won't? The trait-like approach has limitations when one espouses a longitudinal perspective such as the criminal career approach.

These different frames of reference have also contributed to sex offender researchers emphasizing the differences, rather than searching for the commonalities between sexual and nonsexual offending. The study of participation in sex crimes, and the risk factors associated with it, has been largely independent of that of participation in nonsexual crimes. A telling example in this regard is the only "recent" discovery of juvenile sex offenders as a separate population of interest (Van Wijk, Van Horn, Bullens, Bijleveld, & Doreleijers, 2005). Beforehand, explanations of adult sex offending were deemed appropriate for juveniles under the implicit assumption that juvenile sex offenders would eventually grow up to become adult sex offenders; this despite juvenile delinquency being high on the research agenda of criminologists from the very start and in the face of evidence from mainstream criminology that most juvenile delinquents do not become adult criminals (Farrington, 2003). Recognizing that the causal processes that bring juvenile sex offenders to committing their crimes might be age graded and that desistance from sex offending with age is widespread, has opened the door to developmental theories explaining sexual offending that focus on context of adolescence and that allow for developmental trajectories other than the one going from bad to worse.

When considering the criminal careers of sexual offenders, every career feature gets an extra dimension. As recognized by Soothill and colleagues (Soothill, Francis, Sanderson, & Ackerley, 2000), for example, the question of whether offenders are general or specialized in their offending is more complicated if one considers sexual offenses to be a distinct group of offenses. Sex offenders can be either specialized or diverse in their offending in terms of their committing solely sex offenses or a mix of sexual and nonsexual offenses. However, sex offenders can also be specialized in the sense that they only commit one or a group of closely related sex offenses, for example, in terms of whether the offenses involve physical contact or not or in terms of the age or sex of the victims involved. This observation allows for the possibility that sex offenders are generalists in one sense and specialists in the other.

Linked to questions regarding specialization is the issue of escalation: do sexual offending careers tend to follow a "stepping stone" type of development in the sense that sexual offending starts with relatively minor hands-off transgressions and over the course of the offender's career escalates to more severe hands-on offenses with increasing levels of violence? Or do, for example, hands-off offenders rarely cross over to commit hands-on offenses? Again, as with specialization, the question of escalation may also pertain to general offending escalating from minor nonsexual offenses to more severe violent offenses, to severe forms of sexual violence.

These observations have clear theoretical and practical ramifications. If sex offenders are generalists in the sense that they tend to commit both sexual and nonsexual offenses, then the question becomes whether these two types of offending share a common cause, or whether they merely coincide. If sexual offending and nonsexual offending share a common cause, theories explaining sexual offending by referring to derailed sexual development seem to fall short of providing a satisfactory answer. For the therapist working in sex offender treatment programs, the need to consider the sex offender's whole criminal activity might be a futile exercise given that the goal of treatment is to prevent a sexual reoffense. However, if a sex crime is part of a versatile criminal trajectory, the exclusive focus of treatment on factors that are said to be specific to sex offending, as opposed to criminogenic needs that are causing the individual's offending, will not decrease the risk of sex offending. The same argument has been raised for risk assessment and the prediction of recidivism with sex offenders (Lussier & Cortoni, 2008).

However, if sex offenders are generalists in that they commit both sexual and nonsexual crimes, but are nevertheless specialists in terms of their sexual offending, theories that treat sexual offending like any other type of offending might need to be reconsidered to the extent that sexual preoccupations and not merely opportunity factors are at play. Furthermore, if some sexual offending careers tend to escalate, the question becomes whether we are able to predict with an acceptable degree of certainty in which cases this is most likely to happen. While in terms of prevention, much could be learned by studying those that refrain from taking their offending to the next level.

Finally, while a sizable literature addresses the influence of delinquent peers and co-offending among juvenile offenders, for a long time reports of group sex offenses have been limited to the popular media. Recent research, however, shows that group sex offending might be more common than was once believed (Bijleveld, Weerman, Looije, & Hendriks, 2007). To what extent explanations of co-offending derived from mainstream criminology also apply to group sex offending still requires further investigation.

To What Extent Can Life-Course Theories Explain Sex Offenders' Careers?

A contentious issue in life-course criminology is the question of to what extent between-individual differences in criminal careers result from pre-existing individual differences in terms of stable risk factors together constituting the individual's criminal propensity, and to what extent endogenous factors and important life-course transitions exert an independent influence on the individual's criminal trajectory (Hirschi & Gottfredson, 1995; Sampson & Laub, 1995). If the criminal careers of sexual offenders are best understood in terms of stable between-individual differences, this would speak directly to the relevance of the criminal career approach to studying sexual offending – which in that case would be limited. In fact, given that according to maturational theories crime develops similarly for all individuals, sex offending trajectories are expected to follow the general age-crime curve much like any other type of offense. Based on dynamic theories, however, variance in sexual offending trajectories is expected, with some offenders showing developmental patterns that contradict the aggregate age-crime curve. In as far as dynamic explanations apply to sexual offending, both change and continuity in sex offending over time may result from dynamic processes, which are open to outside influence. Combined with the criminal career notion that the causal mechanisms governing each career dimension might differ, dynamic theories urge researchers to study career dimensions of sexual offenders both separately and in tandem and to come up with explanations for not only participation in sex offending, but also the acceleration, escalation, and cessation of sex offending over the individual's life course.

Maturational and dynamic theories both assume that the same mechanism – or mechanisms – underlie the behavior of all offenders. In life-course criminology the distinction between general and typological theories refers to the need to entertain different etiological theories for explaining criminal careers that show distinct features, like an early onset, a high offending frequency, and a long duration (Paternoster et al., 1997). When applied to sexual offending, however, the general/typological distinction can apply to many more plausible divisions between criminal careers, rapidly complicating the theoretical picture.

The most important theoretical question that needs to be answered is whether sex offenders should be regarded as similar or different from nonsexual offenders in terms of the etiology of their offending behavior. If sexual offending is different from nonsexual offending, different theories emphasizing different causal mechanisms might be needed to explain the development of each. Conceptually, development in each trajectory should than be studied separately, each with its own risk factors, while, to the extent development in sexual offending is considered dynamic, allowing transitions in each trajectory to influence development in the other. If, on the other hand, sexual offending is considered as an integral part of a general offending repertoire, than sexual and nonsexual offending are expected to have similar risk factors, and questions of, for example, specialization and escalation of offending would include sex offending together with nonsex offending in the same metric. To complicate things further, one could even ask whether different types of sexual offenses should be considered as stemming from different causal processes and thus best be considered as constituting different developmental pathways. Again this would call for conceptualizing development – participation, frequency, duration – in each of these offense types separately while again allowing interdependence between developments in these different trajectories. In terms of career features, the question of whether different offender types exist could be asked for sexual and for nonsexual offenses separately, or for both combined. In case of the former, researchers might seek to distinguish adolescence-limited from persistent sex offenders, while in the latter the question would be to what extent sexual offending (or which type of sexual offending) is characteristic of a certain overall offending trajectory.

How Can the Criminal Career Approach Inform Policy Decisions Regarding Sex Offenders?

Current policy decisions have been focused on one dimension of the criminal career, that is, persistence. Recent legal and penal dispositions have all pursued the same goal of reducing the risk of sexual reoffending, whether through rehabilitation, deterrent, or neutralization efforts. While policy development has been focused on the "sexual recidivists," other equally important aspects have been neglected. Indeed, this approach does not tackle sexual violence issues such as its prevalence in society or among certain subgroups of the population (i.e., participation), its origins (onset), its volume (individual frequency rate), or its seriousness or termination (desistance). Raising these points is important because it helps to put into perspective the broader issue of sexual violence and its prevention. For example, if prevalence is more important that sexual recidivism, then prevention efforts aimed directly at the general population or the at-risk population might prevent not only sex offending per se, but also sexual recidivism by preventing the onset of sexual criminal careers.

Studying the criminal careers of sex offenders will benefit prevention efforts by explicating the link between sexual and nonsexual offending. If sexual offending and nonsexual offending spring from a common set of risk factors, efforts aimed at preventing general crime among those most likely to be exposed to these risk factors are able to avert nonsexual as well as sexual offending. To the extent, however, that sexual offending trajectories are disconnected from developmental pathways in common crimes, special prevention efforts may be needed to prevent individuals from participating in sexual crimes.

Knowledge on criminal career features, such as escalation, may also benefit decisions about which populations to target to most efficiently prevent certain types of sexual crimes. Criminal career research may, for example, show that violent offenders are more likely to escalate toward rape than are hands-off sex offenders, thus providing guidance as to where rape prevention efforts should best be targeted.

Maturational and typological theories herald early prevention efforts, as prevention is only effective before the tendency to sexually offend is manifest. Dynamic theories in turn recognize that the mechanisms that cause sexual offending may be age-graded and that prevention efforts aimed at different age groups may require a different focus. The answer to the question of whether sexual offending is best explained by maturational or dynamic theories is directly relevant for our efforts to modify sex offenders' criminal careers at different ages and in different career stages.

According to maturational theories, successful efforts – if any – to modify criminal career development are to nip deviant behavioral tendencies in the bud and focus on the very early stages of criminal development, before the tendency to sexually offend becomes sufficiently ingrained in the individual's behavioral repertoire as to withstand any outside influence. Dynamic theories, on the contrary, allow for a greater window of opportunity, and remain positive about possibilities for change even among older sex offenders.

Furthermore, while current interventions aimed at sexual offenders focus mainly on internal factors, like impulse control, sociosexual cognitions, and emotion management, in as far sexual and nonsexual offending are governed by the same causal factors, interventions aimed at sexual offenders could benefit from insights gained from mainstream developmental criminology and also focus on external factors, like increasing the level of social control in the lives of sex offenders.

Maturational theories also speak on incapacitation. On the one hand, maturational theories uphold that those at elevated risk of sexual offending at one point remain at elevated risk throughout their entire life span. While this seems to call for selectively incapacitating those at elevated risk, many maturational theorists have not championed selective incarceration on the grounds that by the time we are able to distinguish the high-risk from the low-risk individuals, the age effect kicks in and the risk of (re)offending starts to decline for everyone (Gottfredson & Hirschi, 1986). Given the decline in offending with age, long prison sentences, even when selectively imposed on those presenting the highest risk, will thus yield increasingly lower gains in terms of the number of offenses diverted.

Dynamic theories also do not favor selective incapacitation and emphasize that while in hindsight there are those that follow a persistent trajectory, it is very difficult to predict beforehand which individuals will follow such a trajectory (Laub & Sampson, 2003). According to dynamic theories, accurate prediction is even principally impossible, as each individual's criminal trajectory is partly shaped by random outside influences. These same outside influences add uncertainty to the benefits of selective incapacitation once applied. While free those incapacitated might have experienced transitions and events that could have curbed their criminal trajectories for the better – or the worse – decreasing – or increasing – the benefits of long-term incapacitation.

Typological theories seem most friendly to the idea of long-term incapacitation selectively imposed on those following a persistent trajectory. While intervening can never be too early, it can, according to the typological point of view, be too late, in the sense that once sexual offending becomes ingrained in the individual's behavioral repertoire these behaviors will resist modification. In fact, depending on the extent to which age has an effect on the criminal trajectory of offenders of the persistent type, the only suitable measure to protect the general public from future offending would seem to entail imprisoning these persistent offenders for life. Given that the empirical evidence on sex offenders' criminal careers needed to test these theories is spotted at best, policies that built on these theoretical insights are still founded on shifting sands, leaving much uncertainty about the effectiveness of these policies to prevent sexual offenders from causing harm and the efficiency by which this goal is reached.

References

Ahlmeyer, S., Heil, P., McKee, B., & English, K. (2000). The impact of polygraphy on admissions of victims and offenses in adult sexual offenders. *Sexual Abuse: A Journal of Research and Treatment, 12 (2)*, 123–138.

Bijleveld, C., Weerman, F. M., Looije, D., & Hendriks, J. (2007). Group sex offending by juveniles: Coercive sex as a group activity. *European Journal of Criminology, 4*, 5–31.

Block, R., Blokland, A., Van der Werff, N., Van Os, R., & Nieuwbeerta, P. (2010). Long-term patterns of offending in women. *Feminist Criminology, 5*, 73–107.

Blokland, A., & Nieuwbeerta, P. (2007). Selectively incapacitating frequent offenders: Costs and benefits of various penal scenarios. *Journal of Quantitative Criminology, 23*(4), 327–354.

Blumstein, A., Cohen, J., & Farrington, D. P. (1988). Criminal career research; its value for criminology. *Criminology, 26*, 1–35.

Blumstein, A., Cohen, J., Roth, J. D., and Visher, C. A. (1986). *Criminal careers and "career criminals": Vol 1. Report of the Panel on Criminal Careers.* Washington, DC: National Research Council, National Academy Press.

Chaiken, J. M., & Chaiken, M. R. (1982). *Varieties of criminal behavior.* Santa Monica, CA: Rand.

Elliott, D. S., Ageton, S. S., Huizinga, B. A., Knowles, B. A., & Canter, R. J. (1983). *The prevalence and incidence of delinquent behavior: 1976–1980.* Boulder, CO: Behavioral Research Institute.

Farrington, D. P. (1986). Age and crime. *Crime and Justice: A Review of Research, 7*, 189–250.

Farrington, D. P. (1992). Criminal career research in the United Kingdom. *British Journal of Criminology, 32*, 521–536.

Farrington, D. P. (2003). Developmental and life-course criminology; key theoretical and empirical issues. The 2002 Sutherland Address. *Criminology, 41*, 221–256.

Farrington, D. P., Lambert, S., & West, D. J. (1998). Criminal careers of two generations of family members in the Cambridge Study in Delinquent Development. *Studies on Crime and Crime Prevention, 7*, 85–106.

Gottfredson, M., & Hirschi, T. (1986). The true value of lambda would appear to be zero: An essay on career criminals, criminal careers, selective incapacitation, cohort studies, and related topics. *Criminology, 24*, 213–234.

Gottfredson, M., & Hirschi, T. (1987). The methodological adequacy of longitudinal research on crime. *Criminology*, 581–614.

Gottfredson, M., & Hirschi, T. (1990). *A general theory of crime.* Stanford, CA: Stanford University Press.

Hirschi, T., & Gottfredson, M. (1983). Age and the explanation of crime. *American Journal of Sociology, 89*, 552–584.

Hirschi, T., & Gottfredson, M. (1995). Control theory and the life-course perspective. *Studies on Crime and Crime Prevention, 4*, 131–142.

Laub, J. H., & Sampson, R. J. (2001). Understanding desistance from crime. *Crime and Justice: A Review of Research, 28*, 1–69.

Laub, J. H., & Sampson, R. J. (2003). *Shared beginnings divergent lives: Delinquent boys to age 70*. Cambridge, MA: Harvard University Press.

LeBlanc, M. (1996). Changing patterns in the perpetration of offenses over time: Trajectories from early adolescence to the early 30s. *Crime and Justice: A Review of Research, 23*, 115–198.

LeBlanc, M., & Fréchette, M. (1989). *Male criminal activity from childhood through youth*. New York, NY: Springer Verlag.

LeBlanc, M., & Loeber, R. (1998) Developmental criminology updated. *Crime and Justice: A Review of Research, 23*, 115–197.

Levenson, J. S., Brannon, Y. N., Fortney, T., & Baker, J. (2007). Public perceptions about sex offenders and community protection policies. *Analyses of Social Issues and Public Policy, 7*, 1–25.

Loeber, R. & LeBlanc, M. (1990). Towards a developmental criminology. *Crime and Justice: A Review of Research, 12*, 375–473.

Lussier, P., & Cortoni, F. (2008). The development of antisocial behavior and sexual aggression: Theoretical, empirical, and clinical implications. In B. K. Schwartz (Ed.), *The sex offender: Offender evaluation and program strategies, Vol. 6* (pp. 2/1 - 2–26). Kingston, NJ: Civic Research Institute.

Lussier, P., & Healey, J. (2009). Rediscovering Quetelet, again: The "aging" offender and the prediction of reoffending in a sample of adult sex offenders. *Justice Quarterly, 28*, 1–30.

Marshall, W. L., & Barbaree, H. E. (1990). Outcomes of comprehensive cognitive-behavioral treatment programs. In W. L. Marshall, R. D. Laws, & H. E. Barbaree (Eds.), *Handbook of sexual assault: Issues, theories, and treatment of the offender* (pp. 363–385). New York: Plenum.

McCord, J., & Conway, K. (2002). Patterns of juvenile offending and co-offending. In E. Waring & D. Weisburd (Eds.), *Crime and social disorganization: Advances in criminological theory, Vol. 10* (pp. 15–30). New Brunswick, NJ: Transaction.

Moffitt, T. E. (1993). Life-course-persistent and adolescence-limited antisocial behavior: A developmental taxonomy. *Psychological Review, 100*, 674–701.

Moffitt, T. E. (1994). Natural histories of delinquency. In E. G. M. Weitekamp & H-J. Kerner (Eds.) *Cross-national longitudinal research on development and criminal behavior* (pp. 3–61). Dordrecht: Kluwer.

Moffitt, T. E. (1997). Adolescence-limited and life-course-persistent offending: A complementary pair of developmental theories. In T. P Thornberry (Ed.), *Developmental theories of crime and delinquency* (pp. 11–54). New Brunswick, NJ: Transaction.

Moffitt, T. E. (2006). Life-course-persistent versus adolescence-limited antisocial behavior. In D. Cicchetti & D. J. Cohen (Eds.) *Developmental psychopathology: Vol. 3. Risk, disorder, and adaption* (pp. 570–598). Hoboken, NJ: John Wiley & Sons, Inc.

Nieuwbeerta, P., Blokland, A., Piquero, A., & Sweeten, G. (2011). A life-course analysis of offense specialization: Introducing a new method for studying individual specialization over the life course. *Crime and Delinquency, 57*(1), 3–28.

Paternoster, R., Brame, R., Piquero, A., Mazerolle, P., & Dean, C. W. (1998). The forward specialization coefficient: Distributional properties and subgroup differences. *Journal of Quantitative Criminology, 14*, 133–154.

Paternoster, R., Dean, C. W., Piquero, A., Mazerolle, P., & Brame, R. (1997). Generality, continuity and change in offending. *Journal of Quantitative Criminology, 13*, 231–266.

Peterson, M. A., & Braiker, H. B. (1980). *Doing crime: A survey of California inmates*. Santa Monica, CA: Rand.

Piquero, A. R. (2004). Somewhere between persistence and desistance: The intermittency of criminal careers. In S. Maruna & R. Immarigeon (Eds.), *After crime and punishment: Pathways to offender reintegration* (pp. 102–128). Devon, UK: Willan Publishing.

Piquero, A. R. (2007). Taking stock of developmental trajectories of criminal activity over the life course. In A. M. Liberman (Ed.), *The long view of crime* (pp. 23–78). New York: Springer Verlag.

Piquero, A. R., Farrington, D. P., & Blumstein, A. (2003). The criminal career paradigm. *Crime and Justice: A Review of Research, 30*, 359–506.

Quinn, J. F., Forsyth, C. J., & Mullen-Quinn, C. (2004). Societal reactions to sex offenders: A review of the origins and results of the myths surrounding their crimes and treatment amenability. *Deviant Behavior, 25*, 215–232.

Sampson, R. J., & Laub, J. H. (1990). Crime and deviance over the life course. The salience of adult social bonds. *American Sociological Review, 55*, 609–627.

Sampson, R. J., & Laub, J. H. (1993). *Crime in the making: Pathways and turning points through life*. Cambridge, MA: Harvard University Press.

Sampson, R. J., & Laub, J. H. (1995). Understanding variability in lives through time: Contribution of life-course criminology. *Studies on Crime and Crime Prevention, 4*, 143–158.

Sampson, R. J., & Laub, J. H. (1997). A life-course theory of cumulative disadvantage. In T. P. Thornberry (Ed.), *Developmental theories of crime and delinquency* (pp. 133–161). New Brunswick, NJ: Transaction.

Soothill, K., Francis, B., Sanderson, B., & Ackerley, E. (2000). Sex offenders: Specialists, generalists, or both? A 32-year criminological study. *British Journal of Criminology, 40*, 56–67.

Spelman, W. (1994). *Criminal incapacitation*. New York: Plenum Press.

Spelman, W. (2000). The limited importance of prison expansion. In A. Blumstein & J. Wallman (Eds.), *The crime drop in America* (pp. 97–129). Cambridge, UK: Cambridge University Press.

Stattin, H., Magnusson, D., & Reichel, H. (1989). Criminal activity at different ages: A study based on a Swedish longitudinal research population. *British Journal of Criminology, 29*, 368–385.

Stemen, D. (2007). *Reconsidering incarceration: New directions in reducing crime*. New York: Vera Institute of Justice.

Tracy, P. E., & Kempf-Leonard, K. (1996). *Continuity and discontinuity in criminal careers*. New York, NY: Plenum.

Van Koppen, V., De Poot, C., & Blokland, A. (2010). Comparing criminal careers of organized crime offenders and general offenders. *European Journal of Criminology, 7*, 356–374.

Van Wijk, A., Van Horn, J., Bullens, R., Bijleveld, C., & Doreleijers, T. (2005). Juvenile sex offenders: A group on its own? *Journal of Offender Therapy and Comparative Criminology, 49*, 25–36.

Wolfgang, M. E., Figlio, R. M., & Sellin, T. (1972). *Delinquency in a birth cohort*. Chicago, IL: University of Chicago Press.

Zimring, F. E. (2004). *An American travesty: Legal responses to adolescent sexual offending*. Chicago, IL: University of Chicago Press.

2

Criminal Career Features in Theories of Sexual Offending

Jo Thakker
University of Waikato, New Zealand

Tony Ward
Victoria University of Wellington, New Zealand

Introduction

Over the last three decades there has been a growing interest in understanding the factors that lead individuals to commit sexual offenses and there have been a number of important theoretical developments in the area of sexual offending. While some researchers have focused on the identification of specific causal variables, such as attachment (Marshall & Marshall, 2010) or negative affect (for instance, McCoy & Fremouw, 2010), others have presented multifactorial models which integrate a number of causal factors (for example, Ward & Beech, 2006). However, a review of the literature in this area indicates that while many theoreticians have considered the factors that lead to sexual offending in general, few have focused on the criminal career or life span features. Such features are important as they provide a different perspective of sexual offending; a perspective that has not been prominent in the sexual offending literature.

This chapter, which serves as a theoretical platform for the rest of this book, examines theories of sexual offending and considers their implications for various criminal career parameters. This approach is considered to be the only approach possible, given that there is very little literature available on this particular topic. Thus, to a large extent, the ideas expressed are speculative and hypothetical. Given the amount of research that has been published in the area of theories of sexual offending, only multifactorial models are included in the discussion. Thus, single factors such as attachment (e.g., Marshall, 2010) that have been shown to be significant are not explicitly covered herein, although they may be alluded to within discussions of the multifactorial models. The chapter begins with listing the criminal career parameters

Sex Offenders: A Criminal Career Approach, First Edition. Edited by Arjan Blokland and Patrick Lussier.

that are included in this discussion. It then examines a number of theories of sexual offending and considers to what extent they shed light on the parameters.

Criminal Career Parameters

The criminal careers approach to the analysis of criminal behavior, as more comprehensively reviewed in the opening chapter of this volume (Blokland & Lussier, this volume), was developed by Blumstein and others (e.g., Blumstein, Cohen, Roth, & Visher, 1986; Blumstein & Cohen, 1987) in the 1980s. As stated by Farrington (1992), "It is not a criminological theory but a framework within which theories can be proposed and tested" (p. 521). As the name suggests, the approach is focused on the characteristics of an offender's career rather than specific instances of offending. For example, a researcher may be interested in the mean age of onset for burglary offenses or the prevalence of violent offending in a specific population. In their discussion of the criminal career paradigm Piquero, Farrington, and Blumstein (2003) include the parameters of prevalence, frequency, specialization, and desistance. It seems that these four are the parameters most commonly referred to in the literature; however, Farrington (1992, 2003) included three more in his discussion, namely, onset, career duration, and continuity. These seven parameters will be considered in relation to each of the theories that are covered in this chapter.

Theories of Sexual Offending

Most theoreticians now agree that sexual offending results from a complex interaction of a range of causal variables. These variables range from more remote influences, such as genetic predisposition (e.g., Siegert & Ward, 2003) and early life experience (e.g., Marshall, 2010), to more proximal causal factors, such as substance abuse (Hanson & Harris, 2000). Obviously, it is not possible within the confines of this chapter to provide a comprehensive overview and analysis of the literature. Therefore five of the most influential theoretical approaches from the last 30 years will be examined, namely: Finkelhor's (1984) Precondition Model of child sexual abuse, Marshall and Barbaree's (1990) Integrated Theory, Hall and Hirschman's (1991) Quadripartite Model, Knight and Sims-Knight's (2004) Three Paths Model, and Ward and Beech's (2008) Integrated Theory. Note that the models are presented in chronological order.

Theories of Child Sexual Offending

Finkelhor's Precondition Model

Finkelhor (1984) suggested that child sexual offenders have four primary psychological problems: emotional congruence, sexual arousal, blockage, and disinhibition. *Emotional congruence* refers to the proposition that individuals who sexually offend against children have difficulties connecting with adults on an emotional level and therefore attempt to meet their emotional needs by associating with children. The *sexual arousal* component of the model is self-explanatory and simply refers to the idea that sexual offending against children is driven, to some extent, by the presence of sexual arousal. The concept of *blockage* encapsulates the suggestion that there are often psychological problems which interfere with child sex offenders' abilities to meet their emotional and sexual needs through normal interaction with other adults. Lastly, Finkelhor suggests that child sexual offending also involves some degree of *disinhibition*, which is conceptualized as reflecting a range of difficulties, such as poor impulse control or substance abuse. Finkelhor dubbed this the Precondition Model because the four components are viewed as being necessary conditions for the commission of a child sexual offense.

Finkelhor's model is one of the earliest multifactorial models of child sexual abuse (Seto, 2008) and since its inception in the mid-1980s it has been widely discussed and critiqued. Ward and Hudson (2001) noted that Finkelhor's theory has a number of strengths. For example, they point out that it provided a conceptual framework for research in the field and that it was one of the first theories to bring together a number of distinct causes within a comprehensive, integrated theory of child sexual abuse. An advantage of a possessing such a comprehensive theory was that clinicians were provided with explicit and theoretically justified treatment targets. However, Ward and colleagues (Ward & Hudson, 2001; Ward & Siegert, 2002) also identified a range of weaknesses within the model. For instance, they argue that it pays undue attention to proximal factors and insufficient attention to more remote causal factors such as early development. Ward and others also assert that Finkelhor's model fails to explain why nonsexual problems such as emotional congruence and blockage lead to inappropriate sexual behavior.

Another problem with Finkelhor's model is its inflexibility. Finkelhor proposes that all four of the aforementioned conditions must be present in order for a child sexual offense to occur. However, this assumes a high degree of homogeneity among child sexual offenders and this does not seem to be consistent with the literature. For instance, although deviant sexual arousal is probably present in a significant proportion of cases, one can imagine situations in which it might not be part of the causal picture. For example, a man might have a preference for an adult woman but might target a young female in certain situations, such as, when an adult female is not available, or when he is under the influence of a substance which impairs his judgement. Furthermore, some men who sexually offend against children are in stable intimate relationships with adults at the time of the offending.

Marshall and Barbaree's Integrated Theory

Marshall and Barbaree (1990) proposed that sexual offending against children has its origins in a range of interacting factors, including early developmental variables and more immediate situational variables. The developmental factors that Marshall and Barbaree identify as being important include problematic parenting (especially, harsh disciplinary methods) and exposure to physical and/or sexual abuse often resulting in insecure attachment. The concept of attachment used by Marshall and Barbaree, which has its origins in the work of Bowlby (1988) and Ainsworth and Bell (1970), refers to the nature of the bond between child and caregiver. According to attachment theory, when a child has a strong and positive bond with his or her caregiver he or she is said to be securely attached. In contrast, there are various types of insecure attachment which arise when there are problems with the bonding process. Note that this concept of attachment is very different from the concept that is used within the criminology literature which ordinarily refers to bonding with social institutions.

Marshall and colleague suggest that these sorts of unpleasant early life experiences can lead to problems with self-regulation and difficulties in negotiating complex social situations. It is theorized that subsequently, during adolescent years, when the individual is experiencing considerable physical (and especially hormonal) changes, sexual experiences and sexually charged emotions combine with the individual's antisocial tendencies leading to inappropriate sexual arousal. Further, it is suggested that a connection is formed between sex and aggression, in part, because they share the same neural pathways.

Marshall and Barbaree propose that later, during early adulthood, the individual's psychological problems (in particular, insecure attachment and limited social skills) lead to difficulties with social interaction and these, in turn, increase the likelihood that the individual will have negative experiences in social settings. Subsequently, the negative experiences, which are typically associated with a range of negative emotions, lead the person to seek sexual gratification and intimacy in inappropriate ways. One of the most important aspects of this model is that adolescence is seen as a critical stage in which development can deviate from its normal trajectory due to the presence of a number of vulnerability factors.

Marshall and Barbaree's model acknowledges the importance of contextual variables in the etiology of sexual offending. For example, factors such as stress and substance use are seen as contributing to the likelihood that an offense will occur via an increase in disinhibition and by impairing an individual's ability to cope. They also state that the presence of a potential victim (which may lead to sexual arousal) could increase the likelihood that an offense will occur. Furthermore, Marshall and colleague examine the role of maintaining factors in child sexual offending and hypothesize that the feelings of sexual gratification that arise from the offending serve as positive reinforcers, thereby making reoffending more likely.

One of the strengths of this theoretical approach is that it includes a detailed examination of early vulnerability factors and considers how these might play out during the adolescent and early adult years. Also, it takes a broad and inclusive approach insofar as it incorporates a range of psychological factors. However, as observed by Ward and Siegert (2002), the model has a number of shortcomings. One problem is that it conceptualizes aggression as playing a key role in the etiology of sexual offending. However, while evidence suggests that aggression is involved in rape, it is not generally considered to play a prominent role in child sexual offending. Further, while the model does a good job of explaining the appearance of sexual offending during adolescence and early adulthood it is less useful in explaining the emergence of sexual offending during adulthood. Ward and Siegert also point out that Marshall and Barbaree's theory overemphasizes the role of disinhibition and in doing so overlooks the importance of alternative offense pathways.

Theories of Adult Sexual Offending

Hall and Hirschman's Quadripartite Model

Unlike the three aforementioned theories, Hall and Hirschman's Quadripartite Model (Hall & Hirschman, 1991) sought to identify the causal factors associated with sexual offending against women. As indicated by the name of the model, Hall and colleague propose that sexual aggression is associated with four "motivational precursors," namely: offense-related sexual arousal, pro-rape cognitions, affective dyscontrol, and "developmentally related personality problems." In discussing the role of sexual arousal in the commission of rape, Hall and Hirschman hypothesize that, "Similar physiological processes may underlie sexual arousal that results in appropriate sexual behaviour as well as sexual arousal that results in sexual aggression" (p. 664). In other words, they make the point that the sexual arousal that is involved in aggressive sexual behavior is not necessarily deviant. In explaining this issue, they refer to research which has shown that sexual arousal to "rape stimuli" is found both in men who commit rape and those who do not (e.g., Malamuth, Check, & Briere, 1986). Thus, these sorts of fantasies are not necessarily indicative of sexual deviance in the way that the fantasies associated with child sexual offending would be. Hall and colleague suggest, therefore, that sexual arousal is necessary but not sufficient for sexual aggression to occur.

Moving on to the cognitive aspect of the model, Hall and Hirschman propose that when an individual experiences sexual arousal he appraises it in terms of its goal relevance, thereby influencing the likelihood that an offense will occur if his judgement confirms its value as a means of achieving a particular goal. In appraising the arousal the man draws on attitudes and beliefs that pertain to the situation, such as rape myths and negative perceptions about women. Moreover, Hall and Hirschman theorize that the individual might also consider the likelihood that an offense will be detected in his appraisal of the situation.

The third factor in the model, affective dyscontrol, refers to the presence of "negative affective states" which the individual is unable to manage in an effective, prosocial manner. In particular, Hall and Hirschman mention anger and hostility, which they state are especially important in rape offenses, compared to sexual offending against children, where depression may be a more prominent emotional feature. In explaining this variable, Hall and colleague state that "... sexually aggressive behaviour occurs when these affective states become so compelling and powerful that they overcome inhibitions" (p. 664).

Developmentally related personality problems, which is the fourth variable in the model, refers to the presence of antisocial traits which Hall and Hirschman propose is related to problematic early life experiences. For example, they state that rapists have often been victims of abuse and neglect, that they often display low levels of educational achievement, and that they frequently exhibit a history of diverse criminal behavior. In discussing the presence of antisocial personality traits, Hall and Hirschman refer to traits such as selfishness, remorselessness, and exploitation of others, which are indicative of psychopathy. Hall and Hirschman assert that along with the above-mentioned psychological or internal causal factors, environmental variables play an important role in determining whether an offense is more or less likely to occur. For example, they state that alcohol use may increase the likelihood of offending while lack of victim availability will decrease it. In clarifying this aspect of their approach they state, "Rather than composing a separate psychological component for explaining sexually aggressive behaviour, environmental contingencies seem to place constraints on a person primed for sexual aggression ..." (p. 665).

In explicating their model, Hall and Hirschman hypothesize that the extent to which each of these four variables predominates is likely to differ across individuals and that this difference may be used to categorize men into various subtypes. Thus, for some offenders, general antisociality may be a prominent causal factor while for others sexual arousal may be especially influential. In this way, Hall and Hirschman's model is quite flexible; although it delineates a number of factors that may lead to sexual aggression, it also allows for variation in the extent to which these factors are present within individuals. This is considered to be an important strength of the model. Another positive feature of the model is the inclusion of environmental variables; in particular, the role of alcohol, which is well known to be associated with aggressive behavior. One could argue that one weakness of Hall and Hirschman's Quadripartite Model is the lack of clarity in regard to the personality aspect of the model. Two questions may be generated in this regard: (1) Do early life experiences always exert their influence on the individual via personality? (2) Can personality problems be present even if there are no problematic early life experiences? This particular aspect of the model seems less clear than the other three components.

Knight and Knight's Three Paths Model

Knight and Sims-Knight's (2004) Three Paths Model is unique among the theoretical approaches that are discussed herein in that it focuses on *pathways* to offending rather than looking only at specific factors. In other words, it is concerned with the trajectory of developmental factors and how these unfold over time, rather than simply identifying the various factors that may play a role. While the model includes a number of factors, these can be arranged in various ways, thereby forming the three different pathways. According to the model, abuse experiences during childhood combined with particular personality characteristics lead to the development of "three latent traits" which contribute to sexual offending against adult females.

These traits are "… (a) arrogant, deceitful personality/emotional detachment, (b) impulsivity/antisocial behaviours, and (c) sexual preoccupation/hypersexuality." Broadly speaking, the first and second of these traits correspond with Factors 1 and 2 (respectively) of Hare's (2003) approach to construing psychopathy. As explained by Benning and colleagues (Benning, Patrick, Hicks, Blonigen, & Krueger, 2003), Factor 1 encompasses "emotional-interpersonal tendencies" and includes characteristics such as superficial charm, deceit, and grandiosity, while Factor 2 encompasses more general antisociality and includes characteristics such as criminal behavior, aggression, and lack of responsibility.

The first pathway in Knight and Sims-Knight's model starts out from physical and/or verbal abuse, tracks through antisocial behavior and/or aggression and leads on to sexual offending. The second pathway leads out from physical and/or verbal abuse, tracks through Factor 1 and then culminates in sexual offending. The third pathway leads out from sexual abuse, tracks through sexual fantasy followed by aggressive sexual fantasy and then leads on to a sexual offense. Knight and Sims-Knight tested the utility of the model on two groups of sexual offenders – adults and juveniles (with a mean age of 15.97 years) – and a group of community controls. They concluded that "The three-path model … not only provided a good fit for the data used to predict sexual coercion in both adult sexual offender and community samples but … also predicted sexual coercion among juvenile sexual offenders" (p. 49).

As noted by Knight and colleague, this model provides a sound theoretical foundation for further exploration of the variables that contribute to sexual offending. Furthermore, the identification of developmental factors is useful in providing preventive interventions to individuals who may be at risk of offending and in the provision of proper treatment. However, as also noted by the researchers, there are likely to be other developmental factors that also play important roles in the development of offending behavior. Moreover, there are obviously other proximal/situational variables that contribute to sexual offending, such as the experience of stress or the availability of potential victims.

A Theory of General Sexual Offending

Ward and Beech's (2008) Integrated Theory differs from the aforementioned theories in that it attempts to explain both child and adult sexual offending. The integrated theory (depicted in Figure 2.1), which is referred to by Ward and Beech as "a network of causal factors," suggests that three clusters of variables converge in the manifestation of a sexual offense. These variables are: *biological factors* (such as genetic predisposition and brain development), *ecological niche factors* (such as sociocultural environment and personal situation), and *neuropsychological factors* (such as emotion, motivation, and memory). In explicating their model, Ward and Beech propose that biological factors and ecological niche factors lead to changes in neuropsychological factors which, in turn, lead to clinical symptoms (also referred

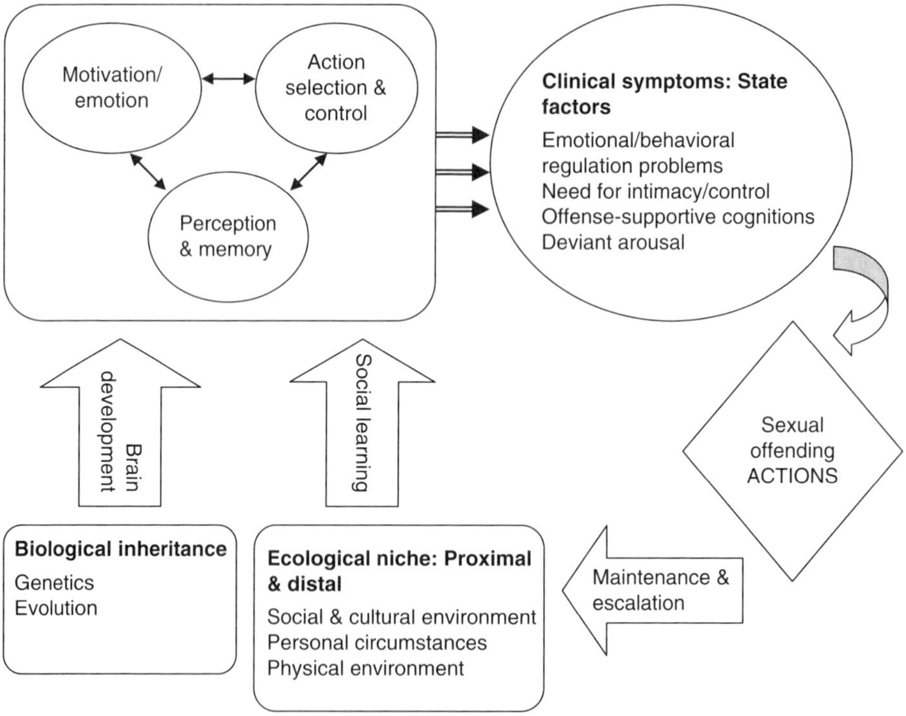

Figure 2.1 Ward and Beech's integrative theory of sexual offending. Adapted from Ward and Beech, 2008.

to as state factors). These symptoms, which include variables such as problems with emotional regulation and offense-related sexual arousal, then contribute to the commission of a sexual offense.

One particularly important aspect of this theory, which sets it apart from others (other than that of Marshall and Barbaree), is that it attempts to explain not just the initial appearance of sexually deviant behavior, but also the continuation of sexual offending over time. Specifically, Ward and colleague suggest that the offense itself and the associated clinical and ecological niche factors comprise part of a "positive feedback loop." In this way, factors that are associated with the sexual offense are construed as maintaining, and perhaps even strengthening, the problematic sexual behavior. In summing up their theoretical approach, Ward and Beech state, "… in our theory brain development (influenced by biological inheritance and genetics) and social learning interact to establish an individual's level of psychological functioning" (p. 23).

One of the strong points of Ward and Beech's model is its scope; it encompasses a wide range of diverse variables, including genetic variables and personal situational factors. Also, it attempts to explain the factors that both initiate and perpetuate sexual offending behavior. The model also allows for a variety of pathways to sexual offending thereby acknowledging that sexual offenders are not a homogeneous group. For example, while some offenders may follow a pathway that begins with exposure to sexual abuse and leads to deviant sexual arousal, others may begin with a genetic predisposition for a particular emotional style (or temperament) which may contribute to emotional problems in later life.

Implications for Criminal Career Parameters

This section explores the implications of each of these theories for each of the parameters. Note that not all of the theories are relevant to all of the parameters; rather some have specific implications and some have none. Also, it appears that generally the aforementioned theories do not neatly map onto the criminal career parameters, thus what follows is a discussion of the possible ways in which the theories may be interpreted according to the parameters. Therefore, it is possible that there are other implications for the parameters which have not been explored. Furthermore, it is equally possible that the authors of the various theories mentioned might argue that their theories have been overinterpreted or misconstrued. Given that this chapter appears to be breaking new ground in bringing together the literatures on sexual offending theory and criminal careers, such weaknesses are probably unavoidable.

Onset

The parameter of onset refers to the first instance of sexual offending. In terms of onset, according to Finkelhor all four of the conditions must be present before child sexual offending can occur, each preparing the etiological ground for the following causal factor. Similarly, Marshall and Barbaree's Integrative Model suggests that sexual offending begins when individuals, who have had certain problematic experiences during their development, are exposed to particular situations. However, according to Marshall and Barbaree, adolescence is a particularly important developmental period, insofar as the physical and psychological changes that take place at this time culminate in a high level of vulnerability for violence. Thus, according to this model, the onset of sexual aggression is probably more likely to occur during adolescence than at any other time, especially in vulnerable individuals.

Hall and Hirschman's theory also emphasizes the importance of problematic development in rape as well as offense-related beliefs. However, importantly, in terms of onset, they also talk about more proximal factors such as affective dyscontrol and offense-related sexual arousal. These latter two factors suggest that the onset of the offending is more probable if the individual is sexually aroused (e.g., if a victim is present) and if he is experiencing unusually high levels of stress, which are likely to tax his ability to cope. Knight and Sims-Knight's pathway model of sexual aggression does not seem to have any specific implications for onset. However, it asserts that there are three different routes by which an individual can arrive at the offense. In other words, onset may arise out of one of three patterns of developmental processes.

According to Ward and Beech, sexual offending starts when biological and ecological (social learning) factors lead to changes in neuropsychological functioning. Then, in turn, these changes lead to the emergence of a number of clinical symptoms – such as self-regulation problems, problematic sexual arousal, and offense-related cognitions – which lead to a sexual offense. Thus, with regard to onset, the model proposes that offending occurs when a range of clinical symptoms are present. These symptoms could probably occur at any time; however, one can theorize that they would be more likely to emerge in times of stress. For example, an individual may have ongoing difficulties with self-regulation; however, this will only become a problem when the man's ability to regulate his emotions is tested.

One particularly important issue in terms of onset is whether the theories described herein apply equally to both juvenile and adult sexual offenders. As mentioned above, Knight and Sims-Knight tested their model on both juvenile and adult sexual offenders and found that it was applicable to both groups. Also mentioned above is Marshall and Barbaree's reference to adolescence as a particularly important period in the development of problematic sexual behavior. However, Marshall and Barbaree do not directly discuss how applicable their theory might be to juvenile-onset versus adult-onset sexual offending. Furthermore, the other theories described in this chapter also make no specific mention of the issue. It should perhaps simply be noted that adolescence is a time of rapid physiological and psychological change for human beings and that therefore behaviors that emerge during that period may not occur beyond that period. In other words, juvenile sexual offending may be part of a short-term pattern of problematic behavior which might bear little relation to behavior during adulthood. It would seem that in light of this view, the theories discussed herein would generally be less applicable to juvenile offenders, especially if those offenders simply commit a one-off offense. Furthermore, in terms of onset, the term only really makes sense if offending continues over time or at least occurs on more than one occasion.

Prevalence

The concept of prevalence in the criminal careers literature is used to examine the occurrence of general offending or specific offenses in particular populations in particular time frames. Also, the age of the offender at the time of the offending is also often considered in assessing prevalence. For example, Farrington (1992) included a table which showed "… the peak age for the annual prevalence of convictions …" which was recorded as 17 years (p. 523). Finkelhor's model of child sexual offending does not seem to have any particular implications for prevalence. In contrast, Marshall and Barbaree's theory suggests that there might be a peak in prevalence in adolescence and early adulthood as an individual is more likely to struggle with social settings during this life period. It may be theorized that if the individual works through his problems and develops social skills then reoffending would be less likely. Furthermore, according to Marshall and Barbaree's theory, sexual offending would be more likely to occur during times of social hardship. For example, during periods of economic recession when large numbers of people are unemployed, sexual offending would be more prevalent because individuals would experience higher levels of stress, and social alienation.

Given the importance of pro-offense cognitions in Hall and Hirshman's model, it may be extrapolated that sexual offending against women would be more prevalent in populations in which such beliefs are endorsed or even promoted. This suggestion is consistent with the view of some media commentators who suggest that using sexualized images of women in advertising contributes to the development of pro-rape attitudes in men (e.g., Malamuth & Check, 1981). Thus, in environments in which such advertising is common it might reasonably be expected that rape would be more prevalent. According to Knight and Sims-Knight, the vulnerability to sexual offending begins with verbal and/or physical abuse or sexual abuse. Thus, they theorize that some sort of abuse is a necessary condition for sexual aggression to occur. It may be assumed, therefore, that sexual offending against women will be more prevalent in populations in which there are particularly high levels of abuse of children.

With regard to prevalence, Ward and Beech's approach has similar implications to those offered by the aforementioned theories. For example, they highlight the importance of early life experiences and offense-related cognitions. However, they also include the impact of evolutionary processes in the biological component of the model. As explained by Ward and Beech, according to evolutionary theory, males are more likely to commit sexual offenses due to "gender linked vulnerabilities." For instance, a man might engage in impersonal sexual interaction if he is unable to find a sexual partner. This occurs because a man's reproductive success is not dependent on a relationship in the same way that a woman's reproductive success is. Therefore, one could hypothesize that sexual offending against adult women would be more common in environments in which it is more difficult for men to find a mate, such as in communities in which men greatly outnumber women.

Frequency

The parameter of frequency refers to the regularity with which an individual offends. With regard to sexual offending, and in particular, child sexual offending, one might also want to know the frequency of offending against one victim as well the frequency across victims. For example, one sexual offender may have just two victims 10 years apart; however, he may have committed scores of offenses against each victim. Thus, simply knowing the frequency with which an offender acquires a victim would provide limited information in regard to the intensity of his offending behavior. Finkelhor's model suggests that the frequency of child sexual offending would depend on the availability of a victim (as this would probably impact on sexual arousal) and the presence of disinhibitors. Thus, an alcoholic would be likely to offend more frequently due to the ongoing disinhibitory effects of chronic alcohol abuse. Similarly, Marshall and Barbaree's theory emphasizes the role of disinhibitors but also includes the role of stress which taxes the person's ability to cope. Therefore, sexual offending would be more frequent in individuals who have ongoing challenges in their daily lives.

With regard to sexual offending against women, Hall and Hirshman's model indicates that offense frequency would be greater in those who experience higher levels of sexual arousal (either more intense or more numerous or both). Also, like the models mentioned above, the component of affective dyscontrol implies that situations that strain a man's ability to regulate his emotions (such as in times of stress) would also lead to an increased frequency of offending. Knight and Sims-Knight's pathway approach seems to suggest that individuals who are preoccupied with sex and have regular antisocial sexual fantasies would be more likely to reoffend at a high rate. The model also indicates that antisocial environments will contribute to higher offense frequency.

Ward and Beech's model emphasizes the cycle of offending; that is, the fact that offending itself increases the likelihood of further offending. As depicted in Figure 2.1, there is a feedback loop such that the sexual offense is viewed as both maintaining and escalating the behavior. Therefore, the model hypothesizes that as an individual amasses convictions for sexual offenses, further offending becomes more likely. This is consistent with literature on recidivism and the research that underlies various risk assessment measures. For example, the Static-99 (Harris, Phenix, Hanson, & Thornton, 2003), which is used to assess risk of sexual reoffending, includes the number of previous offenses and this makes an important contribution to the determination of the final risk category.

Specialization

Specialization refers to the question of whether offenders commit just one type of offense or several different types. For example, one might be interested in whether a violent offender also commits other nonviolent offenses. Finkelhor's model of child sexual offending focuses primarily on personal qualities that are quite specific to sexual offending. For example, emotional congruence and blockage explain why sexual offenders are drawn to interacting with children. Furthermore, there is a sexual arousal component which is also specific to sexual offending. The final component – disinhibition – is the only component aspect of the model that would imply that the individual might also commit other types of offenses. However, given that these are all seen as preconditions, it can be hypothesized that sexual offenders would probably be no more likely than the general population to commit offenses of a more general nature.

Marshall and Barbaree's theory emphasizes the importance of developmental factors, in particular, exposure to physical and/or sexual abuse. This lends weight to the proposition that sexual offenders might also commit other types of offenses insofar as these sorts of developmental experiences are widely believed to increase vulnerability to more general offending (e.g., Burke, Loeber, & Birhamer, 2002; Farrington, 2003). Also, this is consistent with the cycle of violence hypothesis, which proposes that individuals who are exposed to violence as children are at increased risk of becoming perpetrators of violence (e.g., as outlined and evidenced by Fagan, 2005). According to Marshall and Barbaree's theory, these vulnerability factors only lead to a sexual offense if further problems occur during adolescence; however, this says nothing about more general offending. It seems plausible, though, to suppose that general offending would be more likely to accompany the sexual offending if the individual had more aversive early childhood experiences.

Hall and Hirshman's model of sexual aggression against women includes four "motivational precursors," one of which is affective dyscontrol. This precursor is associated with the presence of "negative affective states" which, it is hypothesized, the individual struggles to manage. In particular, Hall and Hirschman highlight the importance of anger and hostility; they propose that these emotions are especially important in rape offenses. Given that anger and hostility are also considered to be important in violent offenses (e.g., Walker & Bright, 2009), it may be hypothesized that individuals who commit rape offenses might also be at increased risk of committing violent offenses. Interestingly, as stated above, Hall and Hirschman state that rapists often have a history of diverse offending and they propose that rapists often have antisocial personality traits. This conjecture is supported by research evidence which indicates rapists frequently have convictions for a wide variety of crimes (Gannon, Collie, Ward, & Thakker, 2008).

Knight and Sims-Knight's model of sexual offending seems to be particularly relevant to discussions of specialization. Like some of the other models mentioned in this section, it emphasizes the importance of aversive early life experiences, especially verbal, physical, and sexual abuse. Thus, it might be reasoned that rapists with more aversive backgrounds would be more at risk of diverse offending. However, this model also takes a pathways approach and one of the pathways is conceptualized as tracking through antisocial behavior. Therefore, Knight and Sims-Knight are suggesting that offenders who take that particular pathway will have strong antisocial tendencies and will be committing other types of offenses besides rape.

Like many of the other models, Ward and Beech's approach incorporates aversive early life events (including social learning and biological factors) and these are linked to clinical symptoms via neuropsychological processes. What is perhaps most pertinent, in terms of specialization, is the list of clinical symptoms that they provide. This list includes emotional regulation difficulties, offense-supportive cognitions, and social problems, all of which are also considered to be important in violent offending (e.g., Wong & Gordon, 2006). Thus, once again, it appears that sexual offenders and violent offenders share some of the same risk factors. Furthermore, Ward and Beech's model incorporates "ecological niche" factors and these cover social, cultural, and environmental variables. It is likely that many of these risk variables are common across violent and sexual offenders. For example, an individual is more likely to commit any sort of offense if he lives in an environment in which offending is commonplace (Pitts, 2008).

Overall, these theories seem to suggest that diverse offending is probably more likely in rapists than in child sexual offenders. While child sexual offenders tend to have a range of psychological problems, some of which are also seen in rapists, these problems are less likely to be associated with general antisocial behavior. In brief, child molesters are much more likely to be specialists (Ward, Polaschek, & Beech, 2006). Furthermore, given the nature of rape, and in light of the theories of rape, it may be hypothesized that violence is a probable addition to this type of sexual offense.

Continuity and Career Duration

The parameter of continuity refers to the tendency for offenders to continue offending over time. For example, Farrington (1992) reported that "Nearly three-quarters of those convicted as juveniles at age 10–16 were reconvicted at age 17–24, in comparison with only 16.0 per cent of those not convicted as juveniles." So, young offenders are at higher risk of further offending. Similarly, evidence suggests that youth is also a risk factor for sexual reoffending. For example, the Static-99 (Harris et al., 2003) takes note of the individual's age in calculating the risk for further sexual offending.

Career duration is simply the time period between the first and the last offense. Interestingly, Farrington reported that in regard to general offending, individuals whose first offense was in the youngest age bracket (namely, 10 to 13 years) had the longest duration of offending. Career duration and continuity are discussed together due to the substantial overlap of the two concepts. Finkelhor's precondition model suggests that child sexual offending is more likely to continue over time if the four preconditions continue. Given the significance of the inability to interact socially and emotionally with adults, it may be hypothesized that an individual will continue offending for longer if these problems continue. Thus, if a sex offender is able to develop his social skills and maintain an age-appropriate intimate relationship then offending would be less likely to continue. Furthermore, Finkelhor's model suggests that the presence of variables that might serve to increase disinhibition (such as alcohol abuse) would also make offending more likely to continue over time. Marshall and Barbaree's theory places special emphasis on adolescence; while early life experiences are considered to be important, adolescence is seen as the time when aversive life experiences begin to impact on the individual due to the biological and other changes that occur in this phase of life. Also, social functioning is seen as important and it is proposed that the man's psychological problems impact on his ability to interact with his peers. Thus, as in Finkelhor's model, it would seem that the offending behavior would be more likely to continue if the social difficulties are not addressed and resolved.

Hall and Hirshman's model of rape incorporates antisocial personality traits (such as selfishness and lack of remorse) as well as environmental variables. Therefore, it would seem to suggest that ongoing sexual offending is likely because personality problems tend to be pervasive and long standing. Interestingly though, evidence suggests that individuals who are identified as having personality problems often show improvement as they age. For example, a recent review of borderline personality disorder (Leichsenring, Leibing, Kruse, New, & Leweke, 2011), which is in the same cluster as antisocial personality disorder, found high rates of remission in follow-up studies. Thus, it is probably best not to assume that a personality problem is going to be enduring.

Knight and Sims-Knight's model includes an antisocial pathway, thus it may be hypothesized that men who arrive at sexual offending via that particular pathway would be more likely to commit further sexual offenses. However, this model also includes a Factor 1–type pathway which similarly suggests inherent personality problems. So, it seems that according to this model two of the three pathways would be likely to be associated with long-term offending behavior. However, the long-term risk for reoffending may simply be for general offending rather than sexual offending, thus it remains unclear whether this model suggests that the presence of antisocial personality traits would increase the duration of the sexual offending behavior.

With regard to continuity and duration, Ward and Beech's theory suggests that the clinical factors are particularly important as to a large extent they serve to maintain the behavior. For example, factors such as offense-related beliefs, deviant sexual arousal, and self-regulation difficulties, which might be referred to as stable dynamic factors, are fundamental to the offending behavior. Note that in the offender literature these factors are contrasted with static and historical factors, such as age and conviction history (see Wong & Gordon, 2006, for a detailed discussion of static and dynamic factors).

It may be theorized that if these dynamic factors continue over time then the offending will be more likely to continue, although this is also dependent on other personal and environmental variables. The point is that if an offender gains knowledge and skills (including more prosocial understandings) and learns to cope with everyday life challenges then his sexual offending will likely be of shorter duration. It is important to note, however, that Ward and Beech's model also takes account of proximal environmental factors, such as the availability of a victim. For example, if a sexual offender is offending against a family member and that member continues to be available then obviously the offending is more likely to continue.

Desistance

Desistance is often defined as a termination point, "the last officially recorded or self-reported offense" (Kazemian, 2007, p. 9). However, it is more properly seen as a dynamic, ongoing process. In essence, it is the state of stopping and staying stopped that we refer to as "desistance" (Maruna, 2001). There are a number of resilience or desistance factors associated with successful crime reduction, including access to social models that promote a nonoffending lifestyle, employment, a stable emotional relationship, good social support, cognitive competencies, development of an adequate self-concept, and the acquisition of a sense of meaning in life (Laws & Ward, 2011; Lösel, 2010; Maruna, 2001). To some extent the issue of when an offender will desist has been covered by the discussion above. Obviously, if an offender continues to offend he is not desisting and the factors that contribute to continuity and duration will be relevant to the question of desistence but in reverse. In other words, a variable that increases duration will thereby decrease the chance of desistance. However, a couple of extra comments can be made in relation to this parameter.

All of the models included herein take into consideration the role of sexual arousal. Given that men's sexual functioning changes with age, there may be significant age-related effects on arousal. Bacon et al. (2003) found, in their follow-up study, that "Many aspects of sexual function (including overall function, desire, orgasm, and overall ability) decreased sharply by decade after 50 years of age" (p. 161). Thus there may be an important relationship between desistance of sexual offending and age-associated physical changes. In actual fact, desistance research has consistently found a drop-off in offending rates as offenders age, arguably due to conflicting values (e.g., values associated with being a parent versus those associated with being a criminal) as well as the physical changes associated with maturation (Laws & Ward, 2011). This evidence indicates that a significant component of desistance probably relates to offenders' construction of alternative narrative identities as much as anything else (Maruna, 2001).

The models also point to the influence of early abuse experiences; therefore, desistance will be more likely to occur if the individual is able to overcome the negative psychological aftereffects of his problematic childhood. According to the models, other factors that would also contribute to desistance would be the acquisition of social skills, establishing and maintaining appropriate intimate relationships, and developing effective coping strategies. One advantage of the Ward and Beech theory is that it is explicit about the importance of approach goals in the offending process: goals that reflect what is important to an individual and what they are seeking via sexual offending, and in their lifestyle more generally. This is useful because identifying the primary good or core value associated with an offense-related goal and finding other ways to achieve it can assist the desistance process (Laws & Ward, 2011). Strength-based approaches to offender rehabilitation, such as the Good Lives Model (GLM; Laws & Ward, 2011), stress the important role of offenders' goals in desistance.

According to the GLM, offenders' core values enable them to capitalize on, or create, objective events that reflect their practical identity. Because of its stress on the importance of the past in fashioning practical identities and the associated socialization and acculturation processes, the GLM also has a strong developmental focus without adopting a fatalistic tone. There is arguably a red thread that runs through offenders' lives from the past to the future, linking core values, life plans, identity, and ultimately meaning. Furthermore, the GLM's stress on agency and the importance of reflectiveness is entirely consistent with desistance theorists' emphasis on "turning points" (Laub & Sampson, 2003) or critical events that create a sense of crisis in offenders and ultimately prompt them to re-evaluate their lives and reconstruct their identities.

Conclusion

This chapter has briefly summarized and critiqued some of the most important theories of sexual offending that have emerged over the last three decades. It has then examined these in light of the various parameters of the criminal careers approach. Theories are important because they explain why individuals commit sexual offenses by identifying the underlying causal processes. They provide maps to guide researchers and practitioners in their respective attempts to understand and to change offenders' harmful behavior. There is little point attempting to change people in ways that are unrealistic and that ignore the way they function. Thus, a viable theory of sexual offending, and its associated rehabilitation initiatives, ought to be naturalistic and pay close attention to what science tells us about the architecture of the mind and the processes that generate and constitute human actions. Intervening therapeutically with offenders presupposes an understanding of the causes of crime, and understanding its causes requires comprehending the nature of human beings. The concept of offender rehabilitation is at its core a deeply normative one that manifests in individual lives in the construction of practical or narrative identities, and at the social level in terms of correctional policy directed at risk reduction and management. To understand criminal careers it is arguably necessary to think developmentally, and to do that, we need comprehensive etiological theories. The ones outlined in this chapter arguably represent the best we have in the field. And, as we have seen, all include developmental variables, and to varying degrees, focus on factors generating criminal careers. What we need now is more data, but the collection of data without ideas to guide it is an inevitably hit-or-miss business.

References

Ainsworth, M. D. S., & Bell, S. M. (1970). Attachment, exploration, and separation: Illustrated by the behavior of one-year-olds in a strange situation. *Child Development, 41*, 49–67.

Bacon, C. G., Mittleman, M. A., Kawachi, I., Giovannucci, E., Glasser, D. B., & Rimm, E. B. (2003). Sexual function in men older than 50 years of age: Results from the health professionals follow-up study. *Annals of Internal Medicine, 139*, 161–168.

Benning, S. D., Patrick, C. J., Hicks, B. M., Blonigen, D. M., & Krueger, R. F. (2003). Factor structure of the Psychopathic Personality Inventory: Validity and implications for clinical assessment. *Psychological Assessment, 15*, 340–350.

Blumstein, A., & Cohen, J. (1987). Characterizing criminal careers. *Science, 237*, 985–991.

Blumstein, A., Cohen, J., Roth, J. A., & Visher, C. A. (Eds.). (1986). *Criminal careers and "career criminals."* Washington, DC: National Academy Press.

Bowlby, J. (1988). *A secure base: Parent-child attachment and healthy human development.* New York: Basic Books.

Burke, J. D., Loeber, R., & Birhamer, B. (2002). Oppositional defiant disorder and conduct disorder: A review of the past 10 years, part II. *Journal of the American Academy of Child and Adolescent Psychiatry, 41*, 1275–1293.

Fagan, A. A. (2005). The relationship between adolescent physical abuse and criminal offending: Support for an enduring and generalized cycle of violence. *Journal of Family Violence, 20*, 279–290.

Farrington, D. (1992). Criminal career research in the United Kingdom. *British Journal of Criminology, 32*, 521–536.

Farrington, D. (2003). Developmental and life-course criminology: Key theoretical and empirical issues – The 2002 Sutherland award address. *Criminology, 41*, 221–256.

Finkelhor, D. (1984). *Child sexual abuse: New theory and research.* New York: The Free Press.

Gannon, T., Collie, R., Ward, T., & Thakker, J. (2008). Rape: Psychopathology, theory, and treatment. *Clinical Psychology Review, 28*, 982–1008.

Hall, G. C., & Hirschman, R. (1991). Toward a theory of sexual aggression: A quadripartite model. *Journal of Consulting and Clinical Psychology, 59*, 662–669.

Hanson, R. K., & Harris, A. J. (2000). Where should we intervene? Dynamic predictors of sexual offence recidivism. *Criminal Justice and Behavior, 27*, 6–36.

Hare, R. D. (2003). *The psychopathy checklist – revised* (2nd ed.). Toronto: Multi-Health Systems.

Harris, A., Phenix, A., Hanson, R. K., & Thornton. D. (2003). *Static-99 coding rules revised – 2003.* Ottawa: Canadian Government.

Kazemian, L. (2007). Desistance from crime: Theoretical, empirical, methodological, and policy considerations. *Journal of Contemporary Criminal Justice, 23*, 5–27.

Knight, R. A., & Sims-Knight, J. E. (2004). Testing an etiological model for male juvenile sexual offending against females. In R. Geffner, K. C. Franey, T. G. Arnold, & R. Falconer (Eds.), *Identifying and treating youth who sexually offend: Current approaches, techniques, and research* (pp. 33–55). New York: Haworth Press.

Laub, J. H., & Sampson, R. J. (2003). *Shared beginnings, divergent lives: Delinquent boys to age 70.* Cambridge, MA: Harvard University Press.

Laws, D. R., & Ward, T. (2011). *Desistance from sex offending: Alternatives to throwing away the keys.* New York, NY: Guilford Press.

Leichsenring, F., Leibing, E., Kruse, J., New, A. S., & Leweke, F. (2011). Borderline personality disorder. *Lancet, 377*, 74–84.

Lösel, F. (2010). *What works in offender rehabilitation: A global perspective.* Keynote given at the 12th Annual Conference of the International Corrections and Prisons Association, Ghent, Belgium.

Malamuth, N. M., & Check, J. V. P (1981). The effects of mass media exposure on acceptance of violence against women: A field experiment. *Journal of Research in Personality, 15*, 436–446.

Malamuth, N. M., Check, J. V. P., & Briere, J. (1986). Sexual arousal in response to aggression: Ideological, aggressive, and sexual correlates. *Journal of Personality and Social Psychology, 50*, 330–340.

Maruna, S. (2001). *Making good: How ex-convicts reform and rebuild their lives.* Washington, DC: American Psychological Association.

Marshall, W. L. (2010). The role of attachments, intimacy, and loneliness in the etiology and maintenance of sexual offending. *Sexual and Relationship Therapy, 25*, 73–85.

Marshall, W. L., & Barbaree, H. E. (1990). An integrated theory of the etiology of sexual offending. In W. L. Marshall, D. R. Laws, & H. E. Barbaree (Eds.), *Handbook of sexual assault: Issues, theories, and treatment of the offender* (pp. 257–275). New York: Plenum.

Marshall, W. L., & Marshall, L. E. (2010). Attachment and intimacy in sexual offenders: An update. *Sexual and Relationship Therapy, 25*, 86–90.

McCoy, K., & Fremouw, W. (2010). The relation between negative affect and sexual offending: A critical review. *Clinical Psychology Review, 30*, 317–315.

Piquero, A. R., Farrington, D. P., & Blumstein, A. (2003). The criminal career paradigm. *Crime and Justice, 20*, 359–506.

Pitts, J. (2008). *Reluctant gangsters: The changing face of youth crime.* Portland, Oregon: Willan Publishing.

Seto, M.C. (2008). *Pedophilia and sexual offending against children.* Washington, DC: American Psychological Association.

Siegert, R. J., & Ward, T. (2003). Back to the future: Evolutionary explanations of rape: In T. Ward, D. R. Laws, & S. M. Hudson (Eds.), *Sexual deviance: Issues and controversies* (pp. 45–64). Thousand Oaks, CA: Sage.

Walker, J. S., & Bright, J. A. (2009). Cognitive therapy for violence: Reaching the parts that anger management doesn't reach. *The Journal of Forensic Psychiatry and Psychology, 20*, 174–201.

Ward, T., & Beech, A. R. (2006). An integrated theory of sexual offending. *Aggression and Violent Behavior, 11*, 44–63.

Ward, T., & Beech, A. R. (2008). An integrated theory of sexual offending. In D. R. Laws & W. T. O'Donohue (Eds.), *Sexual deviance: Theory, assessment, and treatment* (2nd ed.) (pp. 21–36). New York: The Guilford Press.

Ward, T., & Hudson, S. (2001). Finkelhor's precondition model of child sexual abuse: A critique. *Psychology, Crime, & Law, 7*, 291–307.

Ward, T., Polaschek, D., & Beech, A. (2006). *Theories of sexual offending.* Chichester, UK: John Wiley & Sons, Ltd.

Ward, T., & Siegert, R. J. (2002). Toward a comprehensive theory of child sexual abuse: A theory knitting perspective. *Psychology, Crime, & Law, 8*, 319–351.

Wong, S. C. P., & Gordon, A. (2006). The validity and reliability of the Violence Risk Scale. *Psychology, Public Policy, and Law, 12*, 279–309.

3

An Integrated Life-Course Developmental Theory of Sexual Offending

Stephen Smallbone
Griffith University, Australia

Jesse Cale
University of New South Wales, Australia

Introduction

Following his 2003 *Sutherland Award* address to the American Society of Criminology, David Farrington invited leading theorists in the field of developmental and life-course criminology (DLC) to present the latest versions of their theories in an edited volume entitled *Integrated developmental and life-course theories of offending* (Farrington, 2005a). Farrington asked each of the contributors to address in their theoretical expositions a number of theoretical and empirical issues based on 10 "widely accepted conclusions about the development of offending that any DLC theory must be able to explain" (p. 5). In keeping with a longstanding tradition in criminology that opposes the singling out of particular kinds of offenses for special theoretical attention, none of the contributors gave any particular attention to explaining sexual offending. Where sexual offending is considered at all in DLC theories, it is generally understood to occupy a position at the more serious end of a continuum of irresponsible, socially deviant, or unlawful behavior (e.g., LeBlanc, 2005; see also Loeber & Farrington, 1998). Thus DLC theories explicitly or implicitly assume that the same concepts and principles that apply to all other forms of offending apply equally to sexual offending.

Theories of sexual offending have in turn paid little attention to criminological concepts and knowledge, construing the problem instead as a special case of offending requiring its own unique explanations. Specialist sexual offending theories have typically focused on clinical concerns, concentrating on offenders' clinical presentation and its implications for treatment rather than on offending trajectories and their wider implications for prevention and control. Ward and his colleagues (Ward &

Sex Offenders: A Criminal Career Approach, First Edition. Edited by Arjan Blokland and Patrick Lussier.

Beech, 2006; Ward & Hudson, 1998; Ward & Siegert, 2002) in particular have sought to draw from increasingly diverse sources of knowledge to explain sexual offending, and yet even this work pays little attention to the empirical and conceptual connections between sexual offending and other forms of crime. Thakker and Ward (this book) review specialist theories and their contributions to understanding the "criminal careers" of sexual offenders, so we will not deal in detail with these here.

Our aim in the present chapter is to present an integrated theory of sexual offending that incorporates ideas from DLC approaches. We begin by briefly addressing each of the 10 points listed by Farrington as the key empirically confirmed developmental dimensions of offending and antisocial behavior (Table 3.1, left column). We have taken this as our starting point because the theoretical problems Farrington put to his contributors rely on the validity of his empirical conclusions concerning offending in general and, while we do not take issue with that, we cannot take for granted that these empirical conclusions are equally valid for sexual offending. In fact, our analysis leads us to conclude that the developmental dimensions of sexual offending are in part consistent and in part apparently inconsistent with those of offending and antisocial behavior more generally.

This developmental analysis serves as the empirical foundation of our proposed theory of sexual offending. However, like a number of DLC theorists (e.g., Catalano et al., 2005; Farrington, 2005b; Wikström, 2005), we take the view that a developmental theory cannot provide a complete explanation without also considering the role of biological, ecological, and situational factors (see also Ward & Beech, 2006). Our aim is therefore to present an integrated theory of sexual offending that considers the contribution of individual (biological and developmental), ecological (family, peer, organizational, neighborhood, and sociocultural), and situational factors. The theory proposed here is a new iteration of a model originally proposed by Marshall and Barbaree (1990) and later revised and extended by Smallbone, Marshall, and Wortley (2008).

Comparatively little empirical work has been done to directly investigate the criminal careers of sexual offenders. Reports from the major prospective longitudinal studies that have been so important to DLC (e.g., the *Cambridge Study in Delinquent Development*, Farrington, 1994; the *Pittsburgh Youth Study*, Loeber, Van Kammen, & Fletcher, 1996) have had very little to say about sexual offending, and there is no comparable longitudinal study that has focused specifically on sexual offending. Developmental features of sexual offending have instead been examined in retrospective studies of convicted (mostly adult) sexual offenders and in postconviction (usually postprison) follow-up studies concerned mainly with identifying individual-level predictors of recidivism (e.g., Hanson & Bussière, 1998). Even these findings may not be representative, since by all accounts only a small proportion of sexual offenders are ever arrested and convicted, much less included in research studies (see Lussier & Blokland, this book). Our conclusions about the developmental dimensions of sexual offending are therefore necessarily tentative. These are summarized in Table 3.1, alongside the developmental dimensions of general offending as listed by Farrington.

Table 3.1 Ten Developmental Dimensions

General offending	*Sexual offending*
1. The prevalence of offending peaks in the late teenage years – between 15 and 19	Prevalence appears to peak twice: in adolescence & mid- to late 30s
2. The peak age of onset of offending is between 8 and 14 years, and the peak age of desistance is between 20 and 29 years	Adult-onset more prevalent than adolescence-onset; variable desistance patterns depending on onset age and offender type
3. An early age of onset predicts a relatively long criminal career duration and the commission of relatively many offenses	Adolescence-onset offenders generally desist by early adulthood, but early onset common among persistent offenders
4. There is marked continuity in offending and antisocial behavior from childhood to the teenage years and to adulthood	Continuity of general offending and antisocial behavior, but generally low continuity of sexual behavior problems and sexual offending
5. A small fraction of the offending population commits a large fraction of the crimes, and these chronic offenders have an early onset, a high offending frequency, and a long criminal career	A similarly small proportion of sexual offenders responsible for large number of victims, and these chronic sexual offenders similarly have an early onset, a high offending frequency, and a long sexual offending career
6. Offending is versatile rather than specialized	Versatile offending common among sexual offenders
7. The types of acts defined as offenses are elements of a larger syndrome of antisocial behavior, including heavy drinking, reckless driving, sexual promiscuity, bullying, and truancy	Similar patterns observed in sexual offenders
8. Most offenses up to the late teenage years are committed with others, whereas most offenses from age 20 onwards are committed alone	Group offending generally infrequent for both adolescent and adult sexual offenders
9. The reasons for offending up to the late teenage years are variable, including utilitarian (e.g., to obtain material goods or revenge), excitement or enjoyment (or to relieve boredom), and anger (as for violent crimes), whereas from age 20 onwards utilitarian motives become increasingly dominant	Motivations for sexual offending similarly variable, but utilitarian motives do not become more dominant for older offenders
10. Different types of offenses tend to be first committed at different ages (e.g., shoplifting is typically committed before burglary, which in turn is typically committed before robbery). There is an increasing diversification of offending up to age 20, and after age 20 diversification decreases and specialization increases	Sexual offending often preceded by varied nonsexual offending; specialization does not seem to increase in adulthood

Prevalence and Age

Unlike the well-established age-crime curve, age distributions for sexual offenders appear to peak once in the teenage years, and a second time in the mid- to late thirties (Hanson, 2002). The first peak includes both adult-victim and child-victim offenders, and resembles the general age-crime curve. The second, apparently more prominent, peak includes predominantly child-victim offenders. While there is undoubtedly some overlap, low adult sexual recidivism rates among adolescent sexual offenders (Parks & Bard, 2006) and a low prevalence of adolescence-onset among adult sexual offenders (Smallbone & Wortley, 2004a; Zimring, Piquero, & Jennings, 2007) together indicate that adolescent and adult sexual offenders are for the most part two discrete populations. Adults (over 18 years) account for around 80% of the identified perpetrators in sexual offenses reported to police (e.g., United States Department of Justice, 2009). Unlike in general crime, then, participation in sexual crime appears to be considerably more prevalent in adulthood than in adolescence.

Onset and Desistance

Although early clinical studies suggested that adolescence-onset among adult sexual offenders was typical (e.g., Abel et al., 1987; Longo & Groth, 1983), the preponderance of evidence now indicates that adolescence-onset is the exception rather than the rule (Cale, this book; Lussier, Tzoumakis, Cale & Amirault, 2010). Self-report studies (see a detailed review by Lussier, Blokland, Mathesius, Pardini & Loeber, this book) by adult child-victim offenders indicate an average onset age in the mid-twenties (for nonfamilial offenders) and mid-thirties (for familial offenders), but ranging widely from adolescence to the mid-sixties (Marshall, Barbaree, & Eccles, 1991; Smallbone & Wortley, 2004a). Recidivism studies show that, as with general offending, sexual offending persistence declines with age. However, desistance patterns appear to differ for different types of sexual offenders (Hanson, 2002): sexual recidivism for adult-victim offenders declines steadily from early adulthood; sexual recidivism for familial child-victim offenders declines sharply from early adulthood; and sexual recidivism for nonfamilial child-victim offenders declines gradually from the mid- to late twenties.

Onset, Frequency, and Duration

Sexual behavior problems in childhood (under 12 years) apparently are not associated with a longer sexual offending career (Chaffin et al., 2008; Zimring, et al., 2007). Similarly, proportionally few adolescent sexual offenders seem to proceed to a persistent pattern of sexual offending in adulthood. On the other hand, adult sexual offenders whose sexual offending commenced in adolescence or early adulthood are more likely to be persistent (Hanson, 2002; Harris & Rice, 2007; Lussier, LeBlanc, & Proulx, 2005; Prentky, Knight, & Lee, 1997). Some researchers have observed a relationship between late-onset and high-frequency offending for adult child sexual abusers (Lussier, LeBlanc et al., 2005; Proulx, Lussier, Ouimet, & Boutin, 2008). This seems to be particularly the case for familial offenders, who may offend repeatedly against one or two victims, but once caught are likely to desist (Smallbone & Wortley, 2000). Nonfamilial offenders, by contrast, tend to commence offending earlier, have more victims, but offend less often against individual victims (Smallbone & Wortley, 2000), and are more likely to persist post-arrest (Hanson & Bussière, 1998).

Continuity From Childhood to Adulthood

Sexual behavior problems among children have been observed to often occur as part of a wider pattern of disruptive behavior problems, rather than as an isolated or specialized behavioral disturbance (Chaffin et al., 2008; Friedrich, 2007; Lussier & Healey, 2010). In the later developmental periods, 40–60% of both adolescent (Fehrenbach, Smith, Monastersky, & Deisher, 1986; France & Hudson, 2003) and adult sexual offenders (Smallbone & Wortley, 2000) have prior records of nonsexual offenses. Although sexual recidivism rates for adolescent sexual offenders are generally low, nonsexual recidivism rates are typically high (e.g., Nisbet, Wilson, & Smallbone, 2004). Adult sexual offenders are similarly much more likely to be rearrested for nonsexual offenses than for sexual offenses (e.g., Hanson, Gordon, Harris et al., 2002). Thus there seems to be a similar continuity of offending and antisocial behavior among sexual offenders as there is among general offenders, even though sexual offending itself does not exhibit this continuity.

Chronic Offenders

Chronic offenders are characterized by an early offending onset, a high offending frequency, and a long criminal career (Farrington, 2005a). These offenders comprise only a small proportion of the offending population, but are responsible for a large proportion of crime. In the Philadelphia birth cohort study (Tracy, Wolfgang, & Figlio, 1990), 5% of the offenders were responsible for approximately 80% of the total arrests for rape up to age 18. Similarly in the Dunedin birth cohort study, 10% of offenders (labeled "life-course persistent" offenders) were responsible for nearly two thirds of incidents involving physical or sexual violence toward women in adulthood (Moffitt, Caspi, Harrington, & Milne, 2002). In line with these findings, Lussier, Proulx, and LeBlanc (2005) found that an early and persistent antisocial tendency was related to more frequent sexual offending in adulthood. Cale, Lussier, and Proulx (2009) found that these early-onset sexual offenders had a more extensive and more diversified criminal history in adulthood.

Child sexual abuse offending has not been examined in prospective developmental studies. However, criminal history and recidivism studies indicate that offending persistence and frequency are similarly unevenly distributed. Perhaps the most striking illustration is studies where offenders are asked to report confidentially on undetected offending. For example, Abel et al. (1987) found that the mean number of self-reported victims for their nonfamilial sexual abusers was an astonishing 150, but the median number was 4, indicating a highly positively skewed distribution. Similarly, Smallbone and Wortley (2001) found that almost half of a sample of adult sexual abusers reported having had only one victim, 10% reported more than 10 victims, and 1% reported more than 100 victims. The general observation that a small proportion of chronic offenders are responsible for a large proportion of offenses clearly holds true for sexual offenders and sexual offending as well.

Offending Versatility and Specialization

Both adult-victim and child-victim sexual offenders tend to commit nonsexual offenses both before and after their conviction for a sexual offense (Broadhurst & Maller, 1992; Miethe, Olson, & Mitchell, 2006; Soothill, Francis, Sanderson, & Ackerley, 2000). Adult-victim sexual offenders tend to be more versatile than their child-victim counterparts, but child-victim offenders are also criminally versatile (Smallbone & Wortley, 2004b). One study found that more than 80% of recidivist child-victim offenders (those with at least one prior conviction for any offense) were first convicted of a nonsexual offense, and this first conviction typically preceded their first self-reported sexual abuse incident (Smallbone & Wortley, 2004b). Adolescent sexual offenders are similarly likely to have a history of nonsexual offending, and are even more likely than their adult counterparts to go on to further nonsexual offending (Hagan, King, & Patros, 1994; Kahn & Chambers, 1991; Nisbet et al., 2004; Rubinstein, Yeager, Goodstein, & Lewis, 1993). Clearly, sexual offending, like other offending, generally occurs against the backdrop of a much larger and diverse criminal repertoire (Lussier, 2005; Miethe et al., 2006).

Offenses as Part of a Wider Pattern of Antisocial Behavior

The criminal versatility of sexual offenders noted above indicates that, like offending more generally, sexual offending is part of a wider syndrome of antisocial and other irresponsible or reckless behavior (e.g., Lussier, LeBlanc et al., 2005; Lussier, Leclerc, Cale, & Proulx, 2007). Little specific attention has been given to documenting noncriminal problem behaviors among sexual offenders, although significant rates of alcohol problems and relationship problems (Harris, Mazerolle, & Knight, 2009), as well as gambling problems, involvement in automobile accidents, and fathering children out of wedlock (Cleary, 2004) have been observed among adult sexual offenders. General externalizing behaviors and conduct problems have also been widely observed among adolescent sexual offenders (Butler & Seto, 2002). For both adult and adolescent sexual offenders, the extent of noncriminal problem behaviors tends to coincide with diversity and persistence in their criminal behaviors (Butler & Seto, 2002; Harris et al., 2009; Nisbet, Smallbone, & Wortley, 2010).

Group Versus Solitary Offending

Sexual offenses are thought to be among the least likely to be committed with co-offenders or in groups (Van Mastrigt & Farrington, 2009). There are, though, some circumstances in which group sexual offending has been noted, including in college or university settings (Sanday, 2007), wars (Wood, 2006), international pedophile organizations (De Young, 1988), and local child sex rings (La Fontaine, 1993). Internet-based child pornography networks have increasingly become a concern (Wortley & Smallbone, in press), although these seem to be organized more around the distribution of abuse images than around group offending *per se*. Some studies have suggested that as many as one third of adolescent sexual offenders have been involved in group offending (Bijleveld & Hendriks, 2003; Hendriks, Van den Berg, & Bijleveld, this book), but this has not been widely confirmed. Adolescents have been observed to commit group sexual assaults in the context of initiation into street gangs, for example as initiation rituals involving known victims and female gang members (Moore & Hagedorn, 2001). Overall, group sexual offending seems to be unusual for both adolescents and adults.

Motivations for Offending

Drawing conclusions about the motivations for sexual offending, and about offending more generally, involves a much higher level of inference than is required for the other developmental dimensions considered here. Early clinical accounts concentrated on the acquisition and maintenance of deviant sexual preferences (Laws & Marshall, 1990), although a range of other motivations have also been proposed. For example, proposed motivations for rape include opportunism, sadistic and nonsadistic sexual motivations, anger, and vindictiveness (Knight, 1999). Proposed motivations for sexual abuse offending include interpersonal involvement (relationship-seeking), narcissism, sexual fixations on children, and "regression" (Knight, Carter, & Prentky, 1989). Proposed motivations specifically for adolescent sexual offenders include naïve experimentation, sexual aggression, impulsivity and general delinquent motivations, sexual compulsivity, and group-influenced motivations (O'Brien & Bera, 1986). Uncertainty remains about the validity of these motivational schemes, and whether motivations for sexual offending are different at different developmental stages. We can tentatively conclude that, as with general offending up to age 20, motivations for sexual offending are variable. However, unlike for general offending, this variability appears to characterize sexual offending in adulthood as well. Unlike for general offending, sexual offending motivations do not appear to become more utilitarian in later developmental stages.

Diversification and Specialization

Although sexual offenders are now widely recognized to be versatile rather than specialized offenders, little attention has been given to investigating sequences in the activation of different offending types over the life course. DLC researchers have noted that rape tends to be a culmination of a developmental pathway involving progression from less serious to more serious offending (Elliott, 1994; Loeber & Farrington, 1998), but as we have noted, DLC research has generally ignored child sexual abuse offending. Adult sexual abuse offenders seem just as likely to commit nonsexual offenses after their sexual offense convictions as they are before, suggesting that they do not become more specialized over time. Adolescent sexual offenders appear to be much (up to 10 times) more likely to commit further nonsexual offenses following their sexual offense convictions, indicating the opposite trend to that found in general offender populations (i.e., increased diversification, rather than increased specialization).

Other Key Empirical Dimensions of Sexual Offending

There are a number of other important empirical dimensions of sexual offending that do not feature in Farrington's list but that we think require theoretical attention. The most important of these are (1) the overrepresentation of males as offenders, and (2) the settings in which sexual offending occurs. We will deal briefly with each of these before turning our attention to the proposed theory.

Males are overrepresented in most forms of crime; however, the degree of male overrepresentation in sexual crime is particularly striking. By way of illustration, in Australia, reports to police indicate that females are the identified perpetrator in 37% of fraud offenses, 31% of theft offenses (other than motor vehicle theft), 23% of property offenses, 22% of assaults, 12% of robberies, 10% of unlawful entries, and less than 3% of all sexual offenses (Queensland Police Service, 2006). A review of official data from five countries indicated that the average proportion of female sexual offenders was 3.8%. The average from victimization surveys was 4.8% (Cortoni & Hanson, 2005). We think it is crucial to address male overrepresentation in any theory of offending, and especially in a theory of sexual offending.

Unlike most general offending, sexual offending typically occurs in circumstances where the offender and victim are already well known to one another. Most adult victims are female, who are typically victimized in dating, courtship, intimate partner, and familial settings (Amir, 1971; Koss, Dinero, Seibel, & Cox, 1988). Expressive or sadistic violence is unusual, and when it does occur is more likely to accompany either stranger assaults or offenses against intimate partners. The majority of adult-victim cases fall between these extreme ends of the offender-victim familiarity continuum (Ullman & Siegel, 1993).

Child sexual abuse typically occurs in family or analogous settings where adults are in authoritative and care-giving relationships with children, or where adolescents encounter vulnerable younger children in the course of their routine activities. In their sample of adult sexual abusers, Smallbone and Wortley (2000) found that 73% (including 63% of nonfamilial abusers) knew their victim for at least one month prior to the onset abuse incident. More than half had known the child for more than one year. Overt aggression and violence may occur during, or as a means to obtain, sexual contact, but this is atypical. More often the abuse seems to follow a so-called "grooming" process involving a graduation from attention-giving and nonsexual touching, through low-level sexual talk or touching, to increasingly more explicit sexual behaviors (Smallbone et al., 2008). A theory of sexual offending needs to address not only the characteristics of offenders, but also the context of the offending behavior, including how, where, when, and against whom the offending occurs.

The Integrated Theory

Overview of the Theory

Sexual offending encompasses a very diverse set of problem behaviors, including the viewing of child pornography, sexual harassment, and other "noncontact" offenses, as well as "hands-on" offenses ranging from low-level sexual touching through to violent assaults and sexual homicide. Offenders may be relatives, acquaintances, or strangers, who offend against victims ranging in age from infancy to old age. The unifying feature of this otherwise heterogeneous phenomenon is that all sexual offenses, by definition, involve unlawful sexual behavior. Laws prohibiting sexual engagement with children or with nonconsenting adults exist precisely because of human propensities to behave in these ways. What needs to be explained, then, is why some persons fail to observe these legal prohibitions concerning sexual behavior. We attempt below to set out a theory that draws on a wide empirical base, and that integrates individual (biological and developmental), ecological, and situational levels of explanation. We have aimed to achieve parsimony, without losing sight of the complexity of the problem. The theory is set out schematically in Figure 3.1.

Few general DLC theories, and few theories of sexual offending, consider the biological foundations of the problem behavior, and those that do generally take an individual-differences perspective (e.g., Piquero & Moffitt, 2005; Ward & Beech, 2006). We think instead that understanding the *universal* biological foundations of antisocial behavior in general, and of sexual offending behavior in particular, is of fundamental theoretical importance. Otherwise, it is not possible to answer the question of *what it is* that is shaped by individual development, for example. Even if they do consider biological factors, developmental theories may explain how individual criminal potential emerges, but they cannot explain how or why particular

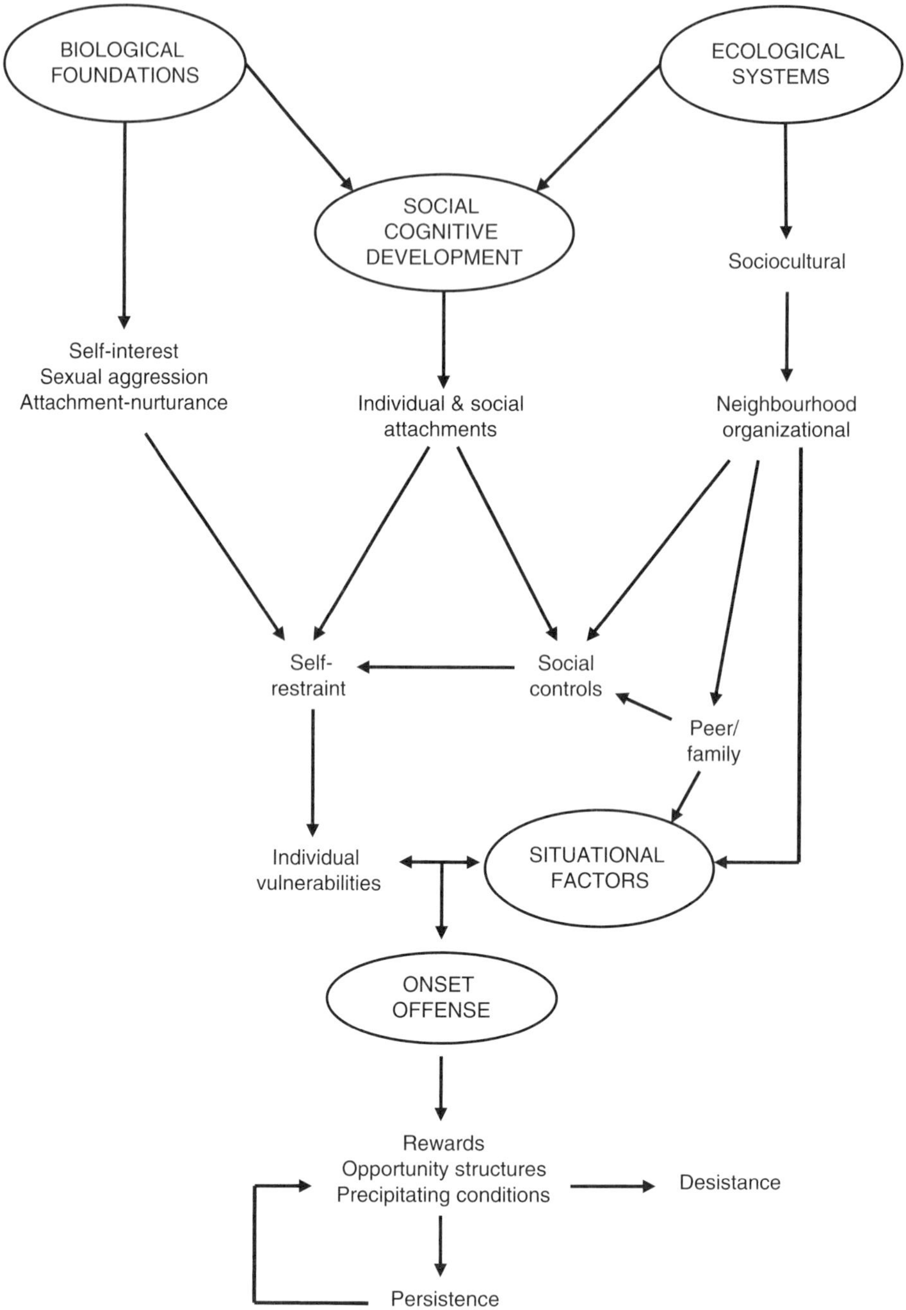

Figure 3.1 Integrated theory of sexual offending.

developmental circumstances or events result in a specific offense at a specific time at a specific location. As Farrington (2005b) points out, we need to keep a clear distinction in this regard between explaining criminal propensities on one hand, and explaining criminal events on the other. Conversely to developmental theories, situational theories may explain why particular kinds of criminal events are more or less likely to occur in specific places at particular times, but cannot by themselves explain why, given precisely the same circumstances, one person commits a crime and another does not. Clearly the way forward is to integrate these developmental and situational perspectives, rather than positioning them as competing paradigms. Finally, an ecological analysis situates sexual offending in the social context within which the offender's development unfolds, and in which sexual offenses themselves occur.

Note that our theory aims first and foremost to explain the *onset* of sexual offending; that is, why a potential offender for the first time sexually assaults or abuses an adult, adolescent, or child. The theory addresses separately the question of why some offenders proceed to further (and in some cases persistent) sexual offending and others do not. One reason for separating these questions is that, just as sexual victimization changes victims, so too does sexual offending change the offender. Thus the abuse-related motivations of a persistent sexual offender may be quite different from those of a novice offender, which may be different again from a potential offender contemplating a first sexual offense. Another reason is that opportunity structures and precipitating conditions are also likely to change. The theory can be set out initially as a list of seven key propositions:

Human evolution provides for a universal human potential for both prosocial and antisocial behavior.

Positive socialization generally constrains, but does not eliminate, the biologically based potential for antisocial motivations and behavior, including sexual violence and abuse. Humans (and especially males) are biologically prepared to employ aggression in the service of sexual goals. Humans (and especially females) are also biologically prepared to nurture and protect vulnerable others, especially children. Nurturing motivations are less biologically compelling and more instrumental for males, and are thus more susceptible to related but competing (e.g., sexual) motivations. Paradoxically, sexual motivations may involve both aggressive and attachment-nurturing emotion-motivation systems.

Positive socialization is required both to constrain the universal potential for (especially) males to engage in sexual violence and abuse, and to enable socially responsible emotional and physical intimacy. Restraining mechanisms include empathic concern, emotional regulation, and moral reasoning; enabling mechanisms include perspective-taking, self-confidence, trust, and social skills.

Primary (parental) attachment relationships provide the developmental foundation for human socialization. Secure individual attachments provide the cognitive and affective foundation for the development of positive peer and social attachments, which serve as important informal social controls on antisocial behavior, including sexual offending. Secure individual attachments also enable emotional intimacy and nurturance.

Risk and protective factors for sexual offending can be located at various levels of the ecological (family, peer, organizational, neighborhood, and sociocultural) systems in which the potential offender and potential victim are socially embedded. More proximal systems (e.g., family and peers) exert a more direct and therefore more powerful effect than more distal systems (e.g., neighborhood; sociocultural norms).

The situational elements that comprise the immediate behavioral setting present the most proximal, and therefore exert the most direct and powerful, influence on sexual offending. Situations present opportunities for offense-related motivations to be enacted. Social situations also contain dynamic properties that precipitate offense-related motivations that would otherwise not occur (or not occur at that time).

Persistence is more likely if the offending behavior is experienced as rewarding, and if favorable opportunities and precipitating conditions continue to be presented. Persistence is less likely if offending becomes unrewarding relative to the effort and risk of continued offending.

Biological Foundations

Humans possess an evolved flexibility to respond adaptively to wide variations in their natural and social environments. According to evolutionary theory, the primary biological goal is to maximize reproductive fitness, which requires individual survival, mating, producing offspring, and ensuring the survival of those offspring. Social behavior strategies involving empathy, trust, nurturance, and social cooperation have been naturally selected because they are highly adaptive in favorable, high-resource social environments. Strategies involving self-interest, deception, coercion, aggression, and opportunism have been naturally selected because they are highly adaptive in unfavorable, low-resource environments. In evolutionary terms, this biological flexibility in human psychological capacities, and the social behavior strategies they serve, allows survival and reproductive fitness in a wide range of natural and social environments. In modern social terms, it provides a universal potential for both prosocial and antisocial behavior.

Since there is no plausible scientific reason to expect that prosocial behavior is the default biological program for humans, we do not need to find individual biological variations or deficits to explain antisocial behavior, including sexual offending. As Marshall and Barbaree (1990) put it, "the (universal) task for human males is to acquire inhibitory controls over a biologically endowed potential for self-interest associated with … sex and aggression" (p. 257). Certainly there are both inherited and acquired individual variations in biological structures and systems, and many associated conditions (e.g., intellectual disability, autism, head injury, drug dependence, and perhaps psychopathy) no doubt present special challenges for the developmental task of acquiring individual controls over sexual violence and abuse. But these individual variations are not a *necessary* condition for sexual offending or other antisocial behavior.

Perhaps the most remarkable variations in human biological characteristics, and the most relevant for our present purposes, are those concerning gender differences. Generally, males are more biologically predisposed to employ aggression in the service of social, and especially sexual, goals. Biological systems underpinning nurturing motivations and behavior are also less developed in males than in females. Certainly males can learn to become very effective caregivers, but nurturing motivations for males are more instrumental (Panksepp, 1998), and are therefore more susceptible to competing motivations, including self-serving and sexual motivations.

Important gender differences are also apparent in the biological organization of human attachment, nurturing, and sexual emotion-motivation systems. Specifically, biological systems associated with attachment-nurturing motivations and behavior are activated in females during sexual arousal (as well as during childbirth and breast-feeding). By contrast, sexual arousal for males involves the activation of neurological systems associated predominantly with aggression. During male sexual arousal the activation of these "aggression" systems declines and is gradually superseded by the activation of attachment-nurturance systems (Murphy, Seckl, Burton, Checkly, & Lightman, 1987). Males are thus likely to experience attachment-nurturing motivations immediately following orgasm, but their pursuit of sexual partners and sexual arousal itself is more likely to involve aggressive motivations.

We are not suggesting a hard biological determinism here – to the contrary, the sexual motivations and behavior of individual males (and females) are undoubtedly shaped by social cognitive development, and activated by situational factors present in the immediate behavioral setting. Nevertheless, we propose that biologically based gender differences are in large part responsible for the overrepresentation of males in most forms of crime, and particularly for the striking overrepresentation of males in sexual crime. We further propose that the universal biological foundations of male social and sexual behavior, particularly their stronger predisposition to sexual aggression and weaker predisposition to nurturing, help to explain why males are more likely than females to exploit vulnerable others for sexual purposes, and indeed why sexual motivations are more likely to arise for males (than for females) in ordinary social interactions with vulnerable others, including children. Biological factors also explain the paradoxical observation that sexual offenses can involve both aggressive and nurturing motivations and behavior.

Social Cognitive Development

The developmental story of sexual offending, as we conceive it, principally involves the acquisition of individuals' general (dispositional) capacity and commitment to exercise self-restraint in order to conform to social rules concerning irresponsible and unlawful sexual behavior. It also involves the acquisition of psychological capacities and skills to engage in responsible sexual conduct, which in sexually mature individuals generally involves negotiating emotional and physical intimacy with consenting others. For us, the key developmental question is not how offenders learn to commit a sexual offense for the first time, as seems to be a common (mis) interpretation of how behavioral and social learning theories might formulate the problem, but rather how it is that offenders *fail* to learn *not to* commit sexual offenses. This is essentially a control theory approach, although we purposely use the term "self-restraint" rather than "self-control" – sexual offending behavior (as with offending generally) may be poorly or highly controlled, but it always involves an absence of restraint, even if only momentarily.

Biological development of course begins before social cognitive development. In addition to genetic variations, there are wide variations in the environmental conditions to which individuals are exposed during gestation (e.g., maternal stressors, nutrition, hormonal conditions, exposure to alcohol or drugs) that may affect subsequent social cognitive development. These variations may introduce special challenges for the later developmental task of acquiring restraining and enabling capacities, although, as we have argued, these biological variations are not necessary conditions for sexual offending. We also need to keep in mind that from birth biological development continues to unfold, and to interact with social cognitive development over the entire life course. Universal within-individual changes involving biological development interact with a range of psychological, ecological, and situational factors relevant to both motivations and opportunities associated with sexual offending. Perhaps the most significant of these are the rapid increase in sexual drive during adolescence, the transitions from intense sexual attraction to potentially more enduring attachment bonds with intimate partners, parenthood and associated child-rearing activities, and the gradual decline of sexual drive in later life.

Primary (parental) attachment relationships provide the developmental foundation for human socialization (Bowlby, 1969). Through warm and responsive parenting, secure primary attachments facilitate the development of individual capacities for empathy, emotional regulation, and moral reasoning. We see these as the key mechanisms of self-restraint. Secure attachment relationships also facilitate the development of key "enabling" mechanisms, namely perspective-taking, self-confidence, trust, and social skills. The experience of these early attachment relationships is carried forward via what Bowlby called the "internal working model of self and other," essentially a cognitive schema concerning one's sense of deservedness of the affections and support of others, and of the reliability and responsiveness of others. Insecure, and especially disorganized, early attachment sets the scene for aggressive, coercive, fearful, or frantic patterns of behavior in attachment, and later also sexual and nurturing, interactions.

Individuals' attachment orientation widens over the course of development to affect expectations of and behavior in a range of other affiliative and social relationships. Thus secure attachments to parents are likely to lead to secure relationships with peers, and later with intimate and sexual partners and (especially one's own) children. These patterns of interpersonal attachment widen further over the course of development, extending to attachments to social institutions and to the community at large. While secure interpersonal attachments establish the foundation for individual self-restraint, both secure interpersonal attachments and strong (pro) social attachments provide individuals with incentives to refrain from irresponsible social and sexual conduct, and therefore act as important informal social controls.

Developmental risk factors for general delinquency and crime have been well documented. The strongest predictors for 6- to 11-year-olds are early delinquent conduct and substance abuse, and for 12- to 14-year-olds involvement with antisocial peers and weak social attachments (Lipsey & Derzon, 1998). Predictors of violent offending include living with a criminal parent, harsh parental discipline, physical abuse and neglect, low parental involvement, high levels of family conflict, parental attitudes favorable to violence, and separation from family (Hawkins et al., 1998). These risk factors are likely to be relevant for sexual offending as well, due primarily to their compromising effect on the developing individual's capacity for and commitment to general and sexual self-restraint (Smallbone, 2006). Other experiences in childhood and adolescence may have more specific relevance for sexual offending, particularly early sexual experiences and sexual abuse (Seto & Lalumière, 2010). However, although sexual offenders are more likely than others to have been sexually abused in childhood, few sexually abused children go on to commit sexual offenses. It seems likely that these early sexual experiences provide a more concrete and realistic model for sexual offending than would otherwise be the case, so that abused persons may more readily recognize an opportunity to abuse. But sexual offending still requires being prepared to exploit such an opportunity, again requiring an absence of self-restraint.

Adolescence appears to be the first of two developmental risk periods for the onset of sexual offending (the other, particularly for child sexual abusers, being early middle age). Interactions between biological and social cognitive development during adolescence are particularly noteworthy. For males, testosterone production increases rapidly from the onset of puberty, reaching adult levels within about two years (Sizonenko, 1978) and coinciding with a dramatic increase both in goal-directed sexual behavior and in the capacity for physical aggression. In early adolescence sexual drive is at its most urgent and perhaps least controlled. Sexual identity and sexual lifestyles are not yet fully formed, the interpersonal skills needed for successful engagement in physical and emotional intimacy are not yet well developed, and social and sexual norms become more influenced by popular and social media than by parents or peers (DeLamater & Friedrich, 2002). It is easy to see how adolescent sexual experimentation can "go wrong," even for well-socialized boys (and girls). For poorly socialized adolescents, it is even less surprising that already-established patterns of under-restrained aggression, coercion, exploitation, opportunism, rule-breaking, sensation-seeking, excessive emotional neediness, and so on, would be extended to the new domain of goal-directed sexual behavior.

Different developmental phases also present different opportunity structures and precipitating conditions for sexual offending. Adolescents, more so than in the adjacent developmental phases of childhood and young adulthood, are likely to spend unsupervised time with younger children in the course of their routine activities. Some may even be called upon by adults to undertake unsupervised care-taking responsibilities with younger children. Some vulnerable youth may be placed with other vulnerable peers or younger children in foster care or institutional environments. Also, more so than in previous developmental phases, adolescents and young adults have greater access to alcohol, illicit drugs, and pornography, become more mobile, and are more likely to spend time with peers without adult supervision. Thus during adolescence certain biological, developmental, ecological, and situational factors converge to significantly increase risks for offending in general, and for sexual violence and abuse in particular.

The second peak risk period for the onset of sexual offending is early middle age, a time when men are first likely to be involved in the care-taking of children who are in turn reaching the peak risk age for sexual victimization. This may be as a parent, step-parent, uncle, family friend, teacher, sports coach, children's activities leader, pastor, and so on. These opportunity structures interact with biological and developmental vulnerabilities of the kind we have already discussed, as well as with transitory mood states (e.g., loneliness; emotional neediness) and disinhibiting factors (e.g., intoxication). Onset in old age is not as common as it is in early middle age, but in adult sexual abuser populations, onset in the fifties and sixties seems to be as common as it is in adolescence. In these senior years men are likely to be first involved with a second generation of children entering the risk age period for sexual victimization, namely grandchildren, step-grandchildren, and their friends.

Ecological Systems

Individual biological and social cognitive development occurs in the context of the ecological systems in which the individual is socially embedded. At any given time, immediate behavior is also influenced by these systems. Thus both developmental and situational risk and protective factors for sexual offending may be located at various levels of the ecological (family, peer, organizational, neighborhood, and broader sociocultural) systems in which both the offender and victim are socially embedded. The influence of distal ecological systems is in effect filtered through successively more proximal systems, with the more proximal systems exerting the more direct and therefore more powerful effect on individual behavior. Because offenders and victims typically know one another, each is likely to share aspects of the other's proximal ecological "space." At the same time, individuals occupy a unique position within these systems. We will comment briefly on how these systems may influence sexual offending, beginning at the most distal level.

Social norms, values, and formal laws concerning sexual offending are determined at a sociocultural level. While virtually all human societies appear to have observed an incest taboo, norms governing sexual engagement with unrelated children and with women have been much more variable. Current norms, values, and laws are no doubt a product of increasing recognition of the rights of women and children, and particularly in modern Western societies there is very little room for ambiguity that sexual violence and abuse are now considered among the most heinous of crimes. Except in the rarest of cases, then, sexual offenders knowingly and intentionally violate laws for which, if caught, they risk severe punishment and ostracization. Formal systems for disseminating and enforcing these laws and for protecting women and children are also established at this sociocultural level. Variations in laws, law enforcement systems, and child protection systems, are therefore likely to have differential effects on the prevalence of sexual violence and abuse.

Variations in social norms and values, and in the effectiveness of formal and informal law enforcement and child protection systems, are also likely to be found at the neighborhood or community level. A stark example is in some remote Australian Aboriginal communities where the capacity of both formal and informal social control systems is severely compromised, and where an unusually high prevalence of sexual violence and abuse (together with other social problems) has been observed (Aboriginal and Torres Strait Islander Women's Task Force on Violence, 1999). More generally, and for a range of reasons, local neighborhoods may contain a higher number of potential sexual offenders, a higher number of vulnerable women and children, and a lower capacity for capable guardianship.

Organizational systems also contain risk and protective factors for sexual offending. There are many potential permutations, but perhaps the most relevant are organizations that serve as convergence settings for potential victims and potential offenders. For child sexual abuse, these may be organizations catering to children with chronic emotional vulnerabilities (e.g., institutional or other out-of-home placements), or more commonly where children are dependent in ordinary ways on unrelated adults as authority figures and caregivers (e.g., schools; recreational organizations; pastoral care settings). Potential offenders in these settings are generally adult males who may be prone to general aggression and rule-breaking, or to emotional over-involvement or other professional boundary slippage with children in their care. Child-focused organizations with weak or corrupted child protection systems present particular risks. For young adults, risks for sexual victimization may be increased in organizational settings where cultures of male sexual conquest and entitlement have taken hold. In Australia, significant media attention has recently been given to cases of sexual harassment and abuse in military establishments and elite sports clubs, for example. Some organizations are even developed for the purposes of sexual exploitation, such as hard-core pornography distribution, prostitution, sex trafficking, sex "tourism," and pro-pedophilia networks.

Families are of course usually a place of safety for adults and the frontline defense for children, and the vast majority of families no doubt provide perfectly adequate protections against sexual offending. Yet it is also in family settings where sexual abuse in particular is by far the most prevalent. Sexual abuse is more likely to occur in families experiencing conflict and separation, and where other kinds of child maltreatment have occurred. There is some evidence that offenders in family settings are more likely to be unrelated to the child victim than to be a biological parent (Simon & Zgoba, 2006), and the presence in the home of a stepfather or mother's boyfriend has been noted as a risk factor (Finkelhor & Baron, 1986). Circumstances in which unrelated males are given unsupervised access to intimate childcare situations (e.g., bathing, dressing, reading in bed) may present avoidable risks. Domestic overcrowding has also been noted as a risk factor for both adolescent and adult sexual offending (Finkelhor, 1984). Sexual abuse of adults in family settings may occur in the context of wider partner abuse and violence.

Finally, peer systems can both protect and endanger young women and children. Peers may help each other to avoid risky situations (e.g., excessive alcohol use, exploitative or violent relationships, unsafe places and unsafe behavior), or provide ready access for safe disclosure if sexual violence or abuse does occur. But peers may also expose each other to risky situations. Some active offenders may even recruit new victims through their peer networks. Peer isolation may place children and young adults at greater risk of succumbing to the attentions of a potential offender. Peer systems may also contain risk and protective factors for potential offenders, for example by providing peer approval or disapproval of abuse-related attitudes and behavior.

Situational Factors

It is in the immediate behavioral setting where these biological, developmental, and ecological factors interact with situational factors to produce a specific behavioral outcome. In Figure 3.1 we have used the generic term "individual vulnerabilities" to denote a general biologically and developmentally based susceptibility to a (chronic, occasional, or momentary) breakdown in sexual self-restraint. We proposed above that the key mechanisms of self-restraint are empathic concern, emotional regulation, and moral reasoning. As depicted in Figure 3.1, these general individual-level vulnerabilities interact with immediate situational factors to produce the onset (and for persistent offenders also subsequent) sexual offense(s). Situational factors generally arise from the more proximal levels of the offender's and the victim's natural social ecologies (family, peer, organizational, and neighborhood systems). This person-situation interaction is at the core of our theoretical model.

The immediate situations in which sexual offenses occur can be understood in two different (but not mutually exclusive) ways. First, situations may present the opportunity for sexual offending motivations to be enacted. In this respect, the minimum requisite conditions are a motivated offender, a suitable "target," and the absence of a capable guardian (Cohen & Felson, 1979). This formulation assumes that the offender brings to the situation an already-formed motivation to commit the offense, and conceives of the situation as little more than a passive backdrop against which the offender's motivations are played out. From the motivated offender's point of view, the most suitable opportunity is one in which the perceived risk of detection is low, committing the offense requires little anticipated effort, and completing the offense is likely to deliver a desired reward (Cornish & Clarke, 1986).

Situations can also be understood to contain dynamic properties that act on the potential offender to produce offense-related motivations in the first place. In this formulation situations are conceived not just as passive locations, but as highly dynamic settings that stimulate criminal behaviors by individuals who would not otherwise have considered committing the crime, at least not at that specific time. Referred to as "crime precipitators" (Wortley, 2001), the mechanisms by which situations may evoke criminal motivations include prompts, temptations, social pressures, permissibility, and perceived provocations. We have described elsewhere some ways in which these mechanisms may evoke sexual abuse motivations (see

Wortley & Smallbone, 2006; Smallbone, Marshall, & Wortley, 2008), and in the interests of brevity we will not elaborate on these here.

This dynamic role of situations may be particularly relevant for explaining the onset sexual offense incident, since at this point many offenders will not yet have formed an unambiguous or stable motivation for sexual offending. Many will have arrived at the onset offense situation with a background of nonsexual offending, so will already have some experience with coercion, rule-breaking, exploiting opportunities for self-interest, and so on, but at the point of the onset sexual offense will not yet have developed a clear intention to commit a sexual offense. Others will have already formed an intention to sexually abuse or assault, either in a general sense or in relation to a specific victim, perhaps even developing elaborate fantasies or plans prior to the onset sexual offense. This group may or may not also have a history of nonsexual offending. A third group will be otherwise law-abiding people whose sexual offense motivations arise more or less spontaneously in response to the onset offense situation itself.

Onset and Beyond

For DLC researchers, the onset of offending is generally conceived of as a process, rather than as a discrete incident; as a time or age period rather than as an event at a specific point in time. Even if offending onset is defined as the first arrest or first conviction, the specific origins of the problem behavior, and especially its proximal causes and consequences, may remain unclear. To be sure, sexual offending may first occur as part of a discernible developmental process involving early behavioral problems and a generalized pattern of irresponsible and antisocial behavior. But while many sexual offenders have early behavioral problems and nonsexual offending histories, few general offenders apparently go on to be convicted of sexual offenses. And even when it is preceded by other offending, adult-onset sexual offending generally does not occur during periods of intensive general offending (which is more likely to occur in adolescence and early adulthood).

One remarkable feature of sexual offending is that postconviction sexual recidivism rates are generally low, and yet a small group of sexual offenders becomes extraordinarily persistent. In some ways this latter group resembles Moffitt's (1993) general life-course persistent offenders, but the unusual aspect of sexual offending is that some offenders, particularly nonfamilial male-victim offenders, develop compulsive and deviant sexual preferences, and some of these do so while refraining from other kinds of offending. We propose that, while certain biological, developmental, and ecological factors interact to produce a general vulnerability for antisocial behavior, including sexual offending, understanding sexual offending and its developmental trajectories requires an analysis of the proximal (as well as distal) antecedents and consequences of the onset offense.

Earlier we proposed that offenders do not learn to commit a first sexual offense, but rather that they fail to learn not to. They may well have learned relevant attitudes and behaviors prior to the onset offense, but offenders learn the most about offending by offending. Thus, in accordance with learning theory, as with any other human behavior, sexual offending behavior is shaped by its consequences, and enabled or constrained by its situational determinants. The development of stable deviant sexual preferences is therefore more likely to follow than to precede the onset of sexual offending.

It is likely that the "dark figure" of sexual offending is very large (e.g., Bouchard & Lussier, this book). Some persistent offenders may succeed in remaining undetected, but persistent offenders are exposed to a much greater risk of detection, and if detected are more likely to be convicted. We can conclude from this that occasional or one-off sexual offenders are more likely to be underrepresented in conviction samples, and that large proportions (perhaps the majority) of sexual offenders commit only one or a few sexual offenses and then desist before being caught. Reasons for spontaneous desistance may include changes in the opportunity structures and precipitating conditions, or the recognition by the offender that continued offending will increase the risk of detection. Perhaps the sexual encounter itself was unsatisfying or aversive, or the offending sensitized the offender to the victim's experience.

Some offenders may be caught after a single sexual offense and then desist from further sexual offending. In many of these cases the sexual offense will occur in the context of contemporaneous general offending, and while the offender refrains from further sexual offending he may go on to be arrested for further nonsexual offenses. This pattern suggests a general antisocial orientation, but perhaps the single sexual offense proved ultimately to be unrewarding, aversive, or risky, and further suitable circumstances for sexual offending do not present themselves. In other cases the single sexual offense may be an aberration in the context of an otherwise conforming lifestyle.

Other offenders offend repeatedly before being caught, but thereafter desist. Familial sexual abusers, for example, often offend repeatedly against one or two (usually female) victims but then desist following detection and arrest. For these offenders the first offense incidents proved rewarding, and opportunity structures remained stable. The offender may at first be apprehensive about being caught, but as time progresses and these fears are unrealized he may become more confident that the risks are remote and manageable. The offending behavior may become increasingly reinforced with successive offenses, but for these offenders external controls nevertheless exert a strong effect on the offending trajectory. In these circumstances desistance involves changes in opportunity structures and precipitating conditions: the offender is likely to be removed from the home or workplace where the offending has occurred (preventing access), others are now alerted to the problem (increasing capable guardianship), and the victim may be afforded support and protection (reducing vulnerability). The arrest may also lead to the offender's treatment and risk management, potentially reducing his individual vulnerabilities and increasing social controls.

A fourth pattern of progression beyond the onset sexual offense involves continued sexual offending prior to and following detection or arrest, sometimes even continuing despite the interruptions of multiple successive arrests. This may be due partly to failures by justice and child protection systems to effect change in the relevant opportunity structures or the offenders' offense-related vulnerabilities and motivations. Persistence for these offenders may be the result of powerful rewards obtained through offending. These cases may involve bald exploitation of others for sexual gratification, or, particularly where the victims are children or youth, the offender's sexual motivations may become confounded with attachment-nurturing motivations. In some cases motivations to sexually assault or abuse become compulsive and increasingly resistant to ordinary situational and social barriers. Many of these persistent sexual offenders will become socially marginalized, both through their sexual lifestyle and through the stigmatization of imprisonment or community notification, and thus become increasingly less influenced by formal and informal social controls.

Ultimately, of course, all sexual offenders desist. As we have proposed, most will do so either before being arrested or immediately following their first arrest. Persistent offenders will eventually desist because opportunity structures and precipitating conditions change, or because the offending ultimately becomes unrewarding relative to the personal effort and potential costs of continued offending. For the most persistent and committed offenders, desistance may ultimately be effected through the incapacitation of aging, illness, indefinite imprisonment, or death.

Conclusions

Criminological research, including DLC theories, have given little specific attention to sexual offending, and at the same time empirical research and specialist theories of sexual offending have paid little attention to the criminal career dimensions of sexual offending. While the empirical base for our theory is therefore in some respects tenuous, we are confident that it is at least consistent with available evidence. Our interpretation of this evidence is that the empirical dimensions of sexual offending are in some respects similar to those of general offending (e.g., criminal versatility; small proportion of offenders responsible for a large proportion of offenses), and in other respects dissimilar (e.g., different onset and desistance patterns). For these reasons we believe a separate theory of sexual offending is required, but that such a theory must maintain conceptual and empirical connections to general theories of crime. Like other DLC (e.g., Farrington, 2005b) and specialist sexual offender theorists (e.g., Marshall & Barbaree, 1990; Ward & Beech, 2006), we think that the way forward is to integrate different levels of analysis. The theory we have proposed in this chapter is essentially a criminological analysis of sexual offending that accordingly aims to integrate multiple theoretical threads (evolutionary, developmental, social ecology, social control, behavioral, and environmental criminology theories).

At the core of our theoretical model is the person-situation interaction. We have argued that biological, developmental, and ecological factors interact to produce general individual vulnerabilities for antisocial behavior, including sexual offending. While we recognize the complexity of human biological and social cognitive development, we have construed these individual vulnerabilities essentially in terms of individuals' capacity and commitment to exercise general and sexual self-restraint. Sexual offending is caused by proximal interactions between these general individual vulnerabilities and the situational factors comprising the immediate behavioral setting. These situational factors in turn arise from the ecological systems in which the offender and victim are socially embedded (family, peer, organizational, and neighborhood systems). While individual vulnerabilities no doubt contribute to the onset sexual offense and are likely to continue beyond that point, sexual offending trajectories are determined by the proximal antecedents and consequences of the offending itself, rather than by distal developmental antecedents.

Moving forward will require new research priorities, and we hope our theory suggests some specific points of focus. We think investigating the proximal antecedents and outcomes of the onset and subsequent sexual offense incidents is one promising direction. An important question in this regard is the extent to which stable sexual offense-related dispositions precede, or develop as a result of, sexual offending. We have assumed the latter is generally more likely, but this requires further empirical testing. Clearly, research directed at understanding the trajectories of undetected sexual offending is also of central importance. Research is also needed to determine the common and possibly distinct developmental antecedents of sexual and nonsexual offending, and the ways in which ecological systems interact with developmental and situational factors. We remain unclear how the role of biological factors might be directly investigated at this stage, but hope that our biological analysis at least contributes to further theoretical debate.

Finally, a theory of sexual offending should contribute to solving applied problems, and in this respect we hope our theory contributes to refinements in treatment and risk management with known offenders, and even more important, to the prevention of sexual offending before it would otherwise occur.

References

Abel, G. C., Becker, M. V., Cunningham-Rathner, J., Mittleman, M. S., Murphy, W. D., & Rouleau, J. L. (1987). Self-reported sex crimes of non-incarcerated paraphiliacs. *Journal of Interpersonal Violence, 2*, 3–25.

Aboriginal and Torres Strait Islander Women's Task Force on Violence. (1999). *Aboriginal and Torres Strait Islander women's task force on violence report*. Brisbane, Australia: Queensland Government.

Amir, M. (1971). *Patterns in forcible rape*. Chicago: University of Chicago Press.

Bijleveld, C., & Hendriks, J. (2003). Juvenile sex offenders: Differences between group and solo offenders. *Psychology, Crime & Law, 9*, 237–245.

Bowlby, J. (1969). *Attachment and loss: Vol. 1. Attachment*. New York: Basic Books.

Broadhurst, R. G., & Maller, R. A. (1992). The recidivism of sex offenders in the Western Australian prison population. *British Journal of Criminology, 32*, 54–80.

Butler, S. M., & Seto, M. C. (2002). Distinguishing two types of juvenile sex offenders. *Journal of the American Academy of Child and Adolescent Psychiatry, 41*, 83–90.

Cale, J., Lussier, P., & Proulx, J. (2009). Heterogeneity in antisocial trajectories in youth of adult sexual aggressors of women: An examination of initiation, persistence, escalation, and aggravation. *Sexual Abuse: A Journal of Research and Treatment, 21*, 223–248.

Catalano, R. F., Park, J., Harachi, T. W., Haggerty, K. P., Abbott, R. D., & Hawkins, J. D. (2005). Mediating the effects of poverty, gender, individual characteristics, and external constraints on antisocial behavior: A test of the social development model and implications for developmental life-course theory. In D. P. Farrington (Ed.), *Integrated developmental and life-course theories of offending* (pp. 93–124). New Brunswick, NJ: Transaction Publishers.

Chaffin, M., Berliner, L., Block, R., Johnson, T. C., Friedrich, W., Louis, D. et al. (2008). Report of the ATSA task force on children with sexual behavior problems. *Child Maltreatment, 18*, 199–218.

Cleary, S. (2004). *Sex offenders and self-control: Explaining sexual violence.* New York: LFB Scholarly Publishing LLC.

Cohen, L. E., & Felson, M. (1979). Social change and crime rate trends: A routine activity approach. *American Sociological Review, 44*, 588–560.

Cornish, D. B., & Clarke, R. V. (1986). *The reasoning criminal: Rational choice perspectives on offending.* New York: Springer-Verlag.

Cortoni, F., & Hanson, R. K. (2005). *A review of the recidivism rates of adult female sexual offenders (R-169).* Ottawa: Research Branch, Correction Service of Canada.

DeLamater, J., & Friedrich, W. N. (2002). Human sexual development. *Journal of Sex Research, 39*, 10–14.

De Young, M. (1988). The indignant page: Techniques of neutralization in the publications of pedophile organizations. *Child Abuse and Neglect, 12*, 583–591.

Elliott, D. S. (1994). Serious violent offenders: Onset, developmental course, and termination. *Criminology, 32*, 1–21.

Farrington, D. P. (1994). Early developmental prevention of juvenile delinquency. *Criminal Behavior and Mental Health, 4*, 209–227.

Farrington, D. P. (Ed.). (2005a) *Integrated developmental and life-course theories of offending.* New Brunswick, NJ: Transaction Publishers.

Farrington, D. P. (2005b). The integrated cognitive antisocial potential (ICAP) theory. In D. P. Farrington (Ed.), *Integrated developmental and life-course theories of offending.* (pp. 73–92). New Brunswick, NJ: Transaction Publishers.

Fehrenbach, P., Smith, W., Monastersky, C., & Deisher, R. (1986). Adolescent sexual offenders: Offender and offense characteristics. *American Journal of Orthopsychiatry, 56*, 225–233.

Finkelhor, D. (1984). *A sourcebook on child sexual abuse.* New York: Free Press.

Finkelhor, D., & Baron, L. (1986). Risk factors for child sexual abuse. *Journal of Interpersonal Violence, 1*, 43–71.

France, K., & Hudson, S. (1993). *The conduct disorders and the juvenile sex offenders.* In H. E. Barbaree, W. L. Marshall, & S. M. Hudson (Eds.), *The juvenile sex offender* (pp. 225–234). New York: Guilford Press.

Friedrich, W. N. (2007). *Children with sexual behavior problems: Family-based, attachment-focused therapy.* New York: W. W. Norton.

Hagan, M. P., King, R. P., & Patros, R. L. (1994). Recidivism among adolescent perpetrators of sexual assault against children. *Journal of Offender Rehabilitation, 21*, 127–137.

Hanson, R. K. (2002). Recidivism and age: Follow-up data from 4,673 sexual offenders. *Journal of Interpersonal Violence, 17*, 1046–1062.
Hanson, R. K., & Bussière, M. T. (1998). Predicting relapse: A meta-analysis of sexual offender recidivism studies. *Journal of Consulting and Clinical Psychology, 66*, 348–362.
Hanson, R. K., Gordon, A., Harris, A., Marques, J., Murphy, W., Quinsey, V. L. et al. (2002). First report of the collaborative outcome data project on the effectiveness of treatment for sex offenders. *Sexual Abuse: A Journal of Research and Treatment, 14*, 169–194.
Harris, D. A., Mazerolle, P., & Knight, R. A. (2009). Understanding male sexual offending: A comparison of general and specialist theories. *Criminal Justice and Behavior, 36*, 1051–1069.
Harris, G. T., & Rice, M. E. (2007). Adjusting actuarial violence risk assessments based on aging or the passage of time. *Criminal Justice and Behavior, 34*, 297–313.
Hawkins, J. D., Herrenkohl, T. L., Farrington, D. P., Brewer, D., Catalano, R. F., & Harachi, T. W. (1998). A review of predictors of youth violence. In R. Loeber & D. P. Farrington (Eds.), *Serious and violent juvenile offenders: Risk factors and successful interventions* (pp. 106–146). Thousand Oaks, CA: Sage Publications.
Kahn, T., & Chambers, H. (1991). Assessing reoffense risk with juvenile sexual offenders. *Child Welfare, 70*, 333–346.
Knight, R. A. (1999). Validation of a typology of rapists. *Journal of Interpersonal Violence, 14*, 303–330.
Knight, R. A., Carter, D. L., & Prentky, R. A. (1989). A system for the classification of child molesters: Reliability and application. *Journal of Interpersonal Violence, 4*, 3–23.
Koss, M. P., Dinero, T. E., Siebel, C. A., & Cox, S. L. (1988). Stranger and acquaintance rape: Are there differences in the victim's experience? *Psychology of Women Quarterly, 12*, 1–24.
La Fontaine, J. S. (1993). Defining organized sexual abuse. *Child Abuse Review, 2*, 223–231.
Laws, D. R., & Marshall, W. L. (1990). A conditioning theory of the etiology and maintenance of deviant sexual preference and behavior. In W. L. Marshall, D. R. Laws, & H. E. Barbaree (Eds.), *Handbook of sexual assault: Issues, theories, and treatment of the offender* (pp. 209–229). New York: Plenum Press.
LeBlanc, M. (2005). An integrated personal control theory of deviant behavior: Answers to contemporary empirical and theoretical developmental criminology issues. In D. P. Farrington (Ed.), *Integrated developmental and life-course theories of offending* (pp. 125–163). New Brunswick, NJ: Transaction Publishers.
Lipsey, M. W., & Derzon, J. H. (1998). Predictors of violent or serious delinquency in adolescence and early adulthood: A synthesis of longitudinal research. In R. Loeber & D. P. Farrington (Eds.), *Serious and violent juvenile offenders: Risk factors and successful interventions* (pp. 86–105). Thousand Oaks, CA: Sage Publications.
Loeber, R., & Farrington, D. P. (1998). *Serious and violent juvenile offenders: Risk factors and successful interventions*. London: Sage Publications.
Loeber, R., Van Kammen, W. B., & Fletcher, M. (1996). *Serious, violent and chronic offenders in the Pittsburgh Youth Study*. Pittsburgh, PA: Western Psychiatric Institute and Clinic.
Longo, R. E., & Groth, A. N. (1983). Juvenile sexual offenses in the histories of adult rapists and child molesters. *International Journal of Offender Therapy and Comparative Criminology, 27*, 150–155.
Lussier, P. (2005). The criminal activity of sexual offenders in adulthood: Revisiting the specialization debate. *Sexual Abuse: A Journal of Research and Treatment, 17*, 269–292.
Lussier, P., & Healey, J. (2010). The developmental origins of sexual violence: Examining the co-occurrence of physical aggression and normative sexual behaviors in early childhood. *Behavioral Sciences and the Law, 28*, 1–23.

Lussier, P., LeBlanc, M., & Proulx, J. (2005). The generality of criminal behavior: A confirmatory factor analysis of the criminal activity of sex offenders in adulthood. *Journal of Criminal Justice, 33*, 177–189.

Lussier, P., Leclerc, B., Cale, J., & Proulx, J. (2007). Developmental pathways of deviance in sexual aggressors. *Criminal Justice and Behavior, 34*, 1441–1462.

Lussier, P., Proulx, J., & LeBlanc, M. (2005). Criminal propensity, deviant sexual interests and criminal activity of sexual aggressors against women: A comparison of explanatory models. *Criminology, 43*, 249–281.

Lussier, P., Tzoumakis, S., Cale, J., & Amirault, J. (2010). Criminal trajectories of adult sexual aggressors and the age effect: Examining the dynamic aspect of offending in adulthood. *International Criminal Justice Review, 20*, 147–168.

Marshall, W. L., & Barbaree, H. E. (1990). An integrated theory of the etiology of sexual offending. In W. L. Marshall, D. R. Laws, & H. E. Barbaree (Eds.), *Handbook of sexual assault: Issues, theories, and treatment of the offender* (pp. 257–275). New York: Plenum.

Marshall, W. L., Barbaree, H. E., & Eccles, A. (1991). Early onset and deviant sexuality in child molesters. *Journal of Interpersonal Violence, 6*, 323–335.

Miethe, T. D., Olson, J., & Mitchell, O. (2006). Specialization and persistence in the arrest histories of sex offenders: A comparative analysis of alternative measures and offense types. *Journal of Research in Crime and Delinquency, 43*, 204–229.

Moffitt, T. E. (1993). Adolescence-limited and life-course-persistent antisocial behavior: A developmental taxonomy. *Psychological Review, 4*, 674–701.

Moffitt, T. E., Caspi, A., Harrington, H., & Milne, B. J. (2002). Males on the life-course persistent and adolescence-limited antisocial pathways: Follow-up at age 26. *Development and Psychopathology, 14*, 179–206.

Moore, J., & Hagedorn, J. (2001). *Female gangs: A focus on research.* Office of Juvenile Justice and Delinquency Prevention. Washington, DC: U.S. Department of Justice.

Murphy, M. R., Seckl, J. R., Burton, S., Checkly, S. A., & Lightman, S. L. (1987). Changes in oxytocin and vasopressin secretion during sexual activity in men. *Journal of Clinical Endocrinology and Metabolism, 65*, 738–741.

Nisbet, I. A., Smallbone, S., & Wortley, R. (2010). Developmental, individual and family characteristics of specialist, versatile, and short duration adolescent sex offenders. *Sexual Abuse in Australia and New Zealand, 2*, 85–96.

Nisbet, I. A., Wilson, P. H., & Smallbone, S. (2004). A prospective longitudinal study of sexual recidivism among adolescent sex offenders. *Sexual Abuse: A Journal of Research and Treatment, 3*, 223–234.

O'Brien, M. J., & Bera, W. H. (1986). *The PHASE typology of adolescent sex offenders.* Salem: Department of Human Resources, Children's Services Division.

Panksepp, J. (1998). *Affective neuroscience: The foundations of human and animal emotions.* New York: Oxford University Press.

Parks, G. A., & Bard, D. E. (2006). Risk factors for adolescent sex offender recidivism: Evaluation of predictive factors and comparison of three groups based upon victim type. *Sexual Abuse: A Journal of Research and Treatment, 18*, 319–342.

Prentky, R. A., Knight, R. A., & Lee, A. (1997). Risk factors associated with recidivism among extra-familial child molesters. *Journal of Consulting and Clinical Psychology, 65*, 141–149.

Piquero, A. R., & Moffitt, T. E. (2005). Explaining the facts of crime: How the developmental taxonomy replies to Farrington's invitation. In D. P. Farrington (Ed.), *Integrated developmental and life-course theories of offending* (pp. 51–72). New Brunswick, NJ: Transaction Publishers.

Proulx, J., Lussier, P., Ouimet, M., & Boutin, S. (2008). Criminal career parameters in four types of sexual aggressors. In B. K. Schwartz (Ed.), *The sex offender: Offender evaluation and program strategies* (Vol. VI, pp. 3/1 - 3–12). New York, NY: Civic Research Institute.

Queensland Police Service. (2006). Queensland Police Service annual report 2005–2006. Retrieved from Queensland Police website: https://www.police.qld.gov.au/corporatedocs/reportsPublications/annualReport/Documents/QPS%202013-14%20Annual%20Report.pdf.

Rubinstein, M., Yeager, C. A., Goodstein, C., & Lewis, D. O. (1993). Sexually assaultive male juveniles: A follow-up. *American Journal of Psychiatry, 150*, 262–265.

Sanday, P. G. (2007). *Fraternity gang rape: Sex brotherhood, and privilege on campus* (2nd ed.). New York: New York University Press.

Seto, M. C., & Lalumière, M. L. (2010). What is so special about male adolescent sexual offending? A review and test of explanations through meta-analysis. *Psychological Bulletin, 136*, 526–575.

Simon, L. M. J., & Zgoba, K. (2006). Sex crimes against children: Legislation, prevention and investigation. In R. Wortley and S. Smallbone (Eds.), *Situational prevention of child sexual abuse* (pp. 65–100). Crime Prevention Studies. Vol. 19. Monsey, NY: Criminal Justice Press.

Sizonenko, P. C. (1978). Endocrinology in preadolescents and adolescents: I. Hormonal changes during normal puberty. *American Journal of Diseases of Childhood, 132*, 704–712.

Smallbone, S. (2006). Social and psychological factors in the development of delinquency and sexual deviance. In H. E. Barbaree and W. L. Marshall (Eds.), *The juvenile sex offender* (pp. 105–127). New York: Guilford Press.

Smallbone, S., Marshall, W. L., & Wortley, R. (2008). *Preventing child sexual abuse: Evidence, policy and practice*. Cullompton, Devon: Willan Publishing.

Smallbone, S., & Wortley, R. (2000). *Child sexual abuse in Queensland: Offender characteristics and modus operandi* (full report). Brisbane, Queensland, Australia: Queensland Crime Commission.

Smallbone, S., & Wortley, R. (2001). Child sexual abuse: Offender characteristics and modus operandi. *Australian Institute of Criminology, Trends and Issues in Crime and Criminal Justice, No.* 193.

Smallbone, S., & Wortley, R. (2004a). Onset, persistence, and versatility of offending among adult males convicted of sexual offenses against children. *Sexual Abuse: A Journal of Research and Treatment, 16*, 285–298.

Smallbone, S., & Wortley, R. (2004b). Criminal diversity and paraphilic interests among adult males convicted of sexual offenses against children. *International Journal of Offender Therapy and Comparative Criminology, 48*, 175–188.

Soothill, K., Francis, B., Sanderson, B., & Ackerley, E. (2000). Sex offenders: Specialists, generalists or both? *British Journal of Criminology, 40*, 56–67.

Tracy, P. E., Wolfgang, M. E., & Figlio, R. M. (1990). *Delinquency careers in two birth cohorts.* New York: Plenum.

Ullman, S., & Siegel, J. (1993). Victim-offender relationship and sexual assault. *Violence and Victims, 8*, 121–134.

United States Department of Justice. (2009). *Crime in the United States, 2008*. U.S. Department of Justice, Federal Bureau of Investigation, Criminal Justice Information Services Division. Retrieved from http://www2.fbi.gov/ucr/cius2008/data/table_43.html.

Van Mastrigt, S. B., & Farrington, D. P. (2009). Co-offending, age, gender and crime type: Implications for criminal justice policy. *British Journal of Criminology, 49*, 552–573.

Ward. T., & Beech, A. (2006). An integrated theory of sexual offending. *Aggression and Violent Behavior, 11*, 44–63.

Ward, T., & Hudson, S. M. (1998). The construction and development of theory in the sexual offending area: A meta-theoretical framework. *Sexual Abuse: A Journal of Research and Treatment, 10*, 47–63.

Ward, T., & Siegert, R. J. (2002). Toward and comprehensive theory of child sexual abuse: A theory knitting perspective. *Psychology, Crime, and Law, 9*, 319–351.

Wikström, P. H. (2005). The social origins of pathways to crime: Towards a developmental ecological action theory of crime involvement and its changes. In D. P. Farrington (Ed.). *Integrated developmental and life-course theories of offending* (pp. 211–246). New Brunswick, NJ: Transaction Publishers.

Wood, E. J. (2006). Variation in sexual violence during war. *Politic Society, 34*, 307–341.

Wortley, R. (2001). A classification of techniques for controlling situational precipitators of crime. *Security Journal, 14*, 63–82.

Wortley, R., & Smallbone, S. (2006). *Situational prevention of child sexual abuse.* Crime prevention studies (Vol. 19). Monsey, NY: Criminal Justice Press.

Wortley, R., & Smallbone, S. (in press). Internet child pornography: Causes, investigation, and prevention. New York: Praeger Publishing.

Zimring, F. E., Piquero, A. R., & Jennings, W. G. (2007). Sexual delinquency in Racine: Does early sex offending predict later sex offending in youth and young adulthood? *Criminology and Public Policy, 6*, 507–534.

Part II

Criminal Career Patterns of Sex Offenders and Associated Issues

4

Criminal Careers for Different Juvenile Sex Offender Subgroups

Jan Hendriks
VU University, the Netherlands

Chantal van den Berg[1] & Catrien Bijleveld[2]
[1] Leiden University, the Netherlands, [2]NSCR and VU University, the Netherlands

Introduction

Recidivism by juvenile sexual offenders (JSO) has attracted a lot of attention in international research over the last two decades. Most studies show that JSO have low base rates of sexual recidivism (Caldwell, 2002, 2010; Hendriks & Bijleveld, 2008; McCann & Lussier, 2008; Vandiver, 2006; Waite et al., 2005; Zimring, Piquero, & Jennings, 2007): a weighted average percentage of between 10 and 13% sexual recidivism is found (Caldwell, 2002, Edwards & Beech, 2005). Recidivism rates also tend to differ widely between studies. Levels of sexual recidivism found in the meta-analysis by McCann & Lussier ranged between 2 and 30%. They concluded that this heterogeneity in results is related to the study design (e.g., nature of sample) and the length of the follow-up period.

The finding that sexual recidivism is generally low is contrary to public belief. Policymakers also seem to believe that juvenile sex offenders, particularly those who have offended against children, are a high risk group, the reason why there are special registration laws for JSO in different countries. In the Netherlands, the country where the study described in this chapter was conducted, JSO are registered in order to ban them for life from working with children or people who are otherwise dependent. At the same time, the international scientific literature also shows that JSO have much higher general than sexual recidivism rates (Caldwell, 2010; Edwards et al., 2005; Hendriks & Bijleveld, 2008; Vandiver, 2006; Waite et al., 2005; Zimring et al., 2007). General recidivism is defined as reoffending that includes any offense (e.g., sexual, violent, drugs, or property crimes). Rates of 50–60% are reported, including recidivism measurements taken during adolescence as well as

Sex Offenders: A Criminal Career Approach, First Edition. Edited by Arjan Blokland and Patrick Lussier.

adulthood; these studies find the likelihood of general recidivism compared to sexual recidivism is roughly fivefold.

Because of the fact that JSO will recidivate mostly to other (nonsexual) offenses, one might question whether JSO are a distinct group or whether their criminal careers are just like those of general offenders. This question is hard to answer as most studies have investigated the criminal careers of JSO over a relatively short time span, often barely into adulthood. Caldwell (2010), for instance, in his meta-analysis of 63 studies, found a weighted mean follow-up period of 59.4 months after the index sex offense. Also, most studies have investigated only the first (sex) offense in a certain follow-up period, thereby disregarding repeat offending and the patterning of offending over the life course. These issues are further complicated by the fact that JSO constitute a heterogeneous group. It is known that motives and backgrounds differ between, for instance, child abusers and peer abusers, the distinction within the group of JSO most commonly made (see Hagan, Cho, Gust-Brey, & Dow, 2001; Hendriks & Bijleveld, 2004; Hsu & Starzynski, 1990; Hunter, Figueredo, Malamuth, & Becker, 2003; Worling, 1995). A further distinction can be made between solo and group offenders (Bijleveld & Hendriks, 2003), that is, those with co-offenders and those without co-offenders. Other distinctions are made on the basis of criminal career aspects. Butler and Seto (2002), for instance, distinguished between "sex-only" and "sex-plus" offenders. The latter group is at higher risk for general offending. Soothill, Sanderson, and Ackerley (2000), who made a distinction between generalists and specialists, came to the same conclusion.

The first aim of this study is to describe the criminal careers of juvenile sex offenders, from adolescence into adulthood. A second aim is to compare these careers for different subgroups: child abusers, peer abusers, and group offenders. Lastly, we aim to investigate the crime mix in these criminal careers.

Literature Review

Despite low overall sexual recidivism, JSO are usually found to be at increased risk of sexual reoffending, though some studies do not find such differences. Caldwell (2007), for example, showed that for JSO (N = 249), the prevalence of a new sex offense charge during a 5-year follow-up period was 6.8%, which was not significantly different from the 5.7% found for nonsexual offenders (N = 1,780). Hendriks and Bijleveld (2008), on the other hand, found that 11% of a sample of JSO (N = 112) who had been treated on an inpatient basis committed a sexual reoffense. Comparatively speaking, Van der Geest, Bijleveld, and Wijkman (2005) found a recidivism percentage of 1.5% for sex offenses in a nonsex offender group (N = 270) who had been treated in the same institution over the same follow-up period as JSO included in the Hendriks and Bijleveld (2008) sample. The difference between the outcomes of Caldwell's study on one hand and those by Van der Geest et al. and Hendriks and Bijleveld on the other hand is possibly due to the fact that Caldwell's sexual offenders were less typical sexual, more violent and antisocial offenders, and that the Hendriks and Bijleveld sex offender sample contained many juvenile child abusers, who may be more likely to persist in committing sex crimes.

Research suggests that different groups of sexual offenders show different offending patterns (Hendriks, 2006; Wiesner & Capaldi, 2003). One problem with looking at the criminal careers of JSO is that, as mentioned before, in many studies, sex offenders are considered as a homogeneous group. Research however indicates that at least two subtypes of JSO can be recognized: child molesters and peer abusers (Hagan et al., 2001; Hendriks & Bijleveld, 2008; Hsu & Starzynsi, 1990; Hunter et al., 2003; Hunter, Figueredo, Malamuth, & Becker, 2004; Worling, 1995). Seto and Lalumière (2010) stress the importance of the age of the victim as moderator. According to them, relatively few studies, however, directly compare JSO who victimized peers or adults with those who victimized children. Adolescent child abusers victimize children who are not sexually mature with an age difference between victim and perpetrator of at least 4–5 years. Peer abusers abuse victims either of their own age or older. These groups can be distinguished by different personality and background characteristics, different risk factors, and different recidivism patterns (Hendriks, 2006). For instance, child abusers are relatively more anxious and depressed and more often a victim of bullying. They manifest greater deficits in psychosocial functioning (see also Hunter et al., 2004). Relatively often they are also a victim of child sexual abuse. Child abusers have both male and female victims. They show less violence in their sexual offending and are less versatile and less violent in their recidivism pattern compared to peer abusers. Peer abusers, on the other hand, mostly offend against females (Hendriks & Bijleveld, 2004, 2008). Bijleveld and Hendriks (2003) included a third subtype, the group offender, who commits his or her sex crime with at least one co-offender. Victims are mostly girls of the offenders' own age. This subtype can be regarded as less psychologically disturbed, but more antisocial than other peer abusers.

An empirical study by Hendriks (2006) suggests that risk factors of sexual recidivism appear to be different for the three groups. Whereas a negative self-image, being bullied at school, and attending special education correlate with sexual recidivism for peer abusers, the absence of neurotic complaints, the presence of court interventions in the past, and a history of sexual offenses correlate with sexual recidivism for child abusers (Hendriks, 2006). For the group offenders no significant risk factors were found in the Hendriks (2006) study. Sexual recidivism was similar (10%) across groups. However, solo offenders were much quicker to reoffended (i.e., 90% of solo offending recidivists reoffended within three years) than group offenders. These findings illustrate the need for relatively long follow-up periods to reveal differences in offending patterns across JSO types.

Lussier, Leclerc, Cale, and Proulx (2007) showed that adult child molesters report lower levels of externalization compared to offenders with adult victims, who are more likely to report higher levels. This result might explain the fact that adult child molesters' criminal activity tends to start late, is less frequent, and is more specialized in sexual crimes compared to those having offended against adults, whose criminal activity tends to mirror that of violent offenders. Skubic Kemper and Kistner (2007) also found that peer abusers, compared to child abusers, had a more extensive criminal history, which is consistent with research showing that peer abusers generally engage in more extensive disruptive behavior than child abusers.

Theory

From criminal career research on general offenders we know that the prevalence of offending peaks in late adolescence (Farrington et al., 2006). Most offenders again desist from crime when in their twenties. Referring to the dual taxonomy introduced by Moffitt (1993), two types of criminal career can be distinguished. The vast majority of juvenile delinquents are adolescence-limited (AL) offenders. AL offenders are characterized by the onset of antisocial behavior in adolescence and desistance in early adulthood. According to the theory, a contemporary maturity gap encourages teens to mimic antisocial behavior of their peers in ways that are normative and adjustive. AL offenders are least likely to initiate victim-orientated offenses such as violence (Moffitt, 1993; Piquero & Moffitt, 2005). Life-course-persistent (LCP) offenders, on the other hand, constitute only a small proportion of all juvenile offenders. This group is characterized by the early onset of antisocial behavior in childhood, its persistence throughout adolescence and adulthood, and diversification and escalation to more serious forms of antisocial behavior. For this latter group, childhood neuropsychological problems interact cumulatively with their criminogenic environment across development, culminating in a pathological personality. A third path, the low-level chronics (LLC), was later added. These individuals have fewer contacts with (antisocial) peers and therefore commit offenses at lower frequencies. Moffitt's taxonomy was developed for general offenders. The question is whether and how juvenile sex offenders fit into this taxonomy. Based both on the seriousness and the interpersonal character of the offense, Moffitt presumed that rape is a manifestation of the LCP syndrome.

The notion of LCP offenders came under attack by Sampson and Laub (2003). These authors stipulated that there is too much heterogeneity in later life outcomes to treat early risk factors as deterministic. They argued that human trajectories are mainly the succession of random processes and events and, therefore, long-term prediction of antisocial behavior cannot be made effectively. Given the fact that random processes are involved, one should not expect to find a high prevalence of LCP offenders among JSO as predicted by Moffitt (1993).

Research on adult and adolescent sexual offenders has produced findings that seem to indicate that there is some similarity between general offenders and sex offenders. Seto and Barbaree (1997) distinguished two types of sexually aggressive men. The first type is persistently antisocial and is characterized by an early onset of problem behavior and developmental stability in the extent and breadth of antisocial behavior, including substance abuse, property offenses, and nonsexual aggression. This type resembles the LCP syndrome described by Moffitt. The second group of rapists, which resembles the AL group, is opportunistic and characterized by sexually coercive activity that mostly is confined to adolescence and young adulthood. These offenders do not show the early onset, extent, and chronicity of other antisocial behavior that is typical for the first group. They may also commit their sexual assaults with co-offenders.

Similar to Moffitt's AL syndrome, the young male syndrome was defined by Lalumière, Harris, Quinsey, and Rice (2005) as a context-dependent phenomenon. Risky tactics like coercion are specifically used during adolescence and young adulthood to obtain sexual gratifications. The LCP syndrome is characterized by an accumulation of early deficits that makes it more difficult for these individuals to succeed in finding suitable partners. The likelihood of using force to acquire sexual gratifications therefore increases. Lalumière et al. (2005) added a third pathway that is characterized by psychopathy. These men have much in common with LCP offenders but the origin of this behavior is different. This subgroup of men uses deceit, manipulation, and coercive tactics to create sexual opportunities. The psychopathic group exhibits a higher frequency of violent offending and recidivates more quickly than LCP offenders (see also Cale, Lussier, & Proulx, 2009).

Other theories concerning the development of sex offending lean less heavily on Moffitt's taxonomy. The pathways model described by Hudson, Ward, and McCormack (1999), for instance, connects rather well with the criminal career approach. One hypothesized pathway has been referred as the "antisocial cognitions" (Ward & Sorbello, 2003). The offenders characterized by this path show antisocial attitudes, and sexual offending is described as another manifestation of their general and versatile criminal behavior pattern. This pathway probably fits best with the group offenders and partly with the peer abusers, because they show, compared to the child abusers, much more general (including violent) offending (Bijleveld & Hendriks, 2003, Hendriks & Bijleveld, 2004; Hunter et al., 2003). Another pathway is that of the multiple dysfunctional scripts. The sex offenders characterized by this path show deviant sexual scripts based on their own child abuse history and/or related to their attachment problems. Relatively, many of these offenders are diagnosed with Attention Deficit Hyperactivity Disorder (ADHD). This pathway probably fits best with the child abusers and some peer abusers (Hendriks & Bijleveld, 2004) although no empirical research has tested these hypotheses.

Shortcomings, Prior Research, and Current Aim

Theories on juvenile sexual offending are seldom empirically tested, meaning that these theories have hardly been validated. Another issue with previous research is that often highly selective samples of juvenile sex offenders are studied, which makes it difficult to generalize findings. Zimring (2004) lists further methodological limitations: besides highly select samples, also short follow-up periods and lack of comparison groups are problematic. As Vandiver (2006) points out, additional research using larger samples and longer follow-up periods is needed to generalize the findings to a larger population. Furthermore, her findings that the age and sex of the victim is related to reoffending indicate that different types of sex offenders may exhibit unique offending patterns over time. In addition, most research on sexual reoffending is restricted to the examination of a new arrest or conviction for a sexual, general, or violent offense. McCann & Lussier (2008) conclude that more research is needed to take into account the criminal activities of JSO over their entire criminal career. By looking only at one or two consecutive crimes over time, only a snapshot of all criminal activity is taken into account.

The aim of this study is, first, to describe the recidivism of JSO, second, to examine their criminal careers well into adulthood, and third, to compare the recidivism and criminal careers for different subgroups of JSO. In doing so, we try to overcome some of the limitations of previous studies by using a relatively large sample of almost 500 JSO. This sample contains three groups: (a) JSO who were considered as highly dangerous and treated in an inpatient treatment center; (b) JSO who were considered as medium risk and treated on an outpatient basis; and (c) low-risk and untreated JSO. The average follow-up period of the current study extends more than a decade, which compared to most studies of JSO can be considered relatively long. The large sample size furthermore enables us to distinguish different subtypes, that is, child abusers, peer abusers, and group offenders, and to compare results across these offender subtypes. Taking into consideration the research mentioned above, it is reasonable to expect that a small proportion of JSO will be characterized by a relatively short period of sexual reoffending, and a much larger proportion by a longer and more intensive period of general offending. Looking at sexual and general offending it is further hypothesized that JSO are, in terms of Moffitt's dual taxonomy (1993), mainly AL offenders. This is in contrast with Moffitt's theory, which states that sexual violence is part of the LCP syndrome. Although the odds that LCP offenders will commit a sexual crime are probably higher than those for AL offenders, it is speculated that, as most juvenile delinquents are AL offenders, LCP offenders in fact constitute a minority of JSO. Furthermore, it is questionable whether child abusers show many similarities with other violent offenders that constitute the LCP group. Variations are expected in these patterns for the different subgroups: child abusers, peer abusers, and group offenders with the latter two probably showing a longer and more serious offending pattern. All in all, the scientific literature leads us to expect three types of developmental pathways among JSO:

1 High-frequency chronics: those antisocially inclined, experiencing an early start and offending at a high rate for a prolonged period of time. For these offenders sex offenses are part of a broader criminal repertoire that includes other types of crimes and violence.
2 Low-frequency chronics: those sexually deviant, who commit few offenses other than sex offenses, but do so for a prolonged period of time.
3 Adolescence-limited offenders: "experimenters" whose sex offending occurs only during early adolescence, and may be accompanied by minor nonsexual offending, like property offending.

Methodology

Sample

The research group consists of 498 male JSO. Of this group, 106 were treated in an outpatient treatment center and 216 did not receive specialized treatment for sex offending. The remaining 176 men were treated for their sex offending in an inpatient treatment center. All the young men in the research group had been convicted for or confessed at least one hands-on sex offense. They all had an active role during this offense. A small part (percentage) of the research group had also committed hands-off sex offenses, like public indecency. At the time of the sampling offense their average age was 14 (range: 10–17). A small number were too young to be prosecuted (in the Netherlands the age of criminal responsibility is 12), and these had been screened under a civil law title. The period in which the sampling offenses had taken place ranges from 1988 to 2001. The men were followed to an average age – when the last data were collected – of 28.7 years (range: 18–40). The average follow-up period is therefore well over 14 years. The Ministry of Justice gave formal consent for the study.

Offending Data

Official records for measuring offending were used and are based on conviction data. The database from which the conviction data were extracted (the so-called judicial documentation or JD) contains information about all cases that are registered for prosecution. Information about the date of perpetration, type of offense, conviction date, and sentence is included as well. All offenses were excluded for which a person was acquitted or when a case was dismissed by the prosecutor for technical reasons, meaning that insufficient proof was deemed present to take the case to court. A small number of cases that had (just before the last data collection) been registered but not yet adjudicated were recorded as registered by the prosecutor. All offenses used in this study were classified according to the standard classification system of Statistics Netherlands (Centraal Bureau voor de Statistiek). Sex offenses are listed in articles 242 to 249 of the criminal code, and entail rape, sexual assault, and various hands-on sex offenses against children or dependent persons. Violent offenses entail (serious) assault, homicide, robbery, and extortion. Property offenses entail theft, burglary, embezzlement, and fraud.

Analysis

Simple frequency counts and percentages are used to describe reoffending after the sampling offense, for sexual offending, violent offending, and property offending. These calculations took into account individual differences in exposure time during the follow-up period of our study. For those who were residentially treated the exposure period commenced when they were discharged: as they were treated in a closed setting, they had much less "exposure" to the risk of committing a new offense. For the remaining JSO the exposure time commenced right after their sampling offense was committed.

Next, the criminal careers of the 498 men from age 12 to the end of the observation period were analyzed using a "semi-parametric group-based trajectory model." This SAS-based procedure enables us to identify a limited number of latent developmental trajectories based on the way offenses are distributed across age (Nagin, 1999, 2005). The group-based model approximates individual developmental variation by a number of discrete groups. The outcome variable is linked to age by a polynomial function, but, unique to the group-based model, the parameters of this function are free to vary across groups. This results in estimated developmental trajectories that differ between groups both in the overall level of offending and in the shape of the trajectory across age. If there are JSO in our data who from an early age continue offending at high rates until far into adulthood, the group-based model will assign these respondents to a "chronic" trajectory; if there are also JSO in our data who offend only during adolescence and then abstain, it will combine these respondents into an "adolescence-limited" group. The technique thus attempts to combine the N respondents into a smaller number of subgroups that share "offending trajectories." In the present analysis we modeled the developmental trajectories based on the number of registered offenses per person per age year. Because the data is count data with excessive zeros – even the most prolific offenders experience many years without registrations – the use of a zero-inflated Poisson model was required (Böhning, 1998; Lambert, 1992).

An important issue in the application of group-based models concerns the determination of the number of distinct groups that define the best solution to fit the data. To choose the optimal number of subgroups in the model, the Bayesian Information Criterion (BIC) can be used (Nagin, 2005). During this procedure the initial one-group model is augmented with additional groups until the BIC score reaches a peak, indicating that adding more groups does not result in a better representation of the underlying data. If the improvement between consecutive models was less than a cut-off value ($2\log_e B_{10}$) (see Jones, Nagin, & Roeder, 2001), this was taken as an indication that model fit was not substantively improved and that a final model had been reached. In addition to the trajectories themselves, the group-based model produces a probability of membership for each of the distinguished trajectory groups for each individual in the sample. High average probability of class membership across all individuals assigned to each class – indicating high classification accuracy when assigning individual JSO to trajectory groups – also indicates good model fit. Nagin (2005) mentions additional criteria – including the odds of correct classification or OCC – that can be used to assess model fit. In the present analysis these other indicators of model fit were in line with the BIC in choosing the final model.

Given the possibility that ethnic background is associated with recidivism as well as the type of sex offense and may therefore act as a confounder, we included ethnic background as a risk factor in the group-based model. The trajectories in this model strongly resembled those in a model without this risk factor, leading us to believe that this did not fundamentally impact on the solution. Furthermore, incarceration time can influence developmental trajectories, because a detainee is not (or is less) able to commit offenses when incarcerated (Piquero et al., 2001). Thus, we corrected for time spent incarcerated by calculating exposure per person per year and taking that into account when estimating the developmental trajectories. The calculation was done by assuming that exposure has a range of 1 (no incarceration) to 0 (the entire year incarcerated). Because there is still a slight chance that a person can commit an offense when incarcerated, we determined exposure as follows:

$$\text{exposure}_{ji} = 1 - (\#\text{ days detained} / 730)$$

for every person j and age i (see Piquero et al., 2001; Van der Geest, Blokland, & Bijleveld, 2009). Within the sample, seven people died and 14 emigrated; after each event these people were coded "missing" so they would not affect the developmental trajectories from that age onward (Eggleston, Laub, & Sampson, 2004).

The group-based technique used in the current analyses has a fundamentally different approach than common recidivism models, such as event history analysis. Instead of only using information on the first offense after the index offense, information on offending over the entire criminal career is used. Thus, we analyze the number of offenses at each age, from age 12 (the earliest age of criminal responsibility) to age 32 (the last age for which data on a sufficiently large proportion of the sample were available). After assigning each individual JSO to the trajectory of their highest probability, we can also investigate whether trajectory membership is associated with background characteristics, for instance whether AL offenders have certain protective factors, or whether chronics committed particular types of sex offenses in adolescence. This technique has the advantage that a long-term view of the criminal career is taken and therefore it is able to distinguish between once-only recidivists and multiple or even chronic recidivists. The longitudinal group-based model therefore provides a much better understanding of the development of criminal careers than standard recidivism models.

For statistical tests on the association between variables (such as group membership and background characteristics) we use adjusted standardized residuals (see Field, 2000). These residuals are generally used to test whether the number of cases in a cell is significantly larger than would be expected if the null hypothesis of no association between the cross-tabulated variables was true.

Results

Recidivism and Group Characteristics

All 498 men had committed a hands-on sex offense. Almost three quarters (72%) are native Dutch. Three subtypes of offenders were distinguished: group offenders (16%), child abusers (52%), and peer abusers (32%). Of all 498 men, 27% committed one offense, the selection offense for this study. The remaining 73% committed at least one more offense after the selection offense; these offenses can vary from another sex offense, to violent and property offenses, but may also be traffic or drugs offenses. For sexual reoffending the recidivism percentage is 12.2%. Almost a third of the total group, 31.7%, reoffended with a violent (nonsexual) offense (as well) and 38.8% committed at least one property offense after the sampling offense. Group, peer, and child abusers did not differ in sexual reoffending patterns (X^2 = 0.036, df = 2, p = .982), nor in property reoffending (X^2 = 3.649, df = 2, p = .161). They did, however, differ on violent reoffending (X^2 = 20.396, df = 2, p < .001), with child abusers reoffending to a violent offense less often than expected (z = -4.5) and peer abusers as well as group abusers reoffending to a violent offense more often (z = 2.7, respectively z = 2.6).

Developmental Offending Trajectories

Next we ran trajectory analyses to investigate the development of offending from age 12 to the end of the follow-up period. Findings of the five-group solution are presented in Table 4.1. Figure 4.1 depicts the trajectories for the model with the best fit to the data.[1]

The first of the five groups was labeled the *late-onset adolescence-limited* (LO AL, N = 28, mean posterior probability = .76) group. The offending trajectory of this group resembles an AL group. The only difference is, as the name implies, a late onset on average at age 15 (range: 11–17) with offending peaking at age 17. On average, the offenders included in this group have 0.7 offenses. The second trajectory type was labeled the *low-level chronics* (LC, N = 165, mean posterior probability = .83). The offending rate for this group is almost constant at about 0.2 offenses per person per age. The third group, the *adolescence-limited* group (AL, N = 248, mean posterior probability = .79), was the one including the highest proportion of JSO. This group starts offending at approximately age 14 (range: 8–17). Offending peaks early at age 15, after which a steep decline sets in until about age 19, and from that point on, individuals from this group appear to desist from offending. This group averages 0.45 offenses per person.

The group called *high-level declining* (HD, N = 19, mean posterior probability = .77) is the fourth and has a peculiar offending trajectory. Their onset is at the young age of 12 at very high frequency with 1.8 offenses per person per year. The offending then declines steadily until age 32 is reached and 0.6 offenses per person per year are committed. Few offenders were characterized by this trajectory. The fifth group, the

[1]The BIC score for this five-group model is –5,094.09, and the $2\log_e B_{10}$ for addition of the fifth group was 12.40; adding a sixth group made the BIC score decline. The BIC score was highest when quadratic curves were chosen for all five groups. The mean group probability was .80, indicating that respondents had a high probability of being assigned to a certain group. To assess that trajectories differed in shape, pairwise Wald tests were performed (Jones & Nagin, 2007). These tests showed that none of the trajectories are parallel. Thus, the solution meets the criteria laid out in the literature.

Table 4.1 Trajectory Model With Five Quadratic Groups

	LC	*HD*	*AL*	*LO AL*	*HC*
N Parameters	165	19	248	28	38
Intercept	1.68999	2.34636	−35.42367	−24.80424	−5.81755
Linear	−1.10883	−0.65619	48.37417	29.40679	6.17697
Quadratic	0.08382	−0.04419	−16.44359	−8.30514	−1.35308
Group assignment					
Mean	.83	.77	.79	.76	.88
Maximum	1.00	1.00	.95	.99	1.00

Note. LC = Low-level chronics. HD = High-level declining. AL = Adolescent-limited. LO AL = Late-onset adolescence-limited. HC = High-level chronics.

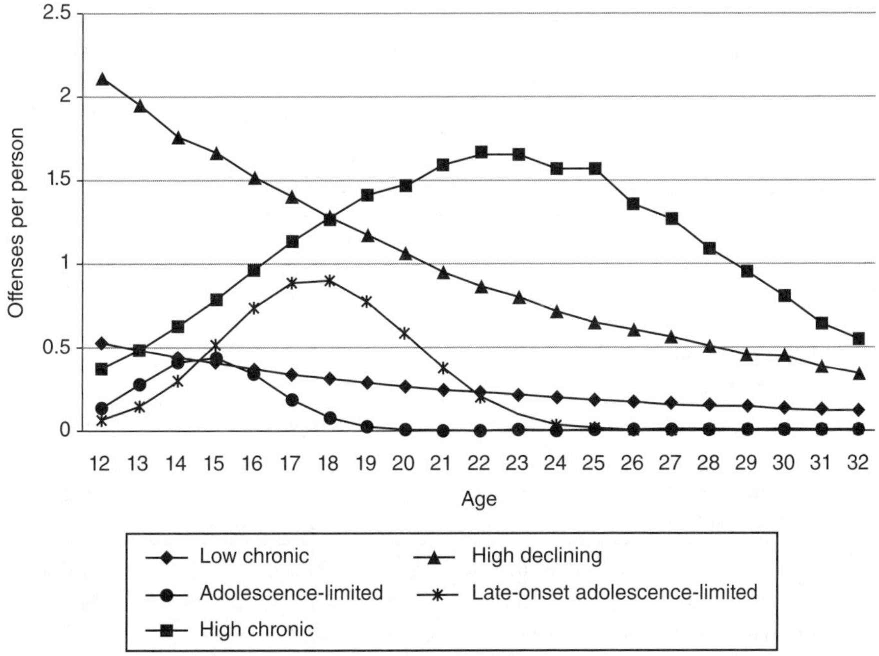

Figure 4.1 Offending trajectories of juvenile sex offenders.

high-level chronic trajectory (HC, N = 38, mean posterior probability = .88), also does not include many offenders: it has a mean onset age comparable to the LO AL and AL trajectory at approximately age 15. After onset, the offending rate increases steeply until age 22, where the peak is at 1.8 offenses per person per year. After reaching their mid-twenties, a steep decline in offending sets in. In spite of this decline, at age 32 they are still the group with the highest offending rate.

In sum, the results show that, within this sample of JSO, a small majority are – contrary to Moffitt's hypothesis – adolescence-/early adulthood–limited offenders: 55% are in adolescence-/early adulthood–limited trajectories (LO AL & AL), against 41% who are in chronic trajectories (LC & HC) at high or low frequency of offending. Almost half (49.6%) of our sample commit (virtually) no more offenses after adolescence.

A subsequent question is whether sex offender types differ or not in terms of their offending trajectory. For instance, are child abusers more likely to be characterized by a chronic offending trajectory than are group sexual offenders? The cross-tabulation of trajectory type and sex offender subtype is presented in Table 4.2. Overall, the association between trajectory group membership and sex offender type is statistically significant ($\chi^2 = 28.060$, df = 8, $p < .001$).

First concentrating on the rows, results in Table 4.2 show that 64% of the child abusers are in either one of the adolescence-limited trajectories, while 5% of the child abusers in our sample follow a high-level chronic trajectory. In contrast, of all peer abusers only 46% are in either one of the adolescence-limited trajectories, while 12% follow a high-level chronic trajectory. Percentages for group offenders are 46 and 6%, respectively. Therefore, while the adolescence-limited pathway is common in all types of sex offenders, the findings also suggest that child abusers are overrepresented in the AL group. Indeed, focusing on the row percentages, we find that 62%

Table 4.2 Cross-Tabulation of Trajectory Type and Sex Offender Subgroup

		Child abuser	*Peer abuser*	*Group offender*
LO AL		46.4 %	46.4 %	7.1 %
	Count	13	13	2
	Expected count	14.6	9	4.4
	Adj. residual	–0.6	1.7	–1.3
LC		44.8 %	35.8 %	19.4 %
	Count	74	59	32
	Expected count	85.8	53	26.2
	Adj. residual	–2.3	1.2	1.5
AL		61.7 %	24.6 %	13.7 %
	Count	153	61	34
	Expected count	129	79.7	39.3
	Adj. residual	4.3	–3.6	–1.3
HD		26.3 %	42.1 %	31.6 %
	Count	5	8	6
	Expected count	9.9	6.1	3
	Adj. residual	–2.3	0.9	1.9
HC		36.8 %	50 %	13.2 %
	Count	14	19	5
	Expected count	19.8	12.2	6
	Adj. residual	–1.9	2.5	–0.5

Note. Percentages presented in this table are row percentages (percentages within trajectory group).

of the offenders included in AL group are child abusers. Next, peer abusers are underrepresented in the AL group, and overrepresented (almost significantly so) in the HC group. In fact, the HC group primarily consists of peer abusers. For group abusers, statistical significance is generally less easily reached because of the small size of this group. Nevertheless, we can tentatively conclude that group abusers are overrepresented in the HD group (standardized residual = 1.9).

Summarizing these findings, we conclude that the three subtypes are spread over the five trajectory groups. We can't conclude, therefore, that a single offending trajectory can represent all JSO. We do, however, note the following trends. Child abusers' offending tends to be limited to the period of adolescence. Peer abusers are typically following a low-level chronic trajectory or an adolescence-limited trajectory. Yet, findings also show that the proportion of AL found is less than is expected by chance alone. Similarly, group abusers are also found primarily in the low-level chronics and the adolescence-limited trajectories. So far, all offenses have been lumped together and we have not distinguished between sexual, violent, or any other offenses. Hence, in the next set of analyses, the type of offenses committed for each offending trajectory are presented. Figures 4.2a, 4.2b, and 4.2c present the average crime mix for each offending trajectory. For ease of inspection, the Y-axes have been adapted to the maximum frequency of offending in each group.

Figure 4.2a shows that most offenses committed by the AL group are sex offenses (0.2 offenses on average per person per year, from age 12 to 17. Some additional violent offenses are committed at ages 14–18 (mean: 0.02 offenses per person in this period), there is some property offending too, but the overwhelming majority of

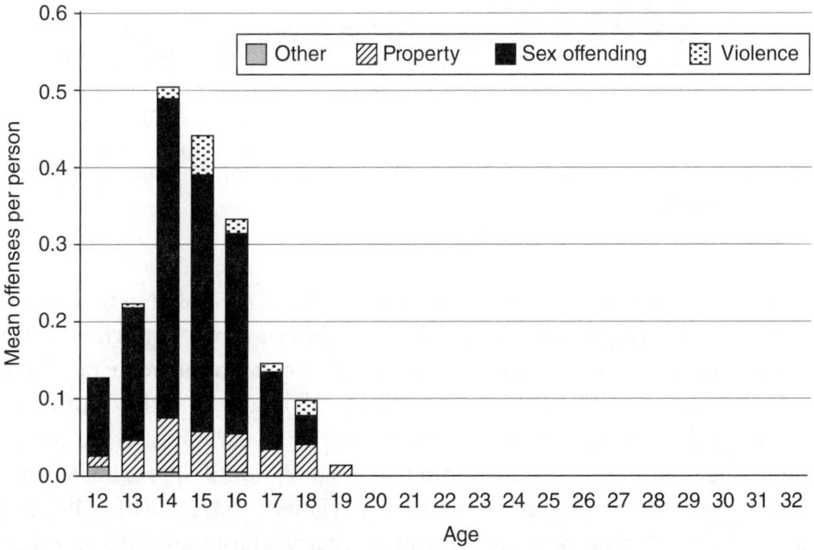

Figure 4.2a Offense types in the AL trajectory (Y-axis max. 0.6 offenses per person).

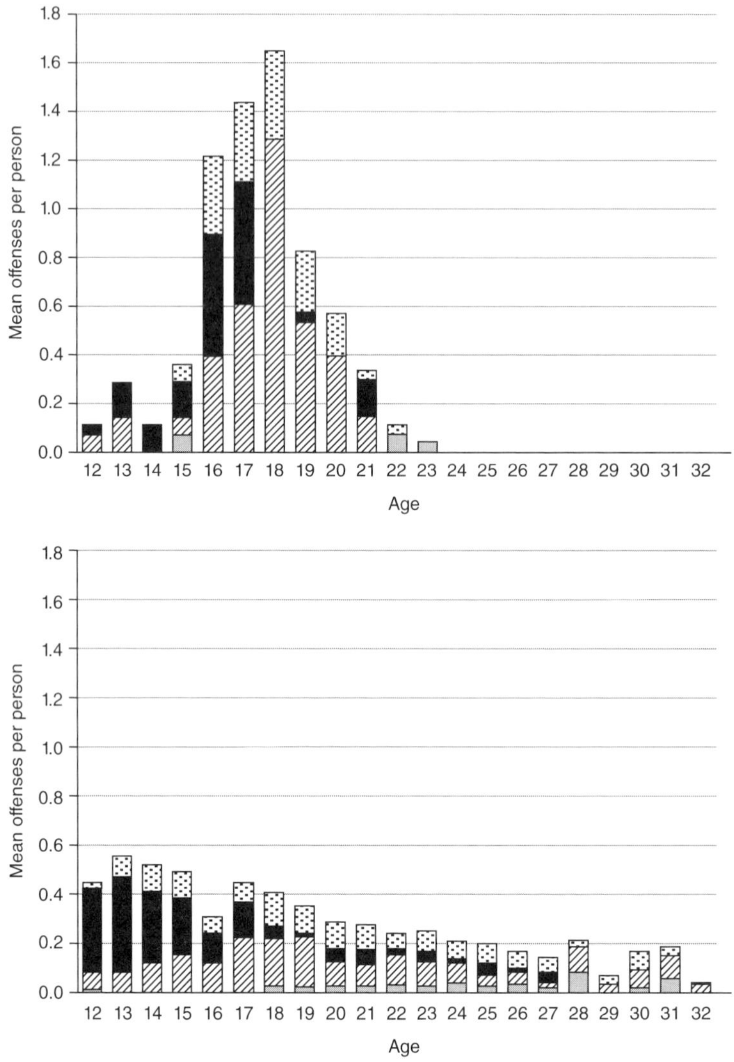

Figure 4.2b Offense types in the LO AL (top) and LC (bottom) trajectory (Y-axis max. 1.8 offenses per person).

offenses are sex offenses. Figure 4.2b shows that the LO AL offenders (on top) not only offend at much higher frequencies, but that the crime mix is much more varied. From age 18 onwards, sex offending continues, though at lower frequency. Violence is prominent from age 15 until age 21, with a peak at age 18 with 0.4 offenses per person. The LC trajectory (on bottom) is marked by an early start of sex offending. Sex offending continues – at much lower frequency – until approximately age 27. The other types of offenses are committed at relatively stable low frequency until about age 24. From then onwards, violent, property, and other types of offending become more frequent.

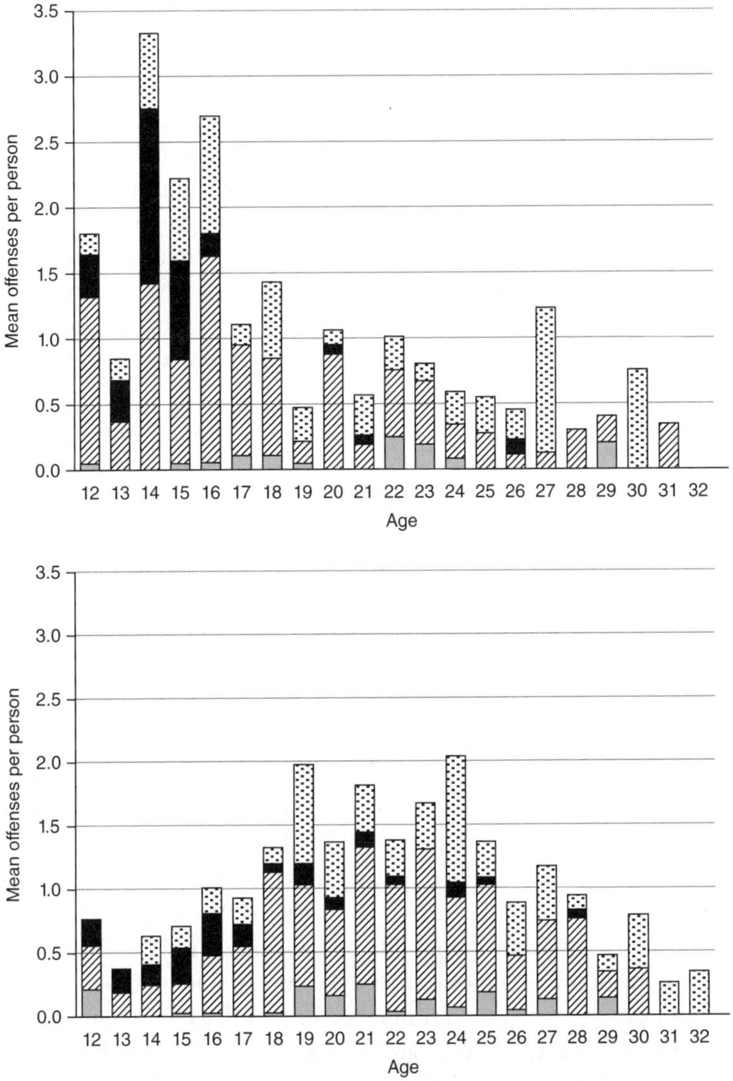

Figure 4.2c Offense types in the HD (top) and HC (bottom) trajectory (y-axis max. 3.5 offenses per person).

Figure 4.2c contains the high-rate offending trajectories, HD (on the top) and HC (on the bottom). Starting out with property and sex offenses, the group of HD offenders increasingly commit violent offenses as they age during which sex offenses appear sporadically. The HC trajectory has a much later peak (at ages 19–24) and the crime mix here is dominated more by property offenses (at the age of 23 the mean property offending per person is 1.3 offenses), with which – until well into adulthood – sex offending occurs occasionally. Violent offending seems a regular feature (at about a third to a quarter of all offending) from age 19 onwards.

Combining these findings with those on the subgroups, it is concluded that – again with the same cautionary note – subgroup membership is not exclusively tied to trajectory membership. The child abuser appears characterized by a short career, with relatively few, predominantly sex offenses. The peer abuser is characterized by a career with different types of offenses, of which sex offending appears in many cases a by-product of a general offending pattern in which property offending and especially violence appear much more prominent. The group abuser is harder to characterize, both in terms of the particular type of trajectory group that this offender is likely to belong to and in terms of the fact that the trajectory group that is, if at all, most characteristic for the group sex offender, also has a very versatile offending pattern with almost equal mixes of property, violent, sex, and other offenses.

Conclusions

The criminal careers of 498 male JSO, who had been treated on either an inpatient or an outpatient basis or had not received any specialized treatment, were described. This group contained high-risk, medium-risk, and low-risk sex offenders. The average follow-up period was more than 14 years, and the average period over which we could describe the criminal career more than 16 years. These are strong points of our study. Our study has limitations too. The most prominent one is probably that we use official data, which is the more problematic as it is well known that sex offending has a relatively high dark number, meaning that most sex offenses remain undiscovered by the authorities (Lisak & Miller, 2002).

First, focusing on the first offense only, we find that, as was expected based on the extant literature, sexual recidivism in our sample of JSO is low (12.2%). Again as expected, general recidivism was found to be much higher (73%). Next, making full use of the long-term follow-up of our study, we were able to look beyond the first reoffense and examine the entire criminal careers of the JSO in our sample. When the findings in our trajectory model are compared to Moffitt's (1993) taxonomy, in our sample of sex offenders an AL trajectory is also retrieved. The trajectory shape of our AL group is in accordance with the AL group described by Moffitt. Possibly the LO AL sex offending group we found in our data could best be seen as a variation of Moffitt's AL group: while the peak occurs later, desistance from age 18 onwards is swift. In our research group almost 50% of JSO are in the AL trajectory; this means that the other 50% continue offending at higher ages and rates. Our findings are in contrast with Moffitt's assumption that sex offending is characteristic for the LCP group. Only 8% were categorized in the high-level chronic group. Although it must be kept in mind that the analysis we conducted cannot be regarded as more than a tool to summarize and interpret the data, and we have to be cautious about taking our findings and the classifications as absolute or "true" (viz. Nagin, 2005), there is a substantial gap between what is to be expected on the basis of Moffitt's theory and our findings. In fact, previously Seto and Barbaree (1997) have relaxed

Moffitt's assumption that sexual offending is always part of the LCP syndrome and argued that AL offenders were also capable of sexual coercion.

Another goal of this study was to compare subgroups of adolescent sexual offenders using the estimated trajectories. Remarkably, and contrary to popular belief, in our data the typical child abuser's offending pattern is one limited to the period of adolescence. In a prior study Hendriks and Bijleveld (2008) had found that within a residentially treated group of JSO, sexual recidivism was concentrated exclusively in the child-abusing subgroup. The analysis conducted here using a larger and more diversified sample of JSO reveals that sexual recidivism by child abusers is quite likely not to extend into adulthood. This immediately shows the advantage of using group-based modeling taking into consideration the whole criminal career over a longer period of time. In doing so, we were able to show that recidivism in youth is not necessarily an indication of permanent failure and persistence of offending in adulthood. The peer abusers are characterized most by chronicity (because of belonging more often to the HC group and not belonging to the AL group).

While both adolescence-limited pathways are also common among peer abusers, relatively speaking, peer abusers are characterized more by chronicity in their offending than are the other JSO types – compared to other offender types they belong more often to the HC group, and less often to the AL group. Besides being persistent in their offending, the criminal careers of the JSO on the high-level chronic trajectory also evidence more diversity in offending. In this respect they seem to resemble the pathway of the antisocial cognitions that was described by Ward and Sorbello (2003). The group offenders are slightly overrepresented in the HD group, a not unexpected finding as most group offending is supposed to be dependent on adolescence-related social contexts that should disappear as people age and mature in adult roles, although the decrease is much slower than in the AL groups.

These results show that different subtypes of adolescent sex offenders are likely to follow different trajectories, although similarities are also evident. The foregoing stresses once again the importance of studying adolescent sex offenders as a heterogeneous group. While this is widely acknowledged in the literature, still many studies – often due to insufficient sample sizes – lump all JSO together thereby obscuring potentially important differences in criminal career development between groups. With respect to criminal careers, these findings also seem to underline that group offenders are not just a variation of the peer-abusing type. As group offenders are responsible for a large proportion of sexual crimes committed by adolescents, this underscores the need for more study into this type of juvenile sex offender.

Looking more closely at Moffitt's theory, it is remarkable that the child abusers are so concentrated in the AL group. Moffitt describes the LCP group as burdened by deficits and psychopathology; at the same time we know from the sex offending literature that child abusers have the highest prevalence of such deficits and psychopathology (Hendriks & Bijleveld, 2004). Also, Moffitt describes that offenders following the AL trajectory tend to commit property-related crimes or statutory offenses. However, both AL and LO AL commit relatively many serious (sexual and violent) offenses. Our research shows that there is a lot of variation between different subgroups of adolescent offenders and that important information about these subgroups is lost when they are studied as one group (cf. Seto & Lalumière, 2010; Zimring, 2004). The advantage of studying and identifying the different criminal careers of subgroups of adolescent sex offenders lies further in the possibilities of developing risk instruments and treatment programs that are tailored to these subgroups.

In sum, more research would be needed to understand the offending patterns in the various trajectory groups. Relations with background characteristics could be investigated, such as personality characteristics, disorders, victimization, and victim choice. Also, as the criminal careers we investigate span a long period, the relevance of such static properties measured in childhood may become less important as people become older. Instead, as Sampson & Laub (2003) argued, factors such as intimate relations, housing, alcohol and drugs use, type of job, and so on, may become more pertinent in understanding why careers develop as they do (cf. Bijleveld, Van der Geest, & Hendriks, 2012).

References

Bijleveld, C. C. J. H. & Hendriks, J. (2003). Juvenile sex offenders: Differences between group and solo offenders. *Psychology, Crime & Law, 9*, 237–245.

Bijleveld, C. C. J. H. , Van der Geest, V. R., & Hendriks, J. (2012). Vulnerable youth in pathways to adulthood. In R. Loeber & M. Hoeve (Eds.), *Persisters and desisters in crime from adolescence into adulthood: Explanation, prevention and punishment* (pp. 105–126). Farnham: Ashgate.

Böhning, D. (1998). Zero-inflated Poisson models and C.A.MAN: A tutorial collection of evidence. *Biometrical Journal, 40*, 833–843.

Butler, S. M. & Seto, M. C. (2002). Distinguishing two types of adolescent sex offenders. *Child and Adolescent Psychiatry, 41*, 83–90.

Caldwell, M. (2002). What we do not know about juvenile sexual reoffense risk. *Child Maltreatment: Journal of the American Professional Society on the Abuse of Children, 7*, 291–302.

Caldwell, M. (2007). Sexual offense: Adjudication and sexual recidivism among juvenile offenders. *Sexual Abuse: A Journal of Research and Treatment, 19*, 107–113.

Caldwell, M. (2010). Study characteristics and recidivism base rates in juvenile sex offender recidivism. *International Journal of Offender Therapy and Comparative Criminology, 54*, 197–212.

Cale, J., Lussier, P., & Proulx, J. (2009). Heterogeneity in antisocial trajectories in youth of adult sexual aggressors of women: An examination of initiation, persistence, escalation, and aggravation. *Sexual Abuse, 21*, 223–248.

Edwards, R., Beech, A. R., Bishopp, D., Erikson, M., & Friendship, C. (2005). Predicting treatment dropout from a residential program for adolescent sexual abusers using pre-treatment variables and implications for recidivism. *Journal of Sexual Aggression, 11*, 139–156.

Eggleston, E. P., Laub, J. H., & Sampson R. J. (2004). Methodological sensitivities to latent class analysis of long-term criminal trajectories. *Journal of Quantitative Criminology, 20*, 1–26.

Farrington, D. P., Coid, J. W., Harnett, L., Holliffe, D., Soteriou, N., Turner, R., & West, D. J. (2006). *Criminal careers up to age 50 and life success up to age 48: New findings from the Cambridge Study in Delinquent Development.* London: Home Office Research Study.

Field, A. P. (2000). *Discovering statistics using SPSS for Windows: Advanced techniques for the beginner.* London: Sage.

Hagan, M., Cho, M., Gust-Brey, K., & Dow, E. (2001). Eight-year comparative analyses of adolescent rapists, adolescent child molesters, other adolescent delinquents, and the general population. *International Journal of Offender Therapy and Comparative Criminology, 45,* 314–324.

Hendriks, J. (2006). *Jeugdige zedendelinquenten: Een studie naar subtypen en recidive. (Juvenile sex offenders: A study on subtypes and recidivism).* Utrecht: Forum Educatief.

Hendriks, J. & Bijleveld, C. C. J. H. (2004). Juvenile sex offenders: Differences between peer abusers and child molesters. *Criminal Behaviour & Mental Health, 14,* 238–250.

Hendriks, J. & Bijleveld, C. C. J. H. (2008). Recidivism among juvenile sex offenders after residential treatment. *Journal of Sexual Aggression, 14,* 19–32.

Hsu, I. K. G. & Starzynski, J. (1990). Adolescent rapists and adolescent sexual assaulters. *International Journal of Offender Therapy and Comparative Criminology, 39,* 23–30.

Hudson, S. M., Ward, T., & McCormack, J. C. (1999). Offense pathways in sexual offenders. *Journal of Interpersonal Violence, 14,* 779–798.

Hunter, J., Figueredo, A., Malamuth, N., & Becker, J. (2003). Juvenile sex offenders: Toward the development of a typology. *Sexual Abuse, 15,* 27–48.

Hunter, J., Figueredo, A., Malamuth, N., & Becker, J. (2004). Developmental pathways in youth sexual aggression and delinquency: Risk factors and mediators. *Journal of Family Violence, 19,* 233–242.

Jones, B. L. & Nagin, D. S. (2007). Advances in group-based trajectory modeling and a SAS procedure for estimating them. *Sociological Research and Methods, 35,* 542–571.

Jones, B. L., Nagin, D. S., & Roeder, K. (2001). A SAS procedure based on mixture models for estimating developmental trajectories. *Sociological Methods & Research, 29,* 374–393.

Lalumière, M. L., Harris, G. T., Quinsey, V. L., & Rice, M. E. (2005). *The causes of rape: Understanding individual differences in male propensity for sexual aggression.* Washington, DC: American Psychological Association.

Lambert, D. (1992). Zero-inflated Poisson regression, with an application to defects in manufacturing. *Technometrics, 34,* 1–14.

Lisak, D. & Miller, P. M. (2002). Repeat rape and multiple offending among undetected rapists. *Violence and Victims, 17,* 73–84.

Lussier, P., Leclerc, B., Cale, J., & Proulx, J., (2007). Developmental pathways of deviance in sexual aggressors. *Criminal Justice and Behavior, 34,* 1441–1462.

McCann, K. & Lussier, P. (2008). A meta-analysis of the predictors of sexual recidivism in juvenile offenders. *Youth Violence and Juvenile Justice, 6,* 363–385.

Moffitt, T. E. (1993). Life-course-persistent and adolescence-limited antisocial behavior: A developmental taxonomy. *Psychological Review, 100,* 674–701.

Nagin, D. S. (1999). Analyzing developmental trajectories: A semi-parametric group-based approach. *Psychological Methods, 4,* 399–424.

Nagin, D. S. (2005). *Group-based modeling of development.* Cambridge: Harvard University Press.

Piquero, A. R., Blumstein, A., Brame, R., Haapanen, R., Mulvey, E. P., & Nagin, D. S. (2001). Assessing the impact of exposure time and incapacitation on longitudinal trajectories of criminal offending. *Journal of Adolescent Research, 16,* 54–74.

Piquero, A. R. & Moffitt, T. E. (2005). Explaining the facts of crime: How the developmental taxonomy replies to Farrington's invitation. In D. P. Farrington (Ed.), *Integrated developmental and life-course theories of offending: Advances in criminological theory* (pp. 51–72). New Brunswick, NJ: Transaction.

Sampson, R. J. & Laub, J. H. (2003). Life-course desisters? Trajectories of crime among delinquent boys followed to age 70. *Criminology, 41*, 319–339.

Seto, M. C. & Barbaree, H. E. (1997). Sexual aggression as antisocial behavior: A developmental model. In D. M. Stoff, J. Breiling, and J. D. Maser (Eds.), *Handbook of antisocial behavior* (pp. 524–533). New York: John Wiley & Sons, Inc.

Seto, M. C. & Lalumière, M. (2010). What is so special about male adolescent sexual offending? A review and test of explanations through meta-analysis. *Psychological Bulletin, 136*, 526–575.

Skubic Kemper, T. & Kistner, J. A. (2007). Offense history and recidivism in three victim-age-based groups of juvenile sex offenders. *Sexual Abuse, 19*, 409–424.

Soothill, K., Sanderson, B., & Ackerley, E. (2000). Sex offenders: Specialists, generalists – or both? A 32-year criminological study. *British Journal of Criminology, 40*, 56–67.

Van der Geest, V., Bijleveld, C. C. J. H., & Wijkman, M. (2005). *Delinquentie na behandeling. Een verkennend onderzoek naar geregistreerde justitiecontacten, persoonlijke en omgevingskenmerken van jongeren uit een behandelinrichting. (Delinquency after treatment. An exploratory study on registered judicial contacts, personality and environmental characteristics of boys treated in an inpatient treatment centre).* (Report # 2005-4). Leiden: NSCR.

Van der Geest, V., Blokland, A. A. J., & Bijleveld, C. C. J. H. (2009). Delinquent development in a sample of high-risk youth: Shape, content, and predictors of delinquent trajectories from age 12 to 32. *Journal of Research in Crime and Delinquency, 46*, 111–143.

Vandiver, D. M. (2006). A prospective analysis of juvenile male sex offenders: Characteristics and recidivism rates as adults. *Journal of Interpersonal Violence, 21*, 673–688.

Waite, D., Keller, A., McGarvey, E. L., Wieckowski, E., Pinkerton, R., & Brown, G. L. (2005). Juvenile sex offender rearrest rates for sexual, violent nonsexual and property crimes: A 10-year follow-up. *Sexual Abuse: A Journal of Research and Treatment, 17*, 313–331.

Ward, T. & Sorbello, L. (2003). Explaining child sexual abuse: Integration and elaboration. In T. Ward, D. R. Laws, & S. M. Hudson (Eds.), *Sexual deviance: Issues and controversies* (pp. 3–20). Thousand Oaks, CA: Sage Publications.

Wiesner, M. & Capaldi, D. M. (2003). Relations of childhood and adolescent factors to offending trajectories of young men. *Journal of Research in Crime and Delinquency, 40*, 231–226.

Worling, J. R. (1995). Adolescent sex offenders against females. Differences based on age of their victims. *International Journal of Offender Therapy & Comparative Criminology, 39*, 276–293.

Zimring, F. E. (2004). *An American travesty: Legal responses to adolescent sexual offending.* University of Chicago Press.

Zimring, F. E., Piquero, A. R., & Jennings, W. G. (2007). Sexual delinquency in Racine: Does early sex offending predict later sex offending in youth and young adulthood? *Criminology & Public Policy, 6*, 507–534.

5

The Childhood Risk Factors of Adolescent-Onset and Adult-Onset of Sex Offending

Evidence From a Prospective Longitudinal Study

Patrick Lussier
Laval University, Canada

Arjan Blokland,[1] Jeff Mathesius,[2] Dustin Pardini,[3] & Rolf Loeber[3]
[1]NSCR and Leiden University, the Netherlands, [2]Simon Fraser University, Canada, [3]University of Pittsburgh, USA

Introduction

The age of onset has received much attention from criminologists with the advent of the criminal career (Blumstein, Cohen, Roth, & Visher, 1986) and the developmental criminology (LeBlanc & Fréchette, 1989; Loeber & LeBlanc, 1990) paradigms. The age of onset of a phenomenon such as sex offending is of particular interest for criminologists because it allows the identification of the potential causal origins but also the possible developmental patterns. Since the advent of these two paradigms, the state of knowledge of the age of onset of delinquency has burgeoned into several areas of research: (a) the description of the age of onset of different forms of antisocial and criminal behaviors and the examination of developmental pathways (e.g., Loeber, Wei, Stouthamer-Loeber, Huizinga, & Thornberry, 1999); (b) the investigation of the developmental correlates of the age of onset and the question of whether the onset of a behavior occurring at a different developmental period is associated with similar or different risk factors (e.g., Farrington & Loeber, 2000; Tibbetts & Piquero, 1999; Tolan, 1987); and (c) the study of the age of onset and whether this criminal career parameter is informative of the unfolding of the criminal career in terms of frequency, persistence, versatility, specialization, and desistance (e.g., Nagin

Sex Offenders: A Criminal Career Approach, First Edition. Edited by Arjan Blokland and Patrick Lussier.

& Farrington, 1992; Piquero, Paternoster, Mazerolle, Brame, & Dean, 1999). These three main areas of research have produced several key empirical findings that have served as a foundation for the elaboration of developmental models of juvenile delinquency. While several conceptual and methodological issues remain unresolved and remain subject to debating (e.g., Thornberry, 2005), the age of onset represents an important aspect of sex offending that has not received much attention from researchers. The current study attempts to fill this gap by examining the age of onset of sex offending and the associated childhood risk factors. In doing so, the current investigation tackles an important assumption in the field of research of sexual violence and abuse: Adult sex offenders are already different from juvenile offenders at a young age.

Clinical researchers and criminologists generally accept the idea that juvenile sex offending and adult sex offending are distinct types (e.g., Zimring, 2004). This difference, however, has been blurred in recent years with the emergence of adult-like legal and penal measures for juvenile sex offenders such as public notification and sex offender registry (e.g., Longo & Calder, 2005). The line has also been blurred between juvenile and adult sex offenders by the use of actuarial risk assessment methods developed for adult sex offenders to assess the risk of reoffending in juvenile offenders. Such practices have been reinforced by the assumption that treatment programs of juvenile sex offenders do not work and that without effective intervention, juvenile offenders will persist in adulthood (Letourneau & Miner, 2005). Clearly, policy developments in recent years, in the USA particularly, suggest that policymakers think of juvenile sex offenders as tomorrow's adult sex offenders. Put differently, juvenile sex offenders are seen as the early starter group at risk of persisting and specializing in sex crimes beyond the period of adolescence. Longitudinal studies have seriously challenged these assumptions by inspecting the risk of recidivism in adolescence but also the continuity of sex offending in adulthood (e.g., see Jennings et al., this book). The current study goes a step further. We posit here that the increased use of adult-like policies with juvenile sex offenders stems in part from the lack of knowledge of the developmental risk factors associated with juvenile and adult sex offending. While emphasis has been put on a tertiary-type approach and intervention (intervention with known sex offenders), secondary type interventions (interventions with individuals at risk of a sex crime) have been seriously neglected (Laws, 2008). The current investigation takes a first step toward filling this gap by examining the childhood risk factors of juvenile-onset and adult-onset sex offending using a prospective longitudinal study. In doing so, the current study attempts to determine the childhood risk factors of juvenile- and adult-onset sex offending, whether such risk factors are similar or different, and to what extent these factors predict the two types of onsets. Stated differently, the current study seeks to determine whether we can identify children at risk of committing a sex crime, and if so, whether the children at risk of committing a sex crime in adolescence are similar or different from those at risk of committing a sex crime in adulthood. In the next section, we review the state of knowledge regarding the onset of sex offending, the developmental correlates of the onset of sex offending, similarities and differences between juvenile and adult sex offenders, and methodological issues of prior studies.

Literature Review

The Onset of Juvenile Sex Offending

Most empirical information about the onset of juvenile sex offending comes from specialized samples of juvenile sex offenders (JSO) in sex offender treatment programs. Interestingly, the age of onset of offending has received little attention from researchers. The average age of onset is typically between 13 and 14 years old in samples of youth in sex offender treatment programs (e.g., Carpentier, Proulx, & Leclerc, 2011; Miner, 2002; Vizard, Hickey, & McCrory, 2007; Waite et al., 2005). However, it is unclear from these studies whether this represents the age at which the initial sex crime was committed, the age at first arrest, the age at first conviction, and so on. It is also unclear whether this information is based on self-report questionnaire, clinical interviews, official records, and so on. For example, in a prospective longitudinal study of the offending behavior of a general sample of adjudicated youth, the mean age of onset of a sex offense was 17 when based on self-report and 19 when based on official data (LeBlanc & Fréchette, 1989). It is unclear from these studies whether the age of onset varies across sex offender types. In that regard, Vizard et al. (2007) showed that early starters (prior age 11) were more likely to have committed the sexually abusive behavior against a male victim but less likely to have offended exclusively against females. Further, some have argued that within the group of JSO there might be an *early starter* group who may be a distinct group of sex offenders. The early onset age has been operationalized differently across studies (e.g., younger than 16; younger than 12, etc.; Carpentier et al., 2011; Prentky & Knight, 1993; Vizard et al., 2007). In that regard, it is unclear whether the onset age of juvenile sex offending is best represented as a continuum or as a bimodal distribution. The general idea stemming from current policies is that the whole group of JSO constitute an early starter group at risk of persisting their sex offending into adulthood. Researchers have examined whether age of onset is a predictor of sexual recidivism and the results have not been consistent across studies (e.g., Långström, 2002; Miner, 2002).

The Continuity of Sex Offending in Adulthood

The lack of homotypic continuity[1] of sex offending from adolescence to adulthood has been documented for quite some time (e.g., Doshay, 1943). It is only in the last two decades, however, that researchers have attempted to replicate these early findings. In fact, in recent years, several empirical studies have looked at the outcome

[1]Homotypic continuity refers to the continuity of the same behavior over time.

of JSO by examining their sexual recidivism following assessment/treatment (for reviews, Caldwell, 2002; Caldwell, 2010; McCann & Lussier, 2008). These empirical studies have highlighted several key findings. The majority of JSO reoffend during adolescence, but when they do it is primarily for a nonsex crime. In fact, only a small fraction of JSO reoffends sexually in adolescence (e.g., McCann & Lussier, 2008). Further, it has been argued that JSO do not continue sex offending in adulthood (Caldwell, 2002; Van den Berg, Bijleveld, & Hendriks, 2011; Zimring, 2004). While this is certainly true for most JSO, empirical studies indicate that a small fraction (between 5 and 10%) may indeed continue their sex offending in young adulthood (e.g., Nisbet, Wilson, & Smallbone, 2004; Sipe, Jensen, & Everett, 1998; Vandiver, 2006; Zimring, Jennings, Piquero, & Hays, 2009; Zimring, Piquero, & Jennings, 2007) and their number gradually increases with a longer follow-up period in adulthood (between 10 and 15%) (e.g., Hagan, Gust-Brey, Cho, & Dow, 2001). Bremer (1992) reported a 6% reconviction rate in a sample of serious JSO, but the recidivism rate rose to 11% when based on self-reports.[2] Therefore, while the use of official data underestimates recidivism rates, it is unlikely to be able to explain the fact that the vast majority are not rearrested or caught again for a sex crime (Bouchard & Lussier, this book). Thus, there appears to be sizeable discontinuity in sex offending from adolescence to adulthood superimposed on a little continuity.

The Onset of Adult Sex Offenders

Criminological studies on antisocial behavior suggest that while most antisocial youth do not become antisocial adults, antisociality in adults almost requires antisocial behavior in youth (Moffitt, 1993; Robins, 1978). The first conclusion seems to apply to JSO as most of them do not become adult sex offenders. What about adult sex offenders? Can we conclude from prior studies that adult sex offending almost always requires sex offending in adolescence? Empirical studies have examined the age of onset of sex offending in clinical and correctional samples of adult sex offenders using retrospective data. Several key findings have emerged from these investigations. First, the age of onset based on self-report data (e.g., Abel & Twigg, 1993; Groth, 1982; Knight & Prentky, 1993) is younger than those based on official data (e.g., Baxter, Marshall, Barbaree, Davidson, & Malcolm, 1984; Gebhard, Gagnon, Pomeroy, & Christenson, 1965; Lussier, LeBlanc, & Proulx, 2005; Smallbone & Wortley, 2004). However, it is difficult to draw a firm conclusion because self-report and official data have rarely been examined in the same study.[3] Second, the age of onset varies across

[2]There is evidence of heterogeneity in the patterns of offending in JSO. In a large sample of JSO, Lussier, Van den Berg, Bijleveld and Hendriks (2012), using semi-parametric group-based modeling, documented two sexual offending trajectories. The first trajectory, the adolescent-limited, included 90% of the sample and represented a pattern of offending, peaking at age 14 and limited to the period of adolescence. The second group, the high-rate slow desisters, included 10% of the sample. The rate of sexual offending peaked in early adolescence, gradually decreasing over time, but persisting into adulthood. Whereas the first group had desisted by age 18, this second group desisted in their early thirties.

sex offender types. Reports suggest that sexual aggressors against women start earlier (i.e., in their twenties) than sexual aggressors against children (i.e., in their thirties) (e.g., Proulx, Lussier, Ouimet, & Boutin, 2008). There are some disparities, however, among sexual aggressors against children. Extrafamilial sex offenders as well as those offending against boys tend to start earlier than those offending against a relative and/or a girl (e.g., Abel et al., 1993; Marshall, Babaree, & Eccles, 1991; Smallbone & Wortley, 2004). Third, the distribution of age of onset and mean age of onset reported in prior studies suggest that most adult sex offenders were not JSO, although some discrepancies are found across studies. The Prentky and Knight (1993) study using self-reported data is informative of the proportion of adult offenders reporting an onset in adolescence. For sexual aggressors against women and aggressors against children, the proportion of JSO was respectively 49 and 62%. This suggests that when looking back in time, most adult sex offenders were JSO.[4] These results have led many scholars to conclude that most adult sex offenders start during adolescence. The high prevalence of juvenile sex offending in adult sex offenders, however, has not been replicated in several studies (e.g., Cale, this book; Lussier, Tzoumakis, Cale, & Amirault, 2010; Marshall et al., 1991; Smallbone & Wortley, 2004; Zimring et al., 2009) and may reflect sampling issues.[5] Based on available evidence, we conclude that adult sex offending does not require juvenile sex offending. This further reinforces the importance of examining the risk factors of adolescent-onset and adult-onset of sex offending.

Developmental Correlates of the Onset of Sex Offending

Theoretical models of juvenile (e.g., Johnson & Knight, 2000; Ryan, 1999; Smallbone, 2006) and adult sex offending (e.g., Knight & Sims-Knight, 2003; Lussier, Proulx, & LeBlanc, 2005; Malamuth, 1998; Marshall & Barbaree, 1990; Ward & Beech, 2006) hypothesize that childhood is a significant period for committing a sex crime (see also Smallbone & Cale, this book; Thakker & Ward, this book). Interestingly, these models have stressed similar key childhood risk factors for both juvenile and adult sex offenders. It is not uncommon to find in theoretical models of juvenile sex offending as well as those of adult sex offending references to risk factors such as poor parent-child attachment, several forms of parental abuse (e.g., violent, sexual, neglect), poor social competence, antisociality, delinquency, impulsivity, poor self-regulation, and atypical sexual development, as well as deviant sexual interests. This overlap raises the question as to whether or not adolescent-onset and adult-onset

[3]The "gap" between the self-reported and official age of onset may be attributable to various factors, such as the offender's ability to avoid/delay detection (Lussier, Bouchard, & Beauregard, 2011).

[4]Similarly, Abel et al. (1987) reported that close to 50% of their sample of adult sex offenders in an outpatient clinic reported an onset of deviant sexual *interests* during adolescence.

[5]The Prentky and Knight study (1993) was based on a sample of serious and/or repetitive sexual aggressors.

sex offenders are characterized by similar and/or different childhood risk factors. Whereas clinical researchers have stressed the importance of distinguishing JSO from ASO, theoretical models have remained relatively silent about the issue. In fact, theoretical models have not been explicit about (a) whether or not the age of onset (adolescence versus adulthood) should be theorized; (b) whether different explanatory factors are responsible for the juvenile- versus the adult-onset of sex offending; and (c) whether the risk factors of onset of sex offending are distinct from the other dimensions of the criminal career (for some notable exceptions, see Laws & Marshall, 1990; Smallbone & Cale, this book; Thakker & Ward, this book). Two lines of empirical research are informative about the childhood risk factors associated with the onset of sex offending: (a) the comparison of developmental background between sex offenders and nonsex offenders; (b) the comparison of the developmental antecedents of clinical and/or correctional samples of juvenile and adult sex offenders.

The Correlates of Adolescent-Onset of Sex Offending

Several empirical studies have compared a clinical/correctional sample of JSO with a purposive sample of non-JSO. For the purpose of the current study, we focus on the findings of the quantitative meta-analysis[6] conducted by Seto and Lalumière (2010), which is based on 59 independent studies conducted between 1975 and 2008 that include more than 3,800 JSO and over 13,000 non-JSO. The findings highlighted that JSO had a less extensive criminal history, were less likely to have antisocial peers and to hold antisocial attitudes and beliefs, and were less likely to show evidence of substance abuse (e.g., alcohol, drugs). Taken together, JSO were less antisocial and delinquent than non-JSO. Yet, no significant differences were found for a history of conduct disorder and age at first criminal justice contact, two indicators typically associated with more extensive history of juvenile delinquency. JSO showed more evidence of atypical sexual interests (e.g., evidence of paraphilic behaviors, such as voyeurism, frotteurism, etc.), and were more likely to have been exposed to pornography, but did not show

[6]Quantitative meta-analyses are useful to minimize the methodological limitations of individual studies. However, the vast majority of those studies are based on retrospective cross-sectional data rather than prospective and longitudinal data, which may lead to biases. For example, because of the context in which JSO were interviewed (often clinical settings), it is possible that they might have been less reluctant than non-JSO to reveal information about their (sexual) victimization and sexual history. Second, most studies rely on purposive samples of juvenile offenders, making it difficult to draw conclusions about the generalization of these findings. In fact, the significant risk factors identified by Seto and Lalumière (2010) showed significant heterogeneity of effect size across studies. Third, the comparison groups are not the same across studies and it is unclear if the findings are truly specific to sex offending, to juvenile offending, or to more serious delinquency. Fourth, meta-analysis allows for the examination of bivariate rather than the multivariate associations between the most important risk factors and the onset of sex offending. Fifth, these studies do not inform about the possibility that different developmental risk factors may differentiate early and late starters.

significant differences in terms of typical and consenting sexual activities (e.g., age at first sexual intercourse, frequency of sexual activities in past 6 months). Finally, JSO were found to show more evidence of anxiety, social isolation, withdrawal, and low self-esteem than non-JSO, but no significant differences were found for general psychopathology, depression, and suicidal tendencies. These findings, while informative, do not take into consideration the presence of different onset groups of JSO.[7] Further, while these findings raise interesting trends about the risk factors of the adolescent-onset of sex offending, they are not informative about the adult-onset of sex offending and whether the risk factors are similar or different.

Juvenile- Versus Adult-Onset of Offending

Empirical studies comparing juvenile and adult sex offenders are scare. Most comparative studies have focused on finding similarities and differences between the sex crime(s) committed by youth and those committed by adults (e.g., Miranda & Corcoran, 2000). Others have compared and contrasted the risk factors of sexual recidivism in youth to those associated with adults (e.g., Chaffin, Letourneau, & Silovsky, 2002; McCann & Lussier, 2008; Worling & Långström, 2006). While such comparisons are informative, these studies are beyond the scope of the current review. Further, other empirical studies have looked at samples of adult sex offenders comparing juvenile- and adult-onset offenders using retrospective data (e.g., Prentky & Knight, 1993; Smallbone & Wortley, 2004). However, it is unclear whether these retrospective studies inform about the risk factors of onset or persistence in offending.

Additionally, these studies typically do not include a comparison group of nonsex offenders. Knight, Ronis and Zakireh (2009) compared a sample of JSO in a residential treatment facility to two groups of adult sex offenders in a prison setting. The two groups of adult sex offenders were subsequently differentiated on the basis of whether or not they had a history of juvenile sex offending. The findings showed that while the JSO and the adult sex offenders with an adolescent-onset did not differ in terms of their juvenile delinquency, they did differ from the adult-onset

[7]In a retrospective study based on a small sample of child and adolescent sex offenders, Vizard et al. (2007), the early-onset group (i.e., starting prior age 11) showed more evidence of hyperactivity, impulsivity, physical aggression, insecure attachment, and difficult temperament along with more evidence of abuse and neglect than the late starters. In a similar study based on a sample of juvenile sex offenders in a sex offender treatment program, Carpentier et al. (2011) showed that the early starters (starting prior age 12) were more likely to have experienced parental neglect and sexual victimization. They were also more likely to be physically aggressive and to manifest evidence of sexual deviance (e.g., compulsive masturbation, voyeurism, deviant sexual fantasizing) as opposed to those starting later in adolescence. Note that the early- and late-onset group were not different in terms of the prevalence of conduct disorder and antisocial personality traits in childhood or consensual sexual activities during adolescence.

group. Hence, both adolescent-onset groups were more delinquent in youth than was the adult-onset group. The same pattern was observed for sadistic fantasies, paraphilia (i.e., voyeurism, atypical behaviors, exhibitionism), and arrogant/deceitful personality traits. No group differences were found for dating and friendships during adolescence. Taken together, these findings suggest that adolescent-onset offenders are more antisocial and more likely to present an atypical sexual development than adult-onset sex offenders. However, the study did not include a comparison group of nonsex offenders and the risk factors and offending data were based solely on self-report.

In sum, the goal of this study is to prospectively examine the similarities and differences between juvenile and adult sex offending using a longitudinal data set that has assessed several domains of childhood risk factors (e.g., family, peer, individual) using a multiple-informants approach (e.g., parents, teachers).

Methodology

Sample

The current study is based on data collected as part of the Pittsburgh Youth Study (PYS), a prospective longitudinal survey of the development of juvenile offending, mental health problems, drug use, and their risk factors in three samples of inner city boys (Loeber et al., 2003). For the purpose of the study, two of the three samples were used to analyze sex offending and the associated risk factors. These two samples of boys were recruited with the collaboration of the board of Pittsburgh public schools who provided the names and addresses of first- (youngest cohort) and seventh-grade (oldest cohort) boys of participating schools. From this list, a random sample of 1,165 first graders and 1,125 seventh graders were selected to participate in the study. The families were then contacted and the participation rate was relatively high (>83%). A screening assessment was then completed with those who agreed to participate using a multi-informant method (i.e., mothers, teachers, boys). The boys who scored at or above the upper 30% on the screening assessment risk ($n \approx 250$), as well as an equal number of randomly selected boys from the remainder, were selected for the follow-up study. At the first follow-up (1987–1988), the first graders averaged 7 years of age ($n = 503$) and the seventh graders averaged 13 years of age ($n = 506$). Of the 1,009 cases included in the study, 25 (2.5%) were removed due to high rates of missing information on the childhood risk indicators included in the study (>50% missing data). All 25 cases were from the youngest cohort. These 25 excluded cases were not statistically different from the included cases in terms of their scores on the initial screening assessment. Hence, the study is based on the remaining 984 cases. More information about the sample and the sampling procedures can be found elsewhere (e.g., Loeber et al., 2003).

Procedures

Interviews were conducted privately at the participant's residence. Interviews were completed biannually for the first 4 years and then annually thereafter. The retention rates for the study sample ranged from 82 to 99% for the youngest cohort and varied between 83 and 99% for the oldest cohort. The analyses did not reveal disproportionate loss of any high-risk group (Stouthamer-Loeber & Van Kammen, 1995). The self-report data on sex offending covered the time period 1987–2001 for the youngest cohort (ages 7–20 or Wave 1–18) and 1987–1998 for the oldest cohort (ages 13–25, or Wave 1–16). For official data on sex offending, four sources of information were used. For juvenile offending, data were obtained from the Allegheny County Juvenile Court Records (age 10–18 for both cohorts) as well as the Pennsylvania Juvenile Court Judges' Commission (age 10–16 for the youngest and age 10–18 for the oldest cohort). The Pennsylvania State Police Repository and the Federal Bureau of Investigation provided state and federal adult criminal record information up to age 29 for the youngest cohort and up to age 36 for the oldest cohort.

Measures

Sex Offending

In total, there were 92 sex offenders included in the study. The youngest cohort included 31 sex offenders while the oldest cohort included 61. All sex offenders were convicted of or self-reported at least one sex crime according to the Criminal Code of Pennsylvania. Sex crimes considered for this study included: rape, indecent assault, indecent assault of a person less than 16 years of age, statutory rape, aggravated indecent assault, indecent exposure, involuntary deviant sexual intercourse, possession of obscene material, or a combination of those. The sample of sex offenders was then divided according to the age of first occurrence of a sex crime. JSO are those whose first sex crime was committed prior age 18 ($n = 52$). Adult sex offenders are those whose first sex crime was committed at age 18 or later ($n = 40$).[8]

[8]The sample of sex offenders differs in a number of ways from that of the Van Wijk et al. (2005) study, which is also based on the PYS data. First, the current study is not limited to juvenile sex offending as was the case in the Van Wijk et al. (2005) study. Second, the youngest and oldest samples were used in the cohort study while the middle and oldest samples were previously used. The middle sample was not included in the current study given that self-reports assessments had stopped at about age 13. Third, a broader, more inclusive definition of sex crimes was used in the current study than that used in the Van Wijk et al. (2005) study. For example, contrary to the current study, Van Wijk et al. (2005) removed all cases of indecent exposure. A broader definition was pursued here considering: (a) the exploratory nature of the study; (b) the relatively small sample of sex offenders found in the two samples; (c) the lack of a theoretical rational for distinguishing offenders based on the legal definition of the crime committed; and (d) the objective of informing about the onset of all types of sex offending. The broader approach taken here is congruent with the strategy used in other longitudinal studies (e.g., Zimring et al., 2007).

Developmental Risk Factors

The study includes a list of 20 indicators tapping into five distinct domains of risk factors. The five domains of risk factors included for this study are: (a) socioeconomic risk factors (7 items); (b) child's behavioral problems (5 items); (c) child's delinquency (2 items); (d) child's psychiatric diagnoses (3 items); and (e) child's sexual behavior (3 items). A description of those indicators, their scoring, and their reliability are presented in Table 5.1. The risk factors were measured with data collected at different waves for the youngest and the oldest cohort. This procedure was used to ensure that risk factors were measured at about the same age for both cohorts. For the oldest cohort, data collected during the first year of the study was used (i.e., study Wave 1 and Wave 2 combined) whereas for the youngest cohort, data collected at later waves were used (i.e., study Wave 11 and Wave 12 combined). In doing so, the youngest cohort averaged 14.0 (SD = .55) years of age at data collection while the oldest was 13.9 (SD = .79) years of age. More details about the assessments, measures, and their coding can be found in Loeber, Farrington, Stouthamer-Loeber, and White (2008).

Analytical Strategy

For the current study, a two-stage process was used. In the first stage, risk factors of the onset of sex offending were analyzed by comparing the sex offenders (n = 92) and the nonsex offenders (n = 892). A series of logit regression models were used. Separate models were run for each of the five domains of risk factors included in the study. Given the exploratory nature of this study (as opposed to theory testing), a backward stepwise approach was selected to identify the most significant risk factors. A backward procedure was selected (over a forward) given the possibility that a suppressor effect could be found. Note that a forward stepwise procedure was also used and the results were consistent with those reported for the backward procedure. The area under the receiver operating characteristics (ROC) curve was analyzed for each model to determine the predictive accuracy. In the second stage, the risk factors associated with a juvenile-onset of sex offending (n = 50) and an adult-onset of sex offending (n = 42) were inspected using a series of multinomial regression models. Separate models were examined for each of the domains of risk factors. For each of these models, a backward stepwise procedure was used to identify the most significant risk factors. The odds ratios were computed by comparing the juvenile-onset and the adult-onset offenders to the nonsex offenders (n = 892). Predictive accuracy of the models was determined using the area under the ROC curve. The sample size varied slightly from one model to another due to missing data. No missing data imputation procedure was attempted due to the low proportion of missing information for each variable. All statistical analyses were completed using SPSS, version 18.0.

Table 5.1 Measures and Coding for the Childhood Risk Factors

Indicators	*Instrument*	*No. of items*	*Scale or cut-off*	*Alpha*
Controls				
Low SES (P)	Demographic questionnaire (Loeber et al., 1998)	6	Hollingshead index	n/a
Family on welfare (P)	Financial information questionnaire (Loeber et al., 1998)	1	(0) No (1) Yes	n/a
African American (P)	Demographic questionnaire (Loeber et al., 1998)	1		n/a
Poorly educated mother (P)	Demographic questionnaire (Loeber et al., 1998)	1	(0) At least 12 years (1) Less than 12 years	n/a
Young mother (P)	Demographic questionnaire (Loeber et al., 1998)	1	(0) At least 20 years (1) Less than 20 years	n/a
Bad neighborhood	1980 U.S. census track information (U.S. Bureau of Census, 2004)	6		n/a
Bad neighborhood (P)	Neighborhood scale (Loeber et al., 1998)	17	3-point Likert scale	.95 (Ys) .94 (Os)
Child's behavior				
Physical aggression (PT)	Child Behavior Checklist (Achenbach & Edelbrock, 1979, 1983; Edelbrock & Achenbach, 1984)	29	3-point Likert scale	.87 (Ys) .86(Os)
Covert behavior (PTY)	Child Behavior Checklist, Teacher Report of the Child Behavior Checklist, Youth self-report (Loeber et al., 1998)	50 (Ys) 54 (Os)	3-point Likert scale	.90 (Ys) .86 (Os)
Shy/withdrawn (PT)	Child Behavior Checklist (Achenbach & Edelbrock, 1979, 1983; Edelbrock & Achenbach, 1984)	14	3-point Likert scale	.79 (Ys) .83 (Os)
Depressed mood	Recent mood and feeling questionnaire (Angold et al., 1996)	13	3-point Likert scale	.80 (Ys) .84 (Os)
Screening risk score (PTY)	Diagnostic interview schedule for Children-Parent version; Youth self-report; Self-reported antisocial behavior scale; Self-report delinquency questionnaire (Loeber et al., 1989, 1998)	21		n/a
Onset of delinquency before age 10 (Y)	Self-report delinquency questionnaire (Loeber et al., 2005)	24		n/a
Total delinquency (Y)	Self-report antisocial behavior scale; Self-reported delinquency questionnaire (Elliott et al., 1985; Loeber et al., 1998)	24		

(*Continued*)

Table 5.1 (*Continued*)

Indicators	*Instrument*	*No. of items*	*Scale or cut-off*	*Alpha*
Child psychiatric diagnoses[a]				
Attention Deficit Hyperactivity Disorder (ADHD) (P)	Diagnostic interview schedule for Children-Parent version (Costello et al., 1982; Costello et al., 1985; Loeber et al., 1998)	28	3-point Likert symptom criteria for DSM-III-R	n/a
Oppositional Defiant Disorder (ODD) (P)	Diagnostic interview schedule for Children-Parent version (Costello et al., 1982; Costello et al., 1985; Loeber et al., 1998)	13	3-point Likert symptom criteria for DSM-III-R	n/a
Conduct Disorder (CD) (P)	Diagnostic interview schedule for Children-Parent version (Costello et al., 1982; Costello et al., 1985; Loeber et al., 1998)	13	3-point Likert symptom criteria for DSM-III-R	n/a
Child sexual behavior				
Age at first heterosexual intercourse	Sexual activity scale (Loeber et al., 1998)	1	Open-ended	n/a
Frequency of sexual intercourse	Sexual activity scale (Loeber et al., 1998)	1	Open-ended	n/a
Number of female sexual partners	Sexual activity scale (Loeber et al., 1998)	1	Open-ended	n/a

Note. P = parent; T = teacher; Y = Youth; Ys = Young sample; Os = Old sample. Based on American Psychiatric Association, 1987.
[a]Based on diagnostic criteria for DSM-III-R.

Results

Prevalence of Sex Offending

The distribution of the age of onset of sex offending can be found in Figure 5.1. Overall, the distribution of the age of onset of sex offending follows the typical age-crime curve. There is a rapid increase between age 11 and age 15. In fact, the peak age of onset is found in adolescence between the ages of 14 and 15. This peak is followed by a sharp decrease. The onset is then relatively stable between age 17 and age 22 before dropping again. Statistical information about the prevalence of sex offending is presented in Table 5.2. In total, 9.3% of this sample committed a

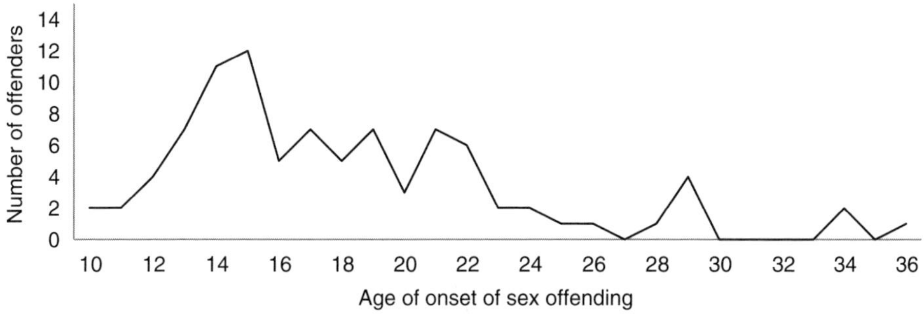

Figure 5.1 Distribution of the age of onset of sex offending.

Table 5.2 Descriptive Information of the Onset of Sex Offending in the PYS

	Total (n = 984)	*Youngest cohort (n = 477)*	*Oldest cohort (n = 506)*
Prevalence of sex offending	9.3%	6.5%	12.1%
Mean age of onset	18.1 (SD = 5.5) Range: 10–36	17.6 (SD = 4.8) Range: 10–29	18.4 (SD = 5.8) Range: 10–36
Prevalence of JSO	5.3%	4.0%	6.5%
Mean age of onset in youth	14.4 (SD = 2.0) Range: 10–17	14.5 (SD = 2.1) Range: 10–17	14.3 (SD = 2.0) Range: 10–17
Prevalence of ASO	4.1%	2.5%	5.5%
Mean age of onset in adulthood	23.0 (SD = 4.7) Range: 18–36	22.5 (SD = 3.7) Range: 18–29	23.2 (SD = 5.1) Range: 18–36

sex crime. The mean age of onset was 18.1, ranging from the ages of 10 to 36. The prevalence varied significantly across the two cohorts. The youngest cohort showed a prevalence of 6.5% as opposed to 12.1% for the oldest cohort [$X^2(2) = 8.94, p < .01$, phi = .10]. While this was statistically different across the two cohorts, the mean age of onset was not. Further analyses revealed that the sample included more JSO than ASO.

Hence, the prevalence of JSO was 5.3% for the whole sample. The prevalence of JSO for the oldest cohort (6.5%) was marginally higher than that of the youngest cohort (4.0%) [$X^2(2) = 3.16, p < .08$, phi = .06]. The prevalence of ASO was 4.1% and the mean age of onset in adulthood was 23 years. The prevalence of ASO was 5.5% for the oldest cohort and 2.5% for the youngest cohort, and the difference

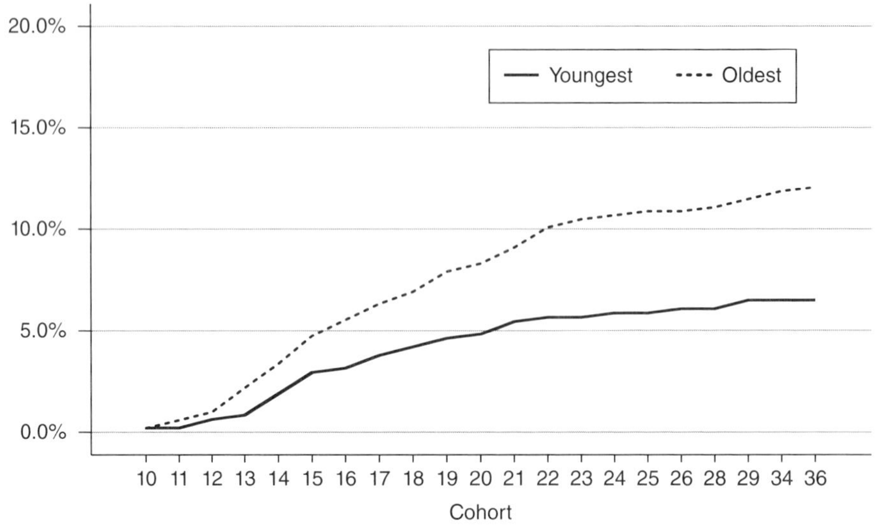

Figure 5.2 Cumulative onset of sex offending (self-reported and official).

was statistically significant [$X^2(2) = 5.73$, $p < .05$, phi = .08].[9] There were no cohort differences as to the age of onset in adolescence and adulthood ($p > .10$).

The cohort effect can also be seen with respect to the cumulative prevalence of sex offending (Figure 5.2). During adolescence, by age 15, the cumulative prevalence of sex offending has already reached the 5% mark for the oldest cohort. For the youngest cohort, however, this cumulative prevalence is only reached in adulthood, or at about age 20.

Onset of Sex Offending

In this section, the developmental childhood risk factors of sex offending were analyzed. Five domains including 20 childhood risk factors were examined: socioeconomic risk factors (7 items), child behaviors (5 items), delinquency (2 items), child psychiatric diagnoses (3 items), and child sexual behaviors (3 items). The association between the risk factors and the onset of sex offending are presented in Table 5.3. To do so, all sex offenders (n = 92) were compared to all other males in the sample (n = 891). Each of the five domains included at least two or more significant risk factors associated with the onset of sex offending. In fact, of the 20 risk factors examined, 16 (80%) were statistically significant at an alpha of .05. All statistically

[9]Note that the oldest cohort had a longer at-risk period given that they were older at last assessment than the men included in the youngest cohort. When removing all onset having occurred at age 29 or older, the effect observed was still significant ($p < .05$). Stated differently, the oldest cohort included a higher proportion of adult-onset sex offenders than the youngest cohort.

Table 5.3 Descriptive Statistics for the Childhood Risk Factors

	Sample statistics	*Risk factors of the onset of sex offending (SO)*	*Risk factors of adolescent-onset (JSO) and adult-onset (ASO) of sex offending*
Socioeconomic indicators			
Family socioeconomic status	N = 980 X = 37.4 (12.3) Range = 6–66	SO: 33.9 (11.4)** NO: 37.7 (12.3)	JSO: 33.7 (10.7) ASO: 34.1 (12.5)
Family on welfare (yes)	N = 941 No = 57.6% Yes = 35.7%	SO: 56.3%*** NO: 36.4%	JSO: 56.0% ASO: 56.8%
African American (yes)	N = 984 No = 45.0% Yes = 55.0%	SO: 67.4%* NO: 53.7%	JSO: 67.3% ASO: 67.5%
Poorly educated mother (no high school degree)	N = 954 Has a degree = 84.3% No degree = 15.7%	SO: 22.1%† NO: 15.1%	JSO: 19.6% ASO: 25.7%
Age of mother at first child	N = 885 X = 20.6 (4.2) Range = 9–37	SO: 19.2 (3.4)** NO: 20.7 (4.2)	JSO: 19.0 (3.3) ASO: 19.4 (3.5)
Bad neighborhood (census data)	N = 976 X = 1.1 (1.6) Range = −1.6–5.27	SO: 1.6 (1.6)** NO: 1.0 (1.6)	JSO: 1.6 (1.6) ASO: 1.6 (1.7)
Bad neighborhood	N = 976 X = 25.6 (8.9) Range = 17–51	SO: 27.5 (9.1)* NO: 25.4 (8.9)	JSO: 27.1 (8.4) ASO: 27.9 (10.0)
Child's behavior			
Physical aggression	N = 983 X = 0.3 (0.8) Range = 0–5	SO: 0.6 (1.1)**[a] NO: 0.3 (0.8)	JSO: 0.6 (1.2) ASO: 0.5 (1.1)
Covert behavior	N = 978 X = 8.3 (5.9) Range = 0–27	SO: 11.2 (6.0)*** NO: 8.0 (5.9)	JSO: 12.1 (5.9) ASO: 10.1 (6.1)
Shy/withdrawn	N = 983 X = 3.0 (1.9) Range = 0–7	SO: 3.0 (1.9) NO: 3.0 (1.9)	JSO: 3.4 (1.8)** ASO: 2.3 (1.8)
Depressed mood	N = 984 X = 2.6 (3.3) Range = 0–24	SO: 2.9 (2.9) NO: 2.5 (3.4)	JSO: 3.1 (3.0) ASO: 2.6 (2.9)

(Continued)

Table 5.3 (*Continued*)

	Sample statistics	*Risk factors of the onset of sex offending (SO)*	*Risk factors of adolescent-onset (JSO) and adult-onset (ASO) of sex offending*
Screening risk score (high score)	N = 984 Low = 48.9 High = 51.1	SO: 63.0%* NO: 50.0%	JSO: 67.3% ASO: 57.5%
Delinquency			
Onset of delinquency before age 10 (yes)	N = 982 No = 45.9% Yes = 51.4%	SO: 43.5%† NO: 52.8%	JSO: 50.0% ASO: 35.0%
Total delinquency	N = 984 X = 1.0 (1.9) Range = 0–14	SO: 1.6 (2.4)**,a NO: 1.0 (1.8)	JSO: 1.8 (2.6) ASO: 1.3 (2.0)
Child psychiatric diagnoses			
Attention Deficit Hyperactivity Disorder (ADHD)	N = 978 X = 3.8 (4.5) Range = 0–25.5	SO: 6.1 (5.8)*** NO: 3.6 (4.2)	JSO: 6.8 (5.8) ASO: 5.1 (5.8)
Oppositional Defiant Disorder (ODD)	N = 978 X = 3.7 (3.0) Range = 0–14	SO: 4.6 (3.1)** NO: 3.6 (3.0)	JSO: 5.0 (3.1)† ASO: 3.6 (3.0)
Conduct Disorder (CD)	N = 978 X = 3.3 (2.3) Range = 0–10	SO: 3.8 (2.6)* NO: 3.3 (2.3)	JSO: 4.2 (2.7) ASO: 3.3 (2.5)
Child sexual behavior			
Early onset of heterosexual intercourse (≤12 y.o.)	N = 970 No = 81.9 Yes = 18.1	SO: 26.4%* NO: 17.3%	JSO: 33.3%† ASO: 17.5%
Frequency of sexual intercourse (past 6 months)	N = 972 X = 2.0 (8.5) Range = 0–150	SO: 5.6 (16.9)***,a NO: 1.6 (7.0)	JSO: 8.0 (21.9) ASO: 2.5 (5.9)
Number of female sexual partners (past 6 months)	N = 974 X = 0.8 (1.9) Range = 0–23	SO: 1.5 (3.0)*** NO: 0.7 (1.7)	JSO: 1.6 (3.1) ASO: 1.5 (2.9)

Note. SO = Sex offenders; NO = Nonsex offenders; JSO = Juvenile sex offenders; ASO = Full sample of adult-onset sex offenders.

[a]Violation of assumption of homogeneity of variance but significant results confirmed using nonparametric test (Mann-Whitney U).

†$p < .10$, *$p < .05$, **$p < .01$, ***$p < .001$.

significant risk factors were in the expected direction (i.e., risk factor increased the likelihood of the onset of sex offending). For this sample, sex offenders were more likely to be African American, coming from a family environment characterized by a poor education (mother), a younger mother (at first child), a lower socioeconomic status, on welfare, and residing in a bad neighborhood.

As a child, sex offenders were also significantly more aggressive, showed more evidence of covert behaviors, were more delinquent (versatile), and presented a higher screening risk score. They also showed more evidence of ADHD, ODD, and CD. Interestingly, shy and withdrawn as well as depressive symptoms were not found to be significant risk factors. Sex offenders were also more likely to have had an early onset of sexual intercourse, to be more sexually active, and to have more sexual partners than nonsex offenders.

Juvenile Versus Adult-Onset of Sex Offending

In this section, the JSO (n = 50) and the ASO (n = 42) were compared on the same 20 risk factors analyzed previously. Of the 20 risk factors inspected, only one emerged as statistically significant at an alpha of .05. The significant finding indicated that the group of JSO were more likely to manifest evidence of being shy and withdrawn compared to the ASO group. Two more factors approached significance ($p < .10$): the presence of ODD and the early onset of sexual intercourse. The findings showed that JSO were marginally more likely to have an early onset of sexual intercourse as well as to present symptoms associated with ODD than the ASO group. The lack of significant difference is probably due to low statistical power given that the whole sample for these analyses was less than 100 cases. Subsequent analyses were conducted by removing all JSO cases (n = 23) for which the onset of sexual offending preceded the year of the childhood risk factor interview. In doing so, several risk factors became significant. Specifically, JSO were showing more evidence of covert behaviors ($p < .001$) and more signs of ODD ($p < .05$), as well as signs of CD ($p < .05$). Note that removing those 23 cases from the first set of analysis (i.e., comparison between SO and NSO) did not change any of the findings.

Multivariate Risk Factors of the Onset of Sex Offending

Next, a series of logit regression models were conducted to identify the most significant risk factors of the onset of sex offending (Table 5.4). For this set of analyses, no distinctions were made as to whether the onset occurred in adolescence or in adulthood. In Model 1, the socioeconomic indicators were analyzed simultaneously. Only one indicator was retained in the model as a risk factor of sex offending, that is, whether or not the family was on welfare (OR = 2.56, $p < .001$). In the second model, looking at behavior in childhood, only covert behavior emerged as a significant risk factor (OR = 1.09, $p < .001$), with sex offenders presenting more evidence of covert behaviors than nonsex offenders. In Model 3, both delinquency

Table 5.4 Logit Regression Analysis of the Childhood Risk Factors of the Onset of Sex Offending (Self-Reported and Official)

	Onset of sex offending	*Model fit*
Model 1: Socioeconomic factors (7 items)		
Family on welfare	2.56*** (1.60–4.10)	−2LL = 518.4 $X^2(1) = 15.5$*** AUC = .60 (.03)
Model 2: Child behaviors (5 items)		−2LL = 586.5
Covert behaviors	1.09*** (1.05–1.13)	$X^2(1) = 23.1$*** AUC = .66 (.03)
Model 3: Delinquency (2 items)		
Delinquency prior age 10	.63** (.40–.98)	−2LL = 595.6 $X^2(2) = 11.7$**
Total delinquency	1.15* (1.06–1.26)	AUC = .61 (.03)
Model 4: Psychiatric diagnosis (3 items)		
Attention Deficit Hyperactivity Disorder (ADHD)	1.16*** (1.09–1.23)	−2LL = 584.1 $X^2(2) = 25.5$***
Conduct Disorder (CD)	.87† (.76–1.00)	AUC = .64 (.03)
Model 5: Sexual behaviors (3 items)		
Frequency of sexual intercourse (past 6 months)	1.02* (1.00–1.04)	−2LL = 583.3 $X^2(2) = 14.7$**
Number of female sexual partners (past 6 months)	1.11* (1.02–1.20)	AUC = .61 (.03)
Model 6: All significant predictors		
Composite risk score (8 items; alpha = .34)	1.18*** (1.12–1.24)	−2LL = 528.5 $X^2(1) = 36.1$*** AUC = .72 (.03)

Note. Multinominal regression models with forward stepwise entry. Each model was run separately. AUC = area under the receiver operating characteristic. The composite risk score includes: family on welfare, covert behaviors, delinquency prior age 10, total delinquency, ADHD, CD (reverse coded), frequency of sexual intercourse, and the number of sexual partners.
†$p < .10$, *$p < .05$, **$p < .01$, ***$p < .001$.

indicators emerged as statistically significant. Sex offenders were least likely to have a child onset of delinquency (prior age 10) (OR = .63, $p < .01$), but were more delinquent than nonsex offenders at the time of the interview (OR = 1.15, $p < .05$). Furthermore, in the next model, both ADHD and CD were retained in the predictive model of the onset of sex offending.

Sex offenders were more likely to show more symptoms of ADHD (OR = 1.16, $p < .001$) while showing a trend of presenting fewer symptoms of CD (OR = .87,

$p < .10$) than nonsex offenders. In the final model, two indicators of sexual behaviors emerged as risk factors of the onset of sex offending. Findings indicate that sex offenders were more sexually active (OR = 1.02, $p < .05$) and had more sexual partners (OR = 1.11, $p < .05$) than nonsex offenders. Note that each logit regression model showed relatively low-to-modest predictive accuracy with the area under the ROC curve varying between .60 and .66. Taken together, the findings indicated that at least one significant risk factor in each of the five domains analyzed significantly contributed to the prediction of the onset of sex offending.

Composite Risk Scale of the Onset of Sex Offending

The scores of the eight identified risk factors were standardized and summed[10] to create a composite risk scale (Mean = –.00; SD = 3.39; Range = –5.6–23.5). Not surprisingly, the alpha of the scale was very low given the indicators summed were measuring different concepts. The score on the composite risk scale was significantly associated with the onset of sex offending (OR = 1.18, $p < .001$). The area under the ROC curve (.72) was relatively higher than that found for individual models. Considering the cohort effect reported earlier, we examined whether it had an effect on the association between the composite risk scale and sex offending (Table 5.5). The findings showed that the strength of the association between the scores of the composite scale and the onset of sex offending was relatively unaffected by the cohort effect. In fact, the cohort effect became marginally

Table 5.5 Cohort, Composite Risk Score, and the Onset of Sex Offending

	Onset of sex offending	*Model fit*
Block 1	1.98**	–2LL = 555.9
Cohort	(1.24–3.15)	$X^2(1) = 8.6$**
(0 = youngest; 1 = oldest)		AUC = .58 (.03)
Block 2	1.52†	–2LL = 525.1
Cohort	(.94–2.47)	$X^2(2) = 39.4$***
(0 = youngest; 1 = oldest)		AUC = .71 (.03)
Composite risk score	1.17***	
	(1.11–1.23)	

Note. Logit regression models with forward stepwise entry. Each model was run separately. AUC = area under the receiver operating characteristic curve (ROC). The composite risk score includes: family on welfare, covert behaviors, delinquency prior age 10, total delinquency, ADHD, CD (reverse coded), frequency of sexual intercourse, and the number of sexual partners.
†$p < .10$, *$p < .05$, **$p < .01$, ***$p < .001$.

[10]Items that were inversely associated to the onset of sex offending (e.g., delinquency prior age 10) were reverse-coded to create this scale.

significant *after* controlling for the composite risk scores. A graphical representation of the link between the score of the composite risk scale and the onset of sex offending is presented in Figure 5.3a. The scores were categorized into six categories with the lowest category (0) representing those with the fewest risk factors, whereas those in the highest category (5) represent those with the highest scores on the composite scale. Nearly half of the sample (47.6 %) had a score of 0 or 1, indicative of a low risk of sex offending. At the other end of the continuum, 38, or just over 4% of the sample, showed the highest score on the composite risk scale (score of 5). Yet, the prevalence of sex offending was 2.5% (score of 0) and 3.8% (score of 1) for the two lowest scores, whereas it gradually increased as the score on the scale increased, reaching 28.9% for those with a score of 5.[11]

Multivariate Risk Factors of the Onset for Juvenile and Adult Sex Offending

The same analytical strategy used in the preceding section was used here. This time, however, a series of stepwise multinominal regression models were conducted to identify the most significant risk factors among the five domains of risk. Results are presented in Table 5.6. The group of nonsex offenders was used as the reference category to which the group of JSO and ASO were compared. Results should be interpreted with caution given the small sample of JSO and ASO analyzed. For the onset of sex offending in youth, at least one significant risk factor was found in each of the five domains of risk. In total, six risk factors were retained by the prediction models: family on welfare (OR = 2.24, $p < .01$), covert behaviors (OR = 1.11, $p < .001$), total delinquency (OR = 1.18, $p < .01$), symptoms of ADHD (OR = 1.12, $p < .001$), frequency of sexual intercourse (OR = 1.02, $p < .01$) and early onset of sexual behaviors (OR = 1.90, $p < .10$). All risk factors were in the expected direction (i.e., increase the likelihood of the onset of juvenile sex offending).

[11]There are at least two known issues with the stepwise regression procedure: (a) the risk of capitalizing on chance, and (b) the assumption of absence of multicollinearity among predictors. Hence an alternative analytical approach pursued here was to reduce the number of risk factors into dimensions (or factors). The factor analysis was conducted with the 20 indicators from the five domains of risk. A six-factor solution emerged. The factors were labeled as follows: (1) behavior problems and psychiatric symptoms; (2) neighborhood risk; (3) socioeconomic adversities; (4) sexual behaviors; (5) early onset; and (6) delinquency and depression. These six dimensions and their associated factor scores were entered into a logit regression model. The first four factors (1–4) were statistically related ($p < .05$) to the onset of sex offending while the other two were not ($p > .10$). The association between the four significant dimensions of risk and sex offending were all in the hypothesized direction. Several findings are worth highlighting here. First, neighborhood indicators were found to be significant risk factors of the onset of sex offending, something not captured with our stepwise regression approach. Second, both delinquency indicators were significantly related to the onset of offending in the stepwise approach but were not in the dimensional approach. Third, the prediction accuracy found for the stepwise approach (AUC = .72) was identical to the one found using the dimensional approach. Complete findings are available upon request from the first author.

(a)

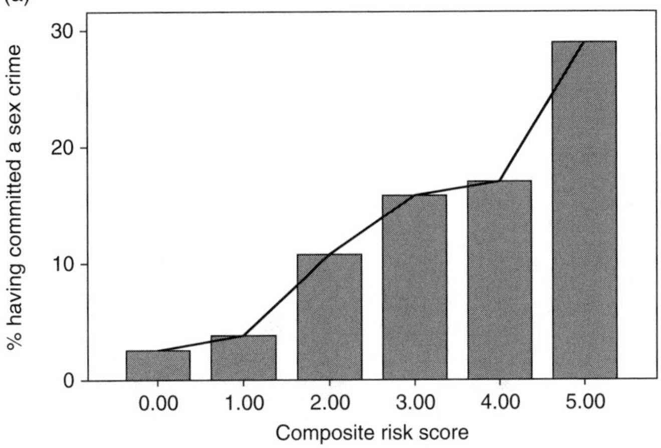

(b)

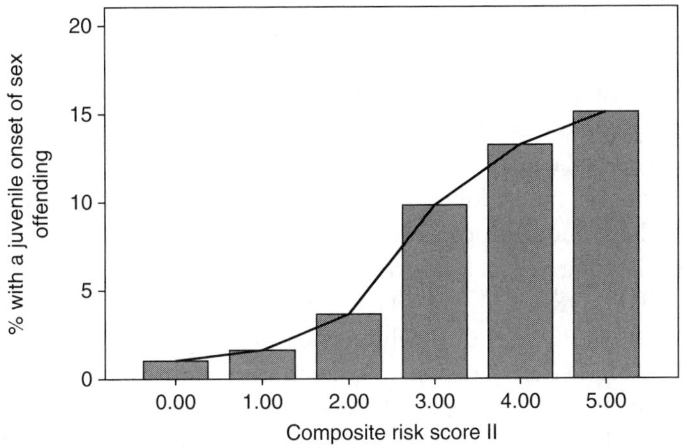

Figure 5.3 Scores for the composite risk scale of sex offending and the prevalence of sex offenders. (a) Composite risk scale and prevalence of sex offending. The composite risk score includes: family on welfare, covert behaviors, delinquency prior age 10, total delinquency, ADHD, CD (reverse coded), frequency of sexual intercourse, and the number of sexual partners. The composite score and sample size for each risk category are as follows: (0) –6.00 to –3.00, n = 118; (1) –2.99 to –1.00, n = 313; (2) –0.99 to 0.99, n = 223; (3) 1.00 to 2.99, n = 120; (4) 3.00 to 5.99, n = 94; (5) 6+, n = 38. (b) Composite risk scale of juvenile-onset of sex offending and the prevalence of juvenile-onset sex offenders. The composite risk score II includes: social welfare, covert behaviors, total delinquency, ADHD, frequency of sexual intercourse and the early onset of heterosexual intercourse. The composite score and sample size for each risk category are as follows: (0) –6.00 to –3.00, n = 193; (1) –2.99 to –1.00, n = 246; (2) –0.99 to 0.99, n = 192; (3) 1.00 to 2.99, n = 112; (4) 3.00 to 5.99, n = 121; (5) 6+, n = 53. (c) Composite risk scales of adult-onset of sex offending and the prevalence of adult-onset sex offenders. The composite risk score III includes: social welfare, shy/withdrawn (reverse coded), delinquency prior age 10 (reverse coded), ADHD, and the number of sexual partners. The composite score and sample size for each risk category are as follows: (0) –6.00 to –3.00, n = 92; (1) –2.99 to –1.00, n = 270; (2) –0.99 to 0.99, n = 259; (3) 1.00 to 2.99, n = 181; (4) 3.00 to 5.99, n = 89; (5) 6+, n = 20.

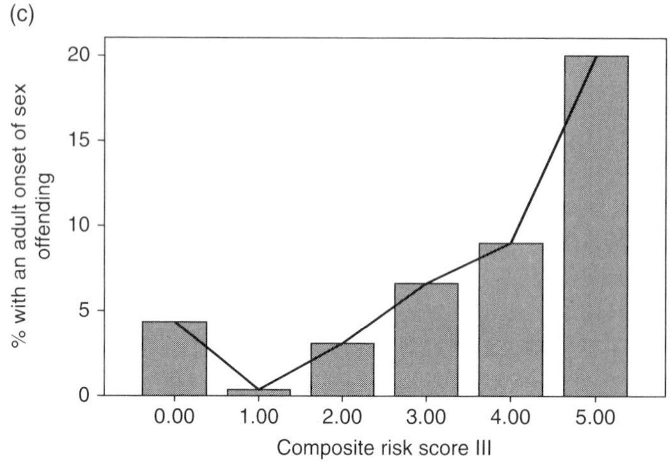

Figure 5.3 (*Continued*)

The predictive accuracy of each domain of factors, as shown by the area under the ROC curve, varied from .59 (Socioeconomic factors: family on welfare) to .69 (Child behaviors: covert behaviors).

When looking at the childhood risk factors of the onset of sex offending in adulthood, at least one significant risk factor was found in each of the five domains of risk. The following risk factors were significantly associated with sex offending: family on welfare (OR = 3.17, $p < .01$), covert behaviors (OR = 1.09, $p < .01$), shy/withdrawn (OR = .75, $p < .01$), delinquency prior age 10 (OR = .45, $p < .05$), symptoms of ADHD (OR = 1.07, $p < .05$), and the number of female sex partners (OR = 1.15, $p < .05$). On the one hand, the individuals with an onset of sex offending in adulthood were more likely to have parent(s) on welfare, to show more covert behaviors, and to have more symptoms associated with ADHD; they were also more likely to report more sexual partners. On the other hand, they were also less likely to be shy and withdrawn and less likely to have had an onset of delinquency prior age 10. The area under the ROC curve for each of the models tested varied from .57 (Psychiatric diagnosis: ADHD) to .67 (Child behaviors: covert behaviors and shy/withdrawn).

Comparing Juvenile-Onset and Adult-Onset of Sex Offending

The series of multinominal regression models allow the contrasting of the similarities and differences found with respect to the childhood risk factor of juvenile-onset and adult-onset of sex offending.[12] First, only three risk factors were found

[12]In line with the rationale and additional findings provided in footnote 11, the association between the six dimensions of risk factors found using factor analysis and the type of onset was examined. In a multinominal regression model, the six dimensions of risk factors were: (1) behavior problems and

Table 5.6 Multinominal Stepwise Regression Analysis of the Childhood Risk Factors of Juvenile and Adult-Onset of Sex Offending

	Juvenile-onset of sex offending (JSO)	*Adult-onset of sex offending (ASO)*	*Model fit*
Model 1: Socioecononomic factors (7 items)			
Family on welfare	2.24 (1.24–4.03)**	3.17 (1.50–6.70)**	–2LL = 623.7 $X^2(2) = 16.1$*** $AUC_{JSO} = .59\ (.04)$ $AUC_{ASO} = .60\ (.05)$
Model 2: Child behaviors (5 items)			
Shy/withdrawn	1.02 (.87–1.20)	.75** (.61–.91)	–2LL = 679.5 $X^2(4) = 34.9$***
Covert behaviors	1.11*** (.106–1.16)	1.09** (1.03–1.15)	$AUC_{JSO} = .69\ (.04)$ $AUC_{ASO} = .67\ (.04)$
Model 3: Delinquency (2 items)			
Delinquency prior age 10	.80 (.46–1.42)	.45* (.23–.88)	–2LL = 117.7 $X^2(4) = 14.2$**
Total delinquency	1.18** (1.06–1.31)	1.11 (.97–1.28)	$AUC_{JSO} = .64\ (.04)$ $AUC_{ASO} = .62\ (.04)$
Model 4: Psychiatric diagnosis (3 items)			
Attention Deficit Hyperactivity Disorder (ADHD)	1.12*** (1.07–1.18)	1.07* (1.01–1.14)	–2LL = 565.2 $X^2(4) = 23.4$*** $AUC_{JSO} = .67\ (.04)$ $AUC_{ASO} = .57\ (.05)$
Model 5: Sexual behaviors (3 items)			
Frequency of sexual intercourse (past 6 months)	1.02** (1.01–1.04)	1.00 (.94–1.05)	–2LL = 185.9 $X^2(6) = 21.3$**
Number of female sexual partners (past 6 months)	1.07 (.96–1.19)	1.15* (1.02–1.31)	$AUC_{JSO} = .63\ (.04)$ $AUC_{ASO} = .61\ (.05)$
Early onset of heterosexual intercourse	1.90† (.99–3.67)	.77 (.31–1.91)	
Model 6: All significant predictors of JSO Composite risk score of JSO (6 items; alpha = .61)	1.22*** (1.14–1.31)	1.12** (1.03–1.22)	–2LL = 663.3 $X^2(2) = 38.4$*** $AUC_{JSO} = .76\ (.03)$ $AUC_{ASO} = .63\ (.04)$
Model 7: All significant predictors of ASO Composite risk score of ASO (6 items; alpha = .19)	1.31*** (1.19–1.43)	1.31*** (1.18–1.45)	–2LL = 679.4 $X^2(2) = 49.2$*** $AUC_{JSO} = .72\ (.04)$ $AUC_{ASO} = .72\ (.05)$

Note. Multinominal regression models with forward stepwise entry. Each model was run separately. AUC = area under the receiver operating characteristic curve (ROC). Composite risk score of JSO includes: social welfare, covert behaviors, total delinquency, ADHD, frequency of sexual intercourse, and the early onset of heterosexual intercourse. Composite risk score of ASO includes: social welfare, shy/withdrawn (reverse coded), delinquency prior age 10 (reverse coded), ADHD, and the number of sexual partners.

†$p < .10$, *$p < .05$, **$p < .01$, ***$p < .001$.

to predict both outcomes: (1) family on welfare, (2) covert behaviors, and (3) symptoms associated with ADHD. Second, even if ADHD was associated with both outcomes, it was more predictive of a juvenile-onset than an adult-onset of offending, as shown by the differential predictive accuracy (AUC for JSO = .67 vs. AUC for ASO = .57). Third, in youth, those with a juvenile-onset of sex offending were more delinquent than nonsex offenders. Such a pattern was not found for those with an adult-onset of sex offending. In fact, this group was least likely to be involved in delinquency prior age 10. Fourth, while both groups of sex offenders were significantly different from the nonsex offenders with respect to their sexual behaviors in adolescence, such differences were manifested differently for the JSO and the ASO groups. More precisely, while the JSO were more sexually active, the ASO were more sexually promiscuous. Fifth, the adult-onset offenders were more likely to be shy and withdrawn than nonsex offenders, but such a difference was not observed for the juvenile-onset offenders.[13] Taken together, there were some similarities and many differences in the childhood risk factors of the onset of sex offending in youth as opposed to those associated with the onset of sex offending in adulthood.

Composite Risk Scales of Juvenile- and Adult-Onset of Sex Offending

Next, composite risk scales were created to predict the juvenile- and adult-onset of sex offending (Table 5.6). The scores for the significant risk factors found for the juvenile-onset of sex offending were standardized and summed to create a composite risk scale of JSO (Mean = .00; SD = 3.52; Range = -4.3 to 25.6). The alpha for this scale was .61, suggesting much covariance between the risk factors included in that scale despite the fact that they were tapping different theoretical constructs and

---

psychiatric symptoms; (2) neighborhood risk; (3) socioeconomic adversities; (4) sexual behaviors; (5) early onset; and (6) delinquency and depression. Three outcomes were compared and contrasted: (a) no onset of sex offending; (b) juvenile-onset of sex offending; and (c) adult-onset of sex offending. The no-onset group served as a reference category for comparison purposes. For juvenile-onset of sex offending, dimension 1 (OR = 1.69, $p < .001$) and dimension 4 (OR = 1.48, $p < .001$) both emerged as significant risk dimensions. Hence, JSO were showing more behavioral problems as well as a more extensive sexual history than the no-onset group. Risk dimension 2 and 3, related to neighborhood (OR = 1.33, $p = .084$) and social adversity (OR = 1.32, $p = .074$) risk, were both marginally related to the juvenile-onset of sex offending. Hence, juvenile-onset offenders had a tendency to come from a poor neighborhood and to be exposed to more social adversity than the no-onset group. Risk dimension 3 (OR = 1.55, $p < .05$) and 4 (OR = 1.38, $p < .05$) were both significant predictors of an adult-onset of sex offending, suggesting that the adult-onset offenders were exposed to more social adversities in childhood and showed a more extensive sexual history than the no-onset group. The neighborhood risk dimension also marginally increased the risk of an adult-onset of sex offending (OR = 1.41, $p = .091$).

[13]The presence of risk factors found to be inversely related to the adult-onset of sex offending (i.e., no prior delinquency before age 10; shy and withdrawn) reinforce our decision to use a variable-based approach rather than a risk dimension approach (see footnotes 11 and 12) as the factorial approach did not capture the inverse relationship between specific indicators and the onset of sex offending.

domains of risk. This suggests that, to some extent, the risk factors identified for JSO were occurring in the same families (multi-risk families). In a similar fashion the significant risk factors found for the adult-onset of sex offending were standardized and summed to create a composite risk scale of ASO (Mean = –.01; SD = 2.69; Range = –6.0 to 13.4).

The two items that were inversely linked to adult-onset of sex offending were reverse-coded and their scores were added to the composite scale. The alpha for this composite scale was very low (.14) and reflective of the independence of these risk factors (as opposed to those found for a juvenile-onset).[14] The composite risk scale of JSO (OR = 1.22, $p < .001$) presented a moderate-to-good predictive accuracy of juvenile-onset of sex offending (AUC = .76). The score of this scale, however, showed a relatively low predictive accuracy of the adult-onset of sex offending (AUC = .63).

Note that the predictive accuracy of the composite risk scale was not affected by the cohort effect reported earlier (Table 5.7). Graphical representation of the link

Table 5.7 Cohort, Composite Risk Score, and the Onset of Juvenile and Adult Sex Offending

	Juvenile-onset of sex offending (JSO)	*Adult-onset of sex offending (ASO)*	*Model fit*
Model 1	1.74†	2.34*	–2LL = 29.0
Cohort	(.98–3.11)	(1.17–4.66)	$X^2(2) = 9.2$**
(0 = youngest; 1 = oldest)			$AUC_{JSO} = .56$ (.04)
			$AUC_{ASO} = .60$ (.04)
Model 2			
Cohort	1.58	2.12*	–2LL = 625.5
(0 = youngest; 1 = oldest)	(.86–2.93)	(1.05–4.28)	$X^2(4) = 45.2$***
Composite risk score of	1.22***	1.12**	$AUC_{JSO} = .76$ (03)
JSO	(1.14–1.31)	(1.03–1.22)	$AUC_{ASO} = .66$ (.04)
Model 3			
Cohort	1.31	1.58	–2LL = 630.3
(0 = youngest; 1 = oldest)	(.70–2.44)	(.77–3.28)	$X^2(4) = 51.7$***
Composite risk score	1.29***	1.29***	$AUC_{JSO} = .72$ (.04)
of ASO	(1.18–1.42)	(1.16–1.44)	$AUC_{ASO} = .72$ (.05)

Note. Multinominal regression models with forward stepwise entry. AUC = area under the receiver operating characteristic curve (ROC). Composite risk score of JSO includes: social welfare, covert behaviors, total delinquency, ADHD, frequency of sexual intercourse, and the early onset of heterosexual intercourse. Composite risk score of ASO includes: social welfare, shy/withdrawn (reverse coded), delinquency prior age 10 (reverse coded), ADHD, and the number of sexual partners.
†$p < .10$, *$p < .05$, **$p < .01$, ***$p < .001$.

[14]The correlation between the scores on the two scales was relatively high and significant (r = .73, $p < .001$).

Table 5.8 Comparison of the Predictive Value of Two Composite Risk Scales

	Juvenile-onset of sex offending (JSO)	*Adult-onset of sex offending (ASO)*	*Model fit*
Cohort (oldest)	.70 (.37–1.33)	.70 (.33–1.47)	−2LL = 614.6 $X^2(6) = 61.5^{***}$
Composite risk score of JSO	1.15** (1.05–1.26)	.91 (.78–1.06)	$AUC_{JSO} = .73\ (.03)$
Composite risk score of ASO	1.12 (.98–1.29)	1.39*** (1.17–1.64)	$AUC_{ASO} = .69\ (.03)$

Note. Multinominal regression models with forward stepwise entry. AUC = area under the receiver operating characteristic curve (ROC). Composite risk score of JSO includes: social welfare, covert behaviors, total delinquency, ADHD, frequency of sexual intercourse, and the early onset of heterosexual intercourse. Composite risk score of ASO includes: social welfare, shy/withdrawn (reverse coded), delinquency prior age 10 (reverse coded), ADHD, and the number of sexual partners.
$^{\dagger}p < .10$, $^{*}p < .05$, $^{**}p < .01$, $^{***}p < .001$.

between the composite score of this scale and the proportion of JSO can be found in Figure 5.3b. Looking at the composite risk scale of factors associated with the adult-onset of sex offending (Table 5.6), scores were found to be associated with both juvenile (OR = 1.31, $p < .001$) and adult-onset (OR = 1.31, $p < .001$) of sex offending. The predictive accuracy found for both outcomes was identical (AUC = .72) and was not affected, once again, by the cohort effect (Table 5.7). Graphical representation of the link between the composite score of this scale and the proportion of adult-onset offenders can be found in Figure 5.3c.

The discriminant predictive value of the two composite risk scales was examined next. Using a multinominal regression analysis, both composite scales were forced simultaneously into a single prediction model, adjusting for cohort membership (Table 5.8). The findings of the model indicated that the scores of the composite risk scale of JSO were significantly related to the juvenile-onset of sex offending (OR = 1.15, $p < .01$), but not to the adult-onset of sex offending (OR = .91, ns). Comparatively speaking, the scores of the composite scale of adult-onset of sex offending were found to be significantly related to adult-onset of sex offending (OR = 1.39, $p < .001$) but not to juvenile-onset of sex offending (OR = 1.12, ns). Clearly, the two composite scales were differently associated to the two types of onset of sex offending. The findings of this analysis suggest that the two types of onset are better predicted by a different configuration of childhood risk factors.

Discussion

The current study examined the childhood risk factors of the onset of sex offending using data from a prospective longitudinal study. The PYS provides a unique opportunity to examine the risk factors associated with the onset of sex offending in two large samples of at-risk boys recruited in elementary schools. This is a departure from clinical-/empirical-based studies on juvenile and adult sex offenders that have relied on (1) highly selective samples of sex offenders; (2) using retrospective data on risk factors (3) that typically exclude the presence of a non-offender and/or a nonsex offender group (4) while not providing the opportunity to compare and contrast the juvenile and adult-onset of sex offending in a single study. Taking into account the unique aspects of the research design of the current study, several key findings emerged:

1 The onset of sex offending follows the typical age-crime curve. The onset of sex offending is abrupt rather than gradual. It peaks in mid-adolescence, between the ages of 14 and 15. In adulthood, the most likely period of adult-onset sex offending was found in young adulthood, between the ages of 18 and 22.
2 By the end of adolescence, only 5.3% of the whole sample had committed a sex crime. By the end of the follow-up period (at about age 32), the prevalence had increased to 9.3%.
3 No single risk factor or single domain of risk factors accurately predicted the onset of sex offending, although some domains of risk factors were slightly more significant than others. The onset of sex offending is the result of an accumulation of risk factors across multiple domains at the individual, familial, and neighborhood level.
4 Measured at about age 13, risk factors associated with the onset of sex offending included living in a poor neighborhood, exposure to socioeconomic adversities, manifesting behavioral problems, and showing symptoms of an externalizing spectrum disorder (i.e., ADHD, ODD), as well as a more extensive juvenile delinquency involvement and a more active sexuality.
5 Childhood risk factors can moderately predict the onset of juvenile sex offending, but the prediction of adult-onset offending is not as accurate. It could be hypothesized (see also Smallbone & Cale, this book) that childhood risk factors are better predictors of juvenile-onset sex offending because they are temporally closer than the adult-onset offending.
6 Some childhood risk factors of juvenile-onset overlap, to some extent, with those associated with an adult-onset of sex offending. For example, the level of covert behaviors was associated with both juvenile- and adult-onset of sex offending.[15] There are significant differences between the childhood risk factors associated with the onset of juvenile and adult sex offending. For example, at age 13, juvenile-onset sex offenders were characterized by a more frequent

[15]It could have been expected that overt behaviors, such as physical aggression, would have been a more important predictor in that sexual offending may be seen as one of the culmination points of an overt pathway. Keep in mind that our outcome, sex offending, is not limited to physically aggressive sex crime. Hence, it could be the case that had we looked at more specific indicators of sex offending (e.g., sexual assault), physical aggression would have emerged more strongly as an indicator of sex offending. The sample size of sex offenders included in the study did not allow for such categorization however.

sexual activity than nonsex offenders while adult-onset sex offenders, at that age, were characterized by having more sexual partners. While apparently similar, these indicators are tapping into two distinct explanatory constructs, sexual drive (i.e., frequency of sex) and sociosexuality or mating effort (i.e., partner diversity).

7 Some hypothesized childhood risk factors were inversely related to adult-onset sex offending. For example, adult-onset sex offenders were *less likely* to be shy and socially withdrawn as well as less likely to have been a child delinquent. Such findings were not observed for juvenile-onset offenders. This may suggest that they may have acted as protective factors, at least in adolescence, against the onset of juvenile sex offending. While this idea has not been tested directly, it should be explored in future research.

Theoretical and Policy Implications

The current findings present baseline information for the need of a developmental-oriented approach to the study of juvenile and adult sex offending. Most discussion on the prevention of juvenile sex offending has focused on tertiary type approaches that focus on the treatment of JSO (e.g., Barbaree & Marshall, 2008; Barbaree, Marshall, & Hudson, 1993). The current study provides baseline information for the implementation of a corpus of research designed to inform policymakers about the development of juvenile and adult sex offending before its occurrence. This corpus of research should be considered a priority for the development and implementation of a primary and secondary prevention approach to the issue of sex offending (see also Basile, 2003; Laws, 2008). The current study is a modest contribution to the elaboration of an evidence-based primary and secondary prevention approach. The study helps to highlight several key findings that can inform policymakers about such an endeavor: There are risk factors that can be screened early. What needs to be clarified here is whether or not this study only picked risk factors associated with general delinquency. It is unlikely to be the case, however, at least for the adult-onset of sex offending, as our findings showed that the level of delinquency in youth was unrelated to it. This matter could be clarified in future studies by comparing JSO to different groups of youth, based on their level of general delinquency.

The pattern of age of onset of sex offending has rarely been discussed from a theoretical perspective (for a discussion on age and sex offending, see Barbaree, Blanchard, & Langton, 2003; Lalumière, Harris, Quinsey, & Rice, 2005). The fact that the age of onset follows the age-crime curve, peaking in mid-adolescence, is of theoretical relevance. Why mid-adolescence rather than early or late-adolescence? Is it related to puberty and elevated testosterone levels during that period, as claimed by some researchers (Marshall & Barbaree, 1990)? Considering that risk factors of juvenile-onset of sex offending do not accurately predict adult-onset of sex offending further reinforces the idea of approaching these two phenomena as distinct issues. This finding may also suggest that the prevention of juvenile sex offending may have limited impact on the prevention of adult-onset sex offending.

The current study further emphasizes the importance of a multifactorial approach to the explanation of sex offending over and above any single-factor models. Intervention strategies targeting multi-risk domains such as individual, social, and neighborhood risk factors may be those that could have the most promising impact on the early prevention of sex offending. Focusing on one domain of risk factors may have limited impact on the early prevention of sex offending due to the cumulative effect found in the current study. The risk factors identified for the juvenile-onset of sex offending are well-known risk factors of antisocial and delinquent behaviors. This further reinforces the reconceptualization of juvenile sex offending as delinquent acts rather than as sexual deviance (Smallbone, 2006). The study findings highlight the difficulty in finding risk factors that distinguish sex and nonsex offenses (see also Van Wijk et al., 2005). It does suggests, however, that effective prevention efforts aimed at reducing antisociality and delinquency may also help reduce the risk of juvenile sex offending.

The juvenile delinquency–juvenile sex offending link observed suggests that greater involvement in delinquency increases the likelihood of committing a sex crime during adolescence. This has several implications for the early screening of youth at risk of juvenile sex offending, less so for the adult-onset of sex offending. The delinquency–juvenile sex offending link is in line with the criminal versatility found in other samples of JSO. While this link has been documented by many, only a few explanations have been provided (for exceptions see, for example, Seto & Barbaree, 1997; Smallbone, 2006). Hence, the reason for such a link remains unclear. For example, the process by which the delinquency–sex offending link exists could be due to a random process, a stepping-stone mechanism, the similarities of risk factors for nonsex and sex offending, and so on. Juvenile sex offending is associated with an early onset of sexual intercourse and a more active sexuality at around age 13. Our results are in line with the meta-analysis conducted by Seto and Lalumière (2010) showing that JSO, as opposed to juvenile nonsex offenders, are more likely to be characterized by an atypical sexual development. From a prevention standpoint, sexual education in schools that addresses, among other things, the issues of consent, coercion, and victimization, as well as false beliefs regarding sex, should be considered.

Practitioners should be aware of the comorbidity between mental health problems and juvenile sex offending. More specifically, youth presenting symptoms of ADHD may be at risk of juvenile sex offending. Of importance, clinicians may pay closer attention to the sexual education and sexual activities and practices of children presenting such symptoms. Future research should clarify if and how ADHD influences the sexual development (see, for example, Lussier & Healey, 2009). It is worth contrasting the prospective predictive accuracy observed in the current study for the onset of sex offending with that observed for the prospective predictive accuracy of juvenile sexual recidivism. The predictive accuracy reported in the current study for the summative risk scale of juvenile-onset offending (AUC = .76) is superior to the predictive accuracy reported for the actuarial risk assessment scale helping to screen for potential juvenile sexual recidivists (AUC ≈ mid .50s) (for a review see Viljoen, Elkovitch, Scalora, & Ullman, 2009). While the findings of the current study should be considered preliminary, they should be seen as promising.

Limitations

The current study is not without methodological shortcomings and the findings should be interpreted accordingly. The study included a small number of juvenile-onset and adult-onset sex offenders. The small number of sex offenders may have limited the current study in identifying the full spectrum of types of juvenile and adult sex offenders. As such, it is reasonable to think that the most common forms of sex offenders were captured by the current research design.[16] Further, the small number of sex offenders prevented analysis of types based on their victim characteristics (e.g., child molesters versus peer abusers), level of violence, or sexual intrusiveness (e.g., rapists versus voyeurs or exhibitionists). It could be reasonably argued, based on prior research, that different developmental risk factors may apply to different types of sex offenders (e.g., Hunter, Figueredo, Malamuth, & Becker, 2003; Johnson & Knight, 2000). The research design was set so that risk factors measured at the same time points for the youngest and oldest cohort were taken into consideration. In doing so, the study was limited to prospective data on risk factors measured at around age 13 for both samples. Since the oldest cohort were initially met for the first time at that age, prospective longitudinal data for the earliest developmental periods were not available for this group. Hence, it can be assumed that the earlier developmental periods may include similar or different risk factors of sex offending. In the same manner, the current study did not examine the developmental period at later developmental stages (e.g., adolescence, emerging adulthood), which may be especially relevant for the understanding of adult-onset sex offending.

The juvenile delinquency–sex offending link should be investigated further. Are there any subtypes of delinquent careers in juvenile sex offending? Emerging research suggests that it is the case (Hendriks, Van den Berg, & Bijleveld, this book; Lussier et al., 2012). Further, is there a subtype (or subtypes) of juvenile offenders at risk of escalating to sex offending (see Van Wijk et al., 2005)? Is it possible to identify developmental pathways leading to sex offending? The sample was followed up to their thirties and the findings may not apply to those whose onset of sex offending

[16]To illustrate, Lussier et al. (2012) found evidence of two meta-trajectories of JSO: (a) the adolescent-limited, and (b) the high-rate slow desisters. The study showed that adolescent-limited offenders represented 90% of the sample of JSO. Hence, in the context of the current study, if 90% of the JSO were adolescent-limited offenders, this suggests that only about five JSO were high-rate slow desisters – a number too low to detect any trends in the data. Therefore, the study findings may apply more to youth at risk of an adolescent-limited track.

occurs later. Onset studies have shown that some offenders do initiate their sex crime careers in their forties and fifties (e.g., Lussier & Mathesius, 2012; Smallbone & Wortley, 2004). We cannot assume that the risk factors identified in the current study also apply to late-onset sex offending. Finally, in the current study the list of potentially relevant and significant risk factors of a juvenile- and adult-onset of sex offending is not exhaustive. For example, past research has shown the importance of childhood sexual victimization as an important precursor of juvenile-onset sex offending (Seto & Lalumière, 2010). Future research should examine a broader range of developmentally informed risk factors, including experiences of abuse.

Conclusion

Using data collected as part of the PYS, a prospective longitudinal study on the causes and correlates of delinquency, the current study examined the onset of sex offending and associated childhood risk factors. The study findings provide preliminary evidence for a developmental approach to the prevention of juvenile and adult sex offending. Further, the study highlights that no single domain, but rather the accumulation of risk factors, is most accurate for the early screening of youth at risk of sex offending. The study findings should be considered preliminary and not definitive. The findings are promising with respect to the elaboration of primary and secondary intervention strategies aiming to prevent sex offending before its onset. More prospective, longitudinally based research studies are needed to describe the onset of sex offending and the developmental causes and correlates.

References

Abel, G. G., Becker, J. V, Mittelman, M., Cunningham-Rathner, J., Rouleau, J. L., & Murphy, W. D. (1987). Self-reported sex crimes of nonincarcerated paraphiliacs. *Journal of Interpersonal Violence, 2*, 3–25.

Abel, G. G., Osborn, C. A., & Twigg, D. A. (1993). Sexual assault through the life span: Adult offenders with juvenile histories. In H. E. Barbaree, W. L. Marshall, & S. M. Hudson (Eds.), *The juvenile sex offender* (pp. 104–117). New York, NY: Guilford.

Achenbach, T. M., & Edelbrock, C. S. (1979). The Child Behavior Profile: II. Boys aged 12–16 and girls aged 6–11 and 12–16. *Journal of Consulting and Clinical Psychology, 47*(2), 223–233.

Achenbach, T. M., & Edelbrock, C. S. (1983). *Manual for the child behavior checklist and revised Child Behavior Profile*. Burlington, VT: University of Vermont, Department of Psychiatry.

American Psychiatric Association. (1987). *Diagnostic and statistical manual of mental disorders* (3rd ed. Rev.)., Washington, DC: Author.

Angold, A., Erkanli, A., Costelo, E. J., & Rutter, M. (1996). Precision, reliability and accuracy in the dating of symptom onsets in child and adolescent psychopathology. *Journal of Child Psychology and Psychiatry, 37*, 657–664.

Barbaree, H. E., Blanchard, R., & Langton, C. M. (2003). The development of sexual aggression through the life span. *Annals of the New York Academy of Sciences, 989*(1), 59–71.

Barbaree, H. E., & Marshall, W. L. (2008). *The juvenile sex offender* (2nd ed.). New York: Guilford Press.

Barbaree, H. E., Marshall, W. L., & Hudson, S. M. (1993). *The juvenile sex offender*. New York: Guilford Press.

Basile, C. K. (2003). Implications of public health for policy on sexual violence. *Annals of the New York Academy of Sciences, 989*(1), 446–463.

Baxter J. D., Marshall, W. L., Barbaree, H. E., Davidson, P. R., & Malcolm, P. B. (1984). Deviant sexual behavior: Differentiating sex offenders by criminal and personal history, psychometric measures, and sexual response. *Criminal Justice and Behavior, 11*(4), 477–501.

Bremer, J. F. (1992). Serious juvenile sex offenders: Treatment and long-term follow-up. *Psychiatric Annals, 22*, 326–332.

Blumstein, A., Cohen, J., Roth, J. A., & Visher, C. A. (1986). *Criminal Careers and "Career Criminals."* (Vol. I). Washington, DC: National Academy Press.

Caldwell, M. (2002). What we do not know about juvenile sexual reoffense risk. *Child Maltreatment, 7*, 291-302.

Caldwell, M. (2010). Study characteristics and recidivism base rates in juvenile sex offender recidivism. *International Journal of Offender Therapy and Comparative Criminology, 54*, 197–212.

Carpentier, J., Proulx, J., & Leclerc, B. (2011). Juvenile sexual offenders: Correlates of onset, variety, and desistance of criminal behavior. *Criminal Justice and Behavior, 38*, 854–873.

Chaffin, M., Letourneau, E., & Silovsky, F. J. (2002). Adults, adolescents, and children who sexually abuse children: A developmental perspective. In J. E. B. Myers, L. Berliner, J. Briere, T. C. Hendrix, C. Jenny, & T. A. Reid (Eds.), *The APSAC handbook on child maltreatment* (2nd ed., pp. 205–232). Thousand Oaks: Sage Publications.

Costello, A., Edelbrock, C., Kalas, R., Kessler, R., & Klaric, S. H. (1982). *The diagnostic interview schedule for children – parent version* (Rev. ed.). Worcester, MA: University of Massachusetts Medical Center.

Costello, E. J., Edelbrock, C., & Costello, A. J., (1985). The validity of the NIMH Diagnostic Interview Schedule for Children (DISC): A comparison between pediatric and psychiatric referrals. *Journal of Abnormal Child Psychology, 13*, 579–595.

Doshay, L. J. (1943). The boy sex offender and his later career. Oxford: Grune & Stratton.

Edelbrock, C., & Achenbach, T. M. (1984). The teacher version of the Child Behavior Profile: I. Boys aged 6–11. *Journal of Consulting and Clinical Psychology, 52*, 207–217.

Elliott, D. S., Huizinga, D., & Ageton, S. S. (1985). *Explaining delinquency and drug use*. Newbury Park, CA: Sage.

Farrington, P. D., & Loeber, R. (2000). Epidemiology of juvenile violence. *Child and Adolescent Psychiatric Clinics of North America, 9*(4), 733–748.

Gebhard, P. H., Gagnon, J. H., Pomeroy, W. B., & Christenson, C. V. (1965). *Sex offenders: An analysis of types*. New York: Harper & Row.

Groth, A. N. (1982). The incest offender. In S. M. Sgrol (Ed.), *Handbook of clinical intervention in child sexual abuse* (pp. 215–239). Lexington, MA: D.C. Heath and Co.

Hagan, M. P., Gust-Brey K. L., Cho, M. E., & Dow, E. (2001). Eight-year comparative analyses of adolescent rapists, adolescent child molesters, other adolescent delinquents, and the general population. *International Journal of Offender Therapy and Comparative Criminology, 45*, 314–324.

Hunter, J. A., Figueredo, A. J., Malamuth, N. M., & Becker, J. V. (2003). Juvenile sex offenders: Towards the development of a typology. *Sexual Abuse: A Journal of Research and Treatment, 15*, 27–45.

Johnson, M. G., & Knight, A. R. (2000). Developmental antecedents of sexual coercion in juvenile sexual offenders. *Sexual Abuse: A Journal of Research and Treatment, 12*(3), 165–178.

Knight, A. R., & Prentky, A. R. (1993). *Exploring characteristics for classifying juvenile sex offenders*. In H. E. Barbaree, W. L. Marshall, & S. M. Hudson (Eds.), *The juvenile sex offender* (pp. 45–83). New York: Guilford Press.

Knight, A. R., Ronis. T. S., & Zakireh, B. (2009). Bootstrapping persistence risk indicators for juveniles who sexually offend. *Behavioral Sciences & the Law, 27*(6), 878–909.

Knight, A. R., & Sims-Knight, E. J. (2003). The developmental antecedents of sexual coercion against women: Testing alternative hypotheses with structural equation modeling. *Annals of the New York Academy of Science, 989*(1) 72–85.

Lalumière, M. L., Harris, G. T., Quinsey, V. L., & Rice, M. E. (2005). *The causes of rape: Understanding individual differences in the male propensity for sexual aggression*. Washington: American Psychological Association.

Långström, N. (2002). Long-term follow-up of criminal recidivism in young sex offenders: Temporal patterns and risk factors. *Psychology, Crime & Law, 8*(1), 41–58.

Laws, D. R. (2008). The public health approach: A way forward? In D. R. Laws & W. T. O'Donohue (Eds.), *Sexual deviance: Theory, assessment, and treatment* (2nd ed.). New York: Guilford Press.

Laws, D. R., & Marshall, W. L. (1990). A conditioning theory of the etiology and maintenance of deviant sexual preference and behavior. In W. L. Marshall, R. D. Laws, & H. E. Barbaree (Eds.), *Handbook of sexual assault: Issues, theories, and treatment of the offender* (pp. 209–229). New York: Plenum Press.

LeBlanc, M., & Fréchette, M. (1989). *Male criminal activity from childhood through youth: Multilevel and developmental perspectives*. New York: Springer-Verlag.

Letourneau, J. E., & Miner, H. M. (2005). Juvenile sex offenders: A case against the legal and clinical status quo. *Sexual Abuse: A Journal of Research and Treatment, 17*(3), 293–312.

Loeber, R., Green S. M., Lahey, B. B., & Stouthamer-Loeber, M. (1989). Optimal informants on childhood disruptive behaviors. *Development and Psychopathology, 1*(4), 317–337.

Loeber, R., Farrington, D. P., Stouthamer-Loeber, M., Moffitt, T. E., Caspi, A., White, H. R., et al. (2003). The development of male offending: Key findings from fourteen years of the Pittsburgh Youth Study. In T. P. Thornberry & M. D. Krohn (Eds.), *Taking stock of delinquency: An overview of findings from contemporary longitudinal studies* (pp. 93–136). New York: Kluwer Academic/Plenum.

Loeber, R., Farrington, D. P., Stouthamer-Loeber, M., & Van Kammen, W. B. (1998). *Antisocial behavior and mental health problems: Explanatory factors in childhood and adolescence*. London: LEA.

Loeber, R., Farrington, D. P., Southamer-Loeber, M., & White, H. R. (2008). *Serious theft and violence: Risk and promotive factors from childhood to early adulthood*. Mahwah, NJ: Lawrence Erlbaum Associates.

Loeber, R., & LeBlanc, M. (1990). Toward a developmental criminology. *Crime and Justice, 12*, 375–473.

Loeber, R., Pardini, D., Homish, D. L., Crawford, A. M., Farrington, D. P., Stouthamer-Loeber, M., Creemers, J. et al. (2005). The prediction of violence and homicide in young men. *Journal of Consulting and Clinical Psychology, 73*(6), 1074–1088.

Loeber, R., Wei, E., Stouthamer-Loeber, M., Huizinga, D., & Thornberry, T. P. (1999). Behavioral antecedents to serious and violent juvenile offending: Joint analyses from the Denver Youth Survey, Pittsburgh Youth Study, and the Rochester Youth Development Study. *Studies in Crime and Crime Prevention, 8*(2), 245–263.

Longo, R., & Calder, M. (2005). The use of sex offender registration with young people who sexually abuse. In M. Calder (Ed.). *Children and young people who sexually abuse: New theory, research and practice developments.* Lyme Regis: Russell Housing Publishing.

Lussier, P., Bouchard, M., & Beauregard, E. (2011). Patterns of criminal achievement in sexual offending: Unravelling the "successful" sex offender. *Journal of Criminal Justice, 39*, 433–444.

Lussier, P., & Healey, J. (2009). Rediscovering Quetelet, again: The "aging" offender and the prediction of reoffending in a sample of adult sex offenders. *Justice Quarterly, 26*(4), 827–856.

Lussier, P., LeBlanc, M., & Proulx, J. (2005). The generality of criminal behavior: A confirmatory factor analysis of the criminal activity of sexual offenders in adulthood. *Journal of Criminal Justice, 33*, 177–189.

Lussier, P., & Mathesius, J. (2012). Criminal achievement, career initiation, and cost avoidance: The onset of successful sex offending. *Journal of Crime and Justice, 35*(3), 376–394.

Lussier, P., Proulx, J., & LeBlanc, M. (2005). Criminal propensity, deviant sexual interests and criminal activity of sexual aggressors against women: A comparison of explanatory models. *Criminology, 43*, 249–282.

Lussier, P., Tzoumakis, S., Cale, J., & Amirault, J. (2010). Criminal trajectories of adult sex offenders and the age effect: Examining the dynamic aspect of offending in adulthood. *International Criminal Justice Review, 20*(2), 147–168.

Lussier, P., Van den Berg, C., Bijleveld, C., & Hendriks, J. (2012). *A Developmental taxonomy of juvenile sex offenders for theory, research, and prevention: The adolescent-limited and the high-rate slow desister. Criminal justice and behavior, 39*(12), 1559–1581

Malamuth, M. N. (1998). The confluence model as an organizing framework for research on sexually aggressive men: Risk moderators, imagined aggression, and pornography consumption. In R. G. Geen & E. Donnerstein (Eds.), *Human aggression: Theories, research, and implications for social policy* (pp. 229–245). San Diego: Academic Press.

Marshall, W. L., & Barbaree, H. E. (1990). An integrated theory of the etiology of sexual offending. In W. L. Marshall, D. R. Laws, & H. E. Barbaree (Eds.). *Handbook of sexual assault: Issues, theories, and treatment of the offender* (pp. 257–275). New York: Plenum Press.

Marshall, W. L., Barbaree, H. E., & Eccles, A. (1991). Early onset and deviant sexuality in child molesters. *Journal of Interpersonal Violence, 6*(3), 323–335.

McCann, K., & Lussier, P. (2008). Antisociality, sexual deviance and sexual reoffending in juvenile sex offenders: A meta-analytical investigation. *Youth Violence and Juvenile Justice, 6*, 363–385.

Miner, H. M. (2002). Factors associated with recidivism in juveniles: An analysis of serious juvenile sex offenders. *Journal of Research in Crime and Delinquency, 39*(4), 421–436.

Miranda, O. A., & Corcoran, L. C. (2000). Comparison of perpetration characteristics between male juvenile and adult sexual offenders: Preliminary results. *Sexual Abuse: A Journal of Research and Treatment, 12*(3), 179–199.

Moffitt, E. T. (1993). Adolescence-limited and life-course-persistent antisocial behavior: A developmental taxonomy. *Psychological Review, 100*(4), 674–701.

Nagin, S. D., & Farrington, P. D. (1992). The stability of criminal potential from childhood to adulthood. *Criminology, 30*(2), 235–260.

Nisbet, A. I., Wilson, H. P., & Smallbone, W. S. (2004). A prospective longitudinal study of sexual recidivism among adolescent sex offenders. *Sexual Abuse: A Journal of Research and Treatment, 16*(3), 223–234.

Piquero, A., Paternoster, R., Mazerolle, P., Brame, R., & Dean, W. C. (1999). *Journal of Research in Crime and Delinquency, 36*(3), 275–299.

Prentky, R. A., & Knight, R. A. (1993). Age of onset of sexual assault: Criminal and life history correlates. In G. C. N. Hall, R. Hirschman, J. R. Graham, & M. S. Zaragoza (Eds.), *Sexual aggression: Issues in etiology assessment, and treatment* (pp. 43–62). Washington, DC: Taylor & Francis.

Proulx, J., Lussier, P., Ouimet, M., & Boutin, S. (2008). Criminal careers of four types of sexual aggressors. In B. Schwartz (Ed.), *Sex Offenders* (Vol. 6, pp. 1–21). New York: Civic Research Institute.

Robins, L. N. (1978). Sturdy childhood predictors of adult anti-social behavior: Replications from longitudinal studies. *Psychological Medicine, 8*, 611–622.

Ryan, G. (1999). Treatment of sexually abusive youth: The evolving consensus. *Journal of Interpersonal Violence, 14*(4), 422–436.

Seto, M. C., & Barbaree, H. E. (1997). Sexual aggression as antisocial behavior: A developmental model. In D. Stoff, J. Breiling, & J. D. Maser (Eds.), *Handbook of antisocial behavior* (pp. 524–533). New York: John Wiley & Sons, Inc.

Seto, M. C., & Lalumière, M. L. (2010). What is so special about male adolescent sexual offending? A review and test of explanations through meta-analysis. *Psychological Bulletin, 136*, 526–575.

Sipe, R., Jensen, L. E., & Everett, S. R. (1998). Adolescent sexual offenders grown up: Recidivism in young adulthood. *Criminal Justice and Behavior, 25*(1), 109–124.

Smallbone, W. S. (2006). Social and psychological factors in the development of delinquency and sexual deviance. In H. E. Barbaree & W. L. Marshall (Eds.), *The juvenile sex offender* (2nd ed., pp. 105–127). New York: Guilford Press.

Smallbone, W. S., & Wortley, K. R. (2004). Onset, persistence, and versatility of offending among adult males convicted of sexual offenses against children. *Sexual Abuse: A Journal of Research and Treatment, 16*(4), 285–298.

Stouthamer-Loeber, M., & Van Kammen, W. B. (1995). *Data collection and management: A practical guide*. Thousand Oaks, CA: Sage.

Thornberry, P. T. (2005). Explaining multiple patterns of offending across the life course and across generations. *The Annals of the American Academy of Political and Social Science, 602*(1), 156–195.

Tibbetts, G. S., & Piquero, R. A. (1999). The influence of gender, low birth weight, and disadvantaged environment in predicting early onset of offending: A test of Moffitt's interactional hypothesis. *Criminology, 37*(4), 843–878.

Tolan, H. P. (1987). Implications of age of onset for delinquency risk. *Journal of Abnormal Child Psychology, 15*(1), 47–65.

Van den Berg, C. J. W., Bijleveld, C. C. J. H., & Hendriks, J. (2011) Jeugdige zedendelinquenten.Lange termijn criminele carrières en achtergrondkenmerken. *Tijdschrift voor Criminologie, 53*, 227–243.

Vandiver, M. D. (2006). A prospective analysis of juvenile male sex offenders: Characteristics and recidivism rates as adults. *Journal of Interpersonal Violence, 21*(5), 673–688.

Van Wijk, A., Loeber, R., Vermeiren, R., Pardini, D., Bullens, R., & Doreleijers, T. (2005). Violent juvenile sex offenders compared with violent juvenile nonsex offenders: Explorative findings from the Pittsburgh youth study. *Sexual Abuse: A Journal of Research and Treatment, 17*(3), 333–352.

Viljoen, J. L., Elkovitch, N., Scalora, M. J., & Ullman, D. (2009). Assessment of reoffense risk in adolescents who have committed sexual offenses: Predictive validity of the ERASOR, PCL:YV, YLS/CMI, and Static-99. *Criminal Justice and Behavior, 36*, 981–1000.

Vizard, E., Hickey, N., & McCrory, E. (2007). Developmental trajectories associated with juvenile sexually abusive behaviour and emerging severe personality disorder in childhood: 3-year study. *The British Journal of Psychiatry, 190*(49), 27–32. doi:10.1192/bjp.190.5.s27.

Waite, D., Keller, A., McGarvey, L. E., Wiechowski, E., Pinkerton, R., & Brown, L. G. (2007). Juvenile sex offender re-arrest rates for sexual, violent nonsexual and property crimes: A 10-year follow-up. *Sexual Abuse: A Journal of Research and Treatment, 17*(3), 313–331.

Ward., T., & Beech, T. (2006). An integrated theory of sexual offending. *Aggression and Violent Behavior, 11*, 44–63.

Worling, J., & Långström, N. (2006). Risk of sexual recidivism in adolescents who offend sexually: Correlates and assessment. In H. E. Barbaree & W. L. Marshall (Eds.), *The juvenile sex offender* (2nd ed., pp. 219–247). New York: Guilford Press.

Zimring, F. (2004). *An American travesty: Legal responses to adolescent sexual offending.* Chicago: University of Chicago Press.

Zimring, F., Jennings, W. G., Piquero, A. R., & Hays, S. (2009). Investigating the continuity of sex offending? Evidence from the Second Philadelphia Birth Cohort. *Justice Quarterly, 26*, 58–76.

Zimring, F. E., Piquero, A. R., & Jennings, W. G. (2007). Sexual delinquency in Racine: Does early sex offending predict later sex offending in youth and young adulthood. *Criminology and Public Policy, 6*, 507–534.

6

Assessing the Continuity of Sex Offending Over the Life Course

Evidence From Two Large Birth Cohort Studies

Wesley G. Jennings
University of South Florida, USA

Alex R. Piquero,[1] Franklin E. Zimring,[2] & Jennifer M. Reingle[3]
[1]*University of Texas at Dallas, USA,*
[2]*University of California, USA,* [3]*University of Texas Health Science Center, USA*

Introduction

Sex offending is a highly publicized and feared crime problem in modern U.S. society (Zimring, 2004). Sex offenders are a distinct criminal population in the sense that special legislation is designed to identify those who will likely reoffend and warn the community of their presence. In general, sex offenders are thought to offend frequently and continually, specialize in sex crimes, and present a threat to the community (Harris, Smallbone, Dennison, & Knight, 2009). This chapter is intended to present research findings on the general recidivism, sexual recidivism, and sexual specialization of juvenile offenders who commit sex crimes. Finally, the chapter ends with an application of the criminal career framework to examine sex offending over the life course, along with a discussion of the implications of these research issues for sex offender registration and community notification policies. Approximately half a million juveniles commit sex crimes in the United States each year, and juveniles comprise an average of 20% of rape arrests and 25% of sexual abuse arrests. The incidence of sexual offending among juveniles varies by community context (e.g., urban center, suburban, rural, etc.), ranging from 0.1 to 1% among females, and approximately 1.5–2% among males (Tracy, Wolfgang, & Figlio, 1990; Zimring, Piquero, & Jennings, 2007). The average age of onset for sexual offending is under age 18 (Abel & Rouleau, 1990). Prior research has

Sex Offenders: A Criminal Career Approach, First Edition. Edited by Arjan Blokland and Patrick Lussier.

indicated that sex offenders are not more likely than nonsex offenders to engage in sex offending behavior over the life course (Zimring et al. 2007; Zimring, Jennings, Piquero, & Hays, 2009). As juveniles, the vast majority of sex offenders (85%) have only one police contact for a sex offense (Zimring et al., 2009). Studies of the continuity of offending among juvenile sex offenders has found that between 4 and 56% (Furby, Wienrott, & Blackshow, 1989; Hagan & Gust-Brey, 1999; Nisbet et al., 2004; Sipe, Jensen, & Everett, 1998; Waite et al., 2005; Zimring et al., 2007, 2009) recidivate; however, there is significant variation in continuity when the type of sexual offense is considered. Specifically, rapists have shown to have relatively low recidivism rates (2.5%) (Langan & Levin, 2002), while child molesters recidivate more frequently (18–35%) (Harris et al., 2009; Quinsey, Lalumière, Rice, & Harris, 1995). These disparities in the continuity, frequency, and specialization among sex offending juveniles compared to nonsex offenders will be discussed in detail in this chapter.

Sex Offending: General Recidivism

A number of researchers have attempted to estimate the general recidivism rates of sex offenders, but it is important to note that the reoffending rates vary across studies with respect to measurement, research design, and length of follow-up. A meta-analysis conducted by McCann and Lussier (2008) found that 60.9% of the juvenile sex offenders recidivated nonviolently, and 28.5% recidivated with a violent crime (average nonsexual recidivism rate = 41.7%). For example, Vandiver (2006) provided a follow-up of juvenile sex offenders 3–6 years after their initial conviction and calculated their recidivism rates. Her results demonstrated that less than 60% of the juveniles were rearrested with 56% not having recidivated for a sex offense. Although age emerged as an important predictor of rearrest, the type of offense committed was not found to be statistically associated with rearrest. In a meta-analysis, Hanson and Bussière (1998) reported that sex offenders had a 36% reconviction rate in general with 12% recidivating for a violent crime. Additional results suggested that the aggressors of women tended to have higher general (46%) and violent (22%) recidivism rates than the child molesters, with 37% general and 10% violent recidivism rates. Subsequent studies have addressed the recidivism rates of sex offenders and compared them to the recidivism rates of other offender types (Caldwell, 2002). For instance, Sipe et al. (1998) examined the recidivism rates for sex and nonsex offenders with regards to violent and property crime. Their results suggested that nonsex offenders had a 12% rearrest rate for violent offenses and a 33% rearrest rate for property offenses. In contrast, sex offenders were rearrested much less frequently, with recidivism rates of only 6% for violent offenses and 16% for property offenses. Also, child molesters have been found to have lower general recidivism rates compared to nonsex offenders. Specifically, Hanson, Scott, and Steffy (1995) reported that 62% of child molesters and 83% of nonsex offenders recidivated at some point during a 15–30-year follow-up. In addition, using prisoner release cohorts, Langan and Levin (2002) found that the general recidivism rates were 41% for sexual assaulters, 46% for rapists, 70% for robbers, 74% for burglars, and 75% for thieves.

Another recent study also found similar results during a 3-year follow-up period where 43% of sex offenders recidivated and 68% of all other types of criminals recidivated (Langan, Schmitt, & Durose, 2003). Sample and Bray (2003) undertook a comprehensive comparison of the recidivism rates for sex offenders relative to a number of other types of offenders and reported the general recidivism rates at 1, 3, and 5 years post initial offense. Their results showed that within 5 years, 75% of robbers, 66% of burglars, 58% of nonsexual assaulters, 53% of larcenists, 45% of sex offenders, 44% of murderers, and 39% of property-damagers were rearrested for another crime. The recidivism rate of sex offenders was considerably lower than many of the other categories, and approximately 93% of the sex offenders were not arrested again for an offense in the 5 years following their initial offense. As expected, recidivism rates increased over time, and the pattern was similar across all offense categories.

Sex Offending: Sex Recidivism

In a classic study, Furby, Wienrott, and Blackshow (1989) reviewed the literature regarding sex offenders' sex crime recidivism and reported that reoffending rates varied from 4 to 56% in both juvenile and adult samples. In another review of the literature, Teir and Coy (1997) reported sex recidivism rates as high as 75%. Despite these seeming high rates of sex offense recidivism, the variability found in the recidivism rates in the earlier studies can generally be attributed to methodological differences. More recent research has since begun to consistently report relatively low sex offense recidivism rates. For example, Vandiver's (2006) analysis found that only 4% of registered male juvenile sex offenders recidivated for a sex offense during young adulthood. In a meta-analysis of 73 studies on sex offending and recidivism, Hanson and Morton-Bourgon (2005) reported a sexual recidivism rate of 13.7% among both juvenile and adult offenders. Another meta-analysis reported similar results, with sexual recidivism rates of juveniles varying from 1.6 to 29.9% (mean rate = 12.2%) (McCann & Lussier, 2008). Similarly, a review by Caldwell (2002) found that the rates of juvenile sex offending recidivism was low, ranging from 1.7 to 18.0%. While sex offenders appear to have relatively low rates of sex recidivism, these rates do appear to increase depending on the length of follow-up. For example, Hagan and Gust-Brey (1999) reported that 8% of adolescent sex offenders had sexually recidivated after 5 years post-release, whereas 16% had sexually recidivated after 10 years.

In contrast, Waite et al. (2005) only found a 5% sex recidivism rate based upon a 10-year follow-up of juvenile sex offenders who were released from sex offender treatment programs. In a longer follow-up study, Teir and Coy (1997) reported a 20% sex recidivism rate for a sample of sex offenders who were followed for 15 years. In a study conducted by Sample and Bray (2003), the pattern of recidivism for sex crimes was substantially different from that of other crimes. Several studies have compared the sex recidivism rates of treated and untreated juvenile and adult sex offenders and found very comparable results. For instance, Hall's (1995) meta-analysis indicated that about 19% of treated and 27% of untreated sex offenders committed future sex offenses. Moreover, Alexander (1999) reported similar findings in his review of the literature, with 13% of treated and 18% of untreated sex offenders recidivating for a sex offense. In addition, Hanson et al. (2002) reported a 5% difference in the sex offense recidivism rate for treated versus nontreated sex offenders. Sex recidivism rates tend to differ within several categories of sex offenders with certain types of sex offenders having a larger number of subsequent arrests. First-time offenders are much less likely to reoffend (10–21%) than habitual recidivists (33–71%) (Marshall, Jones, Ward, Johnston, & Barbaree, 1991). A difference between child molesters and aggressors of women has also emerged in the sex offender/sexual recidivism literature. For instance, child molesters tend to be more persistent offenders with more victims than the assailants of adult women (Parton & Day, 2002). Teir and Coy (1997) reported that child molesters were twice as likely to have had more than one victim and reoffended much more quickly than did aggressors of adults. Quinsey et al. (1995) conducted a study in which they calculated the sexual recidivism rate for homosexual child molesters (35%), aggressors of adult women (23%), heterosexual child molesters (18%), and incest molesters (8%). Their results suggested that homosexual child molesters have the highest probability of being rearrested for a new sex crime. In addition, Prentky, Lee, Knight, and Cerce (1997) demonstrated that 32% of child molesters and 26% of adult female sexual assaulters were rearrested for additional sex crimes based on a 25-year follow-up.

Sex Offending: Specialization

Unlike versatility, which is best regarded as involvement in a diverse range of crimes (Harris et al., 2009, p. 37), specialization is a term used to characterize a particular pattern of offending among offenders who persistently engage in a specific type of offense and/or are inclined to commit offenses within the same offense category (Blumstein, Cohen, Roth, & Visher, 1986). Whenever offenders commit the same crime frequently, they are apt to become more skilled and adept at that particular act (Harris et al., 2009). In general, sex offenders, along with other types of criminals such as drug abusers and white-collar criminals, have long since been viewed as specializing in their particulate genre of offenses (Gottfredson & Hirschi, 1990). However, reviews of current literature have failed to demonstrate that sex offenders are more prone to specialize in sex crimes than any other type of offender (Harris et al., 2009). In one of the earlier specialization studies, Cohen (1986) classified any offender who had more than 50% of their offenses in a particular area as a specialist in that specific crime. Considering this definition, she found that 35% of robbers, 34% of violent, nonsexual aggressors, 25% of burglars, 19% of car thieves, and only 14% of rapists were determined to be specialists. Nearly two decades later, Sample and Bray (2003) calculated the recidivism rates for sex offenders and a number of other types of nonsex offenders. Their results indicated that 39% of nonsexual assaulters and 30% of larcenists were rearrested within 5 years for the same offense type. Furthermore, 18% of robbers, 23% of burglars, 21% of public order disrupters, 6% of murderers, 5% of stalkers, and 3% of kidnappers recidivated within 10 years for the same type of crime. Sex offenders had one of the lowest recidivism rates for the same offense category, at 6.5% after 5 years. Similarly, Langan et al.'s (2003) results demonstrated that 87% of the sex crimes committed after over 270,000 offenders were released from prison were perpetrated by nonsexual offenders. Further, only 13% of subsequent sex crimes were committed by a specialized group of "sex offenders." In one of the more comprehensive studies to date examining sex offender specialization, Miethe, Olson, and Mitchell (2006) analyzed a sample of 38,000 offenders released from prison in 15 states. Their results suggested that sex offenders were noticeably less specialized compared to other offender types. In addition, Miethe et al. (2006) demonstrated that as the length of a sex offender's prior record increased so too did their versatility. Overall, the results led Miethe et al. (2006) to conclude that sex offenders are neither specialists nor persistent offenders.

Despite the consistency of the evidence pointing toward a lack of specialization among sex offenders, it is important to mention that differing degrees of specialization can be observed at times within sex offenders. For example, two groups that often emerge are sex offenders who concentrate their offending either upon adult women or upon children. Rapists of adult women, in general, tend to be more diversified, violent, and frequent in their offending and do not tend to focus predominantly on sex crimes. Child molesters, in contrast, do tend to be more specialized and have a higher frequency of sexual crimes. Nevertheless, neither child molesters nor aggressors of adult women exclusively have a particular type of victim, and many are prone to prey upon people of all ages. Moreover, the majority of both types of sex offenders have typically committed more nonsexual offenses than sexual crimes (Harris et al., 2009; Lussier, 2005; Sample & Bray, 2006). Several other studies have addressed the difference between the specialization of child molesters and rapists. For example, Lussier, LeBlanc, and Proulx (2005) reported that for the 50% specialization threshold, 4% of aggressors of women and 41% of child molesters had the majority of their offenses with either adults or children, respectively. In a recent meta-analysis, Lussier (2005) compared the amount of violent, property, and sexual crimes committed by adult aggressors and child molesters. For adult female rapists, 47% of their offenses were property, 27% were violent, and 14% were sexual. For child molesters, 42% of their crimes were property related, 24% sexual, and 18% violent. In general, child molesters committed similar numbers of property crimes, but more sexual offenses than did aggressors of women. However, the latter were more involved in violent crime. Most recently, Harris et al. (2009) examined the amount of specialization between different categories of sex offenders, including rapists, child molesters, and incest-only offenders. Thirty-four percent of their sample was classified as rapists, 42% were considered child molesters, 6% were incest-only offenders, and 7% had mixed victims. Each category of offender was separated into 50%, 75%, or 100% specialization levels. The results indicated that 11% of rapists, 43% of child molesters, 32% of incest-only offenders, and 49% of mixed-age sex offenders met the criteria for the 50% specialization threshold. However, these percentages dropped considerably when calculating which sex offenders had all of their offenses in a particular specialization area (3% of rapists, 15% of child molesters, 4% of incest offenders, and 8% of mixed offenders). Harris et al. (2009) concluded that child molesters were the most specialized type of sex offenders because even the mixed-age offenders were more likely to molest children than adults. Overall, less than 16% of all of the sex offenders in this study were shown to exclusively specialize in sex crimes.

Sex Offending Continuity

Provided with the background literature reviewed above, two notable and recent studies have been published which follow juvenile sex offenders through young adulthood to determine their sexual and nonsexual reoffending rates (Zimring et al., 2007, 2009). Both of these studies apply the criminal career framework (Piquero, Farrington, & Blumstein, 2003, 2007) to sex offenders and sex offending by examining sex offender recidivism, sex offender specialization, and the ability of juvenile sex offending to predict future sex offending behavior in young adulthood. Importantly, both studies follow similar research designs and rely on large birth cohorts from purposively selected and contrasting locations. Table 6.1 compares and contrasts the two birth cohort sites. Zimring et al. (2007) rely on arrest data from three birth cohorts (1942, 1949, and 1955) of approximately 6,000 boys and girls from the small, racially homogeneous town of Racine, Wisconsin (Middle Town America) (Shannon, 1988, 1991). This study recorded the incidence of a misdemeanor or felony charge, as well as the location, date, and contact number from police contact data. Juvenile and adult police contact information came from the files of the Juvenile Bureau and the Records Division of the Racine Police Department. In this study, sex offending was recorded by the police into the 26 UCR Part I and II offenses, and these groups were then aggregated into "sex felony" and "sex misdemeanor" classifications. The follow-up period ranged from 4 years (1955 cohort) to 14 years (1942 cohort) after the eighteenth birthday. Overall, the amount of offending is low in this area along with having an overall population of less than 90,000 persons according to the 1950 U.S. Census. Similarly, Zimring et al. (2009) used the police contact records of over 27,000 boys and girls in the large metropolitan city of Philadelphia, Pennsylvania (the Big City). This birth cohort (1958) is racially diverse

Table 6.1 "Middle Town America" Versus "the Big City"

Racine, Wisconsin (Middle Town America)	*Philadelphia, Pennsylvania (the Big City)*
1942, 1949, 1955 birth cohorts	1958 birth cohort
Small Midwestern city	Large metropolitan city
Approximately 6,000 boys and girls	Approximately 27,000 boys and girls
Low offending rates	High offending rates
Racially homogeneous (predominantly white)	Racially heterogeneous (predominantly minorities)

with high crime rates in general (Tracy et al., 1990). Police records for cohort members were made available from the Municipal and Court of Common Pleas of Philadelphia during the 8-year follow-up.

In Racine, sex offense types were merely segmented into felonies and misdemeanors. A total of 1.5% of the males and 0.9% of the females in the sample committed a sex crime. Ninety-six percent of the girls and 77% of the boys only had one police contact for a sex offense as a juvenile, while 8.5% (boys) and 3% (girls) registered two or more juvenile sex offense contacts. Regarding the issue of sex offending continuity, Zimring et al. (2007) discovered that only 8.5% of the males and only 10% of females that had a juvenile sex offense also had committed a sex crime in young adulthood. In addition, the factors that were found to significantly predict future adult sex offending in a multivariate context were being nonwhite, male, and having a lengthier juvenile record of police contacts. Surprisingly, being a juvenile sex offender was not significantly related to committing future sex crimes in young adulthood. These results suggested that the best predictor of future sex offending is having knowledge of whether or not the juvenile was an active and versatile offender in adolescence, not whether or not the juvenile had committed a sex offense as an adolescent. Comparatively, the Philadelphia data, which were used in the second Zimring et al. study, were broken down into different categories of sex crimes, with forcible rape and indecent assault being two of the most prevalent and pandering and incest being a couple of the least frequent types of sex offenses. The prevalence of adolescent sexual offending was slightly higher in Philadelphia for the boys, with 1.6% of males having committed a juvenile sex offense, whereas the prevalence of adolescent sexual offending for the girls was slightly lower, with 0.1% of females having committed a juvenile sex offense. Similar to Racine, juvenile sex offender recidivism was noticeably rare and only 10% of the juvenile male sex offenders and none of the juvenile female sex offenders committed a sex offense in young adulthood. Once again, having more police contacts as a juvenile, being male, and being nonwhite were significantly related to adult sexual offending, not having knowledge of whether or not the individual had committed a sexual offense as a juvenile. Table 6.2 provides the overall comparison of the prevalence of juvenile and adult sex offending rates. In sum, both of the studies using large community-based birth cohorts found that juvenile sex offending is noticeably rare.

Among nonsex offenders, most juvenile delinquents do not continue to become career criminals (Piquero et al., 2003). The literature suggests a similar trend among sex offenders, as a small proportion continue offending into adulthood (Zimring et al., 2007). These figures are also detailed in Table 6.2. Youth who offend sexually as a juvenile are just as likely to become adult sex offenders as those who have offended nonsexually as a juvenile. Specifically, the only predictor of becoming a sex offender as an adult was offending frequency as a juvenile (Zimring et al., 2007). These findings indicate that sex offenders are similar to nonsex offenders in their criminal career patterns. Life-course criminology also postulates that a group of "life-course persistent" offenders are responsible for the majority of criminal behavior. Evidence suggests that this paradigm applies to sex offenders, but not to sex offending behavior (Zimring et al., 2007, 2009). Specifically, the number of encounters with police is most predictive of future sex offending rather than a history of juvenile sex offending.

As displayed in Table 6.3, chronic sex offenders (those who have five or more juvenile police contacts with one or more for a sex act) had a 15% rate of sex offending between ages 18 and 26. The next highest sex offending group in adulthood were the males with no juvenile sex offenses but five or more total juvenile police contacts (9.1%), and the difference between these groups was not statistically significant. Nonsex offending juveniles with five contacts were more than twice as likely as juvenile sex offenders without long general records (4.2%) to end up as adult sex offenders, also a nonsignificant difference. Finally, juveniles with fewer than five contacts (including a sex offense, 4.2%) were no more likely to have an adult sex record than juveniles with

Table 6.2 Examining the (Dis)Continuity of Sex Offending

	Racine, Wisconsin (Middle Town America)	*Philadelphia, Pennsylvania (the Big City)*
Juvenile sex offending		
Prevalence		
Males	1.5%	1.6%
Females	0.9%	0.1%
Adult sex offending		
Prevalence		
Males	3.2%	2.4%
Females	0.5%	0.3%
Juveniles with sex contacts and adult sex contacts		
Males	8.5%	10.0%
Females	10.3%	0.0%
Odds of adult sex offense for juvenile sex offender		
No sex contacts	0.52 (ns)	0.89 (ns)
Sex and other offenses	0.35 (ns)	1.76 (ns)

Note. ns = not significant.

Table 6.3 The Relationship Between Chronic Juvenile Offending and Adult Sex Offending

Juvenile offending	*Adulthood sex offenses*
Sex offenders	
Chronic offender with sex offense	15.6%
Sex offender only	4.2%
Nonsex offenders	
Chronic offender	9.1%
Nonchronic	4.1%

fewer than five contacts and no sex offenses (4.1%). Altogether, these findings indicate that the accumulation of a police record is the most potent predictor of sex offending in adulthood, rather than chronic sex offending in adolescence.

It is important to note that these data are not without their limitations. First, both of these studies used the official police records that had true crime codes (i.e., status offenses, traffic offenses, city ordinance violations, etc. were removed) because they are (1) a more accurate official measure of "true" offending and they are (2) closer in time to the actual criminal act than self-reported offending. Second, data were collected in two cities, Racine, and Philadelphia, and may not be generalizable to the population in other cities in the United States and internationally. Finally, these data were collected only through early adulthood, and recidivism may increase in future follow-ups. However, we are confident in the results that are presented in this chapter, as they are concordant with the literature that was collected in other geographic locales, as well as using other methodologies.

Registration and Community Notification

In the United States, sex offenders are forced to register themselves with the state, and depending on state law, community members and organizations are notified of their presence and/or have access to the public registration of their names, addresses, personal characteristics, place of employment, and photographs. This notification process is meant to protect at-risk individuals such as children from the supposedly dangerous sex offenders who may live in their neighborhood. The assumption is that people will be more careful with themselves and their children if they are aware that a sex offender is living nearby. Three types of notification processes exist: broad community notification, notification to those at risk, and passive notification where the information is available but not disseminated. The type of notification used depends on the state regulations and determined danger of the sex offender. Further, all sexual offenders, from violent rapists to voyeurs, are forced to provide blood DNA samples in order to register with police departments, and must update their registration data and place of residence regularly. Even juveniles are sometimes required to register themselves for life because of their sexually deviant acts (Center for Sex Offender Management, 2001; Sample & Bray, 2003; Teir & Coy, 1997; Zimring, 2004). The idea of sex offender notification and registration originated from the brutal murders and sexual assaults of several young children beginning during the 1980s in Washington, Minnesota, and New Jersey by convicted sex offenders who had been released back into the community from prison. These sex offenders had long, violent criminal careers with numerous incidences of sexual abuse. Many members of the state legislatures, police departments, and families of the victims believed that these vicious acts could have been prevented if the parents had known the criminal backgrounds of these repetitive sexual abusers. As a result, Washington became the first of many states to pass sex offender registration laws, which placed the protection of the community above the privacy of the sex offenders.

Congress followed this initiative by enacting in 1994 the Jacob Wetterling Crimes Against Children and Sexually Violent Offender Registration Act, which allocated funding in every state to create a sex offender registry and tracking system.

Since the creation of this act, it has been amended three times with the most notable being in 1996 with the creation of Megan's Law. This law added community notification requirements to the already established sex offender registry (Center for Sex Offender Management, 2001; Lieb, Quinsey, & Berliner, 1998; Sample & Bray, 2003). More recently, sex offenders have received a substantial amount of attention in the popular media, especially given the recent enactment of the Adam Walsh Child Protection and Safety Act (2006), which requires sex offender registration for no fewer than 15 years postconviction, mandatory minimums for kidnapping and sexual assault of children, and the collection of DNA samples and global positioning system information for the physical tracking of child predators. This legislation, along with the policies discussed above, is based upon the assumption that sex offenders are highly specialized, recidivistic, and will continue their sexual behavior over the life course if not treated and constantly monitored. Several problems are associated with sex offender registration and notification laws including the inadequate continuation and enforcement of the system. Many times, the registries are not properly updated or maintained, which renders the information useless (Tewksbury, 2002).

Furthermore, sex offenders have difficulty finding housing and employment because they are stigmatized as being dangerous and likely to recidivate. As a result, they cannot properly reintegrate themselves back into society and live productive lives, especially juveniles who are ostracized by their peers because everyone in their school has been notified that they are a sex offender (Center for Sex Offender Management, 2001; Zimring et al., 2009). Sex offender registration and community notification continues to punish the individual after they have completed their sentence as prescribed by the court system (Sample & Bray, 2003; Teir & Coy, 1997). Moreover, sex offender legislation has an enormous toll on state budgets, and the states are not allotted extra money to maintain the registries by the federal government. For example, in Illinois the sex offender registry on the internet costs 500,000 dollars to sustain without taking into account the salaries of staff and equipment needed for this operation (Sample & Bray, 2003).

Finally, the access to sex offender registries gives some people the opportunity to harass offenders and to act as vigilantes (Center for Sex Offender Management, 2001). The premise of these specialized regulations for sex offenders is based upon the assumption that this type of criminal is a specialized, impulsive, chronic offender who is very dangerous. Criminal justice authorities and legislative bodies believe that registration and notification is necessary so that people can be warned of impending and almost certain peril (Harris et al., 2009; Sample & Bray, 2003).

Notification laws in particular enjoy overwhelming public support. For example, a survey in Washington revealed that 80% of citizens believed that these regulations were important and could reduce crime (Phillips, 1998). Several studies have since addressed the issue of whether sex offender registration and notification laws are effective in preventing future sexual victimization (Caldwell, Ziemke, & Vitacco, 2008).

For example, Schram and Milloy (1995) looked both at the recidivism rates of sex offenders who were released before and those who were released after the notification laws went into effect, and found that 19% of sex offenders under the notification laws were rearrested as opposed to 22% of the sexual offenders who did not face community notification. Although the results were not significant, the notification law did seem to curtail some sexual offending. Further, in a sample of juveniles, Caldwell et al. (2008) evaluated that the impact of the Sex Offender Registration and Notification Act criteria that would require juveniles who committed sexual crimes to register in a national, public database was not associated with future sexual or general recidivism. These findings are problematic, considering the stigmatization to the juvenile, cost to the public, and potential misallocation of time and resources. Further, Sample and Bray (2003) revealed in their review of the literature that around 93% of sex offenders do not recidivate and that creating a registry of robbers would be a better crime prediction tool based on their high recidivism rates. An additional observation made by these authors was that perhaps the sex offender registry was acting as a deterrence mechanism and controlling the actual amount of sex offending that would occur if this type of social segregation was not in place, but they did not test this idea. Similarly, Zimring et al. (2009) noted that 92% of adult sex offenders did not commit sex offenses as juveniles, and more than 85% of juveniles did not recidivate as adult sex offenders. These results, along with the results from the earlier Zimring et al. (2007) study, also suggest that registering adolescents who stole cars would be more productive in predicting who will be more likely to sexually offend during their lifetime.

Conclusion and Suggestions for Further Research

The existing knowledge base – extended in important ways by the two longitudinal studies by Zimring et al. (2007, 2009) – reveals that sex offenders do not appear to be as dangerous as previously assumed, at least with regard to sex offender recidivism. The general recidivism data show that sex offenders were, for the most part, less likely to commit future offenses than other serious criminals (Sample & Bray, 2003; Sipe et al., 1998). Furthermore, many research studies showed that less than 10% of sex offenders would commit a future sexual crime (Meloy, 2005; Sample & Bray, 2003, 2006; Vandiver, 2006). The level of specialization was also quite low for sex offenders, with robbers and burglars having much higher percentages of rearrest for the same type of crime (Sample & Bray, 2003). In addition, the criminal career-informed studies undertaken by Zimring et al. (2007, 2009) suggest that sex offending continuity from adolescence into adulthood is far from the norm. More specifically, their results demonstrated that the more versatile and frequent a juvenile delinquent tends to be the more likely they are to become a future adult sexual offender, much more so than a juvenile who has offended sexually during adolescence. Therefore, in light of these empirical consistencies, it appears that community notification and registration policies seem to overly penalize and misidentify sex offender recidivists (especially among juvenile sex offenders), and may be doing more harm than good. Ultimately, the evidence reviewed in this chapter suggests that, when following juvenile sex offenders into young adulthood, they have a noticeably low rate of continuity, or an apparent discontinuity, in their sex offending behavior. Given the repeatedly observed sets of findings using a wide range of data sources and methodologies, the time is ripe for this body of research to translate into (a more) effective policy, and this appears to be the time when the accumulating research favors a rethinking of the current registration and community notification policies and a refocus on implementing more effective methods for handling sex offenders.

References

Abel, G. G., & Rouleau, J. L. (1990). The nature and extent of sexual assault. In L. Marshall, D. Laws, & H.E. Barbaree (Eds.), *Handbook of sexual assault: Issues, theories, and treatment of the offender* (pp. 9–21). New York: Plenum Press.

Alexander, M. A. (1999). Sexual offender treatment efficacy revisited. *Sexual Abuse: A Journal of Research and Treatment, 11*, 101–116.

Blumstein, A., Cohen, J., Roth, J. A., & Visher, C. A (Eds.). (1986). *Criminal careers and "career criminals"* (Vol. 1). Report of the Panel on Criminal Careers, National Research Council. Washington, DC: National Academy of Sciences.

Caldwell, M. F. (2002). What we do not know about juvenile sexual reoffense risk. *Child Maltreatment, 4*, 291–302.

Caldwell, M. F., Ziemke, M. H., & Vitacco, M. J. (2008). An examination of the sex offender registration and notification act as applied to juveniles. *Psychology, Public Policy, and Law, 14*, 89–114.

Center for Sex Offender Management (2001). *Community notification and education*. Silver Spring, MD: Author

Cohen, J. (1986). Research on criminal careers: Individuals frequency rates and offense seriousness. In A. Blumstein, J. Cohen, J. A. Roth, & C. A. Visher (Eds.), *Criminal careers and career criminals* (pp. 292–418). Washington, DC: National Academy Press.

Furby L., Wienrott, M. R., & Blackshow, L. (1989). Sex offender recidivism: A review. *Psychological Bulletin, 105*, 3–30.

Gottfredson, M., & Hirschi, T. (1990). *A general theory of crime*. Stanford, CA: Stanford University Press.

Hagan, M. P., & Gust-Brey, K. L. (1999). A ten-year longitudinal study of adolescent rapists upon return to the community. *International Journal of Offender Therapy and Comparative Criminology, 43*, 448–458.

Hall, G. C. N. (1995). Sexual offender recidivism revisited: A meta-analysis of recent treatment studies. *Journal of Consulting and Clinical Psychology, 63*, 802–809.

Hanson, R. K., & Bussière, M. T. (1998). Predicting relapse: A meta-analysis of sexual offender recidivism studies. *Journal of Consulting and Clinical Psychology, 61*, 646–652.

Hanson, R. K., Gordon, A., Harris, A. J. R., Marques, J. K., Murphy, W., & Quinsey, V. L. (2002). First report of the collaborative outcome data project on the effectiveness of psychological treatment for sex offenders. *Sexual Abuse: A Journal of Research and Treatment, 14*, 169–191.

Hanson, R. K., & Morton-Bourgon, K. E. (2005). The characteristics of persistent sexual offenders: A meta-analysis of recidivism studies. *Journal of Consulting and Clinical Psychology, 73*, 1154–1163.

Hanson, R. K., Scott, H., & Steffy, R. A. (1995). A comparison of child molesters and non-sexual criminals: Risk predictors and long-term recidivism. *Journal of Research in Crime and Delinquency, 32*, 325–337.

Harris, D. A., Smallbone, S., Dennison, S., & Knight, R. A. (2009). Specialization and versatility in sexual offenders referred for civil commitment. *Journal of Criminal Justice, 37*, 37–44.

Langan, P. A., & Levin, D. J. (2002). *Recidivism of prisoners released in 1994*. Washington, DC: U.S. Department of Justice.

Langan, P. A., Schmitt, E. L., & Durose, M. R. (2003). *Recidivism of sex offenders released from prison in 1994*. Washington, DC: U.S. Department of Justice.

Lieb, R., Quinsey, V., & Berliner, L. (1998). Sexual predators and social policy. *Crime and Justice, 23*, 43–114.

Lussier, P. (2005). The criminal activity of sexual offenders in adulthood: Revisiting the specialization debate. *Sexual Abuse: A Journal of Research and Treatment, 17*, 269–292.

Lussier, P., LeBlanc, M., & Proulx, J. (2005). The generality of criminal behavior: A confirmatory factor analysis of the criminal activity of sex offenders in adulthood. *Journal of Criminal Justice, 33*, 177–189.

Marshall, W. L., Jones, R., Ward, T., Johnston, P., & Babaree, H. E. (1991). Treatment outcome with sex offenders. *Clinical Psychology Review, 11*, 465–485.

McCann, K., & Lussier, P. (2008). Antisociality, sexual deviance, and sexual reoffending in juvenile sex offenders: A meta-analytical investigation. *Youth Violence & Juvenile Justice, 6*, 363–385.

Meloy, M. L. (2005). The sex offender next door: An analysis of recidivism, risk factors, and deterrence of sex offenders on probation. *Criminal Justice Policy Review, 16*, 211–236.

Miethe, T., Olson, J., & Mitchell, O. (2006). Specialization and persistence in the arrest histories of sex offenders: A comparative analysis of alternative measures and offense types. *Journal of Research in Crime and Delinquency, 43*, 204–229.

Nisbet, I. A., Wilson, P. H., & Smallbone, S. W. (2004). A prospective longitudinal study of sexual recidivism among adolescent sex offenders. *Sexual Abuse: A Journal of Research and Treatment, 16*, 3, 223–234.

Parton, F., & Day, A. (2002). Empathy, intimacy, loneliness, and locus of control in child sex offenders: A comparison between familial and non-familial child sexual offenders. *Journal of Child Sexual Abuse, 11*, 41–56.

Phillips, D. M. (1998). *Community notification as viewed by Washington's citizens*. Olympia, WA: Washington State Institute for Public Policy.

Piquero, A. R., Farrington, D. P., & Blumstein, A. (2003). The criminal career paradigm. In M. Tonry (Ed.), *Crime and Justice* (Vol. *30*, pp. 359–506). Chicago: University of Chicago Press.

Piquero, A. R., Farrington, D. P., & Blumstein, A. (2007). Key issues in criminal career research: New analyses of the Cambridge Study in Delinquent Development. Cambridge University Press.

Prentky, R. A., Lee, A. F. S., Knight, R. A., & Cerce, D. (1997). Recidivism rates among child molesters and rapists: A methodological analysis. *Law and Human Behavior, 21*, 635–659.

Quinsey, V. L., Lalumière, M. L., Rice, M. E., & Harris, G. T. (1995). Predicting sexual offenses. In J. C. Campbell (Ed.), *Assessing dangerousness: Violence by sexual offenders, batterers, and child abusers* (pp. 114–137). Thousand Oaks: Sage.

Sample, L. L., & Bray, T. M. (2003). Are sex offenders dangerous? *Criminology and Public Policy, 3*, 59–82.

Sample, L. L., & Bray, T. M. (2006). Are sex offenders different? An examination of rearrest patterns. *Criminal Justice Policy Review, 17*, 83–102.

Schram, D., & Milloy, C. (1995). *Community notification: A study of offender characteristics and recidivism*. Olympia: Washington State Institute for Public Policy.

Shannon, L. W. (1988). *Criminal career continuity: Its social context*. New York: Human Sciences Press.

Shannon, L. W. (1991). *Changing patterns of delinquency and crime: A longitudinal study in Racine*. Boulder: Westview Press.

Sipe, R., Jensen, E. L., & Everett, R. S. (1998). Adolescent sexual offenders grown up. *Criminal Justice and Behavior, 25*, 109–124.

Teir, R., & Coy, K. (1997). Approaches to sexual predators: Community notification and civil commitment. *Criminal and Civil Commitment, 23*, 405–426.

Tewksbury, R. (2002). Validity and utility of the Kentucky Sex Offender Registry. *Federal Probation, 66*, 21–26.

Tracy, P. E., Wolfgang, M. E., & Figlio, R. M. (1990). *Delinquency in two birth cohorts*. New York: Plenum.

Vandiver, D. M. (2006). A prospective analysis of juvenile male sex offenders: Characteristics and recidivism rates as adults. *Journal of Interpersonal Violence, 21*, 673–688.

Waite, D., Keller, A., McGarvey, E. L., Wieckowski, E., Pinkerton, R., & Brown, G. L. (2005). Juvenile sex offender re-arrest rates for sexual, violent non-sexual, and property crimes: A ten-year follow-up. *Sexual Abuse: A Journal of Research and Treatment, 17*, 313–331.

Zimring, F. E. (2004). *An American travesty: Legal responses to adolescent sexual offending*. Chicago: University of Chicago Press.

Zimring, F. E., Jennings, W. G., Piquero, A. R., & Hays, S. (2009). Investigating the continuity of sex offending from the Second Philadelphia Birth Cohort. *Justice Quarterly, 26*, 58–76.

Zimring, F. E., Piquero, A. R., & Jennings, W. G. (2007). Sexual delinquency in Racine: Does early sex offending predict later sex offending in youth and young adulthood. *Criminology and Public Policy, 6*, 507–534.

7

Antisocial Trajectories in Youth and the Onset of Adult Criminal Careers in Sexual Offenders of Children and Women

Jesse Cale
University of New South Wales, Australia

Introduction

A critical line of research pertaining to the criminal careers of sexual offenders has been concerned with the continuity of sexual offending behavior over the life course. Early clinical studies pointed to the hypothesized escalation of sexual deviance in adolescence to sexual offending in adulthood (Abel et al., 1987; Abel, Osborne, & Twigg, 1993; Longo & Groth, 1983). More recent studies have explored the extent to which juvenile sexual offenders continue to sexually offend as adults and have painted a very different picture of sexual offending over the life course (Chaffin et al., 2008; Parks & Bard, 2006; Zimring, Piquero, & Jennings, 2007). Prospective longitudinal studies have produced evidence that juvenile sexual offenders, typically, do not become adult sexual offenders (e.g. Jennings, Piquero, Zimring and Reingle, this volume). Similarly, retrospective studies with adult sexual offenders have also shown that, for the most part, these individuals were not juvenile sexual offenders (Marshall, Barbaree, & Eccles, 1991; Smallbone & Wortley, 2004). Therefore, while there exists an important minority of offenders whose sexual offending starts early in life, and persists into the adulthood years (Nisbet, Wilson, & Smallbone, 2004), the pathway(s) from youth that lead to sexual offending in adulthood remain largely unclear. In effect, if adult sexual offenders were not typically juvenile sexual offenders, then two particularly important questions are: (1) What do their antisocial developmental backgrounds look like in youth? (2) What characterizes the developmental trajectories of these men leading to sexual offending in adulthood?

Recent developmental models of sexual offending have emphasized the role of an antisocial tendency with developmental origins in childhood in explaining sexual

Sex Offenders: A Criminal Career Approach, First Edition. Edited by Arjan Blokland and Patrick Lussier.

offending (Lussier, LeBlanc, & Proulx, 2005). In addition, while there has been debate about the presence of a single or multiple antisocial pathways leading to sexual offending against women (e.g., Cale, Lussier, & Proulx, 2009; Lalumière, Harris, Quinsey, & Rice, 2005; Seto & Barbaree, 1997), developmental models that have explored this question have largely neglected investigating the antisocial trajectories of sexual offenders of children. This is in spite of the fact that sexual offenders of children do demonstrate versatility in their offending behavior (Smallbone & Wortley, 2004), albeit to a lesser extent than sexual offenders of women (Lussier, LeBlanc, et al., 2005). Therefore, the current study has three key aims. First, the characteristics of antisocial trajectories in youth of adult sexual offenders of women and adult sexual offenders of children are examined. Second, the relationship between antisocial trajectories in youth and criminal involvement in adulthood is explored. Third, the relative contribution of antisocial trajectories in youth to the activation of adult criminal careers is examined to investigate the impact of different patterns of youth delinquency on the continuity of offending into adulthood among sexual offenders of children and sexual offenders of women.

Developmental Models of Sexual Aggression

Developmental theories of offending that consider the life course beginning in childhood through to adulthood have identified offender groups characterized by different antisocial trajectories. Antisocial trajectories refer to patterns of onset, course, and desistance from different antisocial behaviors (Loeber & LeBlanc, 1990). One of the first iterations of such theories was Moffitt's pioneering dual taxonomy (1993). She distinguished between *Life-Course Persistent (LCP)* offenders, early-starters who were characterized by the childhood onset of antisocial behavior that persists, escalates, and diversifies into adulthood; and, *Adolescent-Limited (AL)* offenders, late-starters characterized by the adolescent onset of antisocial behavior which is typically followed by desistence in early adulthood. Given that late-starters typically desist, initial developmental models of sexual offending that have emerged mainly emphasize the importance of an early-onset (i.e., childhood-onset) antisocial trajectory that escalates to sexual offending in adulthood (Elliott, 1994; Lussier, LeBlanc, et al., 2005, Moffitt, Caspi, Harrington, & Milne, 2002).

From a developmental perspective, a key question pertaining to sexual offending is how different life stages, beginning in childhood, impact the onset and progression of sexual offending behavior. Only recently have criminological investigations of sexual offenders adopted a developmental approach (Lussier & Cortoni, 2008; Lussier, LeBlanc, et al., 2005; Lussier, Proulx, & LeBlanc, 2005). These studies have centrally focused on the role of an early-onset (i.e., childhood-onset) persistent antisocial tendency in the development of sexual offending behavior later in life. In effect, developmental models attribute sexual offending in adulthood to the manifestation of a more general antisocial tendency with origins in youth (i.e., often referred to as general deviance) (e.g., Lussier, LeBlanc et al., 2005; Lussier, Proulx, et al., 2005; Tedeschi & Felson, 1994). The relationship between an early-onset antisocial tendency characterized by general deviance and sexual offending appears to be important for both sexual offenders of women and sexual offenders of children, albeit to different extents (e.g., Lussier, LeBlanc et al., 2005). Generally speaking, sexual offenders who exhibited more deviant behaviors during childhood and adolescence are also those who display early, frequent, and varied nonsexual and sexual criminal activity in adulthood (Bard et al., 1987; Lussier, LeBlanc et al., 2005; Lussier, Proulx, et al., 2005; Prentky & Knight, 1993).

For serious and violent offenders in general (e.g., LeBlanc & Bouthillier, 2003; LeBlanc & Loeber, 1998), and sexual offenders specifically (e.g., Lussier, LeBlanc, et al., 2005), an early-onset antisocial tendency is characterized in childhood and adolescence by externalizing behaviors, such as behavioral problems/conduct disorders: overt and covert delinquency, recklessness, and authority conflict behaviors (i.e., general deviance). In turn, as this tendency develops through subsequent life stages (e.g., adolescence, early to middle adulthood), it becomes more patterned over time, and manifests as different forms of delinquency, antisocial behavior, criminality, and eventually for some, sexual aggression. One key assumption of developmental models is that this unfolding process represents the process of heterotypic continuity, that is, the continuity of conceptually related behaviors across time and settings (Patterson, 1993). In this regard, both prospective longitudinal studies based on males in the general population (e.g., Elliot, 1994; Moffitt, et al., 2002; Tracy, Wolfgang, & Figlio, 1990) and retrospective studies of adult sexual offenders (e.g., Lussier, LeBlanc, et al., 2005; Lussier, Proulx, et al., 2005; Prentky & Knight, 1993) have provided empirical evidence that the early manifestations of an antisocial tendency are associated with an earlier onset and higher frequency of sexual crimes in adulthood. However, these early antisocial manifestations appear to be more pronounced in the histories of adult sexual offenders of women compared to adult sexual offenders of children (Lussier, LeBlanc, et al., 2005).

Some researchers have hypothesized that the antisocial development of sexual offenders of women may be characterized by a greater degree of heterogeneity than current developmental models of sexual offending imply. More specifically, Seto and Barbaree (1997), and later, Lalumière et al. (2005), hypothesized that early- and late-onset antisocial trajectories might better characterize the antisocial backgrounds of sexual offenders of women. In these developmental models sexual offending represents either the culminating point of the aggravation of an antisocial tendency (i.e., early-onset antisociality) or contextual and state features, such as barriers to sexual activity associated with the biological maturity gap that characterizes typical male adolescent status, such as a lack of access to money, wealth, and goods that make them more attractive sexual prospects (i.e., late-onset antisociality). The latter was hypothesized to explain sexual offending in adolescence, however. Furthermore, while these models make no predictions regarding the late-onset (i.e., adolescent-onset) antisocial trajectory and adult sexual offending, one hypothesis is that for these individuals, sexual offending in adulthood represents the negative long-term implications of delinquency in adolescence (i.e., snares; see Moffitt, 1993). Currently, however, no such studies have empirically examined the presence of antisocial trajectories in youth of sexual offenders of children, and only one empirical study has investigated heterogeneity in antisocial trajectories in youth of adult sexual offenders of women (i.e., Cale et al., 2009).

In our previous study (Cale et al., 2009)[1] we observed that there was substantial heterogeneity in antisocial trajectories in youth of adult sexual aggressors of women. First, two meta-trajectories were evident: one characterized by an early-onset (i.e., childhood-onset) (55% of the sample) of delinquency, and the second, the late-onset (i.e., adolescent/adulthood-onset) (45% of the sample) of delinquency. In other words, just over half of the sample was characterized by the early-onset/persistent antisocial trajectory. Furthermore, within the early-onset meta-trajectory, differential patterns in the unfolding of antisocial behavior were evident (i.e., escalation from minor to serious antisocial behavior, and the persistence of low, moderate, and serious delinquency). Consistent with previous developmental models, these were also the individuals to be more likely characterized by the early adult onset, and a more extensive and diversified criminal history, and violent and sexual offending in adulthood (see also Cale & Lussier, 2011). Contrary to previous developmental models, however, a substantial proportion of the sample reported no delinquent involvement prior to the age of 18. Critically, there have been no subsequent empirical analyses that have examined heterogeneity in the unfolding of early behavioral problems in other populations of sexual offenders (e.g., sexual aggressors of children). Not surprisingly therefore there is also a scarcity of research that has examined the link between antisocial trajectories in youth and criminal career patterns in adulthood of these men.

The past decade has seen substantial advancement in our understanding of the adult criminal careers of sexual offenders. Much of this research has focused on the extent of participation and frequency of involvement in different crimes of sexual offenders, and has shown that their criminal careers are predominately characterized by criminal versatility, with few showing a tendency to specialize in sexual crimes (e.g., Blokland & Lussier, this volume; Harris, Smallbone, Dennison, & Knight, 2009; Lussier, 2005; Miethe, Olson, & Mitchell, 2006; Proulx, Lussier, Ouimet, & Boutin, 2008; Simon, 1997; 2000). Several studies have also measured patterns in the onset of sexual offending in adulthood (e.g., Baxter, Marshall, Barbaree, Davidson, & Malcolm, 1984; Gebhard, Gagnon, Pomeroy, & Christensen, 1965; Groth, Longo, & McFadin, 1982; Lussier, LeBlanc et al., 2005; Smallbone & Wortley, 2004). Studies using self-reported data have indicated the average age of onset for sexual crimes in sexual offenders of women is typically in early adulthood (e.g., 19–22 years old) (Groth et al., 1982; Abel et al., 1993), and officially slightly later (i.e., 22–30 years old) (e.g., Gebhard et al., 1965; Baxter et al., 1984; Lussier, LeBlanc et al., 2005). In terms of sexual offenders of children, the

[1]In this study, the sample consisted of adult males convicted of at least one sexual offence against a woman of 16 years of age or above. In other words, some of these individuals also had convictions for sexual offences against children.

self-reported age of onset is typically older (e.g., early thirties) (Smallbone & Wortley, 2004), and officially slightly later than this (e.g., the mid- to late thirties) (e.g., Gebhard et al., 1965; Lussier, LeBlanc et al., 2005; Smallbone & Wortley, 2004). In other words, the empirical evidence indicates that sexual offenders of children are: (a) significantly older than sexual offenders of women (e.g., Barbaree & Seto, 1997); and (b) unofficially and officially initiate their sexual offending later in adulthood.

We can also draw some general conclusions about patterns in the onset of other crime types of sexual offenders in adulthood. In terms of nonsexual offending, sexual offenders of women tend to initiate both their sexual and their nonsexual adult criminal careers earlier than sexual offenders of children (e.g., Adler, 1984; Baxter, et al., 1984; Lussier, LeBlanc, et al., 2005, Lussier, Proulx, et al., 2005; Proulx, et al., 2008). Furthermore, there also is evidence that nonsexual crimes typically precede, and follow, the commission of sexual crimes (e.g., Broadhurst & Maller, 1992; Hanson & Bussière, 1998; Simon, 1997; Lussier, LeBlanc et al., 2005; Smallbone & Wortley, 2004; Soothill, Francis, Sanderson, & Ackerley, 2000). Importantly, while sexual offenders are for the most part criminally versatile, there are divergent patterns when it comes to the initiation of criminal careers in adulthood between different types of sexual offenders. Therefore, a critical question that remains unanswered is: if heterogeneity characterizes the adult criminal careers of sexual offenders, are there in fact different pathways evident that lead to the onset of both nonsexual and sexual offending of these men in the adult years? Furthermore, while a minority of adult sexual offenders have a history of juvenile sexual offending, it is unclear how juvenile sexual offending fits into the developmental picture of those men who persist. Importantly, understanding the link between offending in youth and criminal careers in adulthood can assist in identifying potential early points of intervention to curtail the development of patterns that lead to sexual offending in adulthood. Currently, however, no empirical studies have investigated the developmental correlates of such patterns.

The overall aim of the current study therefore was to take one step forward in understanding the link between antisocial development in youth and the criminal careers of adult sexual offenders. First, the study explores whether a single or multiple antisocial trajectories characterize the developmental backgrounds of adult sexual offenders. Antisocial trajectories in youth are examined using repeated measures of self-reported delinquency in childhood and adolescence. Hierarchical cluster analyses are used to identify delinquent subgroups in childhood and adolescence and then dynamic classification models are computed by cross-tabulating cluster solutions in each time period. Next, the study examines the extent to which antisocial trajectories in youth are associated with the onset of criminal careers in adulthood. Here, antisocial trajectories are compared in terms of participation in, and the age at first charges for, property, violent, and sexual offending in adulthood. Finally, the study examines the relative contribution of antisocial trajectories to the time to onset of property, violent, and sexual offending in adulthood to explicate the link between antisocial trajectories in youth and the activation of offending careers in adulthood. These analyses are conducted independently for sexual offenders of children and sexual offenders of women to provide a conceptually comparative framework of the respective antisocial development and adulthood criminal careers of these men.

Methodology

Sample

The sample for the current study involved adult males (18 years of age or older at the time of data collection) convicted of a sexual offense who received a federal prison sentence (i.e., of at least two years) between April 1994 and June 2000 in the province of Quebec, Canada, at the Regional Reception Centre of Ste-Anne-des-Plaines, a maximum-security institution operated by the Correctional Service of Canada. The average detention length in this institution is approximately six weeks, during which time correctional assessment procedures are performed to determine the individual's transfer to an institution suited to their risk level and treatment needs. In total, 221 of the participants who committed a sexual crime(s) exclusively against a victim(s) under the age of 16 (i.e., sexual offenders of children), and 155 of the participants who exclusively committed a sexual crime(s) against a victim(s) 16 years of age or older (i.e., sexual offenders of women) were included in the study (n = 376).

Procedures

The data used to measure delinquency in childhood and adolescence were gathered in a semi-structured interview with each participant. Each individual was interviewed once by a member of the research team. Participants were asked a series of question pertaining to their delinquent behaviors prior to adulthood. It was not possible to assess inter-rater reliability, however the scales measuring behavioral antecedents have demonstrated internal consistency elsewhere (i.e., Lussier, LeBlanc et al., 2005; Lussier, Proulx, et al., 2005). The criminal activity in adulthood of the participants in the study was gathered from official police records.

Measures

To investigate the presence of antisocial trajectories prior to adulthood, self-report measures of delinquency in childhood (ages 0–12) and adolescence (ages 13–17) were used. In the current study, five types of indicators were considered in each time period: conduct disorder problems, drug and alcohol use, sexual delinquency, nonviolent delinquency, and nonsexual violent delinquency (see Table 7.1 for a description of the measures). Each of these indicators was coded as either absent (0)

Table 7.1 Sample Description and Measures Used

Variable and description	*Coding*	*Total sample (n = 376) (%)*	*Sexual offenders of women (n=155) (%)*	*Sexual offenders of children (n=221) (%)*	$X^2(df)$| $t(df)$
Control variables					
Level of education	1 = Less than high school	90.6	94.0	90.6	$X^2(1) = 3.3^{\dagger}$, $\Phi = 0.10$
Ethnicity	1 = Non-Caucasian	11.7	15.5	9.0	$X^2(1) = 3.7^{\dagger}$, $\Phi = 0.10$
Employment status	1 = Unemployed	55.9	61.9	51.6	$X^2(1) = 4.0^{*}$, $\Phi = 0.10$
Marital status	1 = Single	40.4	49.0	34.4	$X^2(1) = 3.3^{**}$, $\Phi = 0.10$
Juvenile detention	1 = Juvenile detention	10.1	12.9	8.1	$X^2(1) = 2.3$, $\Phi = 0.08$
Juvenile sexual offenses	1 = Juvenile sex offender	9.8	7.7	11.3	$X^2(1) = 1.3$, $\Phi = 0.06$
Sexual recidivism in adulthood	1 = Prior sexual charges	24.7	25.2	24.4	$X^2(1) = 0.1$, $\Phi = 0.01$
Delinquency measures in youth (Self-reported)					
Conduct disorders:	Childhood	16.8	16.8	16.7	$X^2(1) = 0.0$, $\Phi = 0.00$
2 or more of: frequent lying, rebelliousness, temper tantrums, running away, risk taking	Adolescence	33.5	44.5	25.8	$X^2(1) = 14.3^{***}$, $\Phi = 0.20$
Substance use:	Childhood	4.4	5.8	3.6	$X^2(1) = 1.0$, $\Phi = 0.05$
Regular use of alcohol and/or illicit drugs (e.g., marijuana, cocaine, ecstacy, hallucinogens)	Adolescence	33.2	44.5	25.3	$X^2(1) = 15.1^{***}$, $\Phi = 0.20$
Sexual delinquency:	Childhood	3.5	1.3	5.0	$X^2(1) = 3.7^{\dagger}$, $\Phi = 0.10$
Committed a sexual offense (e.g., sexual assault, exhibitionism)	Adolescence	8.5	7.1	9.5	$X^2(1) = 0.7$, $\Phi = 0.04$
Nonviolent delinquency:	Childhood	8.8	11.0	7.2	$X^2(1) = 1.5$, $\Phi = 0.07$
Minor theft, major theft, robbery, breaking and entering, drug trafficking, fire setting, vandalism	Adolescence	30.3	41.3	22.6	$X^2(1) = 15.0^{***}$, $\Phi = 0.10$

(Contiued)

Table 7.1 (*Continued*)

Variable and description	*Coding*	*Total sample (n = 376) (%)*	*Sexual offenders of women (n=155) (%)*	*Sexual offenders of children (n=221) (%)*	$X^2(df)\| t(df)$
Violent delinquency:	Childhood	1.6	1.9	1.4	$X^2(1)=0.2$, $\Phi=0.02$
Homicide, nonsexual assault, threats and intimidation, armed robbery, weapon offenses	Adolescence	10.1	18.1	4.5	$X^2(1)=18.4^{***}$, $\Phi=0.22$
Criminal career measures in adulthood (official)					
Any prior charges for property crimes[b]		48.7	65.2	37.1	$X^2(1)=28.7^{***}$, $\Phi=0.28$
Age at first charges for a property crime[a,c]	x (sd), range	24.4 (7.4), 15.3–61.5	24.1 (7.4), 16.1–61.5	24.9 (7.5) 15.3–59.3	$t(183)=0.9$, $d=0.12$
Any prior charges for violent crimes		60.9	88.4	41.6	$X^2(1)=83.7^{***}$, $\Phi=0.47$
Age at first charges for a violent crime[a,d]	x (sd), range	30.2 (10.2), 16.1–63.0	27.5 (8.7), 16.1–61.5	34.3 (10.9) 18.6–63.0	$t(164.6)=5.3^{***}$, $d=0.69$
Any charges for sexual crimes		100.0	100.0	100.0	-
Age at first charges for a sexual crime[a]	x (sd), range	37.3 (12.2), 16.5–75.2	31.5 (10.9), 17.6–69.1	41.2 (12.4) 16.5–75.2	$t(368.7)=8.2^{***}$, $d=0.89$

Note. All categorical variables were coded dichotomously.

[a]For some individuals, the minimum value of the range for age at first charges is below 18 years old. The explanation for this is that offenses acquired in youth carry an expiry date and when that date has expired (the expiry date varies according to the severity of the offense), the charges are removed from the criminal record and cannot be accessed. When an individual has been found guilty of a subsequent crime as an adult before the end of the expiry date, the youth offenses are treated as adult charges.

[b] A log transformation was performed on the variable for statistical analyses. The original mean, standard deviation, and range are presented.

[c]Sexual offenders of women (n = 103), sexual offenders of children (n = 82).

[d]Sexual offenders of women (n = 137), sexual offenders of children (n = 92).

$^{\dagger}p < .10$, $^{*}p < .05$, $^{**}p < .01$, $^{***}p < .001$.

or present (1) in each time period. Hence, a total of 10 delinquent manifestations (five in each time period) were considered. For criminal careers in adulthood, official data[2] were obtained pertaining to previous charges, and the age at first charge, for three different types of offending in adulthood including property, violent, and sexual offences.

Analytic Strategy

A dynamic classification strategy was used to identify antisocial trajectories from childhood to adolescence in each sample (i.e., sexual offenders of children and sexual offenders of women). This involved the use of hierarchical cluster analysis (applying Ward's method and squared Euclidean distance; Finch, 2005) to identify nested groups of individuals in each time period (i.e., childhood and adolescence) (see also Cale et al., 2009). Based on the criminological literature (e.g., see LeBlanc, 2002), a two-eight group solution was delineated for the number of clusters allowed within the data for each time period. Two main techniques were applied to determine the most accurate configuration of clusters in each time period. First, scree plots were analyzed to determine the point at which increments of the proximity coefficients produced by the agglomeration schedule indicated that the variance within the clusters was creating heterogeneity within the groups identified (Clatworthy, Buick, Hankins, Weinman, & Horne, 2005). Second, Mojena's (1977) stopping rule was applied, which identifies where a significant increase in the agglomeration schedule occurs as a way to determine the number of clusters when: $X_{j+1} > X + KS_z$.[3]

In the next step of the analysis a dynamic classification model was created (Ayers et al., 1999; LeBlanc & Kaspy, 1998; Loeber, Stouthamer-Loeber, Van Kammen, & Farrington, 1991) by using a turnover table of the frequency distributions (Davis, 1963; Huizinga, 1979) of the clustering solutions found in childhood and adolescence. This allowed for the determination of the antisocial trajectories across the two broad time periods. While there exist several sophisticated techniques for estimating between-individual differences in within-individual change (e.g., onset and course) (i.e., growth curve modeling), these techniques are: (a) designed for prospective longitudinal data; and (b) sensitive to limited repeated measures (i.e., less than three) and the level and distribution of the measures (i.e., continuous and normal) (Curran, Obeidat, & Losardo, 2010). Given the retrospective nature of the current data, and the exploratory aim of the study, a method of cross-sectional

[2]The use of official data concerning the onset of a participant's criminal activity in adulthood was done to avoid problems associated with the use of one source of information for both the independent and the dependent variables.

[3]X_{j+1} refers to the value of the fusion coefficient at stage j+1 of the clustering process. K is a constant, X is the mean of the fusion coefficients, and S_z is its standard deviation. K is set to 1.25 following the recommendations of Milligan and Cooper (1985), given the possibility that only two clusters might characterize the data.

pattern analysis followed by linking across time (i.e., dynamic classification) was applied (see Bergman, Magnusson, & El-Khouri, 2003). Therefore, after the identification of cluster solutions in childhood and adolescence, the childhood solution was cross-tabulated with the adolescent solution. These analyses were performed once using the subsample of sexual offenders of children (n = 221) and again using the subsample of sexual offenders of women (n = 155).

T-tests and chi-square analysis were used to provide descriptive information about delinquency in youth and criminal careers in adulthood of the two subsamples. Two series of three Cox-regression models were then computed, and Hazard Ratios (HR) calculated, to determine whether antisocial meta-trajectories in youth (i.e., early- vs. late-starters) demonstrate postdictive validity regarding the time to onset of property, violent, and sexual crimes in adulthood for sexual offenders of children and sexual offenders of women. The Cox-regression procedure was used to control for those individuals who did not exhibit property or violent offenses in adulthood (i.e., right-censored cases). Therefore, the first step involved creating three variables that indicated whether an individual had a charge in adulthood for property, violent, and/or sexual crime (0 = no, 1 = yes).[4] Next, the follow-up period was determined by calculating the age at first charges in adulthood for each crime type (i.e., property, violent, sexual). For those individuals who did not commit a property or violent offense in adulthood the respective missing data (i.e., age of onset for these crimes) was replaced with the age of the offender at the time of the assessment (i.e., their age at referral for their index/sexual offense) thus representing right-censored cases. Allison's (1995) R^2 was calculated to determine the overall variance explained by the models.[5]

Control Variables Seven control variables were included in the Cox-regression models: (1) level of education (0 = greater than high school; 1 = less than high school); ethnicity (0 = Caucasian, 1 = non-Caucasian); employment status (0 = employed, 1 = unemployed); marital status (0 = not single, 1 = single); whether they self-reported juvenile incarceration (0 = no, 1 = yes), or juvenile sexual offending (0 = no, 1 = yes); and finally, whether participants had previous charges for sexual offenses in adulthood (0 = nonsexual recidivist, 1 = sexual recidivist).[6] Juvenile incarceration was included to serve as a proxy for serious youthful offending (i.e., to control for rival plausible explanations to early-onset antisociality). Furthermore,

[4]Given this is a sample of convicted sexual aggressors, 100% have charges for a sexual crime.

[5]The formula is computed as: $R^2 = 1 - e^{(-G/n)}$ where e is a constant (the base of the natural log), –G is the difference between the log likelihood chi-square statistic for the smaller model (e.g., without the covariates) and the log likelihood chi-square statistic for the larger model (e.g., including the covariates), and n is the sample size for the analysis.

[6]The age at assessment was not controlled for in the current analyses. The high proportion of first-time offenders (i.e., approximately 75%) resulted in strong positive correlations between the age at assessment and age at first sexual offence (i.e., sexual aggressors of children [$r = 0.84$, $p < .001$]; sexual aggressors of women [$r = 0.77$, $p < .001$]).

given that the age of assessment was also the age at the first sexual crime for nearly three quarters of the sample, the sexual recidivist variable was included as a control variable to represent a proxy measurement for age. Finally, juvenile sexual offending was included in the models to explore the relationship between sexual offenses as a juvenile and patterns of onset of sexual offending in adulthood. The sample descriptions and all of the measures used in the current study are presented in Table 7.1.

Results

Sexual Offenders of Children

Two series of hierarchical cluster analyses were first conducted on the subsample of sexual offenders of children (n = 221), one based on measures of delinquency in the childhood period (ages 0–12) and the second in the adolescence period (ages 13–17). For childhood, an analysis of the variance distribution of the proximity coefficients revealed a two-cluster solution from the self-reported measures of delinquency consisting of the following groups: (a) abstainers (79%), which included those individuals who primarily reported no delinquency in childhood;[7] and (b) conduct disordered delinquency (21%), which included those individuals who reported primarily behavioral problems, in addition to a range of nonviolent, violent, and sexual forms of delinquency.

The same procedures were conducted with the data for the adolescence period (ages 13–17). In adolescence, the results of the hierarchical cluster analysis suggested the retention of a three-group solution consisting of: (a) abstainers (49%), who reported no forms of delinquency in adolescence;[8] (b) conduct disordered delinquency and drug use (25%), where only minor forms of behavioral problems and drug use were reported; and (c) a versatile violent delinquency group (26%) where a majority of respondents reported nonviolent delinquency, in addition to varying proportions of respondents who reported the remaining spectrum of delinquent acts in adolescence (i.e., behavioral problems, drug use, violent and sexual delinquency.

The next stage of the analysis involved cross-tabulating the results of the cluster analyses for both time periods to establish within-individual changes in delinquency types across the two time periods representing trajectories of antisocial behavior (Table 7.2 section A). In order to do so, clusters were organized in order of

[7]Nine individuals (5.1%) reported nonviolent delinquency. For the remainder of the delinquency types, 0% was recorded across all individual members of the cluster. These nine individuals remained part of the abstainer group up until the presence of four clusters, at which point two clusters contained each only nine cases. The basis for retaining the two-cluster solution was also based on a two-step clustering procedure which indicated that a two-cluster solution was an appropriate characterization of childhood delinquency of the sexual aggressors of children.

[8]In this cluster solution, one individual reported violent delinquency in adolescence.

seriousness (i.e., abstainers to versatile violent). The results indicated that up to five possible trajectories characterized delinquency prior to adulthood. First, nondelinquents (ND) (45.7%) consisted of those individuals who reported no forms of delinquency in childhood or adolescence. Low-level initiators (LLI) (19.0%) consisted of those individuals who reported no delinquency in childhood, but conduct disordered behavior and drug use in adolescence. Escalators (ES) (17.7%), on the other hand, reported conduct disorder type behaviors in childhood that escalated to include either drug use in adolescence or versatile violent delinquency in adolescence. Next, high-level initiators (HLI) (14.5%) reported no delinquency in childhood, but initiated their delinquency in adolescence with versatile and violent antisocial behavior. Finally, de-escalators (DES) (3.2%) reported conduct disordered behavior in childhood, but displayed no indications of delinquency in adolescence. Due to the small size of the DES group (n = 7), although theoretically important, they were removed from the remaining analyses.

Antisocial Trajectories and Criminal Career Parameters in Adulthood of Sexual Offenders of Children Initial bivariate comparisons were conducted to explore the relationship between antisocial trajectories in youth and involvement and age of onset of offending in adulthood. In total, 37.4% of sexual offenders of children committed a property crime in adulthood. Similar proportions of HLIs (56.3%) and ESs (59.0%) were overrepresented in the property crime category. A smaller proportion of LLIs (31.0%), and NDs (25.7%) had charges for property crimes during adulthood [$X^2(1) = 19.2$, $p < .001$]. The age at first charges for property crimes significantly differed between the groups [*Welch* (3, 34.5) = 5.3, $p < .01$]. NDs (x = 27.8, sd = 7.4) were significantly older than HLIs (x = 21.7, sd = 5.2) ($p < .05$) and ESs (x = 22.3, 4.0) ($p < .05$). LLIs were the oldest on average at 28.5 years old (sd = 11.4) at the time of their first property crime; however, their ages varied substantially within the group. A comparable pattern emerged for violent crime in adulthood. First, 42.1% of sexual offenders of children had committed a violent crime in adulthood. Again, ESs (56.4%), and to a lesser extent, HLIs (46.9%) were slightly over represented in the violent crime category, while slightly smaller proportions of LLIs (38.1%) and NDs (36.6%) had been charged for a violent crime, although these group differences in participation in violent crimes were not statistically significant [$X^2(3) = 5.0$, n.s]. The age at first charges in adulthood significantly differed between the groups [*Welch* (3, 38.8) = 14.8, $p < .001$]. Here, ESs (x = 25.4, sd = 6.0) were significantly younger than NDs (x = 39.8, sd = 11.6) ($p < .001$), and LLIs (x = 35.8, sd = 8.8) ($p < .01$), while HLIs (x = 32.0, sd = 9.0) were marginally younger than NDs ($p < .10$) at the time of their first charge for a violent crime in the adult period. Finally, given that 100% of the sample committed a sexual crime, the age at first charges for a sexual crime was also compared between the trajectory groups of sexual offenders of children and also revealed significant group differences [F (3, 210) = 14.8, $p < .001$]. Here, ESs (x = 31.6, sd = 9.1) were significantly younger than NDs (x = 45.6, sd = 11.9) ($p < .001$) and LLIs (x = 43.6, sd = 10.8) ($p < .001$), while HLIs (x = 37.8, sd = 12.8) were also significantly younger than NDs ($p < .05$).

Table 7.2 Dynamic Classification Models of Self-Reported Delinquency in Youth

A. Sexual offenders of children (n = 221) — *Highest level achieved in adolescence (13–17)*

Highest level achieved in childhood (0–12)	ABSTAINERS	CONDUCT DISORDERED/ DRUG USE DELINQUENCY	VERSATILE VIOLENT DELINQUENCY
ABSTAINERS	Nondelinquents (n = 101; 45.7%)	Low-level initiators (n = 42; 19.0%)	High-level initiators (n = 32; 14.5%)
CONDUCT DISORDERED	De-escalators (n = 7; 3.2%)	Escalators (n = 39; 17.7%)	

$X^2(2) = 34.0$, $p < .000$, Cramer's V = 0.4

B. Sexual offenders of women (n = 155) — *Highest level achieved in adolescence (13–17)*

Highest level achieved in childhood (0–12)	CONDUCT DISORDERED	VERSATILE NONVIOLENT DELINQUENCY	VERSATILE VIOLENT DELINQUENCY
ABSTAINERS	Low-level initiators (n = 54; 34.8%)	High-level initiators (n = 57; 36.8%)	
CONDUCT DISORDERED	Stable-lows (n = 2; 1.3%)	Escalators (n = 21; 13.5%)	
VERSATILE SERIOUS DELINQUENCY	De-escalators (n = 1; 0.6%)	Stable-moderate/highs (n = 20; 12.9%)	

$X^2(4) = 45.1$, $p < .001$, Cramer's V = 0.5

The next step of the analysis involved calculating meta-trajectories according to the timing of onset of delinquency in youth (i.e., childhood versus adolescence). While meta-trajectories based on the onset of delinquency mask some of the evident qualitative differences in the unfolding of trajectories, they provide for a conceptually equivalent base of comparison (i.e., early-starters versus late-starters) between sexual offenders of children and sexual offenders of women. Hence, ESs (n = 39) represented "early-starters" (18.2% of the sample) (i.e., their delinquency first manifested in childhood), while NDs (n = 101), LLIs (n = 42), and HLIs (n = 32) were combined to represent "late-starters" (81.8% of the sample) (i.e., their delinquency was initiated after childhood). Table 7.3 section A displays the prevalence of the specific self-reported delinquency types (i.e., the measures used to compose the clusters in childhood and adolescence) to provide a descriptive profile of the forms of delinquency that characterized the early- and late-starter meta-trajectories of sexual offenders of children.

Table 7.3 includes a comparison between early- and late-starter sexual offenders of children. First, significant differences were evident for participation in property crimes between the early- and late-starters (59.0% versus 32.6%, respectively); approximately one half of the early-starters compared to just over one third of the late-starters had received a charge for a property offense. In addition, early-starters were significantly younger (22.3 years old) than late-starters (26.0 years old) when they committed their initial property offense. The early-starters were also more likely to have charges for violent crimes (56.4%) compared to late-starters (38.9%) and again were also approximately 10 years younger on average (25.5 years old compared to 37.1 years old) at the age of their first charge for a violent crime in adulthood. Finally, early-starter sexual offenders of children were significantly younger (31.6 years old) than the late-starters (43.4 years old) at the time of their first charge for a sexual crime. It is also crucial to note that less than half of the sample of adult sexual offenders of children had charges in adulthood for property or violent crimes.

To examine the postdictive contribution of the meta-trajectories to the time to onset of offending in adulthood, three Cox regression analyses were conducted while controlling for covariates (i.e., less than high school education, non-Caucasian ethnicity, being unemployed, being single, Juvenile detention, juvenile sexual offending, and adult sexual recidivism) (Table 7.4 section A). Juvenile detention was the strongest predictor for the time to onset of property crime [HR = 3.1, 95% CI = 1.5–6.6, $p < .01$], followed by being unemployed [HR = 2.5, 95% CI = 1.5–4.3, $p < .001$], being single [HR = 1.8, 95% CI = 1.1–2.9, $p < .05$]. A previous charge for sexual crimes in adulthood was marginally significant in the model [HR = 1.6, 95% CI = 1.0–2.7, $p < .10$], and the early-onset antisocial trajectory was not a significant predictor. A slightly different pattern was evident for the time to onset of violent crime, where juvenile detention again was the strongest predictor [HR = 3.9, 95% C I = 1.8–8.4, $p < .001$], followed by being non-Caucasian [HR = 3.7, 95% CI = 2.0–7.0, $p < .001$], the early-starter antisocial trajectory [HR = 3.5, 95% CI = 1.8–6.7, $p < .001$], and being unemployed [HR = 2.2, 95% CI = 1.3–3.5, $p < .01$]. Finally, for the time to onset of sexual crime, all of the covariates in the model were at

Table 7.3 Prevalence of Delinquency Types in Childhood and Adolescence, Prevalence and Age of Onset of Criminal Careers in Adulthood Within Early-/Late-Starter Trajectory Groups

	Delinquency in youth									
	Conduct disorders		*Substance use*		*Sexual delinquency*		*Nonviolent delinquency*		*Violent delinquency*	
A. Sexual offenders of children	(0–12) (%)	(13–17) (%)	(0–12) (%)	(13–17) (%)	(0–12) (%)	(13–17) (%)	(0–12) (%)	(13–17) (%)	(0–12) (%)	(13–17) (%)
Early-starter (n = 39)	87.2	76.9	17.4	41.0	20.5	33.3	17.9	59.0	7.7	17.9
Late-starter (n = 175)	0.0	15.4	0.0	22.9	0.0	4.6	5.1	15.4	0.0	1.7
	***	***	***	*	***	***	*	***	**	***
B. Sexual offenders of women	(0–12)	(13–17)	(0–12)	(13–17)	(0–12)	(13–17)	(0–12)	(13–17)	(0–12)	(13–17)
Early-starter (n = 44)	60.5	31.5	18.6	67.4	4.7	16.3	39.5	74.4	7.0	34.9
Late-starter (n = 111)	0.0	76.7	0.0	36.0	0.0	3.6	0.0	28.8	0.0	11.7
	***	***	***	**	†	*	***	***	*	**

	Criminal careers in adulthood					
	Property offending		*Violent offending*		*Sexual offending*	
C. Sexual offenders of children	%	Age of onset[a,b] *x (sd)*	%	Age of onset[c] *x (sd)*	%	Age of onset *x (sd)*
Early-starter (n = 39)	59.0	22.3 (3.9)	56.4	25.3 (6.0)	100.0	31.6 (9.1)
Late-starter (n = 175)	32.6	26.0 (8.3)	38.9	37.1(10.8)	100.0	43.4 (12.1)
	**	*	*	***	-	***

(*Continued*)

Table 7.3 (*Continued*)

	Criminal careers in adulthood					
	Property offending		*Violent offending*		*Sexual offending*	
D. Sexual offenders of women	%	Age of onset[a,d], *x (sd)*	%	Age of onset[a,e], *x (sd)*	%	Age of onset[a], *x (sd)*
Early-starter (n = 44)	81.4	21.7 (3.8)	95.3	24.5 (5.1)	100.0	28.3 (5.6)
Late-starter (n = 111)	60.4	25.4 (8.6)	85.6	28.9 (9.6)	100.0	32.8 (10.1)
	*	**	†	**	-	**

Note. Chi-square analyses were used to compare categorical variables and t-tests were used in comparisons of age between the groups.

[a]A log transformation was performed. Mean and standard deviation of the original variables are presented.

[b]Early-onset (n = 23), late-onset (n = 57).

[c]Early-onset (n = 22), late-onset (n = 68).

[d]Early-onset (n = 35), late-onset (n = 67).

[e]Early-onset (n = 41), late-onset (n = 95).

†$p < .10$, *$p < .05$, **$p < .01$, ***$p < .001$.

least marginally significant, this time with the exception of juvenile detention. The strongest predictors were the early-onset antisocial trajectory [HR = 2.3, 95% CI = 1.3–3.7, $p < .01$], previous charges for sexual crimes in adulthood [HR = 2.2, 95% CI = 1.5–3.2, $p < .001$], being non-Caucasian [HR = 2.1, 95% CI = 1.3–3.5, $p < .01$], and juvenile sexual offending [HR = 1.8, 95% CI = 1.0–3.1, $p < .01$].

Sexual Offenders of Women

The analytic strategy was then repeated using the subsample of sexual offenders of women (n = 148). Two series of hierarchical cluster analyses were conducted based on the childhood (ages 0–12) and adolescent (ages 13–17) self-reported indicators of delinquency. For childhood, the variance distribution of the proximity coefficients revealed that a three-group solution best characterized the data revealing the following groups: (a) abstainers (72%), who were participants that reported no forms of delinquency in childhood; (b) a conduct disordered group (15%), which included those individuals who primarily reported conduct disordered behavior; and (c) a versatile delinquent group (14%), who primarily reported nonviolent delinquency, but also drug use, some violent delinquency, and behavioral problems.

A three-cluster solution also emerged in adolescence; this time the following groups were uncovered: (a) conduct disordered type behavioral problems (37%), consisting of approximately only one quarter of individuals who reported conduct disordered behavior, and no other forms of delinquency; (b) a versatile nonviolent group (27%), who primarily reported drug use and nonviolent delinquency; and (c) a versatile violent group (36%), who also primarily reported drug use and nonviolent delinquency, in addition to violent delinquency.

Next, the results of these two cluster analyses were cross-tabulated to establish antisocial trajectories in youth (refer to Table 7.1 section B). First, low-level initiators (LLI) (34.8%) consisted of individuals who reported no delinquency in childhood and initiated conduct disordered type behavioral problems in adolescence. In contrast, the high-level initiators (HLI) (36.8%) reported no delinquency in childhood, but initiated versatile and violent delinquency in adolescence. Escalators (ES) (13.5%) reported conduct disordered delinquency in childhood with versatile and violent delinquency in adolescence. Stable-lows (SL) (1.3%) represented only two individuals who reported conduct disordered type behavior in the two time periods, whereas the stable-moderate/highs (SMH) (12.9%) represented those individuals who reported serious versatile delinquency in childhood, and versatile violent delinquency in adolescence. Finally, the de-escalator group (DES) (0.6%) represented one individual who reported versatile serious delinquency in childhood, and only conduct disordered behavior in adolescence. Therefore, given that only one individual comprised the DES group, this case was excluded from further analysis. In addition, given the low sample size of the SL group (n = 2), these individuals were merged with the SMH (n = 20) group to represent a "persistent" group (SLMH, n = 22) for the purposes of statistical analyses, considering that within each group there was a similar form of delinquency over the two time periods.

Antisocial Trajectories and Criminal Career Parameters in Adulthood of Sexual Offenders of Women Bivariate comparisons were conducted to explore the relationship between the antisocial trajectories of sexual offenders of women and involvement and age of onset of criminal activity in adulthood. In total, 66.2% of sexual offenders of women had committed a property crime in adulthood. The SLMHs (86.4%) were disproportionally represented for participation in property crime, followed by ESs (76.2%), HLIs (75.4%), and finally LLIs (44.4%) [$X^2(3) = 18.5, p < .001, \Phi = 0.4$]. The age at first charges for property crimes also significantly differed between the groups [*Welch* (3, 47.4) = 4.2, $p < .05$]. ESs (x = 21.0, sd = 3.7) were significantly younger than LLIs (x = 27.9, sd = 9.8) ($p < .01$), as were SLMHs (x = 22.4, sd = 3.8) ($p < .10$); however, the latter difference was moderately significant.

A somewhat similar pattern emerged in terms of violent crime in adulthood. First, a total of 88.3% of sexual offenders of women had committed a violent crime in adulthood. Virtually equal proportions of ESs (95.2%), SLMHs (95.5%), and HLIs (91.2%) demonstrated participation in violent crimes, compared to fewer LLIs (79.6%) [$X^2(3) = 6.5, p < .10, \Phi = 0.2$]. The age at first charges for violent crimes also significantly differed between the groups [F (3, 132) = 3.8, $p < .05$]; ESs (x = 24.0, sd = 5.5) again were significantly younger than LLIs (30.7, sd = 10.3) ($p < .05$). SLMHs (x = 24.9, sd = 4.7) and HLIs (x = 27.4, sd = 8.7) fell between these two extremes and the differences were not statistically significant. Finally, age at first charges for a sexual crime in adulthood also significantly differed between the groups [$F(3, 147) = 3.5, p < .05$]. More specifically, ESs (x = 27.3, sd = 4.8) were significantly younger than LLIs (x = 34.4, sd = 10.6) ($p < .05$). Again, SLMHs (x = 29.3, sd = 6.2) and HLIs (x = 31.2, sd = 9.3) fell between these two extremes and the differences were not significant.

Meta-trajectories were then computed based on the onset of delinquency prior to adulthood; in this case, SLMHs (n = 22) and ESs (n = 21) constituted early-starters (27.9% of the sample). Conversely, LLIs (n = 54) and HLIs (n = 57) constituted late-starters (72.1% of the sample). Table 7.3 section B displays the prevalence of delinquency types between the early- and late-starter meta-trajectories of sexual offenders of women. Early- and late-starters were compared according to participation and age of onset for property, violent, and sexual crimes in adulthood (refer to Table 7.3 section D). The early-starters were significantly more likely than late-starters to have charges for property crimes (81.4% compared to 60.4%, respectively), and were significantly younger then late-starters at the time of the first charge for a property crime (21.7 years old compared to 25.4 years old). A similar pattern emerged concerning participation in violent crimes (95.3% for early-starters compared to 85.6% for late starters), although this relationship was statistically marginal. In terms of the age at first charge for a violent crime, however, early-starters were significantly younger (24.5 years old), compared to late-starters (28.9 years old).

Finally, while 100% of the sample had charges for a sexual crime, early-starters, again, were significantly younger at the age of their first charge for a sexual crime (28.3 years old) compared to late-starters (32.8 years old).

The postdictive contribution of the meta-trajectories to the time to onset of property, violent, and sexual offending in adulthood was examined in a second series of three Cox regression models (refer to Table 7.4 section B). The early-onset meta-trajectory was the strongest predictor of the time to onset for property crimes [HR = 2.3, 95% CI = 1.4–3.6, $p < .001$], followed only by previous charges for sexual crimes in adulthood [HR = 1.6, 95% CI = 1.0–2.5, $p < .05$]. A similar pattern was evident for the time to onset for violent crime; the early-starter meta-trajectory again was the strongest predictor [HR = 1.9, 95% CI = 1.3–2.9, $p < .01$], followed by previous charges for sexual crimes in adulthood [HR = 1.5, 95% CI = 1.0–2.3, $p < .05$]. As for the model predicting the time to onset for sexual offending, the strongest predictor here was juvenile sexual offending [HR = 1.9, 95% CI = 1.0–3.5, $p < .10$], although the relationship was statistically marginal, followed by the early-onset meta-trajectory [HR = 1.7, 95% CI = 1.1–2.6, $p < .05$] and previous charges for a sexual crime in adulthood [HR = 1.8, 95% CI = 1.2–2.6, $p < .01$].

Discussion

The current study adds to a well-established body of literature documenting the extensive heterogeneity in the developmental histories of sexual offenders by demonstrating that their antisocial development is no exception. Heterogeneous patterns of antisocial development in youth are evident between sexual offenders of women and sexual offenders of children, and these patterns are differentially related to criminal activity in adulthood within these two broad groups of sexual offenders. Perhaps most critically, the findings in relation to sexual offenders of women stand in stark contrast to developmental models of offending that emphasize the prevalence of a single early-onset antisocial trajectory that escalates to sexual offending in adulthood (e.g., Moffitt et al., 2002). To the contrary, the results showed that the antisocial development of these men in youth is substantially more complex. Importantly, for both groups there was minimal evidence of juvenile sexual offending in their antisocial histories. However, for the minority of both sexual offenders of children and sexual offenders of women for whom it was present, it was related to an earlier onset of sexual offending in adulthood among the early-starters.

Heterogeneous Antisocial Trajectories in Youth of Adult Sexual Offenders

Only recently have developmental models considered sexual offending as a manifestation of different antisocial trajectories (i.e., *Life-Course Persistent* versus *Adolescent-Limited*), and these models have exclusively focused on sexual offenders of women

Table 7.4 Cox Regression Models for Time to Onset of Property, Violent, and Sexual Offending

	Property offending	*Violent offending*	*Sexual offending*
Sexual offenders of children (n = 208)	*Hazard Ratio (95% CI)*	*Hazard Ratio (95% CI)*	*Hazard Ratio (95% CI)*
Less than high school	2.4 (0.7–7.9)	1.4 (0.6–3.1)	1.7 (1.0–2.6)*
Non-Caucasian	0.9 (0.3–2.2)	3.7 (2.0–7.0)***	2.1 (1.3–3.5)**
Unemployed	2.5 (1.5–4.3)**	2.2 (1.3–3.5)**	1.2 (0.9–1.7)
Single	1.8 (1.1–2.9)*	1.6 (1.0–2.7)†	1.7 (1.3–2.4)**
Juvenile detention	3.1 (1.5–6.6)**	3.9 (1.8–8.4)***	1.5 (0.8–2.6)
Juvenile sex offending	0.7 (0.3–1.6)	0.5 (0.2–1.3)	1.8 (1.0–3.1)*
Adult sexual recidivist	1.6 (1.0–2.7)†	1.1 (0.7–1.9)	2.2 (1.5–3.2)***
Early- versus late-starters	1.6 (0.8–3.1)	3.5 (1.8–6.7)***	2.3 (1.3–3.7)**
−2 Log ML	713.9	759.1	1720.1
X^2 (*df*), *p*-value	89.1 (8)***	86.0 (8)***	122.7 (8)***
R^2	.26	.26	.36
	Property offending	*Violent offending*	*Sexual offending*
Sexual offenders of women (n = 148)	*Hazard Ratio (95% CI)*	*Hazard Ratio (95% CI)*	*Hazard Ratio (95% CI)*
Less than high school	1.8 (0.6–5.0)	1.2 (0.6–2.6)	1.4 (0.7–3.0)
Non-Caucasian	0.9 (0.5–1.7)	1.1 (0.7–1.8)	1.3 (0.8–2.1)
Unemployed	1.2 (0.8–1.9)	1.3 (0.9–1.9)	1.3 (0.9–1.8)
Single	1.5 (1.0–2.3)†	1.0 (0.7–1.4)	1.2 (0.9–1.7)
Juvenile detention	1.3 (0.7–2.7)	1.3 (0.7–2.3)	0.9 (0.5–1.6)
Juvenile sex offending	0.9 (0.4–2.0)	1.2 (0.6–2.3)	1.9 (1.0–3.5)†
Adult sexual recidivist	1.6 (1.0–2.5)*	1.5 (1.0–2.3)*	1.7 (1.2–2.6)**
Early- versus late-starters	2.3 (1.4–3.6)***	1.9 (1.3–2.9)**	1.7 (1.1–2.6)*
−2 Log ML	809.0	1036.0	1129.9
X^2 (*df*), *p*-value	36.1 (8)***	28.7 (8)***	33.9 (8)***
R^2	.20	.15	.18

†$p < .10$, *$p < .05$, **$p < .01$, ***$p < .001$.

(e.g., Cale et al., 2009; Lalumière et al., 2005; Seto & Barbaree, 1997). While sexual offenders of children generally display less involvement in nonsexual offending compared to sexual offenders of women, the current study provides some credence for investigating patterns in their antisocial development in youth as well. First, the extent of involvement in delinquency in youth differed substantially between sexual offenders of women and sexual offenders of children. Virtually all of the sexual offenders of women displayed some degree of involvement in delinquency in youth, and this observation is in line with prospective longitudinal studies based on samples from the general population (e.g., LeBlanc & Loeber, 1998; Moffitt et al., 2002), and clinical studies of adult sexual offenders of women that recognize the extensive antisocial backgrounds of these men (e.g., Bard et al., 1987; Lussier, LeBlanc, et al., 2005; Lussier, Proulx, et al., 2005). Comparatively, just over half of sexual offenders of children demonstrated any evidence of delinquency in youth. Overall, as with their adult nonsexual offending, sexual offenders of children had less delinquent involvement in youth compared to sexual offenders of women.

Second, following from these broad observations, much heterogeneity characterized the unfolding of delinquency within the two broad groups of sexual offenders. The early (i.e., childhood) onset of delinquency was more common in the backgrounds of sexual offenders of women (i.e., approximately 30%) compared to sexual offenders of children (i.e., approximately 20%). The delinquent development of early-starter sexual offenders of women was also more qualitatively diverse as well. For example, these individuals tended to show independent patterns of delinquent development reflecting escalation (i.e., their delinquency became more severe from childhood to adolescence) and persistence (i.e., their delinquency remained stable from childhood to adolescence). On the other hand, the smaller overall proportion of early-starter sexual offenders of children demonstrated a more homogeneous qualitative pattern of delinquent development that was characterized by escalation to more serious delinquency from childhood to adolescence. While to some extent these differences may be attributable to the methodological design of the study, they are generally in line with clinical and descriptive accounts of the more serious and diverse antisocial backgrounds of sexual offenders of women compared to sexual offenders of children (e.g., Lalumière et al., 2005; Lussier, LeBlanc, et al., 2005; Seto, 2008).

While most developmental models of offending since Moffitt's (1993) dual taxonomy highlight the potential negative implications of adolescent- or late-onset antisociality on later life outcomes, they have remained relatively silent about the possibility of sexual offending as one of them. Furthermore, these models have also largely neglected commenting on adult-onset offending (Eggleston & Laub, 2002). Critically, the developmental models of sexual offending have commented little on either of these phenomena. Therefore, from a developmental perspective, perhaps most striking in the current study was the fact that a majority of both sexual offenders of children (i.e., approximately 80%) and sexual offenders of women (i.e., approximately 70%) were not characterized by antisocial manifestations in childhood. For the former group, two patterns of adolescence-onset were evident in approximately equal proportions: a low-level conduct disordered and substance using group, and a high-level serious offending group. Critically, however, nearly half of sexual offenders of children were considered "nondelinquents." While there were no "nondelinquents" among sexual offenders of women, a similar pattern emerged in regard to adolescence-onset delinquency: a low-level conduct disordered group, and a versatile serious and violent group. Importantly, the meta-trajectories encompassing these pathways in youth were differentially related to offending in adulthood.

The Continuity of Offending into Adulthood

For both sexual offenders of children and sexual offenders of women, the findings suggest that the notion of a serious, violent, delinquent youth whose antisocial behavior escalated from a young age and eventually led to sexual offending in adulthood does not characterize the majority of these offenders. To the extent previous developmental models have emphasized the importance of a single, early-onset antisocial trajectory escalating to sexual offending in adulthood, it appeared this pattern may best describe only a certain portion of adult sexual offenders of women. As mentioned above, about one third of these men were characterized by an early-onset antisocial trajectory in youth. Furthermore, there appeared to be a greater continuity of antisocial behavior into adulthood for these individuals compared to other developmental types (i.e., early-starter sexual offenders of children). They began offending almost immediately in early adulthood, and a vast majority of these early-starters reported involvement in both property and violent offending in adulthood. In effect, it would appear that different within-group developmental pathways (i.e., escalation and persistence) characterized the continuity of their offending into adulthood, and that it was this particular group of offenders who best resembled the prototypical early-onset, chronic, serious, and violent offender described by Loeber and Farrington (1998) and Moffitt (1993), among others. Critically, while few of these individuals had histories of juvenile sexual offending (i.e., 7.7%), of those that did, the majority were also early-starters. Taken together, an early-onset antisocial trajectory and juvenile sexual offending were related to the early activation of sexual offending in adulthood.

Importantly, the results suggest that an early-onset antisocial trajectory alone may have slightly less postdictive value when it comes to explaining patterns of offending in adulthood of sexual offenders of children, and this may not necessarily be surprising considering that overall they are typically less antisocial than sexual offenders of women. For example, on the one hand, early-onset antisociality was related to the earlier activation of violent and sexual offending of these men in adulthood. On the other hand, only nearly half of early-onset sexual offenders of children reported any involvement in property or violent offending in adulthood, and juvenile detention was a stronger predictor of nonsexual offending in adulthood above an early-onset antisocial trajectory. Thus, while it appears that a certain proportion of these men likely also represent the prototypical early-onset, serious, and violent adulthood offender, a substantial portion of them displayed a pattern of intermittent offending over the life course that may not be accurately captured by a developmental taxonomy based on the onset of offending prior to adulthood. Nonetheless, based on descriptions of their delinquent profiles, the minority (i.e., 11.3%) that persisted from sexual offending in youth were also likely to be early-starters. The latter findings, in terms of both sexual offenders of children and sexual offenders of women, parallel the much earlier claims of Rice, Harris, and Quinsey (1990) and Rice, Quinsey, & Harris (1991) nearly two decades ago, who described the persistence of sexual offending characteristic of sexually deviant psychopaths. In the context of the current study, the continuity of sexual offending into adulthood was also observed in early-onset antisociality and sexual deviance in youth (see also Cale & Lussier, 2011). Clearly, however, this was not the prevalent developmental pathway leading to sexual offending in adulthood.

In adulthood, approximately between one quarter and one third of late-starters for both sexual offenders of children and sexual offenders of women had any charges for property or violent crimes; significantly less than their early-starter counterparts in both groups. They were also significantly older than their early-starter counterparts at the time of their first charges for any crimes (i.e., property, violent, sexual) in adulthood. In other words, key differences were evident between early- and late-starters on both the age of initiation and the proportion of individuals with various offenses in their histories. As these individuals constituted a majority of this overall sample of sexual offenders, they clearly represent a theoretically important group, and one that has escaped explanation in developmental models of sexual offending. Beyond the identification of these theoretically important groups of offenders in the current study, only some potential hypotheses are raised here regarding their adulthood offending behavior.

Eggleston and Laub (2002) hypothesized that the correlates of initiation of adult offending may be similar to those related to the continuation of offending from adolescence into adulthood. This hypothesis may be especially pertinent in the current study given the virtual parallel activation pattern (with an approximate 4–10-year separation) of adult criminal careers between the early- and late-starters in both groups. In effect, one explanation is that the role of state-related features, such as the breakdown of social bonds, for example, is central to the initiation of nonsexual and eventually sexual offending for late-starter sexual offenders. In adulthood this may mean factors such as unemployment, divorce, and a subsequent inability to achieve prosocial relationships, and intimate ones in particular. In this context, some of the theorized unique motivations for sexual offending may not be at play (i.e., deviant sexual preferences; sexual preferences for children) for these particular individuals when it comes to the onset offense (e.g., Smallbone, Marshall, & Wortley, 2008), thus complicating efforts to identify early precursors specific to sexual offending. On the one hand, these may not be individuals for whom deviant sexual preferences, or sexual preferences for children, are originally present, but rather simply, it may be the case that the motivation for their onset of sexual offending is more closely related to the motivations for nonsexual offending in adulthood (e.g., lack of, or broken, social bonds such as marriages and unemployment, loneliness/boredom, together with opportunities and access to children). On the other hand, these individuals might also be those for whom sexual offending is entering an aggravation process (e.g., Lussier, Tzoumakis, Cale, & Amirault, 2010). One explanation that has been put forward for late-onset and persistent sexual offending is in fact the role of deviant sexual preferences in maintaining the offending behavior (e.g., Lussier, Beauregard, Proulx, & Nicole, 2005; Prentky, Knight, & Lee, 1997). It is also therefore conceivable that for some offenders, the onset sexual offense may have a triggering effect in the activation of deviant sexual preferences. Thus factors typically associated with persistence of sexual offending may not be entirely the same as those associated with onset. Clearly, however, these hypotheses require substantially more empirical investigation.

Conclusion and Limitations

The current study highlighted the differential role of antisocial trajectories in youth on the activation of criminal careers in adulthood between sexual offenders of women and sexual offenders of children. A developmental model emphasizing distinctions between early- and late-onset antisociality provides a picture of the antisocial developmental backgrounds of sexual offenders beyond the scope of early-onset antisociality, suggesting the developmental antecedents of sexual offending can be understood, in part, as the manifestation of early behavior problems and antisocial behavior. For sexual offenders of children, adult onset criminality is far more common, thus suggesting unique developmental precursors for sexual offending between and within groups of sexual offenders that are differentially related to offending patterns in adulthood. Nonetheless, given the study was one of the first to investigate the antisocial development of different sexual offender types, the results should be interpreted as exploratory. Furthermore, the current study suffered from a number of methodological limitations.

First, the sample consisted of federally incarcerated inmates in a treatment facility in the province of Quebec in Canada, and thus cautions are warranted when making generalizations. However, at the same time, the sample also represents a quasi-population over the 6 years across which the data was gathered. In the current study we also excluded individuals who targeted victims across different age groups (i.e., children and adults), who undoubtedly also require important theoretical, empirical, and clinical attention. The study is also based on a combination of self-report retrospective data and official data, and therefore the issues associated with memory recall, and self-report bias given the sample setting, in addition to the limitations of official crime data, need to be taken into consideration. Finally, it was not possible to assess social desirability of responses, or inter-rater reliability of response coding. Nonetheless, despite these limitations, the current study identified important relationships between antisocial development in youth and the criminal careers in adulthood of adult sexual offenders. Importantly, given these preliminary findings, future studies should pursue the examination of the developmental backgrounds of offenders and precursors of offending to build on the results of the current analyses.

References

Abel, G. C., Becker, M. V., Cunningham-Rathner, J., Mittleman, M. S., Murphy, W. D., & Rouleau, J. L. (1987). Self-reported sex crimes of non-incarcerated paraphiliacs. *Journal of Interpersonal Violence, 2*, 3–25.

Abel, G. G., Osborn, C. A., & Twigg, D. A. (1993). Sexual assault throughout the lifespan: Adult offenders with juvenile histories. In H. E. Barbaree, W. L. Marshall, & S. M. Hudson (Eds.), *The juvenile sex offender* (pp. 104–117). New York: Guilford.

Adler, C. (1984). The convicted rapist: A sexual or a violent offender? *Criminal Justice and Behavior, 11*, 157– 177.

Allison, P. D. (1995). *Survival analysis using SAS: A practical guide*. Cary, NC: SAS Institute.

Ayers, C. D., Williams, J. H., Hawkins, J. D., Peterson, P. L., Catalano, R. F., & Abbott, R. D. (1999). Assessing correlates of onset, escalation, de-escalation, and desistance of delinquent behaviors. *Journal of Quantitative Criminology, 15*, 277–306.

Barbaree, H. E., & Seto, M. C. (1997). Pedophilia: Assessment and treatment. In D. R. Laws & W. O'Donohue (Eds.), *Sexual deviance: Theory, assessment, and treatment* (pp. 175–193). New York: Guilford Press.

Bard, L. A., Carter, D. L., Cerce, D. D., Knight, R. A., Rosenberg, R., & Schneider, B. (1987). A descriptive study of rapists and child molesters: Developmental, clinical, and criminal characteristics. *Behavioral Sciences and the Law, 5*, 203–220.

Baxter, D. J., Marshall, W. L., Barbaree, H. E., Davidson, P. R., & Malcolm, P. B. (1984). Deviant sexual behavior: Differentiating sex offenders by criminal and personal history, psychometric measures, and sexual response. *Criminal Justice and Behavior, 11*, 477–501.

Bergman, L. R., Magnusson, D., & El-Khouri, B. M. (2003). *Studying individual development in an interindividual context: A person-oriented approach*. Mahwah, NJ: Erlbaum.

Broadhurst, R. G., & Maller, R. A. (1992). The recidivism of sex offenders in the Western Australian prison population. *British Journal of Criminology, 32*, 54– 80.

Cale, J., & Lussier, P. (2011). Toward a developmental taxonomy of adult sexual aggressors of women: Antisocial trajectories in youth, mating effort, and sexual criminal activity in adulthood. *Violence and Victims, 26*, 16–32.

Cale, J., Lussier, P., & Proulx, J. (2009). Heterogeneity in antisocial trajectories in youth of adult sexual aggressors of women: An examination of initiation, persistence, escalation, and aggravation. *Sexual Abuse: A Journal of Research and Treatment, 21*, 223–248.

Chaffin, M., Berliner, L., Block, R., Johnson, T. C., Friedrich, W., Louis, D. et al. (2008). Report of the ATSA task force on children with sexual behavior problems. *Child Maltreatment, 18*, 199–218.

Clatworthy, J., Buick, D., Hankins, M., Weinman, J., & Horne, R. (2005). The use and reporting of cluster analysis in health psychology. *British Journal of Health Psychology, 10*, 329–358.

Curran, P., Obeidat, K., & Losardo, D. (2010). Twelve frequently asked questions about growth curve modeling. *Journal of cognition and development, 11*, 121–136.

Davis, J. A. (1963). *Panel analysis: Techniques and concepts in the interpretation of repeated measurements*. Chicago: University of Chicago.

Eggleston, E. P., & Laub, J. H. (2002). The onset of adult offending: A neglected dimension of the criminal career. *Journal of Criminal Justice, 30*, 603–622.

Elliott, D. S. (1994). Serious violent offenders: Onset, developmental course, and termination. *Criminology, 32*, 1–21.

Finch, H. (2005). Comparison of distance measures in cluster analysis with dichotomous data. *Journal of Data Science, 3*, 85–100.

Gebhard, P. H., Gagnon, J. H., Pomeroy, W. B., & Christenson, C. V. (1965). *Sex offenders: An analysis of types*. New York: Harper & Row.

Groth, A. N., Longo, R. E., & McFadin, B. (1982). Undetected recidivism among rapists and child molesters. *Crime and Delinquency, 28*, 450–458.

Hanson, R. K., & Bussière, M. T. (1998). Predicting relapse: A meta-analysis of sexual offender recidivism studies. *Journal of Consulting and Clinical Psychology, 61*, 646–652.

Harris, D. A., Smallbone, S., Dennison, S., & Knight, R. A. (2009). Specialization and versatility in sexual offenders referred for civil commitment. *Journal of Criminal Justice, 37*, 37–44.

Huizinga, D. (1979). *Dynamic typologies, a means of exploring longitudinal multivariate data.* Paper presented at the Classification Society meetings, Gainsville, FL.

Lalumière, M. L., Harris, G. T., Quinsey, V. L., & Rice, M. E. (2005). *The causes of rape: Understanding individual differences in male propensity for sexual aggression.* Washington, DC: American Psychological Association.

LeBlanc, M. (2002). The offending cycle, escalation, and de-escalation in delinquent behavior: A challenge for criminology. *Comparative and Applied Criminal Justice, 26*, 53–84.

LeBlanc, M., & Bouthillier, C. (2003). A developmental test of the general deviance syndrome with adjudicated girls and boys using confirmatory factor analysis. *Criminal Behavior and Mental Health, 13*, 81–105.

LeBlanc, M., & Kaspy, N. (1998). Trajectories of delinquency and problem behavior: Comparison of social and personal control characteristics of adjudicated boys on synchronous and nonsynchronous paths. *Journal of Quantitative Criminology, 14*, 181–214.

LeBlanc, M., & Loeber, R. (1998). Developmental criminology updated. In M. Tonry (Ed.), *Crime and justice* (Vol. *23*, pp. 115–198). Chicago: University of Chicago Press.

Loeber, R. and Farrington, D. P. (Eds.). (1998). *Serious & Violent Juvenile Offenders: Risk Factors and Successful Interventions.* London: Sage Publications.

Loeber, R., & LeBlanc, M. (1990). Toward a developmental criminology. In N. Morris & M. Tonry (Eds.), *Crime and justice* (pp. 375–473). Chicago: University of Chicago Press.

Loeber, R., Stouthamer-Loeber, M., Van Kammen, W., & Farrington, D. P. (1991). Initiation, escalation and desistance in juvenile offending and their correlates. *Journal of Criminal Law and Criminology, 82*, 36–82.

Longo, R. E., & Groth, A. N. (1983). Juvenile sexual offenses in the histories of adult rapists and child molesters. *International Journal of Offender Therapy and Comparative Criminology, 27*, 150–155.

Lussier, P. (2005). The criminal activity of sexual offenders in adulthood: Revisiting the specialization debate. *Sexual Abuse: A Journal of Research and Treatment, 17*, 269–292.

Lussier, P., Beauregard, E., Proulx, J., & Nicole, A. (2005). Developmental factors related to deviant sexual preferences in child molesters. *Journal of Interpersonal Violence, 20*, 999–1017.

Lussier, P., & Cortoni, F. (2008). The development of antisocial behavior and sexual aggression: Theoretical, empirical, and clinical implications. In B. K. Schwartz (Ed.), *The sex offender: Offender evaluation and program strategies* (Vol 6. pp. 2/1 – 2–26). Kingston, NJ: Civic Research Institute.

Lussier, P., LeBlanc, M., & Proulx, J. (2005). The generality of criminal behavior: A confirmatory factor analysis of the criminal activity of sex offenders in adulthood. *Journal of Criminal Justice, 33*, 177–189.

Lussier, P., Proulx, J., & LeBlanc, M. (2005). Criminal propensity, deviant sexual interests and criminal activity of sexual aggressors against women: A comparison of explanatory models. *Criminology, 43*, 249–281.

Lussier, P., Tzoumakis, S., Cale, J., & Amirault, J. (2010). Criminal trajectories of adult sex offenders and the age effect: Examining the dynamic aspect of offending in adulthood. *International Criminal Justice Review, 20*, 147–168.

Marshall, W. L., Barbaree, H. E., & Eccles, A. (1991). Early onset and deviant sexuality in child molesters. *Journal of Interpersonal Violence, 6*, 323–335.

Miethe, T. D., Olson, J., & Mitchell, O. (2006). Specialization and persistence in the arrest histories of sex offenders: A comparative analysis of alternative measures and offense types. *Journal of Research in Crime and Delinquency, 43*, 204–229.

Milligan, G. W., & Cooper, M. C. (1985). An examination of procedures for determining the number of clusters in a data set. *Psychometrika, 50*, 159–179.

Moffitt, T. E. (1993). Adolescence-limited and life-course-persistent antisocial behavior: A developmental taxonomy. *Psychological Review, 4*, 674–701.

Moffitt, T. E., Caspi, A., Harrington, H., & Milne, B. J. (2002). Males on the life-course-persistent and adolescence-limited antisocial pathways: Follow-up at age 26. *Development and Psychopathology, 14*, 179–206.

Mojena, R. (1977). Hierarchical grouping methods and stopping rules: An evaluation. *Computer Journal, 20*, 359–363.

Nisbet, I. A., Wilson, P. H., & Smallbone, S. W. (2004). A prospective longitudinal study of sexual recidivism among adolescent sex offenders. *Sexual Abuse: A Journal of Research and Treatment, 3*, 223–234.

Parks, G. A., & Bard, D. E. (2006). Risk factors for adolescent sex offender recidivism: Evaluation of predictive factors and comparison of three groups based upon victim type. *Sexual Abuse: A Journal of Research and Treatment, 18*, 319–342.

Patterson, G. R. (1993). Orderly change in a stable world: The antisocial trait as a chimera. *Journal of Consulting and Clinical Psychology, 61*, 911–919.

Prentky, R. A., & Knight, R. A. (1993). Age of onset of sexual assault: Criminal and life history correlates. In G. C. N. Hall, R. Hirschman, J. R. Graham, & M. S. Zaragoza (Eds.), *Sexual aggression: Issues in etiology, assessment, and treatment* (pp. 43–62). Washington, DC: Taylor & Francis.

Prentky, R. A., Knight, R. A., & Lee, A. (1997). Risk factors associated with recidivism among extra-familial child molesters. *Journal of Consulting and Clinical Psychology, 65*, 141–149.

Proulx, J., Lussier, P., Ouimet, M., & Boutin, S. (2008). Criminal career parameters in four types of sexual aggressors. In B. K. Schwartz (Ed.), *The sex offender: Offender evaluation and program strategies* (Vol. VI, pp. 3/1 – 3–12). New York, NY: Civic Research Institute.

Rice, M. E., Harris, G. T., & Quinsey, V. L. (1990). A follow-up of rapists assessed in a maximum-security psychiatric facility. *Journal of Interpersonal Violence, 4*, 345–448.

Rice, M. E., Quinsey, V. L., & Harris, G. T. (1991). Sexual recidivism among child molesters released from a maximum security psychiatric institution. *Journal of Consulting and Clinical Psychology, 59*, 381–386.

Seto, M. C. (2008). *Understanding pedophilia and sexual offending against children: Theory, assessment, and intervention*. Washington, DC: American Psychological Association.

Seto, M. C., & Barbaree, H. E. (1997). Sexual aggression as antisocial behavior: A developmental model. In D. M. Stoff, J. Breiling, & J. D. Maser (Eds.), *Handbook of antisocial behavior* (pp. 524–533). New York: John Wiley & Sons, Inc.

Simon, L. M. J. (1997). Do criminal offenders specialize in crime types? *Applied and Preventative Psychology, 6*, 35–53.

Smallbone, S. W., Marshall, W. L., & Wortley, R. (2008). Explaining child sexual abuse: A new integrated theory. In S. W. Smallbone, W. L. Marshall, & R. Wortley (Eds.), *Preventing child sexual abuse: Evidence, policy and practice* (pp. 21–45). Cullompton, U.K.: Willan.

Smallbone, S. W., & Wortley, R. (2004). Onset, persistence, and versatility of offending among adult males convicted of sexual offenses against children. *Sexual Abuse: A Journal of Research and Treatment, 16*, 285–298.

Soothill, K., Francis, B., Sanderson, B., & Ackerley, E. (2000). Sex offenders: Specialists, generalists or both? *British Journal of Criminology, 40*, 56–67.

Tedeschi, J. T., & Felson, R. B. (1994). Violence, aggression, and coercive actions. Washington, DC: American Psychological Association.

Tracy, P. E., Wolfgang, M. E., & Figlio, R. M. (1990). *Delinquency careers in two birth cohorts.* New York: Plenum.

Zimring, F. E., Piquero, A. R., & Jennings, W. G. (2007). Sexual delinquency in Racine: Does early sex offending predict later sex offending in youth and young adulthood? *Criminology and Public Policy, 6*, 507–534.

8

Offending Patterns Over Time

An Examination of Specialization, Escalation, and De-escalation in the Commission of Sexual Offenses

Benoit Leclerc
Griffith University, Australia

Patrick Lussier & Nadine Deslauriers-Varin
Laval University, Canada

Introduction

Policy development to tackle the issue and promote the prevention of sexual abuse seems to be driven by the assumption that sexual offenders are characterized by some pathology, which prevents them from controlling their sexual urges and renders them more likely to reoffend if they live close to places where children congregate. This assumption implies that sexual urges and paraphilia will determine how sex offenders behave. From such a perspective, these offenders would always select the same places to approach victims, abuse the same victim type, adopt the same strategies to abuse them, and look for particular sexual behaviors to achieve during the offense. In short, offenses committed by the same offender would all be identical and involve the same victim type. This view, however, is inconsistent with empirical evidence showing that: (1) sexual offenders are likely to take into account risks of apprehension and make decisions when it comes to their offending behavior (e.g., Beauregard & Leclerc, 2007); (2) the immediate environment shapes how sexual offenses are committed, which means that the way an offense is committed varies according to the circumstances found in each crime event (e.g., Leclerc, Beauregard & Proulx, 2008; Wortley & Smallbone, 2006); and (3) the offender-victim interchange in sexual abuse is dynamic and in part determined by victim characteristics, such as age, gender, and their routine activities (e.g., Deslauriers-Varin & Beauregard, 2010; Leclerc, Proulx, Lussier, & Allaire, 2009; Leclerc, Smallbone, & Wortley, 2013).

An investigation of offending patterns takes this body of evidence into consideration, which is essential as prevention initiatives should be based on

Sex Offenders: A Criminal Career Approach, First Edition. Edited by Arjan Blokland and Patrick Lussier.

empirical studies focusing on a detailed analysis of the actual offense, not on anecdotal accounts (e.g., Conte, Wolf, & Smith, 1989; Kaufman et al., 1998; Reppucci & Haugaard, 1989; Wortley & Smallbone, 2006). Building on a previous study (Lussier, Leclerc, Healy, & Proulx, 2008), we extend our analysis of crime-switching patterns to include a wider range of offending strategies employed by the offender to commit the offense and sexual behaviors performed during the offense. A special feature of the current study is the analytic strategy pursued to get a deeper understanding of crime-switching over time. The synchronicity of changes in offending strategies and sexual behaviors performed during the offense over time is assessed and the presence of offense characteristics as covariates of these changes investigated.

Crime-Switching in Sexual Offending

A number of scholars have studied the tendency of sexual offenders to sexually abuse different types of victim over time. This phenomenon has been first referred as victim-choice polymorphia (Guay, Proulx, Cusson, & Ouimet, 2001). If the offender abuses different types of victim over successive offenses, his or her offending pattern is said to be versatile in terms of victim-choice. An example of this is when an offender sexually abuses a child in the first crime event, and an adult woman in the next. If the offender tends to restrict him- or herself to the same type of victim, the victim-choice of the offender is said to be specialized. The conceptualization of victim-choice polymorphia and specialization is important here as it raises a number of issues. First, there are numerous aspects that may distinguish victims, such as their age, gender, ethnic origin, the victim-offender relationship, and so on. Second, the same individual may show evidence of both victim-choice polymorphia and specialization over time. The accumulation of different victim types may characterize a portion of the sex offender's criminal career, while specialization or the tendency to restrict to the same victim type may characterize another (Lussier, 2005). In other words, one offender may abuse children during adolescence and then switch to adults during adulthood. Third, it could also be that offenders might be more versatile for some aspects and more specialized for other aspect of victim-choice. For example, an offender might only target children (i.e., specialization in age) but offend against both boys and girls (versatility in gender). The variety of sources of information used to study the question of victim-choice polymorphia also raises some concerns in terms of reliability. Some studies have relied on only one source of information, such as self-report or police data. Both self-reports and official data have their own limitations, with the former being subject to memory biases and tendency to under-report crimes of this nature (see Heil, Almeyer, & Simons, 2003), while the latter provides a representation of offenses for which the offender has been caught. In sum, the examination of various aspects of the victim-choice over successive victims using complementary sources of information might increase the ability to detect static and dynamic patterns of crime commission in sexual offending over time.

Previous studies have found the presence of both specialization and polymorphia in victim-choice over time. Some studies have found evidence suggesting that specialization is the norm (Cann, Friendship, & Gonza, 2007; Gebhard, Gagnon, Pomeroy, & Christenson, 1965; Guay et al., 2001; Soothill, Francis, Sanderson, & Ackerley, 2000), while others have found that versatility is more common (Heil et al., 2003; Weinrott & Saylor, 1991). Soothill et al. (2000) concluded that while sex offenders are generalists in their criminal offending, they tend to specialize in their sexual offending confining themselves to one victim type. Similarly, Radzinowicz (1957) also found specialization in victim-choice in that only 7% of his large sample of sex offenders had convictions for crimes against both male and female victims, a finding consistent with those of Gebhard et al. (1965). In that regard, Cann et al. (2007) reported that about 25% of their sample of incarcerated sex offenders was versatile when considering three victim characteristics (age, gender, and offender-victim relationship). Empirical studies conducted in clinical settings have shown a divergent picture of the sex offender's crime-switching pattern. Weinrott & Saylor (1991) as well as Heil et al. (2003) have argued that official data hide an enormous amount of sex crimes. Using official data only, Weinrott & Saylor (1991) found that only 15% of their sample of offenders was versatile (see also Abel & Rouleau, 1990). That number rose to 53% when using data from a self-reported computerized questionnaire. Similarly, Heil et al. (2003) reported that incarcerated offenders in treatment are not versatile as to the victim's age (7%) and gender (8.5%) when assessed with official data, but are when interviewed using a polygraph (70 and 36%, respectively). Less dramatic numbers, however, were reported for parolees, which might be explained by sampling differences (i.e., incarcerated offenders were more serious offenders) and the fact that admitting a crime was a prerequisite to enter treatment. These contradictory findings may simply be the result of these empirical studies looking at aggregate information for different aspects of the offender's victim-choice over successive offenses.

In a more recent study, Lussier et al. (2008) extended the notion of victim-choice polymorphia to incorporate the crime event itself, which includes the use of physical force and sexual behaviors performed by the offender. In this context, sexual polymorphia refers to crime-switching and specialization patterns in the perpetration of the offense along several key dimensions, such as victim's age and gender, level of physical force used, and nature of sexual behaviors committed by the offender. Lussier et al. (2008) found that the level of polymorphism in offending varies from one victim to another, but also from one dimension to another. For example, sex offenders tend to limit themselves to the same victim when it comes to gender, suggesting that sexual preferences may come into play in victim-choice decision. At the other end of the continuum, victim's age included much crime-switching across offenders, but this switching was not found to manifest itself in a random fashion. The researchers showed that sex offenders against children who switch victim type will target adolescents, where sex offenders against adults (overwhelmingly against women) who switch will also target adolescents. Hence, switching from a child to an adult victim was rarely seen. In that context, adolescents may be seen as the surrogate choice of both types of offenders (see also Guay et al., 2001). When it comes to the level of physical force used, it was found that when variation did occur, offenders who adopted excessive force to abuse a victim were more likely to only adopt the level of force necessary for subsequent victims rather than not using force at all. Overall, the level of physical force adopted to abuse a victim was quite stable over time. The level of sexual intrusiveness, however, was less stable. Sexual intrusiveness referred to the sexual nature of the offense along a continuum of seriousness from hands-off behaviors (e.g., the offender's exposing his genitals) to penetration of the victim (e.g., anal, vaginal penetration). Offenders who began by touching or masturbating their victim were likely to perform penetration with subsequent victims.

Although the study completed by Lussier et al. (2008) included the use of physical force and the level of intrusiveness achieved during the offense, there is a need to incorporate a much wider spectrum of strategies and sexual behaviors to get a more accurate picture of offending patterns over time. Not including manipulative strategies, for instance, might greatly bias the findings and prevent researchers from detecting patterns of escalation. It should be noted that Lussier et al.'s detailed analysis (2008) also emphasized whether self-control and/or specialization increased offending versatility and created diversity indexes for victim and offense characteristics for that purpose. Therefore, the point of focus of this study is not the offense itself or offending patterns and their dynamic nature over time. Rather, in the current study, offenders are classified as escalators, specialists, or de-escalators based on the strategies and sexual behaviors performed on the victim. Then the synchronicity of changes in strategies and sexual behaviors over time is assessed and the presence of covariates analyzed.

Current Focus

The main purpose of this study is to examine whether or not crime commission patterns in sexual offenders change over time or, more specifically, from one victim to another. By doing so, we also assess, to some extent, whether or not offenders specialize in particular aspects of the crime event. The first aim is to examine whether or not strategies adopted to commit the offense and associated outcomes (sexual behaviors performed during crime) vary across time. Although Sjostedt, Langstrom, Sturidsson, and Grann (2004) completed a study on the stability of offender modus operandi in sexual offending, their conceptualization of offender modus operandi was very broad and not in line with definitions used to define modus operandi. They included offender modus operandi strategies but also victim type, noncontact sex offenses and sexual behaviors. Moreover, only one strategy was examined (i.e., the use of death threat). Kaufman, Hilliker, and Daleiden (1996) define modus operandi as "the pattern of behaviors that perpetrators display in the periods prior to, during, and following illicit sexual contact" (p.18). Douglas, Burgess, Burgess, and Ressler (1997) define modus operandi as "the actions taken by an offender to perpetrate the offense successfully" (p. 353). Following these definitions, we recenter the focus on modus operandi and examine a broad range of strategies used to abuse a victim. In addition, most studies on specialization of offending patterns of sexual offenders over time have looked at crime-switching in terms of victim type only. In this study, we follow Lussier et al.'s (2008) rationale and continue to expand the notion of crime-switching patterns by incorporating a wide range of strategies adopted to sexually abuse a victim. The second aim is to assess the synchronicity of changes in offender strategies and sexual behaviors performed during the offense over time. By synchronicity, we refer to whether or not specialization in one domain of the crime event tends to be associated with specialization in another domain. The third aim is to look at the presence of covariates for both strategies and sexual behaviors in order to help explain the nature of switching over time, if any. Again, this aim is in line with Lussier et al. (2008), but this time covariates are introduced to capture the dynamic nature of the offense itself.

Methodology

Sample

The initial sample consisted of 553 adult males who had been convicted for a sexual offense and who received a prison sentence of at least two years. Because the study of offending patterns from one victim to another requires data from participants who abused at least two victims, a subsample was drawn accordingly. A total of 216 participants had a minimum of two victims and, consequently, were included in this study. At the time of the study, these individuals were incarcerated at the Regional Reception Centre of Ste-Anne-des-Plaines (in the province of Quebec, Canada), a maximum-security federal institution run by the Correctional Service of Canada. They were consecutive admissions between April 1994 and June 2000 at this institution where all individuals sentenced to a minimum of two years are admitted for the purpose of risk and treatment-needs assessment. The average stay in this institution is about six weeks, permitting completion of correctional assessment procedures prior to the individual's transfer to an institution suited to his risk level and treatment needs. The offenders were overwhelmingly Caucasian, and, on average, 43 years old at the time of their admission to the penitentiary. Their criminal history revealed that, on average, they were first convicted at age 35.2 ($s = 15.2$; range = 18.1–73.9). Note that the criminal activity of this sample has been extensively described elsewhere (Lussier, LeBlanc, & Proulx, 2005). One third of this sample had a prior conviction for a sex crime. The age of the victims of these offenders was on average from victim #1 to victim #5 between 12 and 14 years, suggesting that this sample was predominantly composed of child molesters. Also, the victims were primarily females, especially the first two victims (about 70%), but the proportion of males to females changed somewhat for the next three victims considered in the study (between 55 and 60% female). The sample was also composed mainly of extrafamilial offenders (as opposed to intrafamilial), especially for those with four and five victims where the percentage of intrafamilial victim is below 7%.

Procedures

Data used to create scales measuring behavioral antecedents were collected in a semi-structured interview with each subject. Each subject was interviewed only once by a member of the research team unaware of the research questions and hypotheses. Participation in this study was strictly voluntary. Subjects included in this study signed a consent form indicating that the information gathered would be used for research purposes only. Interviewers were all graduate students in criminology and psychology trained by a licensed forensic psychologist to conduct semi-structured interviews using a computerized questionnaire. Quality of data collected from the QIDS (Questionnaire Informatise en Delinquance Sexuelle) was controlled by completing inter-rater agreement. Inter-rater agreement was measured on the basis of 16 interviews conducted jointly by two raters (the principal research assistant and the first author). Ratings were done independently following these interviews, which were conducted by one interviewer in the presence of the other. The mean kappa was .87, which represents very strong agreement. Moreover, as participants granted access to their correctional files, official sources of information (e.g. police reports, victim statements, psychological assessments, etc.) were also used to validate, when possible, information obtained in interview. When disagreements were found between information gathered during the semi-structured interview and that collected from official files, official data were used. Police records were consulted to determine the criminal activity in adulthood. The number of victims refers to the total number of victims for the index offenses. On average, sexual offenders included in this sample have been charged for 3.4 victims (SD = 4.5; range = 2–65).

Measures

Crime Categories

There is no general consensus as to how sex crimes should be categorized. Earlier work has been focused mostly on distinguishing the age and the gender of the victim as well as the nature of the offender-victim relationship (Guay et al., 2001; Abel & Rouleau, 1990; Lussier et al., 2008). Two main dimensions of the sexual criminal activity were considered in the present study: (a) strategies to sexually abuse a victim; and (b) sexual behaviors performed during the offense. The strategies used to abuse a victim reflect behaviors used by the offender to perform or make the victim perform sexual behaviors.

This variable included five categories to reflect the diversity of strategies typically used in such a context. The variable was coded as follows: (1) seduction and persuasion (e.g., convince the victim that sexual behaviors between children and adults are okay); (2) deception (e.g., using drugs and alcohol to intoxicate the victim); (3) direct action (refers to acting on the victim without using seduction, deception, threats, or physical violence); (4) uttering threats (refers to threats of physical violence if the victim does not comply with the sexual behaviors); and (5) physical violence (refers to the use of either instrumental or expressive forms of violence).[1]

The variable was coded to reflect an increase in coercion from a score of 1 to 5. In doing so, the coding allowed the inspection of specialization in strategy used, but also in terms of escalation and de-escalation in coercion over successive victims. As can be seen in Table 8.1, a direct action approach is the most common strategy used by offenders overall (percentage varies from 36.4 to 47.3%). Seduction is also often used by offenders, especially to abuse the fourth and fifth victims. Making threats is not commonly used by offenders. Moreover, percentages of the use of strategies from one victim to another are quite stable, especially for deception, threats, and physical violence, even though some variations are still noticeable (e.g., the percentage of use of deception is 15.1% for the first victim but 23.5% for the third victim). The use of seduction increases from the second to the fifth victim while the use of direct action decreases from the first to the fifth victim.

In line with prior investigations (e.g., Lussier et al., 2008), the sexual behaviors performed were categorized as follows: (1) hands-off behaviors (i.e., exposing genitals); (2) touching, petting; (3) masturbation; (4) oral sex; and (5) anal and/or vaginal penetration. The variables were also coded to reflect an increase in sexual intrusiveness from 1 to 5. This allowed us to examine not only specialization in type of sexual behaviors performed, but also escalation and de-escalation in sexual intrusiveness over successive victims. In the coding of both the strategy and sexual behaviors, important decisions were made where: (a) several strategies or acts may have been performed during the offense; and (b) the victim was offended against over multiple occasions. In both cases, the more serious acts were retained for the coding of the variables. Again looking at Table 8.1, the most common sexual act performed by offenders overall is penetration (percentage varies from 22.9 to 56%). Then oral sex and sexual touching are also commonly performed by offenders. Note that the occurrence of penetration during the offense greatly decreases from the first to the fifth victim. The occurrence of masturbation and sexual touching, however, slightly increases over time.

Covariates

Several indicators were included to determine whether offending patterns were influenced by a victim's characteristics and characteristics of the crime event. Because of the relatively small sample size, these indicators and their association with offending patterns were only analyzed for the first crime transition. Hence, indicators for the first two victims were included here and the descriptive statistics are reported in Table 8.1. The victim characteristics refer to the victim's age and gender. Offense characteristics included two situational factors: offender-victim relationship and victim resistance. Another

[1]Note that certain strategies are not applicable with certain victim types (e.g., seduction with adult victims). It was decided to keep the format as follows as sex offenders against children may move to adolescent and adult victims, and vice versa (see for example, Lussier et al., 2008).

Table 8.1 Descriptive Information on the Sample

Descriptors	*Mean (standard deviation) or percentages*				
Offender characteristics					
Age at prison admission	43.4 (12.7), range: 20–75				
Ethnic origin	Caucasian: 90.4				
	Black: 3.8				
	First Nations: 2.9				
	Other: 2.9				
Past convictions for any crime (Total)	2.9 (4.0), range: 0–19				
Presence of at least one prior conviction for a sex crime (Yes)	33.0%				
Victim characteristics	*$Victim_1$*	*$Victim_2$*	*$Victim_3$*	*$Victim_4$*	*$Victim_5$*
Age	12.4 (10.2)	12.7 (9.4)	13.4 (12.3)	14.4 (14.4)	12.7 (9.9)
Gender (Male)	31.6	31.1	41.0	44.4	40.0
Offense characteristics					
Offender-victim relationship (Intrafamilial)	22.6	18.3	19.0	6.3	2.9
Victim resistance (Physical and verbal)	15.6	14.2	10.3	14.8	2.9
Victim performed acts on offender (Yes)	66.2	56.5	56.1	54.1	51.4
Strategies used to commit the crime	*$Victim_1$*	*$Victim_2$*	*$Victim_3$*	*$Victim_4$*	*$Victim_5$*
Seduction/persuasion (Yes)	13.7	13.7	20.4	24.6	30.3
Deception (Yes)	15.1	14.7	23.5	18.0	15.2
Direct action (Yes)	47.3	46.6	41.8	39.3	36.4
Uttering threats (Yes)	8.3	7.8	5.1	6.6	6.1
Physical violence (Yes)	15.6	17.2	9.2	11.5	12.1
Sexual behaviors performed by the offender	*$Victim_1$*	*$Victim_2$*	*$Victim_3$*	*$Victim_4$*	*$Victim_5$*
Hands-off (Yes)	2.4	5.3	3.1	4.8	11.4
Touching, petting (Yes)	17.7	20.4	26.5	22.6	28.6
Masturbation (Yes)	3.8	7.8	6.1	8.1	11.4
Oral sex (Yes)	20.1	22.8	22.4	30.6	25.7
Penetration (Yes)	56.0	43.7	41.8	33.9	22.9

Table 8.2 Duration of Crime Events Per Victim

	Duration (days)			*Single-day event*[a]	*Overlapping events*[b]
	Mean (SD)	*Median*	*Range*	%	%
Victim #1 (n = 528)	809.5 (1338.3)	92.0	1–8185	39.4	-
Victim #2 (n = 208)	769.2 (1233.2)	222.0	1–7861	23.1	63.0
Victim #3 (n = 100)	911.4 (1392.4)	365.0	1–8328	15.0	65.0
Victim #4 (n = 64)	803.0 (1439.3)	265.0	1–7517	12.5	67.2
Victim #5 (n = 36)	548.6 (772.9)	274.0	1–3164	22.1	52.8

[a]Percentage of crime events that lasted no more than 24 hours.
[b]Percentage of crime events that overlapped in time (at least one day) with the immediately preceding crime event.

offense characteristic, victim participation, measures whether or not the victim was coerced into performing sexual behaviors on the offender. The coding of victim's gender (0 = female; 1 = male) and victim's age (i.e., age at the onset of the event) was relatively straightforward. Offender-victim relationship was dichotomized to reflect the presence or absence of an intrafamilial relationship (i.e., incest). An intrafamilial relationship was present when the victim was the biological child or a biological sibling of the offender. All other offender-victim relationships were coded as extrafamilial. Victim resistance was dichotomized to reflect the presence or absence of resistance (verbal and/or physical). Victim participation was also dichotomized to reflect whether or not the offender made the victim perform sexual behaviors on him during the offense.

The study also included two indicators reflecting the context of the offense in general. One important feature that distinguishes sexual offenses from several other offenses is the fact that an individual can offend against the same victim over several days, several months, and in some cases, several years (see Table 8.2 for descriptive statistics on this matter). Therefore, it was necessary to examine first whether the offense against the victim was a single event or involved multiple events. Hence, the length of the offense refers to the number of days that spanned between the onset and the termination of the crime. Offenses that lasted 24 hours or less were coded as 1. Because offense against a single victim can span over multiple days, we examined the possibility that offenders may have multiple victims at the same time. The measure was simply coded as follows: (0) no victim overlap; (1) at least two victims overlap in time. Hence, we investigated whether offenders having multiple overlapping victims might be characterized by a specific offending pattern.

Transition Matrices

Crime-switching patterns across sexual offenses were investigated in order to examine the tendency for sex offenders to specialize in a particular crime-type. Determining whether offenders act in the same way across victims in different contexts may have several implications for both the prevention and the investigation of sex offenses. Therefore, in keeping with previous studies (Guay et al., 2001; Lussier et al., 2008), the unit of analysis is the victim and we analyzed the sex crime transition for the first five victims. We focused here on the first five victims due to the increasingly smaller sample size as more victims were considered in the analysis.

Due to missing data, it was possible to chronologically order the victims for only 210 individuals. Whereas 210 offenders had two victims, only 36 had at least five victims. Therefore, we only considered here the first four crime transitions. Hence, 210 offenders had one crime transition (from crime #1 to crime #2), 100 had a second transition (from crime #2 to crime #3), 64 had a third transition (from crime #3 to crime #4), while 36 had four transitions (from crime #4 to crime #5). Because of a few cases where there was missing data on the nature of strategies used or the sexual behaviors performed, the sample size varied across those transitions.

Offending Patterns

Using the findings from the crime transition matrices, three offending patterns were measured and analyzed. Each transition matrix gives qualitative information about the specialization, escalation, and de-escalation in offending from one victim to another. While specialization has received much attention from scholars, escalation, and especially de-escalation, have not been the subject of much empirical analyses. The transition matrix, therefore, allowed us to examine these three processes simultaneously from one crime transition to another. The transition matrix can be described as a grid where the offender's behavior against victim_x is cross-tabulated with the offender's behavior against victim_{x+1}. Offenders falling in the diagonal of the matrix are repeating the same behavior from one victim to the next – that is, their behavior is the same. This will be referred to here as specialization. All offenders falling off the diagonal are assumed to be crime switchers – that is, their behavior is changing from one victim to another. Because strategies used and sexual behaviors committed were coded to reflect a level of seriousness, two more offending patterns were examined. Hence, offenders falling above the matrix diagonal manifested a more serious behavior against victim_{x+1} than against victim_x. These offenders were referred to as escalators. Furthermore, some offenders were found below the matrix diagonal, meaning that their level of seriousness has decreased from one victim to another. These offenders were classified as de-escalators. It should be noted that the terminology used here and its operationalization (i.e., specialization) is in line with the criminal career literature and previous studies completed on crime-switching patterns in sexual offending. Therefore, in this study, specialization has been defined as "the tendency of individual offenders to repeat the same offense type as offending continues" (Cohen, 1986, p. 366).

Analysis of Offending Patterns and their Covariates

For each crime transition, offenders were classified as specialist, escalator, or de-escalator for both strategies and sexual behaviors. Because of the small number of offenders with multiple victims and the decreasing sample across transition, only offending patterns for strategies and sexual behaviors for the first crime transition were analyzed. The covariates were analyzed individually by conducting a series of multinominal logit regression models. In each model, the specialization group was identified as the group of reference to which the group of escalators and de-escalators were compared.

Results

Transition Matrices

Table 8.3 shows proportions of offenders who used particular strategies to commit the offense. First, as can be seen in Table 8.3, specialization is somewhat the norm for offenders who use seduction or physical violence from one victim to another (range = .79–1.00; range = .73–1.00, respectively). For instance, a total of 79% of offenders who use seduction to sexually abuse their first victim do not use a different strategy to sexually abuse their second victim. Of those who do use a different strategy, 14% adopt deception and 7% employ a direct action approach. In the second transition, offenders who use a different strategy than seduction adopt a direct action approach (17%).

Of offenders who adopt physical violence to abuse the first victim, 18% de-escalate and use a direct action approach to abuse the second victim while an additional 9% escalate and make threats. Interestingly, there is no evidence of switching between seduction and physical violence across victims overall. Offenders who use seduction to abuse their victims do not use physical violence, and vice versa. Second, looking at other strategies in Table 8.3, versatility is more noticeable. The proportion of offenders using these strategies across victims, especially deception or threats, varies considerably (range = .50–.93; range = .65–1.00, respectively). For instance, offenders who use deception to abuse the first victim but then change for a different strategy to abuse the second victim mostly escalate and adopt a more coercive strategy; that is, direct action (23%). Switching for a direct action approach seems to be more frequent as well for the third and fourth victims (7 and 23%, respectively). Offenders who make threats to abuse the first victim but then change for a different strategy to abuse the second victim tend to use a direct action approach (24%) followed by physical violence (12%).Lastly, of offenders who adopt a direct action approach to abuse the first victim, 10% escalate and employ physical violence, while 9% de-escalate and use seduction (5%) or deception (4%) to abuse the second victim. In Transition 2, offenders who switch to another strategy to abuse the third victim (25%) often de-escalate and adopt either seduction (9%) or deception (15%).

Table 8.3 Crime Transitions of (Most Coercive) Strategies Used to Enact the Offense

Crime T	*Crime T+1*				
	Seduction/ persuasion	Deception	Acting out	Uttering threats	Physical violence
Seduction/ persuasion	T_1 = .79 (22) T_2 = .83 (15) T_3 = .87 (13) T_4 = 1.00 (7)	T_1 = .14 (4) T_2 = .00 (0) T_3 = .07 (1) T_4 = .00 (0)	T_1 = .07 (2) T_2 = .17 (3) T_3 = .07 (1) T_4 = .00 (0)	T_1 = .00 (0) T_2 = .00 (0) T_3 = .00 (0) T_4 = .00 (0)	T_1 = .00 (0) T_2 = .00 (0) T_3 = .00 (0) T_4 = .00 (0)
Deception	T_1 = .07 (2) T_2 = .00 (0) T_3 = .08 (1) T_4 = .33 (2)	T_1 = .71 (22) T_2 = .93 (14) T_3 = .62 (8) T_4 = .50 (3)	T_1 = .23 (7) T_2 = .07 (1) T_3 = .23 (3) T_4 = .00 (0)	T_1 = .00 (0) T_2 = .00 (0) T_3 = .00 (0) T_4 = .00 (0)	T_1 = .00 (0) T_2 = .00 (0) T_3 = .08 (1) T_4 = .17 (1)
Acting out	T_1 = .05 (5) T_2 = .09 (4) T_3 = .04 (1) T_4 = .07 (1)	T_1 = .04 (4) T_2 = .15 (7) T_3 = .09 (2) T_4 = .07 (1)	T_1 = .79 (76) T_2 = .75 (35) T_3 = .87 (20) T_4 = .80 (12)	T_1 = .01 (1) T_2 = .00 (0) T_3 = .00 (0) T_4 = .00 (0)	T_1 = .10 (10) T_2 = .02 (1) T_3 = .00 (0) T_4 = .07 (1)
Uttering threats	T_1 = .00 (0) T_2 = .00 (0) T_3 = .00 (0) T_4 = .00 (0)	T_1 = .00 (0) T_2 = .00 (0) T_3 = .00 (0) T_4 = .33 (1)	T_1 = .24 (4) T_2 = .14 (1) T_3 = .00 (0) T_4 = .00 (0)	T_1 = .65 (11) T_2 = .71 (5) T_3 = 1.00 (4) T_4 = .67 (2)	T_1 = .12 (2) T_2 = .14 (1) T_3 = .00 (0) T_4 = .00 (0)
Physical violence	T_1 = .00 (0) T_2 = .00 (0) T_3 = .00 (0) T_4 = .00 (0)	T_1 = .00 (0) T_2 = .18 (2) T_3 = .00 (0) T_4 = .00 (0)	T_1 = .18 (6) T_2 = .09 (1) T_3 = .00 (0) T_4 = .00 (0)	T_1 = .09 (3) T_2 = .00 (0) T_3 = .00 (0) T_4 = .00 (0)	T_1 = .73 (24) T_2 = .73 (8) T_3 = 1.00 (7) T_4 = 1.00 (3)

T_1 = Transition from victim #1 to victim #2 (n = 205); T_2 = Transition from victim #2 to victim #3 (n = 98); T_3 = Transition from victim #3 to victim #4 (n = 62); T_4 = Transition from victim #4 to victim #5 (n = 34). The shaded area represents specialization trends, the area below represents evidence of de-escalation, while the area above represents evidence of escalation.

Table 8.4 shows proportion of offenders who performed particular sexual behaviors during the offense. As indicated in Table 8.4, contrary to some patterns found for strategies, specialization in a certain type of sexual act across victims is more unusual. The proportion of offenders who repeat sexual touch across victims varies between .38 and .67. For instance, only 38% of offenders who sexually touch their first victim also perform this same sexual act on the second victim. Of those who do a different sexual act, 16% perform oral sex and 38% have sexual intercourse with their victim. The proportion of offenders who repeat oral sex and penetration across victims also varies considerably (range = .48–.54; range = .36–.64, respectively).

A total of 54% of offenders who perform oral sex on the first victim do so for the second victim. Of those who perform a different sexual act to abuse the second victim, 20% perform sexual touch and 20% have sexual intercourse with the victim. Switching to a different sexual act to abuse the third victim is also frequent as only 48% of offenders who perform oral sex to abuse the second victim do so for the third victim.

Table 8.4 Crime Transitions of (Most Serious) Sexual Behaviors Performed During the Offense

Crime T	*Crime T+1*				
	Hands-off	Touching, petting	Masturbation	Oral sex	Penetration
Hands-off	T_1 = .67 (4) T_2 = .75 (3) T_3 = .75 (3) T_4 = 1.00 (3)	T_1 = .00 (0) T_2 = .00 (0) T_3 = .00 (0) T_4 = .00 (0)	T_1 = .00 (0) T_2 = .00 (0) T_3 = .00 (0) T_4 = .00 (0)	T_1 = .17 (1) T_2 = .25 (1) T_3 = .25 (1) T_4 = .00 (0)	T_1 = .17 (1) T_2 = .00 (0) T_3 = .00 (0) T_4 = .00 (0)
Touching, petting	T_1 = .03 (1) T_2 = .00 (0) T_3 = .00 (0) T_4 = .00 (0)	T_1 = .38 (14) T_2 = .67 (12) T_3 = .57 (8) T_4 = .67 (6)	T_1 = .05 (2) T_2 = .00 (0) T_3 = .07 (1) T_4 = .11 (1)	T_1 = .16 (6) T_2 = .11 (2) T_3 = .07 (1) T_4 = .11 (1)	T_1 = .38 (14) T_2 = .22 (4) T_3 = .29 (4) T_4 = .11 (1)
Masturbation	T_1 = .00 (0) T_2 = .00 (0) T_3 = .00 (0) T_4 = .20 (1)	T_1 = .13 (1) T_2 = .50 (4) T_3 = .40 (2) T_4 = .20 (1)	T_1 = .75 (6) T_2 = .25 (2) T_3 = .40 (1) T_4 = .40 (2)	T_1 = .00 (0) T_2 = .00 (0) T_3 = .20 (1) T_4 = .00 (0)	T_1 = .13 (1) T_2 = .25 (2) T_3 = .00 (0) T_4 = .20 (1)
Oral sex	T_1 = .05 (2) T_2 = .03 (1) T_3 = .06 (1) T_4 = .13 (1)	T_1 = .20 (8) T_2 = .14 (4) T_3 = .18 (3) T_4 = .13 (1)	T_1 = .02 (1) T_2 = .03 (1) T_3 = .00 (0) T_4 = .00 (0)	T_1 = .54 (22) T_2 = .48 (14) T_3 = .53 (9) T_4 = .50 (4)	T_1 = .20 (8) T_2 = .31 (9) T_3 = .24 (4) T_4 = .25 (2)
Penetration	T_1 = .04 (5) T_2 = .00 (0) T_3 = .00 (0) T_4 = .00 (0)	T_1 = .16 (19) T_2 = .15 (6) T_3 = .05 (1) T_4 = .18 (2)	T_1 = .06 (7) T_2 = .08 (3) T_3 = .09 (2) T_4 = .09 (1)	T_1 = .16 (18) T_2 = .13 (5) T_3 = .27 (6) T_4 = .36 (4)	T_1 = .58 (67) T_2 = .64 (25) T_3 = .59 (13) T_4 = .36 (4)

T_1 = Transition from victim #1 to victim #2 (n = 208); T_2 = Transition from victim #2 to victim #3 (n = 98); T_3 = Transition from victim #3 to victim #4 (n = 62); T_4 = Transition from victim #4 to victim #5 (n = 34). The shaded area represents specialization trends, the area below it represents evidence of de-escalation, while the area above it represents evidence of escalation.

Indeed, of offenders who perform a different sexual act, 31% perform penetration, 14% touching, and 3% masturbation. Many offenders who perform penetration with the first victim tend to de-escalate and perpetrate a different sexual act to abuse the second victim. For these offenders, sexual behaviors are: oral sex (16%), touching (16%), and masturbation (6%). Lastly, a total of 75% of offenders who perform masturbation do not switch to a different sexual act to abuse the second victim.

Offending Patterns

Findings obtained in crime transition matrices were then used to measure and analyze three offending patterns: specialization, escalation, and de-escalation in offending from one victim to another. Offenders were classified as specialists, escalators, or de-escalators based on transition matrices.

Table 8.5 shows synchronicity of changes in strategies and sexual behaviors over time using the above classification. As observed in Table 8.5, synchronicity in specialization was found. Offenders who specialize and use the same strategy in Transition 1 (i.e., from victim #1 to victim #2) also tend to specialize and perform the same sexual act (58.8%). Remaining offenders who specialize in a strategy can either de-escalate (26.1%) or escalate (15%) in sexual behaviors. Patterns are somewhat similar in Transition 2 (i.e., from victim #2 to victim #3). Specialists in a particular strategy also tend to specialize in a particular sexual act as well (62.7%). Although the number of offenders who abused four or five victims (Transitions 3 and 4, respectively) is small, one trend is noticeable. Specialists in a particular strategy again tend to specialize in a particular sexual act (57.1 and 55.6%, respectively).

Going back to Transition 1, a lack of synchronicity in escalation and de-escalation can also be observed. Offenders who de-escalate and use a less coercive strategy to abuse the second victim tend to specialize in the same sexual act (52.2%). Many de-escalators also de-escalate and perform a less serious sexual act (39.1%). Very few de-escalators, however, escalate in the severity of sexual behaviors committed during the offense (8.7%). Interestingly, offenders who escalate and use a more coercive

Table 8.5 Synchronicity of Changes in Strategies and Sexual Behaviors for Crime

Patterns of strategies used to commit crime	*Patterns of sexual behaviors*		
Transition 1 (n = 202)	De-escalation %	Specialization %	Escalation %
Deescalation (n = 23)	39.1	52.2	8.7
Specialization (n = 153)	26.1	58.8	15.0
Escalation (n = 26)	46.2	30.8	23.1
Transition 2 (n = 95)	De-escalation %	Specialization %	Escalation %
De-escalation (n = 15)	20.0	40.0	40.0
Specialization (n = 75)	22.7	62.7	14.7
Escalation (n = 5)	80.0	20.0	0.0
Transition 3 (n = 59)	De-escalation %	Specialization %	Escalation %
De-escalation (n = 4)	50.0	50.0	0.0
Specialization (n = 49)	20.4	57.1	22.4
Escalation (n = 6)	50.0	33.3	16.7
Transition 4 (n = 33)	De-escalation %	Specialization %	Escalation %
De-escalation (n = 4)	25.0	50.0	25.0
Specialization (n = 27)	25.9	55.6	18.5
Escalation (n = 2)	50.0	50.0	0.0

strategy to abuse the second victim tend to de-escalate and perform a less intrusive sexual act (46.2%). Other escalators can either specialize (30.8%) or escalate (23.1%) in sexual behaviors performed during the offense. In Transition 2, the percentage of offenders who de-escalate in their strategy and who escalate in their sexual behaviors rises to 40%, whereas the percentage of offenders who escalated to a more coercive strategy who de-escalate in sexual behaviors increases to 80%.

Offending Patterns and Covariates

In Table 8.6, a series of multinominal regressions was completed on strategies and sexual behaviors to identify offense characteristics that could be associated with offending patterns over time. Again, classification of offenders as specialists, escalators, or de-escalators was applied. Because of the small sample size, it should be noted that regression analyses were only conducted for the first transition. The models included information on the first and second victims because the dependent variable refers to the (lack of) changes of the offender's behaviors (strategies, sexual behaviors) performed from the first to the second victim. Therefore, the models needed to account for changes in the victim's characteristics from these two "events" to determine whether the offender's behaviors were impacted by the stability and change in the target of the offenses. Such modeling, we believe, allows for an examination of the contextual factors that may impact the offender's decisions and behavior for the first offending transition. Note here that, because of the sample size, all the covariates were analyzed individually in separate regression models.

For strategies, victim resistance emerges as important to explain offending patterns. For instance, Model 4 shows that the combination of the absence of resistance from the first victim (OR = .03) and resistance from the second victim (OR = 19.35) will rather to lead to an escalation than to specialization in the level of coercion of the strategies used. In addition, resistance from the first victim will rather lead to de-escalation than to specialization (OR = 5.75). The victim's age and gender as well as the offense length are also significant covariates. Model 1 indicates that the older the second victim, the more likely the offender is to escalate and use a more coercive strategy to commit the offense than to specialize (OR = 1.06). Model 2 indicates that a male victim for the first victim is more likely to lead to escalation in strategies than to specialization (OR = 3.77). Model 6 also shows that a longer offense period is more likely to lead to escalation and de-escalation as opposed to specialization for the first and second victim.

For sexual behaviors, victim resistance, victim participation (i.e., sexual behaviors performed by the victim), and the offense length are associated with the crime commission pattern found during the first transition. For instance, Model 4 shows that low resistance (OR = .14) for the first victim combined with high resistance (OR = 3.02) for the second victim will rather lead to escalation than to specialization. Model 5 indicates that nonparticipation of the first victim in sexual episodes is more likely to occur in situations where the offender escalates in the first transition compared to those who specialized (OR = .23). In addition, participation of the first

Table 8.6 Multinominal Regression on Patterns of Offending During First Crime Transition

Factor		*Strategies*		*Sexual behaviors*	
		Escalation OR (95% CI)	*De-escalation* OR (95% CI)	*Escalation* OR (95% CI)	*De-escalation* OR (95% CI)
Model 1: Victim's age					
	Victim 1	.98 (.93–1.03)	1.05 (.99–1.10)	.97 (.92–1.03)	.97 (.93–1.01)
	Victim 2	1.06 (1.01–1.10)*	.96 (.89–1.04)	1.02 (.96–1.08)	1.03 (.98–1.07)
	Model fit	9.09 (4)†		2.44 (4)	
	R^2	.057		.014	
Model 2: Victim's gender (male)					
	Victim 1	3.77 (1.15–12.37)*	.58 (.13–2.52)	2.55 (.80–8.14)	.74 (.27–2.03)
	Victim 2	.29 (.08–1.07)†	1.03 (.26–4.15)	.53 (.16–1.75)	.86 (.32–2.32)
	Model fit	6.39 (4)		4.88 (4)	
	R^2	.040		.027	
Model 3: Relationship (extra.)					
	Victim 1	.83 (.19–3.68)	.46 (.12–1.72)	1.71 (.44–6.69)	.57 (.22–1.51)
	Victim 2	8.47 (.83–86.56)†	5.81 (.95–35.52)†	.45 (.12–1.70)	1.72 (.57–5.23)
	Model fit	10.07 (4)*		3.65 (4)	
	R^2	.063		.020	
Model 4: Victim resistance					
	Victim 1	.03 (.00–.29)**	5.75 (1.97–16.80)**	.14 (.03–.71)*	.45 (.17–1.16)†
	Victim 2	19.35 (5.76–64.96)***	.28 (.06–1.28)†	3.02 (.91–10.04)†	2.34 (.90–6.07)†
	Model fit	41.20 (4)***		10.06 (4)*	
	R^2	.245		.057	

Model 5: Victim performed acts				
Victim 1	2.07 (.75–5.72)	1.31 (.44–3.89)	.23 (.09–.62)**	3.27 (1.39–7.69)**
Victim 2	.47 (.19–1.18)	1.58 (.56–4.46)	2.41 (.84–6.91)	.13 (.06–.28)***
Model fit	5.32 (4)		44.68 (4)***	
R^2	.034		.228	
Model 6: Offense length (days)				
Victim 1	1.00 (1.00–1.01)*	1.00 (1.00–1.01)*	.99 (.99–1.00)**	1.00 (1.00–1.00)
Victim 2	.99 (.99–1.00)**	.99 (.99–1.00)*	1.00 (1.00–1.00)	.99 (.99–1.00)**
Model fit	17.10 (4)**		28.52 (4)***	
R^2	.106		.153	
Model 7: Overlapping victims				
	.25 (.10–.60)**	.66 (.27–.1.59)	1.33 (.57–3.06)	1.71 (.89–3.28)
Model fit	10.44 (2)**		2.63 (2)	
R^2	.065		.015	

Note. The reference category here is the specialization pattern. R^2 refers to Nagelkerke.
$^{\dagger}p$ = .10; $^{*}p$ = .05; $^{**}p$ = .01; $^{***}p$ = .001.

victim (OR = 3.27) combined with nonparticipation of the second victim (OR = .13) will rather lead to de-escalation in the nature of sexual behaviors than to specialization. In Model 6,the offense period in the case of the first victim is also associated with an escalation in sexual behaviors as opposed to specialization (OR = .99). On the other hand, the longer the offense period for the second victim, the more likely the de-escalation in sexual behaviors as opposed to specialization (OR = .99).

Discussion

The Dynamic Nature of Offending Patterns

Investigating the tendency to repeat the same offending behaviors from one victim to another was the first step of this study. Strategies adopted to sexually abuse the victim and sexual behaviors performed by the offender during the offense were investigated. Evidence of both specialization and versatility was found. In particular, specialization was found for the use of seduction and physical violence. In addition, no switching occurred between these two strategies from one victim to another. In other words, no offenders who had used physical violence at some point against one victim used seduction to commit another crime, and vice versa. Recall that our sample comprises sexual offenders against children and sexual offenders against women; however, the mean victim age was between 12 and 14 years, suggesting the predominance of sex offenders against children within this sample. One possibility is that offenders against children use different strategies than offenders against women. Seduction relates to the situation where the offender charms, flatters, or uses other seductive ways in order to get a child involved in sexual activity. Manipulative strategies such as seduction and charm are the norm in child sexual abuse, not violence (e.g., Goldstein, 1999; Kaufman et al., 1998; Smallbone & Wortley, 2000). On the other hand, as an adult may be more likely to resist than a child, the use of physical violence to involve the victim in sexual activity is more likely in sexual offenses involving women. It does not mean, however, that some form of seduction has not been used at some point in the offending process of these offenders, such as the victim encounter stage, which was not under investigation here. The victim consent and the ability for the victim to make that consent (e.g., age) therefore are to be considered as well in the offender's decision to rely on a particular strategy type.

Even if specialization was more likely, some evidence of versatility across victims was observed for other strategies. For instance, some offenders who used deception to abuse the first victim used a direct action approach for the second victim. This finding can be explained by the fact that, unlike seduction and physical violence, deception, direct action, and threats can be adopted to abuse a child or a woman. Furthermore, because of their nature, these strategies might be less effective than seduction and physical violence. Therefore, offenders who used one of these strategies to abuse the first victim may have realized that it was not especially effective to make the victim comply for sexual contact and then decided to use another strategy to abuse the second victim. In contrast, seduction and physical violence are likely to be effective if used for the "correct" victim type. Children may not fully understand the situation when an adult tries to involve them in sexual activities, which gives the offender the opportunity to employ manipulation effectively (Berliner & Conte, 1990). A child also has a low capacity to resist mentally and physically. Women are generally not as strong as men physically and may not be capable of physically resisting a violent adult male offender. To some extent, the nature of the strategy used to abuse a victim and associated outcomes could determine whether or not the offender would use another strategy to abuse a subsequent victim.

Evidence of versatility of sexual behaviors was also found across victims. This finding highlights the dynamic nature of offending. Many factors could explain why a different sexual act is performed from one victim to another. First, maybe some offenders are more likely to perform particular acts based on their level of sexual arousal (sexual drive) and the victim's physical appearance or perceived attractiveness. Second, we should expect the situation in which the offense is perpetrated to shape the interchange between the offender and the victim and related outcomes. For instance, it might be easier for an offender to abuse and perform penetration on a victim if he or she were sleeping naked or semi-naked when approached for sexual contact. Another similar example is when the offender gives a bath to a child. The location of abuse (public/private) and the presence of a potential witness/guardian may also determine to some extent what the offender can and cannot do when committing a sexual offense. As the situation is particular to each offense, sexual behaviors performed from one victim to another may vary accordingly. Third, we should expect females to be more at risk of experiencing penetration than males. Simply because of their developmental level, older victims should also be more at risk of penetration. Unfortunately, in this study, we cannot assess to what extent an offender's motivations or situational factors, such as the location of abuse or the presence of somebody else when the offense was committed, influence transitions from one victim to another. Victim characteristics, however, were included as covariates in the final analyses and are discussed below.

The second step of this study was to analyze the synchronicity of changes in strategies and sexual behaviors over time. Recall that strategies used and sexual behaviors committed were coded to reflect a level of seriousness, which allowed us to examine not only specialization but also escalation and de-escalation. Specialization in strategies and sexual behaviors tended to co-occur across victims (around 60% of offenders across victims). Again, this may be explained by a subgroup of offenders who are focused on achieving a particular sexual act by using the same strategy across victims. It also suggests that some offenders may be effective by using a particular modus operandi and decide to keep going with it to abuse subsequent victims. By contrast, a lack of synchronicity was found in escalation and de-escalation. For some other offenders, the level of intrusiveness in sexual behaviors does not increase as the level of coerciveness in strategies increases from one victim to another. De-escalators are likely to perform the same sexual act but also less or more intrusive sexual behaviors. A similar pattern emerges for escalators. Escalators are likely to perform less intrusive sexual behaviors but also to commit the same sexual act from one victim to another. The versatility of these patterns provides good evidence that offenses committed by the same offender may differ in some important ways from one victim to another. The study findings, therefore, suggest that there is much evidence of nonsynchronicity across aspects of crime events. Take into consideration here that only two aspects of the crime event were investigated (strategies to commit the offense, and sexual behaviors performed on the victim). Had we taken into consideration a higher number of components of the crime event, examples of nonsynchronicity might have been even more predominant. This finding, therefore, raises issues about the oversimplification of the issue of whether or not sex offenders are specialists in regard to their offending patterns.

The third and final step of this study was to examine covariates of offending patterns and provide additional evidence about the dynamic nature of offending. Offense characteristics related to the victim were emphasized. On an individual basis all variables were found to be significant, except for offender-victim relationship, showing how dynamic the offense might be once attention is drawn to the offense itself rather than to the offender. First, age and gender of the victim emerged as important covariates for strategies, whereas victim participation clearly has an effect on sexual behaviors performed by the offender, which is consistent with previous studies on sex crime events (Leclerc, Carpentier, & Proulx, 2006; Leclerc et al., 2009; Leclerc et al., 2013). Second, victim resistance emerged as the most important covariate overall. Absence or presence of resistance can lead to escalation or de-escalation in strategies rather than to specialization. Absence of resistance can also lead to escalation in sexual behaviors rather than to specialization across victims. Victim reaction is fundamental if one wants to understand how the offense unfolds (Tedeschi & Felson, 1994). Its importance has been shown for years in research on sexual offenses against women (Ullman, 1997, 2007) and more recently in sexual offenses against children as well (Leclerc et al., 2009; Leclerc, Wortley, & Smallbone, 2011; Leclerc et al., 2013). The current findings clearly show that an offense can take a different route or path once the victim reacts to offender actions. The dynamics of the offending process also involve victim-offender interactions that may change over time and impact the stability of the offender's crime commission dynamics.

It should be noted, however, that it was not possible to perform the analysis on a full model containing all variables. This was due to the small sample size, which renders this analysis exploratory and highlights the need for future research on the subject before any firm conclusions can be reached. Moreover, not taken into account here is the offender's perception as to whether the strategies used had been effective (or not) and whether the sexual behaviors performed had been found to be fulfilling or pleasurable (or not). The outcome of the event as perceived by the offender may impact how subsequent offenses are approached to increase chances of getting away with it while maximizing the benefits of committing the offense. But again, distinguishing offenders against children from offenders against women could have been helpful in further understanding these offending patterns.

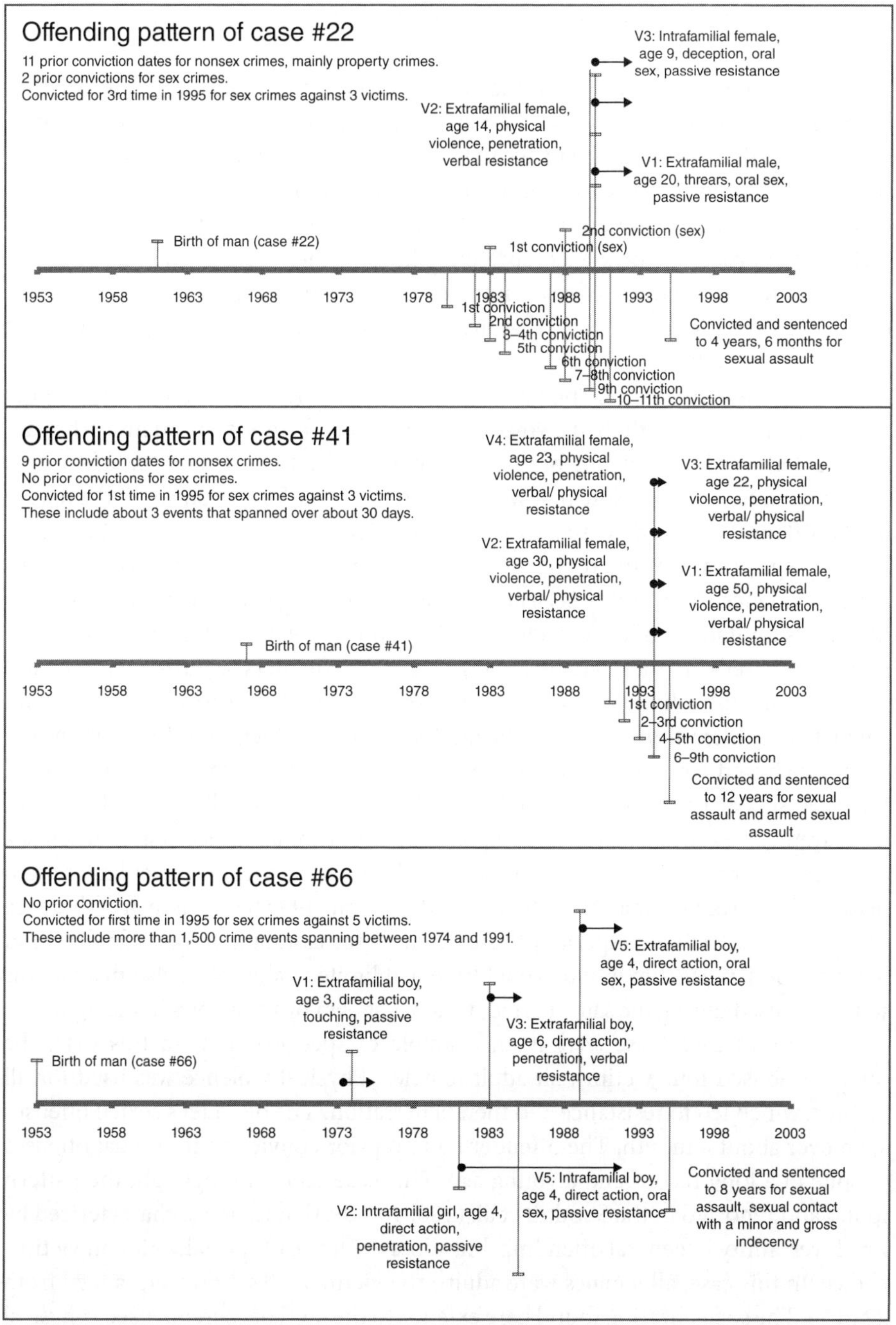
Offending pattern of case #22
11 prior conviction dates for nonsex crimes, mainly property crimes.
2 prior convictions for sex crimes.
Convicted for 3rd time in 1995 for sex crimes against 3 victims.
V3: Intrafamilial female, age 9, deception, oral sex, passive resistance
V2: Extrafamilial female, age 14, physical violence, penetration, verbal resistance
V1: Extrafamilial male, age 20, threars, oral sex, passive resistance
Birth of man (case #22)
2nd conviction (sex)
1st conviction (sex)
1953 1958 1963 1968 1973 1978 1983 1988 1993 1998 2003
1st conviction
2nd conviction
3–4th conviction
5th conviction
6th conviction
7–8th conviction
9th conviction
10–11th conviction
Convicted and sentenced to 4 years, 6 months for sexual assault
Offending pattern of case #41
9 prior conviction dates for nonsex crimes.
No prior convictions for sex crimes.
Convicted for 1st time in 1995 for sex crimes against 3 victims.
These include about 3 events that spanned over about 30 days.
V4: Extrafamilial female, age 23, physical violence, penetration, verbal/ physical resistance
V3: Extrafamilial female, age 22, physical violence, penetration, verbal/ physical resistance
V2: Extrafamilial female, age 30, physical violence, penetration, verbal/ physical resistance
V1: Extrafamilial female, age 50, physical violence, penetration, verbal/ physical resistance
Birth of man (case #41)
1953 1958 1963 1968 1973 1978 1983 1988 1993 1998 2003
1st conviction
2–3rd conviction
4–5th conviction
6–9th conviction
Convicted and sentenced to 12 years for sexual assault and armed sexual assault
Offending pattern of case #66
No prior conviction.
Convicted for first time in 1995 for sex crimes against 5 victims.
These include more than 1,500 crime events spanning between 1974 and 1991.
V5: Extrafamilial boy, age 4, direct action, oral sex, passive resistance
V1: Extrafamilial boy, age 3, direct action, touching, passive resistance
V3: Extrafamilial boy, age 6, direct action, penetration, verbal resistance
Birth of man (case #66)
1953 1958 1963 1968 1973 1978 1983 1988 1993 1998 2003
V5: Intrafamilial boy, age 4, direct action, oral sex, passive resistance
Convicted and sentenced to 8 years for sexual assault, sexual contact with a minor and gross indecency
V2: Intrafamilial girl, age 4, direct action, penetration, passive resistance

Figure 8.1 Graphical representation of the timeline for three different offending patterns in sexual offending.

Timeline of Sexual Offending for Offending Patterns

A more qualitative perspective on the issue of crime commission over time further highlights the complexity of the phenomenon. In Figure 8.1, case studies are presented to further highlight the three main offending patterns analyzed and found in this study. A graphical representation of the timeline of sexual offending over life course of offenders is used to illustrate the dynamic nature of offending over time (calendar approach). The x-axis represents the timeline. Vertical lines above the x-axis indicate: (a) the onset of sex crime; (b) convictions for nonsex crimes; and (c) convictions for sex crimes. Note that the duration of each sex offense is highlighted by the horizontal black arrows.

The first case (case #22) shows the offending pattern of a sexual polymorphic offender. This case study had two prior convictions for a sexual offense (that are represented on the graph) before being convicted for the offenses for which this individual was sampled. Note that we did not have any information about the nature of the offenses that led to the two prior convictions, a limitation of this study. Looking specifically at the three sex offenses for which the offender was last convicted, evidence of versatility is clear. The victims were aged between 9 and 20. This highlights limitations of the current scientific clinical literature that tends to classify offenders based on their victims' ages (i.e., sex offenders against children and offenders against adults). This individual would fit both categories if caught and convicted at different time points during his period of offending. In addition, the offender abused victims of both genders, used different strategies, and performed intrusive sexual behaviors (although sexual behaviors were all of a high level of intrusiveness). Restrictions are also imposed by the criminal justice system when sex offenders return to the community, such as housing restrictions, avoiding certain places. We can see here that if the offender had been caught in between each of these sex offenses, the restrictions, especially those based on the assumption that offenders tend to target the same victim group, would have had limited value. Note also that victims were all abused during the same period, which is shown by the arrows in the figure.

The second case (case #41) is an example of specialization. In this case, the offender abused four victims, all adult females. Physical violence was used for all victims, which led to resistance and then penetration. The offender's sexual offenses span over about a month. The offender had no prior conviction for sexual offenses in spite of a long record and a young age. This case seems to highlight the pattern found and reported in the Soothill et al. (2000) study, that is, one is characterized by much versatility in general offending, but some evidence of specialization in victim-choice. In this case, all females were adults; the victims' ages, however, ranged from 22 to 50. The specialization found here extends to the level of coercion used (physical violence) and the outcome of the crime event (penetration). Specialization and crime-switching within the same offense type (e.g., sex offenses) imply that the persistent offender specializes in one offense type. This case, along with Soothill et al.'s observations, however, suggests instead the presence of a dual track in some adult sex offenders: (a) one associated with a general pattern of offending that extends beyond sexual offending and involves other offense types (i.e., criminal versatility); and (b) specialization within a particular offense type (i.e., specialization in crime commission). The coexistence of this dual track in some offenders across and within offense type could potentially reignite the specialization-versatility debate between scholars, a debate that spanned over several decades. Indeed, researchers have examined the presence of crime-switching across different forms of offense but rarely within a specific form, and the examination of both gives a different and more complete picture of offending and offenders over time.

The third case (case #66) shows no evidence of escalation or de-escalation from one victim to another, even though variations can be identified when examining offending patterns. Rather, this case shows evidence of specialization. This is true for both the offense history and the offending patterns of the offender. This offender had no prior convictions before being convicted for the offenses for which he was recruited in this study initially. This offender was convicted in 1995 for sexual offenses against five children which included more than 1,500 events occurring between 1974 and 1991. In terms of offending patterns, this offender was consistent in victim-choice and modus operandi. A young child was abused in each offense and a direct action approach was also adopted to abuse each victim. Although the offender abused victims of the same age group and used the same strategy, note that the offender also abused victims of both genders (i.e., a young girl once) and used different settings to target victims (i.e., intra- and extrafamilial). In this case, different sexual behaviors were also performed from one victim to another (i.e., touching, oral sex, and penetration). Based on the literature on sexual offending, this case would be the classic case of an offender embedded in chronic child sexual offending. This would also be the case upon which most current policies and legislations aimed at targeting persistent sex offenders would be based. However, as indicated above, there are still some important variations in terms of offending patterns. For instance, this offender abused in both intra- and extrafamilial settings. Again, one could expect policies such as residency restrictions, for which the purpose is to limit the access of convicted offenders to potential victims by imposing minimal distance restrictions between the offender's residence and areas where children congregate (e.g., parks and school), to be mostly ineffective in preventing reoffending.

Limitations of the Study

A larger sample size would be necessary to complete a more focused investigation of offending patterns. In this study, we used a sample of 216 offenders who abused multiple victims. As the number of offenders decreased over transitions, our analysis of covariates of offending patterns was performed for only one transition. It was not possible to complete statistical analysis on a full model containing covariates either. Some of the individual covariates found in this study may prove to be nonsignificant when controlling for all covariates. A larger sample would also permit to separate sexual offenders against children and sexual offenders against women in such an investigation. In this context, we would expect to find variations within offending patterns for each group of offenders, which would be relevant for criminal justice policies. For the reasons above, this study is exploratory. Another limitation is the nature of self-reported data. Some offenders probably minimized the seriousness of the strategies they used or the intrusiveness of the sexual behaviors they performed. Minimization is the most obvious shortcoming of self-reported data. On the other hand, when it comes to understanding offending patterns, collecting data from actors themselves remains an effective way to obtain such information. In addition, the use of official data as well may have reduced limitations associated with self-reported data.

The data set used in this study only provides offense details per victim. An examination of the evolution of strategies and sexual behaviors within victims could prove to be informative for understanding offending patterns. Without data on each episode for a single victim, patterns of escalation might be difficult to detect. At the same time, however, it should be noted that Lussier, Bouchard, and Beauregard (2011) recently showed that the use of physical violence is uncharacteristic of offenders who specialize in sex crimes, are involved in a higher number of crime events over a long period of time, and who remain undetected for a longer period of time. The use of physical violence, therefore, is not typical of sex offenders following an event-oriented strategy that aims to revictimize the same victim over a substantial period of time. A pivotal aspect of their offending is rather to establish a level of trust with the victim (e.g., Leclerc & Tremblay, 2007; Leclerc, Wortley, & Smallbone, 2011) to maintain the victimization, and, as a result, the crime opportunity. Physical violence increases the risk of being reported to the police, which could prevent offenders who seek to secure victims' compliance for repetitive sexual contact from using this strategy. Lastly, an investigation of offending patterns from one victim to another would also benefit from longitudinal data. A specialist might change his offending pattern and escalate (or de-escalate) in the future. Our study only provides a snapshot of offending patterns in sexual offending over time for a group of offenders.

Conclusion

The main purpose of this study was to assess whether or not offending patterns of sexual offenders change from one victim to another. Our investigation was conducted in three steps. The first step consisted of completing transition matrices to examine whether offenders would adopt a particular strategy to sexually abuse a victim and perform the same sexual behaviors from one victim to another. Then the second step consisted of analyzing the synchronicity of change of patterns of strategies and patterns of sexual behaviors over time. The third and final step was to identify covariates that would help explain why offenders change their offending patterns over time. These analyses allowed us to identify not only the presence of specialization in offending patterns, but most important, the presence of versatility.

In particular, apart from an offending pattern characterized by specialization, two other offending patterns characterized by versatility were found: escalation and de-escalation. A number of offense characteristics, such as age and gender of the victim and victim resistance, were also found to co-vary with these patterns. Taken together, these findings point in one direction: Offending patterns in sexual offending over time are likely to be dynamic. The dynamic nature of offending patterns in sexual offending leads us to believe that criminal justice policies should at least consider empirical evidence showing that specialization is not the only offending pattern exhibited by offenders. Considering that this study was somewhat a first of its kind, results should be considered as exploratory. For instance, this study did not include information on the complete sequence of behaviors during the offender-victim interchange (e.g., offender response to victim reactions) and circumstances surrounding each offense (e.g., location for abuse, the use of alcohol and drugs, presence of guardianship). With such information, we could better understand and highlight the dynamic nature of offending patterns in sexual offending. In sum, more studies are needed on the dynamic nature of sexual offending and this should be accounted for in the development (or improvement) of criminal justice policies targeting sexual offenders.

References

Abel, G. G., & Rouleau, J. L. (1990). The nature and extent of sexual assault. In W. L. Marshall, D. R. Laws, & H. E. Barbaree (Eds.), *Handbook of sexual assault: Issues, theories, and treatment of the offender*. Applied Clinical Psychology. New York: Plenum Press.

Beauregard, E., & Leclerc, B. (2007). An application of the rational choice approach to the offending process of sex offenders: A closer look at the decision-making. *Sexual Abuse: A Journal of Research and Treatment, 19*, 115–133.

Berliner, L., & Conte, J. R. (1990). The process of victimization: The victim's perspective. *Child Abuse and Neglect, 14*, 29–40.

Cann, J., Friendship, C., & Gonza, L. (2007). Assessing crossover in a sample of sexual offenders with multiple victims. *Legal and Criminological Psychology, 12*, 149–163.

Cohen, J. (1986). Research on criminal careers: Individual frequency rates and offense seriousness. In A. Blumstein, J. Cohen, J. A. Roth, & C. A. Visher (Eds.), *Criminal careers and "career criminals"* (pp. 292–418). Washington, DC: National Academy Press.

Conte, J. R., Wolf, S., & Smith, T. (1989). What sexual offenders tell us about prevention strategies. *Child Abuse and Neglect, 13*, 293–301.

Deslauriers-Varin, N., & Beauregard, E. (2010). Victims' routine activities and sex offenders' target selection scripts: A latent class analysis. *Sexual Abuse: A Journal of Research and Treatment, 22*, 315–342.

Douglas, J. E., Burgess, A. W., Burgess, A. G., & Ressler, R. K. (1997). *Crime classification manual*. San Francisco: Jossey-Bass Publishers.

Gebhard, P., Gagnon, J., Pomeroy, W., & Christensen, C. (1965). *Sex offenders: An analysis of types*. New York: Harper and Row.

Goldstein, S. L. (1999). Commission of the crime. In S. L. Goldstein (Ed.), *The sexual exploitation of children: A practical guide to assessment, investigation, and intervention* (pp. 113–172). Boca Raton: CRC Press.

Guay, J.-P., Proulx, J., Cusson, M., & Ouimet, M. (2001). Victim-choice polymorphia among serious sex offenders. *Archives of Sexual Behavior, 30*, 521–533.

Heil, P., Ahlmeyer, S., & Simons, D. (2003). Crossover sexual offenses. *Sexual Abuse: A Journal of Research and Treatment, 15*, 221–236.

Kaufman, K. L., Hilliker, D. R., & Daleiden, E. L. (1996). Subgroup differences in the modus operandi of adolescent sexual offenders. *Child Maltreatment, 1*, 17–24.

Kaufman, K. L., Holmberg, J. K., Orts, K. A., McCrady, F. E., Rotzien, A. L., Daleiden, E. L., & Hilliker, D. R. (1998). Factors influencing sexual offenders' modus operandi: An examination of victim-offender relatedness and age. *Child Maltreatment, 3*, 349–361.

Leclerc, B., Beauregard, E., & Proulx, J. (2008). Modus operandi and situational aspects in adolescent sexual offenses against children: A further examination. *International Journal of Offender Therapy and Comparative Criminology, 52*, 46–61.

Leclerc, B., Carpentier, J., & Proulx, J. (2006). Strategies adopted by sexual offenders to involve children in sexual activity. In R. Wortley & S. Smallbone (Eds.), *Situational prevention of child sexual abuse* (pp. 251–270). Crime Prevention Studies, Vol. *19*. Monsey, NY: Criminal Justice Press.

Leclerc, B., Proulx, J., Lussier, P., & Allaire, J.-F. (2009). Offender-victim interaction and crime event outcomes: Modus operandi and victim effects on the risk of intrusive sexual offenses against children. *Criminology, 47*, 595–618.

Leclerc, B. Smallbone, S., & Wortley, R. (2013). Interpersonal scripts and victim reaction in child sexual abuse: A quantitative analysis of the offender-victim interchange. In B. Leclerc and R. Wortley (Eds.), Cognition and crime: Offender decision-making and script analyses. *Crime Science Series*, London, UK: Routledge.

Leclerc, B., & Tremblay, P. (2007). Strategic behavior in adolescent sexual offenses against children: Linking modus operandi to sexual behaviors. *Sexual Abuse: A Journal of Research and Treatment, 19*, 23–41.

Leclerc, B., Wortley, R., & Smallbone, S. (2011). Getting into the script of adult child sex offenders and mapping out situational prevention measures. *Journal of Research in Crime and Delinquency, 48*, 209–237.

Lussier, P. (2005). The criminal activity of sexual offenders in adulthood: Revisiting the specialization debate. *Sexual Abuse: A Journal of Research and Treatment, 17*, 269–292.

Lussier, P., Bouchard, M., & Beauregard, E. (2011). Patterns of criminal achievement in sexual offending: Unravelling the "successful sex offender." *Journal of Criminal Justice, 39*, 433–444.

Lussier, P., Leblanc, M., & Proulx, J. (2005). The generality of criminal behavior: A confirmatory factor analysis of the criminal activity of sex offenders in adulthood. *Journal of Criminal Justice, 33*, 177–189.

Lussier, P., Leclerc, B., Healey, J., & Proulx, J. (2008). Generality of deviance and predation: Crime-switching and specialization patterns in persistent sexual offenders. In M. Delisi & P. Conis (Eds.), *Violent offenders: Theory, public policy and practice* (pp. 97–140). Boston, MA: Jones and Bartlett Publishers.

Radzinowicz, L. (1957). *Sexual offences: A Report of the Cambridge Department of Criminal Justice*. London: MacMillan.

Reppucci, N. D., & Haugaard, J. J. (1989). Prevention of child sexual abuse: Myth or reality. *American Psychologist, 44*, 1266–1275.

Sjostedt, G., Langstrom, N., Sturidsson, K., & Grann, M. (2004). Stability of modus operandi in sexual offending. *Criminal Justice and Behavior, 31*, 609–623.

Smallbone, S., & Wortley, R. (2000). *Child sexual abuse in Queensland: Offender characteristics and modus operandi.* Brisbane, Australia: Queensland Crime Commission.

Soothill, K., Francis, B., Sanderson, B., & Ackerley, E. (2000). Sex offenders: Specialists, generalists – or both? *British Journal of Criminology, 40*, 56–67.

Tedeschi, J. T., & Felson, R. B. (1994). *Violence, aggression, and coercive actions.* Washington, DC: American Psychological Association.

Ullman, S. E. (1997). Review and critique of empirical studies of rape avoidance. *Criminal Justice and Behavior, 24*, 177–204.

Ullman, S. E. (2007). A 10-year update of "Review and critique of empirical studies of rape avoidance." *Criminal Justice and Behavior, 34*, 411–429.

Weinrott, M. R., & Saylor, M. (1991). Self-report of crimes committed by sex offenders. *Journal of Interpersonal Violence, 6*, 286–300.

Wortley, R., & Smallbone, S. (2006). Applying situational principles to sexual offenses against children. In R. Wortley and S. Smallbone (Eds.), *Situational prevention of child sexual abuse* (pp. 7–35). Crime Prevention Studies, Vol. *19*. Monsey, NY: Criminal Justice Press.

9

Criminal Career Features of Female Sexual Offenders

Miriam Wijkman
VU University, the Netherlands

Catrien Bijleveld
NSCR and VU University, the Netherlands

Introduction

This chapter describes a seldom studied group of offenders: females who commit sexual offenses. Female sexual offenders are seldom studied, the most prominent reason probably being that the prevalence of female sexual offending is low. As we will detail below, female sexual offenders make up just a very small fraction of offenders arrested or adjudicated for sexual offenses. Research based on victimization surveys and official data suggest that less than 5% of sexual offenses involve a female perpetrator (Cortoni & Hanson, 2005). From a methodological standpoint, this creates statistical issues due to the small numbers of female offenders typically found in samples of sexual offenders. As a result, female offenders more often than not are excluded from empirical studies rather than analyzed separately from male offenders. A second reason for the lack of research into female sexual offending is that sexual offending is typically not considered feminine behavior. In fact, in the Netherlands until 1991, and similarly so in other countries (e.g., Canada until 1983 and England until 1994), females could by definition not be guilty of rape as the description of the offense was such that only a male could commit the act (Bijleveld, 2007; Horvath, Tong, & Williams, 2011; Tang, 1998).

Over the past years, however, there has been a rising interest in the background and characteristics of female sexual offenders, in all probability, against the backdrop of a general rising interest in female offenders. Research into female sexual offending initially started out viewing female sexual offenders as psychologically disturbed or suffering from some psychiatric disorder. Recent research, however, tends to study female perpetrators' characteristics in such a way that they can be compared to those of male sexual offenders or to those of female offenders in

Sex Offenders: A Criminal Career Approach, First Edition. Edited by Arjan Blokland and Patrick Lussier.

general. The scant literature thus far available shows adult female sexual offenders to constitute a heterogeneous group: some female sexual offenders co-offend with male partners, while others do not, some suffer from mental health issues, while others do not, some offend against (their own) children, while others offend against adult strangers or acquaintances. Some authors have attempted to categorize female offenders into subtypes (e.g., Matthews, Matthews & Speltz, 1991), while others have shown that distinctions between subtypes are fuzzy (see e.g., Wijkman, Bijleveld, & Hendriks, 2010). Empirical research further underscores the high prevalence of (childhood) abuse and mental health disorders, and the prominent role these risk factors are presumed to play in the etiology of female sexual offending (Harris, 2010). Research into criminal careers of adult female sexual offenders has shown sexual recidivism rates to be low, varying between 0 and 2% across empirical studies (for a review see Cortoni, Hanson, & Coache, 2010). The same research, however, highlights that 1 in 5 female sexual offenders reoffend, suggesting that if female sexual offenders persist in criminal behavior it is most likely for nonsex crimes. At the same time, empirical research has also shown that a relatively high proportion of female sexual offenders can be considered as sex crime specialists as their criminal history is composed mainly of sex offenses (Wijkman, Bijleveld, & Hendriks, 2011). This suggests the presence of at least two subgroups in the female sexual offender population: one characterized by just one or a few convictions for sexual crimes and another of more prolific offenders, whose criminal career is composed of a wider variety of crimes, including sexual offenses. Still, given that few empirical studies have been conducted, it is difficult to draw firm conclusions about the criminal careers of adult female sexual offenders. At what age do female sexual offenders generally start offending? Does sexual offending in females coincide with, precede, or lag behind the onset of other types of offending among females? Basic descriptive questions as to how the careers of female sexual offenders can be characterized in terms of standard criminal career parameters, such as age of onset, offending rate (lambda), duration, and desistance, are still in need of answering.

The current lack of empirical knowledge on the criminal careers of female sexual offenders explains, at least in part, why theory development on female sexual offenders' criminal careers has remained rudimentary and untested. To begin to understand the nature and development of female sexual offending, it is important to know to what extent the knowledge gathered on the criminal careers of female offenders generalizes to the female sexual offender population. What are the correlates of persistence and desistance in sexual offending in female offenders? As different kinds of women with different backgrounds commit different kinds of sexual offenses, some of the parameters of female sexual offenders' criminal careers are likely to vary with these background characteristics, and offense types. Predictability of escalation or cessation of sexual crimes is essential to risk assessment and treatment. Over what time span do these female offenders remain involved in crime, and what is the "crime mix" during their criminal careers? Do the criminal careers of female sexual offenders show signs of escalation, starting out with minor crimes and gradually committing more serious offenses (among which sex offenses)? Again, answers to even these basic questions will be of enormous help to practitioners and policymakers in deciding who to target and when to target them, and in tailoring their efforts in a way that is most effective.

For the current study, we will focus on adult female perpetrators of hands-on sexual offenses. A focus on adult offenders was chosen because, just as male juvenile sexual offenders differ from adult male sexual offenders, it is highly likely that juvenile female sexual offenders constitute a group that is etiologically distinct from adult female sexual offenders. Prospective and retrospective research on juvenile and adult male sexual offending does suggest that, for the most part, these two behaviors are committed by two distinct populations (e.g., Lussier, Blokland, Mathesius, Pardini, & Loeber, this book). For now, we deem it reasonable to think that the same may apply to female sexual offenders. In other words, today's juvenile female sexual offenders are most likely not tomorrow's adult female sexual offenders and neither are today's adult female sexual offenders yesterday's juvenile female sexual offenders. In addition, we limit the current effort to hands-on sexual offending. The study uses Dutch data, and under Dutch law hands-off sexual offending comprises a very heterogeneous set of offenses including indecent exposure, producing and possessing child pornography, trafficking of individuals (to work in the sex industry), and brotheling. Given that perpetrators of these types of offenses are likely to differ widely from hands-on sexual offenders – as well as among each other (Laws & O'Donohue, 2008) – in terms of etiology and criminal career characteristics, we discard females convicted for hands-off offenses from our analyses. In an effort to contribute to the sparse but growing literature on female sexual offenders, this chapter will examine the criminal histories of a sample of adult female sexual offenders in order to answer the following research questions:

1 What are the characteristics of criminal careers of female sexual offenders, in terms of age of onset, offending frequency, duration, and desistance?
2 How do these characteristics vary by offender type and prominent background characteristics within the group of female sexual offenders?

These research questions are relevant from an empirical, theoretical, and policy perspective.

Before turning to our data, the next section presents a brief review of the prevalence of female sexual offending as well as offenders' background characteristics based on previous research.

Prevalence

In the Netherlands, for each year between 1999 and 2009 female arrestees constitute around 2–3% of all those arrested for sexual offenses (Heer-de Lang & Kalidien, 2010). Female sexual offenders most often are arrested for sexually offending against children. An even smaller proportion is actually prosecuted: females comprise around 1.5% of all suspects prosecuted for sexual offenses. Similar percentages are reported for Canada, Texas, England, and Wales (Saradjian, 2010). Obviously, official statistics suffer from a number of limitations that victim survey data may be less sensitive to (although, in the area of sexual offending these may be particularly problematic in their own right). For the Netherlands, no general victimization data are available on sexual victimization by females. Some studies, however, have focused on sexual victimization under specific circumstances. A study by Draijer (1988), for example, reported that 1 in 6 women had been sexually abused by a relative (no distinction was made concerning the gender of the relative). Another study on domestic violence also included questions on sexual violence, and victims in this study reported that they were sexually victimized by at least one female family member (Dijk, Veen, & Cox, 2010).

Based on a review of various surveys conducted in a number of countries using different samples (i.e., sexually abused males attending a clinic, childline cases, and incidence studies) Saradjian (2010) estimates that between 14 and 52% of sexually victimized boys were sexually abused by a woman, and that between 1 and 9.3% of sexually victimized girls were sexually abused by a woman. As these studies differed widely in terms of sampled populations and survey methodology, it is hard to derive a more precise prevalence estimate. Cortoni et al. (2010) likely conducted the most comprehensive review of reported prevalence rates to date, covering several countries, including Canada, the United Kingdom, the United States, Australia, and New Zealand, and including data from victim surveys as well as official statistics. These authors conclude that when it comes to sexual offending the male-to-female ratio is about 20:1, with females being responsible for approximately 4–5% of all committed sexual offenses. Thus, it appears that females are responsible for only a small fraction of all sexual offending. A comparison of victim surveys and official statistics shows that the proportion of female perpetrators is consistently higher in victim surveys than in official data (14% compared to 4% on average), pointing to differential disclosure, arrest, and/or prosecution and conviction. The proportion of offenses that does not appear in official statistics thus is higher for female than for male sexual offenders. A separate, though equally scarce, literature exists on sexual coercion. A study by Struckman-Johnson (1988) showed that 22% of women, and 16% of men, had been forced to engage in sexual intercourse on a date at least once during their lifetime. Muehlenhard and Cook (1988) also found a high prevalence of victimization of males. In fact, their findings showed that more men (62.7%) than women (46.3%) had experienced unwanted intercourse. Struckman-Johnson, Struckman-Johnson, and Anderson (2003) reported that 26% of the surveyed women in their study reported having used at least one type of sexually coercive tactic with a person of the opposite sex (compared to 43% of men). Other studies also find that women engage in a wide range of sexual activities with unwilling men, including nonpenetrative and penetrative acts (Krahé, Scheinberger-Olwig, & Bieneck, 2003; Slotboom, Hendriks, & Verbruggen, 2011).

The studies on sexual coercion thus consistently report small differences in the prevalence of sexual offending between females and males, although females do appear to commit less serious or invasive acts than their male counterparts. The sexual coercion literature thus supports our second conclusion that the so-called dark figure, those committed offenses that do not end up in official statistics, is higher for female than for male sexual offenders.

While the above-mentioned studies are typically based on general population, we now turn our attention to empirical studies conducted with convicted female offenders.

Recidivism

Cortoni, Hanson, and Coache (2010) conducted a meta-analysis of female sexual offenders' recidivism. Their study used data on 2,490 female sexual offenders all of whom had officially entered the criminal justice system. These data covered offenders from Australia, Canada, England, the Netherlands, and the United States. Over a follow-up period of approximately 6.5 years, sexual recidivism totaled 3.2%, violent recidivism 6.5%, and general recidivism 24.5%. After removal of one outlier study from the United States that used extremely wide definitions of sexual offending, the sexual recidivism rate dropped to less than 2%. Hanson and Bussière (1998), studying male sexual offenders over a similar period, reported recidivism rates of 13–14% for sex offenses, 25% for violent offenses, and a little over 27% for general offenses. Thus, it appears that, particularly for sexual offenses, female sexual offenders' recidivism rates are much lower than those of their male counterparts. This again may be due to differential reporting and prosecution of sexual offending by females, but given the large discrepancy, it is unlikely that this would explain all of the difference. Freeman and Sandler (2008), however, reported that after controlling for relevant risk factors, the hazard for rearrest for a sexual offense does not differ between males and females. Yet, as Soothill (2010) remarked, given the very low base rate and thus absolute numbers of females (N = 6) actually reoffending sexually, this finding is not to be taken as definitive. We thus tentatively conclude that sexual recidivism is lower for female sexual offenders than for male sexual offenders. These studies also show that if female sexual offenders do persist in offending after having committed their sex crime, their reconviction is most likely for a nonsex crime, which is also a common thing in male sexual offenders. This suggests that, for persistent female offenders, sexual offending may be part of a more general criminal career pattern.

Characteristics of Female Sexual Offenders

While it must be understood that this is still a relatively new area of investigation, the preliminary findings of studies focusing on the characteristics of female offenders have relevance for our current effort. First, these studies suggest that many adult female sexual offenders commit their sex crimes with a co-offender. The prevalence of co-offending varies between 46 and 75% across studies, which suggests that for every two female sexual offenders, one had a co-offender (Faller, 1987; Gannon, Rose, & Ward, 2008; Lewis & Stanley, 2000; Vandiver, 2006; Wijkman et al., 2010). Often, the co-offender is a male and the woman's intimate partner at the time of commission of the offense. Wijkman et al. (2010) found this was so in 63% of all co-offending cases, which is much higher when compared with adult males, for whom sexual co-offending rates for the Netherlands and the United Kingdom ranged between 7 and 23% (Bijleveld & Soudijn, 2008; Woodhams, 2009). Secondly, female sexual offenders are found to often abuse children, in many cases their own. Vandiver and Kercher (2004) report that 37% of the victims of female sexual offenders were somehow related to the offender. Peter (2009) reports that in comparison to male sexual offenders many more victims of female sexual offenders are young children; as many as 92% of female sexual offender victims were under 9 years of age.

Virtually all studies on female sexual offenders report high levels of sexual abuse in childhood, with clinical samples reporting higher levels than prosecution samples. Green and Kaplan (1994), Matthews et al. (1991), and McCarty (1986) reported levels ranging from 60 to 100% in clinical samples, while Wijkman et al. (2010) reported a prevalence rate of childhood sexual victimization of 31% in a prosecution sample. Harris (2010) stated that childhood victimization is a pivotal though not a sufficient factor in the etiology of sexual offending in women, especially for those who offend against young children. Physical abuse (in some cases by the male co-perpetrator) is also reported. Lewis and Stanley (2000) found that 80% of female sexual offenders in their sample had been threatened or actually physically abused by a male sexual partner. Wijkman et al. (2010) reported that a quarter of the women in their study had previously been in a violent relationship while 34% had a violent partner at the time of the offense.

The last striking finding is the high prevalence of mental disorders in female sexual offenders. Depression and suicidal thoughts, post-traumatic stress disorders, anxiety disorders, cognitive disorders, low intellectual functioning, and personality disorders are commonly reported (Bumby & Bumby, 1997; Faller, 1987; Kaplan & Green, 1995; Matthews et al., 1991). In recent research psychotic disorders are rarely reported (Grayston & De Luca, 1999; Vandiver & Walker, 2002), while in older studies psychoses were seen as a distinctive feature of female sexual offenders (Herman & Hirschman, 1981). Wijkman et al. (2010) reported that 40% of the women in their sample were diagnosed with an Axis I disorder included in the DSM (Diagnostic Statistical Manual), 42% were diagnosed with an Axis II disorder, while 23% were diagnosed with a disorder on both Axis I and Axis II.

Many studies on the background of female sexual offenders and the etiology of their offending behavior have employed (sometimes very small) clinical samples. In such clinical samples, it may be the case that women have been referred for psychological or psychiatric complaints and that only while in treatment the sexual offending becomes known. That means first, that findings on the prevalence of personality disorders and trauma should be interpreted with caution. Second, important differences can be expected whenever findings from clinical samples are compared to findings from nonclinical samples, such as from the criminal justice system.

In summary, it seems that the average adult female sexual offender as portrayed in the literature is someone who often suffered from mental disorders. The high prevalence of sexual abuse victimization is prominent, in addition to physical abuse and neglect, which continues sometimes well into adulthood. Furthermore, female sexual offenders remarkably often co-offend with a male (intimate) partner. Finally, it appears that female sexual offenders relatively often abuse (their own) young children. All these aspects may impact the criminal careers of these females. It may be that psychological disorders – if left untreated – lead to chronicity in (sexual) offending. Given that a majority of female sexual offenders appear to offend with a (male) co-perpetrator, sexual offending in females may, on the other hand, be more situational or opportunistic, which would suggest that desistance could occur swiftly once the deviant partner (in crime) disappears from the scene. Yet, the fact that many women are involved in the abuse of their own children may, on the other hand, result in a relatively extended criminal career, as underage children remain vulnerable targets in a secluded family setting.

Still, not all female sexual offenders have been traumatized, nor do all co-offend with a (male) partner, and not all abuse young children, suggesting there might be different types of female sexual offenders, with distinct etiologies, and distinct developmental pathways. A number of studies have attempted to address the heterogeneity within the group of female sexual offenders by searching for distinct subtypes (Matthews et al., 1991; Sandler & Freeman, 2007; Sarrel & Masters, 1982; Vandiver & Kercher, 2004; Wijkman et al., 2010). Such studies have generated partly overlapping, partly different subtypes of female sexual offenders. Most have produced fuzzy profiles that have not been strongly empirically linked to criminal career aspects. A prominent and recurrent subtype is that of a woman involved in a relationship (often reciprocal) with a (much) younger man, such as a "teacher-lover" relationship, or a sexual relationship between a therapist and a patient. A second subtype is that of female offenders with a history of physical and/or sexual abuse who by themselves or together with a partner abuse their own children or a child acquaintance. A third is the male-coerced subtype, women who either participate under force in the abuse of their child or children or who do not protect their children against the abuse, initiated by their husband or intimate partner. A fourth subtype is a young and solo-operating woman, without marked mental disturbances, who commit acts like fondling and/or oral sex on often young male relatives or acquaintances. Finally, a small subgroup is made up of women who, acting alone, have intercourse with or sexually penetrate their usually older (male or female) nonfamily victims.

The "subtypes" of female sexual offenders mentioned above are distinguished based on a number of characteristics, or "themes." A first characteristic is whether the sexual offenses occurred with the (presumed) approval of both partners, though without legal consent. A second aspect is whether the woman operates alone or with a co-offender (almost always male). A third, partially overlapping, aspect is whether the woman offends with her male intimate partner. A fourth aspect is the presence of mental disturbances in the offender. A final aspect is the age of the victim. In the below description of the criminal careers of the female sexual offenders in our sample, we will use these characteristics to make comparisons and examine the extent to which these characteristics are related to the various criminal career dimensions.

Method

Sample

The sample used in this study is comprised of all 135 adult females who had been prosecuted in the Netherlands for at least one hands-on sexual offense between 1994 and 2007 and was originally presented in a previous study conducted by Wijkman et al. (2011). In that sense, the current sample constitutes the entire population of known female sex offenses in the Netherlands during that 14-year period. Given that the Netherlands does not have the judicial practice of plea bargaining, the offense categorization under which an offense is registered at the Public Prosecutors Office can be assumed to reflect the actual nature of the offense that has taken place. All women who were acquitted or whose case was dismissed by the public prosecutor for "technical reasons" (understood to imply in the Netherlands that the prosecutor drops the case as he or she expects the case to end in acquittal) have been removed. All remaining women were either convicted or had their case dismissed by the prosecutor for policy reasons, such as that the defendant had started therapy or had paid damages to the victim. Cases under this uniquely Dutch system of prosecutorial expediency are counted as "convictions" in academic research in the Netherlands (Wartna, Blom, & Tollenaar, 2008).

Variables and Measuring Instruments

For all women, complete criminal career information was available based on the General Documentation Files (GDF) of the Dutch Criminal Record Office. The GDFs contain all offenses ever registered by the Dutch Public Prosecutor's Office, starting at age 12, which is the minimum age of criminal responsibility in the Netherlands. Only those offenses for which the women had been convicted or which ended in a "policy dismissal" by the public prosecutor were retained for analysis; the reasons for this being that in these cases, according to the judgement of the last official who assessed the case, these women had committed the offense. Both guilty verdicts and policy dismissals were labeled as "convictions" in reconstructing the women's criminal careers. The last date of retrieval of criminal career information was December 2011. The prospective follow-up time thus ranged from 4 to 17 years, with an average of 13.7 years after the index offense. At the time criminal history information on these women was last retrieved, the female sexual offenders in our sample were 48.9 years old on average. The average total observation period for which we have criminal history information starting at age 12 up to the offenders' age in 2011 was almost 37 years.

In addition, prosecution and court files for all 135 females were analyzed. From these, offender and offense variables were scored using a scoring tool that was previously developed by Hendriks and Bijleveld (2006), and which has shown reasonable to good reliability and has been used extensively in various studies by Hendriks (2006; see also Hendriks for specific information on reliability of coding). For the current purpose, this scoring tool was supplemented with a number of variables deemed particularly important for female sexual offenders, such as the nature of the relationship and other characteristics of any co-offender(s). Court files in the Netherlands always contain the charge and the judicial decision, in which it is specified what offense the defendant was charged with and, in the case of a court verdict, found guilty of, as well as a verbal description of what behavioral acts were determined proven by the court. Each court file contains a detailed charge by the prosecutor, which lists the acts purportedly committed by the defendant, entailing a factual description of the physical acts committed, and against which victims. Psychological or psychiatric screening reports may be included if they were requested, carried out by certified psychologists/psychiatrists by appointment of the Ministry of Justice. Clinical judgments are included. For more on the data collection procedure for this specific study, see Wijkman et al. (2011).

For our current analysis purposes, we use the following variables: (a) *age of onset* – defined as the age at which the first conviction for any offense, starting at age 12, was incurred; (b) *criminal career duration* – defined as the age at which the last conviction was incurred minus the onset age, with time spent incarcerated and/or in secure hospital treatment subtracted. For women with only one offense (the sampling offense) criminal career duration is set as missing; (c) *lambda* – defined as the total number of convictions for any crime divided by total criminal career duration. A small number of women were convicted for a very large number of offenses (e.g., twice-weekly abuse of two children over a large number of years) but were first convicted sometime after the sexual abuse had commenced. As including these extreme cases would spuriously inflate lambda and cause outliers at certain ages, we truncated the number of convictions in these cases at 104, denoting a twice-weekly abuse spanning 1 year; (d) *desistance* – defined as having remained conviction-free for any crime for at least 5 years before the last date of criminal career data extraction, that is, December 2011. From the court files, it was inferred whether the sexual offending had taken place during a purportedly reciprocal relationship (approved of by both partners, but without the possibility of legal consent), whether the woman had had one or more co-offenders, whether any co-offender(s) had been her intimate partner, the age of the victim(s), the presence of mental disorders as diagnosed by screening psychologists and/or psychiatrists, and whether the offender had reported herself having been abused sexually and/or physically.

Analyses

To analyze the extent to which offender subtypes were related to criminal career dimensions, t-tests were performed for interval level variables, and chi-square tests for nominal variables. We tested one-sided when a hypothesis allowed so. Given that we conducted a large number of tests, we might have tested more conservatively. As we carried out our study on a relatively small sample, we have, however, stuck to a standard 5% alpha.

Results

General Description: Background, Criminal Career Characteristics, and Sentences

A description of our sample in terms of demographics and criminal history characteristics at the time of the sampling offense is given in Table 9.1. The vast majority of perpetrators were ethnic Dutch (84%, N = 113). At the time of commission of the sampling offense the women were on average 35 years, which seems relatively old given that general offending peaks during late adolescence. The most common final educational level was elementary school, which is exceptionally low for the Netherlands, or special education (N = 64).

For almost two thirds of the women in our sample, the sampling sex offense was the first offense these women were convicted for. For all but one woman, the sampling sex offense was the first sex offense they had been prosecuted for. This, however, is not to say that a large majority had committed only one sex offense upon being prosecuted for the sampling offense. The court files of these women reveal that one charge could pertain to the repeated abuse of one child, or the abuse of several victims that came to light when they were arrested for the sampling sex offense. Almost one third (31%) of the women included in our sample received a prison sentence, with the average length of that prison sentence being 2.1 years.

Criminal Career Dimensions

The average age at which the women had started their criminal career – as measured by their age at commission of the first offense (any offense) they were prosecuted for – was over 33 years, and is given in Table 9.2. The average age at which they had first committed a sexual offense was approximately 35 years. Over their entire career, more than half (51%) of the women committed other offenses besides sex offenses. After the sampling offense, very few committed other offenses: 131 desisted (defined as staying free from offending for a period of at least 5 years before the last date the offending data were collected, i.e., 2011). Average criminal career duration was 3.7 years for all women (SD = 5.3). Thus, we conclude that the vast majority of female

Table 9.1 Associations Between Typological Aspects, Background Characteristics, and Criminal Career Parameters

	%	*Mean*	*SD*
Personal characteristics			
Ethnicity			
Dutch	84		
Netherlands Antilles	4		
Surinam	3		
Turkey	2		
Other West-European	7		
Age		35	
Married	55		
Children	41		
Type of sampling offense			
242 (rape)	24		
243 (sexual intercourse with incapacitated)	2		
244 (sexual intercourse with person <12 years)	13		
245 (sexual intercourse with person 12–16 years)	9		
246 (sexual assault)	8		
247 (sexual abuse of a minor)	27		
249 (sexual acts with abuse of authority)	17		
Co-offender	62		
Not present partner	12		
Present partner	88		
Sentence following sampling offense			
Prison term	32		
Length of prison term		2.1 year	2.9 year
Criminal history			
Prior offenses	36.30		
Sexual	0.1		
Violent	5.2		
Property	18.5		
Other	12.5		

sexual offenders tend to desist after prosecution for the sex offense. This ties in with what was found in the literature regarding sexual recidivism: very few reoffend to a sexual offense. About half had committed other offenses as well, mostly before the sampling sexual offense.

Using latent class analysis, Wijkman et al. (2011) summarized the criminal careers of the women in our sample based on the mix of crimes these women had been convicted for. About 16% had committed only one sexual offense and no other offenses. These were labeled as "once-only offenders." Two other groups were distinguished: a group of generalists (27%, who combine sexual offending with relatively many

Table 9.2 Criminal Career Characteristics of Female Sexual Offenders (N = 135)

	Range	*Mean*	*SD*
Age of onset	15.9–58.5	33.1	10.7
Sexual	15.9–60.1	35.2	10.4
Violent	17.6–40.2	28.2	8.9
Property	16.6–49.0	28.3	10
Other	18.0–51.4	32.6	9.8
Duration criminal career (year)	0–28.5	3.7	5.3
Age at desistance	20.9–65.5	40.1	10.5
Frequency	N		
Sexual	2		
Violent	16		
Property	29		
Other	55		
Crime mix	%		
Sex only	44.4		
Sex and nonsex	55.6		
Criminal career	%		
Only index offense	49.0		
Prior and index	25.2		
Index and recidivism	14.8		
Prior, index, and recidivism	11.1		

serious other, often violent, offenses) and specialists (57%, who commit relatively many sex offenses next to some minor offenses). The analysis thus showed that quite a number of female sexual offenders specialize in sexual offending.

As the authors noted, the group of female sex crime specialists may actually comprise further, qualitatively different types of specialist sexual offenders. A qualitative analysis of their file information showed that some of the female sexual offenders in the group of sex crime specialists had abused their own child repeatedly, in a similar fashion, over a number of years. Other female sexual offenders had lured various neighborhood children at different occasions to their home and abused them. Again others had abused handicapped children who had been entrusted to them. These women – while all repeatedly committing sexual abuse – exhibit different modus operandi, and differ in victim choice and possibly motive. Generalists tended to offend more often against unknown victims compared with the two other groups of offenders. They started offending at younger ages than specialists, had been maltreated as a child more often, and had more often used drugs. Specialists, on the other hand, offended most often against victims who were acquaintances or family/children, had more often themselves been sexually abused, had a delinquent partner more often, and more often than the other groups offended with a male co-offender.

Thus, it appears from these studies that specialists, generalists, and once-only offenders differed in victim choice, negative childhood experiences, drug abuse history, co-offending, and delinquency of the romantic partner.

Next, we examined the extent to which the different "aspects" of female sexual offender typologies were related to criminal career characteristics. In this, we distinguished five such aspects. The first was whether the sexual offenses had occurred within the context of a "reciprocal" romantic relationship between victim and perpetrator. To distinguish this type of female sexual offender, we included only those cases where the victim was over 12 years of age and both the victim and the offender had declared that their sexual contact was desired and approved by both parties involved[1] – although consent is obviously problematic given the age of the victim or the relationship between victim and perpetrator, for instance in the case of a secondary school teacher and a pupil. Next, we distinguished female solo sexual offenders from those whose offending had involved co-offenders. A third relevant distinction was whether the woman had offended with her (in all cases in our data, male) romantic partner. The fourth and fifth test was the age of the victim: below 12 or above 16. We also distinguished offenders who were diagnosed as suffering from Axis I/II disorders according to DSM-IV from those without such disorders. Finally, we compared offenders with victimization experiences like physical abuse, neglect, sexual abuse, and any abuse. We made comparisons for age of onset for any offense and for the index sex offense, lambda for any offense and for the index sex offense, criminal duration, and the age at desistance. In these analyses we compared each subgroup as defined by the above-mentioned characteristics with all other remaining female sexual offenders in our sample who do not show the particular characteristic under scrutiny. So, for our first comparison, we contrasted the criminal careers of those women who offended against a minor or otherwise dependent person (not being a child under 12) within the context of a reciprocal romantic relationship with all other sexual offenders who did not report such a relationship between them and their victim(s). The findings are summarized in Table 9.3.

Women who committed sex offenses within the context of a romantic relationship with their victim differ from other female sexual offenders in several criminal career parameters. Our tests showed that these women started offending at significantly younger ages. Their lambda is – unexpectedly – much, though not significantly, lower than that of the other offenders. This shows that the consensual relationship may have been short-lived. Next we examined female sexual offenders who committed the sexual abuse with a co-offender. A co-offender is defined as a second offender who has an active share in the offense for which he or she has been found guilty. Female sexual offenders who committed the abuse with a co-offender(s) at times do not commit the hands-on offense themselves and then do not play active or initiating roles but follow or do not resist the behavior initiated by their (mostly male) co-offender. Also, a number of those who are convicted of hands-on offending state that they were forced or felt pushed into it. The tests showed that – even though all

[1]The age of consent in the Netherlands is 16 years.

Table 9.3 Comparative Analysis of Criminal Career Parameters Based on Individual Characteristics. Associations Between Typological Aspects, Background Characteristics, and Criminal Career Parameters

	"Consensual" relationship	*All other sexual offenders*		*Co-offenders*	*All other sexual offenders*		*Intimate partner as co-offender*	*All other sexual offenders*	
	Mean (N = 14)	Mean (N = 121)	sign.	Mean (N = 85)	Mean (N = 39)	sign.	Mean (N = 73)	Mean (N = 62)	sign.
Onset age (any offense)	27.2	33.8	**0.028**	31.8	34	0.293	34	32	0.286
Onset age (sex offense)	30.0	35.8	**0.045**	33.3	36.3	0.137	35.9	34.4	0.414
Lambda (any offense)	0.5	9.6	0.371	14.7	5	0.225	5.7	12.6	0.234
Lambda (sex offense)	0.2	8.6	0.411	14.3	4	0.206	4.8	11.9	0.234
Duration (any offense)	4.5	3.6	0.539	3.5	3.8	0.713	3.4	3.9	0.533
Age at desistance	34.9	40.7	0.051	37.8	41.1	0.109	40.9	39.2	0.391

	Victim <12 years	*All other sexual offenders*		*Victim >16*	*All other sexual offenders*		*Axis I and/or Axis II*	*All other sexual offenders*	
	Mean (N = 47)	Mean (N = 68)	sign.	Mean (N = 25)	Mean (N = 90)	sign.	Mean (N = 65)	Mean (N = 70)	sign.
Onset age (any offense)	33.5	32.9	0.745	33	33.6	0.798	31.2	34.9	**0.046**
Onset age (sex offense)	34.8	35.7	0.646	34.9	36.7	0.449	33.2	37.1	**0.031**
Lambda (any offense)	14.7	3.4	0.1	1.7	9.9	**0.028**	8.5	9.1	0.91
Lambda (sex offense)	14.3	2.0	0.08	0.6	9.2	**0.022**	7.6	8.3	0.897
Duration (any offense)	3.4	3.9	0.58	3.6	3.9	0.785	3.3	4.1	0.377
Age at desistance	39.8	40.6	0.7	39.9	41.4	0.538	38	42.1	**0.026**

	Physically abused	*All other sexual offenders*		*Neglected*	*All other sexual offenders*		*Sexually abused*	*All other sexual offenders*	
	Mean (N = 17)	Mean (N = 118)	sign.	Mean (N = 35)	Mean (N = 100)	sign.	Mean (N = 30)	Mean (N = 105)	sign.
Onset age (any offense)	27.1	34	**0.013**	31	33.8	0.185	34.1	29.6	**0.038**
Onset age (sex offense)	30.2	36	**0.033**	33.4	35.9	0.234	36.0	32.5	0.105
Lambda (any offense)	9.4	8.7	0.927	10.5	8.1	0.686	9.4	7.6	0.762
Lambda (sex offense)	9	7.7	0.857	10.1	7	0.596	8.6	6.5	0.734
Duration (any offense)	4.7	3.5	0.388	4	3.6	0.673	3.6	4.1	0.622
Age at desistance	35.2	40.8	**0.038**	38.1	40.9	0.19	41.0	37.1	0.078

differences were in the expected direction – these women do not differ from the other female sexual offenders on any of the criminal career parameters.

Next, we investigated whether female sexual offenders who commit the sex offense with their intimate partner differ from female sexual offenders who do not co-offend with their intimate partner. This group obviously has a substantial overlap with the previous group and it is therefore not surprising that both the results (the differences are again in the expected direction) and the significance tests are similar. Subsequently, we tested whether women abusing either young (<12 years) or older (>16 years) victims differed from the other female sexual offenders. For those abusing younger victims, results were either not statistically significant or not in the expected direction. Women abusing older victims were significantly less active offenders than women abusing victims under the age of 16.

Women with mental health problems started offending (any offense including but not restricted to sexual offenses) at significantly younger ages, and they desisted at a significantly younger age. Women with histories of sexual or physical abuse started offending with any offense at significantly younger ages and those with experiences of physical abuse also started earlier with sexual offending. Further, the criminal careers of those physically abused were significantly shorter. There were no significant results for the women who had experiences of neglect in childhood.

Conclusion and Discussion

Integrating findings from the literature and the analyses conducted for this chapter we conclude the following. Women are responsible for a small fraction of sexual offenses, and for an even smaller fraction of those sexual offenses that are dealt with by the criminal justice system. Most female sexual offenders are not prolific offenders. A little above half commit no other offenses. One in six women included in the study sample committed only one single (sex) offense in their life time. It appears as if almost all desist from offending (defined as staying free from offending for a period of at least 5 years before the last date the offending data were collected, i.e., 2011) after being prosecuted for a sex offense, although – as they are such sporadic offenders – longer follow-up periods might be needed to assess whether this is truly so. Sexual recidivism is very low. Thus, it is reasonable to conclude that female sexual offenders appear to be at a generally low rate if not sporadic offenders.

On average, female sexual offenders start offending well into adulthood. It is reasonable to think that at the time of their onset of offending, these women are in a stable relationship and, possibly, have children. As our previous research has shown (Wijkman et al., 2010), a large proportion of women offended with their male partner and abused their own children. This could explain their late average starting age, and the fact that for a substantial proportion their criminal careers contain only one sexual offending charge (at times, however, pertaining to multiple sex offenses). Thus, female sexual offending appears, to a certain extent, influenced by contextual and situational factors. Obviously, this raises the question of whether this is a matter of choice or of selection by the offender. Did these women "choose" antisocial partners in order to continue their antisocial lifestyle, which includes deviant sexual behaviors within the family setting. Or, were these women "chosen" by abusive men for their gullibility, low IQ, or lack of resistance against the abuse of (their) children? Using court data, such issues are hard to resolve as (co-)offenders will use defense strategies that imply "blaming" the other perpetrator(s) or claiming duress.

We investigated whether recurring "aspects" of typologies and prominent characteristics of female sexual offenders were associated with criminal career aspects. Here, although most differences were in the expected direction, we found few significant differences. This is partly due to the fact that – even though we studied an entire population of offenders during a specific time period – we conducted the statistical analyses on a small group of women. This may not be the entire reason, as comparisons of generalist and specialist offenders on the same sample (Wijkman et al., 2011) generate a number of significant differences. Thus we conclude that some "aspects" of typologies that we investigated here have only modest relevance for the criminal career parameters for female sexual offenders. However, with appropriate care, we conclude that it appears that women who have committed sex offenses within a relationship that they and the victim reported as consensual start at earlier ages. This can be explained by the fact that these women likely do not have very large age differences with their underage, mostly male victims. The fact that these are not prolific offenders does not clarify the picture: If they are less antisocial than "nonconsensual" sexual offenders, we would expect their careers to be shorter rather than longer and their lambda, on the other hand, to be higher. The reverse is true. This raises the question of whether the consensuality of the relationship may not in fact have been a neutralization technique of legal defense strategy. Women burdened by trauma or mental disturbances start offending relatively early. This can be understood from their background and is therefore what we expect. The offenders victimizing sexually mature victims are less prolific, as we expected them to be. The fact that these women victimize others who will – when they are male – generally be physically stronger than themselves could also be argued to point to antisociality, and could perhaps also have led us to postulate the opposite.

In order to be able to investigate female sexual offenders better – and for associations to emerge as statistically significant – it is vital that larger samples of female sexual offenders, their offenses, victims, and characteristics be collected. Given the low prevalence of female sexual offending, this can probably be achieved only through concerted international collaborative effort, in which definitions and data collection procedures are synchronized, and data sets combined to achieve greater statistical power. Unless such databases are constructed, female sexual offending will likely remain an obscure, underresearched, and little-understood phenomenon. Future studies should also focus in more (qualitative) detail on the role of the co-offender in the sexual offending of adult women, as much of these women's (sexual) offending appears directly tied in with that of their (romantic) partners. Some women may have been instrumental in their partners' offending and the study of these women's characteristics may in fact have less explanatory power than those of their partners. More systematic study of the dynamics and motivation behind female sexual offending complements our understanding of the etiology of female sexual offending and these women's criminal careers. Given the variation, and sometimes the committing of sexual offenses year after year, further research about female sexual offenders is a necessity.

References

Bijleveld, C. C. J. H. (2007). Sex offenders and sex offending. In M. Tonry & C. C. J. H. Bijleveld (Eds.), *Crime and justice* (Vol. 35, pp. 319–389). Chicago: The University of Chicago Press.

Bijleveld, C. C. J. H., & Soudijn, M. (2008). Verdachten van een groepszedendelict [Suspects of a group sex offence]. *Tijdschrift voor seksuologie, 32*, 80–89.

Bumby, K. M., & Bumby, N. H. (1997). Adolescent female sexual offenders. In B. K. Schwartz & H. R. Cellini (Eds.), *The sex offender: Corrections, treatment, and legal practice* (pp. 1–16). Kingston: Civic Research Institute.

Cortoni, F., & Hanson, R. K. (2005). *A review of the recidivism rates of female sexual offenders.* Public Safety and Emergency Preparedness Canada.

Cortoni, F., Hanson, R. K., & Coache, M. E. (2010). The recidivism rates of female sexual offenders are low: A meta-analysis. *Sexual Abuse: A Journal of Research and Treatment, 22*(4), 387–402.

Dijk, T., Veen, M., & Cox, E. (2010). *Slachtofferschap van huiselijk geweld: Aard, omvang, omstandigheden en hulpzoekgedrag* [Victimisation of domestic violence: Characteristics, volume, circumstances and helpseeking behavior]. Hilversum: Intomart.

Draijer, N. (1988). *Een lege plek in mijn geheugen. Seksueel misbruik van meisjes door verwanten* [A blank in my memory. Sexual abuse of girls by family members]. Den Haag: Ministerie van Sociale Zaken en Werkgelegenheid.

Faller, K. C. (1987). Women who sexually abuse children. *Violence and Victims, 2*(4), 263–276.

Freeman, N. J., & Sandler, J. C. (2008). Female and male sex offenders: A comparison of recidivism patterns and risk factors. *Journal of Interpersonal Violence, 23*(10), 1394–1413.

Gannon, T. A., Rose, M. R., & Ward, T. (2008). A descriptive model of the offense process for female sexual offenders. *Sexual Abuse: A Journal of Research and Treatment, 20*(3), 352.

Grayston, A. D., & De Luca, R. V. (1999). Female perpetrators of child sexual abuse: A review of the clinical and empirical literature. *Aggression and Violent Behavior, 4*(1), 93–106.

Green, A. H., & Kaplan, M. S. (1994). Psychiatric impairment and childhood victimization experiences in female child molesters. *Journal of the American Academy of Child and Adolescent Psychiatry, 33*(7), 954–961.

Hanson, R. K., & Bussière, M. T. (1998). Predicting relapse: A meta-analysis of sexual offender recidivism studies. *Journal of Consulting and Clinical Psychology, 66*(2), 348–362.

Harris, D. A. (2010). Theories of female sexual offending. In T. Gannon & F. Cortoni (Eds.), *Female Sexual Offenders* (pp. 31–51). Chichester: John Wiley & Sons, Ltd.

Heer-de Lang, N. E. d., & Kalidien, S. N. (2010). *Criminaliteit en Rechtshandhaving* [Crime and law enforcement]. Den Haag: WODC.

Hendriks, J., & Bijleveld, C. C. J. H. (2006). Juvenile sexual delinquents: Contrasting child abusers with peer abusers. *Criminal Behavior and Mental Health, 14*(4), 238–250.

Herman, J. L., & Hirschman, L. (1981). *Father-daughter incest*. Cambridge, MA: Harvard University Press.

Horvath, M. A. H., Tong, S., & Williams, E. (2011). Critical issues in rape investigation: An overview of reform in England and Wales. *The Journal of Criminal Justice Research, 1*(2).

Kaplan, M. S., & Green, A. (1995). Incarcerated female sexual offenders: A comparison of sexual histories with eleven female nonsexual offenders. *Sexual Abuse: A Journal of Research and Treatment, 7*(4), 287–300.

Krahé, B., Scheinberger-Olwig, R., & Bieneck, S. (2003). Men's reports of nonconsensual sexual interactions with women: Prevalence and impact. *Archives of Sexual Behavior, 32*(2), 165–175.

Laws, D. R., & O'Donohue, W. T. (2008). *Sexual deviance: Theory, assessment, and treatment*: New York: Guilford Press.

Lewis, C. F., & Stanley, C. R. (2000). Women accused of sexual offenses. *Behavioral Sciences and the Law, 18*(1), 73–81.

Matthews, J. K., Mathews, R., & Speltz, K. (1991). Female sexual offenders: A typology. In M. Q. Patton (Ed.), *Family sexual abuse: Frontline research and evaluation* (pp. 199–219). Newbury Park, NJ: Sage Publications, Inc.

McCarty, L. M. (1986). Mother-child incest: Characteristics of the offender. *Child Welfare, 65*(5), 447.

Muehlenhard, C. L., & Cook, S. W. (1988). Men's self-reports of unwanted sexual activity. *Journal of Sex Research, 24*(1), 58–72.

Peter, T. (2009). Exploring taboos: Comparing male- and female-perpetrated child sexual abuse. *Journal of Interpersonal Violence, 24*(7), 1111–1128.

Sandler, J. C., & Freeman, N. J. (2007). Typology of female sex offenders: A test of Vandiver and Kercher. *Sexual Abuse: A Journal of Research and Treatment, 19*(2), 73–89.

Saradjian, J. (2010). Understanding the prevalence of female-perpetrated sexual abuse and the impact of that abuse on victims. In T. Gannon & F. Cortoni (Eds.), *Female sexual offenders. Theory, assessment and treatment* (pp. 9–31). Chichester: John Wiley & Sons, Ltd.

Sarrel, P. M., & Masters, W. H. (1982). Sexual molestation of men by women. *Archives of Sexual Behavior, 11*(2), 117–131.

Slotboom, A. M., Hendriks, J., & Verbruggen, J. (2011). Contrasting adolescent female and male sexual aggression: A self-report study on prevalence and predictors of sexual aggression. *Journal of Sexual Aggression, 17*(1), 15–33.

Soothill, K. (2010). Sex offender recidivism. *Crime and Justice, 39*(1), 145–211.

Struckman-Johnson, C. (1988). Forced sex on dates: It happens to men, too. *The Journal of Sex Research, 24*, 234–241.

Struckman-Johnson, C., Struckman-Johnson, D., & Anderson, P. B. (2003). Tactics of sexual coercion: When men and women won't take no for an answer. *Journal of Sex Research, 40*(1), 76–86.

Tang, K. (1998). Rape law reform in Canada: The success and limits of legislation. *International Journal of Offender Therapy and Comparative Criminology, 42*(3), 258–270.

Vandiver, D. M. (2006). Female sex offenders: A comparison of solo offenders and co-offenders. *Violence and Victims, 21*(3), 339–354.

Vandiver, D. M., & Kercher, G. (2004). Offender and victim characteristics of registered female sexual offenders in Texas: A proposed typology of female sexual offenders. *Sexual Abuse: A Journal of Research and Treatment, 16*(2), 121–137.

Vandiver, D. M., & Walker, J. T. (2002). Female sex offenders: An overview and analysis of 40 cases. *Criminal Justice Review, 27*(2), 284–300.

Wartna, B. S. J., Blom, M., & Tollenaar, N. (2008). *De WODC-recidivemonitor.* Den Haag: WODC.

Wijkman, M. D. S., Bijleveld, C. C. J. H., & Hendriks, J. (2010). "Women don't do such things!" Characteristics of female sex offenders and offender types. *Sexual Abuse: A Journal of Research and Treatment, 22*, 135–156.

Wijkman, M. D. S., Bijleveld, C. C. J. H., & Hendriks, J. (2011). Female sex offenders: Specialists, generalists and once-only offenders. *Journal of Sexual Aggression, 17*(1), 34–45.

Woodhams, J. A. (2009). *Juvenile sex offending: An investigative perspective.* University of Leicester.

10

Mayhem by Occupation

On the Relevance of Criminal Careers to Sexual Homicide Offenders

Matt DeLisi

Iowa State University, USA

> *If only it were all so simple! If only there were evil people somewhere insidiously committing evil deeds, and it were necessary only to separate them from the rest of us and destroy them. But the line dividing good and evil cuts through the heart of every human being. And who is willing to destroy a piece of his own heart?*
>
> Aleksandr Solzhenitsyn (1973, p. 168)

> *A single instance of multiple homicide can be cited in support of divergent rhetorical messages, and none is self-evidently correct or objectively true.*
>
> Philip Jenkins (1994, p. 2)

Introduction

Bizarre, grotesque, and pathological, sexual murder has challenged behavioral scientists, law enforcement personnel, and the lay public alike in their quest for a causal explanation and coherent conceptual framework. Various authors, investigators, and audiences have developed around sexual murder, and these diverse communities have promoted and digested many theoretical explanations for it. These explanations vary in terms of their sophistication, their popularity, their usefulness to criminal justice personnel, and the degree to which they seem to match the empirical existence of sexual murder. Although the extant literature on sexual murder contains much useful information, it also contains a set of crippling problems and misguided views that limit the scientific understanding of sexual murder. This is unfortunate because it deserves a better, more scientific explanation.

Sex Offenders: A Criminal Career Approach, First Edition. Edited by Arjan Blokland and Patrick Lussier.

The first problem is captured in the outstanding quotation from Solzhenitsyn, the content of which is lyrical, powerful, and when applied to an evil deed such as sexual murder, incorrect. Although feelings of good and evil are universal, evil deeds are not; the more extreme the criminal behavior, the more exceedingly rare its incidence. To illustrate, serial murder, the repeated act of killing in conjunction with sexual violence that is embodied by sexual murder, constitutes less than 1% of the total number of murders in a society, and many classic offender data sets in criminology contain little to no homicide offenders, let alone serial and/or sexual murderers (DeLisi, 2001; McNamara & Morton, 2004). Quinet (2007) calculated an annual serial murder victim count in the United States and produced a lower estimate of 182 serial murder victims per year, and an upper estimate of 1,832 serial murder victims per year; however, 17,034 persons were murdered during the publication year of her study. Among juveniles, serial/sexual murder is also exceedingly rare, evidenced by a review study that found just six cases among children or adolescent offenders occurring in the past 150 years (Myers, 2004).

Using the Solzhenitsyn quotation further, there is a vast incongruity between feelings of malice and the perpetration of malice. Although virtually everyone entertains thoughts or feelings of doing wrong (or evil), virtually no one acts on them – except extraordinarily violent and clinically disturbed offenders. Substantively, Solzhenitsyn's quotation conveys a fundamental distrust of the notion that individuals are differentially capable of evil deeds, or the use of violence, or the commission of crime, or in the current case, the perpetration of sexual murder. If we are all equally susceptible to malice as Solzhenitsyn suggests, then we can easily discard the simplistic notion that those who commit heinous violent acts are in some ways different.

A second problem ironically stems from the empirical truth that severe forms of violent criminal offending – principally serial and/or sexual murder – are pathological. In this view, the rare and markedly abnormal nature of serial murder means that it is not truly deserving of study, and instead, *serious* scholars should focus on forms of crime that are more common and presumably addressable by policy. Long a tradition in sociological criminology, this shunning of serial murder genuinely questions whether serial murder even exists to instead assert that the phenomenon is a social construction. As discussed previously (see DeLisi & Wright, in press), for instance, Edwin Sutherland (1950) argued that sexual psychopath laws – which were designed to socially control instrumentally violent criminals such as serial murderers – were based on false, questionable knowledge based in popular literature as opposed to science. Indeed, as the chapter-opening quotation from Jenkins suggests, sensationalistic "constructs" such as serial murder, if they exist at all, are too aberrant to study. I call this the social construction error.

Although this is just one example, it is largely representative of an unfortunately petty, dismissive tone that too many professional criminologists harbor toward the study of serial murder. As a result, explorations of the causes of serial murder have been abdicated to other literary communities such as true crime genres and works by expert practitioners, most notably professionals from within the Federal Bureau of Investigation (FBI; i.e., scholar-practitioners like

Hazelwood, Ressler, Burgess, and Douglas). And the latter authors have produced volumes of articles, treatises, and other products that have informed the public on the lives and crimes of serial murderers, and provided law enforcement with the investigative tools to catch them. But few of these works rise to the level of an actual theoretical explanation of serial murder, particularly one substantiated by rigorous empirical research.

Another substantively meaningful problem is that the scientific understanding of serial/sexual murder has frankly become stagnant. The MacDonald Triad of enuresis or chronic bed wetting, animal cruelty, and fire setting has been discovered in the childhoods of many serial murderers, and has achieved a sort of lore in the popular understanding of serial murderers (MacDonald, 1963; Hellman & Blackman, 1966). However, these symptoms are just three of many behavioral disturbances and psychopathological symptoms demonstrated by serial/sexual homicide offenders. In the same way, the roster of serial and/or sexual homicide offenders that diffuses through popular media – featuring names like Ted Bundy, Richard Ramirez, John Wayne Gacy, Aileen Wuornos, and others – have become part of our cultural lexicon. But what more can be gleaned from poring over the biographies of serial murderers? I call the lack of innovation in scholarly thought on serial and/or sexual murder the stagnancy error.

Current Focus

By now it is understood that serial/sexual murderers represent the apotheosis of what can happen when individuals with a host of severe behavioral and neuropsychological deficits are subjected to the most depraved, abusive, and criminogenic environments in early life. The family backgrounds of most sexual killers are not pretty, and the abuses and deprivations that they have endured are so tortuous that it nearly rivals the atrocious violence they will later commit. Their victimization experiences are commonly of a psychosexual nature, which contribute to a range of abnormal sexual disorders, paraphilias, which then often serve to drive their homicide offending (see Purcell & Arrigo, 2006). But unfortunately, there are many research gaps. As Nicole and Proulx (2007, p. 32) observed, "Few studies have investigated whether the authors of sexual crimes with objectively high severities have a more active, more varied or more serious criminal career. The criminal career of sexual murderers has not been extensively investigated, and what little is known comes from case studies."[1]

[1]To illustrate the paucity of studies linking criminal careers to sexual homicide, consider the relatively small literature on the broader content area of sexual homicide. For instance, Chan and Heide's (2009) systematic review of the sexual homicide literature from 1986 to 2008 produced just 32 studies. The bulk of these studies were psychiatric and psychological in scope and mostly focused on the personality traits of offenders, their modus operandi and signature, victim selection, and developmental patterns occurring pre-, per-, and post-crime.

The current chapter explores the emergence and course of serial/sexual homicide offenders as they relate to the criminal careers paradigm. I intend to demonstrate that one of the most influential and popular areas of research in criminology (e.g., criminal careers) can fruitfully be used to study a topic that has historically been studied outside of mainstream criminology. Moreover, there are meaningful inroads between these content areas, and criminal careers research can bolster the nomological network relating to lethal violence.

Criminal Careers and Sexual Homicide Offenders

Case Studies and Targeted Clinical Samples

In February 2010, Arizona death row inmate Viva Leroy Nash, the oldest condemned offender in the United States, died at age 94. Born in 1915, Nash had an extensive criminal record dating to the 1930s with multiple stints in state and federal prisons for an assortment of violent and property crimes. He was convicted of the attempted killing of a police officer in Connecticut during the 1940s and spent the next 25 years in prison. In 1977, he was convicted again for murder and armed robbery and given two consecutive life sentences. Nash escaped from prison custody in October 1982 and less than one month later committed still another murder and armed robbery, crimes for which he was sentenced to death in 1983 (Associated Press, 2010).

A similar profile exists for Richard Biegenwald who died in March 2008. Biegenwald had a long and murderous odyssey in New Jersey that included multiple death sentences that waxed and waned with the state's own statutes on capital punishment. When he died, New Jersey had already abolished capital punishment, thus reducing his sentences to life imprisonment. Biegenwald led an extraordinarily violent and antisocial life characterized by setting fire to his family home at age 5, childhood onset of alcohol abuse, and diverse criminal offending and periods of confinement throughout childhood and adolescence. At age 18, he was convicted of murder and armed robbery. During that criminal episode, Biegenwald fled New Jersey to Maryland where he shot a police officer and was captured. Despite receiving a life sentence in 1958, he was paroled in 1974. Over the next several years, he was suspected in a range of rapes, weapons, and drug charges culminating in nine murders in the early 1980s, although he was only convicted of five of the murders (Associated Press, 2008).

The life histories of career criminals who happen to commit serial and/or sexual murder are characterized by a litany of severe risk factors that individually are pernicious and when congealed within a single person are seemingly a blueprint for extreme violence. These background factors are consistent with the modal risk factors for sexual homicide offending among adolescents. In their seminal investigation of 36 sexual murderers, Burgess, Hartman, Ressler, Douglas, and McCormack (1986) reported severe antisocial behavioral histories during the childhood, adolescence, and adulthood of the murderers, including behaviors such as fire setting, destruction of property, cruelty to children, stealing, assault and battery against adults, cruelty to animals, and other forms of maladaptive behaviors. The behavioral, interpersonal, and affective profiles of these offenders were consistent with diagnostic criteria for severe forms of psychopathology including Oppositional Defiant Disorder, Conduct Disorder, Antisocial Personality Disorder, and psychopathy.

Myers (2004) identified the "Big Ten" warning signs of sexual murder among adolescents as impaired capacity to feel guilt (the call sign of psychopathy), neuro-psychiatric vulnerabilities, serious school problems, child abuse, family dysfunction, history of interpersonal violence, prior arrests, sadistic fantasy, psychopathy, and other personality disorder diagnoses, such as schizoid or schizotypal. Although case studies of murderers and/or serial murderers have a venerable history, it is important that criminologists study sexual murderers similarly to other offenders in order to assess their overall criminal careers. The rationale for doing this is twofold. First, there is tension in the literature regarding the criminal careers of serial and/or sexual killers. On one hand is the view that, given its clandestine nature, these types of crimes are perpetrated by offenders who manage to avoid police detection and thus have minimal official criminal history. On the other hand is the view of a career criminal who also mixes sexual murder into his offending repertoire, as illustrated by the historical examples described earlier in this chapter. Thus whether serial and/or sexual murderers are the putative boy next door who engages in extreme violence in a shadowy other life or a remorseless thug cycling in and out of prison is an empirical question. The second rationale is theoretical and attempts to examine whether mainstream criminological theories of crime, and statistical models that contain conventional measures used to predict crime, also have validity among criminals who kill for sexual gratification. To the degree that sexual homicide offenders behave like garden variety criminals, there is support for general theories of crime. The degree to which they differ from mundane criminals suggests the need for specialized theories of violence (cf., Amirault & Lussier, 2011; Harris, Mazerolle, & Knight, 2009; Harris, Smallbone, Dennison, & Knight, 2009).

Broadening the Study of Sexual Homicide Offenders

Although case studies and targeted convenience samples of extreme offenders have been the modal approach to studying sexual homicide offenders, there has also been concerted effort to sample adequate numbers of sexual murderers to compare them to other types of offenders and understand the parameters of their offending career. Firestone, Bradford, Greenberg, Larose, and Curry (1998) compared the antisocial history and psychopathology of 17 extrafamilial homicidal child molesters to 35 extrafamilial child molesters who had not murdered their victims. Although both groups presented with severe risk profiles, the sexual homicide offenders presented with characteristics that were much worse. Nearly 87% of the homicidal child molesters had previous history of interpersonal violence and nearly 63% had been placed in a confinement or psychiatric facility prior to age 16. Over 82% of the homicidal child molesters met diagnostic criteria for sexual sadism and 53% were co-morbid for pedophilia and sexual sadism (prevalence of sexual sadism and co-morbid pedophilia and sexual sadism was zero for the nonhomicidal child molesters). The homicidal child molesters were also acutely psychopathic and scored in the 93rd percentile on Factor 1 of the Hare Psychopathy Checklist, revised (Hare, 1991), and the 82nd percentile on Factor 2. The presence of a personality disorder, sexual sadism, and pedophilia, three mental health disorders, might be explained by the fact that the study was conducted with a sample of homicidal child molesters having been sent to a psychiatric clinic for a clinical assessment. In other words, they might have been sent to the clinic for assessment because such disorders were suspected by criminal justice practitioners.

Trojan and Salfati (2010) compared 137 single-victim homicide cases drawn from the Cincinnati, Ohio, Police Department and 17 closed serial murder cases obtained from the FBI. Whereas the single homicide offenders averaged 13 arrests and eight convictions, serial murderers averaged five arrests and three convictions. Although this seems comparatively less severe, five or more arrests are a standard measure of habitual or chronic criminality (the most prolific serial killer had 25 prior arrests). The criminal histories of serial murderers also demonstrated more instrumental offenses suggesting a specific targeting of a victim. Langevin, Ben-Aron, Wright, Marchese, and Handy (1988), and more recently Langevin (2003), compared the antisocial histories of 33 sexual homicide offenders to 80 sexually aggressive offenders, 23 sexual sadists, and 611 general sex offenders. Similar to the Firestone et al. (1998) study, all these men had been seen for psychiatric assessments either for pre-trial or as part of parole evaluation. Overall, the criminal careers and antisocial pasts of sexual homicide offenders were significantly worse than even these other severe risk groups. More than 27% of the homicide offenders had been committed to reform school, more than 21% were gang members, over 15% had been expelled from school for behavioral problems, and more than 30% had prior history of animal cruelty, vandalism, and/or fire setting.

The interrelations between criminal careers and sexual murder are also an object of study beyond the United States. For example, Andreas Hill and his colleagues (Hill, Habermann, Klusmann, Berner, & Briken, 2008) studied the forensic reports of 139 sexual homicide offenders in Germany who had served time in prison and 90 of whom had been released. The mean number of sexual homicide victims per offender was 3.7. Twenty years after their release, more than 23% of offenders recommitted sexual offenses and more than 18% committed nonsexual violent offenses, such as armed robbery and aggravated assault. Three men, or more than 3%, were subsequently convicted of attempted or completed murder. They found that the earlier that an offender committed his first sexual homicide the more likely he was to be convicted of a sexual crime, which included extremely violent sexual offenses (i.e., sexual homicide, rape, sexual abuse of a child, and sexual assault) as well as nonsexual violent offenses. Nearly 1 in 5 defendants convicted of sexual homicide have prior convictions for homicide and more than half have other violent crimes in their criminal history (Häkkänen-Nyholm, Repo-Tiihonen, Lindberg, Salenius, & Weizmann-Henelius, 2009).

Based on data from 101 sexual aggressors and 40 sexual murderers selected from Canada, Nicole and Proulx (2007) extensively studied the criminal careers of these high-risk groups, and found few behavioral differences between them. Although sexual murderers had an earlier self-reported age at first crime and more severe crimes against persons, sexual aggressors accumulated more severe property offenses and total crimes. On 18 other measures of the criminal career, including total and offense-specific annual offending rates or lambda, offense-specific onset, and other indices of chronic offending, the groups were comparably severe. Beauregard, Stone, Proulx, and Michaud (2008) explored the offending careers of 11 sexual murderers of children and 66 sexual murderers of adult women, using data from incarcerated Canadian offenders. They found extensive criminal history among both types of homicide offenders. Among sexual murderers of children, 50% had prior convictions for nonsexual nonviolent crimes and 40% had prior convictions for nonsexual violent crimes. Thirty percent had prior convictions for contact sexual offenses and 20% had prior convictions for noncontact sexual crimes. Slightly more than 18% were drug or alcohol dependent and more than 27% frequently abused drugs or alcohol. The criminal careers of sexual murderers of women were generally worse, with 71% having prior convictions for nonsexual, nonviolent crimes and 51% having prior convictions for nonsexual violent crimes. More than 22% had prior convictions for contact sexual crimes and just over 3% had prior convictions for noncontact sexual crimes. Drug and alcohol use was also significantly higher, evidenced by 62% reporting frequent drug/alcohol abuse and 49% reporting drug or alcohol dependence. An interesting study based on offenders from Finland estimated the risk of violent offending and general criminality among the children of homicide offenders. Compared to matched controls of children whose parents were not murderers, the children of homicide offenders were a staggering 24 times more likely to one day commit violent crime and 17 times more likely to be criminals (Putkonen, Ryynänen, Eronen, & Tiihonen, 2002).

Recently, DeLisi and Lussier (in press) examined sexual homicide offending in a criminal career context, drawing on data from 618 convicted male homicide offenders selected from eight U.S. states. They compared the criminal careers of different classifications of sexual homicide offenders, including child-murderers, rape-murderers, multiple rape-murderers, and nonsexual homicide offenders (single and multiple victims). They found differences across groups in terms of criminal career parameters, demographic characteristics, and other offending measures. For instance, multivariate logistic regression models indicated that prior arrests/convictions for rape, kidnapping, and child molestation predicted a subsequent sexual murder, and prior rape arrests/convictions predicted diverse forms of subsequent sexual multiple homicide offending. ROC-AUC models further indicated that prior rape convictions predicted all forms of sexual homicide and that other indicators of prior criminal convictions were significantly predictive of subsequent homicide offending, albeit at varying levels of sensitivity and specificity. These and other studies increasingly demonstrate the utility of a criminal careers framework for understanding a range of sexual aggressors (cf., Beauregard & Bouchard, 2010; Beauregard

& Leclerc, 2007; Beauregard, Proulx, Rossmo, Leclerc, & Allaire, 2007; Lussier, Bouchard, & Beauregard, 2011; Lussier, LeBlanc, & Proulx, 2005; Lussier, Proulx, & LeBlanc, 2005; Lussier, Tzoumakes, Cale, & Amirault, 2010).

Incorporating Theory into the Study of Sexual Homicide Offenders

Just as there is recent criminological interest in studying various sex offenders – putatively considered to be specialized, pathological offenders – within a conventional criminal career framework, there is also relatively new interest in exploring sex offenders with mainstream, general criminological theory.[2] To illustrate, DeLisi and Wright (in press) explored Gottfredson and Hirschi's (1990) self-control theory and its relation to sexual homicide offending. Sexual homicide offending is defined as the predatory perpetration of murder in conjunction with some sexually oriented offense, such as rape, sodomy, or other type of sexual assault. In some ways, self-control theory provides a useful framework for understanding the lives of predatory sexual murderers, particularly those who leave disorganized crime scenes. However, in other ways, the offending behavior of these offenders is characterized by an extremely high level of self-control and self-regulation, particularly those who leave organized crime scenes. Thus, according to DeLisi and Wright, a self-control paradox exists when studying the apex of violent criminals.

DeLisi and Wright sought to utilize Ressler, Burgess, and Douglas' (1988) typology of sexual homicide offending. One prototype was a disorganized sexual murderer whose offense was spontaneous, whose victim was known but depersonalized, and who engaged in minimal conservation during the attack. The disorganized killer's murder scene was random and sloppy, characterized by sudden violence with minimal use of restraints, and sexual acts after death. The victim's body was left in view at the death scene and importantly, weapons and other forensic evidence were often present at the scene. In contrast, the second prototype, the organized sexual murderer, committed a planned killing of a targeted stranger who was personalized. There was controlled conservation during the killing, use of restraints, aggressive acts before death, and demand for submission. The entire crime scene of the organized killer reflected control. The victim's body was hidden, often transported, and there was an absence of weapons or other forensic physical evidence.

According to DeLisi and Wright (in press), the disorganized-organized typology essentially reflects the distribution of self-control from low to high, respectively. In many respects, the disorganized offender's behavior contemporaneous to their

[2]Despite the criticisms of the criminal career paradigm by Gottfredson and Hirschi during the 1980s, there is convergent validity between criminal careers and self-control theory. For example, DeLisi and Vaughn (2008) reported that self-control was a strong indicator of career criminality, a status that is disproportionately responsible for the most serious crimes in a society. Using data from a statewide sample of institutionalized delinquents, they found that those scoring 1 SD above the mean on a low self-control scale were over five times more likely to become a career criminal and disproportionately likely to commit violent crimes.

homicide event is consistent with the conduct of the modal criminal offender. The murder is unplanned, hasty, and represents a poorly contemplated, rash action to satisfy an underlying desire (recall that the victim is known to the offender). The crime scene of the disorganized sexual homicide offender is, simply, sloppy. In contrast, the organized sexual homicide offender seemingly exudes self-control in certain respects. The crime scene evinces self-control: forensic evidence is cleaned up, weapons and other physical evidence are removed from the scene. The murder itself is premeditated and reflects considerable planning and control, it is a well-executed plan. Planning is not the strong suit of offenders with low self-control. All of these conditions of the organized sexual homicide offender intimate a paradoxical relationship between self-control and violence, one that could not be anticipated by self-control theory.

DeLisi and Wright's thesis is thought-provoking, but self-control theory is certainly not the only criminological work that could be used to supply conceptual/theoretical heft to the career study of sexual homicide offenders. Another theory that immediately comes to mind is Moffitt's (1993) developmental taxonomy. The neuropsychological deficits that contribute to life-course-persistent offending potentially comport with the neuropsychiatric disturbances that sexual homicide offenders differentially display. Other criminologists have applied a social learning framework toward the study of serial and/or sexual homicide offending and the possible mechanisms whereby exposure to violence potentially contributes to learning how to kill (see Wright & Hensley, 2003). Of course, there is much work that is needed to provide linkages between criminological theories and sexual murder.

Conclusion

Nearly 20 years ago, during my graduate training, criminology was limited by a camp mentality that segregated content areas of research, such as criminal careers, the study of homicide offenders, the study of sex offenders, and criminological theory. In recent years, a salvo of research has demonstrated the utility of studying all criminal offenders – from the normative to the pathological – with mainstream theory and methods. As this chapter has made clear, there is clear relevance of the criminal career paradigm to the most violent of offenders, such as those who commit sexual homicide. It is exciting to anticipate how much further this research will progress, especially given the human and policy import of sexual homicide.

References

Amirault, J., & Lussier, P. (2011). Population heterogeneity, state dependence, and sexual offender recidivism: The aging process and the lost predictive impact of prior criminal charges over time. *Journal of Criminal Justice*, *39*, 344–354.

Associated Press. (2008). New Jersey serial killer Biegenwald dies. Retrieved January 19, 2010, from http://www.freerepublic.com/focus/f-news/1983667/posts.

Associated Press. (2010). Oldest death row inmate dies at 94 in Arizona. Retrieved April 23, 2010, from http://rss.msnbc.msn.com/id/35396284.

Beauregard, E., & Bouchard, M. (2010). Cleaning up your act: Forensic awareness as a detection avoidance strategy. *Journal of Criminal Justice, 38*, 1160–1166.

Beauregard, E., & Leclerc, B. (2007). An application of the rational choice approach to the offending process of sex offenders: A closer look at the decision-making. *Sexual Abuse: A Journal of Research and Treatment, 19*, 115–133.

Beauregard, E., Proulx, J., Rossmo, K., Leclerc, B., & Allaire, J. F. (2007). Script analysis of hunting process in serial sex offenders. *Criminal Justice and Behavior, 34*, 1069–1084.

Beauregard, E., Stone, M. R., Proulx, J., & Michaud, P. (2008). Sexual murderers of children: Developmental, precrime, crime, and postcrime factors. *International Journal of Offender Therapy and Comparative Criminology, 52*, 253–269.

Burgess, A. W., Hartman, C. R., Ressler, R. K., Douglas, J. E., & McCormack, A. (1986). Sexual homicide: A motivational model. *Journal of Interpersonal Violence, 1*, 251–272.

Chan, H-C., & Heide, K. M. (2009). Sexual homicide: A synthesis of the literature. *Trauma, Violence, & Abuse, 10*, 31–54.

DeLisi, M. (2001). Extreme career criminals. *American Journal of Criminal Justice, 25*, 239–252.

DeLisi, M., & Lussier, P. (in press). Sexual homicide offenders and their criminal careers: An exploratory empirical examination. In Nadya Gotsiridze-Columbus (Ed.), *Psychology of Violence*. Hauppauge, NY: Nova Science.

DeLisi, M., & Vaughn, M. G. (2008). The Gottfredson-Hirschi critiques revisited: Reconciling self-control theory, criminal careers, and career criminals. *International Journal of Offender Therapy and Comparative Criminology, 52*, 520–537.

DeLisi, M., & Wright, J. P. (in press). A self-control paradox? The case of sexual homicide offending. In G. Bruinsma & D. Weisburd (Eds.), *Encyclopedia of criminology and criminal justice*. New York: Springer-Verlag.

Firestone, P., Bradford, J. M., Greenberg, D. M., Larose, M. R., & Curry, S. (1998). Homicidal and nonhomicidal child molesters: Psychological, phallometric, and criminal features. *Sexual Abuse: A Journal of Research and Treatment, 10*, 305–323.

Gottfredson, M. R., & Hirschi, T. (1990). *A general theory of crime*. Stanford, CA: Stanford University Press.

Häkkänen-Nyholm, H., Repo-Tiihonen, E., Lindberg, N., Salenius, S., Weizmann-Henelius, G. (2009). Finnish sexual homicides: Offence and offender characteristics. *Forensic Science International, 188*, 125–130.

Hare, R. D. (1991). *The Hare Psychopathy Checklist-Revised*. Toronto, Ontario, Canada: Multi-Health Systems.

Harris, D. A., Mazerolle, P., & Knight, R. A. (2009). Understanding male sexual offending: A comparison of general and specialist theories. *Criminal Justice and Behavior, 36*, 1051–1069.

Harris, D. A., Smallbone, S., Dennison, S., & Knight, R. A. (2009). Specialization and versatility in sexual offenders referred for civil commitment. *Journal of Criminal Justice, 37*, 37–44.

Hellman, D. S., & Blackman, N. (1966). Enuresis, firesetting and cruelty to animals: A triad predictive of adult crime. *American Journal of Psychiatry, 122*, 1431–1435.

Hill, A., Habermann, N., Klusmann, D., Berner, W., & Briken, P. (2008). Criminal recidivism in sexual homicide perpetrators. *International Journal of Offender Therapy and Comparative Criminology, 52*, 5–20.

Jenkins, P. (1994). *Using murder: The social construction of serial homicide*. Hawthorne, NY: Aldine de Gruyter.

Langevin, R. (2003). A study of the psychosexual characteristics of sex killers: Can we identify them before it is too late? *International Journal of Offender Therapy and Comparative Criminology, 47*, 366–382.

Langevin, R., Ben-Aron, M. H., Wright, P., Marchese, V., & Handy, L. (1988). The sex killer. *Annals of Sex Research, 1*, 263–301.

Lussier, P., Bouchard, M., & Beauregard, E. (2011). Patterns of criminal achievement in sexual offending: Unravelling the "successful" sex offender. *Journal of Criminal Justice, 39*(5), 433–444.

Lussier, P., LeBlanc, M., & Proulx, J. (2005). The generality of criminal behavior: A confirmatory factor analysis of the criminal activity of sex offenders in adulthood. *Journal of Criminal Justice, 33*, 177–189.

Lussier, P., Proulx, J., & LeBlanc, M. (2005). Criminal propensity, deviant sexual interest and criminal activity of sexual aggressors against women: A comparison of explanatory models. *Criminology, 43*, 249–281.

Lussier, P., Tzoumakis, S., Cale, J., & Amirault, J. (2010). Criminal trajectories of adult sexual aggressors and the age effect: Examining the dynamic aspect of offending in adulthood. *International Criminal Justice Review, 20*, 147–168.

MacDonald, J. M. (1963). The threat to kill. *American Journal of Psychiatry, 120*, 125–130.

McNamara, J. J., & Morton, R. J. (2004). Frequency of serial sexual homicide victimization in Virginia for a ten-year period. *Journal of Forensic Sciences, 49*, 529–533.

Moffitt, T. E. (1993). Adolescence-limited and life-course-persistent antisocial behavior: A developmental taxonomy. *Psychological Review, 100*, 674–701.

Myers, W. C. (2004). Serial murder by children and adolescents. *Behavioral Sciences and the Law, 22*, 357–374.

Nicole, A., & Proulx, J. (2007). Sexual murderers and sexual aggressors: Developmental paths and criminal history. In J. Proulx, É. Beauregard, M. Cusson, & A. Nicole, (Eds.), *Sexual murderers: A comparative analysis and new perspectives* (pp. 29–50). Hoboken, NJ: John Wiley & Sons, Inc.

Purcell, C. E., & Arrigo, B. A. (2006). *The psychology of lust murder: Paraphilia, sexual killing, and serial homicide*. San Diego, CA: Academic Press/Elsevier.

Putkonen, A., Ryynänen, O-P., Eronen, M., & Tiihonen, J. (2002). The quantitative risk of violent crime and criminal offending: A case-control study among the offspring of recidivistic Finnish homicide offenders. *Acta Psychiatrica Scandinavica, 106*, 54–57.

Quinet, K. (2007). The missing missing: Toward a quantification of serial murder victimization in the United States. *Homicide Studies, 11*, 319–339.

Ressler, R. K., Burgess, A. W., & Douglas, J. E. (Eds.). (1988). *Sexual homicide: Patterns and motives*. New York: Simon and Schuster.

Solzhenitsyn, A. I. (1973). *The gulag archipelago, 1918–1956* (Vol. 1). New York: Harper & Row.

Sutherland, E. H. (1950). The sexual psychopath laws. *Journal of Criminal Law and Criminology, 40*, 543–554.

Trojan, C., & Salfati, C. G. (2010). A multidimensional analysis of criminal specialization among single-victim and serial homicide offenders. *Homicide Studies, 14*, 107–131.

Wright, J., & Hensley, C. (2003). From animal cruelty to serial murder: Applying the graduation hypothesis. *International Journal of Offender Therapy and Comparative Criminology, 47*, 71–88.

11

Changing Prevalence of Sex Offender Convictions

Disentangling Age, Period, and Cohort Effects Over Time

Brian Francis[*]
Lancaster University, UK

Claire Hargreaves & Keith Soothill
Lancaster University, UK

Introduction

There has been much interest over the past few decades in sexual crime, but remarkably little research into possible changes of the prevalence of sex crimes over time. There have, of course, been legislative and criminal justice changes that are recognized. Thus, in many jurisdictions, consenting sexual relations between males is no longer a crime, while rape is a crime that is now taken much more seriously by the justice system, with an acknowledgment that both females *and* males can be raped. Beyond this, research into changes over time has been strangely neglected. Figure 11.1 shows the number of offenders either found guilty in a court or cautioned[1] in England and Wales for three specific sexual offenses – rape of a female, indecent assault on a male, and indecency between males – for each year over the period 1970–2009. We notice that there are different trajectories for each of the three offenses. Rape of a female convictions and cautions show a steady increase over the period, rising from around 300 in 1970 up to just under 1,000 in 2009. In contrast, indecent assaults against males (which excludes rape) have shown a steady decrease, from around

* We acknowledge the support of the Economic and Social Research Council under research grant number RES-576-25-0019. We are very grateful for the insightful and useful comments of the referees.

[1] The Home Office states that "Police caution can be given when there is sufficient evidence for a conviction and it is not considered to be in the public interest to institute criminal proceedings. Additionally, the offender must admit guilt and consent to a caution in order for one to be given" (Home Office, 2001). Taken with offenders found guilty in a court, the two categories make up known offenders in a specific year.

Sex Offenders: A Criminal Career Approach, First Edition. Edited by Arjan Blokland and Patrick Lussier.

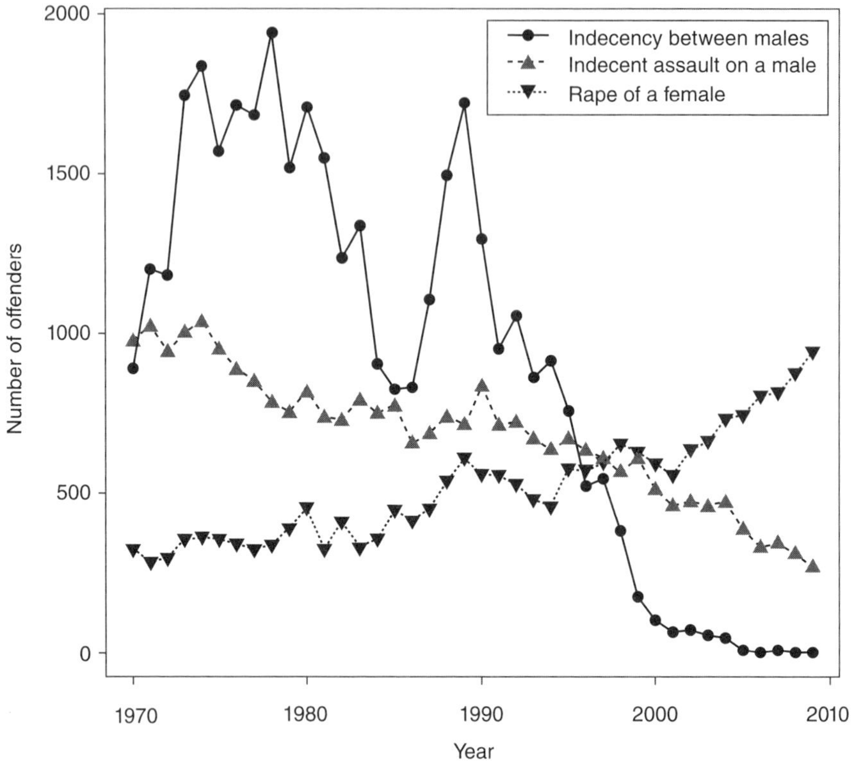

Figure 11.1 Sexual convictions in England and Wales 1970–2009, for three different sexual offenses.

1,000 in 1970 to under 300 in 2009. Indecency between males[2] offenses show a more irregular pattern from 1970 until up to the mid-1990s, varying from 1,000 to 2,000 convictions and cautions per year, followed by a dramatic decrease to near zero by 2009. It is clear that there are considerable changes over time, and moreover, different offense types show different trajectories. However, the explanations for such changes have, to date, been lacking.

More generally, there have been some dramatic declines in the rate of general crime over the past two decades in many Western countries. Much of the focus has been on the decline in the rate of crime in the United States in the decade between 1991 and 2001, and this phenomenon has attracted various explanatory theories from commentators (e.g., Conklin, 2003; Levitt, 2004; Zimring, 2007), with some pointing to increased incarceration, whilst others noted strong economic conditions. Some researchers have suggested changing demographics, whilst others credit the increased access to legal abortion (Levitt, 2004). Recently, however, Soothill and Francis (2011) have pointed to some limitations with the explanatory frameworks

[2]"Indecency between Males" was a legal offence established in 1885 and used to prosecute men engaged in consensual homosexual acts, usually in public places.

that have been posed. In fact, the focus that Conklin (2003), Levitt (2004) and Zimring (2007) are embracing is essentially on how to deal with the relatively small percentage of persons (roughly 3%) who commit much crime – the problem of incidence. An alternative approach is to consider the numbers of persons involved in crime, which may also change over time – the problem of prevalence.

The core of the prevalence issue is to try to determine what proportions of the population are committing at least one crime. As reviewed by Bouchard and Lussier (this book), only a small fraction of individuals are caught, charged, and convicted for their sex crime. In this chapter, we use official conviction data which provide us with the long criminal careers for a variety of offenders of different ages; such data is needed to fully investigate changing rates. Moreover, looking at official data produces "official" prevalence rates, which are important in their own right as they underpin much of the social policy in this area. These changing official prevalence rates over time will reflect both actual changes in behavior and changes in societal response to sexual crime. Additionally, from a criminal justice standpoint, prevalence can be seen as the proportion of the population who have been convicted at least once. However, one needs to recognize that trying to get fewer convicted at all (that is, increasing the figure of around two thirds who are not currently convicted) is a very worthwhile goal, but presents a long-term effort. Changing social circumstances and improving life chances are not things that can be achieved overnight. In short, the results and outcomes are likely to be generational rather than instant. Those who are interested in long-term change are on a different mission from those who appeal to short-term measures.

This chapter is specifically about the prevalence of sex offending and sex offenders, which is a type of offending that has not been considered by the three commentators above. In fact, there are some ready, but contrasting, explanations in trying to interpret the changes over time identified in Figure 11.1. Perhaps younger generations are committing more rape than older generations and so the rise in rape convictions reflects a generational change in behavior – what we will later term a "cohort effect." Perhaps victims of all ages are more willing to report rape, and so more offenders are being convicted – what we will later term a "period effect." Or perhaps such a yearly change simply reflects changes in public opinion about the seriousness of rape and, thus, there is an increased focus on catching rape offenders, which is reflected in officially registered data. In this scenario – also a period effect – the importance is not so much placed on behavior changes but on system changes that are reflecting the increased concern about rape. It is also important to distinguish between changes in the *number of individuals* committing a sex offense, and changes in the *rate at which such individuals* commit sexual offenses. Increases in convictions over time can be caused by more people committing a sexual offense or by an increase in the rate of offending among a constant population of sexual offenders – or indeed both. Finally, demographic changes will also be important and an increase in the population size of those more likely to be involved in rape, that is, those in their late teens to late twenties, will also be relevant. The possibilities need careful consideration and disentangling the age, period, and cohort effects is crucial in understanding what is actually happening.

While the focus of this chapter is on sex offender prevalence, we will be using methodology which has been applied to other types of offending, where we have also attempted to disentangle age, period, and cohort effects. So, for example, Francis, Soothill, and Ackerley (2004), in looking at the risk of criminal conviction in England and Wales, found that age and period were the most important of the three effects, and that only a weak cohort effect was found. Francis and Soothill (2005) have reported on burglary, identifying that when analysis is restricted to the first burglary conviction, there are no strong year or cohort effects. Soothill, Ackerley, and Francis (2004), in contrast, and using a graphical approach, identified *strong* cohort effects when looking at the risks of a robbery and a violence first conviction. The approach of the separation of age, period, and cohort effects is frequently used in medical research, and we will refer to this later in the chapter.[3] The research questions addressed in this paper are therefore:

1 Are there changes in the rate of those first convicted of a sexual offense by age, period, or cohort in England and Wales?
2 If so, what is the nature of such changes and why have they occurred?

The Need for Sociological Explanations of Sex Crime

In examining this fundamental issue of whether there is actually change in those convicted of a sexual offense over time, a shift of approach is needed. Historically, psychiatrists and, more recently, psychologists have tended to be the dominant disciplines in theorizing about sex offending. However, both psychiatry and psychology tend to individualize social problems and regard the source of the problems for the individual as usually wrapped in some form of psychopathology, which certainly cannot explain why there are significant variations in the rates of sex offending over time and between societies. While more work certainly still needs to be done in relation to the issues raised by the disciplines of psychiatry and psychology, system and behavioral changes at the societal level need to be considered as much as behavioral changes at the individual level. In other words, while psychology has been dynamic at the individual level, recognizing changes over the life course, criminology needs to be much more dynamic at the societal level, recognizing social and cultural changes that may lead to changes in sex offending.

There is scope within a traditional sociological approach to develop theorizing that embraces this recognition of social and cultural changes. One will need to probe further important concepts, such as opportunity, capital, and social bonds. There has only been limited effort in applying such concepts to potential changes in sex

[3]A related issue is that of public perception of change. Sadly, most of the public discourse about sex crime is generated from media attention. These public discourses help to give the impression that there is more prostitution, rape, or child sexual abuse around at a particular time, but rarely is the coverage based on much evidence. In truth, media interest is largely about shifting public perceptions in a particular direction and may be far apart from what is actually happening in reality. However, this is what this chapter will be trying to confront. It attempts to move away from the media headlines and to consider the routine enactment of sex crime and the changing number of sex offenders over time.

offending over time, but the possibility is there. For example, situational crime prevention which discusses the importance of opportunity has been applied to child sexual abuse (e.g. Wortley & Smallbone, 2006), while the increase or decrease in social bonding (e.g., Sampson and Laub, 1993) or differences in personal and social capital (e.g., Nagin & Paternoster, 1994) will clearly have a relevance to sexual offending. However, we are pursuing a more modest journey in this paper in charting the empirical material on which theorizing can be developed.

Measuring Sexual Offending

It is notoriously difficult to measure sex crime. Victim surveys are the usual method, and are relatively straightforward, although care needs to be taken in understanding that respondents may not wish to admit to being a victim of a sex offense to the interviewer. As an example of such work, Baker and Duncan (1985) produced the first report, based on a nationally representative sample, to estimate the national prevalence of child sexual abuse in Great Britain. This study reveals the scale at which child sexual abuse is a problem in Great Britain. Of the 2,019 participants in the study, involving both males and females aged 15 years and over, 206 (10%) reported sexual abuse. If the results were generalized to the general population, a possible 4.5 million adults (15 years and over) will have been sexually abused as a child. In turning to offenders, progress has been made in recognizing the *range* of persons engaged in illicit sexual activity. Slater (2003), for example, has through the use of interviews with convicted sex offenders discovered that sex offending can start from an early age, with numerous sex offenders disclosing that they began to sexually abuse even before they reached puberty. Further, Slater (2003) notes a recurring theme that sex offenders mentioned during their interviews, namely, the ability to live multiple lives. In one life they were well-respected members of society and in the other they groomed and raped children.

Estimating the *number* of sex offenders is more complex. Victim surveys provide little information about the number of offenders at large, as 20 victims reporting being raped could involve 20 different rapists or just one serial rapist. Self-reported offending is often styled as the way to get nearer to the truth of offending, but who is likely to admit that they have raped a female or sexually abused a child? The focus of most offender studies is therefore on official data. However, there are numerous issues to consider and it is likely that those convicted do not represent the totality of sex offenders in a community. In order to proceed, we need to understand the progression from sex crime to conviction. There are two current debates on this topic – namely, the reporting of a sexual offense to the criminal justice system, and what happens after a crime is reported within the criminal justice system. First, it is a truism to say that, in order for predators to be prosecuted, they must be reported, recorded, and apprehended. However, as the literature reveals (Van Wijk, Mali, & Bullens, 2007; Langevin et al., 2004), it is only a minority of sexual crimes that are actually reported. Victims are often too scared to report the crime or, as children or being mentally incapable, they may even be unaware that a crime has been committed. Hence, reporting a sex crime is certainly an issue. Second, in recent years there has been a focus on the ineffectiveness of the judicial system in dealing with reported sex crime. The last couple of decades in the United Kingdom have seen an increasingly heated public debate on the falling conviction rate of sexual offenders and the inadequacy of the judicial system to protect women and children from violence (Gregory & Lees, 1999, p. 211).

When a crime is reported, the police and prosecutors will use their discretion to record and act on the report. Harris and Grace (1999), Kelly, Lovett, and Regan (2004) and Feist, Ashe, Lawrence, McPhee, and Wilson (2007) have variously studied the hurdle race of a report of a rape in England and Wales. They concur in reporting numerous reasons why police may take no further action. The offender may be unknown, the complaint may be withdrawn, there may be insufficient evidence to prosecute, or the victim may be unwilling to testify or cooperate. In a minority of cases there may be a false or malicious allegation. Even if the allegations are followed through and a suspect determined, apprehending and prosecuting the suspect can prove extremely difficult. Thomas (2000) identifies a number of factors that can influence an unjust prosecution. These include prosecutors downgrading charges to improve the chances of a successful prosecution, unfair treatment of victims in court hearings, and victims being too scared to testify.

Changes in Sexual Offenders – Official Data and the Offenders Index

To examine changes in the number of sexual offenders, there are two approaches that can be taken. The self-report route will take general samples of the population reporting on their own sexual offending behavior and perhaps will give the closest match to the true prevalence rate of sexual offenders in the population. However, as pointed out in the last section, respondents are unlikely to be honest about their illicit sexual behavior. Moreover, large surveys able to follow offenders through time are rare. In addition, sexual offending is most probably a comparatively rare event and large samples would be needed. The closest such survey in England and Wales is the Offending, Crime and Justice survey (Budd, Sharp, & Mayhew, 2005), but although questions are asked on sexual assault victimization, no questions are asked on sexual *offending*.

Thus, self-report data that might help to fully investigate the changes and the variations in the incidence of sexual offending do not exist. There are no data sources that get close to actual behavioral changes over time – that is, including sexual offending which does not come to the attention of public agencies. The crucial point to recognize is that obtaining a conviction is hazardous and our subsequent analysis based on convictions is some way from measuring actual changes in sexual behavior. Indeed, measuring changes in prevalence of sexual offending through convictions may represent changes in the *social response* toward the behavior as well as changes in the behavior itself. In short, variations in conviction data may be related to a whole variety of factors and we return to this issue later.

However, while recognizing the shortcomings of data sources, cohort conviction studies do help in providing evidence of change over time. The crucial advantage of using official conviction data is that data is available over long periods of time at the individual level. Moreover, large numbers of cases convicted of sexual offending can be accumulated, which would be impossible with self-report data. In this respect, the Home Office has developed a unique set of comparable data sets for England and Wales. The Offenders Index[4] cohorts consist of six data sets. These data sets contain the complete criminal records as found on the Offenders Index for all offenders with a date of birth falling in four pre-selected weeks of the years 1953, 1958, 1963, 1968, 1973, and 1978, giving an approximate 1 in 13 sample of the population of offenders. The six cohorts provide the complete criminal history of standard-list offenses[5] for a total of 47,000 male offenders and more than 10,000 female offenders born in the six sample years. Convictions on the Offenders Index go back to 1963 and so, with the age of criminal responsibility in England and Wales being 10 years, the full range of the "official" criminal career is captured for all offenders in the six cohorts up to the end of 1999. Our analysis will focus on all convictions for all sex offending that has been documented for the members of the six data sets. So what do we hope to learn? The main focus, as mentioned, will be on changes in terms of the patterning of sexual offenders that have taken place. The aim is for the analysis to provide some evidence for theorizing about the extent to which one should appeal to behavioral or system changes to explain the actual changes in sex offending over time.

In using official data, understanding definitions is crucial. In other words, one needs to appreciate what is recognized as sexual offending. In England and Wales, for example, offenders who steal ladies' underwear from washing lines may have a sexual motivation for the act but the offense will be charged as "theft." The official definition is a narrower one and focuses on those convicted of a sexual offense[4] in the courts of England and Wales. Hence, not only will the ladies' underwear thief be excluded, but the most serious sexual crime, such as murders with a sexual motivation, will also be excluded. From the outset, therefore, one needs to recognize that, if we can identify changes in sex offending over time, it will be in relation to a specific band of sexual behavior. Having said that, however, our operational definition still includes what most people would regard as the staple diet of sex crimes. Using our operational definition, 3.8% (n = 1,819) of all the male offenders in the six series have been convicted of a sexual offense and 0.14% (n = 15) of all the female offenders have been convicted of a sexual offense. Owing to the small number of female cases, only convicted male offenders will be analyzed.

[4]Advantages of the Offenders Index include: provision of a complete standard list conviction history of all offenders born in the six cohorts; long conviction histories that range (for the earliest cohort) from age 10 to age 46 and which are difficult to obtain from any other source; and large numbers of offenders. Disadvantages include the fact that there is no information on arrests, cautions, police warnings, or when the offence actually occurred. There is also no information on whether and when an offender moved outside England and Wales or died, and thus observed periods of nonoffending may in fact not be so.

[5]Standard list offences are all indictable offences plus the more serious summary offences (i.e., common assault, criminal damage).

Approaches to Analyzing Offending Behavior Over Time

Systematic analyses of whether the prevalence of being a sexual offender changes over time are complex. As pointed out earlier, we can either focus on the number of convicted sexual offenders (the prevalence) or the number of convicted sexual offenses. The latter quantity is a mix of the prevalence of sexual offending convictions and the varying incidence of sexual convictions among those convicted. This chapter takes the former approach and models the changing prevalence of sexual offending in 5-year age groups. By modeling age-specific prevalence rates, we control for changes in the underlying age distribution. Thus, for example, if rape offenders are most common in the 16–20 age group, then the number of rapes is likely to decrease if the numbers in this age group decline. Cohen and Land (1987) find that age distribution trends, together with other variables such as opportunity, business cycles, and imprisonment rates, explain most of the variation in U.S. homicide and motor vehicle crime. However, Levitt (1999) introduces a note of caution, identifying that changes in age structure explain no more than a one percentage point change per year.

In the subsequent statistical analysis, we will model the prevalence of *a first conviction* for a sexual offense. This is akin to approaches in medicine, where the prevalence of the *first occurrence* of a specific illness will be of interest. We categorize the age-specific prevalence rates into 5-year age periods – with six different birth cohorts of offenders; this means that for a specific cohort, a particular age period will belong to a distinct 5-year period in calendar time. Thus, prevalence rates for those males first offending aged 16–20 for the 1963 cohort will belong to the period 1979–1984. We will then be able to determine risk of first offending as a function of age group, cohort membership, and historical period category.

This approach recognizes the importance of age in sex offending. The age-crime curve is thought to be the oldest relationship in criminology, being first reported by Quetelet (1831). Farrington (1986) identifies the main features of the age-crime curve – the rate of offending increases with age from the age of criminal responsibility, reaching a peak at between 18 and 20, and then declines slowly and, most important, Farrington identifies that different offenses peak at different times. Steffensmeier, Allan, Harer, and Streifel (1989) showed that the median age for sexual offending is 28, substantially higher than the median age for burglary (18), vandalism (18), and robbery (20). As well as age effects, period and cohort effects must also be considered and a suitable analysis strategy chosen that can disentangle the three effects. These effects are formally described by Smith (2002, pp. 715–716) as follows:

> Age effects are termed as changes that occur as an individual proceeds through the life cycle regardless of time period or location. Year (or period) effects are described as changes over a historic time that affect all individuals regardless of age, and cohort effects are seen as effects affecting all individuals sharing a common experience such as being born at the same time and passing through changing society at the same ages. Cohort effects might be observed when younger generations are

committing more crime more frequently than other generations, whereas period effects might be observed when proportionately more crime is being committed by all ages in recent years.

In terms of sexual offending, age effects may be due to factors such as gaining skills and knowledge (e.g., to groom children), biological factors (e.g., testosterone levels, physical abilities), confidence (e.g., to be able to capture and control victims), and changing opportunity for different types of sexual offenses over the life course. Period effects may be due to changes in legislation or to changes in social structure (e.g., the introduction of the general use of the internet would be a contemporary example), and cohort effects may be due to the cohort population size (increasing competition in some cohorts compared to others) or changing societal views on gender relationships, which will affect attitudes acquired in childhood.

As with many problems of this kind, attempting to disentangle age, period, and cohort effects is not a recent issue. In short, there has been a history of criminological work to probe this conundrum. Wilkins (1960) was the first to attempt systematically to explain offending behavior through both year and generational effects. His work initiated the classic criminological debate on the alleged phenomenon of "delinquent generations," that is, whether there are some generations which are more delinquent than others. He was particularly concerned with the paternal and maternal deprivation suffered by many young children during World War II (1939–1945) and whether this experience had lasting effects on their delinquent behavior. Wilkins used cross-tabulations to analyze the conviction rates of English males from age 8 to 20 in each year from 1946 to 1957. After comparing the observed conviction rates with those expected on the basis of row and column totals (of year and age averages), Wilkins found that males who were aged 4–5 at some time during World War II were especially crime-prone at later ages. From these results, Wilkins argued that World War II had produced a "delinquent generation." Wilkins's work inspired researchers in several countries to conduct similar work (e.g., Christiansen, 1964; Jasinsky, 1966; Slater, Darwin, & Ritchie, 1966). However, Wilkins's work attracted a number of criticisms largely led by Walters (1963), who argued that Wilkins's results reflected two trends in conviction rates of those aged 8–11 and 17–20 due to changes in police activity.

Age, Period, and Cohort Modeling

Criticisms of Wilkins's work appeared to close the debate on "delinquent generations" but, more recently, various pieces of research (e.g., Francis et al. 2004; Francis & Soothill, 2005) have been conducted using a statistical technique known as age, period, and cohort modeling. This statistical technique can determine whether there are in fact changes in criminal activity over time and allows the investigator to specify the relative importance of the three effects. For example, Francis et al. (2004) investigated the effect of birth cohort membership on the risk of criminal conviction. They found weak cohort effects for males and a very weak effect for females after controlling for age, year, previous convictions, and interactions between them. Various statistical approaches have been used to investigate age, period, and cohort effects in data. One of the most common is to fit a linear model to the rates, assuming normality of the residuals, and fitting age, period, and cohort as factors (e.g., Menard and Huizinga, 1989). A better approach, which we adopt here, is to use log-linear modeling, which assumes an underlying Poisson distribution for the counts of offenders. Additionally, the log-linear modeling approach allows for a varying population size at risk over time (due to immigration, emigration, and death), takes account of the increasing variability as the counts increase, and also allows the overall goodness of fit to be assessed. Each Poisson log-linear model will take as a response variable the number of convicted offenders for a particular type of sexual offense, modeling effects for categorical age, period, and cohort through sets of dummy variables, and using a log link or transformation to relate the linear model to the response. The size of the relevant population at risk is used as an exposure variable. To proceed, we group the data into 5-year age groups and periods, using the age groups 11–15, 16–20, 21–25, 26–30, 31–35, 36–40, and 41–45, and the year groups 1964–1968, 1969–1973, 1974–1978, 1979–1983, 1984–1988, 1989–1993, and 1994–1998 to classify each first conviction date. The data can be visualized as an age-by-period table of counts, with empty cells. Thus we have convictions for the age group 11–15 in the year 1964–1968 but not for age group 31–35, as this would belong to an earlier birth cohort.

Limitations to Age, Period, and Cohort Modeling

Although age, period, and cohort (APC) modeling allows us to analyze change over time, there is one major limitation. Age, period, and cohort are interrelated and if all three effects are in the model, then one of the main effect parameters cannot be determined (Robertson & Boyle, 1998). Knowing the value on two of the variables provides complete knowledge of the third. For instance, if the age of an offender was born in 1963 and they were convicted in 1983 then age group can be determined. This dependency is present whether age, period, and cohort are fitted as categorical factors or as continuous linear effects.[6] It must be remembered that the identification problem only comes into play if all three factors are found to be significant. If one or two factors are found to be nonsignificant, and are removed from the model, the problem is eliminated. It turns out that this lack of identifiability is not a problem in the study reported here, but it may be in other studies.

[6]Various researchers have tried to overcome this problem using a variety of techniques (Robertson & Boyle, 1998; Glenn, 2005; Hall *et al.* 2005; Okamoto, Hata, Kobayashi, & Hayashi, 2007). One common approach is that of imposing an additional constraint based on prior knowledge (Kupper, Janis, Karmous, & Greenberg, 1985), and software packages for log-linear modeling often impose a constraint without the user being explicitly informed. Applying different forms of constraint will in general yield different parameter estimates. Using constraints is always an arbitrary method of solving the identifiability problem, unless prior or external information is available to enable the constraint to be chosen with consideration.

Types of Sexual Offending and Initial Analysis

Sex offending covers a wide variety of activity. The Home Office codebook (Home Office, 1998) identified 75 distinct sexual offenses then on the statute book which they have grouped into 19 broader types under two headings: "Sexual Offences with Victim" and "Sex-related Offences" (see Appendix A). There is a need in this study to group into fewer categories that remain meaningful, so as to provide sufficient numbers in each category for analysis. We also wanted to identify offenses by age of victim. The 75 offenses have therefore been regrouped by us into a compact set of seven categories determined also by the age and the gender of victim, and are presented as Table 11.1 along with an example of an offense contained in each category.

In Table 11.1 there are essentially two types of groupings of offenses. There are sexual offenses grouped by the victim's age and sexual offenses grouped by the victim's gender. However, these two groupings cannot be directly compared as they are not mutually exclusive. Deciding on groups is constrained by the amount of information available, but identifying meaningful groupings is also the aim. Both age- and gender-determined categories have been chosen for a number of reasons. Certainly there is a recognition that sexual offenders may offend against victims of a certain age but with any gender, whilst other offenders may offend against victims of a certain gender but with no age restriction. In other words, sex offenders may exhibit versatility in their sex offending, whilst others may specialize in one particular type of sexual offense (Cann, Friendship, & Gonza, 2007; Soothill, Francis, Sanderson, & Ackerley, 2000).

The two remaining categories of "consensual sexual offenses" and "other sex-related offenses" are rather different. As the term implies, "consensual sexual offenses" contains offenses where the participants consented to the act, while the "other sex-related offenses" category contains all remaining sexual offenses.

Our initial analysis examined the frequency of male offenders and offenses by males in each birth cohort (Table 11.2). The decline in the number of convicted sexual offenders over the six cohorts seems quite dramatic from 527 offenders in the

Table 11.1 Categories of Sexual Offenses

Sexual offense type	*Example of offense*
Sexual offense against a victim under the age of 16	Rape of a female aged under 16
Sexual offense against a victim aged 16 or over	Indecent assault on a male person 16 years or over
Sexual offense against a victim but age unknown	Incest; Indecent assault on a male with age not stated
Sexual offense where the victim is male	Gross indecency with boys
Sexual offense where the victim is female	Indecent assault on a female
Consensual sexual offenses	Indecency between males
Other sex-related offenses	Possessing obscene material for gain

Table 11.2 Frequency of Male Offenders and Offenses Type of Sexual Offending and Birth Cohort

Birth cohort	*1953*		*1958*		*1963*		*1968*		*1973*		*1978*	
Type of offense	*Offenders*	*Offenses*	*Offenders*	*Offenses*	*Offenders*	*Offenses*	*Offenders*	*Offenses*	*Offenders*	*Offenses*	*Offenders*	*Offenses*
All sexual offenses	527	998	453	793	404	720	241	416	140	272	54	85
Victim under 16	227	461	205	360	178	313	112	182	77	153	29	49
Victim 16 and over	107	142	108	138	88	119	71	103	40	49	18	25
Victim age unknown	161	241	134	219	138	217	60	96	31	43	6	8
Male victim	70	125	54	92	49	98	27	45	21	38	5	6
Female victim	376	696	344	608	322	537	194	328	112	185	47	74
Consensual	54	64	46	49	32	36	19	19	2	2	3	3
Other	56	90	21	27	19	35	12	16	8	25	0	0

1953 cohort to only 54 offenders in the 1978 cohort but, whereas the 1953 cohort is followed up to age 45, the 1978 cohort only reach age 20 by the end of 1999. Female victims always outnumber male victims, but the later cohorts have a higher proportion of female victims. However, this difference may be age-related. The decline in consensual offenses seems likely to be a real difference over time as the effect of the 1967 Act legalizing homosexual acts in private between consenting adults aged 21 or over comes into play, followed by further legislation in 1994 reducing this age of consent to 18.

Table 11.2 also identifies that the 1978 cohort has a relatively small number of offenses (partially due to this cohort only having 10 years of conviction data) and it was decided to restrict the analysis to the first five cohorts.

Population Estimates for Age Groups

Male population estimates for each birth cohort and for each 5-year age group are required to model age-specific rates of first offending correctly. Male population estimates for England and Wales were obtained from the Office of National Statistics (2010). These estimates are mid-year population estimates for every age and for every study year from 1963 to 1999 and allow correct rates standardized by the relevant population to be calculated. As we are grouping offending into 5-year periods, the average of the five population estimates must be calculated for each age group in each cohort. In addition, this average should be multiplied by 28/365 to form an *adjusted* population estimate, as the cohort data set is a 4-week sample of those in the data set born in the target years.[7]

Results

As already mentioned, age, period, and cohort modeling has been conducted to try to disentangle the effects that seem to drive changes in the conviction rates of sexual offenses. In fact, the results of the sexual offenses with victims (victim aged under 16, victim aged 16 and over, victim male, and victim female) will be looked at in more detail as these offenses are generally regarded as being more serious than consensual and other-related sex offenses. Appendix B contains the adjusted population estimates, the number of first male sexual offenders, and the male prevalence rate of convicted first sexual offending per 10,000 population for each 5-year period and for each cohort. First, we note that the within cohort *population* is changing over year groups. For the 1953 birth cohort, for example, the estimated population size is increasing

[7]If $p_1 \ldots p_5$ are the five base population estimates for each age in the specified age group then the adjusted average population per age group $= \left(\frac{(p_1+p_2+p_3+p_4+p_5)}{5}\times\frac{28}{365}\right)$.

until the late 1970s, and then decreasing to allow for differential effects of immigration, emigration, and death. Second, we note the relative sizes of conviction rates – rates of first male convictions against a male are about a tenth of the rates of offending against a female. Similarly, male rates of first conviction against those under 16 are about three times higher compared to rates against those 16 and over, although the large size of the unknown age group makes this interpretation less reliable. The rates for consensual and other types of offending are in general smaller.

Table 11.3 contains the results of the age, period, and cohort modeling, and shows the final model for each type of sexual offending. For example, the final model for "victim aged under 16" is age + period, thus showing age and period affect the rate of sexual convictions. For each model, the deviance and degrees of freedom (d.f.) are presented together with the goodness of fit test p-value (GOFT) calculated from the deviance and d.f. The results show two features. First, there are different effects for different subcategories of sexual offending prevalence – age only, age + period, and age + cohort. This indicates that there are different drivers for changes in sexual conviction prevalence rates for different types of sexual offending. However, it is important to notice that age affects all categories of sexual conviction. In addition, there are period but not cohort effects for sexual offenses against those under 16, offenses against males, and offenses against females, and cohort but not period effects for consensual sexual offenses. The category of sexual offenses against those 16 and over shows only age effects and no evidence of any other changes due to period or cohort. Second, we notice that the APC model fits well for nearly all categories of sexual offending. For "victim under 16" and "victim 16 and over" as well as for female and consensual sexual offenses, the APC model fits well, with p-values substantially greater than 0.05. For the "male victim" category the model fits less well, with variability left to explain. This lack of fit for male victims probably indicates that further subdivision within male victims is necessary. Even though age is important in all sexual offense categories, the effects differ substantially.

Figure 11.2 shows the age estimates for four of the major categories, demonstrating the varying effects, some of which do not follow the well-known bell shaped curve of the age-crime curve for general offending. Figure 11.2 reveals different age effects for sexual offenses with a male victim compared to with a female victim. The

Table 11.3 Final Model, Deviance, Degrees of Freedom, and Goodness of Fit Test When Modeling the Prevalence Rate of First Conviction for Specific Types of Sexual Offense

Type of sexual offending	*Final model*	*Deviance*	*d.f.*	*Goodness of fit p value*
Victim under 16	Age + period	11.40	12	0.495
Victim 16 and over	Age	22.99	18	0.190
Male victim	Age + period	23.060	12	0.027
Female victim	Age + period	12.031	12	0.443
Consensual	Age+ cohort	16.060	14	0.310

Note. Age, period, and cohort are included as categorical explanatory variables in the various models. The "Other" category was excluded from analysis as it was too diverse in offending types.

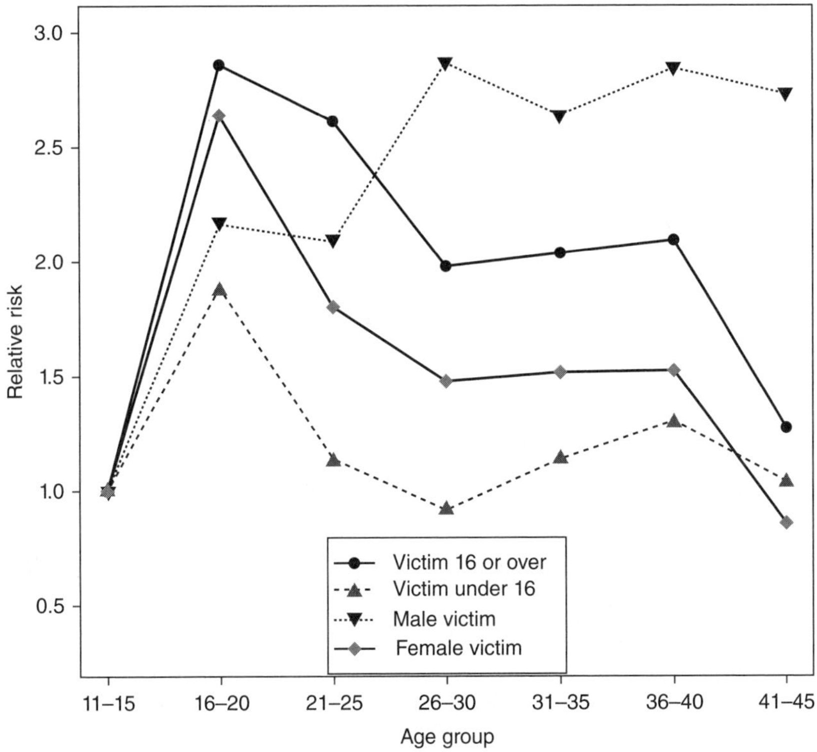

Figure 11.2 Age effects in terms of 5-year relative risks for different types of sexual offenses by males. Relative risks are relative to age group 11–15.

relative risk for a first sexual conviction with a male victim increases gradually by age to 2.87 at age 26–30 and then remains relatively stable at that value. In contrast, this final increase in relative risk does not occur when the victim is female; instead, the relative risk gradually decreases from the first initial peak at age 16–20, with a plateau between ages 26 and 40, and then a further sharp decrease at age 41–45 to the initial level. Figure 11.2 also shows different offender age effects when disaggregating by age of victim rather than by gender of victim. The "victim under 16" relative risk increases from 11–15 to 16–20, then declines, then increases again, reaching a maximum relative risk of around 1.25 by the offender age of 36–40. On the other hand, the "victim 16 and over" relative risk increases more steeply from 11–15 to a relative risk of 2.86 at age 16–20, and declines to a plateau, staying relatively unchanged between the ages of 26 and 40, after which there is a further decline.

As well as age effects, period and cohort effects are also identified. Most remaining categories of sexual offenses are also driven by period effects. Figure 11.3 shows the period effects for these three types of sexual offending, and shows rather different changes over time. For the male victim category, and compared to the reference period of 1964–1968, there is an increase in relative risk of a first conviction up to the 1984–1988 period, after which the relative risks decline steeply, with the risk in 1994–1998 being half that of the

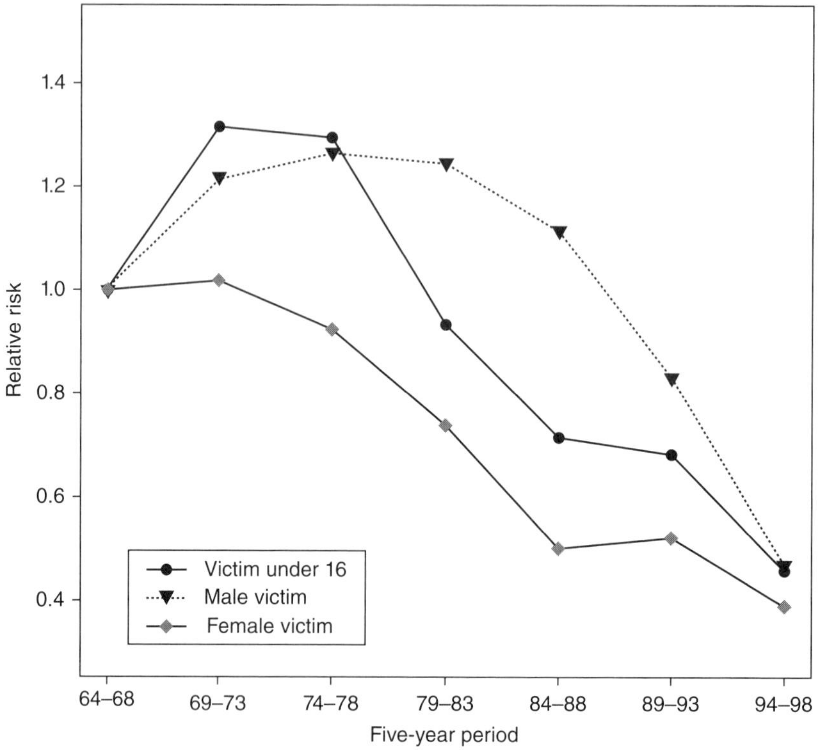

Figure 11.3 Period effects in terms of 5-year relative risks of first conviction by males for victim under 16, and for male and female victim offenses. Relative risks are relative to the period 1964–1968.

reference period. For the victim under 16 category, there is a similar but shorter lived increase up to the 1974–1978 period, followed by a steady decline over subsequent periods. For offenses against a female, the relative risks exhibit a steady decline from 1964 to 1968. In all three categories, the relative risk is lower than the reference period after 1988. Cohort effects play a part only in consensual sexual crimes.

Figure 11.4 shows that the relative risk declines steadily by birth cohort. In particular, the most recent birth cohort of 1973 has a relative risk of 0.08 compared to the 1953 cohort.

In summary, age and period effects drive changes in the conviction rate of most categories of sexual offenses, whilst age and cohort effects drive changes in the conviction rates only for consensual sexual offenses.

Discussion and Conclusions

The academic analysis of sexual offending has been dominated by contemporary practice. However, it is important to consider sexual offending as a dynamic process, as massive changes have taken place over time. By understanding past changes, we

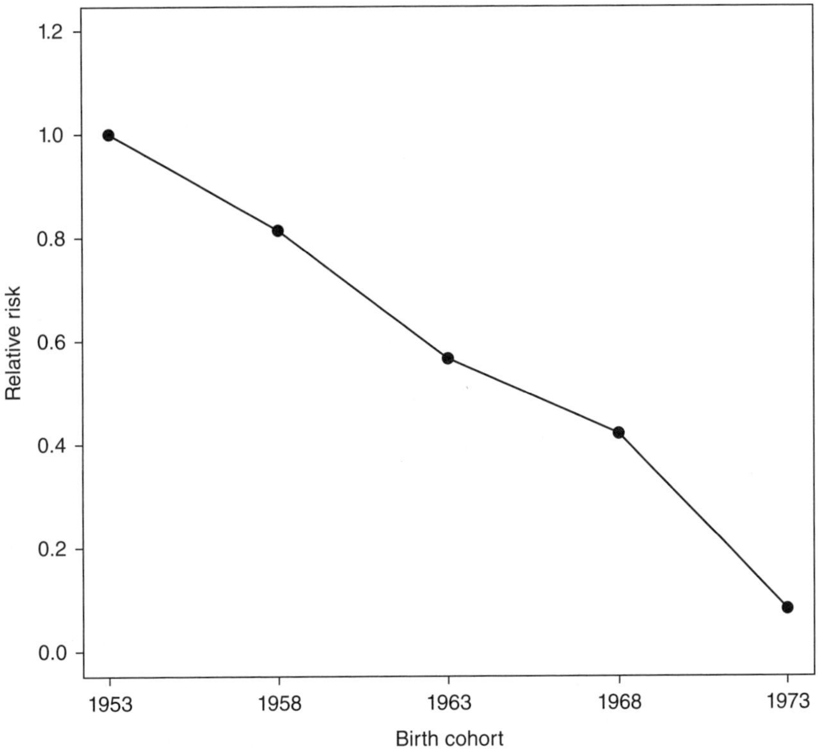

Figure 11.4 Birth cohort effects presented as 5-year relative risks of first conviction by males for consensual sexual offenses.

will gain an insight into future changes, and possible effects which may influence such changes.

In this chapter, we have considered changes over the past 40 years. Examination of official data on cautions and convictions in England and Wales has identified trajectories for different types of sexual crime. Cautions and convictions for rape have increased, whereas indecency between males has had a much more volatile trajectory, before finally decreasing to near zero. However, identifying changes in the number of cautions and convictions does not tell us what the likely drivers for such changes are. We have focused on court data and the risk of being first convicted of a sexual offense. One factor to consider is age – the changing age distribution of the male population may well affect offending rates if younger males are more likely to offend than older males. A second set of drivers relates to changes by year which affect all offenders equally – such drivers would be legislation, changing prosecution policy, and economic conditions. A final set of drivers will relate to generational changes – factors which affect the behavior of each new generation and which are specific to that generation.

Before summarizing the results, it is important to stress the nature of our data. In investigating changes over time, we are limited to examining conviction data as it is only conviction data which can give us information on offenders disaggregated by age over a long historical period. However, there is a well-known danger of using court convictions as a measure of sexual criminal behavior. A court conviction comes at the end of a long criminal justice process, and a change in convictions may reflect a change in the criminal justice processes. Thus, changes in police and prosecution practices may make certain offenses easier or harder to prosecute; there may additionally be moves to police caution, for example, for less serious offenses committed by minors. Such changes would cause increases or decreases in convictions even if the underlying rate of offending were constant.

While previous literature has examined different aspects of sexual offending, the statistical technique of age, period, and cohort modeling has not hitherto been used to analyze change in sexual offender prevalence over time. Such changes that have been identified will represent changes in the underlying risk of becoming a sex offender, but of course will also reflect procedural changes in the criminal justice system toward sexual offending, which in turn will reflect attitudinal changes in society toward sexual offending. In addition, convictions do not represent the totality of sexual crime – many crimes are not reported, and only a small proportion of those reported are convicted. Care is therefore needed in interpreting the results. Nevertheless, examining sexual offending convictions over time is a valuable exercise as it allows us both to examine *offender* characteristics such as age, and to investigate changes over a long period of time.

We now turn to the major influences that might influence changes in risk over time and the life course. Age effects are predominately related to maturity and opportunity. Maturity effects will be partly biological. Thus, Gove (1985) identified the changing levels of testosterone in males over age. Maturation effects will also be developmental – with changing social bonds and responsibilities as an individual ages – and, specifically for sexual crime, will also reflect the ability of an individual to control a victim through physical strength and confidence. Opportunities for committing sexual crime will also change over the life course. At younger ages opportunities are high, but will decrease as an individual gains family responsibility. However, at older ages opportunities again rise, specifically with access to children increasing both within and outside the family.

Period or year effects are risk factors which affect all ages equally. These are partly due to structural factors such as changes in legislation. Over the period of our data there have been two such changes in England and Wales in relation to sexual offending – the Sexual Offences Act of 1967, which decriminalized male homosexual sex between consenting males aged 21 or over, and the Criminal Justice and Public Order Act 1994 Act, which made rape within marriage an offense, also specifying that men as well as women could be victims of rape, and reduced the age of consent for homosexual sex to 18.

Period effects will also be caused by changing social attitudes among the victims of sexual crime, leading to an increased willingness to report such crime. For example, there will be changes in individuals reporting a serious sexual assault to the police and changes in the proportion of cases the police label as "no crime." Changing social behavior may also cause period effects. One such behavioral change is the availability of pornography (Malamuth, Addison, & Koss, 2000); another is the rise of the internet and the anonymity it offers to sexual predators in finding those of like mind and in grooming young victims. Their effect on sexual offending is, however, unknown. Other year effects may be cultural – some commentators (e.g., Armstrong, 2001) have blamed gangsta rap music and its hatred against women as a "celebration of rape culture." The more traditional period effects described by Conklin (2003) and Zimring (2007) of changing police numbers, the changing availability of drugs, economic conditions, and social policies are probably of less relevance for sexual offending, but changing policies on incarceration may well play a part.

Finally, cohort effects affect new generations of individuals and are primarily concerned with the upbringing of children. Of interest here are changing social mores between the genders, and the changing attitudes of respect toward others and the equality agenda. Others may point to the declining influence of religion in new generations. Easterlin (1978, 1987) suggested that the size of the cohort itself will affect offending, with larger cohorts having more competition for resources. Finally, there is the changing policy on cautioning. This increasing tendency to divert sexual offenders away from courts and to offer a police caution will be a period effect. If, however, the policy is targeted at the youngest in society, specifically those who may have been convicted of indecent assault and unlawful sexual intercourse with a girl under 16 and who are themselves under 16, then this will manifest itself as a cohort effect.

Our analysis indicated that sexual offending does change over time. However, a complex analysis also produces some complex answers. In short, it was found that the significant effects differed depending on the category of offense. Age is a crucial variable and provides an interesting start. The age effect was always found to significantly influence changes in prevalence rates of first conviction no matter what the type of sexual offense. The analysis found two distinct trends for age offending. The first – for victims aged 16 or over and for female victims – shows an increasing risk to 16–20, followed by a decline, and then a nearly flat risk until age 40, when there is a further decline. The second trend pattern, in contrast, which is evident for victims under 16 and for offenses against males, shows two peaks – a first peak at age 16–20, followed by a decline, and then an increasing trend to a second peak between the ages of 30 and 40. This echoes work carried out by the Canadian Centre for Justice Statistics on accused offenders based on police-reported crime incidents, where two peaks on sexual offending convictions were found – one at age 13 and the second at age 36 (Canadian Centre for Justice Statistics, 1999). Hanson (2002) suggests that this shows a qualitative difference between juvenile sex offenders and adult sex offenders, and identifies the first peak with antisocial youth becoming sexually active, and the second, later peak with increasing opportunities available to older adult males via relatives and friends. We, in contrast, suggest that it is the nature of the victim that is important – the increasing risk at later ages is dominant in those targeting children and those males targeting other males. An alternative explanation for the second peak would therefore be that older adult males are gaining experience in being able to groom victims and gaining increasing access to specific groups.

A second point relates to whether the peaks in activity are caused by changing activity among the same individuals, or by new offenders becoming sexual offenders at a later age. Our analysis, with its focus on risk of first offending, suggests that there are certainly a large number of new individuals gaining sexual convictions at later ages, and the "new offenders" explanation is strongly supported for specific victim groups. It does not, however, preclude the possibility that there will be individuals with long sexual offending histories.

Changes over time are also crucial. We identified significant period effects for the under 16, male, and female victim groups. Each of the conviction prevalence rates for these offense types is likely to be driven by different factors. For male victims, the increase up to 1979–1983, followed by a decline after that period, may well have been caused by police policy of prosecuting illegal homosexual activity. Following the Sexual Offences Act of 1967, consenting homosexual acts between two men in private were legal if both were aged 21 or over, but the age of consent still differed from that for heterosexual sex. Not until 1994 was the male homosexual age of consent lowered. Tatchell (1998) gives a commentary of police behavior against young gays in the 1970s and 1980s: "Queers were seen as criminals, undeserving of police protection. Gay men who reported being queer-bashed in parks and toilets often found themselves under investigation for homosexual offences and accused by officers of provoking the attack by dressing flamboyantly." He goes on to say that not until the late 1980s "did hard-line police homophobia give way to PR-conscious roundtable discussions." For the female victim group, the risk of a sexual conviction for an offense against a female has been declining since the earliest period of 1963–1967. This may well be related to the declining number of sexual convictions for the offense of "unlawful sexual intercourse with a girl under 16," where there is less willingness to report and the police may increasingly decide not to prosecute if there is evidence of consent. Thus in 1963 there were 4,179 reported offenses; this declined to 1,133 by 1998/9. Finally, the decline in risk for victims under 16 may also be affected by the same phenomenon.

Cohort effects are identified in only one type of sexual offending – that of consensual sexual offenses. This sexual category is dominated by the offense of "indecency between males," which decreased dramatically before finally being repealed in 2004.[8] The prosecuted offense is essentially one of having sex in a public place, most usually a public lavatory. Interestingly, the change over time is identified as a cohort effect, suggesting that new generations were taking advantage of gay bars and internet services as an alternative way of meeting men, and avoiding risk of prosecution. The analysis suggests that establishing ways to overcome the age effect should be a top priority if authorities are to begin to tackle sexual offending. Moreover, as the effects of age differed depending on the category of offense, then the criminal justice system should additionally take this into account when constructing new approaches to reducing sexual offending. Identifying the increased risk posed by older males,

[8] A new gender-neutral offence of "sexual activity in a public lavatory" was introduced in the 2003 Act. Most offenders are male.

specifically against male victims and victims under 16, could lead to more targeted policies in sex offender registration laws. However, as a cautionary point, while we argue that both the conceptual framework and the methodological approach are relevant outside of England, the results may not be applicable elsewhere. In other words, we are stressing that this is a case study and there is a need to replicate the approach in other countries where the context may be different – perhaps leading to rather different results.

In conclusion, it seems unwise to focus on sex offending or sex offenders as a homogeneous entity. Appreciating the heterogeneity of sex offending is pivotal and, as a consequence, different approaches to tackling sexual offending are required depending on the category of the sexual offender. This follows from the recognition that different influences are driving changes in conviction rates. Finally, we make a general plea that criminologists begin to take on board much more the social context and social changes over time in relation to sex crime.

References

Armstrong, E. G. (2001). Gangsta misogyny: A content analysis of the portrayals of violence against women in rap music, 1987–1993. *Journal of Criminal Justice and Popular Culture*, *8*(2), 96–126.

Baker, A. W., & Duncan, S. P. (1985). Child sexual abuse: A study of prevalence in Great Britain, *Child Sexual Abuse & Neglect*, *9*(4), 457–467.

Budd, T., Sharp, C., & Mayhew, P. (2005). *Offending in England and Wales: First results from the 2003 Crime and Justice Survey*. Home Office Research Study 275. London: Home Office.

Canadian Centre for Justice Statistics. (1999). Sex offenders. *Juristat* (Vol. *19*, no. 3). Catalogue no. 85-002-XIE. Ottawa: Statistics Canada.

Cann, J., Friendship, C., & Gonza, L. (2007). Assessing crossover in a sample of sexual offenders with multiple victims. *Legal and Criminological Psychology*, *12*(1), 149–163.

Christiansen, K. (1964). Delinquent Generations in Denmark. *British Journal of Criminology*, *4*(3), 259–264.

Cohen, L. E., & Land, K. (1987). Age structure and crime: Symmetry versus asymmetry and the projection of crime rates through the 1990s. *American Sociological Review*, *52*(2), 170–183.

Conklin, J. E. (2003). *Why crime rates fell*. New York: Allyn and Bacon.

Easterlin, R. A., (1987). *Birth and fortune: The impact of numbers on personal welfare* (2nd ed.). New York: Basic Books.

Easterlin, R. A., (1978). What will 1984 be like? *Demography,15*, 397–432.

Farrington, D. P. (1986). Age and crime. *Crime and Justice* (Vol. *7*, pp. 189–260).

Feist, A., Ashe, J., Lawrence, J., McPhee, D., & Wilson, R. (2007). *Investigating and detecting recorded instances of rape*. Home Office online report 18/07.London: Home Office. Retrieved from http://socialwelfare.bl.uk/subject-areas/services-activity/criminal-justice/homeoffice/144173rdsolr1807.pdf

Francis, B., & Soothill, K. (2005). Explaining changing patterns of crime: A focus on burglary and age-period-cohort models. In M. Peelo & K. Soothill (Eds.), *Questioning crime and criminology* (pp. 102–119). Cullompton: Willan Publishing.

Francis, B., Soothill, K., & Ackerley, E. (2004). Multiple cohort data, delinquent generations, and criminal careers. *Journal of Contemporary Criminal Justice*, *20*(2), 103–126.

Glenn, N. D. (2005). *Cohort analysis* (2nd ed.). California: Sage Publications.

Gove, W. R. (1985). The effect of age and gender on deviant behavior: A biopsychosocial perspective. In A. S. Rossi (Ed.), *Gender and the life course*. Hawthorne, NY: Aldine.

Gregory, J., & Lees, S. (1999). *Policing sexual assault*. London: Routledge.

Hall, B. H., Mairesse, J., & Turner, L. (2004). Identifying age, cohort and period effects in scientific research productivity: Discussion and illustration using simulated and actual data on French physicists. NBER working paper 11739. Retrieved from http://www.nber.org/papers/w11739

Hanson, R. K. (2002). Recidivism and age: Follow-up data from 4,673 sexual offenders. *Journal of Interpersonal Violence*, *17*(10), 1046–1062.

Harris, J., & Grace, S. (1999). *A question of evidence? Investigating and prosecuting rape in the 1990s*. Home Office Research Study 196. London: Home Office.

Home Office. (1998). *The offenders index: Codebook*. London: Home Office. Retrieved from doc.ukdataservice.ac.uk/doc/3935/mrdoc/word/oicodes.doc

Home Office. (2001). *Criminal statistics 2000*. London: Home Office. Retrieved from http://www.archive.official-documents.co.uk/document/cm53/5312/crimestats.pdf

Jasinsky, J. (1966). Delinquent generations in Poland. *British Journal of Criminology*, *6*(2), 170–182.

Kelly, L., Lovett, J., & Regan, L. (2005). *A gap or a chasm? Attrition in reported rape cases*. Home Office Research Study 293. London: Home Office. Retrieved from http://webarchive.nationalarchives.gov.uk/20110218135832/rds.homeoffice.gov.uk/rds/pdfs05/hors293.pdf

Kupper, L. L., Janis, J. M., Karmous, A., & Greenberg, B. G. (1985). Statistical age-period-cohort analysis: A review and critique. *Journal of Chronic Diseases*, *38*(10), 811–830.

Langevin, R., Curnoe, S., Fedoroff, P., Bennett, R., Langevin, M., Peever, C., Pettica, R., & Sandhu, S. (2004). Lifetime sex offender recidivism: A 25-year follow-up study. *Canadian Journal of Criminology and Criminal Justice*, *46*(5), 531–552.

Levitt, S. D. (1999). The limited role of changing age structure in explaining aggregate crime rates. *Criminology*, *37*(3), 581–598.

Levitt, S. D. (2004). Understanding why crime fell in the 1990s: Four factors that explain the decline and six that do not. *Journal of Economic Perspectives*, *18*(1), 163–190.

Malamuth, N. M., Addison A., & Koss, M. (2000).Pornography and sexual aggression: Are there reliable effects and can we understand them? *Annual Review of Sex Research*, *11*, 26–91.

Menard, S., & Huizinga, D. (1989). Age, period, and cohort size effects on self-reported alcohol, marijuana, and polydrug use: Results from the National Youth Survey. *Social Science Research*, *18*(2), 174–194.

Nagin, D. S., & Paternoster, R. (1994). Personal capital and social control: The deterrence implications of a theory of individual differences in criminal offending. *Criminology*, *32*(4), 581–606.

Office of National Statistics. (2010). *Mid-year resident population estimates for England and Wales*. Population Estimates Unit, Personal Communication (July 23, 2010).

Okamoto, E., Hata, E., Kobayashi, M., & Hayashi, K. (2007). Age-period-cohort analysis of asthma prevalence among school children. *Environmental Health and Preventive Medicine*, *12*(3), 119–128.

Quetelet, A. (1831). *Research on the propensity to crime of different ages.* Brussels: Hayez.

Robertson, C., & Boyle, P. (1998). Age-period-cohort analysis of chronic disease rates. I: Modelling approach. *Statistics in Medicine, 17*(12), 1305–1323.

Sampson, R. J., & Laub, J. H. (1993). *Crime in the making.* Cambridge, MA: Harvard University Press.

Slater, A. C. (2003). *Predators, pedophiles, rapists, & other sex offenders: Who they are, how they operate, and how we can protect ourselves and our children.* New York: Basic Books.

Slater, S., Darwin, J., & Ritchie, W. (1966). Delinquent generations in New Zealand. *Journal of Research in Crime and Delinquency, 3*(2), 140–146.

Smith, D. J. (2002). Crime and the life course. In M. Maguire, R. Morgan, & R. Reiner (Eds.), *The Oxford handbook of criminology* (3rd ed.). Oxford: Oxford University Press.

Soothill, K., Ackerley, E., & Francis, B. (2004). Profiles of crime recruitment: Changing patterns over time. *British Journal of Criminology, 44* (3), 401–418.

Soothill, K., & Francis B. (2011). Considering paradigms of crime reduction in different contexts. In C. Gould (Ed.), *National and international perspectives on crime and policing* (pp. 477–505). Pretoria: Institute of Security Studies.

Soothill, K., Francis, B. J., Sanderson, B., & Ackerley, E. (2000). Sex offenders: Specialists, generalists – or both? A 32-year criminological study. *British Journal of Criminology, 40*(1), 56–67.

Steffensmeier, D. J, Allan, E. A., Harer, M. D., & Streifel, D. (1989). Age and the distribution of crime. *American Journal of Sociology, 94* (4), 803–831.

Tatchell, P. (1999). Policing with prejudice. In P. Francis & P. Fraser (Eds.), *Building safer communities: Selected papers from a conference.* London: The Centre for Crime and Justice Studies.

Thomas, T. (2000). *Sex crime: Sex offending and society.* Cullompton: Willan Publishing.

Van Wijk, A. Ph., Mali, S. R. F., & Bullens, R. A. R. (2007). Juvenile sex-only and sex-plus offenders: An exploratory study on criminal profiles. *International Journal of Offender Therapy and Comparative Criminology, 51*(4), 407–419.

Walters, A. (1963). Delinquent generations? *British Journal of Criminology, 3*(4), 391–395.

Wilkins, L. (1960). Delinquent generations. *Studies in the causes of delinquency and the treatment of offenders* (Vol. 3). London: HMSO.

Wortley, R., & Smallbone, S. (2006). *Situational prevention of child sexual abuse.* Boulder, CO: Lynne Rienner Publishers.

Zimring, F. E. (2007). *The Great American Crime Decline.* New York: Oxford University Press.

Appendix A. Home Office Categorisation of Sexual Offences (Home Office, 1998)

Sexual offences with "victims"

Buggery
Indecent assault on a male
Indecency between males
Rape
Indecent assault on a female
Unlawful sexual intercourse with girl under 13
Unlawful sexual intercourse with girl under 16
Incest
Abduction
Abuse of Trust-sexual offences
Gross indecency with a child
Indecent exposure

Sex-related offences

Procuration of males and females
Bigamy
Soliciting by a man
Possession of obscene material
Keeping a brothel
Offences by prostitutes
Living on prostitutes earnings

Appendix B. Adjusted Population Estimates, and the Number of First Sexual Offender Convictions and Rate Per 10,000 of the Population, for Each Age Group and Cohort. Males only.

				All sexual offenses		*Victim under 16*		*Victim 16 or over*		*Victim age unknown*		*Consensual*		*Other*		*Male victim*		*Female victim*	
Cohort	*Period*	*Age at first conviction*	*Adjusted population Size*	*N*	*Rate*	*N*	*Rate*	*N*	*Rate*	*N*	*Rate*	*N*	*Rate*	*N*	*Rate*	*N*	*Rate*	*N*	*Rate*
1953	64–68	11–15yr	25928.8	75	28.93	32	12.34	11	4.24	13	5.01	1	0.39	18	6.94	4	1.54	51	19.67
1953	69–73	16–20yr	26297.0	185	70.35	83	31.56	25	9.51	62	23.58	6	2.28	9	3.42	13	4.94	155	58.94
1953	74–78	21–25yr	26501.0	179	67.54	58	21.89	35	13.21	56	21.13	14	5.28	16	6.04	18	6.79	128	48.30
1953	79–83	26–30yr	26101.3	142	54.40	34	13.03	12	4.60	49	18.77	21	8.05	26	9.96	24	9.19	69	26.44
1953	84–88	31–35yr	25769.0	136	52.78	74	28.72	20	7.76	22	8.54	16	6.21	4	1.55	19	7.37	93	36.09
1953	89–93	36–40yr	25558.1	180	70.43	105	41.08	26	10.17	34	13.30	5	1.96	10	3.91	22	8.61	135	52.82
1953	94–98	41–45yr	25346.0	91	35.90	69	27.22	13	5.13	2	0.79	1	0.39	6	2.37	23	9.07	61	24.07
1958	69–73	11–15yr	28116.6	76	27.03	47	16.72	12	4.27	16	5.69	0	0.00	1	0.36	6	2.13	69	24.54
1958	74–78	16–20yr	28132.0	198	70.38	85	30.21	30	10.66	67	23.82	12	4.27	4	1.42	12	4.27	166	59.01
1958	79–83	21–25yr	28096.2	162	57.66	62	22.07	22	7.83	57	20.29	11	3.92	10	3.56	29	10.32	107	38.08
1958	84–88	26–30yr	27671.7	127	45.90	52	18.79	28	10.12	33	11.93	11	3.98	3	1.08	23	8.31	87	31.44
1958	89–93	31–35yr	27526.0	99	35.97	48	17.44	24	8.72	17	6.18	7	2.54	3	1.09	9	3.27	76	27.61
1958	94–98	36–40yr	27511.7	127	46.16	63	22.90	21	7.63	29	10.54	8	2.91	6	2.18	13	4.73	99	35.98
1963	74–78	11–15yr	31857.1	71	22.29	49	15.38	7	2.20	15	4.71	0	0.00	0	0.00	4	1.26	67	21.03
1963	79–83	16–20yr	32128.6	223	69.41	96	29.88	35	10.89	79	24.59	8	2.49	5	1.56	25	7.78	183	56.96
1963	84–88	21–25yr	32073.9	139	43.34	48	14.97	24	7.48	52	16.21	10	3.12	5	1.56	14	4.36	110	34.30
1963	89–93	26–30yr	31579.2	132	41.80	55	17.42	26	8.23	32	10.13	12	3.80	7	2.22	23	7.28	83	26.28

(*Continued*)

(Continued)

				All sexual offenses		Victim under 16		Victim 16 or over		Victim age unknown		Consensual		Other		Male victim		Female victim	
Cohort	Period	Age at first conviction	Adjusted population Size	N	Rate	N	Rate	N	Rate	N	Rate	N	Rate	N	Rate	N	Rate	N	Rate
1963	94–98	31–35yr	31199.2	127	40.71	47	15.06	27	8.65	30	9.62	6	1.92	17	5.45	18	5.77	81	25.96
1968	79–83	11–15yr	30787.1	59	19.16	40	12.99	16	5.20	2	0.65	0	0.00	1	0.32	11	3.57	47	15.27
1968	84–88	16–20yr	30719.6	136	44.27	54	17.58	28	9.11	38	12.37	6	1.95	10	3.26	12	3.91	106	34.51
1968	89–93	21–25yr	30565.1	134	43.84	53	17.34	28	9.16	40	13.09	10	3.27	3	0.98	10	3.27	108	35.33
1968	94–98	26–30yr	30564.2	84	27.48	34	11.12	30	9.82	16	5.23	2	0.65	2	0.65	12	3.93	65	21.27
1973	84–88	11–15yr	26578.3	29	10.91	21	7.90	5	1.88	3	1.13	0	0.00	0	0.00	7	2.63	22	8.28
1973	89–93	16–20yr	26758.5	132	49.33	87	32.51	19	7.10	24	8.97	0	0.00	2	0.75	28	10.46	102	38.12
1973	94–98	21–25yr	26780.2	86	32.11	20	7.47	25	9.34	16	5.97	2	0.75	23	8.59	3	1.12	57	21.28

12

Life-Course Transitions and Desistance in Sex Offenders

An Event History Analysis

Arjan Blokland
NSCR and Leiden University, the Netherlands

Victor van der Geest
VU University, the Netherlands

Introduction

Contrary to many early studies in criminology, life-course criminology focuses not on the advent of crime, but instead on explaining desistance from offending in the post-adolescent period. The basic premise of the life-course approach to crime, taken from criminal career research, is that the criminal career has many dimensions – for example, onset, frequency, crime mix, and duration – and that each dimension is governed by different causal influences emanating from different life-course domains (Blumstein & Cohen, 1987). What causes individuals to engage in crime (e.g., want of peer status) is assumed to be different from what makes them persist in crime (e.g., financial strain), which in turn is different from – and not merely the absence of – what eventually makes a person stop offending (e.g., ill health). It is the latter process – referred to as desistance – that is a focal concern in life-course criminology (Laub & Sampson, 2001). Desistance is a universal process in the sense that even the most active offenders eventually cease offending (Laub & Sampson, 2003). Cross-sectional research – research examining many different offenders at one point in time – finds offending to be related to age in a predictable manner: Criminal behavior steeply increases to a peak from late childhood to late adolescence, after that crime slowly decreases reaching trivial levels during old age (Farrington, 1986). Longitudinal research – research that examines a limited number of offenders for a prolonged period of time – however, has found this cross-sectional age-crime curve to obscure much individual variability in criminal trajectories (Piquero, 2008; Van Dulmen, Goncy, Vest, & Flannery, 2009). Desistance may very well be universal, but the timing, pace, and duration of the desistance process differs widely from one offender

Sex Offenders: A Criminal Career Approach, First Edition. Edited by Arjan Blokland and Patrick Lussier.

to the next. Some theorists tend to disregard individual variability in the parameters of desistance, and ascribe desistance from crime to general processes like maturation – the biological and psychological aging of the individual (Hirschi & Gottfredson, 1983). Others, however, have sought for explanations that could incorporate both the general downward trend in offending, as well as its between-individual variability. While a number of theories have been offered, most common are theories that explain desistance from crime from a control perspective (Laub & Sampson, 2003; Moffitt, 1993; Sampson & Laub, 1993). Control theorists reverse the typical criminological question and do not seek to explain why a person engages in crime. Instead they ask why he or she refrains from acting on the selfish impulses which are assumed to be ever present in all of us. Building on Hirschi's classic social control theory (Hirschi, 1969), present-day life-course theories view the bond to conventional institutions, like work and marriage, as pivotal in understanding both the universality and the variability of the desistance process (Sampson & Laub, 1995). In their efforts to explain why offenders stop offending, life-course theorists have posited that the frequency of offending diminishes with age as a result of offenders increasingly becoming encapsulated in conventional society (Blokland & Nieuwbeerta, 2010). As offenders transition to and invest in adult social roles the potential costs of offending rise and are argued to progressively deter offenders from continued offending. In their study of 500 former pupils of a Massachusetts reformatory, Laub and Sampson (2003; Sampson & Laub, 1993), for example, find that a steady job and a good marriage independently contribute to desistance from crime. In the qualitative part of their study, the boys, now in their seventies, pinpoint these transitions as turning points in their criminal careers. As William, one of the boys interviewed in old age, states: "The thing that changed me was marriage. That turned me straight down the line. She won't put up with any baloney" (Laub & Sampson, 2003, p. 134). However, while with age adult obligations and responsibilities tend to increase, not all youths simultaneously find that one-in a-million job or happen to run into their long-term partner, giving rise to the variability in individual desistance patterns found in longitudinal studies.

Unlike Sampson and Laub, Moffitt (1993; 1994) explicitly states that the effect of these life-course transitions on crime is conditional on the offender's individual characteristics. For some, temperamental difficulties and failed parent-child interactions have led them to adopt antisocial interaction patterns from an early age onward. By the time these children reach adolescence their antisocial manners have become so much ingrained in their behavioral repertoire that they defy any outside influence, including that of the transitions that cause other offenders to desist (Moffitt, 1997). These persistent and often violent offenders continue to offend long into their adult years. The majority of offenders, however, not burdened by individual or familial risks, may explore offending as a way to obtain personal autonomy, but are expected to refrain from further offending as with age opportunities other than crime arise (Moffitt, 2006). Theorists looking at desistance from a maturation perspective, however, maintain that the decrease in offending with age is a given, not caused by the fulfillment of adult social roles, but merely coinciding with these life-course transitions. These theorists dismiss any association between life-course circumstances and crime as spurious (Hirschi & Gottfredson, 1995). While some efforts have been made to apply the life-course criminological perspective to specific types of offenders, like organized crime offenders (Van Koppen, De Poot, & Blokland, 2010) or homicide offenders (Vaughn, Delisi, Beaver, & Howard, 2009), today much of life-course criminology has dealt with common crimes and the majority of research has been conducted on general population samples or samples with a generally increased risk of offending (Farrington, 2003; Piquero, Farrington, & Blumstein, 2003). As a result, it is still unclear to what extent current theoretical knowledge on the development of crime over the life span generalizes to less common or more serious forms of crime, like sexual offenses.

Only recently have the concepts and analytical tools from life-course criminology been applied to study the criminal careers of sex offenders, and has the analytical focus in sex offending research broadened beyond theories explaining the etiology and onset of sexual offending, to research and theories that also cover the maintenance and desistance of sexual offending across the sex offender's life span (e.g., Proulx, Lussier, Ouimet, & Boutin, 2008; Ward & Beech, 2006). The aim of the current study is to gain insight in the mechanisms influencing desistance from sex offending and to establish the extent to which insights from mainstream criminological theories generalize to specific offender populations. In this chapter we seek to test life-course explanations of desistance and ask to what extent important life-course transitions are associated with reoffending rates in convicted sex offenders. More specifically, we examine whether, whilst controlling for stable risk factors, being married, being divorced, or being a parent postpones reconviction in convicted sex offenders.

Age and Desistance From Sexual Offending

A handful of studies have focused on the way age affects sexual offending. Contrary to the once – and even still – widely held belief that sexually deviant behavior can be expected to continue across the life span, the results of these studies mount to a conclusion that is similar to that of mainstream criminology, namely that, like for other forms of crime, there is desistance from sex offending with age (Laws & Ward, 2011). Combining data on over 4,500 sex offenders, Hanson (2002) showed the frequency of sexual offending to rise to a peak and subsequently show a more gradual decline when plotted against age; a shape very similar to the age-crime curve found for general offending. The age-sex crime curve for rapists most closely resembled the general age-crime curve with rapists' sexual offending peaking in their late twenties. For child molesters and incest offenders, however, the zenith of the age-sex crime curve was not reached until these offenders were in their thirties, which is much later than the peak age period for general offending (Farrington, 1986; 2003). Despite differences in peak age, all curves evidenced desistance, and by age 60 sexual offending declined to a near zero rate for all sex offenders. At first glance, the finding that the age-crime curve peaks at an older age for sex offenders goes against the logic of the life-course explanation of desistance from crime. Life-course theory argues that crime peaks in the relatively roleless adolescent period, but starts to decline again when young adults increasingly transition into adult social roles (Laub & Sampson, 2003; Moffitt, 2006). Despite the fact that in recent years the average ages of marriage and parenthood have increased (Arnett, 2004), the peak in sex offending – especially that for child molesters – seems to occur at a time when the majority of adolescents have already started taking up adult responsibilities. This might signal that either sex offenders do not transition into adulthood at the same pace as nonsex offenders, or that these transitions do not affect recidivism in a similar manner. The empirical landscape on the (emerging) adult development of sex offenders is spotted and precludes drawing definitive conclusions. Some studies do address issues related to relationship formation. With regard to conventional sexual experience, adolescent sex offenders have been found to score higher, rather than lower than nonsexual offenders (Chewning, 1991). Contrary to explanations referring to sex offenders' social incompetence (e.g., Finkelhor, 1984; Marshall & Barbaree, 1990; Ward & Siegert, 2002) adolescent sex offenders also do not seem to differ on heterosocial skills that might keep them from forming intimate romantic relationships (Seto & Lalumiere, 2010). Loneliness, on the other hand, is commonly reported among sex offenders (Seidman, Marshall, Hudson, & Robertson, 1994).

An alternative explanation for the age–sex crime curve peaking at a later age might be that the transitions that influence common crime do not affect sexual offending or do so only to a lesser extent. While the consequences of sexual offending in terms of loss of social capital are likely to match or – given public opinion with regard to sexual offenders – top the costs associated with common delinquency, these transitions might also change the incentive structure for sex offending in a way that makes it more instead of less likely. Conflicting interpersonal relationships can give rise to frustration and anger; negative emotions that may set the stage for sexual violence (Malamuth, 1996). Becoming a (step)parent leads to intensified interaction with underage children – both one's own child and nonfamilial children, for example, classmates, neighborhood friends – thereby increasing the opportunity to offend against minors. However, if sex offenders resemble Moffitt's persistent offenders and their sexual offending is rooted in some stable characteristic that is not influenced by contextual factors, life-course transitions are unlikely to affect sexual offending. If sexual offending, for example, results from neurobiological functioning or deviant sexual interests (e.g., Kafka, 2003), life-course transitions may simply offer new opportunities to commit sexual crimes instead of deterring offenders from future offending, causing desistance from sex offending to be postponed. Finally, the age–sex crime relationship might be governed by maturational factors. Prior research, for example, has shown the libido to decline with age. Like the frequency of consensual sexual intercourse, sexual offending may similarly decline with age (Bacon et al. 2003; Langstrom & Hanson, 2006). If desistance from sex offending is caused by waning sexual interest, than important life-course transitions merely coincide with desistance from sex offending, but exert no causal influence (Barbaree, Blanchard, & Langton, 2003; Blanchard & Barbaree, 2005).

Prior Research

Reviews on sex offender recidivism contradict the popular belief that sex offenders are specialized and persistent offenders (Furby, Weinrott, & Blackshaw, 1989; Hanson & Bussière, 1998). A recent meta-analysis by Hanson and Morton-Bourgon (2005), pooling data from 73 studies involving 19,276 sex offenders in total, found that over a 5–6-year follow-up, the average observed sexual recidivism rate was 13.7%. The average violent nonsexual recidivism rate was 14.3% (24 studies, 6,928 sex offenders in total), while, on average, 36.2% of sex offenders reoffended with any offense (56 studies, 12,708 sex offenders in total). Observed recidivism tends to increase with the length of the follow-up (Furby, Weinrott, & Blackshaw, 1989; Harris & Hanson, 2004), suggesting that sex offenders' criminal careers may show substantial periods of intermittency. While caution is needed given that these averages are based on studies using diverse samples, different operationalizations of what constitutes recidivism (e.g., arrest, charge, conviction, self-report), and different follow-up periods, we can safely conclude that extant knowledge suggests that sex offenders are more likely to recidivate with a nonsexual than a sexual offense. Prior research also has identified a number of risk factors that are associated with both sexual and nonsexual recidivism in sex offenders (Hanson & Bussière, 1998; Hanson & Morton-Bourgon, 2005). In the parlance of sex offender research, variables that reflect stable historical between-individual differences are labeled static risk factors. Static risk factors, or predictors, are unchangeable and include variables such as childhood behavioral problems, criminal history, and age.

Dynamic risk factors, on the other hand, refer to changeable variables. Dynamic risk factors are further subdivided into stable dynamic risk factors and acute dynamic risk factors, reflecting the time frame in which changes in these risk factors may manifest themselves. Stable dynamic risk factors, like a drug addiction, are in principle changeable, but are expected to remain unchanged for months or even years. Acute dynamic risk factors, like being high on drugs or being angry, change far more rapidly, and can be regarded as situational factors influencing the occurrence of an offense, but not the individual's overall risk potential (Hanson & Harris, 2000). Adult social roles like the ones studied here can be regarded as stable dynamic factors, as even for the most capricious of offenders, marriage duration is best expressed in months or years rather than days or hours.

Much of the earlier research into sex offender recidivism focused on static risk factors, such as age, offense type, and criminal history. Hanson and Bussière (1998) find that sex offenders' age is related to violent and general recidivism. These findings corroborate studies among general offenders (Grendreau, Tittle, & Goggin, 1996). Age also affects sexual recidivism, be it to a lesser extent. Sexual recidivism is lower among older offenders, with fewer than 5% of offenders over the age of 60 recidivating, compared to over 20% of those in their twenties (Hanson, 2002). Still, other studies find that there is little change in recidivism rates during most of the adult period, suggesting that the effect of age on recidivism is far from linear (Doren, 2006). In fact, Hanson (2002) found that extrafamilial child molesters maintained a high risk of recidivism longer than did other sex offenders, before it rapidly declined to near zero at old age (but see Barbaree, Blanchard, & Langton, 2003). Offender type also predicts recidivism. Offenders classified as rapist tend to have higher recidivism rates for violent offending than do child molesters (Hanson & Bussière, 1998). A recent study of 2,785 males arrested for the first time in Western Australia between 1984 and 1994, however, did not find such differences (Broadhurst & Loh, 2003). Sex offender type also predicts sexual recidivism rates, with sexual recidivism being highest in exhibitionists and child molesters, and with extrafamilial child molesters having higher recidivism rates than incest offenders (Hanson & Bussière, 1998; Soothill, Francis, Sanderson, & Ackerley, 2000). A history of nonsexual offending predicts general reoffending in sex offenders (Hanson & Bussièrre, 1998). The total number of prior offenses is also a reliable, but modest, predictor of sexual recidivism. Violent nonsexual recidivism is predicted by a history of violent crimes (Hanson & Morton-Bourgon, 2005). Sexual recidivists, those already having a history of sexual offending, have an elevated risk of recidivating to a sexual offense. A history of prior sexual offending does not predict violent reoffending and seems only weakly related to general recidivism (Hanson & Bussière, 1998).

While in life-course criminology the association between an early onset of problem behavior and a frequent and prolonged criminal career is considered a "widely accepted conclusion" that needs theoretical interpretation (Farrington, 2003, 2005), the association between an early onset and sexual recidivism is much more equivocal. Though consistent with predictions derived from the Moffitt taxonomy, an early onset of problematic behavior is sometimes associated with an increased risk of reoffending (Hanson & Morton-Bourgon, 2005), an early onset of sexual offending does not always predict a persistent sexual criminal career (e.g., Zimring, Jennings, & Piquero, 2007). While Harris and Rice (2007), combining multiple data sources into a sample of 1,338 sex offenders, concluded that age of onset of the criminal career predicted recidivism in sex offenders, Lussier and Healy (2009), in their Canadian study on 553 incarcerated sex offenders, instead found that age of onset was not related to recidivism after controlling for age of release, suggesting that desistance is the default for late- as well as early-onset offenders. Recently, researchers have increasingly begun to focus on dynamic risk factors of recidivism in sex offenders.[1] Stable dynamic risk factors appear most relevant for policies aimed at reducing individuals' long-term risk for reoffending. While both Hanson and Bussière (1998) and its update (Hanson & Morton-Bourgon, 2005) review research pertaining to the effect of marital status, neither includes information on potential effects of parenthood. Prior research finds that being single increases the risk of sexual recidivism, but that current marital status in not related to sexual reoffending (Hanson & Bussière, 1998). In contrast, Scalora and Garbin (2003) did

[1]To date a handful of studies have focused on acute dynamic risk factors. Given the nature of our data and the focus of the current analyses, here only research on stable dynamic risk factors is discussed; the interested reader is referred to Hanson and Harris (2000) and Mann, Hanson, and Thornton (2010) for examples of recent efforts to also chart acute predictors of recidivism in sex offenders.

find current marital status to be significantly associated with sexual recidivism in a sample of 194 convicted child molesters. Using data from 437 probationed sex offenders, Hepburn and Griffin (2002) found married sex offenders to be less likely to subsequently commit a technical violation, reoffend with any offense, or fail parole. More recent studies also indicate that conflicts in intimate relationships increase the likelihood of sexual reoffending (Hanson & Morton-Bourgon, 2005). However, most studies only included static indicators of these dynamic variables, for example, whether the offender had been married or was married at the time of the offense or not. Therefore, what remains unknown is whether changes in these dynamic risk factors are related to changes in recidivism. In one of the few studies on sex offender recidivism explicitly taking a life-course perspective, Kruttschnitt, Uggen, and Shelton (2000) examined the effects of formal and informal controls on sexual reoffending in a sample of 556 sex offenders placed on probation in 1992. Their study focused on the effects of employment and marriage. Employment stability was measured as working for at least six months with the same employer. Marital stability was operationalized as being married both at the time of the offense and at the time of sentencing. Overall about 35% of the sex offenders reoffended with any offense, while 5.6% of the sample reoffended with a new sex offense within the 5-year follow-up. Those with stable employment were about 37% less likely to reoffend and this effect extended to all types of reoffending. The effect of a stable marriage was also negative, but did not reach statistical significance. However, note that in this study employment and marital stability reflect a history of stability, rather than stability over the observation period. Consequently, the above findings may to some unknown extent result from individual differences – for example, heterogeneity in the extent to which these offenders were "marriage material" – rather than from genuine effects of these informal social controls on the rate of reoffending. The finding that sex offender treatment was most successful in sex offenders with stable work histories might reflect this bias. The current study examines the effect of stable dynamic factors and focuses on the way marriage, divorce, and parenthood are associated with recidivism of registered sex offenders over a 25-year period. Like Kruttschnitt, Uggen, and Shelton (2000), we use event history analysis to examine sex offender recidivism. However, unlike these authors, the data allows us to assess the impact of marriage, divorce, and parenthood as they vary over time.

Data and Method

Sample

This study uses data from the Criminal Career and Life-Course Study (CCLS), a large-scale, longitudinal study of a cohort of individuals who had their criminal case adjudicated in 1977. These data have been previously used to map criminal development up to age 72 (Blokland, Nagin, & Nieuwbeerta, 2005; Blokland & Van Os, 2010), to study the impact of life-course transitions of these trajectories (Blokland

& Nieuwbeerta, 2005), and most recently to study the impact of imprisonment (Apel, Blokland, Nieuwbeerta, & Van Schellen, 2010; Nieuwbeerta, Nagin, & Blokland, 2009). The current study is primarily based on a subsample of 500 individuals whose criminal case adjudicated in 1977 pertained to a sexual offense. The entire CCLS sample constitutes a 4% sample of all criminal cases adjudicated in 1977; however, a number of serious crimes, including all sexual crimes, were oversampled. As a result, the current sample is based on all criminal cases involving a sexual offense adjudicated in that year. As such, in a statistical sense we do not study a sample, but rather the entire population of adjudicated sex offenders in the Netherlands in 1977. In some of the analyses a control group is used. The control group for this study consists of all offenders convicted solely for a nonsexual offense in 1977 who also did not have any convictions for sexual offenses prior to 1977.

Measures

The criminal careers of the sampled people were reconstructed using information from the General Documentation Files (GDF) of the Criminal Record Office ("rap sheets"). The GDFs contain information on every criminal case registered by the police at the Public Prosecutor's Office. Information on the final decision is sent to the Criminal Record Office by the Public Prosecutor's Office, the court in first instance, and the higher court, respectively. The GDFs contain information on all adjudications that led to any type of outcome (not guilty, guilty, sentence, prosecutorial decision to drop due to lack of evidence, prosecutorial decision to drop for policy reasons, and prosecutorial fines). Criminal careers in the present analysis include only those cases with a guilty finding by a judge, a prosecutorial waiver due to policy reasons, or a prosecutorial fine, combining these three outcomes as "conviction." For each criminal case, data were obtained on the type of crime and way the case was dealt with. Based on the separate sections of the Dutch criminal code, we were able to distinguish between those convicted for indecent exposure (i.e., flashing) (art. 239 WvSr), sexual assault (art. 246 WvSr), rape (art. 242 WvSr), child molestation (art. 244–245 WvSr), and a miscellaneous category of "other sexual" offenses (art. 240, 243, 247–250 WvSr), including possession of child pornography and forcing someone into prostitution (for a complete listing of all hands-on sex offenses and the corresponding maximum sentences in the Netherlands, see Bijleveld, 2007). Sections 247–249 of the Dutch criminal code pertain to sexual assault involving persons unable to express their will because of impairment or unequal power relations between perpetrator and victim. While technically these offenses could be perpetrated against children, most cases of child molestation will be prosecuted under sections 244–245 WvSr. However, given the unknown age of the victim, cases registered under sections 247–249 were coded in the "other" category. In the 25-year period that the follow-up period of the CCLS covers, the scope of some of these sections has changed substantially. Prior to 1991, for example, forcible sexual intercourse between married partners did not entail rape. As of 1991, all sex offenses were also made gender neutral in the sense that both females and males could be victimized. These legal changes, however, have not led to major prosecutorial changes or quantitative changes in the type of sex offenses registered (Bijleveld, 2007, p. 323).

Analytic Strategy

We use event history analyses to assess the time stable and time varying correlates of the occurrence of an event, in our case being registered for a subsequent offense. Event history models are used to study the duration until the event of interest (Allisson, 1982; Blossfeld & Rohwer, 2002; Yamaguchi, 1991). Duration is measured from the time the individual becomes at risk of experiencing the event. In the current analysis, individuals in our sample become at risk either directly after their 1977 offense, or after the incarceration period they were sentenced to following the 1977 offense. The maximum follow-up is the 25-year period between 1977 and 2003, which is shortened if individuals die prior to that year. The dependent variable in event history analysis is said to be right censored, because not all individuals will have experienced the event under scrutiny within the temporal boundary of the follow-up period. Instead of excluding these cases from further analyses, which would lead to biased results, event history models retain right-censored observations under the assumption that censoring times are independent of event times. That is, these models assume that individuals are not withdrawn from the sample because they are more or less likely to experience the event. In our case, this assumption is reasonable since censoring is determined by the end of the follow-up, which is random with respect to instances of offenders' reoffending. Event history models permit us to assess the correlates of event occurrences by entering time-stable risk factors as variables into the model. Besides adding time-stable covariates, event history models also allow for entering time-varying covariates. This enables us to explore how the timing of the event relates to changes in the value of the covariate.

In the present analysis we assess the impact of transitioning to marriage, marital dissolution, and parenthood on the risk of reoffending. Some methodological considerations are appropriate at this point. First, event history models are sensitive to frailty, or unobserved population heterogeneity. Failure to account for frailty may lead to inconsistent parameter estimates, incorrect standard errors, and misleading estimates of duration dependency. The schoolbook example illustrating the effects of frailty includes a population that consists of two subgroups – a high-risk and a low-risk group. Because individuals of the most failure-prone – more frail – group tend to fail first, the overall hazard rate may appear to decline even if the group-specific hazards are flat (Blossfeld & Rohwer, 1995). Prior research suggests that different types of sex offenders may differ with respect to their reconviction rates (e.g., Soothill et al., 2000). Furthermore, prior offending is also known to influence subsequent offending (Hanson & Morton-Bourgon, 2005). Therefore, to combat the potential influences of frailty we included a range of demographic information as well as characteristics of the criminal history of the offenders prior to their 1977 offense that are known from prior research to be associated with recidivism and desistance as time-stable variables in our models. Second, in an event history model the time-varying variables are assumed exogenous. That is, the values of the time-variable variables are assumed to be generated by a process that is completely independent of the rate of occurrence of the dependent event, the occurrence of a future offense. In our case, this assumption is likely to be violated. To the extent maturational theories are correct, stable individual characteristics that influence the likelihood of getting married are also likely to affect reoffending.

To be able to examine possible independent effects of marriage, divorce, and parenthood on desistance, individual differences in marriage, divorce, and parental "propensity" need to be controlled for. In order to do so, and following Osgood (2010), we apply a technique known as group-mean centering, in which we include the overall proportion of the time at-risk individuals spent in a certain demographic state as time-stable covariates in the model. In addition, we construct the time-varying variables such that they indicate yearly variation from the individual's overall mean. In this way, time-varying variables only pertain to within individual variation in the outcome variable (see Blokland & Nieuwbeerta, 2005; Horney, Osgood, & Marshall, 1995; Laub & Sampson, 2003, for previous applications of this method in criminal career research). Making full use of the information available in the CCLS study, our analyses proceed in the following steps. First, we describe our sample of convicted sex offenders in terms of demographic and criminal history characteristics. Next, we examine general, special, and specific recidivism in this sample over the 25-year period from 1977 to 2003. Finally, we estimate event history models to assess the extent to which reconviction rates for different types of offenses are influenced by between-individual characteristics and within-individual differences in life-course circumstances.

Results

Sex Offenders Convicted in 1977

Table 12.1 describes the characteristics of the sample of 500 sex offenders convicted in 1977. The age of the sex offenders convicted in 1977 ranged from 13 to 62, with a mean of 27.3. Of the total, 37.4% of the sex offenders could be regarded as first-time offenders; these offenders did not have any convictions prior to 1977. Those that did had a criminal history totaling an average of 3.3 convictions. The average age of onset for any offense was 21.0. Of the 1977 sex offenders 67.4% could be regarded as first-time sex offenders; their 1977 conviction was their first conviction for a sexual offense, though they might have had prior convictions for other types of offenses. Those that already were sexual recidivists in 1977 had an average of 1.0 prior convictions for sexual offenses. Average age of onset for sex offending was 22.4. Considering sexual offenders' bond to conventional society we found that, in 1977, 37.2% of sex

Table 12.1 Descriptive Statistics of the Sample of Sex Offenders (N = 500) Convicted in 1977

	Type of sexual offense in 1977					
	Indecent exposure	*Sexual assault*	*Rape*	*Child molestation*	*Other sexual*	*Total*
%	21.4%	23.6%	23.0%	31.2%	.8%	100%
N	107	118	115	156	4	500
Age in 1977						
Age	32.3 (sd = 9.6)	21.8 (sd = 6.8)	22.0 (sd = 5.8)	33.0 (sd = 11.8)	29.8 (sd = 15.4)	27.3 (sd = 10.3)
Criminal history in 1977						
% any offending	72.0%	53.4%	62.6%	62.8%	75.0%	62.6%
# any offending	4.7 (sd = 8.2)	2.1 (sd = 3.5)	3.1 (sd = 5.0)	3.2 (sd = 4.9)	4.3 (sd = 3.8)	3.3 (sd = 5.6)
Age onset any offending	23.6 (sd = 9.6)	18.0 (sd = 4.5)	17.8 (sd = 3.4)	23.9 (sd = 10.8)	19.8 (sd = 9.5)	21.0 (sd = 8.5)
% nonsex nonviolent	67.3%	49.2%	58.3%	50.6%	75.0%	55.8%
# nonsex nonviolent	3.9 (sd = 7.2)	1.7 (sd = 3.1)	2.5 (sd = 4.3)	2.3 (sd = 4.2)	2.8 (sd = 3.6)	2.6 (sd = 4.9)
Age onset nonsex nonviolent	24.4 (sd = 9.8)	19.2 (sd = 6.2)	19.4 (sd = 5.3)	22.2 (sd = 8.7)	23.3 (sd = 8.2)	21.4 (sd = 8.1)
% violence	17.8%	7.6%	22.6%	13.5%	75.0%	15.6%
# violence	.4 (sd = 1.1)	.1 (sd = .5)	.4 (sd = .9)	.2 (sd = .6)	1.3 (sd = 1.3)	.3 (sd = .8)
Age onset violent	21.2 (sd = 4.6)	24.3 (sd = 6.9)	20.9 (sd = 5.4)	21.6 (sd = 6.8)	22.3 (sd = 10.1)	21.6 (sd = 5.9)
% sex	57.0%	18.6%	20.0%	35.9%	25.0%	32.6%
# sex	2.4 (sd = 4.6)	.4 (sd = 1.2)	.3 (sd = .8)	.9 (sd = 1.9)	.3 (sd = .5)	1.0 (sd = 2.6)
Age onset sex	24.0 (sd = 8.1)	17.7 (sd = 4.7)	18.7 (sd = 4.7)	23.8 (sd = 8.8)	39 (N = 1)	22.4 (sd = 8.1)
Risk factors in 1977						
Unemployed 1977	19.6%	52.5%	46.1%	30.1%	75.0%	37.2%
Alcohol 1977	11.2%	22.0%	34.8%	12.2%	25.0%	19.6%
Drugs 1977	0%	0%	3.5%	0%	0%	.8%
Life-course status in 1977						
% married	55.1%	14.4%	14.8%	29.5%	25.0%	28.0%
% divorced	8.4%	3.4%	4.3%	8.3%	25.0%	6.4%
% children	48.6%	11.0%	17.4%	26.3%	50.0%	25.6%

offenders were unemployed and roughly one fifth were regarded by the police as having addiction problems.

Municipal data also provided information about the offenders' marital and parental status at the time of their 1977 conviction. These data show that 72% of the offenders were single, while 25.6% had fathered at least one child prior to their conviction in 1977. When we compared age and criminal history variables across sex offender types, we found that on average those convicted for sexual assault were the youngest, followed by those convicted for rape. Those convicted for indecent exposure were least likely to be first offenders in 1977. Many have a criminal history of nonviolent nonsexual offenses and over half have been previously convicted for a sexual offense. Rapists are most likely to have a history of violent offending. On average, those convicted for rape also experience the earliest onset of their criminal careers. Note, however, that this is partly due to rapists and those convicted for sexual assault being the youngest in 1977: for them to have a criminal history prior convictions had to be at a relatively early age, whereas prior convictions for those convicted for indecent exposure could have also occurred when these individuals were in their twenties. With regard to risk factors and life-course status, we found that those convicted for indecent exposure were least likely to be unemployed or to be categorized as having problems with alcohol or drugs, and were most likely to be married and have children at the time of their conviction. Rapists, on the other hand, seem the most unadjusted group, with over one third being categorized as alcohol or drug dependent. Note that while 14.8% of the rapists are married, 17.4% have fathered children, which, when compared to the other offender types, suggests that rapists are most likely to have fathered children out of wedlock. As with criminal history, however, employment and marital and parental status again need to be considered in light of the average age of these offenders in 1977.

Recidivism

In the 25-year period following their conviction in 1977, 331 out of the total 500 sex offenders (71.0%) were convicted for at least one subsequent offense. For nearly two thirds of the sample their post-1977 convictions included at least one nonsexual nonviolent offense (63.2%), for 26.2% it included a violent offense. During the 25-year follow-up between 1977 and 2003, 30.2% of the sex offenders were eventually reconvicted for at least one sexual offense (special recidivism). Taking time in prison into account, average time between conviction in 1977 and reconviction was 6.5 years for any offense, and 4.8 years for a sexual offense (see Table 12.2). Sexual offense recidivism was over nine times more prevalent among sex offenders compared to the comparison group (N = 3,495 men convicted for a nonsexual offense in 1977, and never convicted for a sexual offense prior to 1977). Nonsexual offense recidivism did not differ between the two groups. In the comparison group, average time between conviction in 1977 and reconviction was reduced, but only for less serious offenses. Within the group of sexual offenders, those convicted for rape

Table 12.2 Recidivism Rates of Sex Offenders and Control Group

			General recidivism		*Special recidivism*	*Specific recidivism*				
		Any offending	*Nonsexual nonviolent*	*Violent*	*Any sexual*	*Indecent exposure*	*Sexual assault*	*Rape*	*Child molestation*	*Other sexual*
Those convicted of a sexual crime in 1977										
Total	Percentage convicted	71.0%	63.2%	26.2%	30.2%	11.0%	8.0%	7.0%	10.4%	3.0%
	Average survival time	6.46	4.40	7.37	4.79	4.61	5.47	5.34	5.39	8.64
Indecent exposure	Percentage convicted	62.6%	57.0%	15.0%	41.1%	33.6%	4.7%	2.8%	8.4%	2.8%
	Average survival time	6.80	5.02	8.87	4.43	3.94	10.82	7.34	6.36	8.64
Sexual assault	Percentage convicted	70.3%	62.7%	22.0%	28.0%	6.8%	13.6%	5.9%	5.9%	1.7%
	Average survival time	6.33	4.22	5.64	4.31	4.97	4.00	5.09	3.98	12.2
Rape	Percentage convicted	86.1%	80.0%	48.7%	26.1%	4.3%	11.3%	17.4%	1.7%	.9%
	Average survival time	4.91	3.53	7.50	4.40	5.70	4.67	4.52	6.91	12.0
Child molestation	Percentage convicted	65.4%	54.5%	19.2%	28.2%	3.8%	3.8%	3.2%	21.8%	5.8%
	Average survival time	7.92	5.08	7.70	5.77	7.26	6.64	7.78	5.33	7.48
Other sexual	Percentage convicted	100%	100%	75.0%	0%	0%	0%	0%	0%	0%
	Average survival time	4.24	4.24	8.65	–	–	–	–	–	–
Control group										
	Percentage convicted	72.4%	70.4%	30.4%	3.2%	0.5%	1.0%	1.4%	0.8%	0.4%
	Average survival time	4.66	4.09	6.82	9.07	7.21	8.53	8.06	13.13	15.35

were most likely to recidivate, with 86.1% obtaining at least one additional conviction during the 25-year follow-up. Recidivism to nonsexual nonviolent offenses and to violent offenses was most common in rapists, with nearly half (48.7%) of the rapists being subsequently convicted for a violent offense. Sexual recidivism, however, was most prevalent in those convicted for indecent exposure, with 41.1% of this group reconvicted for a sexual offense, compared to between 26.1 and 28.2% of the other sexual offender subtypes. Compared to the comparison group, sexual recidivism in those convicted for indecent exposure was almost 13 times more prevalent.

Finally, the outer right panel of Table 12.2 gives insight into specific recidivism among the different types of sex offenders. Specific recidivism pertains to the extent to which sex offenders recidivate to the exact same type of sexual offense they were convicted for in 1977. As such, specific recidivism rates provide insight into the extent sex offenders tend to specialize in certain offense types (see Blokland & Lussier, this volume, for a more thorough discussion of specialization). The extent to which sex offenders tend to specialize can be assessed by comparing the percentages on the diagonal to those in the upper and lower part of the panel. The outer right panel of Table 12.2 indeed shows the percentages on the diagonal are greater than the off-diagonal percentages, indicating that sex offenders in the current sample tend to specialize in a certain type of sexual offense. Specific recidivism is high for those convicted for indecent exposure – with 33.6% of the total group, or 81.8% ([33.6/41.1]*100) of the sexual recidivists, subsequently convicted for a similar sex offense. Specialization is also found in the recidivism patterns of child molesters. While 28.2% of child molesters recidivate to a sexual offense, of those sexually recidivating 77.3% are again convicted for the sexual abuse of a minor at least once during our follow-up. At the same time these figures also show a considerable amount of cross-over. Twenty-eight percent of those convicted for sexual assault eventually recidivate to a sexual offense: 13.6% recidivate to sexual assault, 5.9% recidivate to rape, and 6.8% of the total group of sexual assaulters, or nearly 1 in 4 sexually recidivating sexual assaulters, recidivate to the hands-off offense of indecent exposure. Similarly, of those convicted for (hands-off) indecent exposure, 8.4%, or one fifth of the sexual recidivists in this group, are subsequently convicted for (hands-on) child molestation. These figures can also be seen as indicating escalation and de-escalation within sex offenders' criminal careers. When we consider the hands-off offense of indecent exposure as the least serious sexual offense, followed by sexual assault, and consider rape and child molestation as the most serious of sexual offenses distinguished here, we can conclude that for 15.9% of those convicted for indecent exposure, or approximately 4 in 10 sexual recidivists in this group, the criminal career escalates from hands-off to hands-on offending following the 1977-conviction. Similarly, 4 in 10 sexually recidivating sexual assaulters progress to either rape of child molestation during the 25-year follow-up.

Recidivism for any offense for both the sex offender and the control group is depicted by the survival curves in Figure 12.1. These curves show similar declines (Log-rank test; $\chi^2 = .29$, df = 1, $p = .59$) indicating that sex offenders and nonsex offenders recidivate at similar rates. Within 1 year, almost one quarter of all sex

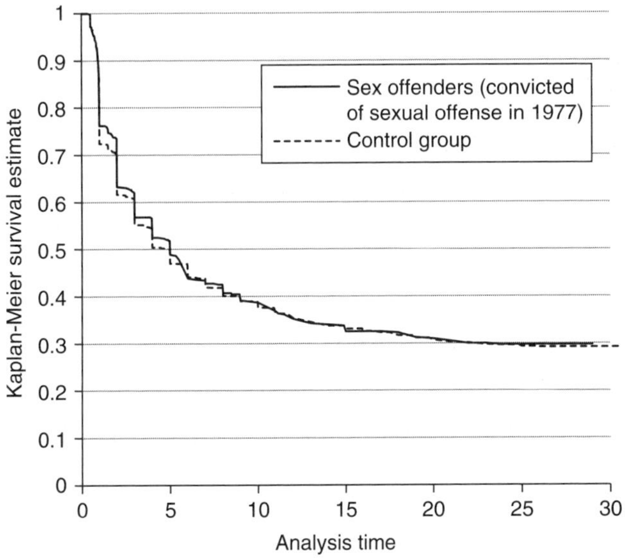

Figure 12.1 Kaplan-Meier survival analysis for all offending.

offenders (23.8%) – compared to 27.6% within the control group – were convicted for any offense. Within 5 years, more than half of the sex offenders (51.2%) were convicted for any offense (compared to 53.0% within the control group).

Figures 12.2a to 12.2c provide the survival curves for both the sex offender group and the control group by type of recidivism. Inspection of nonsexual nonviolent recidivism shows a slightly more gradual decline for sex offenders (Log-rank test; $\chi^2 = 8.22$, df = 1, $p = .004$). Violent offense recidivism develops similarly in both groups. As expected from the recidivism rates in Table 12.2, sexual offense recidivism follows a much steeper decline for sex offenders (Log-rank test; $\chi^2 = 509.07$, df = 1, $p < .001$). Within 5 years, 17.9% of all sex offenders were reconvicted of a sexual offense, within 10 years this accumulates to almost one quarter (24.3%). In sum, we find that sex offenders convicted in 1977 are no different from nonsex offenders convicted in 1977 in terms of their overall recidivism during the 25-year follow-up period of our study. However, when we split recidivism according to the type of offense, we find that sex offenders are more likely than nonsex offenders to be convicted for a subsequent sexual offense. While there is some indication for specialization in particular types of sexual offending in our sample, we also find evidence for crossover – and escalation – to other sexual offense types.

Demographic Transitions

Can differences in the pace with which sex offenders and nonsex offenders take on adult social roles explain differences in desistance between these groups? To address this question we next compare the timing and occurrence of demographic transitions

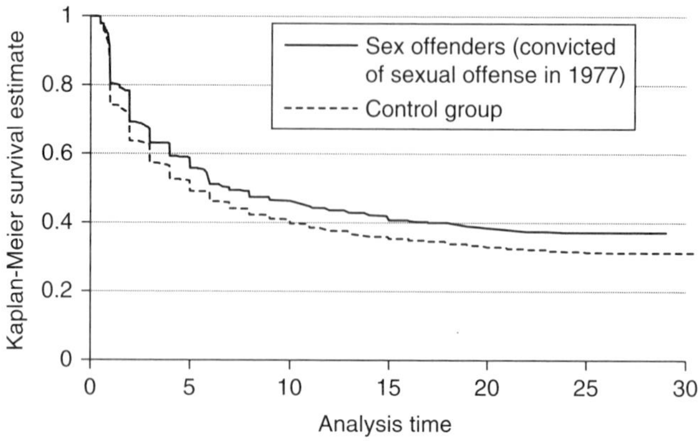

Figure 12.2a Kaplan-Meier survival analysis for nonsexual nonviolent offending (Log-rank test; $\chi^2 = 8.22$, df = 1, $p = .004$).

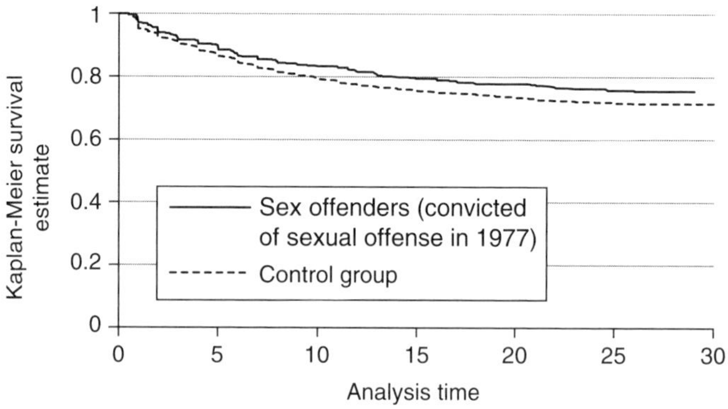

Figure 12.2b Kaplan-Meier survival analysis for violent offending (Log-rank test; $\chi^2 = 3.51$, df = 1, $p = .06$).

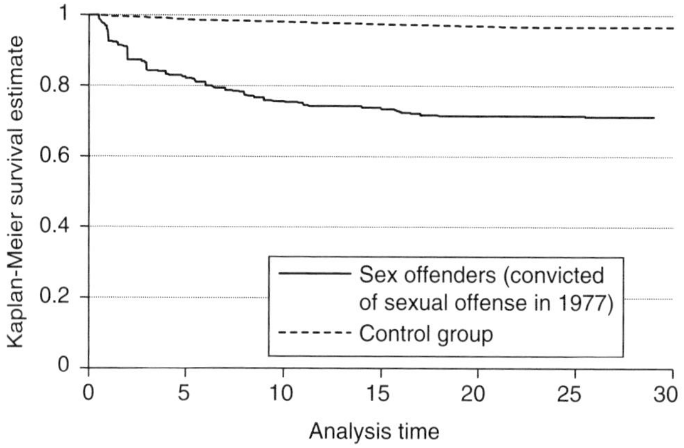

Figure 12.2c Kaplan-Meier survival analysis for sexual offending (Log-rank test; $\chi^2 = 509.07$, df = 1, $p < .001$).

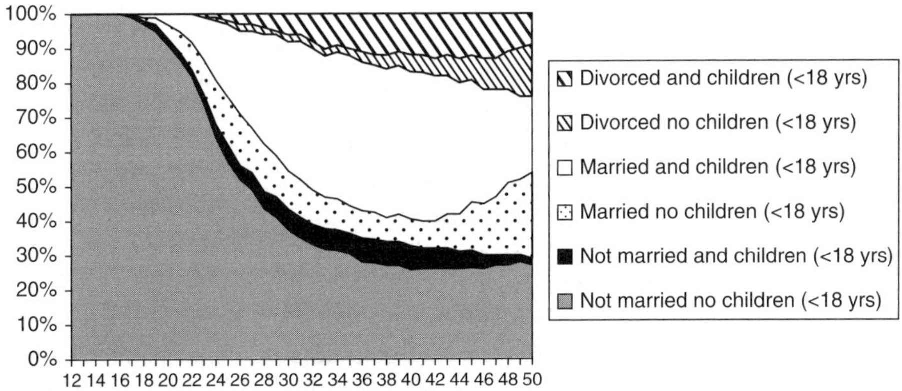

Figure 12.3a Demographic transitions in sexual offender group by age.

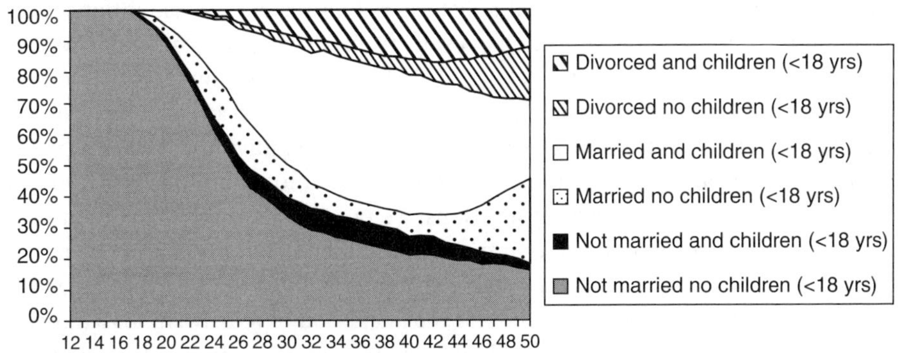

Figure 12.3b Demographic transitions in the control group by age.

over the life course in both groups. Figures 12.3a and 12.3b refer to the different life-course states individuals can be in, in terms of marriage and parenthood, for each separate group, depicted by stacked percentages by age. As Figure 12.3a shows, between ages 20 and 40 the majority of sex offenders transition into marriage (70%) and have children while being married (43%). By age 50 about one quarter (27%) have remained single and childless. In the control group more men end up divorced (29% instead of 24%). Although the overall demographic pattern for sexual offenders is rather similar to that of the control group, sex offenders' transition to family life seems to flatten out by their late thirties and is eventually less frequent than among nonsexual offenders.

The Impact of Life-Course Transitions on Nonsexual Nonviolent Recidivism

To what extent do marriage, divorce, and parenthood – and the restrictions and obligations that accompany these transitions – affect recidivism in sexual offenders? To investigate the impact of these demographic transitions on recidivism, we carried out a Cox regression analysis that allows us to examine the incidence of offending as a function of time-varying demographic status. The onset of risk of recidivism is 1977, the follow-up period is our analysis time (1977–2003, controlling for prison time), and the first failure outcome to be considered here is being convicted for a nonsexual nonviolent offense. In the first Cox model we estimate the effects of life-course transitions on nonsexual nonviolent recidivism, whilst controlling for the effects of age in 1977. The results of the first Cox model are given in three columns of Table 12.3. Table 12.3 gives the exponentials of the proportional hazards which may be interpreted in terms of relative risks. Thus, with every year the age of the offender in 1977 increases, the rate of reconviction for a nonviolent nonsexual offense drops by 3.4%. Of the time-varying indicators of offenders' life circumstances, only being divorced significantly influences the rate of nonsexual nonviolent reconviction; when divorced, the rate of reconviction increases with 77.6%, compared to those who remain single and childless. However, as it is likely that stable individual characteristics that affect the risk of recidivism also influence the likelihood of demographic transitions, results from Model 1 are vulnerable to bias. That is, hazard ratios in this model are likely to reflect not only the time-varying influence of being in a certain demographic state, but also – to an unknown extent – the effect of time-stable characteristics that increase the individual's risk of being in a particular state at any given moment in time. In order to reduce this bias resulting from selection into certain adult transitions, we ran two alternative Cox models. A first strategy to reduce bias resulting from unobserved heterogeneity in our data is to include information on as many stable characteristics as can be hypothesized to affect both the life-course transitions and the likelihood of recidivism. Based on the available data, we were able to include information on the criminal history of the sexual offenders, which we separated by the type (nonsexual nonviolent, violent and sexual) of prior convictions. Not only are prior convictions predictive of future offending, offense history has also been shown to be related to life-course transitions (e.g., Blokland, Nagin, & Nieuwbeerta, 2005). In addition, we added dummy variables indicating the type of sex offense the offender was convicted for in 1977. Finally, we included information on risk factors (unemployment, addiction) as available from the police file pertaining to the 1977 case. Results from the model including time-stable risk factors are presented under Model 2 in Table 12.3. We find that of the stable risk factors entered in the model, only the extent of the offender's nonviolent nonsexual conviction history and being categorized as either alcohol or drug dependent at the time of the 1977 arrest significantly increase reconviction rates for nonsexual nonviolent offenses. Other variables, like the type of sexual offense convicted for in 1977, do not influence the reconviction rate. Entering time-stable risk factors into the model reduces the effect of being divorced and renders it only marginally significant. This tells us that part of the time-varying effect of being divorced observed in Model 1 is due to stable offender characteristics that influence both the likelihood of divorce and the rate of reconviction. In an effort to further control for unobserved heterogeneity, we applied a second strategy and estimated a Cox model using a method known as group mean centering (Osgood, 2010). In this

Table 12.3 Parameter Estimates for the Cox Regression Analysis for Nonsexual Nonviolent Recidivism

	Model 1			*Model 2*			*Model 3*		
	Hazard ratio (e^b)	*p-value*	*95% CI*	*Hazard ratio (e^b)*	*p-value*	*95% CI*	*Hazard ratio (e^b)*	*p-value*	*95% CI*
Age in 1977									
Age	.966*	< .001	.952–.979	.948*	< .001	.930–.966	.949*	< .001	.931–.967
Type of offense in 1977									
Indecent exposure or other (reference)				–	–	–	–	–	–
Sexual assault				.788	.224	.537–1.157	.783	.211	.533–1.149
Rape				.983	.928	.672–1.436	.929	.711	.631–1.369
Child molestation				1.026	.889	.717–1.468	1.005	.980	.700–1.442
Criminal history in 1977									
Nonsexual nonviolent (log[x + 1])				4.740*	< .001	3.183–7.058	4.421*	< .001	2.940–6.648
Violent (log[x + 1])				1.171	.699	.526–2.605	1.148	.737	.512–2.571
Sexual (log[x + 1])				.921	.738	.571–1.487	.968	.895	.595–1.575
Age onset (prior to age 16) yes/no				1.013	.930	.764–1.343	1.031	.832	.775–1.373
Risk factors in 1977									
Employed				.915	.505	.704–1.189	.918	.524	.706–1.194
Alcohol/drugs				1.708*	< .001	1.277–2.284	1.722*	< .001	1.284–2.308
Time stable life-course status (individual average)									
Married							.606	.109	.329–1.118
Children							1.194	.599	.616–2.312
Divorced							1.890	.090	.906–3.939
Time varying life-course status (mean centered Model 3)									
Married	.775	.175	.536–1.120	.801	.236	.555–1.156			
Children	1.237	.229	.874–1.751	.965	.841	.682–1.365			
Divorced	1.776*	.016	1.111–2.838	1.530	.076	.957–2.447			
Married (mean-centered)							.857	.515	.539–1.364
Children (mean-centered)							.910	.623	.627–1.323
Divorced (mean-centered)							1.324	.376	.711–2.464

approach we subtract the individual means of each time-varying explanatory variable. This results in a model in which the time-varying explanatory variable has a mean of zero for all individuals so it cannot explain between individual variation, but rather only within individual variation in the outcome. In this model, we add the individual means as time-stable explanatory variables to also capture the effects of between-individual differences in average life circumstances (Blokland & Nieuwbeerta, 2005; Horney, Osgood, & Marshall, 1995; Osgood, 2010).

While only marginally significant, results from Model 3 suggest that those more likely to be married tend to be less likely to reoffend, while those more likely to be divorced seem to experience an increased risk of reoffending. Model 3 further shows that introducing controls for between-individual differences in the propensity to marry, have children, and divorce, renders the time-varying within-individual effect of being divorced insignificant. In sum, in the current sample of convicted sex offenders, the reconviction rate for nonsexual nonviolent offending decreases with age and increases with the extent to which these offenders had prior records for nonsexual nonviolent offending. Sex offenders categorized by the police as being alcohol or drug dependent show an increased risk of reoffending. Demographic transitions do not seem to influence nonsexual nonviolent reoffending once between-individual differences in the propensity to experience these transitions are accounted for.

The Impact of Life-Course Transitions on Violent Recidivism

The results of the Cox models for violent recidivism are given in Table 12.4. These models show that, as for nonsexual nonviolent offending, recidivism rates for violent offending decline with age. The results in Table 12.4 further show that the extent of the offender's violent criminal history, but not his nonsexual nonviolent criminal history, influences his rate of reconviction for violent offenses. Being employed in 1977, compared to being unemployed in 1977, reduces the rate of reconviction by 34%. Considering the effects of life-course transitions we find that though Model 1 initially indicates that being married reduces violence reconviction rates, while being divorced increases reconviction rates, in the full model only between-individual differences in divorce propensity significantly influence the rate of reconviction for violent offenses. As for nonviolent nonsexual recidivism, differences in reconviction rates seem to stem primarily from between-individual rather than within-individual differences.

The Impact of Life-Course Transitions on Sexual Recidivism

Finally, Table 12.5 presents the results for the Cox models estimating the effects of time-stable and time-varying risk factors on sexual recidivism. Results of these models show that the offender's age in 1977 does not significantly influence sexual reconviction rates. This means that in our sample a 20-year-old sex offender is no

Table 12.4 Parameter Estimates for the Cox Regression Analysis for Violent Recidivism

	Model 1			*Model 2*			*Model 3*		
	Hazard ratio (e^b)	*p-value*	*95% CI*	*Hazard ratio (e^b)*	*p-value*	*95% CI*	*Hazard ratio (e^b)*	*p-value*	*95% CI*
Age in 1977									
Age	.952*	< .001	.928–.976	.934*	< .001	.906–.968	.938*	< .001	.907–.970
Type of offense in 1977									
Indecent exposure or other (reference)				–	–	–	–	–	–
Sexual assault				.745	.433	.356–1.556	.736	.416	.351–1.542
Rape				1.733	.101	.898–3.344	1.684	.125	.866–3.274
Child molestation				1.215	.559	.632–2.333	1.188	.606	.616–2.291
Criminal history in 1977									
Nonsexual nonviolent (log[x+1])				1.707	.111	.884–3.296	1.587	.176	.813–3.099
Violent (log[x+1])				14.544*	<.001	4.723–44.792	14.471*	<.001	4.667–44.867
Sexual (log[x+1])				1.432	.384	.637–3.219	1.470	.357	.647–3.341
Age onset (prior to age 16) yes/no				1.386	.132	.907–2.119	1.411	.117	.917–2.169
Risk factors in 1977									
Employed				.664	.050	.440–1.000	.660*	.048	.437–.997
Alcohol/drugs				1.124	.648	.681–1.854	1.138	.614	.669–1.881
Time stable life course status (individual average)									
Married							.454	.116	.170–1.214
Children							.764	.577	.297–1.965
Divorce							3.679*	.017	1.268–10.671

(Contiunued)

Table 12.4 (*Continued*)

	Model 1			*Model 2*			*Model 3*		
	Hazard ratio (e^b)	*p-value*	*95% CI*	*Hazard ratio (e^b)*	*p-value*	*95% CI*	*Hazard ratio (e^b)*	*p-value*	*95% CI*
Time varying life course status (mean centered models 3)									
Married	.500*	.027	.271–.923	.575	.073	.314–1.054			
Children	.918	.744	.548–1.538	.701	.170	.423–1.163			
Divorced	2.466*	.004	1.344–4.526	2.418*	.005	1.299–4.500			
Married (mean-centered)							.585	.194	.260–1.314
Children (mean-centered)							.716	.268	.396–1.293
Divorced (mean-centered)							1.843	.216	.670–4.856

Table 12.5 Parameter Estimates for the Cox Regression Analysis for Sexual Recidivism

	Model 1			*Model 2*			*Model 3*		
	Hazard ratio (e^b)	*p-value*	*95% CI*	*Hazard ratio (e^b)*	*p-value*	*95% CI*	*Hazard ratio (e^b)*	*p-value*	*95% CI*
Age in 1977									
Age	1.005	.621	.987–1.023	.986	.243	.962–1.010	.983	.207	.960–1.009
Type of offense in 1977									
Indecent exposure or other (reference)				–	–	–	–	–	–
Sexual assault				1.001	.997	.569–1.763	.974	.928	.555–1.711
Rape				.944	.852	.518–1.721	.891	.708	.487–1.631
Child molestation				.849	.526	.513–1.407	.785	.350	.473–1.303
Criminal history in 1977									
Nonsexual nonviolent (log[x+1])				1.753	.062	.973–3.161	1.540	.155	.849–2.792
Violent (log[x+1])				1.087	.875	.384–3.079	1.108	.847	.390–3.151
Sexual (log[x+1])				4.570*	<.001	2.400–8.700	4.482*	<.001	2.343–8.574
Age onset (prior to age 16) yes/no				.882	.564	.577–1.349	.910	.665	.594–1.394
Risk factors in 1977									
Employed				1.215	.341	.814–1.812	1.189	.394	.799–1.770
Alcohol/drugs				.715	.191	.433–1.182	.772	.315	.466–1.279
Time stable life-course status (individual average)									
Married							.401*	.033	.173–.930
Children							.834	.695	.336–2.068
Divorce							2.363	.077	.911–6.134
Time varying life-course status (mean centered models 3)									
Married	.683	.139	.412–1.132	.622	.079	.366–1.057			
Children	1.354	.186	.864–2.123	1.167	.521	.728–1.871			
Divorced	1.179	.598	.639–2.174	1.041	.902	.554–1.955			
Married (mean-centered)							.874	.729	.406–1.878
Children (mean-centered)							1.274	.394	.729–2.227
Divorced (mean-centered)							.789	.622	.307–2.028

more or less likely to recidivate to a sexual offense than a 40-year-old sex offender. The type of sexual offense convicted for in 1977 does not influence sexual reconviction rates. A prior history of sexual offending does; those having multiple sexual offenses in their registered criminal history show an elevated rate of sexual reoffending. Lastly, life-course circumstances do not seem to influence sexual reconviction rates. However, those sex offenders who are more likely to be married during their life course show lower sexual recidivism rates than sex offenders who are less likely to be married. While only marginally significant, those sex offenders more likely to be divorced show an increased risk of sexual reoffending compared to those having lower divorce propensities.

In sum, using two different statistical approaches to detect and reduce unobserved bias resulting from selection into adult life-course transitions, we found no evidence for an effect of demographic transitions on the risk of recidivism among convicted sexual offenders. Individual means for these variables – indicating the overall proportion of time being in a specific demographic status – reflected an effect of between-individual differences in marital and divorce propensity on, respectively, sexual and violent recidivism outcomes only. With regard to other stable risk factors, the extent of the offense-type-specific criminal history was positively related to recidivism, with more extensive criminal histories predicting increased reoffending rates. Alcohol and drug dependence influenced only nonsexual nonviolent offending, while being employed reduced violent reoffending. Finally, age was related to recidivism rates, but not for sexual reoffending.

Conclusion

In this chapter we focused on the long-term criminal recidivism of 500 sex offenders convicted in the Netherlands in 1977. The first part of our analyses gave a description of the various types of criminal recidivism in our sample, comparing reconviction rates in sex offenders to that of a control group of nonsex offenders and distinguishing between different kinds of sex offenders based on the type of offense these offenders were convicted for in 1977. We found that, considering overall reconviction rate, sex offenders were very much like nonsex offenders. During the 25-year follow-up, 71.0% of sex offenders were reconvicted. However, convicted sex offenders differed considerably from nonsex offenders with regard to sexual recidivism: the rate of sexual reconviction for sex offenders was 30.2%, which was nine times that of nonsex offenders.

The message these figures convey is twofold: on the one hand, the popular image of sex offenders being perpetual predators needs adjusting; the majority of sex offenders do not recidivate to a sexual offense even over a long follow-up such as ours. On the other hand, the likelihood of a subsequent offense being a sexual offense is far greater for sexual offenders, compared to other types of offenders. In this sense, prior behavior does predict future behavior. Comparing different types of sex offenders, we found that of all distinguished types of sex offenders, rapist have the highest reconviction rate, with 86.1% being reconvicted for any offense. Consistent with prior theoretical and empirical work, rapists especially displayed high rates of nonsexual recidivism – both nonviolent and violent – suggesting that rape is often part of an extensive criminal repertoire. Those convicted for indecent exposure displayed the highest sexual reconviction rates (41.1%) but were in turn least likely to reoffend with a violent offense. Finally, when we considered rates of specific recidivism, offenders recidivating to an offense similar to that of their 1977 conviction, we found evidence for specialization: of those that did recidivate to a sexual offense many offenders recidivated to a sexual offense similar to that of their 1977 conviction. Yet, we also found that a substantial minority of offenders crossed over during our 25-year follow-up, for example, from hands-on to hands-off offending.

With regard to the effects of stable and dynamic risk factors, we found that recidivism in sex offenders, be it nonsexual nonviolent, violent, or sexual recidivism, is best predicted by stable risk factors. If fact, once we controlled for stable unobserved characteristics that cause some sex offenders to be more prone to experience certain life states than others, being married or divorced, or having children, did not alter the risk of reoffending. While this finding is not inconsistent with conclusions from prior meta-analyses (Hanson & Bussière, 1998; Hanson & Morton-Bourton, 2005), it is at odds with many studies in life-course criminology that do find changes in life circumstances to have an independent effect on criminal career development (Blokland & Nieuwbeerta, 2010; Sienick & Osgood, 2008). Plotting the timing and occurrence of life-course transitions for sex offenders and nonsex offenders against age resulted in relatively similar patterns, showing that many convicted sex offenders do make these transitions within normative age boundaries.

The absence of an effect of these transitions on sex offending could be explained by conflicting changes in the incentive structure. For example, the obligations and responsibilities that accompany the transition into parenthood may deter future offending on the one hand, while on the other the increased access to underage children that also accompanies this transition may promote rather than decrease future offending, nullifying any overall effect. Yet, this kind of explanation seems unlikely since, if this were the case, we would arguably still have found a deterring effect for nonsexual offending, as increased access to children is unlikely to also significantly influence the opportunity structure for nonsexual offending. Alternatively, the absence of a marriage effect could result from the nature of the marital relationship or characteristics of the marriage partner with whom the men in our sample were involved. Sampson and Laub (1993) stress that it is not the marriage per se, but rather the quality of the marriage that promotes desistance, by offering the offender a stake in conformity. Unstable marriages, for instance, are unlikely to result in diminished offending (Laub, Nagin, & Sampson, 1998). Previous research also indicates that the effect of marriage may be conditional on the type of partner. While marriage to a noncriminal partner did reduce general offending, marriage to a previously convicted partner did not. Given that all of the men in the current sample were convicted sex offenders, one could ask what kind of women would be willing to date and wed a known sex offender and how this would resonate in the strength of the marital attachment. It could also be that sex offenders are best regarded as "life-course persistent" offenders, in terms of Moffitt's taxonomy. Stable individual characteristics and a history of early problem behavior might render sex offenders immune to the effects of life-course transitions by the time they have reached adulthood. While this might explain the absence of an effect of the time-varying variables in our study, this kind of interpretation is difficult to reconcile with both the average age of onset for general offending – which was 21 – and the discontinuity in offending displayed by many sex offenders in our sample, especially with regard to sexual offending. At this point the analyses seem to be most in line with maturational theories of offending that ascribe differences in recidivism risk to between-individual differences. For these theories, the individual's criminal history simply reflects the past materializations of his latent criminal tendencies, thus explaining criminal history's predictive value with regard to future offending. Prior studies that find deviant sexual interests predict sexual reoffending (Hanson & Bussière, 1998) are also in line with a maturational approach to sexual offending over time, although deviant sexual interest could also be a result rather than a cause of sexual offending. Following from their focus on between-individual differences, maturational theories consider the age effect as a given, left unexplained by exogenous variables. While we did find that the risk of recidivism declined with age for both nonviolent nonsexual and violent offenses, in the current study we did not find the risk of sexual recidivism to decline with age. This is contrary to the meta-analytic results from Hanson and Bussière (1998), which found a significant, be it modest, negative effect of age on sexual recidivism. The lack of an age effect on sexual recidivism in the present study may result from this effect being modeled as linear. Some prior research suggests that recidivism rates for sex offenders reach a plateau during much of adulthood, not to show a significant decline until older ages (Hanson & Morton-Bourgon, 2005; Langan, Smitt, & Durose, 2003; Thornton, 2006). Future studies may therefore experiment with different operationalizations of age in 1977 – for example, using age brackets. However, despite the size of the current sample, sex offenders aged over 50 constitute a relatively small group, limiting the statistical power of such analysis.

Like any other study, the current study has its limitations. For one, this study is based on officially registered data and thus recidivism – and aspects of the offender's criminal history – only pertain to those sex offenses that came to the attention of, and lead to a reaction from, the criminal justice system. Prior research indicates the proportion of undisclosed offenses, or the "dark number," is especially high for sex offenses, and therefore our estimated recidivism rates are likely to underestimate actual offending behavior (e.g., Weinrott & Saylor, 1991). Even for those sex offenses that are officially registered, recidivism rates may differ as a function of disposition, with rates being highest for charges, followed by convictions and imprisonment (Prentky, Lee, Knight, & Cerce, 1997). Still, in absence of self-reports, given that plea bargaining is unknown in the Dutch criminal justice system, officially registered offenses may better represent actual behavior in the Netherlands than in countries where sex offenders might eventually be charged with a nonsexual offense in exchange for a guilty plea. Second, while we were able to distinguish between several different types of sex offenders, the sections of the Dutch penal code these distinctions were based upon do not offer us the possibility for a more fine-grained distinction in sex offender subtypes. Prior research, for example, suggests that extrafamilial child molesters differ from incest offenders in terms of their risk of sexual recidivism (Hanson & Bussière, 1998). Given the changes in the opportunity structure that accompany the transition to marriage and parenthood, the distinction between extrafamilial child molesters and incest offenders might have been especially relevant in the current context. Third, of all life-course transitions that might affect reoffending we were only able to address the effects of marriage, divorce, and parenthood. Prior research suggest that other transitions, like moving house or stable employment, might also foster desistance (e.g., Averdijk, Elffers, & Ruiter, 2012; Uggen & Wakefield, 2008), even among high-risk offenders (Verbruggen, Blokland, & Van der Geest, 2012). In addition, given that information on adult social roles was also gathered from official records, those role transitions that go unregistered, like cohabitation without marriage, were unaccounted for in our analyses. With regard to parenthood, we were not able to tell whether the children in question actually lived with the father or were, for instance, raised by family members or placed in foster care. Finally, it might be that the effects of life circumstances on subsequent criminal career development are conditional on offender type. Dynamic risk factors might not operate in the same way or have the same effect for all offenders (Kruttschnitt, Uggen, & Shelton, 2000). The current study did not examine interaction effects between static and dynamic factors, and this may have obscured any group-specific effects.

With the above caveats in mind, the results of our study offer valuable insights for sex offender policy and treatment. Even when considering a very long follow-up period, desistance from sex offending is the norm among our sample of convicted sex offenders. The penal climate in the Netherlands can be considered lenient – according to European standards – for the majority of the follow-up period and, given the absence of sex offender registries or community notification during this period, desistance cannot simply be ascribed to these types of measures. In all types of sex offenders, nonsexual recidivism is much higher than sexual recidivism. Especially for rapists, sexual offending seems part of a more extensive criminal career. This raises the question of whether programs aimed at reducing general offending could also be effective in reducing sexual offending.

Although dynamic risk factors were found to have no effect on recidivism in our study, it would be too easy to conclude that efforts aimed at changing sex offenders' life circumstances in order to reduce their reoffending risk are missing the point. First, many life-course studies do find transitions into adult social roles to deter offenders from subsequent offending. While there might be theoretical reasons to expect that sexual recidivism is relatively insensitive to exogenous influences, there is far less reason to expect that sexual offenders are different from nonsexual offenders when it comes to the processes giving rise to their nonsexual offending.

Second, in the current study, indications of alcohol or drug dependency were found to predict nonviolent nonsexual recidivism, while being employed in 1977 reduced violent reoffending. Given a lack of longitudinal information, these variables were treated as stable risk factors in the current analyses. This leaves open the possibility that if we had been able to model changes in these risk factors over time, these changes might have influenced reoffending risk.

Finally, official data offer only a crude insight into the effects of life circumstances on offending. As Laub and Sampson (Laub, Nagin, & Sampson, 1998; Laub & Sampson, 2003) have argued in the context of the marriage effect on offending, it is not so much being married as such, but the attachment and level of involvement in the relationship that counts when it comes to reducing offending. When using official data, levels of social bonding necessarily need to be inferred from simply being in a certain state. While this is common practice in life-course research, studies that were able to assess more qualitative aspects of the social bond find that these do often play an important role in desistance from offending.

Currently, the weapons of choice to combat the perils caused by sexual offenders are incapacitation and surveillance. Sex offenders are sentenced to stiff penalties, face prolonged periods of registration, and have their movements restricted. While recognizing the harm caused by sex offenders, these policies to us seem at least partly misguided. First, these policies are based on an image of sex offenders as persistent and specialized offenders. Results from this study add to a substantive body of research that shows that this is not the case and that desistance is default, even among sex offenders. Second, policies' sole focus on sex offender recidivism overlooks the fact that a large part of all sex offenses committed are committed by those who have not previously engaged in sex offending. While in the current study the risk of being reconvicted for a sexual offense was nine times greater for already convicted sex offenders, in absolute numbers the sex offenses committed by the comparison group make up over 40% of all sex offenses committed during the follow-up period of this study. Policies focusing on sex offender recidivism, even if 100% successful, will thus leave a substantial amount of sexual offending unaddressed. Finally, these policies seem to take as vantage point that the state is the designated and only body to provide surveillance of (ex-)sex offenders in the community. Life-course research, however, indicates that institutions like school, work, and intimate relationships can act as important sources of informal social control that deter offenders from committing additional crimes. As informal controls tend to cumulate over the life course, they potentially provide a more durable – and less expensive – reaction to offending than do state-initiated formal controls. To the extent that current sex offender policies lead to the exclusion rather than the inclusion of sex offenders in society, these policies may backfire and increase rather than decrease the risk of recidivism. For informal controls to be effective, the offender's ties to conventional society have to be meaningful and fertile for rehabilitation. This will not only require a change of policy, but also a change in the way the public writ large thinks of sex offenders.

References

Allison, P. D. (1982). Discrete-time methods for the analysis of event histories. *Sociological Methodology, 13*, 61–98.

Apel, R., Blokland, A. Nieuwbeerta, P., & Van Schellen, M. (2010). The impact of imprisonment on marriage and divorce: A risk set matching approach. *Journal of Quantitative Criminology, 26*, 269–300.

Arnett, J. J. (2004). *Young adulthood: The winding road from late teens through the twenties.* Oxford, UK: Oxford University Press.

Averdijk, M., Elffers, H., & Ruiter, S. (2012). Disentangling context effects on criminal careers. In R. Loeber, N. W. Slot, M. Hoever, & P. Van der Laan (Eds.), *Persisters and desisters in crime from adolescence into adulthood: Explanation, prevention and punishment* (pp. 51–76). Farnham: Ashgate.

Bacon, C. G., Mittleman, M. A., Kawachi, I., Giovannucci, E., Glasser, D. B., & Rimm, E. B. (2003). Sexual function in men older than 50 years of age: Results from the health professionals follow-up study. *Annals of Internal Medicine, 139*, 161–168.

Barbaree, H. E., Blanchard, R., & Langton, C. M. (2003). The development of sexual aggression through the life span: The effect of sexual arousal and recidivism among sex offenders. In R. Prentky, E. Janus, & M. Seto (Eds.), *Understanding and managing sexually coercive behavior. Annals of the New York Academy of Sciences* (Vol. *989*, pp. 59–71). New York Academy of Sciences.

Bijleveld, C. C. J. H. (2007). Sex offenders and sex offending. In M. Tonry, & C. Bijleveld (Eds.), *Crime and justice in the Netherlands. A review of research* (Vol. *35*, pp. 319–387). The University of Chicago Press.

Blanchard, R., & Barbaree, H. E. (2005). The strength of sexual arousal as a function of the age of the sex offender: Comparisons among pedophiles, hebephiles, and teleiophiles. *Sexual Abuse: A Journal of Research and Treatment, 17*, 441–456.

Blokland, A., Nagin, D., & Nieuwbeerta, P. (2005). Life span offending trajectories of a Dutch conviction cohort. *Criminology, 43*(4), 919–954.

Blokland, A., & Nieuwbeerta, P. (2005). The effects of life circumstances on longitudinal trajectories of offending. *Criminology, 43*(4), 1203–1240.

Blokland, A., & Nieuwbeerta, P. (2010). Life-course criminology. In S. G. Shoham, P. Knepper, & M. Kett (Eds.), *International handbook of criminology* (pp. 51–93). Boca Raton: CRC Press.

Blokland, A., & Van Os, R. (2010). Life span offending trajectories of convicted Dutch women. *International Criminal Justice Review, 20*(2), 169–187.

Blossfeld, H. P., & Rohwer, G. (1995). *Techniques of event history modeling.* Mahwah, NJ: Lawrence Erlbaum.

Blossfeld, H. P., & Rohwer, G. (2002). *Techniques of event history modeling: New approaches to causal analysis* (2nd ed.). Mahwah, NJ: Lawrence Erlbaum.

Blumstein, A., & Cohen, J. (1987). Characterizing criminal careers. *Science, 237*, 985–991.

Broadhurst, R. G., & Loh, N. (2003). The probabilities of sex offender rearrest. *Criminal Behaviour and Mental Health, 13*(2), 121–139.

Chewning, M. F. (1991). A comparison of adolescent male sex offenders with juvenile delinquents and nonreferred adolescents. Doctoral dissertation, Virginia Commonwealth University. *Dissertation Abstracts International, 51*(7), 3557. (UMI No. 9034117).

Doren, D. M. (2006). What do we know about the effect of aging on recidivism risk for sexual offenders? *Sexual Abuse: A Journal of Research and Treatment, 18*, 137–157.

Farrington, D. P. (1986). Age and crime. In M. Tonry & N. Morris (Eds.), *Crime and justice: An annual review of research* (Vol. *7*, pp. 189–250). University of Chicago Press.

Farrington, D. P. (2003). Developmental and life-course criminology: Key theoretical and empirical issues – The 2002 Sutherland award address. *Criminology, 41*(2), 221–256.

Farrington, D. P. (2005). Introduction to integrated and life-course theories of offending. In D. P. Farrington (Ed.), *Integrated developmental and life-course theories of offending* (pp. 1–14). New Brunswick: Transaction.

Finkelhor, D. (1984). *Child sexual abuse: New theory and research.* New York: Free Press.

Furby, L., Weinrott, M. R., & Blackshaw, L. (1989). Sex offender recidivism: A review. *Psychological Bulletin, 105*(1), 3–30.

Grendreau, P., Tittle, T., & Goggin, C. (1996). A meta-analyses of the predictors of adult offender recidivism: What works! *Criminology, 34*(4), 575–607.

Hanson, R. K. (2002). Recidivism and age. Follow-up data from 4,673 sexual offenders. *Journal of Interpersonal Violence, 17*(10), 1046–1062.

Hanson, R. K., & Bussière, M. T. (1998). Predicting relapse: A meta-analysis of sexual offender recidivism studies. *Journal of Consulting and Clinical Psychology, 66*(2), 348–362.

Hanson, R. K., & Harris, A. J. R. (2000). Where should we intervene? Dynamic predictors of sexual offense recidivism. *Criminal Justice and Behavior, 27*(6), 6–34.

Hanson, R. K., & Morton-Bourgon, K. E. (2005). The characteristics of persistent sexual offenders: A meta-analysis of recidivism studies. *Journal of Consulting and Clinical Psychology, 73*(6), 1154–1163.

Harris, A. J. R., & Hanson, R. K. (2004). *Sex offender recidivism: A simple question.* Ottawa: Public Safety and Emergency Preparedness Canada.

Harris, G. T., & Rice, M. E. (2007). Adjusting actuarial violence risk assessments based on aging or the passage of time. *Criminal Justice and Behavior, 34*, 297–313.

Hepburn, J. R., & Griffin, M. L. (2002). *An analysis of risk factors contributing to the recidivism of sex offenders on probation.* Report submitted to the Maricopa County Adult Probation Department and the National Institute of Justice.

Hirschi, T. (1969). *Causes of delinquency.* University of California Press.

Hirschi, T., & Gottfredson, M. (1983). Age and the explanation of crime. *American Journal of Sociology, 89*(3), 552–584.

Hirschi, T., & Gottfredson, M. (1995). Control theory and the life-course perspective. *Studies on Crime and Crime Prevention, 4*(2), 131–142.

Horney, J., Osgood, D. W., & Marshall, I. H. (1995). Criminal careers in the short term: Inter-individual variability in crime and its relation to local life circumstances. *American Sociological Review, 60*, 655–673.

Kafka, M. P. (2003) The monoamine hypothesis for the pathophysiology of parafillic disorders. In R. Prentky, E. Janus, M. Seto, & A. W. Burgess (Eds.), *Understanding and managing sexually coercive behavior. Annals of the New York Academy of Sciences* (Vol. *989*, pp. 86–94). New York Academy of Sciences.

Kruttschnitt, C., Uggen, C., & Shelton, K. (2000). Predictors of desistance among sex offenders: The interaction of formal and informal social controls. *Justice Quarterly, 17*(1), 61–87.

Marshall, W. L., & Barbaree, H. E. (1990). An integrated theory of the etiology of sexual offending. In W. L. Marshall, D. R. Laws, & H. E. Barbaree (Eds.), *Handbook of sexual assault: Issues, theories, and treatment of the offender* (pp. 257–275). New York: Plenum Press.

Langan, P. A., Smitt, E. L., & Durose, M. R. (2003). Recidivism of sex offenders released from prison in 1994. Washington, DC: U.S. Department of Justice, Office of Justice Programs, Bureau of Justice Statistics.

Langström, N., & Hanson, R. K. (2011). High rates of sexual behavior in the general population: Correlates and predictors. *Archives of Sexual Behavior, 35*(1), 37–52.

Laub, J. H., Nagin, D. S., & Sampson, R. J. (1998). Trajectories of change in criminal offending: Good marriages and the desistance process. *American Sociological Review, 63*(2), 225–238.

Laub, J. H., & Sampson, R. J. (2001). Understanding desistance from crime. *Crime and Justice: A Review of Research, 28*, 1–29.

Laub, J. H., & Sampson, R. J. (2003). *Shared beginnings, divergent lives: Delinquent boys to age 70*. Cambridge, MA: Harvard University Press.

Laws, D. R., & Ward, T. (2011). *Desistance from sex offending: Alternatives to throwing away the keys*. New York: Guilford Press.

Lussier, P., & Healy, J. (2009). Rediscovering Quetelet, again: The "aging" offender and the prediction of reoffending in a sample of adult sex offenders. *Justice Quarterly, 26*, 827–856.

Malamuth, N. (1996). The confluence model of sexual aggression: Feminist and evolutionary perspectives. In D. M. Buss & N. Malamuth (Eds.), *Sex, power, conflict: Evolutionary and feminist perspectives*. New York: Oxford University Press, 269–295.

Mann, R. E., Hanson, R. K., & Thornton, D. (2010). Assessing risk for sexual recidivism: Some proposals on the nature of psychologically meaningful risk factors. *Sexual Abuse: A Journal of Research and Treatment, 22*, 191–217.

Moffitt, T. E. (1993).Adolescence-limited and life-course-persistent antisocial behavior: A developmental taxonomy. *Psychological Review, 100*(4), 674–701.

Moffitt, T. E. (1994). Natural histories of delinquency. In E. G. M. Weitekampand & H-J. Kerner (Eds.), *Cross-national longitudinal research on development and criminal behavior* (pp. 3–61). Dordrecht: Kluwer.

Moffitt, T. E. (1997). Adolescence-limited and life-course-persistent offending: A complementary pair of developmental theories. In T. P. Thornberry (Ed.), *Developmental theories of crime and delinquency* (pp. 11–54). New Brunswick: Transaction.

Moffitt, T. E. (2006). Life-course persistent versus adolescence-limited antisocial behavior. In D. Cicchetti & D. J. Cohen (Eds.), *Developmental psychopathology* (Vol, 3, pp. 570–598). Hoboken, NJ: John Wiley & Sons, Inc.

Nieuwbeerta, P., Nagin, D., & Blokland, A. (2009). Assessing the impact of first-time imprisonment on offenders' subsequent criminal career development: A matched samples comparison. *Journal of Quantitative Criminology, 25*(3), 227–257.

Osgood, D. W. (2010). Statistical models of life events and criminal behavior. In A. R. Piquero & D. Weisburd (Eds.), *Handbook of quantitative criminology* (pp. 375–398). New York: Springer.

Piquero, A. R. (2008). Taking stock of developmental trajectories of criminal activity over the life course. In A. M. Liberman (Ed.), *The long view of crime. A synthesis of longitudinal research* (pp. 23–78). New York: Springer.

Piquero, A. R., Farrington, D. P., & Blumstein, A. (2003). The criminal career paradigm. *Crime and Justice: A Review of Research, 30*, 359–506.

Prentky, R. A., Lee, A. F. S., Knight, R. A., & Cerce, D. (1997). Recidivism rates among child molesters and rapists: A methodological analysis. *Law and Human Behavior, 21*(6), 635–659.

Proulx, J., Lussier, P., Ouimet, M., & Boutin, S. (2008). Criminal career parameters in four types of sexual aggressors. In B. K. Schwartz (Ed.), *The sex offender: Offender evaluation and program strategies* (Vol. 6, pp. 3/1-3–12). New York: Civic Research Institute.

Sampson, R. J., & Laub, J. H. (1993). *Crime in the making. Pathways and turning points through life*. Cambridge: Harvard University Press.

Sampson, R. J., & Laub, J. H. (1995). Understanding variability in lives through time: Contributions of life-course criminology. *Studies on Crime and Crime Prevention, 4*(2), 143–158.

Scalora, M. J., & Garbin, C. (2003). A multivariate analysis of sex offender recidivism. *International Journal of Offender Therapy and Comparative Criminology, 47*(3), 309–323.

Seidman, B., Marshall, W. L., Hudson, S. M., & Robertson, P. J. (1994). An examination of intimacy and loneliness in sex offenders. *Journal of Interpersonal Violence, 9*, 518–534.

Seto, M. C., & Lalumiere, M. L. (2010). What is so special about male adolescent sexual offending? A review and test of explanations through meta-analysis. *Psychological Bulletin, 136*(4), 526–575.

Sienick S. E., & Osgood, D. W. (2008). A review of research on the impact on crime of transitions to adult roles. In A. M. Liberman (Ed.), *The long view of crime: A synthesis of longitudinal research* (pp. 161–187). New York: Springer.

Soothill, K., Francis, B., Sanderson, B., & Ackerley, E. (2000). Sex offenders: Specialists, generalists – or both? *British Journal of Criminology, 40*(1), 56–67.

Thornton, D. (2006). Age and sexual recidivism: A variable connection. *Sexual Abuse: A Journal of Research and Treatment, 18*(2), 123–135.

Uggen, C., & Wakefield, S. (2008). What have we learned from longitudinal studies of work and crime? In A. M. Liberman (Ed.) *The long view of crime: A synthesis of longitudinal research* (pp. 191–219). New York: Springer.

Van Dulmen, M. H. M., Goncy, E. A., Vest, A., & Flannery D. J. (2009). Group-based trajectory modeling of externalizing behavior problems from childhood through adulthood: Exploring discrepancies in the empirical findings. In J. Savage (Ed.), *The development of persistent criminality*. Oxford, UK: Oxford University Press.

Van Koppen, M. V., De Poot, C. J., & Blokland, A. (2010). Comparing criminal careers of organized crime offenders and general offenders. *European Journal of Criminology, 7*, 356–374.

Vaughn, M. G., Delisi, M., Beaver, K. M., & Howard, M. O. (2009). Multiple murder and criminal careers: A latent class analysis of multiple homicide offenders. *Forensic Science International, 183*(1), 67–73.

Verbruggen, J., Blokland, A., & Van der Geest, V. R. (2012). Effects of employment and unemployment on serious offending in a high-risk sample of men and women from ages 18 to 32 in the Netherlands. *British Journal of Criminology, 52*(5), 845–869.

Ward, T., & Beech, A. (2006). An integrated theory of sexual offending. *Aggression and Violent Behavior, 11*, 44–63.

Ward, T., & Siegert, R. J. (2002). Toward a comprehensive theory of child sexual abuse: A theory knitting perspective. *Psychology, Crime, and Law, 9*, 197–248.

Weinrott, M. R., & Saylor, M. (1991). Self-report of crimes committed by sex offenders. *Journal of Interpersonal Violence, 6*, 286–300.

Yamaguchi, K. (1991). *Event history analysis*. Applied Social Research Methods, 28. Newbury Park, CA: Sage.

Zimring, F. E., Piquero, A. R., & Jennings, W. G. (2007). Sexual delinquency in Racine: Does early sex offending predict later sex offending in youth and young adulthood? *Criminology & Public Policy, 6*(3), 507–534.

13

Offending Trajectory and Residual Offending of Adult Sex Offenders

A Person-Oriented Approach to Risk Prediction

Patrick Lussier
Laval University, Canada

Garth Davies
Simon Fraser University, Canada

Introduction

There is a long tradition of criminological research on persistence in crime (e.g., Glueck & Glueck, 1930; LeBlanc & Fréchette, 1989; Robins, 1978; West & Farrington, 1977). Over the years, the relationship between past and future offending has received much attention from theoretical, empirical, and methodological standpoints (e.g., Nagin & Paternoster, 2000). These research contributions can be organized into four main research perspectives and research agendas: (a) the sociology of crime and research on criminal achievement, the role of mentorship, criminal network, professionalization and the study of the "successful criminal" (e.g., Lussier, Bouchard, & Beauregard, 2011; Morselli & Tremblay, 2004; Tremblay, 2010); (b) the criminal career approach, which has been concerned with the modeling of offending, the longitudinal sequence of crimes, crime specialization, and the study of the "chronic offender" (e.g., Blumstein, Cohen, Roth, & Visher, 1986; Loeber & Farrington, 1998; Piquero, Farrington, & Blumstein, 2003); (c) the life-course perspective, which has focused on life events, life transitions, informal controls, and the study of the "desistor" (e.g., Laub & Sampson, 2003; Sampson & Laub, 2005); and (d) developmental criminology, which has contributed to the understanding of criminal persistence by examining the role of formative years, early life stages, and the study of the "early onset" offender (e.g., LeBlanc & Loeber, 1998; Loeber & LeBlanc, 1990; Moffitt, 1993). Understanding the processes by which offending becomes persistent has been central to each of these perspectives, whether

Sex Offenders: A Criminal Career Approach, First Edition. Edited by Arjan Blokland and Patrick Lussier.

it is because sometimes crime pays off, whether crime can generate negative life circumstances conducive to further criminal activities, or because crime and its various manifestations are driven by a series of cumulative deficits taking place over several developmental stages. This is in contrast to the atheoretical risk-factor approach taken by actuarialists and instruments that generate risk scores.

The current study claims that the inability to take into account crime and persistence as a process leads to the underestimation of risk for some and overestimation of risk for others. In doing so, the study departs from the traditional operationalization of "risk" typical to the construct used by actuarialists by examining the offending trajectories of a sample of adult sex offenders. The study, therefore, approaches recidivism from a different perspective than the one actuarialists have been using for several decades. Actuarialists have relied on a variable-oriented perspective; that is, on "risk factors" which emphasize between-individual differences in offending. This approach has been utilized in the clinical research of risk assessment and risk prediction, as most actuarial instruments are based on this perspective. This focus on between-individual differences is somewhat at odds with the rationale of risk assessment, which is intended to assess the risk of an individual, but also to take into account any changes in the level of risk over time for a specific individual. Researchers have introduced "dynamic" risk factors to account for the possible change in risk of recidivism over time (e.g., Dempster & Hart, 2002; Hanson & Harris, 2001), but the operationalization and measurement of these factors are still embedded in the between-individual perspective only. An approach that builds risk assessment on both between- and within-individual changes in offending over time has never really been adopted in this field of research. This approach requires a longitudinal perspective more commonly used by criminologists studying crime persistence. This gap in actuarial-based instruments is central to hypotheses about the mismeasure of risk in the context of risk assessment of sexual recidivism in convicted adult sex offenders (Lussier & Davies, 2011). The study adopts a different focus by relying on a person-oriented perspective and, in doing so, examines the heterogeneity of criminal careers of adult sex offenders, the importance of within-individual changes in offending over time, and the dynamic aspects of offending over life course.

Person-Oriented Perspective

Over the years, clinical researchers have criticized actuarial tools for not allowing a more individualized, nonlinear approach to risk assessment and risk prediction (e.g., Cote, 2001; Monahan et al., 2005; Silver, Smith, & Banks, 2000; Steadman et al., 2000). More specifically, there are different types of offenders and risk profiles which may not be accounted for by a single, variable-oriented instrument. This limitation has also been raised in a different context – that is, by developmental psychologists who suggest that the dynamic changes of individuals over time may not be well reflected by a variable-centered approach. More specifically, developmentalists have coined the term "person-oriented approach" to describe a paradigm that shifts the focus from variables to individuals (Bergman & Magnusson, 1997). The variable-oriented approach is based on aggregate data and average series across individuals, which can misrepresent individual patterns of development (Von Eye & Bergman, 2003; Von Eye & Bogat, 2006). Consequently, conclusions from variable-oriented studies might not apply to all or most individual cases. Therefore, to better account for the heterogeneity of individual development, the person-oriented approach focuses on the disaggregation of information and the identification of individual patterns, with the understanding that some patterns occur more often than others (Bergman, 2002). In this regard, development can be conceptualized as a process characterized by states that can change over time (Bergman & Magnusson, 1997). Therefore, repeated measurements become pivotal to the identification of continuity and change as individuals age. As such, this modeling needs to account for the diversity of intercepts (i.e., initial level of the behavior) and slopes (i.e., trends) representing human development. To this end, nonlinear modeling becomes crucial to detect trends in individual development over time. Configurations of variables, longitudinal data with repeated measurements, nonlinear patterns of continuity, and changes over time best characterize the person-oriented approach. This perspective is in sharp contrast to the cross-sectional nature of actuarial tools designed to examine the number of risk factors, which are described as linearly related to reoffending. This is not to say that the person-oriented approach is superior to the variable-oriented one, but that it provides a different perspective on human development (Bergman & Trost, 2006). Current actuarial tools were not developed to accommodate a person-oriented perspective on criminal behaviors, risk, and recidivism.

Person-Oriented Approach and Sex Offenders

The heterogeneity of adult sex offenders is one of the most agreed-upon clinical observations. Several classification models of sexual offenders have been proposed over the years. In the main, these models have been developed using cross-sectional data and situational and contextual information to represent: (a) the diversity of offenders' motivation to commit a sexual crime (Gebhard, Gagnon, Pomeroy, & Christenson, 1965; Groth, 1979; Knight & Prentky, 1990); (b) the diversity of pathways of sexual reoffending (e.g., Laws, Hudson, & Ward, 2000; Ward & Hudson, 1998); and (c) the diversity of the offenders' modus operandi and offending scripts (Beauregard, Proulx, Rossmo, Leclerc, & Allaire, 2007; Beauregard, Rossmo, & Proulx, 2007; Deslauriers-Varin & Beauregard, 2010). While providing insights into the contextual and situational aspects as well as the offender's decision-making processes linked to the sexual crime event, these models are not well-suited for a developmental and life-course understanding of the unfolding of criminal activities. More specifically, these models were not developed to characterize the entire criminal activity of sex offenders. In that regard, two perspectives have been pursued: the pathway and the trajectory approaches. The pathway approach has been used to describe the qualitative changes in the behavioral development of sex offenders over time. Few empirical studies conducted with adult sexual aggressors of women have examined their developmental pathways (Cale, this volume; Cale & Lussier, 2011; Cale, Lussier, & Proulx, 2009). The modeling of developmental pathways can be achieved using a dynamic classification system allowing for the identification of patterns of behaviors that can escalate and de-escalate in seriousness over time by taking into consideration the timing of onset of a series of behavioral manifestations. The Cale et al. studies helped identify three groups of early-onset and two groups of late-onset offenders with different criminal activity patterns. In contrast, the trajectory approach is more concerned with quantitative changes of one behavior over time, typically frequency of offending over time. This approach, therefore, is concerned with the rate and shape of offending across time periods, parameters which are typically analyzed using group-based modeling.

Trajectories of Offending

While developmental and life-course criminologists have not fully embraced the person-oriented perspective as proposed by Bergman and Magnusson (1997), several of its concepts have been theoretically developed and empirically examined. The interest for a person-oriented perspective in criminology was largely initiated by developmental criminologists (Fréchette & LeBlanc, 1987; LeBlanc & Fréchette, 1989; Loeber & LeBlanc, 1990). The approach gained popularity following the introduction of developmental theories of offending and developmental taxonomies of offenders (Farrington, 2003; LeBlanc, 2005; Moffitt, 1993; Patterson & Yoerger, 1993; Thornberry & Krohn, 2005). The person-oriented approach was also facilitated by the rapid emergence of statistical techniques developed to handle longitudinal data such as group-based modeling (Nagin, 2005; Nagin & Tremblay, 2005) and latent-growth curve modeling (Curran, 2000; Curran & Hussong, 2002). This theoretical and methodological movement has stressed the importance of disaggregating offending data to help identify different individual-level patterns of offending. In the last two decades, several longitudinal studies have been launched in various countries to examine individual-level trajectories of offending (Farrington, 2005; Thornberry & Krohn, 2003).[1] In spite of methodological variations across studies, we can conclude that there are a multiplicity of offending patterns in terms of rate and shape of offending. When looking at known offenders and official offending data, this

[1]Drawing general conclusions is a challenge considering that these studies differ in various methodological aspects, such as the nature of the sample (e.g., general population, at-risk individuals, known offenders), the behavior analyzed (e.g., general offending, violent offending), the source of information (e.g., self-reports, official data), the developmental period covered (e.g., childhood, adolescence, adulthood), the length of the follow-up, and the number of measurement periods.

multiplicity of patterns can be characterized by between three and five offending trajectories (e.g., Piquero, 2008). These trajectories are characterized by an activation phase, a plateau, and a desistance phase, all of which vary in terms of rate, level, and speed. Until recently, these empirical studies have not examined the offending patterns of sex offenders specifically, or general offending trajectories and their relation to sexual offending.

Offending Trajectories of Sex Offenders

Barbaree and colleagues (2009) have recently called researchers' attention to the issue of aging and whether sex offenders' recidivism is driven by stable dynamic traits over time. Actuarial tools are based on the assumption that stable dynamic traits are operating, reminiscent of the population heterogeneity hypothesis that criminology theorists have put forward (e.g., Nagin & Paternoster, 2000). However, this assumption requires, first and foremost, the inspection of criminal career and offending trajectories to examine the stability of offending over time. The call to examine longitudinal patterns of offending in adult sex offenders has been made for quite some time now (e.g., Lussier, 2005; Soothill & Gibbens, 1978), but, until recently, the call has gone unanswered. Few empirical studies have been conducted to examine the presence of offending trajectories of sexual offenders using longitudinal data (Lussier & Davies, 2011; Lussier, Tzoumakis, Cale, & Amirault, 2010). The Lussier et al. studies have examined the offending histories of older adult sex offenders (past age 35) using a semi-parametric group-based modeling. One of the rationales for focusing on older offenders was that they tend to be targeted by the criminal justice system for the most stringent penal/legal dispositions, such as civil commitment (USA), and dangerous offender status (Canada). Lussier et al. (2010) identified four offending trajectories: (a) high-rate; (b) low-rate desistors; (c) late-bloomers; and (d) the very low-rate. Close examination of the offending trajectories revealed that they were, for the most part, parallel for the study period. There were also significant changes, more specifically when the offenders reached their early thirties. At that stage, escalators were found to be offending at the same rate as the high-rate offenders. Second, the two most criminally active trajectories (i.e., high-rate, and low-rate desistors) followed what is commonly known as the age-crime curve, suggesting that the aging factor is applicable to higher-risk offenders, contrary what has been proposed earlier (Harris & Rice, 2007). Current actuarial tools for sex offenders do not adjust for within-individual changes in offending over time, the aging factor of offenders, or the fact that the aging factors might function differently for different offenders (e.g., Lussier & Healey, 2009). While the Lussier et al. study (2010) was informative regarding the general offending trajectories of adult sex offenders, it only examined the prior criminal history without linking these four offending patterns to recidivism.

Lussier and Davies (2011) examined violent and sexual offending trajectories of older adult sex offenders and their predictive values for risk assessment purposes. The analyses revealed the presence of two sexual offending trajectories – a very low-rate group and a high-rate group, the latter representing only 3.7% of the sample. For this sample, the findings suggested that a sex crime was more reflective of a transitory phase of the criminal career rather than evidence of a "sexual criminal career" in the making. Similar findings were observed when looking at nonsexual violent crimes in that two offending trajectories were found, a very low-rate group and a high-rate group, with the latter group representing about 20% of the sample. Furthermore, the trajectories were found to show promising predictive accuracy when looking at the post-release reoffending of this sample. More specifically, the high-rate sexual offending group were more than three time more likely to be reconvicted for any crime or a violent/ sexual crime than the very low-rate group. On the other hand, when looking at sexual recidivism specifically, of the 13 recidivists found, none of them were high-rate sex offenders; that is, they were all very low-rate offenders. Taken together, the findings showed that, first, there is much crime-switching at play as high-rate offenders were most likely to be reconvicted for nonsexual offenses, and, second, the group most criminally active in one time period was not necessarily the group most likely to reoffend in another time period, supporting the idea that offending is more dynamic than what actuarial studies have shown in the past. The current study builds on these last recent findings – that is, offending trajectories, crime-switching, and competing risk of recidivism following prison release.

The Current Study

The main objective of the current study is to examine the longitudinal sequence of offending in adult sex offenders, in terms of both between-individual and within-individual changes in offending rate. To accomplish this, the current study proposes to do three things. First, the study aims to identify and describe the violent/sexual offending trajectories between the ages of 18 and 35. The selected period is the one where sex offenders tend to be at most risk of recidivism. Second, the study is set to examine whether offending trajectories are informative of post-release recidivism. In other words, is the pattern of offending between 18 and 35 informative about the risk of post-release recidivism past age 35? Put differently, are there any changes in the risk of offending from one period to another? Third, the study aims to determine the impact of age and the passage of time on the link between past offending pattern and the risk of recidivism. In other words, are the most active offenders in one period (18–35) also the most active offenders in another (past age 35)? This, for example, could help to determine whether the high-rate offenders in one period remain the high-rate offenders in a subsequent period. In doing so, the study aims to examine whether prior criminal records lose their predictive value with the passage of time and aging.

Methodology

Sample

As part of a research project on recidivism, all individuals consecutively admitted to a federal penitentiary for a sex crime between April 1994 and June 2000 were recruited for a study.[2] All individuals were incarcerated for at least 2 years in a federal penitentiary in the province of Quebec, Canada. In total, 93% of individuals approached (n = 553) agreed to participate in the study. At the time of the study, all participants were incarcerated in a maximum security institution operated by the Correctional Service of Canada. On average, participants stayed at the reception center for 6 weeks while their level of risk and rehabilitative needs were assessed. After their assessment, participants were transferred to an institution that best suited their risk and needs. Detailed accounts of criminal activity allowing for the computation of the criminal trajectory were obtained only for the first 393 cases recruited as part of that study. Of those 393 cases, only information on offenders older than 35 at the time of their prison release (n = 246) was used for the purposes of this study. The decision to keep only these offenders is in line with the focus of the study to: (a) examine older sexual offenders often targeted by the criminal justice system; (b) inspect the adult criminal career of those offenders having had a substantial time period to offend (from age 18 to 35, or 17 years); and (c) examine the criminal trajectories of offenders when they are at most risk of reoffending (i.e., prior age 35). Indeed, the analytical framework of this study requires a sufficiently long period to evaluate criminal trajectories of offenses with low base rates. Detailed information about the sample is presented in Table 13.1.

Procedures

Participation in this study was strictly voluntary, and all subjects signed a consent form indicating that the information collected would be used for research purposes only. The participants signed an additional consent form allowing access to their correctional files. When participants granted their consent, Correctional Service of Canada allowed inspection of their correctional files. Correctional files were used to code information on the criminal history of each individual included in the study. All files included information about the participants' official records based on the Royal Canadian Mounted Police (RCMP) record. RCMP data was then use to establish offenders' criminal histories. Recidivism data was collected in June 2004 using the same source of information.

[2]The authors are grateful to Dr Jean Proulx and the Correctional Service of Canada for granting access to this data.

Table 13.1 Descriptive Information of the Sample of Sexual Aggressors (n = 246)

Descriptive information	
Age at intake	45.1 (sd = 9.8; range: 26–74)
Age at first conviction	33.9 (sd = 14.2; range: 15–74)
Age at release	47.9 (sd = 9.4; range: 36–77)
Current conviction(s)[a]	
Sexual assault	58.2%
Sexual assault with weapon	8.2%
Sexual assault causing bodily harm	4.9%
Aggravated sexual assault	1.6%
Sexual interference	21.1%
Invitation to sexual touching	18.0%
Victim type[b]	
Male child victim (0–12 y.o.)	16.0%
Female child victim (0–12 y.o.)	43.9%
Male adolescent victim (13–17 y.o.)	13.1%
Female adolescent victim (13–17 y.o.)	26.2%
Adult female victim (18+ y.o.)	26.2%
Adult male victim (18+ y.o.)	1.2%
Criminal history – Sexual crimes	
18–23	.09 (sd = .40; range: 0–3)
24–29	.14 (sd = .68; range: 0–6)
30–35	.35 (sd = 1.74; range: 0–19)
Criminal history – Violent crimes	
18–23	.36 (sd = 1.36; range: 0–16)
24–29	.27 (sd = .78; range: 0–7)
30–35	.36 (sd = 1.26; range: 0–13)
Post-release recidivism (New charge) (n = 237)	
Any	19.8%
Violent, excluding sexual	9.7%
Violent, including sexual	14.3%
Sexual	7.2%

[a]Some offenders were convicted for multiple type of sexual crimes.
[b]Offenders can have more than one victim type.

Measures

Criminal History

The examination of offending trajectories was based on official data on offending. The decision to focus on official data only was justified on the basis that actuarial tools use official data on prior offending to determine the level of future offending. In keeping with actuarial studies, the number of charges for any violent and sexual crime was determined over a 17-year period. More specifically, all charges for a violent crime and/or a sex crime between the ages of 18 and 35 were coded according to three distinct 6-year time periods: (a) ages 18 to 23; (b) ages 24 to 29; and (c) ages 30 to 35. Note that for comparison purposes, a second approach was also used using shorter time periods: (a) 18–20; (b) 21–23; (c) 24–26; (d) 27–29; (e) 30–32; and (f) 33–35. The two coding schemes allowed us to determine whether smaller, and therefore more precise, time-periods produced similar or divergent findings in terms of both offending trajectories and prediction of reoffending. All analyses were conducted with these two coding schemes. For each of the three time periods, the total number of charges for sex crimes, the total number of charges for violent crimes, and the total number of charges for both violent and sexual crimes were determined. Four factors led us to merge violent and sexual crimes for data analyses: (a) the criminal versatility of adult sexual aggressors (Lussier, 2005); (b) the relatively low base rate of prior convictions for violent or sexual crimes in the criminal history of convicted sex offenders (Hall, 1988; Lussier, 2005); (c) the fact that an underdetermined number of sexual crimes have been registered as convictions for a violent crime due to plea bargaining (Proulx, Tardif, Lamoureux, & Lussier, 2000; Quinsey, Harris, Rice, & Cormier, 1998); and (d) the inspection of sexual offending trajectory for this sample showed a lack of heterogeneity (Lussier & Davies, 2011). (Additional information about the coding of criminal career information can be found in Lussier, LeBlanc, & Proulx, 2005; Lussier et al., 2010). Descriptive data about this sample are presented in Table 13.1.

Follow-Up Period

The follow-up period refers to the length of time for which each offender was at risk of recidivism in the community after their prison release for their index crime. To establish this period, the date of release for each offender included in the study was identified. Recidivism data was collected in June 2004, marking the end of the follow-up period for all individuals. Of the 246 cases included in the study, nine were excluded from the analysis of recidivism. Of those nine cases, six had not been released by the time the post-release recidivism data was collected and three cases were excluded because it was not possible to determine the length of their follow-up period due to missing data. For those 237 cases, the average follow-up period was 60.6 months (sd = 20.5). Keep in mind that the length of the follow-up period was influenced by: (a) the date of admission to prison, (b) the length of the prison sentence, (c) the length of time served in prison, and (d) whether the offender had reoffended before the end of the follow-up period.

Post-Release Recidivism

For the purpose of this study, recidivism refers to the presence of a new charge during the follow-up period. Limitations to the use of official data as a criteria of recidivism are well known, most importantly that they underestimate the true recidivism rate (e.g., Friendship & Thornton, 2001). Four definitions of recidivism were used for the current study. First, any recidivism refers to the presence of a new charge for any crime. This includes any nonviolent and nonsexual crime, as well as any violent and/or sexual crime for which the individual was charged during the follow-up period. Second, violent/sexual recidivism refers to the presence of a new charge for a violent crime or a sex crime. Third, sexual recidivism refers to the presence of a new charge for a sex crime. Fourth, violent recidivism refers to the presence of a new charge for a violent crime during the follow-up period. See also Lussier & Davies (2011) for additional coding information.

Analytical Strategy

First, semi-parametric group-based modeling (Nagin, 2005) was used to identify trajectories. Complete charge data was available for 246 individuals. Because official data are normally deleted from an offender's file once the offender turns 18, this study focused on adult offending. Consequently, convictions were aggregated across three time periods: (a) ages 18–23; (b) ages 24–29; and (c) ages 30–35. The analyses were conducted in SAS 9.2 using the PROC TRAJ add-on (Jones, Nagin, & Roeder, 2001). PROC TRAJ offers a variety of analytic capabilities, including zero-inflated Poisson (ZIP) modeling, which was best suited to the analysis of charge counts. For each charge type, the Bayesian Information Criterion (BIC) was used to select the model with the most appropriate number of trajectories. Second, survival analyses were used to examine post-release recidivism. Empirical analyses of the role of age at release on reoffending have used mainly two types of multivariate statistical techniques: logistic regression and Cox regression. Cox regression (Cox proportional hazards; Cox & Oakes, 1984) is a statistical technique that allows for examining whether survival time (i.e., not reoffending) is influenced by specified factors. Cox regression controls for censored data, something that cannot be achieved through logistic regression. In the present study, right censoring is important because it refers to nonrecidivist cases who might reoffend given a longer follow-up period. Recidivism studies have favored using Cox regression because failing to control for the length of the follow-up period could create biases in assessing and interpreting parameter estimates. Using SPSS, version 18.0, a series of Cox regression analyses were performed to determine the association between the offending trajectories and post-release recidivism.

Results

Modeling the Trajectories

Trajectory models were examined for violent/sexual offending between the ages of 18 and 35. Models allowing for one to five offending trajectory groups were estimated.[3] When looking at the number of violent and sexual charges combined,

[3]The findings for all semi-parametric group-based modeling can be obtained from the authors.

the three-group model best fit the data based on the BIC. No improvement in fit was found by allowing a four-group solution. Each individual was then assigned to their most likely trajectory group using posterior probabilities. The average posterior probabilities varied between .84 and .86. For comparison purposes, both the solution with three time points and that with six time points are represented in Figure 13.1. Note here that the overlap between the classification obtained from the three and six time points was considerable (Pearson's Phi = .91, $p < .001$). Only the solution based on three time points is used for the next set of analyses.

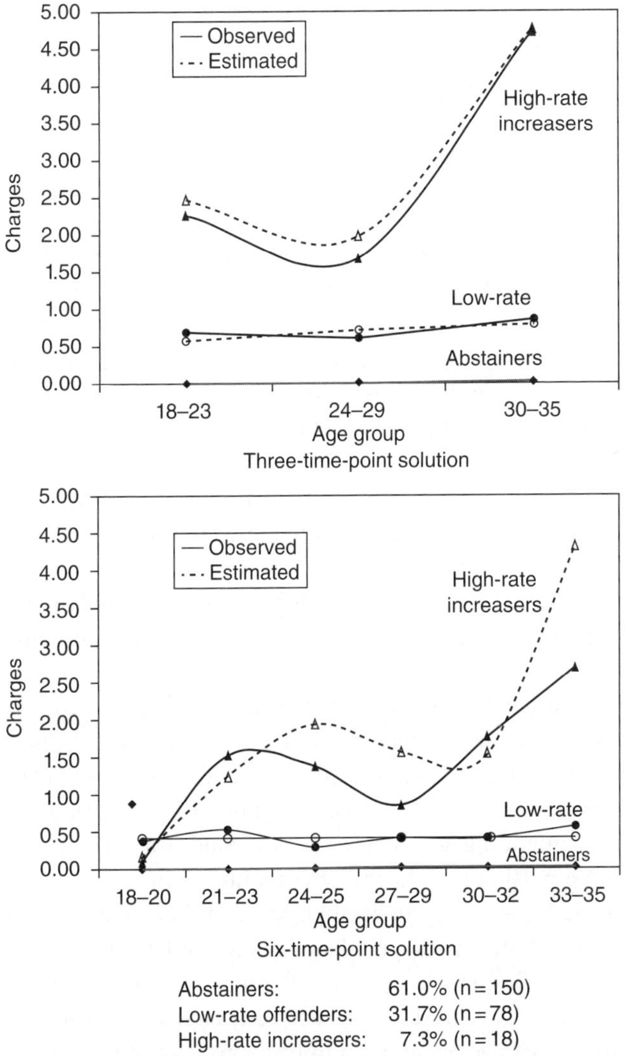

Figure 13.1 Violent/sexual offending trajectories of offenders between 18 and 35 years old.

Rate and Shape of Offending

The violent/sexual offending trajectories identified revealed the presence of three trajectories varying in frequency and shape of the distribution of offending over time (Figure 13.1). The first group (61.0 %), the abstainers, is characterized by the absence of violent/sexual offending between ages 18 and 35. The second pattern, representing 31.7% of the sample, was characterized by a pattern of low-rate violent/sexual offending frequency. They showed an average of about one violent/sexual offense per time period, or more specifically .82 (between ages 18 and 23), .77 (between ages 24 and 29), and .95 (between ages 30 and 35) charges. Finally, the third pattern, the high-rate increasers (7.3 %), showed a pattern of offending that varied, on average, between two and six violent/sexual crimes per time period, with the highest offending period being between ages 30 and 35. Analysis of variance revealed that the three offending patterns were statistically different on the three time points [$F = 351.70, p < .001$].

The Abstainers

Table 13.2 presents descriptive information on aggregate indicators of the criminal career for the three offending trajectory identified. The first group, the abstainers, were late-onset offenders, being first charged for a crime, on average, at age 40 and first charged for a sex crime at 47. Their volume of offending was more limited and the least diversified among the three identified trajectories. On average, these men have been convicted three times, while having been charged for close to five counts of sex crimes. Recall that between the ages of 18 and 35, these men were significantly less active than the low-rate and high-rate groups. This suggests that their offending exploded after that time period. Their record shows an average of about two victims, but a mean number of 356 sex crime events (median = 77). Hence, they did not have more victims than the other two groups of offenders, but repeatedly revictimized their victims more often than the other two groups.

Their higher number of crime events appears to be linked to two things: (a) the fact that they were primarily targeting children (as opposed to adult victims) who are less likely to report an abuse; and (b) their ability to avoid detection. Indeed, their record also shows that 122.7 months (about 10 years) elapsed between the onset of their sex offending and their detection. Since turning 18, these men spent 73% of their time outside prison, in the community. In sum, the abstainers were typically older, perhaps due to their ability to avoid/delay detection longer. This group were child molesters with a tendency to reoffend against the same victim on multiple occasions. The nature of their offending was also highlighted by their criminal record, which was more limited and restricted to sex crimes. The explosion of their offending, past age 35, appears to be an artefact of their ability, at least for some of these men, to avoid detection and apprehension.

Table 13.2 Offending Trajectories and Aggregate Criminal Career Information

	Offending trajectories between ages 18 and 35				
	Abstainers (n = 150) AB	*Low rate (n =78) LR*	*High-rate increasers (n = 18) HR*	*F statistic*	*Post-hoc test*
Age at prison admission (index)	48.6 (10.0)	40.1 (6.6)	37.2 (3.9)	28.8***	AB > LR, HR
Onset					
Age at first charge	40.4 (14.2)	23.8 (5.6)	24.1 (6.3)	52.1***	AB > LR, HR
Age at first sex charge	47.0 (10.4)	34.3 (8.2)	31.6 (6.0)	53.0***	AB > LR, HR
Volume					
Total number of convictions	2.9 (2.7)	6.9 (4.3)	8.7 (5.1)	43.1***	AB < LR, HR
Total number of sex charges	4.8 (4.2)	3.3 (3.7)	8.1 (7.3)	8.8***	AB > LR
Total number of violent (nonsex) charges	0.8 (1.7)	3.2 (2.7)	8.1 (7.2)	61.4***	AB < LR < HR
Number of victims (index)	2.2 (1.7)	1.5 (0.9)	2.1 (2.2)	6.3**	AB > LR
Number of child victims (index)	1.3 (1.4)	0.5 (0.8)	0.8 (1.2)	9.4***	AB > LR
Number of adult victims (index)	0.2 (0.7)	0.5 (0.7)	0.9 (2.2)	5.3**	AB < LR
Number of sex crime events (index)	356.4 (686.2) (Md = 77)	101.2 (299.2) (Md = 2)	23.4 (49.9) (Md = 6)	6.5**	AB > LR, HR
Diversity					
Total criminal versatility	2.8 (1.9)	6.3 (3.1)	7.2 (3.5)	59.5***	AB < HR
Cost avoidance					
Time-to-detection (months) (index)	122.7 (120.8) (Md = 83.5)	41.0 (64.2) (Md = 17)	25.2 (32.9) (Md = 10)	19.4***	AB > LR, HR
Percentage time free of incarceration since turning 18 y.o.	73.1 (34.1)	71.2 (21.4)	57.6 (65.5)	2.0	

Note. Md refers to the median score. Child victims refer to those who are 12 years old or younger. Adult victims are those who are at least 18 years old. Index refers to a parameter specific to the index crime. Levene test was analyzed for all group comparison and all tests showed heterogeneity of variance. Therefore, robust (Welch) tests of equality of means were analyzed. Nonparametric tests were also inspected. The findings of all additional tests were in line with those reported in the Table. All significant post-hoc tests were significant at $p < .05$. Versatility scores vary between 0 and 14 with a higher score indicating higher crime versatility. Time-to-detection was computed by calculating the time elapsed between the actual onset of sex offending (based on victim statement, police report, offender self-report) for the index crimes and the date at prison admission for the index crimes (see Lussier, Bouchard, & Beauregard, 2011). It refers to the proportion of time between turning 18 (birthday) and date at prison admission for the index crime. A higher proportion indicates that the offender has spent less time incarcerated since turning 18 years old. $^{\dagger}p < .10$, $^{*}p < .05$, $^{**}p < .01$, $^{***}p < .001$.

The Low-Rate Offenders

The second group, the low-rate offenders, were statistically different from the abstainers on most of the criminal career indicators examined. They were first charged in young adulthood (Mean = 23.8), but first charged for a sex crime a decade after their official onset (Mean = 34.3). Hence, their criminal activity was well established by the time they were first charged for a sex crime. This is reflected by the volume of their offending (Mean = 6.9 convictions), which was more important and violent (Mean = 3.2 charges) than that of the abstainers, although sexual offending (Mean = 3.3 charges) was less important than that of the abstainers. On average they had fewer charges for a sex crime, offended against fewer victims, had fewer child victims, and had fewer sex crimes events than the group of abstainers. Although they had more adult victims than the abstainers, they were more indiscriminate in the victims they offended against, showing the same number of child and adult victims. They were detected on average 41 months after the onset of their index offense, or just over 3 years, which contrasts with the abstainer group. Since turning 18, they spent 71.2% of their time free of incarceration. In sum, this group were more criminally active than the abstainers, and had been criminally active for a longer period, having started a younger age, but their sex offending was more indiscriminate (victim selection) and more limited than the abstainers.

The High-Rate Increasers

The third group, the high-rate increasers showed the most serious, diversified, and violent offending pattern. Like the low-rate group, the men included in the high-rate increaser group were first charged in young adulthood (Mean = 24), and were first charged for a sex crime soon after turning 30. This group had the more important volume of offending, in terms of total number of convictions, and total number of violent and sexual crimes. Their general offending was similar to that of the low-rate group, but they were more often charged for violent crimes (Mean = 8.1). Their sexual offending was similar to the abstainers in terms of the number of charges and number of victims (child and adults), but they were involved in fewer sex crime events. Keep in mind that, while the volume of their sex offending was similar to the abstainers, they were 10 years younger than the abstainers at prison admission, suggesting that they were indeed offending at a much higher rate. Their high offending rate might explain why they were caught about 2 years after the onset of their index offense, which is much sooner than the abstainers. More precisely, their rate might be indicative of a stronger inclination for short-term gratification at the costs of more long-term consequences. Together, these findings suggest that the high-rate increaser group were criminally active at a younger age, their offending was serious, diversified, and violent, and their sex offending was probably more impulsive and opportunistic, as shown by their tendency to be caught and apprehended sooner after the act.

Post-Release Recidivism

Table 13.3 presents the percentages of recidivists for each of the three offending trajectory groups. Clearly, the low-rate and the high-rate increasers include a higher proportion of recidivists for any reoffense, violent reoffense, and violent/sexual reoffense, but not for a sexual reoffense. For example, 37.5% of the high-rate increasers, 33.8% of the low-rate offenders, but only 10.9% of the abstainers were charged for a new crime during the follow-up period. Although the sexual recidivism rate of abstainers is noticeably lower, it is not statistically significant, which appears to be related to statistical power issues. Similar findings were observed for a new charge for violent/sexual crimes where 31.3% of high-rate increasers, 24.3 % of low-rate offenders, but only 5.4 % of the abstainers were recidivists. That said, the high-rate increasers represented only 5 of the 34 (14.7 %) of the violent/sexual recidivists identified in the study. Further, 12.5 % of the high-rate increasers, 9.5 % of the low-rate offenders, and 5.4% of the abstainers were charged again for a sex crime during the follow-up period. It is interesting to note that only two of the 17 (11.8 %) sexual recidivists identified in this study were high-rate increasers.

Length of Survival

Table 13.4 provides an overview of the length of survival when considering four outcome measures of recidivism. When looking at a new charge for any crime, the length of survival of abstainers averaged 100.9 months (about 8 years). For low-rate and high-rate abstainers, the mean length of survival without a new charge was, respectively, 71.3 and 73.2 months (or about 6 years). In other words, the two most active groups of offenders in terms of their offending between the ages of 18 and 35,

Table 13.3 Descriptive Information About Post-Release Recidivism

	Offending trajectories between ages 18 and 35			
Post-release recidivism	*Abstainers (n = 150)*	*Low rate (n = 78)*	*High-rate increasers (n = 18)*	*Group comparison*
Any new charge	10.9 (16)	33.8 (25)	37.5 (6)	$X^2(2) = 19.6^{***}$
A new charge for a violent (excluding sexual) crime	3.4 (5)	20.3 (15)	18.8 (3)	$X^2(2) = 17.6^{***}$
A new charge for a sexual crime	5.4 (8)	9.5 (7)	12.5 (2)	$X^2(2) = 1.9$
A new charge for a violent and/or sexual crime	7.5 (11)	24.3 (18)	31.3 (5)	$X^2(2) = 15.4^{***}$

Note. % and (n) are presented in the table.
$^{\dagger}p < .10$, $^{*}p < .05$, $^{**}p < .01$, $^{***}p < .001$.

Table 13.4 Post-Release Survival Time (Months) Without Reoffending for Each Offending Trajectory

	Offending trajectories between ages 18 and 35			
Post-release recidivism	*Abstainers (n = 150)*	*Low rate (n = 78)*	*High-rate increasers (n = 18)*	*Group comparison (Mantel-Cox)*
Any new charge	100.9 (2.5)	71.3 (3.7)	73.2 (8.6)	AB > LR***, AB > HR**
A new charge for a violent (excluding sexual) crime	108.2 (1.4)	79.3 (3.7)	85.8 (8.7)	AB > LR***, AB > HR*
A new charge for a sexual crime	106.3 (1.7)	87.6 (2.8)	85.8 (6.1)	n.s.
A new charge for a violent and/or sexual crime	104.6 (2.0)	76.8 (3.8)	76.8 (8.8)	AB > LR***, AB > HR**

$^{\dagger}p < .10$, $^{*}p < .05$, $^{**}p < .01$, $^{***}p < .001$.

spent about 2 years less in the community without reoffending past age 35 compared to the least active group. Similar trends were observed for violent recidivism as well as violent/sexual recidivism where low-rate offenders and high-rate increasers survived a shorter time period in the community without a new charge compared to the abstainers. Note that the low-rate offenders and the high-rate increasers, in spite of their significant differences in prior offending, did not differ in terms of their length of survival in the community without a new charge. Note also that, while a similar trend was observed for sexual recidivism, the differences were not statistically significant. The absence of a significant effect is probably attributable to the statistical power of the analysis due to the small number of sexual recidivists in the study. Survival curves are presented in Figure 13.2.

Hazard Rate and Age at Release

Table 13.5 presents the findings of a Cox proportional hazards modeling on the link between offending trajectories and the four recidivism outcomes. In Model 1, the three trajectories are compared in terms of their risk of recidivism. For the purpose of the analysis, the low-rate offenders and the high-rate increasers were compared to the group of abstainers. The findings show that the low-rate offenders and the high-rate increasers were more likely to reoffend for any crime, for a violent crime, and for a violent/sexual crime than the abstainer group. Note that the hazard ratios found for the low-rate offenders and the high-rate increasers were quite similar across outcomes, suggesting that the low-rate group, past age 35, were reoffending at the same rate as the high-rate increasers. Interestingly, there were no statistical differences between groups for when sexual recidivism was analyzed specifically. These results, therefore, mirrored those observed in the previous section. Of importance,

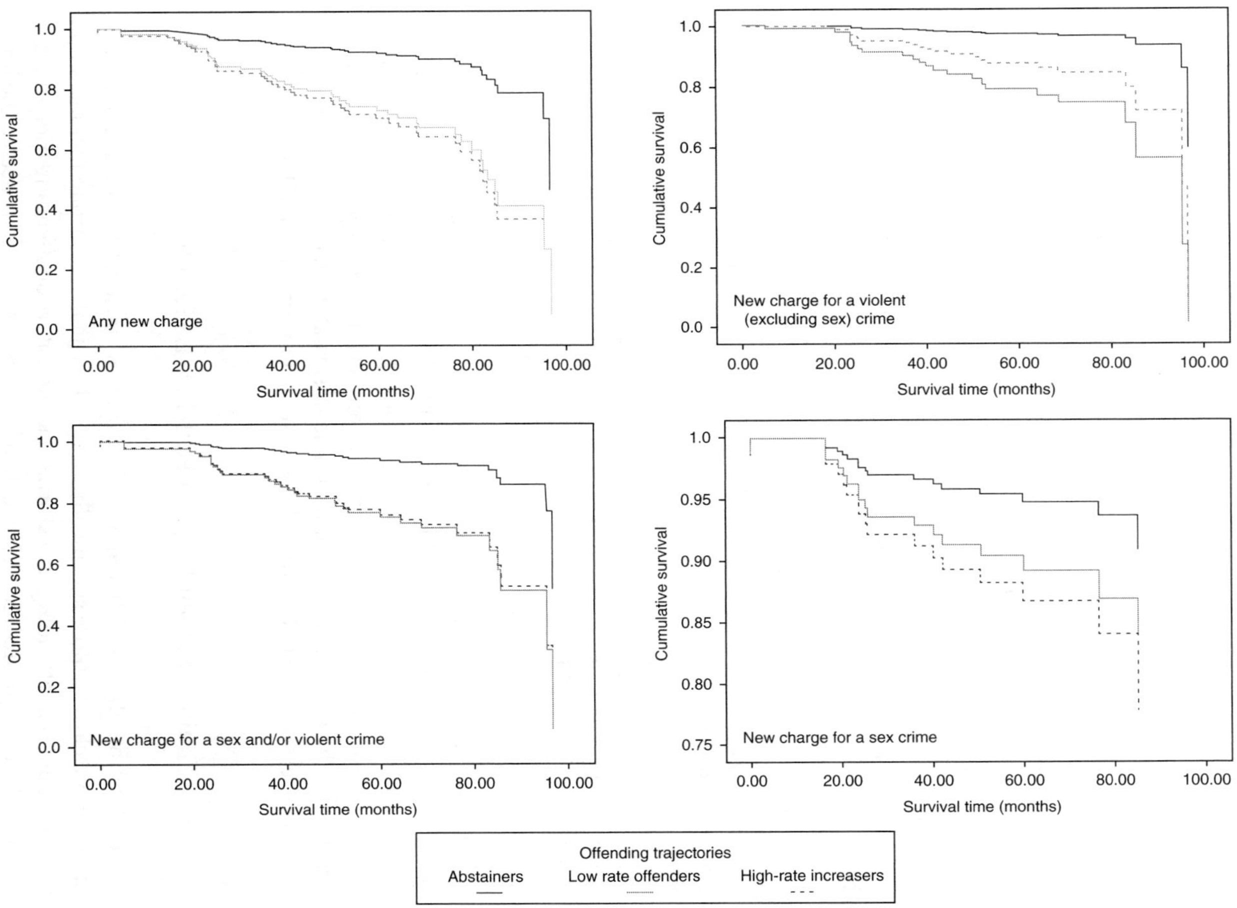

Figure 13.2 Survival curves for post-release recidivism according to offending trajectories.

Table 13.5 Cox Proportional Hazards Prediction Model of Post-Release Reoffending

	Post-release recidivism (New charge)			
Covariates	*Any new charge*	*New charge for a violent crime*	*New charge for a sex crime*	*New charge for a violent and/ or sex crime*
Model 1: Baseline model				
Offending trajectory				
Low-rate offenders	4.2 (2.2–7.9)***	8.4 (3.0–23.3)***	2.1 (0.8–5.9)	4.4 (2.1–9.4)***
High-rate increasers	3.7 (1.4–9.9)**	4.8 (1.0–22.7)*	2.7 (0.6–12.7)	4.3 (1.4–12.9)*
Model 2: Adjusted for age at release				
Offending trajectory				
Low-rate offenders	3.5 (1.8–6.9)***	5.3 (1.9–15.1)**	1.7 (0.5–5.0)	3.5 (1.6–7.9)**
High-rate increasers	3.3 (1.1–9.8)*	2.5 (0.4–14.1)	1.9 (0.4–10.0)	3.3 (1.0–11.2)†
Age at release (linear)	0.9 (0.9–1.0)	0.9 (0.8–1.0)	1.0 (0.9–1.0)	1.0 (0.9–1.0)
Age at release (quadratic)	0.5 (0.3–0.9)*	0.5 (0.2–1.4)	1.0 (0.6–1.6)	0.7 (0.4–1.2)
Contribution of the age effect of the prediction model	$X^2(2) = 8.88$*	$X^2(2) = 5.68$†	$X^2(2) = 1.12$	$X^2(2) = 3.54$

Note. The group of abstainers were used as the reference category to compute the hazard ratios. Hazard ratios with 95% confidence intervals are shown.
†$p < .10$, *$p < .05$, **$p < .01$, ***$p < .001$.

the hazard rates for the low-rate offenders and the high-rate increasers were adjusted for the offender's age at release. To do so, a linear and a quadratic term were entered in Cox proportional hazards models. A significant age effect (quadratic, or inverted U-shaped) was found for a new charge for any crime. The age effect was not significant for the other three outcomes (violent, sexual, violent/sexual), although the trends observed were in line with those observed in previous studies.

Timing of Offending and Post-Release Recidivism

In Table 13.6, the effect of offending trajectories on post-release recidivism was examined more closely. More specifically, rather than analyzing group membership of the three identified offending trajectories, the indicators of offending used to create the trajectories were analyzed. Hence, in a baseline model, we inspected the link between the number of charges at three time points (18–23; 24–29; 30–35) and the four outcome measures of recidivism. When entered simultaneously, the findings show that the number of charges between ages 30 and 35 is the only indicator significantly related to all four outcome measures (Hazard ratios vary between 1.12

Table 13.6 Offending, Timing of Offending, and Post-Release Recidivism

	Post-release recidivism			
	Any new charge	*New charge for a violent crime*	*New charge for a sex crime*	*New charge for a violent and/or sex crime*
Baseline model				
Number of charges 18–23	1.07 (.92–1.25)	1.07 (.86–1.32)	1.05 (.81–1.37)	1.07 (.91–1.27)
Number of charges 24–29	1.22 (1.06–1.40)**	1.19 (.96–1.47)	1.04 (.71–1.53)	1.13 (.92–1.40)
Number of charges 30–35	1.12 (1.04–1.21)**	1.14 (1.04–1.26)**	1.14 (1.02–1.27)*	1.15 (1.07–1.24)***
Hierarchical modeling	**Relative improvement provided by the volume of offending at different time points to the prediction of recidivism**			
Adding charges 18–23[a]	$X^2(1) = .87$, ns	$X^2(1) = .44$, ns	$X^2(1) = .12$, ns	$X^2(1) = .67$, ns
Adding charges 24–29[b]	$X^2(1) = 6.65$, $p < .05$	$X^2(1) = 2.60$, ns	$X^2(1) = .13$, ns	$X^2(1) = 1.88$, ns
Adding charges 30–35[c]	$X^2(1) = 5.53$, $p < .05$	$X^2(1) = 4.80$, $p < .05$	$X^2(1) = 3.36$, $p = .067$	$X^2(1) = 8.47$, $p < .01$
	Relative improvement provided by the age (linear and quadratic) effect to the prediction of recidivism			
Adding age effect[d] (linear and quadratic)	$X^2(2) = 12.36$**	$X^2(2) = 10.49$**	$X^2(2) = 1.84$	$X^2(2) = 6.34$*

Note. Cox proportional hazard models (Cox regression). Hazard ratios with 95% confidence intervals are presented in the table.

[a]Adding the number of charges between 18–23 y.o. to a prediction model without any covariate.

[b]Adding the number of charges between 24–29 y.o. to a regression model with only the number of charges between 18–23 y.o. as the other covariate.

[c]Adding the number of charges between 30–35 y.o. to a regression model where the number of charges between 18–23 y.o. and the number of charges between 24–29 y.o. are the covariates.

[d]Adding a linear and a quadratic age effect to the baseline model including the number of charges at all three time periods.

†$p < .10$, *$p < .05$, **$p < .01$, ***$p < .001$.

and 1.15). Offenders who were more active during that time period were at higher risk of being charged again for a new crime, for a violent crime, for a sexual crime, and for a violent/sex crime. Therefore, the most recent time period considered in the analysis, which also corresponds to the time period closest to the offender's index crime, was more indicative of their risk of post-release recidivism, irrespective of the nature of the reoffense. When using a hierarchical modeling procedure,[4] the findings highlighted that offending between the ages of 18 and 23 was not predictive of reoffending. The same situation was observed for offending between the ages of 24 and 29, to the exception of a new charge for any crime [$X^2(1) = 6.65, p < .05$].

Therefore, for sex offenders who were more than 35 years old at the time of their prison release, the number of prior charges for violent and sexual crimes was not predictive of violence and sexual post-release recidivism. Again, the hierarchical procedure highlighted that the level of violent and sexual offending between the ages of 30 and 35 was the most predictive of violent and sexual post-release reoffending. Finally, we tested the age effect, after controlling for the level of offending for three time points (Baseline model). In other words, all three indicators of violent and sexual offending were entered in a model to control for the effect of prior offending, to which we added a linear and quadratic age effect. A significant age effect was found for three of the four outcomes examined. The age effect was significant for any reoffense, violent reoffense, and violent/sexual reoffense, but not for sexual reoffense, suggesting that the risk of reoffending decreased as offenders aged, with the exception of sex offending. The small number of sexual recidivists, and statistical power issues, may explain the absence of a significant effect.

Discussion

The current study aimed to accomplish three things. First, the study aimed to identify and describe the violent/sexual offending trajectories of adult sex offenders. Second, the study was set to determine whether these trajectories were informative of post-release recidivism to inform risk assessors. Third, the study aimed to determine the impact of age and the passage of time on the link between past offending pattern and the risk of post-release recidivism. In doing so, the study merged two traditions of research: (a) the criminal career perspective and the identification of offending patterns over time; (b) the study of post-release recidivism and using survival modeling. The findings, while preliminary, provide new insights into the

[4]The hierarchical procedure used refers to the fact that three indicators of violent/sexual offending were entered in a series of nested models. First, a model with only offending between ages 18 and 23 was compared to a baseline model without any covariates. Then, a model including offending between ages 24 and 29 and ages 18 and 23 was compared to one including only offending in the latter period. Finally, a model including the three offending indicators was compared to one including only offending between ages 24 and 29 and ages 18 and 23. The ordering of the predictors in the model was based on chronological order.

understanding of the long-term patterns of offending in adult sex offenders, but also set an agenda for research to understand the mechanisms responsible for such patterns. We review here the main findings and discuss their practical implications for future research using a criminal career approach.

The Offending Trajectories of Adult Sex Offenders

The study identified three underlying violent/sexual offending trajectories in a sample of older adult sex offenders: the abstainers, the low-rate offenders, and the high-rate increasers. When analyzing offending trajectories, the first two key elements of interest are the intercept (onset) and the slope (development) of the trajectory. The intercept of the trajectory, marking the onset of violent/sexual offending in adulthood, varied across the three groups; by age 23, differential patterns of offending are already emerging.[5] The factors associated with differential intercepts across these offenders remains unknown. The rate and shape of offending also across the three identified trajectories varied significantly between the ages of 18 and 35. It is interesting to note that none of the identified pattern follows, for the 18–35 period, the typical age-crime curve pattern. In fact, during that time period, one pattern had yet to start (abstainers), one was constantly low (low-rate offenders) and the other one was on the rise (high-rate increasers). The factors associated with differential rate of violent/sexual offending were not investigated here and have not been examined in prior research studies. Such heterogeneity in the life course in terms of onset, rate, and shape of offending should be a priority of future research. While such heterogeneity is informative about the underlying patterns of offending in adult sex offenders, the prevalence of each of the patterns found is equally important for policy development. Indeed, in spite of using a sample of federal inmates (the most serious among incarcerated Canadian offenders), our study showed that a trajectory of abstainers represented 61% of the sample. Hence, the most prevalent trajectory characterized a group of sex offenders who were not charged for any violent and/or sexual crimes between the ages of 18 and 35.

At the other extreme, it also interesting to note that the group who were the most active offenders between the ages of 18 and 35, the high-rate increasers, represented only 7% of this sample. Depiction of sexual offenders' offending trajectory as one characterized by a fixed high rate of sexual offending is clearly at odd with our findings. The three offending trajectories identified varied, not only in terms of their rate and shape of violent/sexual offending between the ages of 18 and 35, but also in terms of various additional aggregate criminal career markers. The inspection of aggregate criminal career markers (onset, volume, diversity, and cost avoidance) helps in putting each of the three violent/sexual offending trajectories into the context of their entire criminal career. The analyses revealed that abstainers were first

[5]Analysis of the trajectories using six time points revealed that if the three groups are quite similar from age 18 to 20, their onset pattern emerges soon after (Figure 13.1).

charged for a sex crime well into their forties. This raises the question as to why this group started their sex offending much later in adulthood compared to the other two groups. In that regard, the abstainers were typically child molesters first charged in their forties, thus suggesting that this group were late-onset offenders. Their criminal activity was more restricted and limited to sexual offending, suggesting some evidence of specialization in their offending. Hence, while an analysis of their offending based solely on number of charges depicts these men as abstainers between 18 and 35 years old, other sources of information suggest that these men where more effective at avoiding and delaying detection.[6] In fact, they avoided detection for a decade or so after activating their sexual offending. The results are in line with those of Lussier and Mathesius (2012), which show that the gap between actual and official onset of sex offending in child molesters is about 10 years.

A more detailed analysis of their offending also revealed that this group had been involved in the highest number of crime events due to their tendency to revictimize the same victim several times. It could be reasonably argued that their criminal record, or lack thereof, contributed to their gaining access to potential victims by presenting a more conventional and prosocial image (e.g., to a single mother, to both parents, to employers, to victims). The other two trajectories identified, the low-rate offenders and the high-rate increasers, were not reflective of a pattern of specialized sexual offending or reflective of a sexual criminal career in the making. Rather, these trajectories within the context of their entire criminal career suggest that the sexual offending of these men was part of a more general criminal activity varying in volume, seriousness, and diversity. These two groups are more likely to be subject to increased attention for classification risk at their prison admission, as well as from parole board members, compared to abstainers, given their history of violence as well as their more extensive criminal record. In spite of their criminal history showing a more extensive criminal record for violent and sexual offending, a finer analysis of their sex offending revealed that these men had been involved in significantly fewer sex crime events than had abstainers. The ability of low-rate offenders and high-risk increasers to delay detection may partly explain the differential criminal record separating these men from the abstainers. It is unclear whether and how risk assessment procedures took into account these offenders' differential cost avoidance ability. In fact, actuarial tools are typically based on official indicators of crime (charges, convictions) and are, therefore, biased toward offenders who are more likely to get caught and get caught more often.

Post-Release Recidivism

The findings regarding post-release recidivism are not surprising and are in line with prior empirical investigations, having examined similar samples of offenders. For an average follow-up period of about 5 years, only 19.8% of this sample were

[6]These findings alone highlight the importance of combining several sources of information to provide a more accurate depiction of the offending pattern of sex offenders.

charged again for any crime, while 9.7% were charged for a violent crime and 7.2% were charged for a new sex crime. Recidivism was relatively low, lower perhaps than what is typically reported in empirical studies given that: (a) our sample was older than other samples found in the literature; and (b) having removed younger sex offenders from our sample, we removed a somewhat sizeable proportion of recidivists. This should not be interpreted as a limitation, given that several researchers have urged researchers to look at the recidivism for specific age-groups due to the age-crime curve effect (e.g., Wollert, 2006). In that sense, this sample is older and more heterogeneous in terms of age and risk of recidivism. With that in mind, the risk of post-release recidivism was relatively in line with the offending trajectories observed for the period ranging between the ages of 18 and 35. The abstainers were different from the other two groups in terms of the post-release likelihood of reoffending and the speed at which they reoffended. Both the low-rate offenders and the high-rate increasers survived about 2 years less in the community without being charged again than the abstainers. We can't preclude that abstainers had a lower risk of recidivism and survived longer in the community without reoffending due to (a) their ability to delay detection for long periods, (b) their late-onset of official sex offending, well into their forties, and (c) their older age at the time of their prison release, which is associated with lower sexual recidivism rates. This result suggests at least some fixed propensity to the likelihood of offending across different time periods. This observation is in line with the actuarial prediction of recidivism, which emphasizes the role of static predictors of reoffending, such as the number of prior charges for a violent crime or a sex crime, in assessing the risk of recidivism. That being said, we also found evidence that departs from a fixed-propensity approach to offending.

The Dynamic Aspect of Offending

Aging and the passage of time was a critical aspect of this study and the study findings suggest that its role highlights the dynamic aspect of offending over time. First, and in line with prior studies (e.g., Lussier & Healey, 2009), age was found to be related to recidivism in spite of the exclusion of younger offenders from the study, suggesting that the age effect was still captured even among a more heterogeneous group of offenders. Second, significant differences were found between the low-rate offenders and the high-rate increasers between the ages of 18 and 35 in terms on their violent/sexual offending rate. Such differences were not associated with differential post-release recidivism rates or length of survival in the community without reoffending. In fact, the risk of post-release recidivism for the low-rate offenders and the high-rate increasers was not statistically different. Hence, past age 35, the low-rate group represented the same "risk" for any, violent, and sexual crime as the high-rate increaser group. This could reflect the possibility that: (a) the low-rate offenders caught up with the high-rate increasers; (b) the high-rate increasers started slowing down; (c) our measure of recidivism was too imprecise given that it did not take into account the number of new charges (only the presence of at least one new charge for each of the four outcome measures). Third, it is also noteworthy that the majority of this group of older offenders were described as following an abstainer trajectory, and were not reconvicted during the follow-up period. If persistence in violent/sexual offending is important in younger adult sex offenders, then some of this would have been captured in our study. Instead, less than 10% of this sample was characterized by an active offending trajectory in young adulthood. Finally, it is noteworthy that the high-rate increaser group, or the most prolific offenders between ages 18 and 35, represented only 12% of the sexual recidivists and about 15% of the violent and/or sexual recidivists past age 35. The findings suggested the presence of a state-dependent process, suggesting that the more recent indicators are better indicators of reoffending than long-term ones. When we broke down the level of offending at different time points, it allowed us to determine whether the level of offending at different time points predicted post-release recidivism at a later time point. In doing so, it allowed us to test whether an early onset of sex offending in adulthood predicted recidivism. It also allowed us to examine the propensity hypothesis, which suggests that the level of offending at different time points captures the same underlying propensity to commit acts of violence and sexual crimes.

The findings did not show evidence of an "early-onset" factor as the level of offending between ages 18 and 23 was not predictive of reoffending past age 35. One could argue that this is not truly a test of the early-onset hypothesis, given that offending in youth was not included in the study. However, according to the propensity hypothesis, past the period of adolescence (some would claim much earlier) such propensity is fixed and stable. Therefore, based on that hypothesis, we could reasonably argue that offenders with a higher propensity would be more likely to start early in adulthood. When we compared the level of offending at different time points, it is the level of offending closest to prison admission for their index crime that was most predictive of reoffending. We are not saying that there is not early-onset effect, but rather that with the passage of time and aging, the early-onset effect seems to disappear. In other words, more recent criminal activity, rather than older criminal records, are more indicative of the likelihood of reoffending. Therefore, we could assume that, with the passage of time, the predictive value of a prior criminal record is significantly reduced (see also Amirault & Lussier, 2011). In fact, it is the level of offending in the time period (ages 30–35) closest to the post-release period studied that predicted recidivism. Future research should examine, for this age group, whether the level of offending during that time period is more indicative of post-release recidivism because is it closer in time to the outcome being predicted, or, perhaps, because there is something more specific during that time period for which the level of offending might be more indicative of later or future offending.

Presentation of Three Cases

In order to illustrate the findings, one case is outlined for each of the three trajectories identified. The three cases are detailed in terms of their offending pattern and their criminal career, but also in terms of the nature of their sexual offending.[7] Even a brief description of these cases illustrates the complexities of the issues at hand.

Case #9: The Abstainer

Mr X had no criminal record between the ages of 18 and 35. In fact, Mr X was first charged at age 58 for sexual assault and gross indecency. The analysis of his correctional file revealed that this man was convicted for sex crimes committed against two young females. According to the police report and the victim statement, the offenses started when the offender was 39 years old. The first victim was 7 years old at the time. The abuse of this victim spanned over a 10-year period. Mr X started abusing the second victim when he was 40 years old, and the offenses spanned over a 3-year period. The second victim was also 7 years old when the abuse started. The sexual abuse stopped when the offender was 49, about 9 years before being charged and convicted for his crimes. It could be argued that this man had desisted or was in the process of desisting before being first charged for his sex crime. Both victims were Mr X's stepdaughters and were living under the same roof with the offender and their mother. The first victim was raped, while the second was coerced into noncoital acts. Mr X denied any deviant sexual fantasies, instead blaming the victims, stating that they were asking for such sexual contacts. According to the victims, they were sexually abused about 15 times. Mr X never used any physical violence against them while committing the abuse. When the offenses started, Mr X was physically disabled due to a work-related accident, and, as a result, could not work, spending most of his time at home. He had marital conflicts, and such conflicts appeared to be related to the nature/frequency of his sexual activities with his partner. The offender was sentenced to a 3-year prison term. He was released at age 60. In the seven and a half years since his release, his record indicates that he has not been charged for a new crime. This is not surprising, given that he had remained crime-free for almost a decade before being charged for his offenses. While recidivism is based on official statistics, it remains to be seen whether self-report data would provide the same picture.

[7]The selection of these cases was made as follows. For each trajectory, all cases presenting the highest probability of group membership were identified using posterior probabilities. Once these cases were identified, one case was randomly selected from among them for each of the three offending trajectories.

Case #164: A Low-Rate Offender

Mr Y was first charged at 23, then multiple times at ages 29, 31, and 33. In total, Mr Y was convicted five times for any crime; two of those convictions led to prison terms. In total, Mr Y's criminal record shows a total of six charges, four of which were for violent (mainly assault) or sexual crimes. Looking more specifically at his violent/sex offending, he was charged once between the ages of 18 and 23 and again at three different times between the ages of 30 and 33. Hence, Mr Y's criminal activity was serious and persistent, but his offending rate was relatively low and intermittent. At 33, he was sentenced to 7 years of prison for armed sexual assault (index crime). It marked the first time he was charged (and convicted) for a sex crime. During day-time, armed with a knife, he forced his victim to perform oral sex. The victim was a 24-year-old female he had never met before. The crime was unplanned and opportunistic, and he was caught in the act. The offender used more than necessary violence during the event and inflicted severe physical injuries to the victim. At the time of the events, Mr Y was unemployed and intoxicated (alcohol and drugs). He was released on parole at age 37, about 4 years into his prison sentence. Two years after his prison release, he was charged and convicted for two counts of sexual assault and sentenced to 13 years of prison. Between the ages of 18 and 32, the criminal record suggests that this man was mainly a low-rate, violent offender. From age 33 onward, the criminal activity of this man became limited to acts of sexual violence, and he became a sexual recidivist in the process. Hence, snapshots at two different time points showed a different pattern in the nature of the offending, while its rate remained relatively constant.

Case #339: A High-Rate Increaser

In adulthood, Mr Z was first charged soon after turning 18. He was 19 when he was first charged for a property crime. His criminal record showed from then on a pattern of chronic offending. In total, between the ages of 19 and 37 (time of his index crime), his police record showed 48 charges for which he was convicted and sentenced to a prison term 10 times. During that period, he was charged on 19 counts of violent crimes and three counts of sex crimes. His offending showed a clear pattern of escalation, moving from property crimes, to violent crimes, and finally to sexual crimes. Indeed, Mr Z was first charged for a violent crime at age 26, while he was 32 when first charged for a sex crime. At age 32, Mr Z was charged for two counts of sexual assault against two adult females. This escalation pattern was accompanied by an increasing rate of violent/sexual offending with 15 of his violent/sexual charges having occurred between the ages of 30 and 35. At age 37, he was charged for uttering threats, assault, and sexual assault, all for the same incident involving one adult female. At night, he raped a 44-year-old female using physical violence. Mr Z had met the victim a few times prior the offense. Both the offender and the victim were intoxicated (alcohol) at the time of the offense. His crime involved some planning and the offender admitted to having deviant sexual fantasies involving the victim in the days prior the rape. At that time, he was unemployed and married, but was having significant marital difficulties. He was sentenced to 3 years in prison but was released on parole 2 years later. He was 39 years old at the time of his prison release. Four years after being released, Mr Z was charged again (five counts) for uttering threats, for which he was convicted and sentenced to 5 months of prison. The offending pattern of this sexual recidivist suggests that his sexual offending is part of a chronic and violent offending pattern which might have peaked in his thirties, both in terms of rate and seriousness.

Implications of the Person-Oriented Approach

This chapter is part of a series of empirical studies designed to uncover the offending trajectories of sexual offenders (Lussier et al., 2010; Lussier & Davies, 2011). This new corpus of research is in line with the criminal career approach in that it aims to improve our understanding of the longitudinal sequence of crimes committed by sex offenders. While the findings do not have immediate policy implications, they do highlight the benefits of adopting a person-oriented perspective to disentangle the patterns of offending of sex offenders. The potential policy, clinical, and research implications are significant and important. Current risk management policies, actuarial assessment, and treatment programs do not typically adjust their criminal justice response, risk prediction about long-term offending, and treatment interventions according to sex offenders' offending trajectory, stage of the criminal career at the time of assessment, or the time elapsed since the last arrest/charges. They also do not give more weight to the most recent level of offending. While the role and importance of age and aging on offending patterns are gradually making their way in various research circles, they have yet to influence the criminal justice response, risk assessment, and treatment in a systematic and coordinated manner. Future research should determine how best to approach such adjustment to take into account the dynamic aspect of offending and the importance of a state-dependence process. Several questions that should be addressed in future research should concern the role and importance of life events, life transitions, and turning points across life stages in adulthood. For example, what factors are responsible for the differential patterns of activation found for the abstainers, low-rate offenders, and high-rate increasers? What factors are responsible for the differential rate of offending across the identified offending trajectories? What factors are responsible for the increasing rate observed for the high-rate increasers? Among each of the three trajectories, who are the individuals most likely to reoffend, and are those factors similar or different across offending trajectories? In other words, are the risk factors associated with sexual recidivisms for low-rate offenders the same as those for sexual recidivists following a high-rate pattern?

Limitations and Considerations for Future Research

This is one of the first studies to examine offending trajectories in adult sex offenders and the study findings should be interpreted accordingly. The sample composition might have influenced the number and shape of trajectories identified. Because the focus of the study was federally sentenced Canadian inmates, it was based on a group of men who had been convicted mostly for hands-on behaviors. Federally sentenced sex offenders probably include an overrepresentation of individuals having committed more serious sex crimes, as well as those with more extensive criminal histories. Furthermore, the majority of this sample had been convicted for sexual assault and close to the majority of this sample had offended against a female child. Also, this study is based on a sample of sex offenders who were older than 35 at the time of their prison release. It is unlikely that this study uncovered all trajectories of violent/sexual offending given our decision to focus on older convicted sex offenders. More patterns are likely to emerge by analyzing the younger adult sex offenders. Moreover, the study only took into consideration violent/sexual offending. Clearly, as the criminal career data presented and as our case example illustrated, the criminal activity of these men was not limited to violent and sexual crimes. Extending the analysis of offending trajectories to nonsex crimes could provide a fruitful avenue to better contextualize the offending of adult sex offenders and their risk of reoffending (see Lussier et al., 2010). Further, the computation of the offending trajectory did not take into account time incarcerated (or opportunity to offend).[8] The findings highlight the importance of examining the offending trajectory of sex offenders by extending the observational period beyond the mid-thirties and examining the trajectories up to ages 50 and 60. It is unlikely the study of offending past age 60 would provide meaningful findings as previous studies have shown that recidivism past that age is extremely rare (e.g., Wollert, 2006).

Conclusion

The current study represents an additional step toward a more individualized, nonlinear approach to risk assessment and risk prediction. The study findings highlight that the offending trajectories of adult sex offenders go through dynamic changes in adulthood, in terms of rate and nature of offending, changes that are not captured by the traditional actuarial methods. The study aims to stimulate research in the area of offending trajectories by introducing a person-oriented approach to better understand the criminal career of adult sex offenders. The study also aims to inform risk assessors and policymakers about the limitations of approaching the criminal activity of adult sex offenders as something inevitably fixed and static. Such perceptions will lead to the overestimation of risk for some and the underestimation of risk

[8]Yet, our findings also showed that the three groups were not statistically different in terms of total time spent incarcerated since turning 18 years old (Table 13.2).

for others. In fact, the study highlights that the most active sex offenders in one period may not be the most criminally active in a subsequent period. Future research should investigate the role of life events, life transitions, and turning points that may impact the course of offending over time.

References

Amirault, J., & Lussier, P. (2011). Population heterogeneity, state dependence and sexual offender recidivism: The aging process and the lost predictive impact of prior criminal charges over time. *Journal of Criminal Justice, 39*, 344–354.

Barbaree, H. E., Langton, C. M., Blanchard, R., & Canton, J. M. (2009). Aging versus stable dynamic traits as explanatory constructs in sex offender recidivism: Partitioning actuarial prediction into conceptually meaningful components. *Criminal Justice and Behavior, 36*, 444–465.

Beauregard, E., Proulx, J., Rossmo, K., Leclerc, B., & Allaire, F. (2007). Script analysis of the hunting process of serial sex offenders. *Criminal Justice and Behavior, 34*, 1069–1084.

Beauregard, E., Rossmo, D. K., & Proulx, J. (2007). A descriptive model of the hunting process of serial sex offenders: A rational choice perspective. *Journal of Family Violence, 22*, 449–463.

Bergman, L. R. (2002). Studying processes: Some methodological considerations. In L. Pulkkinen & A. Caspi (Eds.), *Paths to successful development: Personality in the life course*. Cambridge, UK: Cambridge University Press.

Bergman, L. R., & Magnusson, D. (1997). A person-orientated approach to research on developmental psychopathology. *Development and Psychopathology, 9*, 291–319.

Bergman, L. R., & Trost, K. (2006). The person-orientated versus the variable-orientated approach: Are they complementary, opposites, or exploring different worlds? *Merrill-Palmer Quarterly, 52*, 601–632.

Blumstein, A., Cohen, J., Roth, J. A., & Visher, C. A. (1986). *Criminal Careers and "Career Criminals." (Vol. I)*. Washington, DC: National Academy Press.

Cale, J., & Lussier, P. (2011). Toward a developmental taxonomy of adult sexual aggressors of women: Antisocial trajectories in youth, mating effort, and sexual criminal activity in adulthood. *Violence and Victims, 26*(1), pp. 16–32.

Cale, J., Lussier, P., & Proulx, J. (2009). Heterogeneity in antisocial trajectories in youth of adult sexual aggressors of women: An examination of initiation, persistence, escalation, and aggravation. *Sexual Abuse: A Journal of Research and Treatment, 21*, 223–248.

Cote, G. (2001). Les instruments d'évaluation du risque de comportements violents: mise en perspective critique. *Criminologie, 34*, 31–45.

Cox, D. R. & Oakes, D. (1984). *Analysis of survival data*. London: Chapman and Hall.

Curran, P. J. (2000). A latent curve framework for the study of developmental trajectories on adolescent substance use. In J. S. Rose, L. Chassin, C. C. Presson & S. J. Sherman (Eds.), *Multivariate applications in substance use research: New methods for new questions*. Mahwah, NJ: Lawrence Erlbaum Associates, Inc.

Curran, P. J., & and Hussong, A. M. (2003). The use of latent trajectory models in psychopathology research. *Journal of Abnormal Psychology, 112*, 526–544.

Dempster, R. J., & Hart, S. D. (2002). The relative utility of fixed and variable risk factors in discriminating sexual recidivists and nonrecidivists. *Sexual Abuse: A Journal of Research and Treatment, 14*, 121–138.

Deslauriers-Varin, N., & Beauregard, E. (2010). Victims' routine activities and sex offenders' target selection scripts: A latent class analysis. *Sexual Abuse: A Journal of Research and Treatment, 22*, 315–342.

Farrington, D. P. (2003). Developmental life-course criminology: Key theoretical and empirical issues – The 2002 Sutherland award address. *Criminology, 41*, 221–255.

Farrington, D. P. (Ed.). (2005). *Integrated life-course theories of offending. Advances in criminological knowledge* (Vol. 14). London: Transaction.

Fréchette, M., & LeBlanc, M. (1987). *Délinquances et délinquants.* Montreal: Gaétan Morin.

Friendship, C., & Thornton, D. (2001). Sexual reconviction for sexual offenders discharged from prison in England and Wales. *The British Journal of Criminology, 41*, 285–292.

Gebhard, P. H., Gagnon, J. H., Pomeroy, W. B., & Christenson, C. V. (1965). *Sex offenders: An analysis of types.* New York: Harper & Row.

Glueck, S., & Glueck, E. (1930). *500 criminal careers.* New York: Knopf.

Groth, N. A. (1979). *Men who rape.* New York: Plenum Press.

Hall, G. C. N. (1988). Criminal behavior as a function of clinical and actuarial variables in a sexual offender population. *Journal of Consulting and Clinical Psychology, 56*, 773–775.

Hanson, R. K., & Harris, A. J. R. (2001). A structured approach to evaluating change among sexual offenders. *Sexual Abuse: A Journal of Research and Treatment, 13*, 105–122.

Harris, G. T., & Rice, M. E. (2007). Adjusting actuarial violence risk assessments based on aging or the passage of time. *Criminal Justice and Behavior, 34*, 297–313.

Jones, B. L., Nagin, D. S., & Roeder, K. (2001). A SAS procedure based on mixture models for estimating developmental trajectories. *Sociological Methods & Research, 29*(3), 374–393.

Knight, R. A., & Prentky, R. A. (1990). Classifying sexual offenders: The development and corroboration of taxonomic models. In W. L. Marshall, D. R. Laws, & H. E. Barbaree (Eds.), *Handbook of sexual assault: Issues, theories and treatment of the offender* (pp. 23–54). New York: Plenum.

Laub, J. H., & Sampson, R. J. (2003). *Shared beginnings, divergent dives: Delinquent boys to age 70.* Cambridge, MA: Harvard University Press.

Laws, D. R., Hudson, S. M., & Ward, T. (Eds.). (2000). *Remaking relapse prevention with sex offenders: A sourcebook.* Thousand Oaks, CA: Sage.

LeBlanc, M. (2005). An integrative personal control theory of deviant behavior: Answers to contemporary empirical and theoretical developmental criminological issues. In D. P. Farrington (Ed.), *Integrated developmental and life-course theories of offending* (pp. 125–163). London: Transaction.

LeBlanc, M., & Fréchette, M. (1989). *Male offending from latency to adulthood.* New York: Springer-Verlag.

LeBlanc, M., & Loeber, R. (1998). Developmental criminology updated. *Crime and Justice: A Review of Research, 23*, 115–198.

Loeber, R., & Farrington, D. P. (Eds.). (1998). *Serious and violent juvenile offenders: Risk factors and successful interventions.* Thousand Oaks, CA: Sage.

Loeber, R., & LeBlanc, M., (1990). Toward a developmental criminology. *Crime and Justice: A Review of Research, 12*, 375–473.

Lussier, P. (2005). The criminal activity of sexual offenders in adulthood: Revisiting the specialization debate. *Sexual Abuse: A Journal of Research and Treatment, 17*, 269–292.

Lussier, P., Bouchard, M., & Beauregard, E. (2011). Patterns of criminal achievement in sexual offending: Unravelling the "successful sex offender." *Journal of Criminal Justice, 39*, 433–444.

Lussier, P., & Davies, G. (2011). A person-oriented perspective on sexual offenders, offending trajectories, and risk of recidivism: A new challenge for policymakers, risk assessors, and actuarial prediction? *Psychology, Public Policy, and Law, 17*(4), 530--561.

Lussier, P., & Healey, J. (2009). Rediscovering Quetelet, again: The "aging" offender and the prediction of reoffending in a sample of adult sex offenders. *Justice Quarterly, 28*, 1–30.

Lussier, P., LeBlanc, M., & Proulx, J. (2005). The generality of criminal behavior: A confirmatory factor analysis of the criminal activity of sexual offenders in adulthood. *Journal of Criminal Justice, 33*, 177–189.

Lussier, P., & Mathesius, J. (2012). Criminal achievement, career initiation, and cost avoidance: The onset of successful sex offending. *Journal of Crime and Justice, 35*(3), 376–394.

Lussier, P., Tzoumakis, S., Cale, J., & Amirault, J. (2010). Criminal trajectories of adult sex offenders and the age effect: Examining the dynamic aspect of offending in adulthood. *International Criminal Justice Review, 20*, 147–168.

Moffitt, T. E. (1993). Adolescence-limited and life-course-persistent antisocial behavior: A developmental taxonomy. *Psychological Review, 4*, 674–701.

Monahan, J., Steadman, H. J., Clark Robbins, P., Appelbaum, P., Banks, S., Grisso, T., Heilbrun, K. et al. (2005). An actuarial model of violence risk assessment for persons with mental disorders. *Psychiatric Services, 56*, 810–815.

Morselli, C., & Tremblay, P. (2004). Criminal achievement, offender networks and the benefits of low-self-control. *Criminology, 42*, 773–804.

Nagin, D. S. (2005). *Group-based modeling of development*. Cambridge, MA: Harvard University Press.

Nagin, D. S., & Paternoster, R. (2000). Population heterogeneity and state dependence: State of the evidence and directions for future research. *Journal of Quantitative Criminology, 16*, 117–144.

Nagin, D. S., & Tremblay, R. E. (2005). Developmental trajectory groups: Fact or statistical fiction? *Criminology, 43*, 873–904.

Patterson, G. R., & Yoerger, K. (1993). Developmental models for delinquent behavior. In S. Hodgins (Ed.), *Mental Disorder and Crime* (pp. 140–172). Newbury Park, CA: Sage.

Piquero, A. R. (2008). Taking stock of developmental trajectories of criminal activity over the life course. In A. M. Liberman (Ed.), *The long view of crime: A synthesis of longitudinal research*. New York: Springer.

Piquero, A. R., Farrington, D. P., & Blumstein, A. (2003). The criminal career paradigm. *Crime and Justice, 30*, 359–506.

Proulx, J., Tardif, M., Lamoureux, B., & Lussier, P. (2000). How does recidivism risk assessment predict survival? In D. R. Laws, S. M. Hudson, & T. Ward (Eds.) *Remaking relapse prevention with sex offenders: A sourcebook* (pp. 466–484). Newbury Park, CA: Sage.

Quinsey, V. L., Harris, G. T., Rice, M. E., & Cormier, C. A. (1998). *Violent offenders: Appraising and managing risk*. Washington, DC: American Psychological Association.

Robins, L. N. (1978). Sturdy childhood predictors of adult antisocial behaviour: Replications from longitudinal studies. *Psychological medicine, 8*, 611–622.

Sampson, R. J., & Laub, J. H. (2005). A life-course view of the development of crime. *Annals of the American Academy of Political and Social Science, 602*, 12–45.

Silver, E., Smith, W. R., & Banks, S. (2000). Constructive actuarial devices for predictive recidivism: A comparison of Methods. *Criminal Justice and Behavior, 27*, 733–764.

Soothill, K. L., & Gibbens, T. C. N. (1978). Recidivism of sexual offenders: A re-appraisal. *British Journal of Criminology, 18*, 267–276.

Steadman, H. J., Silver, E., Monahan, J., Appelbaum, P. S., Clark Robbins, P., Mulvey, E. P., Grisso, T. et al. (2000). A classification tree approach to the development of actuarial violence risk assessment tools. *Law and Human Behavior, 24*, 83–100.

Thornberry, T. P., & Krohn, M. D. (2003). *Taking stock of delinquency: An overview of findings from contemporary longitudinal studies*. New York: NY: Kluwer/Plenum Publishers.

Thornberry, T. P., & Krohn, M. D. (2005). Applying interactional theory to the explanation of continuity and change in antisocial behavior. In D. P. Farrington (Ed.), *Integrated developmental and life-course theories of offending advances in criminological theory* (Vol. *14*). Piscataway, NJ: Transaction.

Tremblay, P. (2010). *Le délinquent idéal (The ideal offender)*. Montreal: Liber.

Von Eye, A., & Bogat, G. A. (2006). Person-orientated and variable-orientated research: Concepts, results and development. *Merrill-Palmer Quarterly, 52*, 390–420.

Von Eye, A., & Bergman, L. R. (2003). Research strategies in developmental psychopathology: Dimensional identity and the person-orientated approach. *Development and Psychopathology, 15*, 553–580.

Ward, T., & Hudson, S. M. (1998). A model of the relapse process in sexual offenders. *Journal of Interpersonal Violence, 13*, 700–725.

West, D J., & Farrington, D. P. (1977). *The Delinquent Way of Life*. London: Heinemann.

Wollert, R. (2006). Low base rates limit expert certainty when current actuarials are used to identify sexually violent predators. *Psychology, Public Policy, and Law, 12*, 56–85.

14

The Concentration of Sex Offenses in British and Dutch Families

Steve van de Weijer
NSCR and VU University, the Netherlands

Sytske Besemer,[1] Catrien Bijleveld,[2,3] & Arjan Blokland[2,4]

[1]*University of California, USA,* [2]*NSCR, the Netherlands,* [3]*VU University, the Netherlands,* [4]*Leiden University, the Netherlands*

Introduction

It is well established in criminological research, that a small group of offenders is responsible for a large share of total crime (Fox & Tracy, 1988; Piquero, 2000). This offending pattern does not only appear within cohorts of individuals but in cohorts of families as well. Previous research shows that criminal behavior in general (Farrington, Barnes, & Lambert, 1996; Farrington, Jolliffe, Loeber, Stouthamer-Loeber, & Kalb, 2001), and violent crime in particular (Van de Weijer, Bijleveld, & Blokland, 2014), is highly concentrated within families. Little is known about the concentration of sexual offending within families, as, to our knowledge, no study has focused on this topic before. In this chapter we will use prospectively collected data on the male family members in 397 British nuclear families and 140 Dutch extended families to examine the concentration of sexual offending in families, as well as possible explanations for such a concentration. We will also examine whether the degree of concentration differs for different types of sex offenses. In addition to the research indicating a concentration of crime within families, there is also empirical evidence of intergenerational transmission of crime, from father to son (e.g., Besemer, 2012; Bijleveld, & Wijkman, 2009; Van de Weijer et al. 2014), and intragenerational transmission of crime, between siblings (Farrington et al., 1996; Van de Rakt, Nieuwbeerta, & Apel, 2009). This inter-, and intragenerational transmission of crime implies a concentration of crime within families, as multiple criminal family members are necessary for the transmission to occur. Studies that examined the intergenerational transmission of sex offenses have focused on the transmission of victimization rather than on the transmission of sexual offending

Sex Offenders: A Criminal Career Approach, First Edition. Edited by Arjan Blokland and Patrick Lussier.

(e.g., Avery, Hutchinson, & Whitaker, 2002; Faller, 1989; Testa, Hoffman, & Livingston, 2011). These studies show that children are at increased risk of being sexually abused if their parents were victims of (childhood) sexual abuse. For example, one pattern that illustrates this link is that of mothers who have been sexually abused, who marry men who will later sexually abuse their/her child(ren) (Faller, 1989). Prior researches, however, do not estimate the risk of becoming a sex offender for those with a sexually abusive parent. On theoretical grounds, it can also be expected that children from sexually abusive parents are at increased risk of committing sexual crimes themselves even if these children themselves were not victimized, as they might have been otherwise exposed to their parents' deviant sexual behavior. Therefore, in this study, we will examine the transmission of sex offending instead of the transmission of victimization. Because sex offenses include several types of behavior for which the intergenerational transmission might operate differently, different types of sexual crime will be analyzed (e.g., Gebhard, Gagnon, Pomeroy, & Christenson, 1965). Previous research showed that exhibitionists, rapists, and child abusers differed from each other in the degree and timing of recidivism (Blokland & Van der Geest, this volume; De Vogel & De Ruiter, 2003; Nieuwbeerta, Blokland, & Bijleveld, 2003) and treatment effectiveness (Alexander, 1999). In this chapter, the data allow us to examine differences in the degree of concentration within families for hands-off offenses, hands-on offenses, and sex offenses committed against victims aged under 16.

Theory

Concentration of Sex Offenses Within Families

As previous research shows that both general (Farrington et al., 1996; Farrington et al., 2001) and violent offending (Van de Weijer et al., 2014) cluster in families, we hypothesize that sexual offending will be concentrated within families as well (Hypothesis 1a). We go on to discuss five possible explanations for such a concentration of sex offenses within families. As we detail below, some of these explanations might be more applicable for hands-on offending, particularly for sex offending against minors, and we thus expect these types of sex offending to be more concentrated within families than hands-off offending (Hypothesis 1b).

Transmission of Sex Offenses Within Families

Several mechanisms may cause transmission of sexual offending between family members. Van Beek and Mulder (2002) argue that children who are exposed to pornography, sexual violence, and abuse (including their own victimization) in their family are at increased risk of developing cognitive distortions. These cognitive distortions may imply rationalization and normalization of the abnormal sexual behaviors to which they were exposed. Such distortions facilitate deviant sexual behavior and decrease the step toward these children's own sexual offending. In a similar vein, Ward and Siegert (2002) argue that individuals who experience sexual abuse or are exposed to sexual material or activity at a young age and who do not receive appropriate feedback from their parents, family, or others, can develop distorted sexual scripts. If distorted sexual scripts are developed, individuals may interpret deviant sexual behaviors as normative, which in turn leads to an increased risk of becoming a sex offender. Sexual offending might also be transmitted intergenerationally by social learning mechanisms; this suggests that children learn and imitate a (deviant) behavioral repertoire from their parents or other relatives (Bandura, 1977; Burton, Miller, & Shill, 2002; Marshall, Laws, & Barbaree, 1990). In line with these mechanisms, previous research reported that adolescent sex offenders who had been sexually abused tended to perpetrate the same types of sexually abusive acts they had experienced themselves (Bijleveld & Hendriks, 2007; Burton, 2003; Veneziano, Veneziano, & LeGrand, 2000). While a comprehensive examination of all possible mechanisms underlying the intergenerational transmission of sexual offenses is beyond the scope of the current study, we will test to what extent the intergenerational transmission of sexual offending explains the clustering of sex offenses within families. Based on the mechanisms just discussed, intergenerational transmission of sexual offending might explain the clustering of sex offenses within families in two ways. First, those who have been sexually abused by a family member may experience an increased risk of becoming sex offenders themselves, since having been a victim of sexual abuse in childhood is an often-cited risk factor for becoming an abuser in later life (Salter et al., 2003). In addition, meta-analyses based on retrospective data show that both adolescent sex offenders (Seto & Lalumière, 2010) and adult sex offenders (Jespersen, Lalumière, & Seto, 2009) more often have a history of childhood sexual abuse than nonsex offenders. Therefore, we hypothesize that the concentration of sexual offending within families is (partly) due to incest victims being at higher odds of becoming sex offenders (Hypothesis 2a). We argue that this explanation is especially relevant for the concentration within families of sex offending against minors, as previous research shows that juvenile as well as adult sex offenders who commit crimes against children are more likely to report a history of childhood sexual abuse than sex offenders who commit crimes against adults or peers (Bijleveld & Hendriks, 2007; Jespersen et al., 2009). In addition, victims of childhood sexual abuse appear to be likely to commit the same kinds of sexual crimes as they experienced as a victim (Burton, 2003; Veneziano et al. 2000). Second, sexual offending might also be transmitted intergenerationally without the younger generation being abused. As the above described mechanisms responsible for the intergenerational transmission of sexual delinquency indicate, exposure to deviant sexual behavior by family members may also lead to sexual offending without the offender having been victimized as a child. Previous research showed that during their youth, adolescent sex offenders were significantly more often exposed to sex, pornography, or sexual violence in the family than were adolescent nonsex offenders (Seto & Lalumière, 2010). Although it remains unknown whether for sexually mature persons exposure to sex and pornography precedes rather than follows deviant sexual behavior,[1] we assume that childhood exposure to sexually deviant behavior may lead to sexual delinquency. Therefore we expect that the concentration of sexual offending within families can (partly) be explained by the intergenerational transmission of sexual delinquency, without being mediated by the offender himself having been victimized (Hypothesis 2b). Moreover, we expect that these first two mechanisms will be stronger when the older sex offender is a parent or sibling of the younger sex offender, rather than when it is another relative.

Previous research shows that if the perpetrator is relationally closer to the victim, the victim is more likely to model the person's victimizing behaviors (Burton et al., 2002). One could therefore expect children who have been sexually abused by their parents or siblings to be more likely to become sex offenders than children who have been sexually abused by other relatives, such as uncles, aunts, or cousins. The intergenerational transmission of sexual offending for offenders who have not been victimized may also be stronger if the older sex offender is a parent or sibling. Children are probably more intensively, and for longer periods of time, exposed to their parents and siblings sexually offending behavior than to the sexually offending behavior of other family members. In addition, in case of a sexually offending extended family member, parents can intervene and explain to their children that such behavior is abnormal, while such interventions are unlikely when the parent him/herself is a sex offender. Supporting this argument, studies on the transmission of general delinquency also show that the odds of becoming delinquent are higher when ones parents or siblings are delinquent than when extended family members are delinquent (Farrington et al., 2001). For these reasons, Hypothesis 2c states: the transmission of sexual offending will be stronger between nuclear family members than between extended family members.

Transmission From Serious and Violent Offenses to Sex Offenses Within Families

A third possible explanation for the concentration of sexual offending within families is that sexual crimes are a manifestation of more general antisocial and violent tendencies. Gottfredson and Hirschi's (1990) general theory of crime, for example, suggests that offenders, due to their low self-control, have difficulties resisting the immediate gratifications that criminal opportunities provide. Consequently, individuals with low self-control engage in many different types of crime, including sexual crimes. Concurrent with this notion, several typologies of both child abusers and rapists distinguish such antisocial sex offenders, whose sexual crimes are believed to be part of their general antisocial lifestyle (Lussier, Proulx, & Leblanc,

[1]Marshall and colleagues (1990), for example, argue that juvenile sex offenders, following the onset of their sexual offending, are more likely to seek pornographic material to support their masturbatory activities.

2005; Robertiello & Terry, 2007; Seto & Barbaree, 1997). Hall and Hirschman's (1991, 1992) theory of sexual offending, for example, suggests that sex offenders primarily motivated by affective dysregulation are likely to commit both sexual and nonsexual offenses. Based on these theories, we would assume that there might be no specific transmission of sexual offending between generations. Instead, general antisocial and violent tendencies might be transmitted intergenerationally, and sexual offending appears in multiple generations as a byproduct of these tendencies. In support of this hypothesis, previous research shows that sex offenses constitute a relatively small proportion of the criminal activity and criminal repertoire of sex offenders (Lussier, 2005). The majority of adolescent sex offenders also commit nonsexual offenses (France & Hudson, 1993). Moreover, when adolescent sex offenders recidivate, they are more likely to commit a nonsexual crime than another sexual crime (Caldwell, 2002; Worling & Långström, 2006). In addition, it has been shown that adolescent sex offenders and nonsex offenders were, as groups, similar to each other in terms of self-reported conduct problems, antisocial personality traits, family problems (such as parental separation or divorce, familial substance abuse, familial criminality), and IQ scores (Seto & Lalumière, 2010). Finally, Harris and colleagues (2009) show that in a sample of convicted male sex offenders, 88% of rapists and 57% of child molesters had committed more nonsexual crimes than sexual crimes. Based on the above theories and prior empirical results, we hypothesize that the concentration of sexual offending within families can (partly) be explained by the intergenerational transmission of serious and violent crimes (Hypothesis 3). We argue that this explanation especially pertains to the concentration of hands-on offending (both sex crimes against minors and rape and sexual assault) since these sexual crimes entail physical contact with victims that might involve violence, while this is not the case for hands-off offending.

Co-offending Relatives

The fourth possible explanation is that sex offending concentrates within families because sexually abusive family members do not intervene, and might even cooperate or facilitate the sexual abuse. Bijleveld and colleagues (Bijleveld, Weerman, Looije, & Hendriks, 2007) estimated that approximately a third of all registrations of Dutch juveniles for a sex offense had been committed within a group. Other studies show that group sex offending is not a recent phenomenon nor exclusively committed by juveniles: In Renaissance Florence 1 in 3 heterosexual rapes was a group rape (Smith, 2004), 80% of all rapes in Moscow between 1928 and 1929 were committed by a group (Oseretzky, 1929), and Bijleveld and Soudijn (2008) showed that more than half of the suspects of group sex offending in the Netherlands are aged 18 or older. Little is known, however, about the prevalence of relatives within sex offending groups. Bijleveld and Soudijn (2008) estimated that a maximum of 25% of all group sex offenses committed by persons above the age of 26 concerned a married couple who sexually abused a child. In addition, Bijleveld and colleagues (2007) showed that, in a Dutch sample of male juvenile sex offending groups, 12% of the co-offenders were relatives. Based on these earlier studies, we hypothesize that the concentration of sexual offending within families can (partly) be explained by the co-offending of relatives (Hypothesis 4). We expect that this leads to the concentration within families of sex offenses against minors, as children might be more likely to be victimized by multiple family members because: (a) they live in the homes of (relatives of) these perpetrators; (b) children generally are more vulnerable than more mature individuals; (c) children are less able to resist such abuse and may not even recognize it as abuse (let alone a crime) and thus not report it; and (d) children may passively or actively take part in their own abuse and may fear that revealing the abuse may result in negative consequences for their perpetrator(s), especially if the perpetrator is a family member. This makes it more difficult for children to escape from such abuse.

Incest Victims Mating With Sexually Abusive Men

Finally, the nonoffending parent, usually the mother, may have an unintended mediating role. Faller (1989) showed that half of the nonoffending mothers of sexually abused children had a history of sexual abuse in their family of origin. In addition, Avery and colleagues (2002) found that if nonoffending parents had been sexually abused as children, their children were more likely to be sexually abused as well. This might be a consequence of the fact that women who were raised in incestuous families are likely to mate with a partner displaying a similar degree of role and boundary confusion. When such partners form their own family, they may end up in a family environment similar to that of their families of origin (Estes & Tidwell, 2002), in which the next generation of children is victimized. In addition, Faller (1989) argues that sexually abused women may mate with men who will not make sexual demands upon them. Some of those men do not make sexual demands upon adult women because their real sexual interest is in children. According to this hypothesis, women with a history of sexual abuse would be more likely to mate with a sexually abusive partner. If the nonoffending mothers were abused by a family member during childhood this leads to a concentration of sexual crimes within families since both these abusive family members and the husbands of the women commit sexual crimes. Our final hypothesis, therefore, is: the concentration of sexual offending within families is (partly) caused by the fact that female incest victims mate with sexually abusive men (Hypothesis 5). We argue that this especially leads to a clustering of sexual crimes against minors, since the mothers are more likely to have been abused as a child, while their husbands abuse their children as well. In sum, we will test the following hypotheses:

Hypothesis 1a: Sexual offending concentrates within families. Hypothesis 1b: The concentration of hands-on offending within families, and sex offending against minors in particular, will be larger than the concentration of hands-off offending.

Hypothesis 2a: The concentration of sexual offending within families is (partly) caused by incest victims being at higher odds of becoming sex offenders.

Hypothesis 2b: The concentration of sexual offending within families can (partly) be explained by the intergenerational transmission of sexual delinquency, without the mediating effect of the younger generation having been victimized.
Hypothesis 2c: The transmission of sexual offending will be stronger between nuclear family members than between extended family members.
Hypothesis 3: The concentration of sexual offending within families can (partly) be explained by the intergenerational transmission of serious and violent crimes.
Hypothesis 4: The concentration of sexual offending within families can (partly) be explained by co-offending of relatives.
Hypothesis 5: The concentration of sexual offending within families is (partly) caused by female incest victims who mate with sexually abusive men.

Method

In this study we use two samples from two prospective intergenerational studies: a sample of British families from the Cambridge Study in Delinquent Development (CSDD), and a sample of Dutch families from the Transfive study.

Sample From the CSDD

The intergenerational transmission of sex offenses in England was investigated using data from the CSDD, a prospective longitudinal study that has followed 411 London males born around 1953. At the time they were first contacted, in 1961–1962, these males were all living in a working-class inner-city area of South London. The sample was chosen by taking all of the boys who were then aged 8–9 and on the registers of six state primary schools within a 1-mile radius of a research office that had been established. Hence, the most common year of birth for these males was 1953. In nearly all cases (94%), their family breadwinner in 1961–1962 (usually the father) had a working-class occupation (skilled, semi-skilled, or unskilled manual worker). Most of the boys were Caucasian and of British origin. Donald J. West originally directed the study and David P. Farrington, who has worked on it since 1969, has directed it since 1982. The males have been studied at frequent intervals between the ages of 8 and 50. Information about criminal convictions and self-reported delinquency was collected over the course of these years. Additionally, convictions records for the parents and siblings of these 411 males have been collected. For the current study, only the official records were used, because self-reports were not available for parents and siblings. For more information and major findings see West (1969, 1982), West and Farrington (1973, 1977), Farrington and West (1990), Farrington (1995, 2003), Farrington et al. (2006) and Farrington, Coid, and West (2009). The current investigation studies the original men, their parents, and their siblings. Because the data collection started with families that had at least one boy born about 1953, the data set did not contain families with girls only. Therefore the proportion of males to females in the current sample was approximately 2:1. The most recent criminal record search for the original men took place in December 2004, for their full biological siblings in September 2002, and for their biological parents in December 1994. At the time of data collection the original men were on average 51 years old, siblings were on average 48 years old, and parents were on average 70 years old. In total, the British sample consisted of 1,296 men and 916 women.

Variables From the CSDD

Convictions for sexual offenses were searched in the Criminal Record Office in London (Farrington et al., 1996). Sexual offenses against males as well as females ranged from rape, indecent assault, and indecent exposure, to indecent telephone messages.

Sample From the Transfive Study

The intergenerational transmission of sex offenses in the Netherlands was studied using the youngest three generations from the Transfive study, which contains data on five consecutive generations. Data collection of this study started with the first 198 boys who were placed in a Dutch Catholic reform school between 1911 and 1914. Some boys were placed in this institution because of general concern about their character and problem behavior, including minor delinquency. Others were in the reform school because their parents, according to guardian organizations, were not able to take proper care of them. Therefore, these 198 boys can be said to constitute a high-risk sample in terms of delinquency. The parents and all descendants of these boys were traced in Dutch genealogical and municipal records, with a retrieval rate of 100%. Emigrated sample members and their descendants were not traced further. The parents of the 198 boys are the oldest generation in the sample and are called Generation 1 (G1). The 198 boys are called G2, while their children, grandchildren, and great-grandchildren are called G3, G4, and G5, respectively. The G3 to G5 were studied prospectively.[2] On average, the G3 were born in 1932, the G4 in 1960, and the G5 in 1986. At the moment of data collection, the surviving G3 were approximately 75 years old, on average. The surviving G4 were about 47 years old and the G5 were approximately 21 years old. Figure 14.1 summarizes the sample from the Transfive study. In addition to the respondents shown in Figure 14.1, all partners to whom these respondents were ever married or with whom they were

[2]Although data collection started when the G3, G4, and G5 were already, respectively, 75, 47, and 21 years old, information on their offending behavior is collected prospectively since we did not know how their offending behavior would develop over time. For the older generations, the data is not collected prospectively because we knew that the G2 showed problem behavior, including minor delinquency.

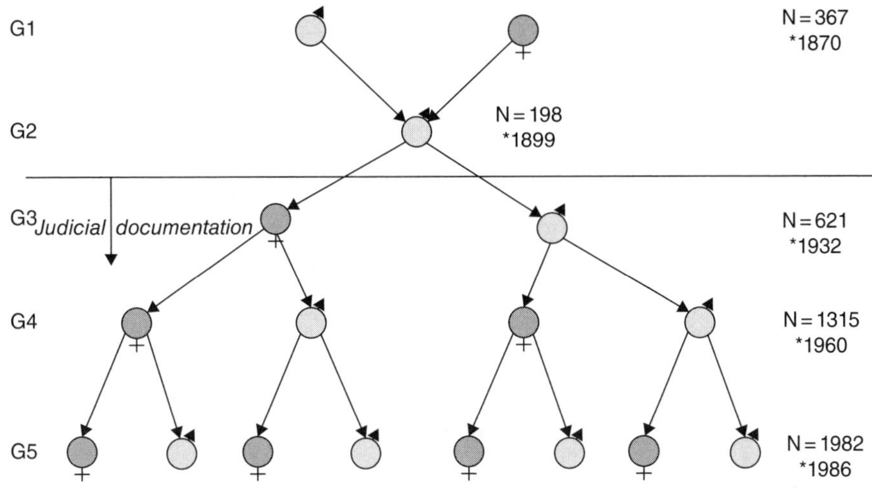

Figure 14.1 Design of the sample from the Transfive study.

ever in a registered partnership are included in the data set as well. Family members of these partners, however, are not included in the data set. More detailed information may be found in Bijleveld and Wijkman (2009).

For this current study we included all G3, G4, and G5 who were 12 years or older at the moment of data collection, and their partners, in the analyses. Persons under the age of 12 were not taken into account because people in the Netherlands can only be prosecuted from age 12 onward. Since 58 of the 198 G2 men did not have any children, our sample consists of 140 extended families. Within these 140 extended families there are 550 nuclear families consisting of the G3 and, if any, their partners and children, and 1,204 nuclear families consisting of the G4 and, if any, their partners and children. In total, the Dutch sample for this study includes 2,661 men and 2,516 women. The persons in this sample were predominantly ethnic Dutch, Catholic, and from families that were part of the lower social strata of Dutch society around the 1900s.

Variables From the Transfive Study

The demographic variables for each sample member were obtained from the Dutch population registration data (GBA). These data include the dates of birth, death, marriage, and divorce or separation. Information on delinquency was obtained from the archives of the Dutch Criminal Records Documentation Service (judicial documentation) in December 2007. Since these records do not contain data on individuals born before 1912 and may miss people born between 1912 and 1916, we have excluded all G3 and their partners born before 1916 from the analysis. The records are complete for the remaining respondents, apart for those sample members born in the Almelo arrondissement before 1967, which applies to no more than 3% of the

G3 and G4. Offenses have been classified based on the Statistics Netherlands standard classification for offenses (Eggen & Van der Heide, 2005). Exhibitionistic offenses are considered as hands-off crimes, (attempted to) sexual assaults and rape are considered as hands-on crimes, and sexual crimes against persons under the age of 16 are considered as (hands-on) sexual crimes against minors. Moreover, all violent offenses, property offenses, arson, and drugs and weapons offenses are considered as serious crimes. All registrations that did not result in an acquittal or technical dismissal were taken into account. Because the judicial documentation does not have any information about victims, we obtained this information from the court file of each sexual offense. Unfortunately, sometimes the court files of the old criminal cases had been destroyed or did not contain specific victim information. In total, we retrieved and studied court files for 54% of the sexual offenses. Of the court files studied, 67% contained enough information to trace the relationship between the victim and the perpetrator.

Analyses

We will start our analyses by aggregating the individual conviction data to the family level. This enables us to examine to what extent sexual crimes are concentrated in families. Kolmogorov-Smirnov tests will be estimated to test whether the concentration of sex offending within families differs significantly from a Poisson distribution with sex offenses per family. We use Poisson distributions in these tests since (sexual) offending takes the form of an event count. Thereafter, we will use the individual data to calculate odds ratios in order to test whether the concentration of sex offending within families can be explained by an intergenerational transmission of sexual offending from parents to children, between siblings, or between extended family members. Odds ratios are simple to interpret and widely used in intergenerational studies to assess the transmission of delinquency. However, odds ratios do not enable us to control for the fact that parents with more offspring appear more often in the equation. Therefore, GEE (Generalized Estimating Equation) models will be estimated to control for this intracluster correlation (Ghisletta & Spini, 2004). All odds ratios and corresponding confidence intervals that are displayed in the following section are those from the GEE models. Differences between two odds ratios are tested for significance by estimating a ratio between the two odds ratios, with a corresponding confidence interval (Altman & Bland, 2003). The significance of those RORs should, however, be taken as not more than indicative, as there is dependency between the samples compared. In order to test our third hypothesis, which states that the concentration of sex offenses within families can be explained by the intergenerational transmission of violent crimes, we will use an ANOVA to test whether families that include one or more sex offenders commit more serious and violent offenses than families that do not include any sex offenders. In addition, GEE models will be used to estimate whether persons with violent family members are at increased risk of committing sex offenses.

Results

Prevalence of Sexual Crimes Within Families

In Table 14.1 the total number of sex offenses and sex offenders in both the British CSDD sample and the Dutch Transfive sample are shown. In the sample from the CSDD, 26 persons from 22 nuclear families committed a total of 40 sex crimes. Since the CSDD sample did not include information about extended family members, it is unknown to how many extended families the 26 sex offenders belong. Moreover, the CSDD computerized offense file did not distinguish between different types of sex offenses. For the Transfive sample this information is present. For this sample there are 72 sex offenders from 64 nuclear families within 38 extended families who committed 101 sex crimes. More than half of these sex offenses were committed against minors, more than a quarter involved a rape or sexual assault, and less than 1 in 5 was a hands-off sex offense. The child abusers most often committed more than one sex offense, as shown by the large difference between the number of offenses and the number of offenders. Hands-off offenders and rapists mostly committed a single sex offense over the course of their criminal career.

In the CSDD sample, there were only three nuclear families that included multiple sex offenders. In one family both father and son committed sexual crimes, in another family two brothers were convicted for a sex crime, and the third family included three brothers who were all sex offenders. In the Transfive sample, eight nuclear families included two sex offenders. In three cases both father and son committed sex crimes, in the five other cases two brothers were both sex offenders. Thus, in both the British and the Dutch samples, relatively few nuclear families include more than one sex offender. When we also take the extended family members from the Dutch sample into account, we see much more clustering of sex offenders within families.

Table 14.2 summarizes all combinations of sex offenders that were found within the extended families from the Transfive study. The relationship between two sex

Table 14.1 Overview of the Distribution of Sex Offenses Within Both Samples

Sample	*CSDD*	*Transfive*				
Crime	*All sex crimes*	*Child abuse*	*Rape*	*All hands-on*	*Hands-off*	*Total*
Offenses (N)	40	55	27	82	19	101
Offenders (N)	26	34	26	58	16	72
Nuclear families (N)	22	29	25	50	16	64
Extended families (N)	–	18	18	29	15	38

Note. The total number of offenders in the Transfive sample is not the sum of the number of hands-off offenders, child abusers, and rapist since some offenders committed multiple types of sex crimes.

Table 14.2 Overview of all Combinations of Sex Offenders Within Extended Families From the Transfive Study

Relationship	*N*	*Relationship*	*N*
Uncle and a nephew	7	Father and son	3
Uncle-by-marriage and a nephew	6	Brother-in-law and brother-in-law	3
Brother-in-law and a brother	6	Aunt and nephew	1
Brother and brother	5	Father and son-in-law	1
Cousin and cousin	4	Brother-in-law and sister	1
Cousin-by-marriage and cousin	4		

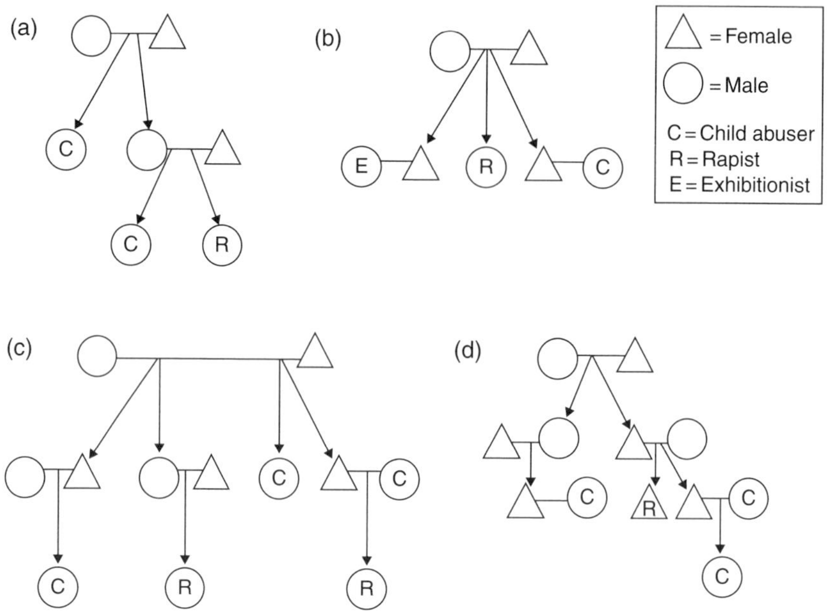

Figure 14.2 Four extended families from the Transfive study that include multiple sex offenders. Only those family members who are necessary to illustrate the familial relationships are displayed.

offenders within one extended family found most often was that between an uncle and a nephew, which occurred seven times. Other relationships between sex offenders within the same family that were found often were: an uncle-by-marriage and a nephew (6 times), a brother-in-law and a brother (6), two brothers (5), two cousins (4), and a cousin-by marriage and a cousin (4).

Figure 14.2 illustrates four such extended families that include multiple sex offenders. Family A is an example of a family that includes three adolescent sex offenders: two brothers and their uncle. The uncle committed a sex crime against a minor at the age of 17. Almost 24 years later, the oldest son of his brother was convicted for a rape he committed when he was 15 years old. More than 6 years after this conviction, one of his four younger brothers committed a sex crime against a minor at the age of 17. Within family B there are three sex offenders, convicted for three different types of offenses. The parents of family B have five children: three daughters and two brothers. In 1970, their oldest daughter married a man who would be convicted for exhibitionistic crimes twice: after 12 and 14 years of marriage. Her youngest sister married a sex offender as well. However, this man was convicted for this crime before this marriage; he committed a sex crime against a minor when he was 15 years old. More than 20 years after these sisters married, their youngest brother was convicted for sexual assault at age 41. Family C includes five sex offenders from two generations. The two sex offenders in the older generations were brothers-in-law. The first of them committed two sex crimes against minors at the ages of 24 and 29. The second committed two sex crimes against minors at the age of 38. Fourteen years later, his son was convicted for rape at the age of 16. Two older cousins of this son were convicted for sex offenses as well. One of them raped someone at the age of 18; the other abused a child when he was 32. Finally, family D includes three male sex offenders and one female sex offender. This woman was the first in the family to commit a sexual crime when she raped someone at the age of 23. Two years after this crime, her nieces' husband committed a sex crime against a minor, at the age of 22. Three years later, this woman's brother-in-law abused a child when he was 33 years old. At that moment, one of his sons was almost 5 years old. At the age of 25, this son followed in his father's footsteps and also committed a sexual crime against a minor. These examples of the four families in Figure 14.2 illustrate that sex offenses might cluster in families in various ways: between relatives or in-laws, within the same generation or between different generations, by transmission of the same or a different type of sex offense, and with sex offenses committed at various ages. Only one of the sex offenders from the families in Figure 14.2 was a woman. In total, there were only five female sex offenders in the CSDD sample and the Transfive sample combined. The only female sex offender who was included in the CSDD sample committed three sex offenses. The four sex offending females in the Transfive study all committed one sex offense. Given this low prevalence of female sex offenders in the samples, we have excluded all females from further analyses.

Concentration of Sexual Crimes Within Families

In order to test our first hypothesis, we used Kolmogorov-Smirnov tests to examine whether sex offenses significantly concentrate within families. For the nuclear families from both the CSDD and the Transfive study, the Kolmogorov-Smirnov tests indicated that the sex offenses were not significantly concentrated in these nuclear families. For the extended families from the Transfive study, however, we did find significant results, which are shown in Table 14.3.

The results from the upper part of Table 14.3 illustrate that sex offenses significantly concentrate within extended families. This concentration can be attributed to the fact that hands-on offenses, and then particularly sex offenses against minors, cluster within extended families, as shown by the significant Kolmogorov-Smirnov

Table 14.3 Concentration of Sexual Offenses and Offenders Within Extended Families from the Transfive Study

Type of crime	*Hands-off*	*Rape and sexual assault*	*Child abuse*	*All hands-on*	*All sex crimes*
λ Offenses	0.129	0.186	0.379	0.564	0.693
Kolmogorov-Smirnov Z	0.244	0.484	2.208	2.821	2.956
Significance	1.000	0.973	0.000	0.000	0.000
λ Offenders	0.107	0.179	0.229	0.393	0.486
Kolmogorov-Smirnov Z	0.021	0.414	0.896	1.562	1.594
Significance	1.000	0.996	0.398	0.015	0.012
N	140	140	140	140	140

test in Table 14.3. No significant results were found for the concentration of hands-off offenses or of rape and sexual assault within families. We also tested whether the number of sex offenders concentrates within the extended families to control for the possibility that the concentration of sex offenses within families is caused by a single family member committing multiple sex offenses. The lower part of Table 14.3 shows that the concentration of child abusers within families is not statistically significant, while the concentration of all hands-on offenders and all sex offenders remains significant. The concentration of sex offenses against minors within families is significant, while the concentration of child abusing offenders is not. It seems, therefore, that the concentration of sex offenses against minors is caused by child abusers who commit multiple sex offenses against minors, as we have seen in Table 14.1. In addition, the significant concentration of all sex offenders within extended families is probably driven by the concentration of hands-on offenders, since hands-off offenders do not concentrate within families at all. These results are in line with Hypothesis 1a, that sexual offending would cluster within families. Hypothesis 1b, which stated that hands-on offenses, and sex offenses against minors in particular, would cluster more within families than hands-off offenses, can only partly be confirmed with the results from Table 14.3.

Transmission of Sexual Crimes Within Families

After we showed that sex offenses concentrate within the extended families from the Transfive study, we examined how this concentration of sex crimes, and especially hands-on crimes, can be explained.

Table 14.4 shows the results from the GEE models that estimated the degree of transmission of sex offenses from fathers, brothers, any nuclear family member (i.e., father and brothers), any extended family member (i.e., grandfathers, uncles, nephews, in-laws), and any family member (i.e., nuclear and extended family members). These GEE models are estimated for men from each generation

Table 14.4 GEE Models for Intergenerational Transmission of (Hands-on) Sex Offending Among Males From the Transfive Study

	Transmission of hands-on offending			
Transmission from:	*Generation 3*	*Generation 4*	*Generation 5*	*All generations*
Father	[a]	**7.20 (1.46–35.55)**	5.91 (0.70–49.60)	**6.95 (1.96–24.70)**
Brother	**8.93 (2.70–29.55)**	**6.20 (1.88–20.45)**	[b]	**8.08 (3.78–17.25)**
Any nuclear family member	**8.93 (2.70–29.55)**	**8.75 (2.99–25.66)**	3.69 (0.45–30.17)	**8.92 (4.42–17.98)**
Any extended family member	**18.17 (3.88–85.11)**	**5.64 (1.77–17.92)**	3.24 (0.94–11.18)	**5.95 (2.87–12.33)**
Any family member	**13.78 (2.95–64.39)**	**27.17 (3.55–208.10)**	3.14 (0.91–10.80)	**8.73 (3.82–19.97)**
	Transmission any sex offending			
Transmission from:	*Generation 3*	*Generation 4*	*Generation 5*	*All generations*
Father	[a]	4.61 (0.97–21.91)	3.33 (0.41–26.95)	**4.20 (1.22–14.51)**
Brother	**4.42 (1.49–13.17)**	**6.09 (1.89–19.65)**	[b]	**5.91 (2.83–12.35)**
Any nuclear family member	**4.42 (1.49–13.17)**	**7.20 (2.58–20.15)**	2.12 (0.27–16.86)	**5.86 (3.00–11.47)**
Any extended family member	**6.09 (2.01–18.43)**	**3.37 (1.25–9.10)**	1.59 (0.53–4.77)	**2.83 (1.54–5.20)**
Any family member	**3.98 (1.32–11.98)**	**7.74 (2.22–27.00)**	1.48 (0.49–4.44)	**3.35 (1.77–6.32)**

Note. Odds ratios in bold are significant.
[a]The transmission from father to son is not estimated for the G3s since their fathers are not included in the sample.
[b]The odds ratios for the transmission between G5 brothers could not be estimated since there were no G5 brothers who were both sex offenders.

separately, and for men from all generations taken together. The GEE models are not estimated for the partners of the G3 and G4 since our data does not include information on the members of their family of origin. Table 14.4 shows that none of the odds ratios for the men in the youngest generation (G5) were significant. For example, the odds ratio for transmission from the father is 5.91. However, the fact that the lower bound of the confidence interval is below 1, while the upper bound of the confidence interval is far above 1, indicates that this odds ratio is not statistically significant. Male G5 who have a father who has been convicted for a hands-on offense, thus, do not have a significantly higher risk of committing a hands-on offense themselves. These insignificant odds ratios for the G5 are likely caused by the low number of sex offenders in this generation (N = 13), which is not surprising given their relatively young age. All but one of the odds ratios for the men from the other two generations (G3 and G4) are significant. In the last column of Table 14.4, the transmission to men from all three generations is shown. As expected, all odds ratios in this column are significant, indicating that having a sex offending father, brother, or other male relative increases the probability that one becomes a sex offender. However, most odds ratios have wide confidence intervals which could be caused by the low prevalence of sex offenders in the sample. The results should, therefore, be interpreted with some caution.

Although the results from Table 14.4 provide evidence for transmission of sexual offending between family members, these results do not tell us whether this transmission is caused by sex offenders being sexually victimized by their relative, as proposed in Hypothesis 2a, or whether victimization is not necessary for the transmission to occur, as proposed by Hypothesis 2b. Information from the court files about the victims of the sex offenses, on which we will elaborate later on, shows that none of the sex offenders was the victim of a sex crime for which a family member was convicted. This suggests that sex offenses are transmitted between family members without the relative victimizing the other. Based on these results, we reject Hypothesis 2a and confirm Hypothesis 2b. In order to test Hypothesis 2c, whether the transmission from nuclear family members is stronger than the transmission from extended family members, we estimated a ratio between odds ratios (ROR). Although the odds ratio for the transmission of hands-on offending between nuclear family members is larger than that for the transmission of hands-on offending between extended family members, the difference is not significant [ROR: 1.50 (0.55–4.12)]. Also the difference between transmission of any sex offending between nuclear family members and between extended family members is not significant [ROR: 2.07 (0.84–5.12)]. These insignificant RORs might be caused by the large confidence intervals of the odds ratios in Table 14.4. Hypothesis 2c can thus not be confirmed for hands-on offending nor for any sex offending. Table 14.4 further shows that all odds ratios are higher for the transmission of hands-on offending than for the transmission of any sex offending, which would indicate a stronger transmission effect for hands-on offending than for any sex offending. However, these differences between odds ratios for hands-on offending and any sex offending are not significant. Finally, one should note that any sex offending includes hands-on offending, and that the transmission of any sex offending between family members is more likely when hands-on offenses are committed.

Transmission From Serious and Violent Crimes to Sexual Crimes Within Families

Next, to test our third hypothesis, we calculated the average number of serious and violent offenses committed by family members of families with none, one, or multiple hands-on sex offenders. Families for which the members did not commit any serious offense are excluded from the analysis in order to compare between offending families. As Table 14.5 shows, the number of serious crimes as well as the number of violent crimes is much higher in families with one or multiple hands-on offenders than in criminal families with no hands-on offenders. An ANOVA showed that these differences are significant. In order to control for differences in family size, we also calculated the percentage of male family members who were convicted for a serious or violent crime in each family. Again, families with one or multiple hands-on sex offenders included a significantly higher percentage of men who were convicted for serious or violent crimes than families with no hands-on sex offenders. We also repeated these analyses for any sex offenders instead of hands-on offenders (not shown in Table 14.5). This led to similar results, except for the difference in percentages of family members who were convicted for violent crimes, which was not significant.

As we have shown that families with sex offenders commit more serious and violent crimes than families without sex offenders, we would expect the sex offenders themselves to be more antisocial and violent as well. In Table 14.6 we present the average number of serious and violent crimes committed by nonsex offenders and hands-on offenders. Hands-on offenders, on average, commit significantly more serious and violent crimes than do nonsex offenders. Also the percentage of hands-on offenders convicted for serious and violent crimes is significantly higher than the percentage of nonsex offenders convicted for such crimes.

However, when we compared the average number of crimes of the hands-on offenders with only the nonsex offenders who were convicted for a serious crime (i.e. excluding the nonoffenders), we did not find a significant difference anymore (not shown in Table 14.6). The hands-on offenders in the Dutch sample are, thus, not significantly different from other serious offenders in terms of the average number of serious and violent crimes. We also repeated these analyses for all sex

Table 14.5 The Average Number of Serious and Violent Crimes Within Criminal Families From the Transfive Study

	Average number of crimes		*Percentage convicted*	
Offending within family	*Serious crimes*	*Violent crimes*	*Serious crimes*	*Violent crimes*
No hands-on offenders (N = 92)	14.24	2.95	28.7%	11.3%
One hands-on offender (N = 12)	58.75	12.17	32.6%	12.5%
Multiple hands-on offenders (N = 15)	127.47	19.93	39.7%	19.6%
All families (N = 119)	33.00***	6.02***	30.5%*	12.4%*

Note. Only the convictions from male family members are taken into account; sex offenses are excluded from the total number of crimes.
$^{*}p < .05$, $^{**}p < .01$, $^{***}p < .001$.

Table 14.6 The Average Number of Serious and Violent Crimes of Nonsex Offenders and Hands-on Offenders

	Average number of crimes		*Percentage convicted*	
	Serious crimes	*Violent crimes*	*Serious crimes*	*Violent crimes*
Nonsex offenders (N = 2606)	1.37	0.26	27.6%	11.2 %
Hands-on offenders (N = 55)	6.55	0.80	63.6%	23.6%
All respondents (N = 3111)	1.48***	0.27***	28.3%***	11.5%**

Note. Sex offenses are extracted from the total number of crimes.
$^{*}p < .05$, $^{**}p < .01$, $^{***}p < .001$.

Table 14.7 GEE Models for the Intergenerational Transmission From Violent Offending to (Hands-on) Sex Offending

	Violent offending → hands-on offending	*Violent offending→ any sex offending*
Transmission from:		
Father	1.52 (0.51–4.53)	1.20 (0.41–3.50)
Brother	**2.68 (1.31–5.48)**	**2.32 (1.19–4.55)**
Any nuclear family member	**2.35 (1.19–4.65)**	**1.91 (1.01–3.60)**
Any extended family member	**3.86 (1.18–12.62)**	2.20 (0.93–5.22)
Any family member	3.15 (0.96–10.29)	1.79 (0.75–4.25)

Note. Odds ratios in bold are significant.

offenders (not shown in Table 14.6), which led to similar results. Although the sex offenders were shown to commit more serious and violent crimes, 36.4% of the hands-on offenders and 39.7% of all sex offenders did not commit any serious crimes, while, respectively, 76.4 and 72.1% did not commit any violent crimes. In additional analyses (not shown in Table 14.6), we tested whether the sex offenders who also commit serious or violent crimes belong, more often than sex offenders who do not commit other serious or violent crimes, to families whose members commit more serious and violent crimes. However, no significant difference was found. Families in which many violent and serious crimes are committed thus include both versatile sex offenders, who also commit other serious and violent crimes, and specialized sex offenders, who only commit sex offenses.

Finally, we estimated GEE models to test whether persons with violent family members are at increased risk of becoming sex offenders, which we would expect based on earlier results (see Table 14.5). Table 14.7 shows that individuals with a violent brother, any violent nuclear family member, or any violent extended family member have a significantly higher chance of being a hands-on sex offender. The odds ratio for having any violent extended family member is larger than the odds ratio for having any violent nuclear family member, but the difference is not significant [ROR: 1.64 (0.42–6.44)]. In addition, those with a violent brother or any violent nuclear family member are at increased risk of being a sex offender.[3] The same analyses were repeated for transmission from serious offending to (hands-on) sex offending. This showed significant odds ratios for having a serious offending brother, father, or any nuclear family member (not shown in Table 14.7). Odds ratios for serious offending by extended family members could not be estimated because all hands-on offenders had at least one serious offending extended family member. In short, the results from Table 14.5, Table 14.6, and Table 14.7 show that sex offenders come from families in which serious and violent crimes are more prevalent than in (criminal) families without any sex offenders, that sex offenders themselves commit on average many serious and violent crimes, and that individuals with criminal and violent family members are at increased risk of becoming a sex offender. For these reasons, we confirm our third hypothesis that the concentration of sex offenses within families is partly explained by the transmission of serious and violent crimes.

Victims of Sexual Abuse

Our final two hypotheses postulated that sexual crimes cluster in families through co-offending family members (Hypothesis 4) or because female incest victims mate with sex offenders (Hypothesis 5). Table 14.8 summarizes the relationship between the victims and perpetrators of the sex crimes. In 31.15% of the cases, the victim was a family member of the perpetrator, most often a niece or the (step)daughter of the

Table 14.8 Overview of the Relationship Between Perpetrator and Victim of Sex Offenses

Victims within family	*N*	*Percentage*	*Other victims*	*N*	*Percentage*
Daughter	5	8.20	Neighbor	3	4.92
Step-daughter	3	4.92	Acquaintance	9	14.75
Spouse	1	1.64	Stranger	11	18.03
Sister	1	1.64	Total	23	37.70
Granddaughter	1	1.64			
Niece	6	9.84			
Nephew	2	3.28			
Total	19	31.15	Unknown	19	31.15

Note. The number of victims is higher than the number of convictions since in some cases there were multiple victims; victims are considered as unknown if the court files did not include victims' names, if the relationship between the victim and the perpetrator is unknown, and if there is no specific victim (e.g., in the case of exhibitionism).

[3]Table 14.7 shows the odds ratios for all generations together. Odds ratios were also estimated for each generation separately, but this resulted in only a couple of significant odds ratios for G5. This is probably the consequence of the low prevalence of sex offenders in each generation, while having a violent family member is much more likely.

sex offender. Victims from outside the family are most often strangers and acquaintances. Not much empirical support was found for our hypothesis that the concentration of sex offending within families can be explained by co-offending family members. In only one case, two family members from the Dutch sample committed a sex offense together: two brothers, under influence of alcohol, raped a woman whom they met in a bar that night. Besides that, there is only one other victim who was abused by multiple family members: a father and son both abused their granddaughter/niece. However, information from the court files made clear that this was not an offense that they perpetrated together, since the perpetrators had not been in contact with each other for decades. In some other cases, sex offenders from our sample co-offended with nonfamily members. However, since the perpetrators came from different families this cannot explain the concentration of sex offending within families. In sum, these results give little support for the hypothesis that the concentration of sex offending can be explained by co-offending family members. Lastly, based on the court files, we know that one woman in our data set who was abused by her father married a man who, later on, sexually abused her 13-year-old daughter. However, since this father is not included in our sample,[4] it does not explain the concentration of sex offending within the families in our sample. None of the other known sexually abused women in our sample married a man who was or became a sex offender. Thus, our fifth hypothesis, which states that sex offending concentrates within families because female incest victims marry sex offenders, cannot be confirmed either.

Discussion

In this chapter we examined the degree of concentration of sex offending within Dutch and British families. In addition, we examined whether the degree of concentration differs for different types of sex offenses and we tested five possible explanations for this concentration. We used data from the Cambridge Study in Delinquent Development (CSDD) that includes 2,212 persons from 397 British nuclear families, and data from the Transfive study that includes 5,177 persons from 140 Dutch extended families. Our analyses showed that there is no significant concentration of sex offenses within the nuclear families from either the CSDD or the Transfive study. However, sex offenses, more specifically hands-on offenses and offenses against minors, were shown to cluster significantly within the extended families from the Transfive study; the clustering of sex offenses against minors driving the overall clustering effect observed. This clustering of sex offenses against minors within families can by itself be explained by the fact that many child abusers commit multiple sex offenses. Moreover, the concentration of all sex offenses within

[4]This man is not included in the sample because he is the father of the partner (i.e., the sexually abused woman) of one of the G4 males (i.e., her husband, who sexually abused her daughter). As mentioned in the method section, such family members of the partners are not included in the sample.

families is mainly driven by the concentration of hands-on offenses, as we found that hands-off offenses do not concentrate within families at all. We found support for two possible explanations for the concentration of hands-on offending and any sex offending within the Dutch extended families. First, we found support for transmission of any sex offending and hands-on offending from father to son, between brothers, and between other male relatives.

Transmission between nuclear family members was larger than transmission between extended family members, but the difference was not significant. This transmission is not mediated by childhood sexual abuse victimization of sex offenders. Second, we found support for the hypothesis that sex offending clusters within families due to a transmission of serious and violent delinquency. Families that include one or more sex offenders commit much more serious and violent crimes than (criminal) families without any sex offenders. This is partly due to the fact that sex offenders themselves commit relatively many serious and violent crimes. Also, persons with violent family members are at increased risk of being a sex offender. It thus seems that sex offending within these families is a manifestation of general antisocial and violent tendencies. Against our expectations, we did not find a concentration of specific types of sex offending, such as hands-off offending, sex offending against minors, and rape or sexual assault. This might be a consequence of the relative low prevalence of each of these specific types of sex offending, which makes it hard to reach statistical significance. On the other hand, generalized social learning mechanisms might be at work instead of specific social learning mechanisms.

Specific modeling assumes that one exactly imitates the behavior of their model, while generalized antisocial modeling might also lead to other forms of antisocial behavior (Bandura, 1977; Kalmuss, 1984). Criminal family members may not transmit their exact behavior, but rather more general antisocial scripts that include a more broad disregard of behavioral conventions and that justify letting one's own needs take precedence over the welfare of others. In turn, such general antisocial scripts could result in violent, but also in sexual offending, thus explaining the link between violent family members and sexual offending. Furthermore, even sexually distorted scripts could be versatile in the sense that these scripts convey more general cognitions – for example, denial of injury, blaming the victim – that aim to justify sexual transgressions, regardless of the specific type of offense. This might be an explanation for the fact that we did find concentration of any sex offending and all hands-on offending within families, but not of specific types of offending. Moreover, we did not find support for our hypothesis that the concentration of sex offending within families was caused by incest victims becoming sex offenders. This is in contrast with earlier research that showed that many sex offenders experienced childhood sexual abuse (e.g., Faller, 1989; Jespersen et al., 2009; Seto & Lalumière, 2010).

A possible explanation might be the use of official data. The actual number of victims of sexual abuse is largely underestimated by these data because only a small minority of victims report their victimization. The court files of some cases contained more extensive information about the sex offenders, including information about their history of sexual abuse. These court files showed that some sex offenders indeed stated to be sexually abused as a child, but not by a relative, or that the relative was not convicted for the crime. While this might be interpreted as supportive of the hypothesis that child abuse victims are more likely to evolve into sex offenders themselves, caution remains warranted. First, the available data on child sexual abuse are retrospective only and give no information about the number of abused children that do not continue the assumed cycle of sexual abuse. Second, offenders' claims of being themselves victimized may also result from their efforts to rationalize or exculpate their offending behavior, either in their own eyes or in the eyes of clinicians or criminal justice officials. Our results further showed that the Dutch sample includes both versatile sex offenders, who also commit violent and serious offenses, and specialized sex offenders, who only commit sex offenses. This is in line with typologies for sex offenders that distinguish nonsexual subtypes from sexual subtypes (Robertiello & Terry, 2007), and with previous research on the (lack of) specialization of sex offenders (e.g. Harris et al., 2009). More remarkable is our finding that both the versatile and the specialized sex offenders have family members who commit relatively many serious and violent offenses. We would have expected that only the versatile sex offenders come from antisocial and violent families, as their sex offenses are part of a general antisocial and violent behavioral repertoire which might be transmitted from family members. However, the specialized sex offenders were also shown to come from antisocial and violent families. These findings may result from an official bias against members of known criminal families and persons. If antisocial and violent families are monitored more intensively by the police and the criminal justice system, sex offenses committed by family members from known antisocial families might more often result in a conviction – rather than, for example, a referral to outpatient treatment without a conviction – even in the absence of a criminal history. Consequently, specialized sex offenders from such families might be more likely to be convicted for the sex offenses they commit than specialized sex offenders from nonantisocial families.

Like any other study, this study has its limitations. The most important limitation is the use of official judicial information. As mentioned before, only a small minority of sex offenses is reported to the police, which leads to a large "dark number" (see Bouchard & Lussier, this volume). Next, relatively more sex offenses than other offenses are acquitted or end in a technical dismissal. We discarded all such cases as we could not be sure of the level of certainty possible using official data – that the offender had actually committed the abuse. More support might have been found for our hypothesis that incest victims become sex offenders if self-reported data had been used. As mentioned above, the court files showed that, in some cases, sex offenders were sexually abused in their youth by a family member who was never convicted for such acts. The use of self-reported data might provide more information on the history of sexual abuse of sex offenders. But also the concentration itself might be under- or overestimated by the use of conviction data. On the one hand, it might be overestimated if families in which sexual offending occurred are more intensively monitored by police and justice. This increases the probability of detecting sex offending within such families, while sex offending in other families remains undetected. On the other hand, the concentration might be underestimated, as information from the court files showed that in some families much more sexual offending occurred than was reflected by the official documentation. Another disadvantage of the use of conviction data is the fact that the prevailing definitions of sexual offending have changed over time (i.e., marital rape was not defined as a crime in the Netherlands until 1991; brotheling has been legal in the Netherlands since 2000). As a consequence, the odds of being convicted for a sex crime might differ among the generations in our samples. Our findings should thus be interpreted with some caution since they might be influenced by the use of conviction data.

Another limitation of our study design is that we do not have information on the criminal history of all extended family members. The data from the CSDD only contained information about the nuclear family members, while in the Transfive study, information about the family members of partners is missing. Consequently, the Transfive study does not contain any information about approximately half of the grandparents, uncles, aunts, and cousins. Given how rare sex offending is, even in this high-risk sample, such data might have strengthened our findings. In addition, it would have been interesting to examine whether persons from families in which sex offenses occur mate with persons from similar families. Unfortunately, we could not test this with the data sets we used. For these reasons, it would be good if future studies replicate this study whilst including information on the offense history of all extended family members from both partners' side. Finally, given the rarity of sexual offending even in comparatively large data sets such as the ones used here, the absolute number of sex offenders remains low. Bijleveld and Hendriks (2007) showed that there is much heterogeneity in families in which juvenile sex offenders live, varying from hypersexual families that frequently expose children to pornography and sexual behavior to sexually repressed families in which no one talks about sex. This heterogeneity is probably not reflected in our data sets because of the low number of sex offenders and the homogeneous character of our samples (i.e., mainly Caucasian families living in a working-class inner-city area of South London; and predominantly ethnic Dutch Catholics). The generalizability of our findings is, therefore, limited, especially to cases of sexual offending that take place in families living under very specific circumstances, for example, urban ghettos, or in families that adhere to particular traditional or cultural norms.

Despite these limitations, our study contributed to the existing literature on sex offenders in various ways. First of all, we used prospectively collected data to study the concentration of sex offenses within Dutch and British families, a topic which has to our knowledge never been studied before. Moreover, we examined the intergenerational transmission of the perpetration of sexual offenses, whereas earlier studies focused on the transmission of sexual victimization. Finally, for the Transfive data set, we were able to distinguish between different types of sex offending. A meta-analysis on evaluations of sex offender treatment showed that interventions aimed at reducing recidivism not only lead to less sexual recidivism but also decrease levels of violent and general recidivism as well (Lösel & Schmucker, 2005). Based on our findings that families with a broader antisocial and violent tendency include more sex offenders, it might be expected that interventions aimed at reducing violent and general recidivism could also decrease the risk of sex offending for the offenders' family members. In order to design effective interventions for at-risk families, it would be desirable if more knowledge were to become available about the causal mechanisms that underlie the transmission of sex offending between sexually offending and criminal and violent family members. In this study we were able to show that sex offenses are transmitted from such family members, but, at this time, leave it up to future studies to address the issue of possible underlying mechanisms (e.g., social learning mechanisms or genetic influences) in more detail.

References

Alexander, M. A. (1999). Sexual offender treatment efficacy revisited. *Sexual Abuse: A Journal of Research and Treatment, 11*(2), 101–116.

Altman, D. G. & Bland, J. M. (2003). Interaction revisited: The difference between two estimates. *BMJ,326*, 219.

Avery, L., Hutchinson, K. D., & Whitaker, K. (2002). Domestic violence and intergenerational rates of child sexual abuse: A case record analysis. *Child and Adolescent Social Work Journal, 19*(1), 77–90.

Bandura, A. (1977). *Social learning theory*. Englewood Cliffs, NJ: Prentice-Hall.

Besemer, S. (2012). Specialized versus versatile intergenerational transmission of violence: A new approach to studying intergenerational transmission from violent versus non-violent fathers: Latent class analysis. *Journal of Quantitative Criminology, 28*(2), 245–263.

Bijleveld, C. C. J. H., & Hendriks, J. (2007). Gezin en seksueel misbruik: Overdracht van daderschap en slachtofferschap van seksueel misbruik. *Tijdschrift voor Criminologie, 49*(2), 123–136.

Bijleveld, C. C. J. H., & Soudijn, M. (2008). Verdachten van een groepszedendelict. *Tijdschrift voor Seksuologie, 32*, 80–89.

Bijleveld, C. C. J. H., Weerman, F. M., Looije, D., & Hendriks, J. (2007). Group sex offending by juveniles: Coercive sex as a group activity. *European Journal of Criminology, 4*(1), 5–31.

Bijleveld, C. C. J. H., & Wijkman, M. D. S. (2009). Intergenerational continuity in convictions: A five-generation study. *Criminal Behaviour and Mental Health, 19*, 142–155.

Burton, D. L. (2003). Male adolescents: Sexual victimization and subsequent sexual abuse. *Child and Adolescent Social Work Journal, 20*(4), 277–296.

Burton, D. L., Miller, D. L., & Shill, C. T. (2002). A social learning theory comparison of the sexual victimization of adolescent sexual offenders and nonsexual offending male delinquents. *Child Abuse & Neglect, 26*, 893–907.

Caldwell, M. F. (2002). What we do not know about juvenile sexual reoffense risk. *Child Maltreatment, 7*, 291–302.

De Vogel, V., & Ruiter de, C. (2003). Recidive bij behandelde zedendelinquenten. *Tijdschrift voor Criminologie, 45*, 378–390.

Eggen, A. T. J., & Van der Heide, W. (2005). *Criminaliteit en rechtshandhaving 2004*. Den Haag: WODC/Boom Juridische uitgevers.

Estes, L. S., & Tidwell, R. (2002). Sexually abused children's behaviours: Impact of gender and mother's experience of intra- and extra-familial sexual abuse. *Family Practice, 19*(1), 36–44.

Faller, K. C. (1989). Why sexual abuse? An exploration of the intergenerational hypothesis. *Child Abuse & Neglect, 13*, 543–548.

Farrington, D. P. (1995). The development of offending and antisocial behaviour from childhood: Key findings from the Cambridge Study in Delinquent Development. *Journal of Child Psychology and Psychiatry, 36*, 929–964.

Farrington, D. P. (2003). Key results from the first forty years of the Cambridge Study in Delinquent. In T. P. Thornberry & M. D. Krohn (Eds.),*Taking stock of delinquency: An overview of findings from contemporary longitudinal studies*. New York: Kluwer.

Farrington, D. P, Barnes, G.C., & Lambert, S. (1996). The concentration of offending in families. *Legal and Criminological Psychology, 1*, 47–63.

Farrington, D. P., Coid, J. W., Harnett, L., Jolliffe, D., Soteriou, N., Turner, R., & West, D. J. (2006). *Criminal careers up to age 50 and life success up to age 48: New findings from the Cambridge Study in Delinquent Development*. Home Office Research Study No. 299. London: Home Office.

Farrington, D. P., Coid, J. W., & West, D. J. (2009). The development of offending from age 8 to age 50: Recent findings from the Cambridge Study in Delinquent Development. *Monatsschrift fur Kriminologie und Strafrechtsreform [Journal of Criminology and Penal Reform]*, (2/3), 160–173.

Farrington, D. P., Jolliffe, D., Loeber, R., Stouthamer-Loeber, M., & Kalb, L. M. (2001). The concentration of offenders in families, and family criminality in the prediction of boys' delinquency. *Journal of Adolescence, 24*, 579–596.

Farrington, D. P. & West, D. J. (1990). The Cambridge Study in Delinquent Development: A long-term follow-up of 411 London males. In H.-J. Kerner & G. Kaiser (eds.), *Kriminalitat: Personlichkeit, lebensgeschichte und verhalten [Criminality: Personality, life history and criminal behaviour]*. Berlin: Springer-Verlag.

France, K. G. & Hudson, S. M. (1993). The conduct disorders and the juvenile sex offender. In H. E. Barbaree, W. L. Marshall, & S. M. Hudson (Eds.), *The juvenile sex offender* (pp. 264–277). New York: Guilford Press.

Fox, J. A. & Tracy, P. E. (1998). A measure of skewness in offense distributions. *Journal of Quantitative Criminology, 4*(3), 259–273.

Gebhard, P. J., Gagnon, J. H., Pomeroy, W. B., & Christenson, C. V. (1965). *Sex offenders: An analysis of types*. New York: Harper and Row.

Ghisletta, P., & Spini, D. (2004). An introduction to generalized estimating equations and an application to assess selectivity effects in a longitudinal study on very old individuals. *Journal of Educational and Behavioral Statistics, 29*(4), 421–437.

Gottfredson, M. R., & Hirschi, T. (1990). *A general theory of crime*. Stanford, CA: Stanford University Press.

Hall, G. C. N., & Hirschman, R. (1991). Toward a theory of sexual aggression: A quadripartite model. *Journal of Consulting and Clinical Psychology, 59*, 662–669.

Hall, G. C. N., & Hirschman, R. (1992). Sexual aggression against children: A conceptual perspective of etiology. *Criminal Justice and Behavior, 19*, 8–23.

Harris, D. A., Mazerolle, P., & Knight, R. A. (2009). Understanding male sexual offending: A comparison of general and specialist theories. *Criminal Justice and Behavior, 36*(10), 1051–1069.

Jespersen, A. F., Lalumière, M. L., & Seto, M. C. (2009). Sexual abuse history among adult sex offenders and non-sex offenders: A meta-analysis. *Child Abuse & Neglect, 33*, 179–192.

Kalmuss, D. (1984). The intergenerational transmission of marital aggression. *Journal of Marriage and Family, 46*(1), 11–19.

Lösel, F., & Schmucker, M. (2005). The effectiveness of treatment for sexual offenders: A comprehensive meta-analysis. *Journal of Experimental Criminology, 1*, 117–146.

Lussier, P. (2005). The criminal activity of sexual offenders in adulthood: Revisiting the specialization debate. *Sexual Abuse: A Journal of Research and Treatment, 17*(3), 269–292.

Lussier, P., Proulx, J., & LeBlanc, M. (2005). Criminal propensity, deviant sexual interests and criminal activity of sexual aggressors against women: A comparison of explanatory models. *Criminology, 43*, 249–281.

Marshall, W. L., Laws, D. R., & Barbaree, H. E. (1990). *Handbook of sexual assault: Issues, theories, and treatment of the offender*. New York: Plenum Press.

Nieuwbeerta, P., Blokland, A. A. J., & Bijleveld, C. C. J. H. (2003). Lange termijn recidive van daders van seksuele delicten. *Tijdschrift voor Criminologie, 45*, 369–377.

Oseretzky, N. J. (1929). Die Sexualkriminalität der Minderjährigen. *Monatschrift für Kriminalpsychologie und Strafrechtsreform, 20*, 705–732.

Piquero, A. R. (2000). Assessing the relationships between gender, chronicity, seriousness, and offense skewness in criminal offending. *Journal of Criminal Justice, 28*, 103–115.

Robertiello, G., & Terry, K. J. (2007). Can we profile sex offenders? A review of sex offender typologies. *Aggression and Violent Behavior, 12*(5), 508–518.

Salter, D., McMillan, D., Richards, M., Talbot, T., Hodges, J., Bentovim, A., Hastings, R. et al. (2003). Development of sexually abusive behavior in sexually victimized males: A longitudinal study. *The Lancet, 361*, 471–476.

Seto, M. C., & Barbaree, H. E. (1997). Sexual aggression as antisocial behavior: A developmental model. In D. M. Stoff, J. Breiling & J. D. Maser (Eds.), *Handbook of antisocial behavior* (pp. 524–533). Hoboken, NJ: John Wiley & Sons, Inc.

Seto, M. C., & Lalumière, M. L. (2010). What is so special about male adolescent sexual offending? A review and test of explanations through meta-analysis. *Psychological Bulletin, 136* (4), 526–575.

Smith, M.D. (2004). *Encyclopedia of rape*. Westwood, CT: Greenwood.

Testa, M., Hoffman, J. H., & Livingston, J. A. (2011). Intergenerational transmission of sexual victimization vulnerability as mediated via parenting. *Child Abuse & Neglect, 35*, 363–371.

Van Beek, D., & Mulder, J. (2002). De rol van cognitieve vervormingen in het plegen van pedoseksuele delicten en hun plaats in de behandeling. *Tijdschrift voor Seksuologie, 26*, 79–86.

Van de Rakt, M., Nieuwbeerta, P., & Apel, R. (2009). Association of criminal convictions between family members: Effects of siblings, fathers and mothers. *Criminal Behaviour and Mental Health, 19*, 94–108.

Van de Weijer, S. G. A., Bijleveld, C. C. J. H., & Blokland, A. A. J. (2014). The intergenerational transmission of violent delinquency. *Journal of Family Violence, 29*(2), 109–118.

Veneziano, C., Veneziano, L., & LeGrand, S. (2000). The relationship between adolescent sex offender behaviors and victim characteristics with prior victimization. *Journal of Interpersonal Violence, 15*(4), 363–374.

Ward, T., & Siegert, R. J. (2002). Toward a comprehensive theory of child sexual abuse: A theory knitting perspective. *Psychology, Crime & Law, 8*, 319–351.

West, D. J. (1969). *Present conduct and future delinquency*. London: Heinemann.
West, D. J. (1982). *Delinquency: Its roots, careers and prospects*. London: Heinemann.
West, D. J., & Farrington, D. P. (1973). *Who becomes delinquent?* London: Heinemann.
West, D. J., & Farrington, D. P. (1977). *The delinquent way of life*. London: Heinemann.
Worling, J. R., & Långström, N. (2006). Risk of sexual recidivism in adolescents who offend sexually: Correlates and assessments. In H. E. Barbaree, W. L. Marshall, & S. M. Hudson (Eds.), *The juvenile sex offender* (pp. 264–277). New York: Guilford Press.

Part III

The Criminal Career Approach and Associated Policy Issues

15

Estimating the Size of the Sexual Aggressor Population

Martin Bouchard*
Simon Fraser University, Canada

Patrick Lussier
Laval University, Canada

Introduction

Several key parameters were introduced by criminal career researchers to better understand the longitudinal sequence of offenses committed by individuals. Two of the four key parameters defined and described by criminal career researchers, participation and frequency, stir much controversy among criminologists. Participation refers to the "fraction of a population ever committing (or 'doing') at least one crime before some age *a* (D_a) or currently active during some observation period *(d)*" (Blumstein, Cohen, Roth, & Visher, 1986, p. 31). Frequency (or individual frequency) refers to the number of crimes committed by the active criminal population within a given time period. Criminal career researchers posited that participation and frequency are two distinct phenomena that may be driven by different motives and explained by different causal mechanisms. In other words, the factors leading someone to embark on a criminal career may be different from the explanation for why offending becomes frequent or chronic. The controversy was fueled by propensity theorists arguing about the theoretical importance of distinguishing between the two concepts (e.g., Gottfredson & Hirschi, 1986; Hirschi & Gottfredson, 1995). For propensity theorists, the distinction was conceptually and empirically unnecessary as participation and frequency were part of a continuum of criminality subject to the age effect. Of importance, they argued that both participation and frequency vary similarly by age. Criminal career theorists responded that the age-crime curve reflected more a drop in participation than in frequency

*The authors would like to thank Pierre Tremblay as well as the reviewers for the many helpful comments made on an earlier version of this manuscript.

Sex Offenders: A Criminal Career Approach, First Edition. Edited by Arjan Blokland and Patrick Lussier.

of offending, further reinforcing the need to distinguish between the two (Blumstein, Cohen, & Farrington, 1988). The importance of distinguishing between participation and frequency, and the debate that ensued, led to various interpretations among scholars. Some built on the criminal career assumptions to elaborate two types of young offenders, one reflecting the participation and the age-crime curve, the other reflecting frequency and the relative stability of offending over time (Moffitt, 1993). Others proposed a conceptual and empirical model integrating the two dimensions (Rowe, Osgood, & Nicewander, 1990). In the process, the policy implications brought forth by the distinction made by criminal career researchers were somewhat left aside (Visher & Roth, 1986). Yet, at the core of the concept of participation lies the idea of the size of a criminal population, something that frequency of offending is not capturing. While much work has been undertaken to monitor and analyze trends in the amount of crimes committed, almost never raised is the issue of the size of the underlying population involved in committing those crimes. Either this issue is overlooked by researchers, or the implicit assumption is made that the underlying population of offenders simply follows crime trends; if crime is increasing, there are more criminals. And vice versa.

It is entirely plausible, however, to imagine that the size of the criminal population follows a different trend from those reflected in official crime figures (e.g., see Bouchard, 2007). Nothing prevents a stable population of offenders from increasing their individual crime frequencies in any given year, especially if they stumble upon or create an especially profitable crime opportunity (Tremblay, 2010). When those offenders are among the heaviest contributors to crime statistics – say, chronic offenders – such changes may have a significant impact on crime trends. Those issues are particularly relevant in the context of analyzing trends in a behavior involving a great deal of social stigma such as sexual aggression. Ever since Gene Abel's studies on the self-reported sexually deviant behaviors of adult men referred to his clinic, it has been assumed that official data are useless to examine the criminal activity of sex offenders because such data only capture a small proportion of their criminal activity (e.g., Abel, Becker, Cunningham-Rathner, Rouleau, & Murphy, 1987; Abel & Rouleau, 1990). For example, the 224 heterosexual child molesters interviewed revealed a total of 4,435 victims, the 153 homosexual child molesters were responsible for 22,981 victims, while the 126 rapists interviewed reported 882 victims. Ever since the publication of these oft-cited findings, such numbers have never been fully replicated (but see Weinrott & Saylor, 1991)[1] and researchers have questioned their validity (Marshall, Barbaree, & Eccles, 1991). Using a similar procedure, Marshall et al. (1991) reported that the mean number of victims of their

[1]Weinrott & Saylor (1991) subsequently analyzed the self-reported behaviors of 99 convicted sex offenders who were committed for an indeterminate period in a psychiatric hospital. The 37 rapists included, who had been charged for 66 offenses of this type, reported a total number of 433 rapes and a median number of six victims (Mean = 11.7). By comparison, the 67 child molesters surveyed reported a total of 959 victims (Mean = 14.3; Median = 7). These numbers are somewhat in line with those reported.

sample (n = 57) of extrafamilial child molesters against female victims was 4.7, while it was 3.3 for their sample (n = 34) of extrafamilial child molesters against male victims. While Marshall et al.'s (1991) numbers are more conservative, they do suggest, however, that several sex crimes go undetected, and, by extension, that many men who have used some form of coercion in a sexual context, get away with it.

This chapter draws on recent advances in capture-recapture modeling (i.e., Bohning and Van der Heijden's 2009 extension of Zelterman's (1988) estimator) to estimate the size of the sexual aggressor population. Doing so also allows us to estimate the risks of incarceration for the sex offenders in Quebec. Although researchers have been concerned by the extent of sexual victimization and perpetration for quite some time, the size of the sexual aggressor population remains unknown. Social scientists have pursued different avenues to establish the extent and nature of the problem of sexual aggression, and three main strategies have been chosen over the years: victimization surveys, self-report studies, and official statistics.

Strategies to Estimate the Prevalence of Sexual Offending

Prevalence and Victimization Surveys

Victimization surveys are not helpful to estimate the size of the sexual aggressor population for several reasons. First, while these surveys are helpful to obtain information about the prevalence of victimization, they are less suited to the estimation of the perpetration rate in a given population. Victimization surveys do not take into account the impact of individuals offending against multiple victims and the fact that a small group of offenders are responsible for a high proportion of victims (e.g., Abel & Rouleau, 1990). Similarly, victimization surveys often do not control for multiple victimization by different offenders. Furthermore, such studies do not survey tourists and visitors who may be sexually victimized during their stay. Also, individuals who are more difficult to reach (e.g., no fixed address, no phone access, hospitalized, incarcerated) are not included in most surveys but may have a higher victimization rate than those who are. The long recall period often used in these surveys (i.e., "have you ever...") does not allow the estimation of the population of sexual aggressors in a given time period. The difficulties in establishing the prevalence of victimization is due in part to the definition of the behavior being measured. The behaviors included in some surveys are vague and/or not defined, which may lead to various interpretations by those surveyed, or by researchers. For example, rape refers to sexual intercourse subsequent to the use of force or physical violence, but studies showed variations in the lower boundary age included in the definition (sexual victimization since age 14, 16, or 18) (e.g., Koss, 1993). Others have used the broader concept of sexual assault that refers to being pressured or forced into have sexual contact (e.g., Sorensen, Stein, Siegel, Golding, & Burnam, 1987). These definitions lead to different prevalence rates. For example, in an oft-cited study based on a large sample of college women, Koss, Gidycz, and Wisniewski (1987) reported that the prevalence of sexual victimization since age 14 was 53% (unwanted sexual contacts: sexual coercion, attempted rape, rape); this number dropped to 15% when considering rape alone. While the compartmentalization is desirable to address specific research questions, it limits the possibility of estimating the size of the offender population as the same individual may be involved in different crime types. This point has been empirically shown in several studies examining the crime-switching patterns of sexual aggressors (e.g., Leclerc, Lussier, & Deslauriers-Varin, this book; Lussier, Leclerc, Healey, & Proulx, 2008).

Prevalence and Self-Reported Sexual Aggression

The scientific literature on the prevalence of sexual aggression has come a long way since Brownmiller (1975) claimed that rape was a "conscious process of intimidation by which *all* men keep *all* women in a state of fear" (emphasis added). Self-report studies have been typically conducted with a highly selected group of young men, most often undergraduate university students. Malamuth (e.g., Malamuth, 1981, 1989) questioned a group of male undergraduate university students about their likelihood of committing a series of behaviors if they could get away with it without any negative consequences. In total, 74% said they would not rape under any circumstances, thus suggesting that 26% were at least open to the idea under some circumstances. Among those, about 2% of the men surveyed by Malamuth (see also Greendlinger & Byrne, 1987) said they would very likely rape someone under such circumstances. While this study did not measure the percentage of men who actually raped someone, it did highlight the fact that 1 out of 4 men may contemplate the idea if given the opportunity to do so. This further called researchers' attention to the issue of sexual aggression in young college men. In the Koss et al. (1987) study, 25% of college men surveyed reported having engaged in at least one form of behavior defined as sexual aggression (which included unwanted sexual contacts: pressuring someone into sex, sexual coercion, rape, and attempted rape). When narrowing down the definition to sexual coercion (i.e., sexual intercourse subsequent to pressure, threats, or misuse of authority), that prevalence dropped to 7%, while it was found to be 4% for behaviors meeting the legal definition of rape. Similar findings have been reported elsewhere (Abbey & McAuslan, 2004; Greendlinger & Byrne, 1987; Senn, Desmarais, Verbeg, & Wood, 2000; Spitzberg, 1999).

The bulk of research on sexual aggression perpetration has been focused on adult victims, and, consequently, few studies have asked men to self-report the perpetration of sexual aggressive behaviors against children. The scarcity of research is of interest here considering that victimization rates of child sexual abuse found in epidemiological studies are quite substantial. A meta-analysis based on retrospective studies conducted with college students found that about 17% of men (range: 3–37%) and 28% of women (range: 8–71%) had been sexually abused as a child (Rind, Tromovich, & Bauserman, 1998). The lower victimization rates found for child sexual abuse as opposed to those reported for sexual aggression against women appear to be in line with a generally lower interest by adult males for sexual contacts with children. In Malamuth's (1989) study, 91% of men responded that it would be very unlikely that they would commit an act of pedophilia if they could get away with it. Similarly, Templeman and Stinnett (1991) found that 5% of their community sample of men reported a sexual interest for children. Briere and Runtz (1989) reported that 9% of their college students had had sexual fantasies involving a child, and 7% (of the whole sample) would act on them if they could get away with it. Futhermore, Fromuth, Burkhart, and Jones (1991) found that 3% of their sample of men had had a "sexual experience" with a child. The focus of these self-report studies on young adult males enrolled in a university program makes it difficult to generalize findings to other subgroups of adult males (e.g., older, less educated), but does point out the pervasive nature of sexual aggression. Note that self-report studies did not ask these men whether they had been caught, arrested, or convicted for the behaviors they reported, thus not allowing researchers to estimate the actual risks of apprehension/conviction.

Prevalence and Official Statistics

The prevalence of sexual offending has also been examined using official statistics on crime. Several key findings have been highlighted by those studies, especially those based on prospective longitudinal data which allowed the examination of prevalence rates across time for the same group of individuals. For example, using Gluecks' longitudinal arrest data for a sample of adjudicated juvenile delinquents, Cline (1980) reported that the prevalence rate for sex crimes steadily increased from 0.3% in early adolescence (ages 11–15) to 1.6% in late adolescence (ages 16–20), 2.4% in early young adulthood (ages 21–25), and 2.6% in late young adulthood (ages 26–30). These numbers are interesting for various reasons. First, the self-reported retrospective data reported by Koss et al. (1987) in a sample of college men (averaging 21 years old) suggested that self-reported rates were *10 to 15 times higher* than those based on arrests. It is also interesting to note that data from Koss et al. underestimate the cumulative prevalence rate, considering that older men were not sampled and Cline's data suggest that either (a) they are offending more, or (b) they are getting caught more often than young adult men. Firm conclusions cannot be drawn as Koss and Cline had different operationalization of sex offenses and different populations sampled. Interesting comparisons can also be drawn with findings from the 1945 Philadelphia birth cohort conducted by Wolfgang, Figlio, and Sellin (1972). They reported that 0.43% of their sample had been arrested for rape in adolescence while 1.44% had been arrested for a sex offense. In spite of the sampling differences, the Wolfgang et al. prevalence data are in line with those reported by Cline (1980). Tracy, Wolgang, and Figlio (1990) conducted a second birth cohort (1958) study in Philadelphia allowing for the examination of cohort/period effects. Hence, for youth born 13 years later than in the original study, the prevalence of being arrested for rape increased to 0.66% (1.5 times higher) while that for sex offenses dropped to

0.43% (3.4 times lower). The Tracy et al. 1958 arrests data for "rape" are interesting because they allow direct comparison with the Koss et al. data on self-reported "rape" by college men born around 1963–1964. Hence, when only considering rape, the self-reported prevalence rate found by Koss et al. is *6.7 times higher* than the prevalence arrest rate provided by Tracy et al. This rate may vary across ethnic groups as both Koss et al. and Tracy et al. reported that nonwhites had higher a prevalence rate than whites.

Prevalence and Cohort Studies

To our knowledge, only one study tried to estimate the population of sex offenders at a given place in a given time using a series of birth cohorts. Marshall (1997) used five cohorts of individuals born in 1953, 1958, 1963, 1968, and 1973 to estimate the participation rate and the cumulative participation rate in sex crimes. One in 70 men born in 1953 and followed up to age 40 had been convicted for a sexual offense involving a victim, 1 in 90 men had been convicted for a serious sexual crime (i.e., hands-on behaviors against children and/or adults), while about 1 in 140 men had been convicted of a sexual crime against a child (Marshall, 1997). Furthermore, Marshall reported that about 10% of these men sexually reoffended within the first 5 years of their first conviction, a number in line with recidivism studies using a comparable follow-up period (e.g., Lussier, 2005; Lussier & Healey, 2009). Looking at the cumulative participation rate up to age 20 is interesting as it allows comparisons to be made with the Koss et al. studies on undergraduate university students. In that regard, the Marshall study showed that 1 in 200 men (about 0.5%) up to the age of 20 had been convicted for a sexual crime involving a victim. This is a far cry from the self-reported 25% prevalence estimate reported by Koss et al. (1987), but closer to the 1.6% arrest rate in late adolescence reported by Cline (1980). Granted, these cumulative participation rates are based on national estimates of different countries. Yet they do suggest that men's self-report rate of sexual aggression is *50 times* higher than the rate based on official data. The discrepancy is considerable, especially considering that the Koss et al. study did not include acts of sexual aggression against children.

Using the cohort data, Marshall (1997) estimated the population of known sexual offenders in 1993 in England and Wales. In total that year, it was estimated that 260,000 individuals had been convicted for a sexual offense (210,000 when limiting it to those crimes involving a victim). The estimated population of sex offenders, however, included a broad definition that encompassed crimes such as prostitution, possession of obscene material, and indecent exposure. That population was then broken down into age groups. Interestingly, the participation rate (not to be confused with the cumulative participation rate) steadily increased from the 20–24 age group (0.3%) to the 40 and older group (1.8%), thus suggesting that older men might be either more active, or more at risk of being caught. This trend is reminiscent of the one reported by Cline (1980) using arrest data on a sample of adjudicated juvenile delinquents. The same increasing trend was observed when looking specifically at sex crimes against children. This result is surprising as it suggests that the participation rate in sex crime may not vary by age in a traditional fashion (Farrington, 1986; Hirschi & Gottfredson, 1983). This finding may also shed some light on the discrepancies found between victimization and perpetration rates found in college students. The lower perpetration rate reported by men, as opposed to the victimization rate reported by women, was reflective of men underreporting perpetration. While this is certainly a factor, the discrepancy might also be due to the fact that the victimization rate reported by college women included both crimes perpetrated by young males and those perpetrated by men from other age groups. Unfortunately, Marshall (1997) stopped short of estimating the total size of the sex offender population as he focused strictly on known offenders. In other words, Marshall's estimated population did not include individuals who had not been caught or convicted for their crimes.

Methodology

Sample

As part of a research project on recidivism, all individuals consecutively admitted to a federal penitentiary for a sex crime between 1994 and 2000 were recruited for a study. All individuals were incarcerated for at least two years in a federal penitentiary in the province of Quebec, Canada. In total, 93% of individuals approached (n = 553) agreed to participate in the study. At the time of the study, all participants were incarcerated at the Regional Reception of Ste-Anne-des-Plaines, a maximum-security institution operated by the Correctional Service of Canada. On average, participants stayed at the reception center for 6 weeks while their level of risk and rehabilitative needs were assessed. After assessment, participants were transferred to an institution that best suited their needs. Detailed criminal activity and previous conviction history was obtained only for the first 387 cases recruited as part of that study. Keeping only those offenders admitted consecutively was important to preserve the validity of the capture-recapture experiment. In other words, meaningful capture-recapture estimates could not have been produced if a large component of the population had been captured but not identified as such.[2] For the purpose of this study, we used a fixed period with interviews starting in January 1995 and ending exactly at mid-year in 1998. The first official conviction date is December 22, 1994, and the last is June 28, 1998, almost exactly 3 years and 6 months. Detailed information about the sample is presented in Table 15.1.

[2]In other words, the consecutive admission criterion provides a systematic build-up to the sample that allows us to interpret the results within the confines of a relatively well-defined population (offenders at risk of being convicted to a federal prison sentence between January 1, 1995, and June 30, 1998) as opposed to a sampling procedure where the logic of inclusion is unknown.

Table 15.1 Description of the Sample (N = 387)

	Mean (SD)
Total convictions	4.6 (4.3)
Total convictions for sexual offenses	1.4 (0.7)
Age at first conviction	30.1 (13.3)
Age at window period conviction	39.3 (11.9)
Number of offenders recaptured during window period	N = 9

Procedures

Participation in this study was strictly voluntary, and all subjects signed a consent form indicating that the information collected would be used for research purposes only. The participants signed an additional consent form allowing access to their correctional files. When participants granted their consent, Correctional Service of Canada allowed inspection of the individual's correctional file. Correctional files were used to code information on the criminal history of each individual included in the study. All files included information about the participants' official records based on the Royal Canadian Mounted Police (RCMP) record. RCMP data was then use to establish offenders' criminal histories. Recidivism data was collected in June 2004 using the same source of information.

Defining the Population to be Estimated and the Time Period

We rely on consecutive admissions to a federal establishment, which means that every offender in our sample has been convicted and given a prison sentence of a minimum of 24 months. This means that the population to be estimated involves offenders whose offenses are serious enough to warrant a sentence of 2 years or more.

We also have to decide what the proper time period to estimate the size of the population is. One way to do this is to examine the amount of time between convictions for those who have more than one during the window period. Another way is simply to examine the conviction distribution for different time periods and see how much time is needed to get suitable distributions. For drug dealing and cannabis cultivation, a period of 3 years proved to be the most suitable for capture-recapture estimates (Bouchard, 2007; Bouchard & Tremblay, 2005). It provided enough time for dealers and growers to be incarcerated, released, and get back into the game in order to be at risk again.

For sex offenders, a period of 3–4 years is likely to be enough. The time between convictions varies, ranging between 1.5 and 34 months, for a mean of 22 months between convictions. Using 12 or 24 months as a baseline would not provide enough time for the majority of convicted offenders to be incarcerated and released, and thus at risk of being recaptured and reconvicted. In addition to jail time, the court procedures should be taken into account. Too long a time period violates the assumption of a closed population as more offenders may move in and out of the population of interest. Too short a time period will affect the probability of recapture. A period of 2 years would not provide enough time for offenders to get rearrested *and* convicted. Because many sequences were over 24 months, a period of 3–4 years is safest. The data available for the first 387 convictions goes from January 1995 to June 1998, a period of 3 years and 6 months. Those 42 months will be used to estimate the size of the sex offending population at risk of conviction specifically for this time period.

For the sample, the average prison sentence received for the index crime was 4.49 years (SD = 3.84). It is unlikely that sex offenders will serve their entire sentence in prison. The court can impose a condition that requires the offender to serve at least 50% of his sentence in prison. This condition was imposed on only three cases included in this sample. The few empirical studies on the topic suggest that federal inmates will spend about 40% of their sentence in prison, spending the remaining portion in the community on parole (Solicitor General of Canada, 1999). Hence, if the average sentence is about 4 years and 6 months, after 21 months these individuals will most likely be on parole. Those numbers exclude provincial prison sentences that are for less than 2 years, which are more likely to be imposed on offenders having committed a less serious sex offense (e.g., sexual nuisance, gross indecency, voyeurism, etc.).[3]

Estimation Model

Truncated Poisson methods such as Zelterman's (1988) estimator (Z) provide the necessary framework for estimating hidden populations of offenders. If data on known convictions and reconvictions follow the Poisson distribution specified by Z's model, the missing cell in the distribution should be estimated correctly, that is, the number of offenders with zero convictions. For data to follow a general Poisson distribution, a number of assumptions must be respected: (1) the population under study must be closed (no movement in the population); (2) the population has to be homogeneous; (3) the probability for an individual to be observed and reobserved must be held constant during the observation period (the independence assumption).

Such assumptions when using data on criminal populations may not be respected. The first and second assumptions pose obvious difficulties. Offenders tend to go in

[3]There are no data available specifically for the time spent incarcerated for sex offenders having received a provincial sentence. Only one report was found that showed that, in Quebec, inmates serve on average between 45 and 52% of their prison sentence (Service Correctionnel du Québec, 1993). Hence, for these individuals, after 6 months and up to 1 year, they may be on parole in the community.

and out of offending at different periods of their lives; some are more active than others, and they may trigger different probabilities of convictions. This is especially the case when using conviction data as we do here, something discussed in more details below. Moreover, offenders may modify their behavior after release, and the police may also be tempted to over-target them following a successful apprehension, leaving the third assumption unsatisfied. Zelterman (1988) derived a truncated Poisson estimator designed to be robust to departures from these assumptions (see also Collins & Wilson, 1990; Smit, Reinking, & Reijerse, 2002; Smit, Toet, & Van der Heijden, 1997). It is given by:

$$Z = N / \left(1 - e(-2 * n2 / n1)\right)$$

where Z is the total population, N is the total number of individuals convicted with a sexual offending charge, n1 is the number of individuals convicted once, and n2 is the number of individuals convicted twice in a given time period.

Zelterman Regression

One issue with Zelterman's estimator above is the impossibility of controlling for observed heterogeneity in the data. For example, it is entirely conceivable that younger and older offenders have differential probabilities of being convicted, a situation that would affect the Poisson parameter and thus the population estimates. A recent study by Bohning and Van der Heijden (2009) provides an interesting extension to Zelterman's estimator for use with covariates in a regression model. The authors noticed Zelterman's compatibility with standard logistic regression, notably its reliance on a binary outcome, and proceeded to extend the estimator for use with covariates in a logistic regression, a procedure that can be labeled "Zelterman regression." Bohning and Van der Heijden (2009) published a STATA program in supplementary materials provided with the article that has been adapted for use with the present data. Note that running the procedure without covariates is equivalent to using Equation 1 presented above. An added benefit to using the program is the calculation of confidence intervals for every estimate provided, including the no covariate estimate. The addition of covariates to the estimation procedures can account for observed heterogeneity in the data, something the simpler model cannot. However, to the extent that the covariates are not significantly related to the probability of recapture, the total population estimates won't be significantly affected. In other words, if the added covariate is not associated with the probably of recapture, there is little need for covariates and the parsimonious model may be preferred. This procedure does not account for or detect unobserved heterogeneity that may still be present in the models. Zelterman's (1988) estimator, however, has been shown to be robust under potential unobserved heterogeneity (Bohning and Van der Heijden, 2009).

The one covariate of substantive interest in the current study is the age of sexual offenders at time of first conviction. To facilitate the interpretation of risks of incarceration in a situation with few recaptures, we used the median age (36) to divide the sample in two: (1) younger offenders (18–35) and (2) older offenders (36+).

Zelterman's Poisson estimator has a number of attractive features for estimating criminal populations. First, it can minimize the impact of population heterogeneity in arrest risks by eliminating the minority of high-rate offenders with multiple arrests. In fact, Equation 1 shows that only those offenders arrested once (n1) or twice (n2) are considered for establishing the arrest rate (Poisson) parameter, something that is reproduced in the regression model. Zelterman (1988) and other researchers who derived similar models (Chao, 1989), base their approach on the rationale that estimation models should be complex enough to be meaningful, but simple enough to contain only the parameters that are necessary, and close to the quantity to be estimated. In other words, using information on those offenders who are not convicted very often should be more meaningful in assessing the prevalence of nonconvicted offenders.

Another advantage of the model is that it can be used on only one sample (as with conviction data), whereas other capture-recapture approaches require three or more samples to derive estimates. The use of multiple samples is warranted in many situations. For example, someone interested in estimating the total population of drug users should not strictly consider only treatment data (entry and re-entry into treatment), but also possibly arrest and hospital records (Hser, 1993). Using only conviction data confines the interpretation to prevalence estimates of offenders "at risk of being convicted," which may safely be assumed to concern the majority of active sexual offenders.

The Z estimator, however, assumes that the hidden population of interest is a "closed" population. On the one hand, the likelihood of severe departures from this assumption is minimized by the analysis of convictions at an aggregate level (e.g., province of Quebec) rather than at a city or neighborhood level. This procedure does not account for the fact that some offenders may move in and out of the criminally active population, but it reduces the possibility of offenders being excluded from the sample simply because they moved to another city or neighborhood. There is also some indication from the literature that, in most cases, using closed population models on open populations is not a major sin. Kendall's (1999) simulations showed that animal prevalence estimates from closed population models are only minimally affected when movements in the population occur randomly, and when there is no sign of a massive emigration or immigration during the period under study. If the period under study is short enough, criminal population movements are unlikely to be swift and massive enough to have an impact on the prevalence estimates derived from closed population models such as Zelterman's.

One possibility remains, however, for a major violation of the closed population assumption: we rely on incarceration data where offenders are effectively not at risk of recapture for significant periods of time – half the time, on average (21 months incarcerated out of a 42 month follow-up period). This issue cannot be fully resolved here, but we take steps to verify the extent to which it potentially affects our findings. We created a variable "year of first conviction within window period" and use it as a control in our estimation model. If the timing of incarceration has an effect on the probability of recapture (i.e., the later the conviction, the lower the probability of recapture), this variable would emerge as significant in the model. At the same time, controlling for it would reduce some of the potential bias. As shall be seen below, the results show that year of first conviction is not significantly associated with the probability of recapture.[4]

Results

Among our sample of 387 offenders, a total of nine offenders (2.3%) were convicted twice, and none were convicted three times or more during the 42-month window period (WP). The first question of interest is whether reconvicted offenders are any different from others. If they are too different, this may violate the assumption of homogeneity of population. Although too few offenders are found in the reconviction sample to lead to any meaningful separate analyses, the results of comparisons with the various variables found in Table 15.1 (not shown) indicate that these offenders are similar on all characteristics, except one: number of sex-related convictions. The nine offenders who were reconvicted during the window period had significantly more sex-related convictions that others (2.7 vs. 1.4), a difference that disappears once we remove the second WP conviction. Nothing else indicates that this subsample is any different from the other.

How many sex offenders were active but not convicted for a sexual offense during the window period?[5] To answer this question, we applied Zelterman's estimator (first with no covariates) on the frequency distribution of convictions on our sample (Table 15.2). An important criterion in the choice of a model is that it provides a good fit to the data, that is, the distribution of convictions estimated by the model should resemble the observed distribution derived from the data. Results of the goodness-of-fit analysis (Neyman's chi-square test) show that Zelterman's model provides a perfect fit for the data distribution (X2 = 0.00). The estimator performs well with the data because the distributions analyzed have no cases of three or more convictions, parameters that are not captured by the Z model (see Equation 1). In other words, the smaller the proportion of multiple

[4]We don't think it's a complete nonfactor because of this, however. Instead, we feel that this is a statistical power issue. With a larger sample and more recaptures, it would approach significance, in the direction expected: the earlier the first conviction, the higher the probability of reconviction (and vice versa).

[5]Note that the time period considered is important to understand the meaning of the estimate. Here we are solely concerned with offenders who were active during the whole time period of January 1995 to June 1998 where the cumulative incarceration process was taking place.

Table 15.2 Frequency Distribution for Sexual Offense Convictions in Quebec (January 1995 to June 1998) and Estimated Prevalence of Sexual Offending at Risk of Conviction

	Observed	*Theoretical*
Z estimate[a]	8,322	–
CI[b]	(2,890–13,754)	–
N convictions		
0[c]	7,935	–
1	378	378
2	9	9
3+	0	0
Risk of conviction	4.8%	–
Neyman's X^2	–	0.00

[a]As estimated by Equation 1.
[b]Confidence intervals, as estimated using Bohning and Van der Heijden's (2009) procedure.
[c]Z estimate – number of arrested offenders.

arrests (3+), the better the fit.[6] Although goodness-of-fit tests are not truly decisive criteria in the choice of a model (Coull & Agresti, 1999), such a good performance supports the use of the Z estimator and other similar models (e.g., Chao, 1989) in this particular case.

$$\text{Neyman's X2 is given by } X^2 = \frac{\sum\left(n_j - \hat{u}_j\right)^2}{{}^{j-1}n_j}$$

Importantly, Table 15.2 shows that a substantial number of sex offenders were active and never convicted during the window period. Our results indicate that the 387 offenders convicted during the 42-month period were active among a much larger population of 8,322 sex offenders (95% CI = 2,890–13,754), including 7,935 who were active but never convicted. If this estimate proves to be valid, this would mean that over 95% of all sex offenders were allowed to roam free between January 1995 and June 1998, for a risk of conviction of 4.8%.

The model presented in Table 15.2, however, assumes that the incarceration rate is equal for every sexual offender at risk of incarceration. It is entirely conceivable, however, that risks of incarceration vary by age within the sexual aggressor population. For example, prior research has shown that the prevalence of sex offending has a tendency to increase as offenders become older (Cline, 1980; Francis,

[6]It should also be noted that Zelterman's estimator has been shown to perform well as an estimator of hidden populations, even in circumstances where the model fit is weaker than is the case in the present analysis (Bohning, Suppawattanabodee, Kusolvisitkul, & Viwatwongkasem, 2004; Collins & Wilson, 1990; Wilson & Collins, 1992). Other criteria in model evaluation include an estimation of the intervals of confidence generated by the model. Those estimated in the present analysis (using Zelterman, 1988) are narrow enough to be considered meaningful.

Hargreaves, & Soothill, this volume; Marshall, 1997). Unresolved, however, is whether these results are due to differential risks of apprehension – it could well be that younger offenders are simply better at avoiding arrest and conviction, and are thus more rarely found in incarcerated populations.

Bohning and van der Heijden's (2009) extension of Zelterman's model accepts the integration of covariates into the model presented in Table 15.2, such as age. This allows us to (1) verify whether age is significantly associated with the probability of recapture, and (2) estimate separate populations by age group. Using Zelterman regression also allows us to partially assess violation of the closed population assumption by controlling for year at first conviction (the later the conviction, the less likely offenders are released in time to be considered again for a recapture). The Zelterman regression results are presented in Table 15.3. Four models were estimated. The Null model is the no covariate model also presented in Table 15.2. Then we provide estimates for age alone, year of first conviction alone, and both combined in one model (the full model). For each set of estimates,[7] Akaike's information criterion (AIC) indicates which model is a better fit to the data (the smaller the AIC, the better the fit). The logic of AIC will make it biased toward choosing the best fitting, most parsimonious model possible. In other words, it penalizes the addition of nonsignificant variables to models. For each model with covariates, we report whether the model (G^2) is significant (p), the population estimate ($\widehat{\boldsymbol{N}}$), and the 95% confidence interval. The smaller the interval, the more confidence one can have in the $\widehat{\boldsymbol{N}}$ estimate. Although the intervals are strictly based on statistical fit, there are no guarantees that they are more or less on target.

Table 15.3 first shows that none of the models with covariates are statistically significant at the .05 level. None of the variables emerged as significant predictors of the probability of recapture in any models (performance of each separate variable not shown). The best fitting model is the one with year of first conviction added as the only control ($G^2 = 2.86$, $p = .09$). The later the year of first conviction, the lower the probability of recapture. This model yielded an estimate of 11,133 sexual offenders, approximately 3,000 more than the Null model estimate. The confidence

Table 15.3 Capture-Recapture Regression (Zelterman) Estimates of the Number of Serious Sex Offenders in Quebec, January 1995 to June 1998

	AIC	*G^2*	*P*	$\widehat{\boldsymbol{N}}$	*95% CI*
Null[a]	87.49	–	–	8,322	2,890–13,754
Age	88.68	0.81	0.37	9,053	2,270–15,836
Year 1st conviction	86.63	2.86	0.09	11,133	673–21,594
Age + year	87.49	4.0	0.14	12,599	−583–25,780

[a]Same as estimated from Equation 1.

[7]The exception being the Null model where G^2 and p cannot be calculated.

interval, however, is wide (673–21,594), suggesting instability in the estimates when the violation in the closed population is partially taken into account. The full model (age + year) performs even worse as the confidence interval crosses zero (−583–25,780). Overall, however, the prevalence estimates are very close to each other, even to the no covariate (null) model where the confidence intervals are tighter.[8] The Null model, in this case, appears to perform just as well as the others and may be preferred, especially given the potential for overestimation due to violation of the closed population assumption.

Although age is not a significant predictor of the probability of recapture (something we suspect would change should we consider a larger sample), the regression coefficient (not shown) is negative. This suggests that the risks of incarceration may actually decrease – not increase – with age. To illustrate, Table 15.4 presents the prevalence estimates and the risks of incarceration divided by age group. Estimates are extracted from both the age model and the full model where year of first conviction is controlled for.

The results of the age-group analysis in Table 15.4 are consistent with past studies indicating that the prevalence of sex offending increases with age. Although our categories are not exactly comparable (18–35 vs. 36+[9]), older offenders were relatively less likely to be found in the reconvicted category (even if the total number of convictions was larger), leading to a 2.7 times larger population at risk of conviction (9,202 v. 3,397 – full model). The results also show that risks are not equally distributed among sex offenders. Table 15.4 indicates that the risks of conviction are almost twice as high for younger offenders: 4.7% compared to 2.5% for older offenders in the full model.

These results are consistent with the risk assessment literature, suggesting that younger convicted sex offenders are at greater risk of being reconvicted. Studies typically suggest that adult sex offenders between 18 and 24 years of age (Hanson &

Table 15.4 Prevalence Estimates and Risks of Incarceration for Younger and Older Sex Offenders for "Age" and "Age + Year" Models

	Younger (18–35)	*Older (36+)*
	$\widehat{N}$	$\widehat{N}$
Age model	2,494	6,556
Risks of incarceration	6.3 %	3.5%
	$\widehat{N}$	$\widehat{N}$
Age + year model	3,397	9,202
Risks of incarceration	4.7%	2.5%

[8] As noted by a reviewer, the effect of the violation of the closed population, in this case, would lead to a potential overestimation of the total population of sex offenders by superficially decreasing the probability of recapture (because incarcerated) and thus increasing the population at risk of incarceration.

[9] The oldest offender in the sample was 74 years old at time of conviction.

Thornton, 2000) is the group most likely to be reconvicted (although others studies refer to a larger age band to represent the "high-risk" group, e.g., 18–27; 18–30) (see Doren, 2006). The risk of reconviction steadily decreases (about 2% yearly) as the offender's age increases (Lussier & Healey, 2009). Several researchers have stressed the importance of risk assessors recognizing that the risk of reconviction follows the age-crime curve effect in suggesting risk estimates of sexual recidivism for different age groups (Wollert, 2006; Wollert, Cramer, Waggoner, Skelton, & Vess, 2010). A recent study, however, shed a different light on these findings. Lussier, Bouchard, and Beauregard (2011) examined the differential cost avoidance in adult sex aggressors or, in the context of that study, the ability to delay detection and sanction. They found much heterogeneity in sexual aggressors' ability to delay detection, with age being significantly associated with it. The study findings showed that older offenders were better at delaying detection, with some offenders delaying detection for more than 15 and up to 40 years. Hence, it could be argued that the lower risk of reconviction for older sexual aggressors may be attributable to the age effect for most, but also the ability to delay detection for others. Finally, note that the only prior capture-recapture study to examine the differential risks among juvenile and adult offenders also found that younger offenders faced higher risks of detection. Collins and Wilson's (1990) study of the prevalence of auto thieves in Australia found that the smaller population of juvenile thieves was nonetheless overrepresented in court cases because of a collectively higher risk of detection.

Assessing the Plausibility of the Estimates

Assessing the plausibility of the estimates is important, especially in regards to the uncertainty associated with capture-recapture modeling with small samples (Bouchard, 2007). First, consider the ratio of nonconvicted to convicted offenders: the Null model estimate of 8,322 suggests that there would be 20.5 times more non-convicted than convicted serious offenders in Quebec. Although no comparison is truly satisfying given the different samples and methodologies involved, this ratio can be compared to the ones previously found in studies comparing studies based on self-reported information and official data. Recall that Koss et al (1987) found a self-reported rate of sexual offending in the order of 25% for their sample of college men – a rate that was found to be 6–7 times higher than the official conviction rate found in Tracy et al. (1990), 10–15 times the one found in Cline (1980), and 50 times the one found in Marshall (1997). Our rate of 20.5 is right in between those.[10]

Another way to assess the estimate is to consider the rate for the general population of males in Quebec. There were approximately 2,129,136 males in Quebec between the ages of 20 and 64 – a reasonable range as a target population. Our estimate

[10]Variations are expected considering that comparison estimates stem from different studies with different definitions of sex crimes (e.g., Koss's estimates excluded child sexual abuse; Tracy's estimates refers to juvenile sexual offending; Cline's estimates are based on a sample of adjudicated youth).

means that 0.4% (8,322/2,129,136) of Quebec adult males were active sex offenders at risk of conviction between 1995 and 1998. Is this a small or a large number? It's hard to tell, as no prior studies estimated the size of the sexual offending population. Marshall's (1997) study is our closest comparable study, but comparisons are unfair on a number of levels, including the length of the follow-up period. Marshall estimated that in 1993, there were 165,000 males of at least 20 years of age with at least one conviction for a serious sex crime[11] in England and Wales. Considering the size of the male population in 1993, it could be concluded that about 0.89% of the male population had been convicted at least once for a serious sex crime that year. Marshall's estimate, however, is based on the cumulative prevalence rate. In the current study, the prevalence rate at a specific time point was determined, making the comparison difficult.

Conclusion

Both researchers and practitioners typically deal with data or populations found within the criminal justice system. Theoretically, however, we both are interested in all active individuals, not simply the ones who were apprehended and sanctioned within the system. This is the typical problem of the "dark figure" of crime. The proportion of active offenders not passing through the criminal justice system is of considerable interest for many reasons, including knowledge of (a) the success of law enforcement agencies at capturing a sizeable proportion of offenders, and (b) the number of potential victims of a crime, including the ones who never reported their victimization to the authorities. Statistical techniques developed mainly in biology to estimate the size of animal populations have increasingly been used and adapted to the study of human populations, including criminal populations.

In this chapter, we use one such capture-recapture model (Zelterman, 1988) and its extension to consider covariates (Bohning and van der Heijden, 2009) that have been validated in prior studies to estimate the number of serious sexual offenders at risk of incarceration in a Canadian province (Quebec). The data consist of a sample of 387 individuals convicted for a serious sexual offense between January 1995 and June 1998 in Quebec (a quasi-population). The study findings indicate that the 387 incarcerated individuals were active among an estimated 8,000 other sex offenders between January 1995 and June 1998. The risk of being incarcerated was 4.8% for offenders during that time period. We also estimated differential populations and risks for younger (18–35) and older (36+) offenders. The results indicate that 36+ offenders were at least close to three times as numerous as younger ones, with a risk of incarceration twice as small. These results were consistent with past research on

[11]Serious sexual offenses exclude offenses involving obscene materials and indecent exposure but do include the following: rape, buggery, indecent assault on a male or a female, unlawful sexual intercourse, incest, abduction, gross indecency with a child.

age (e.g., Francis et al., this volume; Marshall, 1997) and risk differentials (e.g., Doren, 2006; Hanson & Thornton, 2000; Lussier & Healey, 2009) in sex offending.

Despite those promising results, the current study shares the same limitation as prior capture-recapture studies, namely that the true size of the hidden population is unknown. As much as we consider the use of capture-recapture models as a true contribution in assessing the size of criminal populations, the precision of the estimates remains hard to assess. The current study has a few other limitations that should be taken account, including the fact that only nine offenders managed to get reconvicted for a federal (2+ years) sentence over the course of 42 months. This reconviction rate is dependent on a variety of factors, including court-related factors that may influence the recapture process in a way that arrest data are not subjected to.[12] Relying on a sample of offenders who were incarcerated on average for close to half the window period considered may lead to a potentially serious violation of the closed population assumption. Although we attempted to partially control for the effect of this violation, the solution is hardly fully satisfying and not the last word on this issue. There is a clear need for future studies relying on similar samples of incarcerated offenders to assess the validity of the exercise, and of the solutions provided.

The fact that we relied on conviction data only for offenders sentenced to 2 years or more also influences the meaning of our estimates. As such, we are not estimating the full population of sexual aggressors in the province of Quebec, but only the ones whose offense is serious enough to warrant a sentence to a federal penitentiary. Note, however, that many of the 8,000 sexual aggressors estimated for the purpose of this study may have been captured in other contexts, but simply not a context that led to federal incarceration. The inclusion of provincial court data, and general arrest data, in future studies should lead to the estimation of a potentially much larger pool of active sexual offenders in Quebec.

Notwithstanding those limitations, the study provides the first attempt to estimate the size of the sexual offending population drawing from capture-recapture methods. In doing so, we hoped to spark the interest of the scientific community in undertaking similar efforts locally in search of innovative and informative ways to monitor trends in the criminal careers of sexual offenders.

References

Abbey, A., & McAuslan, P. (2004). A longitudinal examination of male college students' perpetration of sexual assault. *Journal of Consulting and Clinical Psychology*, *72*, 747–756.

Abel, G. G., Becker, J. V., Cunningham-Rathner, J., Rouleau, J. L., & Murphy, W. D. (1987). Self-reported sex crimes of nonincarcerated paraphiliacs. *Journal of Interpersonal Violence*, *2*, 3–25.

[12]Even if an arrest does not lead to a court conviction, it will be officially recorded in police databases. Whether such a police contact related to a nonsuccessful charge for a similar crime qualifies as a "recapture" or not in a given study will have a potentially important impact on the estimates.

Abel, G. G., & Rouleau, J.-L. (1990). The nature and extent of sexual assault. In W. L. Marshall, D. L. Laws, & H. E. Barbaree (Eds.), *Handbook of sexual assault: Issues, theories, and treatment of the offender* (pp. 9–21). New York: Plenum Press.

Blumstein, A., Cohen, J., & Farrington, D. P. (1988). Criminal career research: Its value for criminology. *Criminology, 26*, 1–35.

Blumstein, A., Cohen, J., Roth, J. A., & Visher, C. A. (1986). *Criminal careers and "career criminals"*(Vol. 1). Washington, DC: National Academy Press.

Bohning, D., Suppawattanabodee, B. Kusolvisitkul, W., & Viwatwongkasem, C. (2004). Estimating the number of drug users in Bangkok 2001: A capture-recapture approach using repeated entries in one list. *European Journal of Epidemiology, 19*, 1075–1083.

Bohning, D., & van der Heijden, P. G. M. (2009). A covariate adjustment for zero-truncated approaches to estimating the size of hidden and elusive populations. *The Annals of Applied Statistics, 3*(2), 595–610.

Bouchard, M. (2007). A capture-recapture model to estimate the size of criminal populations and the risks of detection in a marijuana cultivation industry. *Journal of Quantitative Criminology, 23*, 221–241.

Bouchard, M., & Tremblay, P. (2005). Risks of arrest across markets: A capture-recapture analysis of "hidden" dealer and user populations. *Journal of Drug Issues, 34*, 733–754.

Briere, J., & Runtz, M. (1989). University males' sexual interest in children: Predicting potential indices of "pedophilia" in a nonforensic sample. *Child Abuse and Neglect, 13*, 65–75.

Brownmiller, S. (1975). *Against our will: Men, women and rape*. New York: Simon & Schuster.

Chao, A. (1989). Estimating population size for sparse data in capture-recapture experiments. *Biometrics, 45*, 427–438.

Cline, H. F. (1980). Criminal behavior over the life span. In O. J. Brim, Jr. & J. Kagan (Eds.), *Constancy and change in human development* (pp. 641–674). Cambridge: Harvard University Press.

Collins, M. F., & Wilson, R. M. (1990). Automobile theft: Estimating the size of the criminal population. *Journal of Quantitative Criminology, 6*, 395–409.

Coull, B. A., & Agresti, A. (1999). The use of mixed logit models to reflect heterogeneity in capture-recapture studies. *Biometric, 55*, 294–301.

Doren, D. M. (2006). What do we know about the effect of aging on recidivism risk for sexual offenders? *Sexual Abuse: Journal of Research and Treatment, 18*, 137–157.

Farrington, D. P. (1986). Age and crime. In M. Tonry & N. Morris (Eds.), *Crime and justice: A review of research* (Vol. 7, pp. 189–250). Chicago: Chicago University Press.

Fromuth, M. E., Burkhart, B. R., & Jones, C. W. (1991). Hidden child molestation: An investigation of adolescent perpetrators in a nonclinical sample. *Journal of Interpersonal Violence, 6*, 376–384.

Gottfredson, M., & Hirschi, T. (1986). The true value of Lambda would appear to be zero: An essay on career criminals, criminal careers, selective incapacitation, cohort studies, and related topics. *Criminology, 24*, 213–234.

Greendlinger, V., & Byrne, D. (1987). Coercive sexual fantasies of college men as predictors of self-reported likelihood to rape and overt sexual aggression. *The Journal of Sex Research, 23*, 1–11.

Hanson, R. K., & Thornton, D. (2000). Improving risk assessments for sex offenders: A comparison of three actuarial scales. *Law and Human Behavior, 24*, 119–136.

Hirschi, T., & Gottfredson, M. R. (1983). Age and the explanation of crime. *American Journal of Sociology, 89*, 552–584.

Hirschi, T., & Gottfredson, M. R. (1995). Control theory and the life-course perspective. *Studies on Crime and Crime Prevention, 4*, 131–142.

Hser, Y. (1993). Population estimation of illicit drug users in Los Angeles county. *Journal of Drug Issues, 23*, 323–334.

Kendall, L. W. (1999). Robustness of closed capture-recapture methods to violations of the closure assumption. *Ecology, 80*, 2517–2525.

Koss, M. P. (1993). Rape: Scope, impact, interventions, and public policy responses. *American Psychologist, 10*, 1062–1069.

Koss, M. P., Gidycz, C. A., & Wisniewski, N. (1987). The scope of rape: Incidence and prevalence of sexual aggression and victimization in a national sample of higher education. *Journal of Consulting and Clinical Psychology, 55*, 162–170.

Lussier, P. (2005). The criminal activity of sexual offenders in adulthood: Revisiting the specialization debate. *Sexual Abuse: A Journal of Research and Treatment, 17*, 269–292.

Lussier, P., Bouchard, M., & Beauregard, E. (2011). Patterns of criminal achievement in sexual offending: Unravelling the "successful sex offender." *Journal of Criminal Justice, 39*, 433–444.

Lussier, P., & Healey, J. (2009). Rediscovering Quetelet, again: The "aging" offender and the prediction of reoffending in a sample of adult sex offenders. *Justice Quarterly, 28*, 1–30.

Lussier, P., Leclerc, B., Healey, J., & Proulx, J. (2008). Generality of deviance and predation: Crime-switching and specialization patterns in persistent sexual offenders. In M. Delisi & P. Conis (Eds.), *Violent offenders: Theory, public policy and practice* (pp. 97–140). Boston, MA: Jones and Bartlett Publishers.

Malamuth, N. (1981). Rape proclivity among males. *Journal of Social Issues, 37*, 138–157.

Malamuth, N. (1989). The attraction to sexual aggression scale: Part I. *Journal of Sex Research, 26*, 26–49.

Marshall, P. (1997). *The prevalence of convictions for sexual offending*. Research Findings, No. 55. London, UK: Home Office Research and Statistics Directorate.

Marshall, W. L., Barbaree, H. E., & Eccles, A. (1991). Early onset and deviant sexuality in child molesters. *Journal of Interpersonal Violence, 6*, 325–335.

Moffitt, T. (1993). Adolescence-limited and life-course-persistent antisocial behavior: A developmental taxonomy. *Psychological Review, 100*, 674–701.

Rind, B., Tromovich, P., & Bauserman, R. (1998). A meta-analytic examination of assumed properties of child sexual abuse using college samples. *Psychological Bulletin, 124*, 22–53.

Rowe, D. C., Osgood, D. W., & Nicewander, W. A. (1990). A latent trait approach to unifying criminal careers. *Criminology, 28*, 237–270.

Senn, C. Y., Desmarais, S., Verbeg, N., & Wood, E. (2000). Predicting coercive sexual behavior across the lifespan in a random sample of Canadian men. *Journal of Social and Personal Relationships, 17*, 95–113.

Service Correctionnel du Québec. (1993). Analyse de l'effet de certains facteurs sur la durée de la peine purgée. *Faits and Chiffres: Bulletin d'Information sur la Recherche Correctionnelle, 1*, 1.

Smit, F., Reinking, D., & Reijerse, M. (2002). Estimating the number of people eligible for health service use. *Evaluation and Program Planning, 25*, 101–105.

Smit, F., Toet, J., van der Heijden, P. (1997). Estimating the number of opiate users in Rotterdam using statistical models for incomplete count data. In European Monitoring Centre for Drugs and Drug Addiction (EMCDDA), *1997 Methodological Pilot Study of Local Prevalence Estimates*. Lisbon: EMCDDA.

Solicitor General of Canada. (1999). Corrections and conditional release statistical overview. Ottawa, Ontario: Public Works and Government Services Canada.

Sorensen, S. B., Stein, J. A., Siegel, J. M., Golding, J. M., & Burnam, M. A., (1987). The prevalence of adult sexual assault: The Los Angeles epidemiological catchment area project. *American Journal of Epidemiology, 126*, 1154–1164.

Spitzberg, B. H. (1999). An analysis of empirical estimates of sexual aggression victimization and perpetration. *Violence and Victims, 14*, 241–260.

Templeman, T. L., & Stinnett, R. D. (1991). Patterns of sexual arousal and history in a "normal" sample of young men. *Archives of Sexual Behavior, 20*, 137–150.

Tracy, P. E., Wolfgang, M. E., & Figlio, R. M. (1990). *Delinquency careers in two birth cohorts.* New York: Plenum Press.

Tremblay, P. (2010). *Le délinquant idéal.* Montreal: Liber.

Visher, C. A, & Roth, J. A. (1986). Participation in criminal careers. In A. Blumstein, J. Cohen, J. A. Roth, & C. A. Visher (Eds.), *Criminal careers and "career criminals"* (Vol. 1, pp. 211–291). Washington. DC: National Academy Press.

Weinrott, M. R., & Saylor, M. (1991). Self-report of crimes committed by sex offenders. *Journal of Interpersonal Violence, 6*, 286–300.

Wilson, R. M., Collins, M. F. (1992). Capture-recapture estimation with samples of size one using frequency data. *Biometrika, 79*, 543–554.

Wolfgang, M. E., Figlio, R. M., & Sellin, T. (1972). *Delinquency in a birth cohort.* Chicago: University of Chicago Press.

Wollert, R. (2006). Low base rates limit expert certainty when current actuarials are used to identify sexually violent predators. *Psychology, Public Policy, and Law, 12*, 56–85.

Wollert, R., Cramer, E., Waggoner, J., Skelton, A., & Vess, J. (2010). Recent research (n = 9,305) underscores the importance of using age-stratified actuarial tables in sex offender risk assessments. *Sexual Abuse: A Journal of Research and Treatment, 22*, 471–490.

Zelterman D. (1988). Robust estimation in truncated discrete distributions with applications to capture-recapture experiments. *Journal of Statistical Planning and Inference, 18*, 225–237.

16

Potential for Redemption for Sex Offenders

Kiminori Nakamura
University of Maryland, USA

Alfred Blumstein
Carnegie Mellon University, USA

Introduction

As a response to the public's concerns about the potential risk of sex predators, sex offender registration laws were originally developed and designed to control and monitor offenders who had been convicted of violent sex offenses. In the United States, the well-publicized sex offender laws named after victims, such as Jessica's Law in 2005 and Megan's Law in 1996, are based on incidents where children were violently victimized by previously convicted sex offenders.[1] Sex offender laws in other countries have been enacted in similar circumstances. For instance, in Canada, the well-publicized case of 11-year-old Christopher Stephenson, who was sexually assaulted and murdered by a person with a history of violent sex crimes, led to Christopher's Law in Ontario, and provided impetus to enact the federal Sex Offender Information Registration Act in 2004. In the United Kingdom, following the public outrage over the murder of 8-year-old Sarah Payne by a convicted pedophile, tougher measures for child sex offenders were introduced as part of the Sexual Offenses Act 2003.[2]

[1]In 1994, the Congress passed the Jacob Wetterling Crimes Against Children Act, which required all 50 states to establish a system of sex offender registration. The Wetterling Act was amended in 1996 to allow for community notification (Megan's Law). Jessica's Law was first passed in Florida and then subsequently passed by a total of 24 states by 2006, which increased penalties for sex offenders, including mandatory minimum sentences, electronic monitoring, and residence restrictions.

[2]Compared with the United States, Canada and the United Kingdom have taken more cautious measures to control sex offenders by weighing the public safety risk posed by sex offenders and the human rights of the offenders and by implementing pilot projects to test the effectiveness of such measures (Lieb, Kemshall, & Thomas, 2011; Petrunik, Murphy, & Fedoroff, 2008).

Sex Offenders: A Criminal Career Approach, First Edition. Edited by Arjan Blokland and Patrick Lussier.

Those cases involving a murder of a child by a person with a history of violent sex offenses have surely increased the public fear about sex offenders. According to a 2005 U.S. Gallup poll, 66% of people surveyed were "very concerned" about child molesters, compared to 52% who were concerned about violent crime, and 36% who were concerned about terrorism (Carroll, 2005; see also the *Economist* August 24, 2006). As the public demands that more has to be done about managing sex offenders, legislatures, with their limited repertoires, can only respond by increasing the breadth and length of registration and imposing more restrictions on the lives of sex offenders.

In the United States, the breadth of offenses covered by sex offense registries, which are now adopted by all 50 states, is expansive.[3] According to the National Center for Missing and Exploited Children (2010), about 728,000 sex offenders are currently registered in the United States.[4] In many states, those who commit not only offenses that are of violent nature, but also nonviolent, relatively minor crimes, such as urinating in public, prostitution, and consensual sex between teenagers, are required to register as sex offenders (Human Rights Watch, 2007).[5] Moreover, an increasing number of states seem to be expanding sex offender laws to include nonsexual offenders based on the assumption that some nonsexual offenses, such as burglary and robbery, signify leading indicators of future sex offenses (Sample & Bray, 2003).

The length of time for which those who were convicted of sex offenses are required to register is often very lengthy as well. For example, in the State of New York, from where the data for the analysis presented in the current study come, sex offenders must stay on the registry for 20 years to life.[6] New York is not alone in imposing a permanent registration requirement in the United States: in 17 states, the length of registration is now for life (Human Rights Watch, 2007). Once registered, sex offenders will be under continuous public scrutiny (Matson & Lieb, 1997). Online registries post not only their names and the nature of the offenses they committed, but also their photos and current address. As the fear and hostility against sex offenders increase, those who are registered as sex offenders face harassment and a lack of privacy, difficulties in finding housing and employment, and potentially diminished chances of reintegration into society (Levenson & Cotter 2005; Levenson, Zgoba, & Tewksbury, 2007; Socia, 2011; Tewksbury, 2005; Tewksbury & Lees 2006).

[3]The trend in recent legislation is to increase the number of covered offenses subject to registration (Adams, 2002; Harris & Lobanov-Rostovsky, 2010; Harris, Lobanov-Rostovsky, & Levenson, 2010).

[4]The number more than doubled from about 386,000 registered sex offenders in 2001 (Adams, 2002).

[5]Likewise, in the United Kingdom and Canada, since underage teenagers engaged in consensual sex can be convicted under those countries' respective sex offender laws, they could possibly be placed on the sex offender registry as well.

[6]Based on a variety of factors, such as the use of force, weapons, alcohol, or drugs, and the victim's age, sex offenders in New York are assigned a risk level (1 for low risk of repeating the offense, 2 for moderate risk, and 3 for high risk). Level 2 and Level 3 sex offenders, as well as those who have special designations of "sexual predator," "sexually violent offender," or "predicate sex offender," are required to register for life (for more information, see the website of the New York State Division of Criminal Justice Services: http://criminaljustice.state.ny.us/nsor/risk_levels.htm).

The severity of restrictions imposed upon sex offenders' lives is considerable; also, the length of registration seems to be set arbitrarily and does not seem to be based on any empirical assessment of their risk to public safety.[7] If the justification for the registration is the concern about sex offenders' risk of committing another crime (sexual in nature or otherwise), then it seems reasonable to base the length of registration on the assessment of that recidivism risk.

Recidivism of Sex Offenders

The justification for the measures that severely handicap sex offenders' lives seems to hinge upon the belief that sex offenders are inherently compulsive recidivists, and without close monitoring their recidivism is almost inevitable (Sample & Bray, 2003; Simon, 2003; Zimring, 2004). In contrast, however, there is reasonable consensus among studies that only a minority of sex offenders recidivate (e.g., Hanson & Bussière, 1998; Lussier, 2005; Sample & Bray 2003). There are several factors that are important to consider in reviewing past studies on the recidivism of sex offenders. First, depending on the base population of sex offenders, the recidivism rate varies significantly. The base population can be defined as those who are arrested, convicted, incarcerated, treated, or even self-reported for sex offenses. The choice of the base population has important implications. For example, convicted sex offenders who were referred to psychiatric assessment and treatment (Langevin et al., 2004) are likely to have a different level of recidivism risk from those who are simply arrested or convicted for sex offenses. Also, since the sex offender registration is not limited to those who are incarcerated as a result of sex crime conviction, and those who are convicted but are not sentenced to prison or jail are still required to register, examining the recidivism based on only incarcerated sex offenders addresses a population of sex offenders that could well be considerably different from all those required to register.

Second, the overall recidivism rate (cumulative proportion of sex offenders who recidivate), which is often used as a measure of sex offenders' recidivism risk, may not be as informative as one might think in examining the level of recidivism risk for sex offenders. The recidivism rate varies as a function of the length of the follow-up. More specifically, as Soothill (2010) points out, the longer the follow-up, the larger the recidivism rate becomes because there is more time for the offenders to commit a new crime. Prentky, Lee, Knight, and Cerce (1997) report findings from a 25-year follow-up study of sex offender recidivism. Not surprisingly, the cumulative recidivism rate is higher at later time points during the follow-up. The recidivism (reconviction) rate for rapists was 11, 16, 20, 23, and 24% after 5, 10, 15, 20, and 25 years, respectively. What is more interesting and important than the increasing

[7]The United Kingdom's Sexual Offences Act 2003 and Canada's Sex Offender Information Registration Act both require subsets of sex offenders to register for an indefinite length of time. Similar to the situation in the United States, the length does not seem to be based on any empirical evidence of risk posed by the registered offenders (Thomas, 2009).

recidivating proportions is that the *changes* in the proportions are smaller as time passes (5, 4, 3, and 1%). This suggests that the longer the rapists stayed without reconviction, the lower their risk of recidivism became. This is consistent with the findings of many recidivism studies: the risk of recidivism declines with time clean since the last arrest, conviction, or incarceration. The rate of eventual recidivism cannot adequately characterize the recidivism risk of those who have stayed crime-free for a long time, and it is important to examine the *conditional* recidivism risk as a function of the law-abiding period.

Third, it is important to assess sex offenders' recidivism in comparison with the recidivism of other types of offenders. The justification for imposing especially lengthy registration requirements and other restrictions specifically on sex offenders is based on the presumption that sex offenders must have a higher risk of recidivism than other offenders, especially in terms of recidivism for sex crimes. Several studies have compared the recidivism risk of sex offenders against that of nonsex offenders. A study by the Bureau of Justice Statistics compared the recidivism of sex offenders and nonsex offenders who were all released from state prisons in 1994 (Langan, Schmitt, & Durose, 2003). The study shows that within a 3-year follow-up, released sex offenders were much less likely to be rearrested for any type of offense than released nonsex offenders (43 vs. 68%). The study also shows, however, that sex offenders were four times more likely to be rearrested for a sex offense than released nonsex offenders (5.3 vs. 1.3%). Other studies have also shown the same pattern: while sex offenders have a lower risk of overall recidivism (committing any type of offense) than nonsex offenders, sex offenders have a higher risk of sex offense recidivism than nonsex offenders (e.g., Hanson, Scott, & Steffy, 1995; Sipe, Jensen, & Everett, 1998). The literature on offense specialization also offers some insights into the tendency of sex offenders to repeat sex crimes over their criminal careers. In general, studies tend to suggest that sex offenders are no more specialized than other types of offenders (e.g., Harris, Smallbone, Dennison, & Knight, 2009; Miethe, Olson, & Mitchell, 2006; Simon, 2000). However, there is variety across subtypes of sex offenders in their tendency to specialize; for example, child molesters tend to specialize more than rapists (Harris et al., 2009; Miethe et al., 2006).

Finally, there is considerable evidence that sex offenders are not a homogeneous group with regard to recidivism risk (Hanson, 2002; Lussier, 2005; Rice & Harris, 1997; Sample & Bray 2006; Soothill, 2010). As discussed earlier, the label of sex offender provokes a strong perception among the public that sex offenders are violent recidivists. As an increasing number of offenses, from forcible rape to public urination, are all categorized as sex offenses and universally subject to harsh restrictions, it is crucial to examine the heterogeneity of sex offenders with respect to their recidivism. In particular, since violent sex crime is of primary concern, analyzing the recidivism of violent compared to nonviolent sex offenders could be informative. If only an identifiable subset of sex offenders is shown to have the level of recidivism risk that the public should be concerned about, then the laws should be"recalibrated to more closely reflect the empirical realities of recidivism among sex offenders" (Sample & Bray 2006, p. 98).

Relevance of Past Criminal Record and Potential for Redemption

One major rationale behind the law that requires sex offenders to register and that allows law enforcement as well as the public to monitor the sex offenders' whereabouts closely is that there is a general recognition among stakeholders (law enforcement, policymakers, the public) that a strong positive relationship exists between past and future criminal offending. The continuity in criminal behavior has been validated by many studies (Blumstein, Farrington, & Moitra, 1985; Brame, Bushway, & Paternoster, 2003; Farrington, 1987; Piquero, Farrington, & Blumstein, 2003). While these studies lend support to policymakers who would support life-long registration requirements for sex offenders, these policymakers would also be well advised by some interlinked lines of research in criminology, which present equally strong evidence of desistance from crime in a subpopulation of those with past offenses. One line of research argues that changes in the life course of offenders affect their risk of future involvement in crime. For example, it is well established that a stable marriage and employment are powerful predictors of such desistance (Sampson & Laub, 1993; Sampson, Laub, & Wimer, 2006; Uggen, 1999; Warr, 1998). Also, in another line of research, the age-crime curve demonstrates a steady decline in criminal activity after a peak in the late teens and young-adult period, and aging is one of the most powerful explanations of desistance (Farrington, 1986; Hirschi & Gottfredson, 1983; Sampson & Laub, 1993, 2003).

Most importantly for the current study, time clean since the last offense strongly affects the relationship between past and future offending behavior. Studies on recidivism consistently demonstrate that those who have offended in the past will have the highest probability of reoffending within several years, and the probability will decline steadily afterwards (Beck & Shipley, 1997; Gottfredson, 1999; Langan et al., 2003; Langan & Levin, 2002; Maltz, 1984; Schmidt & Witte, 1988; Visher, Lattimore, & Linster, 1991). A study that tracked released U.S. prisoners shows that of all those who were rearrested in the first 3 years, approximately two thirds were arrested in the first year, indicating the declining recidivism rate over time (Beck & Shipley, 1997; Langan & Levin, 2002). Based on the same study on released U.S. prisoners, of all released sex offenders who were rearrested in the first 3 years, more than half (56%) were arrested in the first year (Langan et al., 2003).[8]

There have been numerous other studies showing that recidivism occurs relatively quickly. However, little attention has been paid to the smaller population of ex-offenders who stay crime-free for an extended period of time. Recent papers have shed some light on the population characterized by long-time avoidance of crime (Blumstein & Nakamura, 2009; Bushway, Nieuwbeerta, & Blokland, 2011; Kurlychek, Brame, & Bushway, 2006, 2007; Soothill & Francis, 2009). Examining the hazard, they show that the risk of offending for those with criminal records converges toward the risk for those without a record as substantial time passes. Blumstein and Nakamura (2009) used the concept of "redemption" to describe

[8]Similar recidivism patterns are found among registered sex offenders in New York (Krueger, 2007).

the phenomenon that the recidivism risk of those with a prior criminal record declines to appropriate benchmarks. These authors estimated redemption times as time points when the recidivism risk falls below the arrest risk of the general population and when it becomes "close enough" to the risk of those without a prior record. It is important to note that the process of redemption has been demonstrated using data from different contexts: Kurlychek et al. (2006, 2007) relied on birth-cohort data from two U.S. cities (Philadelphia, Pennsylvania and Racine, Wisconsin), Blumstein and Nakamura (2009) used criminal-history record data from one U.S. state (New York), and Soothill and Francis (2009) and Bushway et al. (2011) used data from an entire country (England and Wales, and the Netherlands, respectively).

The idea of redemption and redemption time is relevant to the policy and laws concerning sex offenders. In particular, the length of sex offender registration can take into consideration the redemption time. If the risk of recidivism for sex offenders is sufficiently low beyond the redemption time, it may be appropriate for sex offenders who stay clean longer than redemption times established for sex offenders to be a priority for lifting registration requirements, public notification, and other restrictions that incur implementation and administration costs and require scarce resources from law enforcement agencies, probation, and parole.

In the current research, we first examine the relatively long-term recidivism risk of sex offenders and compare it with the recidivism risk of nonsex offenders. To begin to address the possible recidivism heterogeneity among sex offenders, we distinguish violent and nonviolent sex offenders. We then address the question of redemption: when an old record of a sex crime may sufficiently lose its relevance as an indicator of future sex-crime recidivism.

Data

The data we used consist of the criminal history of first-time adult arrestees in 1980, 1985, and 1990 in New York State, with the total of approximately 198,000 individuals (70,000, 63,000, and 65,000 individuals in the 3 years, respectively).[9,10] We focus

[9]We focus on those who were arrested for sex offenses instead of those who were convicted mainly because the measurement error associated with the use of arrest (error of commission or false positive) is likely to be smaller than the error associated with the use of conviction (error of omission or false negative) (Blumstein & Cohen, 1979). Because offenders are likely to plead to nonsexual offenses in order to avoid the long-lasting stigma of being registered as sex offenders, arrest data have been used in sex offender recidivism studies (Sample & Bray, 2003, 2006).

[10]The data from three sampling years (1980, 1985, and 1990) are combined to secure a sample size that is sufficient for reasonably precise estimation. This is especially necessary for this study, which focuses on sex offenders, who constitute a small portion of the entire first-time arrestee population. It should be noted that, based on a separate analysis (Nakamura & Blumstein, 2011), there is reasonable robustness in recidivism patterns across the three sampling years, especially after about 5 years from the first arrest, where redemption is more relevant. This provides some justification for aggregating data from the three sampling years and estimating recidivism risk based on the combined data. There may be a possibility

on individuals whose age at first arrest (A_1) is between 19 and 50 and whose crime type of arrest (C_1) was categorized as violent sex (VS), nonviolent sex (NVS), violent (V), property (P), drug (D), and public-order crimes (PO), and a remaining group of "others."[11,12] VS is represented by forcible rape, which involves forcible sexual intercourse without the victim's consent. NVS crimes are represented by non-rape sexual assault and non-prostitution sex offenses, which, under the Uniform Crime Report (UCR) coding, include offenses such as incest, indecent exposure, statutory rape, and other forms of sexual abuse.[13]

As discussed above, several past studies have found that sex offenders are not homogeneous with respect to their recidivism patterns (Hanson, 2002; Lussier, 2005; Rice & Harris, 1997; Sample & Bray, 2006; Soothill, 2010). In particular, within a short follow-up, rapists exhibit a higher recidivism rate than child molesters, whereas molesters show a higher recidivism rate than rapists as the follow-up time increases (Hanson, 2002; Rice & Harris, 1997). This suggests that the recidivism risk of rapists declines with age, while the recidivism risk of child molesters declines more slowly (Hanson, 2002; Rice & Harris, 1997).

Findings from previous studies showed that the relationship between recidivism risk and A_1 might be quite different depending on C_1. To address this interaction, we used two ranges of A_1 (19–30, 31–50) in estimating recidivism risk and designated them as "Younger" and "Older" offenders, respectively.[14] Table 16.1 provides the distribution of the sample by A_1 and C_1. It is important to first observe that sex crime (VS or NVS) is rare, and only about 3% of the first-time arrestees were arrested for sex crimes. Figures 16.1a–16.1d show the distributions (histograms) of A_1 for C_1 = V, P, VS, NVS, with an exponential fit to the histograms. The exponential relationship between A_1 (x) and relative frequency (y) is expressed by the two-parameter

that the recidivism of sex offenders is affected by the sex offender laws, which may increase the recidivism risk by limiting their legitimate opportunities or may decrease the recidivism risk by the threat of further restrictions on their life as deterrence. Although the issue regarding the effects of sex offender laws on recidivism is beyond the scope of this study, based on the fact that a major sex offender law in New York (the Sex Offender Registration Act) was enacted in 1996, the majority of the follow-up time in this study does not overlap with the time during which the sex offender law in New York was in effect. Thus, the effect of the law on the estimates of recidivism risk should be minimal.

[11]The reason to focus on the 19 and above age range is that the arrestees whose ages are between 16 and 18 are considered "youthful offenders" in New York and their criminal records are often sealed.

[12]Violent crimes are designated to include robbery, aggravated assault, and simple assault. Property crimes are designated to include burglary, larceny, motor vehicle theft, stolen property, forgery, fraud, and embezzlement. Drug crimes include both possession and sales of any controlled substance. The category "All" is for all crime types except driving under the influence (DUI).

[13]There are other characteristics of the offenders that can affect the recidivism risk. Most notably, race has been shown to be an important predictor of recidivism (e.g., Beck & Shipley 1997; Langan & Levin 2002). However, the differentiation of redemption by race is not central to the issue addressed in this study, which is the length of sex offender registration and notification.

[14]These two age ranges are used to characterize "Younger" and "Older" offenders in order to contrast potential differences in recidivism patterns by age at first arrest and also to secure large enough sample sizes for reasonable estimation.

Table 16.1 Initial Sample Size (Arrested), by Age at First Arrest (A_1) and First Offense (C_1) (Row Percentages in Brackets)

	C_1							
A_1	*VS*	*NVS*	*V*	*P*	*D*	*PO*	*Others*	*Total*
A_1 = 19–30	410 (.5)	1,466 (1.9)	14,243 (18.2)	29,230 (37.3)	14,443 (18.4)	11,550 (14.7)	6,975 (8.9)	78,317
A_1 = 31–50	268 (.8)	1,330 (4.0)	6,105 (18.2)	12,509 (37.2)	5,076 (15.1)	4,937 (14.7)	3,383 (10.1)	33,608
Total	678	2,796	20,348	41,739	19,519	16,487	10,358	111,925

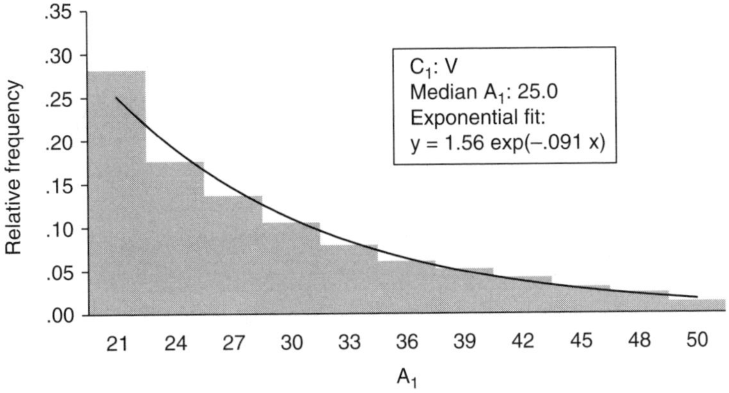

Figure 16.1a A_1 distribution for C_1 = V.

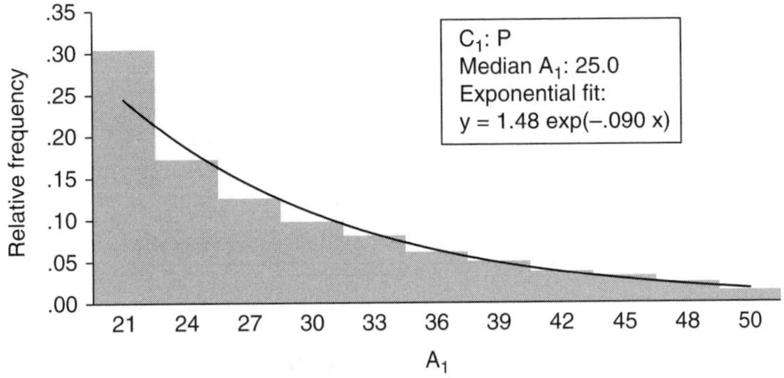

Figure 16.1b A_1 distribution for C_1 = P.

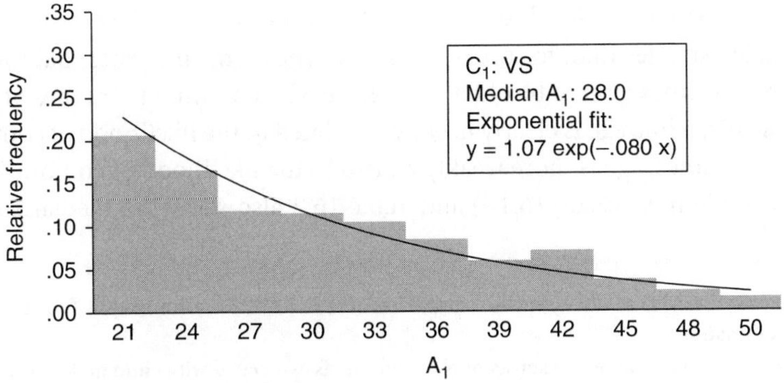

Figure 16.1c A_1 distribution for C_1 = VS.

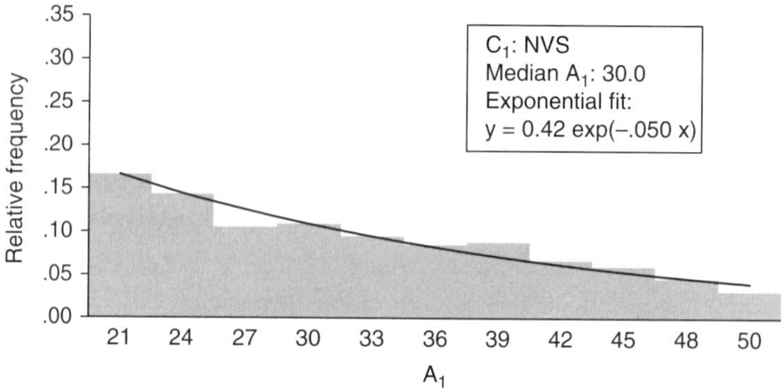

Figure 16.1d A_1 distribution for C_1 = NVS.

Table 16.2 Exponential Parameter Estimates and Median of A_1 Distribution

	Parameter estimates		
C_1	*a*	*b*	*Median* A_1
V	1.56	−.091	25.0
P	1.48	−.090	25.0
VS	1.07	−.080	28.0
NVS	.42	−.050	30.0

equation: $y(x) = a \cdot e^{bx}$, where $a = y(0)$, the relative frequency of the youngest A_1, and b is the constant rate of change by a factor e.[15] The estimated parameter values in Table 16.2 shed light on the similarities and differences of these crime types' age distributions.

First, the estimates of *b* for V and P are strikingly similar, which indicates that the participation rate of those two crimes declines with age in a very similar way. The estimate of *b* for VS is quite close to those of V and P, whereas the estimate for NVS is appreciably smaller than for the other crime types. This indicates that those who commit NVS crimes tend to be older than those who commit other types of crime.[16] In other words, while age is clearly negatively related to the likelihood of committing V, P, and VS crimes, age is more weakly related to the likelihood of committing NVS crimes. The Figures (16.1a–16.1d) and Table 16.2 also show the median ages, and

[15]The equation: $\ln y(x) = \ln a + bx$ (the natural log of $y(x) = a \cdot e^{bx}$) is estimated by OLS to obtain the parameter estimates.

[16]This may suggest that at least a subset of NVS offenses is associated with child molestation, which is shown to be committed by offenders who are older than other sex offenders such as rapists (Hanson, 2002).

they confirm the fact that sex offenders, particularly NVS offenders, tend to be older than other types of offenders.

Analytic Strategy

In order to characterize and compare the recidivism patterns of arrestees, we make use of two statistics that are commonly used in survival analysis: survival probability and hazard. Survival probability is the probability of surviving beyond time *t* without a subsequent arrest. We define *T* as the random variable that represents the time to the subsequent arrest. Survival probability, *S(t)*, is calculated as:

$$S(t) = \Pr(T > t) = \frac{\text{\# of arrestees who have not had a new arrest by the end of time period } t}{\text{Total number of arrestees in the 1980, 1985, and 1990 samples}}$$

Survival probability can be used to describe the proportion of those who have not recidivated by some time point, which is 1 minus the "recidivism rate" used in most recidivism studies.

While survival probability is useful in describing the cumulative rate of recidivism, we use hazard to understand how the risk of recidivism varies with time clean. Hazard is defined as the conditional probability of a new arrest at time *t*, given survival to *t* without an arrest (Hess, Serachitopol, & Brown, 1999; Wooldridge, 2002).[17] This is the quantity that describes the *conditional* risk of recidivism for those who have remained crime-free since the initial arrest.[18]

In calculating *h(t)*, we count a new arrest (after their initial arrest in 1980, 1985, or 1990) for *any* offense type.[19,20] Thus, for example, a new arrest is marked

[17]More precisely, hazard, *h(t)*, can be expressed as follows: $h(t) = \lim_{\Delta \downarrow 0} \frac{\Pr(t \le T < t + \Delta t | T \ge t)}{\Delta t}$. Thus *h(t)* is the instantaneous rate of a new arrest at time *t*. For small values of Δt, $\Pr(t \le T < t + \Delta t | T \ge t) \approx h(t)\Delta t$. Thus, the hazard can approximate the conditional probability.

[18]In order to reduce random fluctuations that prevent us from capturing the overall trend of the hazard, we smooth hazard estimates using kernel smoothing (Klein & Moeschberger, 2005; Wang, 2005). The kernel-smoothed estimator of *h(t)* is a weighted average of crude hazards over the interval (*t–b*, *t+b*) where *b* is the bandwidth or window width that controls the smoothness of the hazard estimates. The weights are provided by kernel functions such as uniform, Gaussian, and Epanechnikov; the uniform kernel assigns an equal weight to the points in the interval, while other kernels assign more weights to the points closer to t. It's been shown that the choice of kernel does not affect the resulting hazard estimate (Hess et al., 1999). The Epanechnikov kernel is most commonly used, and it is used in our analysis.

[19]Throughout our analyses, we ignore all DUI arrests because DUI arrests are so prevalent that including them would distort our results.

[20]In some cases, we find that an arrest is followed quickly by another arrest. We are concerned that what seems to be a new "arrest" might be related to the same crime event as the prior arrest (e.g., transfer to a different jurisdiction), so we count an arrest as a new arrest only if it occurs at least 30 days after the prior arrest.

when a person whose first arrest occurred in 1980 for a sex offense is rearrested for any offense (sex offense or otherwise). We estimate the hazard, given conditions at the first arrest, namely the arrestee's age A_1 and the crime type C_1 of the first arrest.

Results

Survival probabilities for sex offenders and other types of offenders are shown in Figure 16.2a and Figure 16.2b (the horizontal bold line of *S(t)* = .7 is added as a reference). It is first important to note that the Younger offenders have lower survival probabilities than the Older offenders. Regardless of offense type, 70% of the Younger offenders were rearrested within 6 years after the first arrest, whereas 70% of only V and P offenders were rearrested after 10 years. This is consistent with the criminological literature that those with an early onset have a more serious criminal career (Piquero, Farrington, & Blumstein, 2007).

NVS offenders have the highest survival probability for both age groups. The Younger VS offenders have a relatively low survival probability similar to V offenders, so it suggests that despite the sexual nature of their offense, the Younger VS offenders are just like other types of violent offenders. The Older VS offenders, on the other hand, have a relatively high survival probability similar to NVS offenders, so even among VS offenders, there may be differences in recidivism patterns depending on their age.

The analysis of survival probability illustrates the strong effect of A_1, which is that the Older offenders have a much higher probability of surviving without rearrest. While survival probability is informative about the cumulative probability of recidivism, hazard is informative about the instantaneous rearrest risk at *t*.

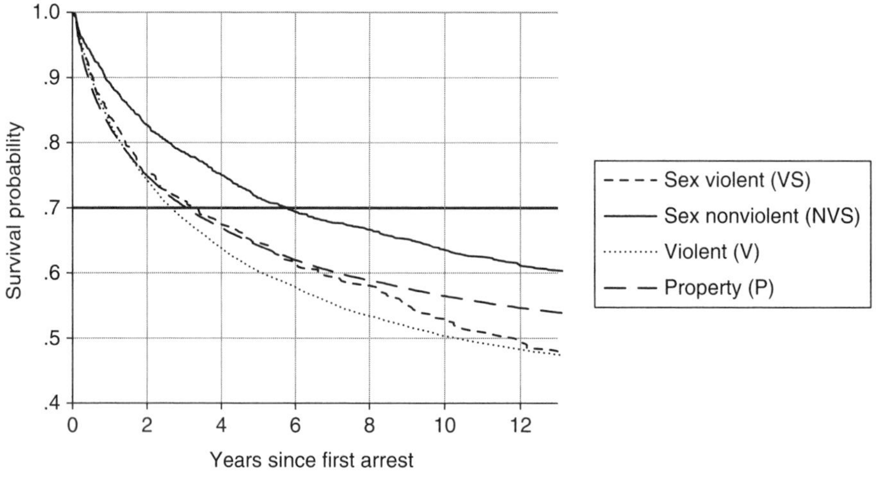

Figure 16.2a Survival probability (*S(t)*) as a function of C_1 for A_1 = 19–30.

Figure 16.3a and Figure 16.3b show the hazards for the two A_1 groups (19–30, 31–50) as a function of C_1.[21] Importantly, the hazards decline as time since the first arrest increases for all crime types. This means that, just as for other types of offenders, for sex offenders, the longer an offender stays crime-free, the lower the risk of recidivism becomes.

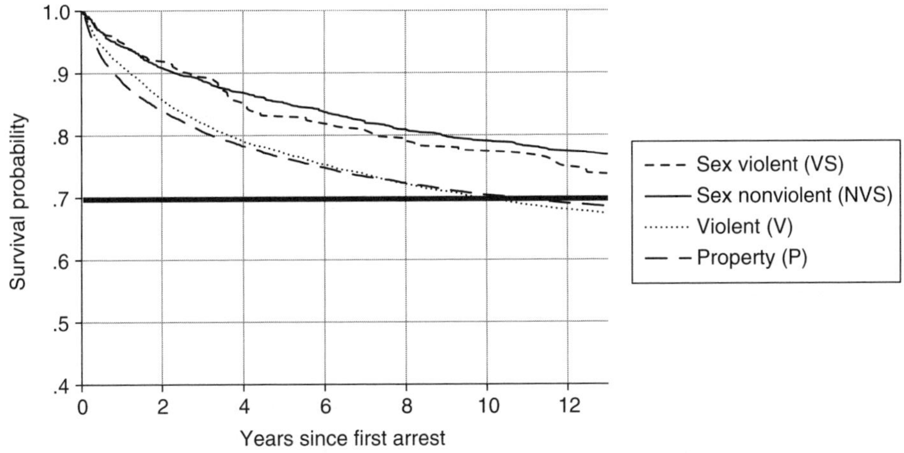

Figure 16.2b Survival probability (*S(t)*) as a function of C_1 for A_1 = 31–50.

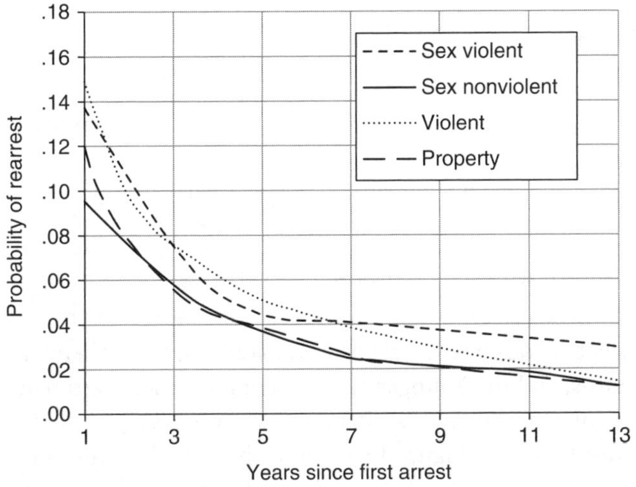

Figure 16.3a *h(t)* for A_1 = 19–30 by C_1.

[21]It should be noted that the maximum on the vertical axis (probability of rearrest) is .18 in Figure 16.3a and .10 in Figure 16.3b, which illustrates that, in general, younger A_1 is associated with higher *h(t)*.

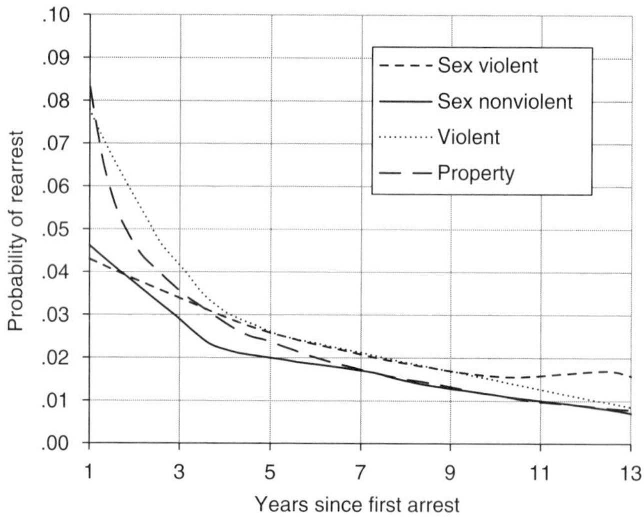

Figure 16.3b *h(t)* for A_1 = 31–50 by C_1.

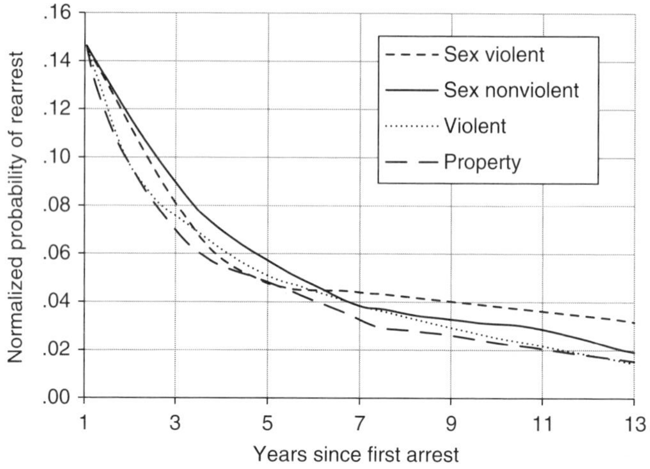

Figure 16.4a Normalized hazard *h(t)* for A_1 = 19–30 by C_1.

Similar to what we observe in survival probabilities, NVS offenders tend to have the lowest hazards, and the Younger VS offenders show a hazard pattern similar to V offenders, while the Older VS offenders are more similar to the Older NVS offenders. Figure 16.4a and Figure 16.4b show the same hazards but normalized to the hazard of V offenders at $t = 0$. These normalized hazards demonstrate the hazards' rate of decline relative to that of the hazard of V offenders. Although, as Figure 16.3a and Figure 16.3b show, the hazards of sex offenders are lower than those of V and P offenders, the normalized hazards show that the hazards of sex offenders tend to decline more slowly than other types of offenders, and this pattern is more pronounced for the Older offenders. This is implied by the relatively flat age

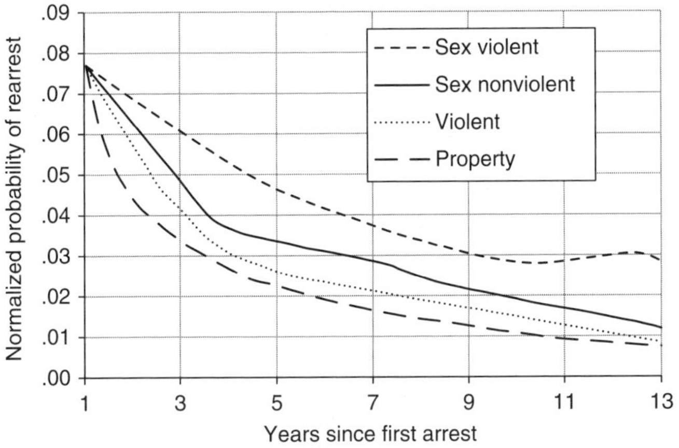

Figure 16.4b Normalized hazard *h(t)* for A_1 = 31–50 by C_1.

distribution of sex offenders (Figure 16.1c and Figure 16.1d). What these might suggest is that the time clean has a smaller effect on reducing the recidivism risk of sex offenders than that of nonsex offenders.

While the previous analysis of hazard sheds light on the sex offenders' recidivism patterns in comparison with the recidivism of other types of offenders, we considered only the recidivism for any crime (C_2 = any). Thus, the recidivism could be not only for sex offenses, which we are most concerned about, but also for other types of offenses, which may not amount to a risk of major concern. As discussed earlier, the justification for imposing stringent restrictions on sex offenders is the concern that they could be likely to recidivate and commit another sex offense. Thus, it is important to consider the crime types of both the first arrest (C_1) and the second arrest (C_2) and probabilistically quantify the risk of a particular C_2 of concern that may follow from any C_1.

Table 16.3a and Table 16.3b show the crime-switch matrices, which display the probability of different crime types of second arrest (the columns)[22] as a function of the crime type of first arrest (the rows). This allows us to examine what proportion of those who were first arrested for each of the seven C_1 categories were rearrested for the same crime category, or for a different category. The values in the diagonals of the matrix represent the proportion recidivating to the same crime type as that for which they were first arrested. The values in the off-diagonals represent the proportion committing different crime types from their first one. The second from bottom row, Prevalence, is the proportion (of those who do recidivate) recidivating to each of the seven C_2 categories. Since the diagonals are influenced by the

[22]The crime-switch matrices inform about the probability of switching from the crime type of the first arrest to different crime types for the second arrest. It is important to note that the matrices take no account of the crime types of the third and later arrests for those who have more than two arrests. In this sense, the information that the matrices contain is consistent with the hazard, which is the risk of having a second arrest.

Table 16.3a Crime-Switch Matrix for Arrestees for A_1 = 19–30

	C_2							
C_1	*VS*	*NVS*	*V*	*P*	*D*	*PO*	*Others*	*No rearrest*
VS	**3.4**	2.9	13.9	12.9	9.8	7.8	6.8	42.4
NVS	1.3	**9.4**	8.5	11.0	5.2	3.9	6.0	54.8
V	0.3	0.9	**19.7**	13.6	8.7	7.3	6.6	42.9
P	0.2	0.7	8.0	**24.6**	6.2	4.9	5.2	50.2
D	0.2	0.4	8.5	9.9	**26.5**	5.1	3.9	45.6
PO	0.3	0.7	11.9	11.4	8.9	**16.5**	5.4	44.9
Others	0.2	1.0	10.0	14.3	6.1	6.1	**10.0**	52.2
Prevalence	.5	1.6	21.0	31.8	20.5	13.7	10.9	
Diag/Prevalence	6.5	5.7	.9	.8	1.3	1.2	.9	

Table 16.3b Crime-Switch Matrix for Arrestees for A_1 = 31–50

	C_2							
C_1	*VS*	*NVS*	*V*	*P*	*D*	*PO*	*Others*	*No rearrest*
VS	**2.6**	3.7	8.6	5.6	4.5	2.2	3.0	69.8
NVS	0.7	**8.3**	3.9	5.4	2.0	2.3	4.7	72.9
V	0.3	1.0	**14.5**	7.0	3.7	4.1	5.7	63.8
P	0.1	0.5	4.5	**20.5**	2.9	2.3	3.3	66.0
D	0.3	0.3	5.2	6.5	**24.9**	3.7	3.2	56.0
PO	0.1	0.6	7.6	5.7	4.7	**14.9**	3.8	62.7
Others	0.3	1.2	6.0	9.3	3.6	4.0	**8.5**	67.3
Prevalence	0.6	2.7	19.5	33.1	18.5	13.4	12.1	
Diag/Prevalence	4.3	3.1	0.7	0.6	1.3	1.1	0.7	

prevalence of each C_2, the last row, which is the diagonals divided by Prevalence, represents the propensity to repeat the same crime type ($C_1 = C_2$) after accounting for the prevalence of each particular C_2.

Just as sex offenses have low prevalence among the crime types of the first arrest, it is clear that sex offenses (VS, NVS) are also rare as C_2. Among those offenders who recidivate, only 2.1% (.5 + 1.6) of the Younger offenders and 3.3% (.6 + 2.7) of the Older offenders recidivate to sex offenses. As shown by the survival probabilities earlier, for the Younger offenders, the probability of no rearrest for VS offenders is very similar to that for V offenders (42.4% for C_1 = VS, 42.9% for C_1 = V). For the Older offenders, the probability of no rearrest for VS offenders is closer to that for NVS offenders than to that for V offenders.

This again illustrates that age is an important factor in understanding the recidivism patterns of violent sex offenders. For both A_1 groups, NVS offenders have the highest probability of no rearrest. Based on the diagonal values, among the Younger offenders, sex offenders are more likely to recidivate to nonsex crimes. A larger proportion of both VS and NVS offenders commit property crimes than repeat the same crime type as the first one.[23] However, this observation does not correctly describe the sex offenders' true propensity to repeat sex crimes due to the low prevalence of sex crimes. The higher diagonals/Prevalence values for sex offenders indicate that, in fact, once the prevalence of each is accounted for, sex offenders seem to show a much higher propensity to repeat the same types of crime than other types of offenders. The patterns are similar for the Older offenders: once the low prevalence of sex crimes is considered, sex offenders seem to exhibit a high tendency to repeat the same crime types.

While a crime-switch matrix is informative in characterizing the crime types to which the sex crime arrestees recidivate, it is useful to examine more explicitly how the risk of recidivism to certain C_2s changes over time. In order to estimate the hazard for recidivism to a particular crime type, type-specific hazard (Allison, 1995; Kalbfleisch & Prentice, 2002) is estimated. Type-specific hazard approximates the conditional probability of having a new arrest for a particular crime type at time *t* given surviving without any new arrest until time *t*.

Figure 16.5a and Figure 16.5b show the hazards of rearrest for a violent sex offense for each of four C_1s (VS, NVS, V, P) for A_1 = 19–30, 31–50. First, we notice that for both A_1 groups, the hazard of rearrest for violent sex crime is below .01, much lower

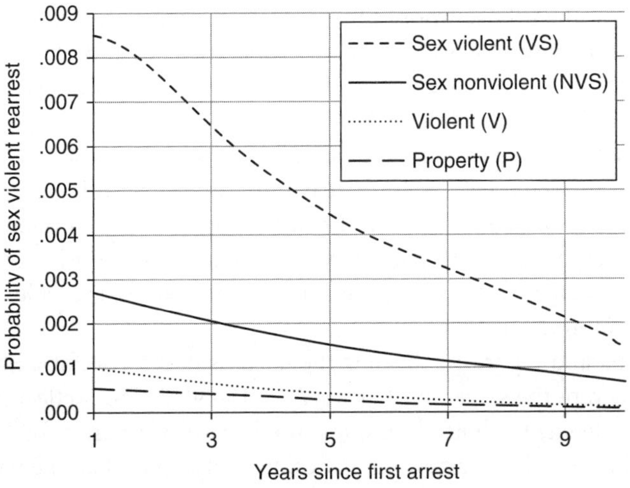

Figure 16.5a *h(t)* for C_2 = VS by four types of C_1; A_1 = 19–30.

[23]It should also be noted that the Younger VS offenders have the lowest probability of no rearrest, and have the highest nondiagonal values for most types of C_2, indicating that the Younger VS offenders have a relatively high recidivism risk and tend to be versatile in terms of the offense type for the recidivism.

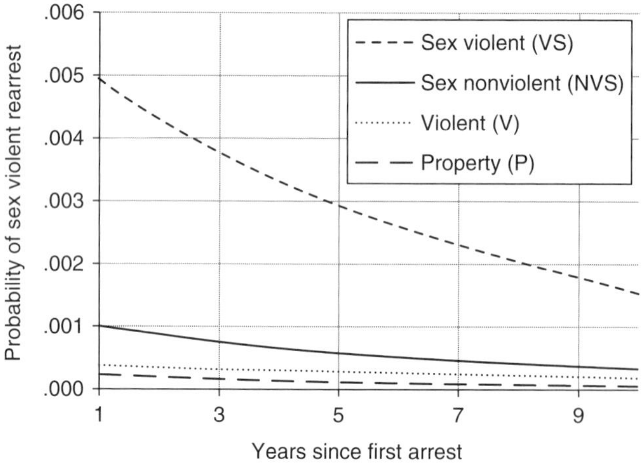

Figure 16.5b *h(t)* for C_2 = VS by four types of C_1; A_1 = 31–50.

than the hazard of rearrest for any crime, which we estimated earlier. Thus, policymakers and the public should be aware that the risk of future crime by someone with a prior record of a particular crime (C_1) is less if they are only concerned about a specific set of crimes such as only VS crimes.

As implied by the crime-switch matrices above, those whose first arrest was for VS crime tend to have a higher recidivism risk of VS crime for at least 10 years from their first arrest than those whose first arrest was for the other three crimes. This suggests that for those who are particularly concerned about the risk of a future VS offense, a prior record of VS crime, which could be as old as 10 years, indicates at most a probability of .0016 if C_1 = VS and 50% less, or .0008, if C_1 = NVS for the Younger offenders. For the Older offenders, the probability is still .0016 if C_1 = VS and 80% less, or .0003, if C_1 = NVS. It is interesting that although the Older VS offenders initially have a lower risk of committing another VS offense than their younger counterparts, after 10 years they have about the same risk of VS recidivism. This suggests that the recidivism risk declines more slowly for the Older VS offenders than for the Younger offenders.[24]

Figure 16.6a and Figure 16.6b show the hazards of rearrest for a nonviolent sex offense for each of the same four C_1s for A_1 = 19–30, 31–50. Reflecting the differences in prevalence, for both A_1 groups, the hazard of rearrest for NVS crime is lower than the hazard of rearrest for any crime, but higher than the hazard of rearrest for VS crime.

[24]This is not necessarily contradictory to the fact that the Older offenders have a higher survival probability (Figure 16.2a and Figure 16.2b) and a higher probability of No rearrest (Table 16.3a and Table 16.3b). The two probabilities are based on the overall (cumulative) proportion of the initial arrestee population who are rearrested, while the hazard represents a conditional probability of rearrest.

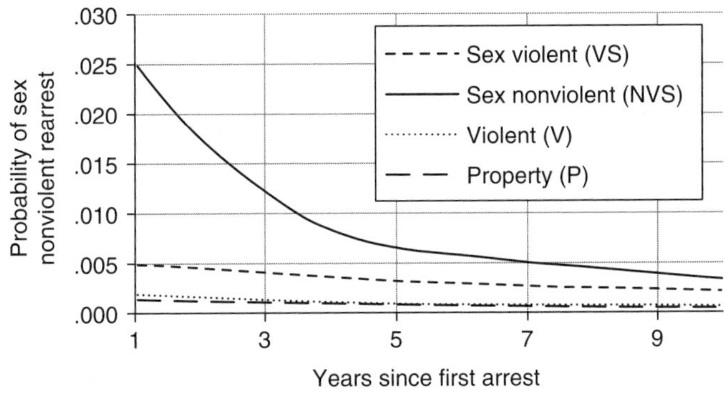

Figure 16.6a *h(t)* for C_2 = NVS by four types of C_1; A_1 = 19–30.

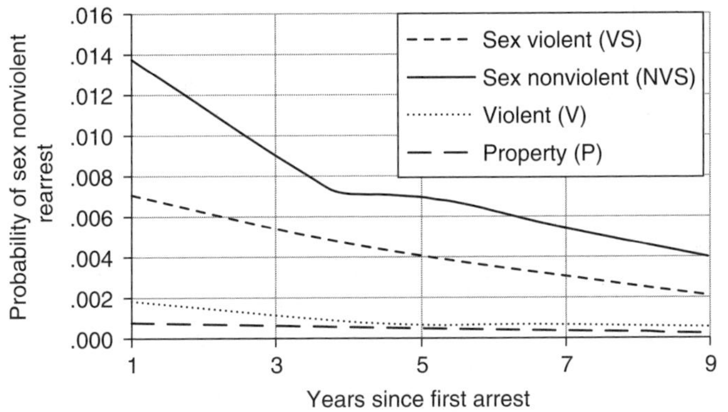

Figure 16.6b *h(t)* for C_2 = NVS by four types of C_1; A_1 = 31–50.

Consistent with the crime-switch matrices, those whose first arrest was for NVS crime tend to have a higher recidivism risk of NVS crime for at least 10 years than those whose first arrest was for the other three crimes. However, unlike for C_2 = VS, where VS offenders have a clearly higher hazard than NVS offenders for both A_1s, for C_2 = NVS, the difference in hazards between VS and NVS is smaller for the Older offenders. This suggests that, compared to their younger counterparts, the Older VS offenders are more similar to NVS offenders in terms of their propensity to recidivate to an NVS offense.

The findings from the survival probability analysis and the crime-switch matrices indicate that VS offenders and V offenders, especially younger ones, show similar recidivism patterns. Thus, it is important to examine the extent to which a prior record of VS offense may be related to the future risk of V recidivism. The hazards of rearrest for a V offense for each of the four C_1s for the Younger and Older offenders are estimated and shown in Figure 16.7a and Figure 16.7b.

The figures show that for the Younger offenders, V offenders have the highest risk of recidivism for violence, followed fairly closely by VS offenders. VS offenders and

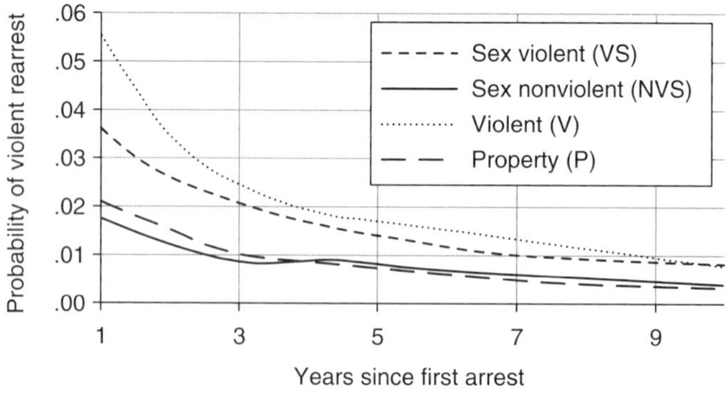

Figure 16.7a $h(t)$ for A_1 = 19–30, C_2 = V by four types of C_1.

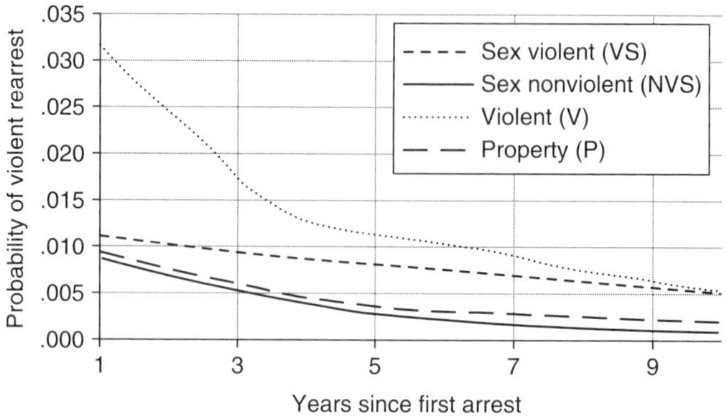

Figure 16.7b $h(t)$ for A_1 = 31–50, C_2 = V by four types of C_1.

V offenders have fairly similar risk of recidivism for violence.[25] Because V offense is more prevalent than VS or NVS crimes, VS offenders tend to have a higher hazard of rearrest for V offense than rearrest for VS offense.

Among the Older offenders, V and VS offenders show very different recidivism patterns. V offenders have a much higher hazard of rearrest for violence than VS offenders. It is, however, interesting to note that, despite the relatively large difference in early hazards between C_1 = V and C_1 = VS, the hazard for C_1 = VS declines more slowly than the hazard for C_1 = V. At $t = 1$, the ratio of the hazard for C_1 = V to the hazard for C_1 = VS is about 3.0; at $t = 5$, the ratio becomes about 1.3, less than half; and at $t = 10$, the ratio is down to about 1.0. This suggests that the recidivism risk of V offenders becomes about the same as the recidivism risk of VS offenders after 10

[25]In light of evidence on the relationship between age and offending specialization (Piquero, Paternoster, Brame, Mazerolle, & Dean, 1999), this may indicate Younger offenders' relative versatility within violent offenses (sexual or otherwise).

years since the first arrest. This observation can be missed if just survival probability is considered as a measure of recidivism risk: Survival probability for V would be much lower than that for VS based on the observation that the initial hazard for V is much higher than that for VS.

It is also important to note that for both A_1 groups, NVS offenders have a very low risk of V recidivism.

Approach to Estimating Redemption Times

Even though past wrongdoings are a useful sign of future trouble, this information has decreasing value over time because the risk of recidivism decreases monotonically with time clean, and there can come a point where we can be confident that redemption has been reached, where the risk of reoffending has subsided to the level of a reasonable benchmark. The problem here is that there has been very little empirical information that can help to establish that point. In the context of sex offender registration, the absence of reliable empirical guidelines has left policymakers with little choice but to set their own arbitrarily selected cut-off points for the length of registration based on some intuitive sense of how long is long enough, inevitably with a conservative bias responding to the public's concerns. Given the importance of this issue, particularly for sex offenders who are faced with an increasing amount of public scrutiny and official surveillance, it becomes important to explore empirical estimates of a reasonable point of redemption or "redemption time."

One such point, which we denote as T*, is where the recidivism risk of someone with a prior criminal record (arrest or conviction) declines and matches the risk of arrest for the general population of the same age, and so can serve as a point of redemption.[26] The risk of arrest for the general population is represented by the age-crime curve whose horizontal axis is age (*A*) and whose vertical axis is the age-specific arrest rate of people of age *A*, the ratio of the number of arrests of age *A* to the population of age *A*.

[26]Prior studies on redemption used the risk of arrest for those who have no prior record (nonoffenders) as well as the risk of arrest for the general population as a benchmark (Blumstein & Nakamura, 2009; Bushway et al., 2011; Kurlychek et al., 2006, 2007; Soothill & Francis, 2009). The issue addressed in this study is when the recidivism risk of sex offenders falls to a sufficiently low level where registration and other measures of monitoring may not be required. The appropriate comparison group which corresponds to this benchmark is not necessarily nonoffenders, and the general population benchmark may be more appropriate. This policy has clearly responded to a public uproar that has escalated the burden placed on sex offenders, even the NVS, to a level well above that of all other offenders, who have no such reporting requirement, even when their offense could well be seen as far more serious than those of many sex offenders.

Arrest Risk for the General Population of the Same Age as a Benchmark

The value of the age-crime curve in year *t* after the first arrest of persons of A_1 in 1980, 1985, and 1990 is given by the number of arrests of people of age ($A_1 + t$) divided by the population of that age in those years. The sample cohort is from New York, so the age-crime curve as a comparison is also from New York.[27] To generate a comparable benchmark for the hazard estimates based on the three sampling years (1980, 1985, and 1990), the average of the three age-crime curves from the three years is used.[28]

In order to estimate redemption time for each of the three A_1 examined above, we create three A_1-specific age-crime curves. For the three age-crime curves, we count arrests for (1) VS crime (forcible rape in UCR), (2) NVS crime (sex offenses in UCR), and (3) V (robbery, aggravated assault, and simple assault in UCR), respectively. Figure 16.8a shows the age-crime curves for C_2 = VS and

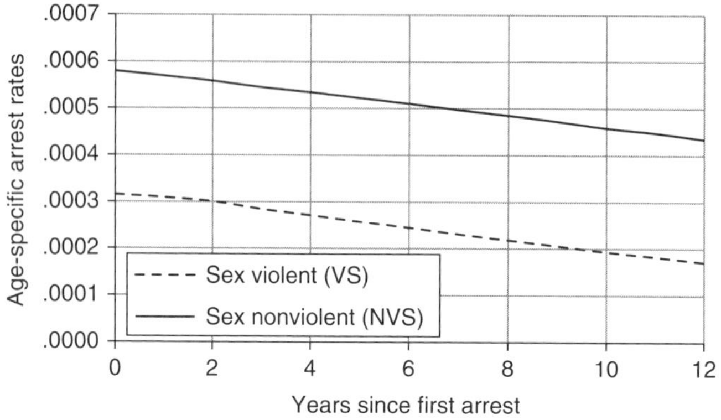

Figure 16.8a Age-crime curves, C_2 = VS, NVS, A_1 = 19–30.

[27]The number of arrests by age in New York in 1980, 1985, and 1990 is from the Uniform Crime Reports (Federal Bureau of Investigation, 1981, 1986, 1991; National Consortium on Violence Research, n.d.), and the population of New York State in the 3 years is from the census (U.S. Census Bureau, 1996).

[28]The number of arrests reported in the Uniform Crime Reports is greater than the number of individuals arrested because an individual can have multiple arrests in a year. As a result, the age-crime curve that is based on the number of arrests is an overestimate of the probability of arrest for a member of the general population. In order to adjust for these redundant arrests, we first calculate the ratio of the number of arrestees to the number of arrests as a function of A_1 in 1980, from the data of the 1980 New York arrestee cohort. We then estimate the number of arrestees by multiplying the A_1-specific ratio by the number of arrests from the UCR. In general, the ratio is smaller for younger ages (for example, for A_1 = 16, the ratio = .80, while for A_1 = 40, the ratio = .97), which is consistent with the fact that younger ages are associated with higher hazards and higher offending frequency.

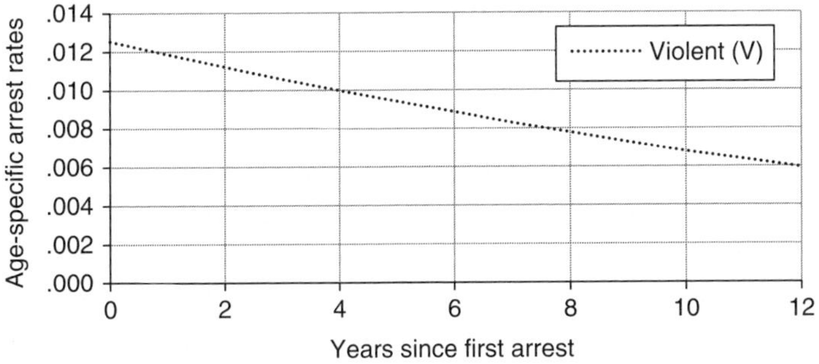

Figure 16.8b Age-crime curve, C_2 = V, A_1 = 19–30.

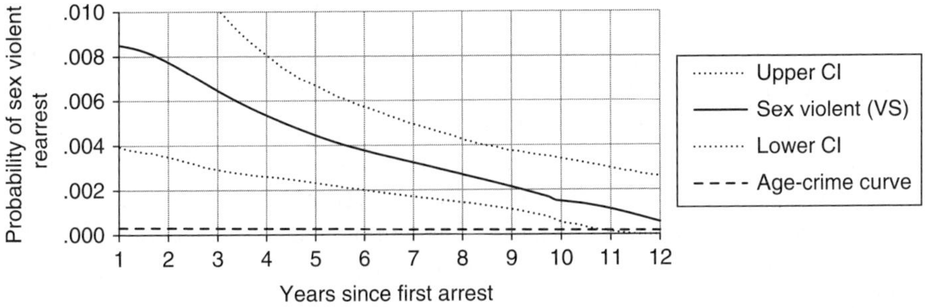

Figure 16.9 Comparison with the general population (Younger VS).

C_2 = NVS for the Younger offenders. Figure 16.8b shows the age-crime curve for C_2 = V. The violent age-crime curve is higher than the sex offense age-crime curves by an order of magnitude, reflecting the higher prevalence of V crime in the general population.

Consideration of Risk Tolerance

Figure 16.9 shows the hazard curve for C_1 = VS, C_2 = VS, A_1 = 19–30 along with the 95% confidence intervals, and the corresponding age-crime curve. The confidence intervals are based on the method of bootstrap, with the number of bootstrap samples, B = 2001. The hazard of VS offenders is clearly much higher than the risk of arrest for a VS crime among the general population. This can be explained by the fact that although the recidivism risk of VS offenders we are considering is very small (.2–.8%), the prevalence of VS crime in the general population is even smaller. The lower confidence interval of the hazard estimate crosses the age-crime curve just over 10 years after the first arrest, so there is some evidence that the risk of rearrest by a VS offender can become comparable to this general population benchmark. However, since the upper bound of the confidence interval (conservative estimate of the hazard) is far from the age-crime curve, within the 10-year follow-up, the likelihood that the Younger VS offenders' risk becomes comparable to the risk of the general population is low. The results are similar for the case of C_1 = NVS, C_2 = VS, and for the Older offenders.

In contrast, the hazard of V offenders crosses the age-crime curve about 8 years after the first arrest, and even the upper bound of the confidence interval becomes comparable to the age-crime curve after 10 years. Thus, if the type of recidivism we are concerned about is VS offense, and we use the prevalence of such crime in the general population as a benchmark, the risk of sex offenders (violent or otherwise) does not seem to come down to the benchmark until about 10 years after their first arrest.

The patterns are also similar for C_2 = NVS: the hazard of sex offenders remains higher than the age-crime curve of NVS offenses for at least 10 years after the first arrest. For the recidivism for C_2 = V, in which case the primary concern is the risk of rearrest for a V offense, the patterns are different. The hazard for sex offenders, especially of the Older NVS offenders, is very close to the age-crime curve, and for the Older offenders, the upper bound of the confidence interval crosses the age-crime curve at about t = 8, as shown in Figure 16.10. The crossover could occur for two reasons: First, NVS offenders have a low hazard of violent offense as evident in Figure 16.6b. Second, the prevalence of violent offense in the general population is much higher than the prevalence of sex offenses as shown in Figure 16.7a and Figure 16.7b.

Given these observations, we could quantify how close the sex offenders' risk is to the age-crime curve and whether they can be considered "close enough." Our approach first invokes the use of δ, a risk difference that can be tolerated (Blumstein & Nakamura, 2009). The parameter δ allows us to find a point estimate of a time when the hazard intersects the tolerable level of risk compared with a benchmark, which is in this case the age-crime curve (i.e., when the hazard falls below (age-crime curve + δ)). As Figure 16.11 shows, with δ = .0025 the upper bound of the confidence interval crosses the benchmark. The use of the upper bound provides a more conservative approach to answering the redemption question (Blumstein & Nakamura,

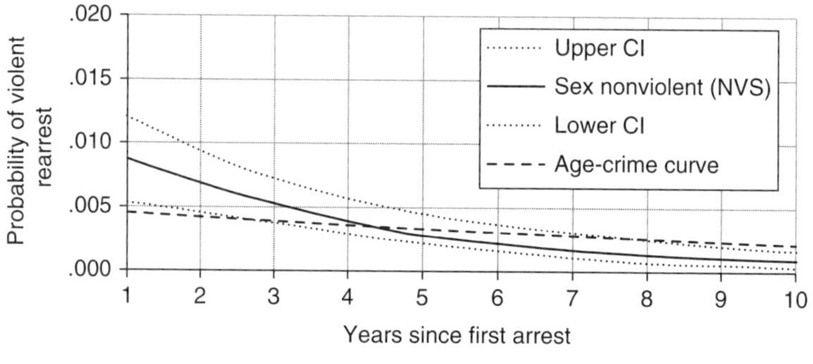

Figure 16.10 Comparison with the general population (Older V).

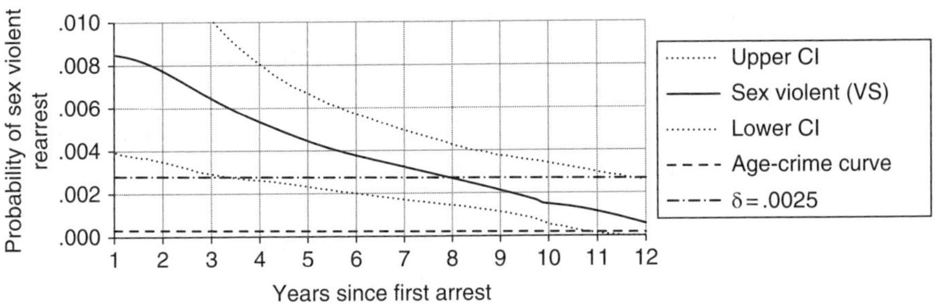

Figure 16.11 Comparison with the general population (Younger VS) with risk tolerance, δ.

2009).[29] Thus, if the additional .25% risk is acceptable, the recidivism risk of VS offenders is considered sufficiently close to the risk of arrest for the general population. The concept of additional tolerable risk may be useful if one considers the fact that the sex offender registration requirement and surveillance for a prolonged length of time incur costs to law enforcement agencies, who need to allocate resources to register sex offenders, track their residences, notify the public of where they are, and arrest and punish them when they fail to register annually as required. Moreover, in many states, sex offenders are barred from living within close proximity (usually 1,000–2,500 feet) to places where children congregate, such as schools, daycare centers, and parks (Human Rights Watch, 2007; National Conference of State Legislatures, 2006). In some instances, such residency restrictions can make the residential area of almost an entire city off limits and often lead to sex offenders concentrating in areas with high poverty and crime, and thus it is doubtful whether severely limiting housing options for sex offenders could help reduce their recidivism risk (Durling, 2006; Human Rights Watch, 2007; Levenson & Cotter, 2005; Levenson et al., 2007). Thus, a sensible question is, once such costs are considered, whether the risk posed by sex offenders who stay clean for 10 years or more warrants the same level of surveillance and registration requirements as the sex offenders who recently offended and thus have a relatively high risk of recidivism.

Conclusions and Discussion

There have been an increasing number of restrictions and sanctions imposed on the lives of sex offenders, ranging from direct ones such as sex offender registration requirements, public notification, and housing restrictions, to more indirect and less

[29]The use of upper bound also provides a more statistically appropriate approach. The lower bound is often used in determining when a declining hazard becomes "indistinguishable" from some benchmark, which represents a sufficiently low risk. However, the use of the lower bound is problematic in the sense that smaller sample sizes inevitably make confidence intervals wider, and the lower confidence bound would inappropriately make it easier to conclude that the hazard drops to the benchmark level of risk.

visible yet equally unforgiving ones such as lack of privacy, loss of job, family ostracism, and public humiliation (Levenson & Cotter, 2005; Levenson et al., 2007; Tewksbury, 2005; Tewksbury & Lees, 2006). It is important to recognize that all the restrictions are imposed upon sex offenders after they fully serve their sentences, and these restrictions in many states can last forever (Tewksbury, 2005). Given that there seems to be little evidence that sex offender registration and community notification reduce recidivism (Maddan, Miller, Walker, & Haen-Marshall, 2011; Zgoba, Witt, Dalessandro, & Veysey, 2008), there seems to be no empirical basis to justify the magnitude of these collateral sanctions associated with the registration. Given that the imposition of the restrictions is at least in part based on the belief that sex offenders are compulsive recidivists (Sample & Bray, 2003; Simon, 2003; Zimring, 2004), it is important to understand the limited magnitude of sex offenders' recidivism patterns. In the current research, we examined the level of sex offenders' recidivism risk relative to other types of offenders, and addressed the question of how their recidivism risk varies with time clean and whether it can be considered sufficiently low at some point in time.

We analyzed the hazard and survival probability of those who were arrested for the first time as adults in New York in 1980, 1985, or 1990. The results show that in terms of the recidivism for any offense, sex offenders tend to have a lower risk than other types of offenders, confirming the findings from most prior studies on sex offense recidivism (e.g., Hanson & Bussière, 1998; Lussier, 2005; Sample & Bray, 2003). We also found that sex offenders, especially those arrested for NVS offenses, tend to be older, and despite their lower level, their recidivism risk declines more slowly with time clean than other types of offenders. We also examined the recidivism risk for the specific crimes of concern: violent offenses in general and violent sex offenses. For violent recidivism, Younger VS (rapists) and V offenders have similar patterns. This is congruent with prior studies showing that rapists and other violent offenders share underlying characteristics, such as low self-control, and thus show similar recidivism patterns (Lussier, Proulx, & LeBlanc, 2005; Prentky, Knight, Lee, & Cerce, 1995; Rice, Harris, & Quinsey, 1990). In terms of the recidivism for sex offenses, sex offenders tend to show a higher recidivism risk than other types of offenders for at least about 10 years after their first arrest. Further, it was found that the risk of repeating the same crime type for the Older VS offenders does not decline as fast as for the Younger VS offenders. Also for the NVS recidivism, the Older sex offenders (VS and NVS) seem to show similar recidivism patterns. These observations suggest some interesting characteristics of those who are arrested for VS offense at older ages. Despite the low level in magnitude, the risk of recidivism for those older violent sex offenders declines slowly as the law-abiding time increases, and, when they do recidivate, those older offenders engage in both violent and nonviolent sex crimes. Given that child molesters tend to be older (Hanson, 2002), our finding that older violent sex offenders remain at a relatively high risk of sex offense recidivism could be explained by prior studies which show that recidivism of child molesters tends to be driven by characteristics unique to the nature of their offending, such as sexual preoccupation toward children

(Prentky et al., 1997), and that they exhibit a higher level of specialization (Harris et al., 2009; Miethe et al., 2006).

It is important to note that the risk of sex offense recidivism is much smaller than the risk of recidivism for any offense, largely due to the low prevalence of sex crime (2–3% of all rearrests). Compared to the risk of sex offense arrest for the general population that is represented by the sex-offense-specific age-crime curve, the sex offenders' risk of recidivism remains higher during the 10-year follow-up. Although the sex offenders' recidivism does not seem to become comparable to the risk of the general population, we consider the concept of risk tolerance to be potentially useful. By setting an additional risk for the sex offenders that can be tolerated over the general population arrest risk, one can estimate a redemption time.

While this study provides important information in considering the appropriate length of time for registration and monitoring of sex offenders, some important issues should still be pursued. This study focuses on longer term recidivism patterns and redemption for first-time offenders. However, many of those who are on sex offenders registries could have more than one prior crime. Those with multiple priors are likely to have a higher risk of recidivism than first-time offenders (Gendreau, Little, & Goggin, 1996), and Bushway et al. (2011) address the relationship between the number of prior convictions and redemption. In light of the evidence that an increasing number of convictions in a relatively short period of time can lead to escalation in offense seriousness (Liu, Francis, & Soothill, 2011), future research should address the relationship between the nature and the number of prior records and redemption for sex offenders.

The amount of resources allocated to register and monitor sex offenders should be taken into consideration in determining how high the risk tolerance should be and for how long the registration should be required. This is sensible, especially in light of the recent evidence that questions the effectiveness of registration and notification laws in reducing recidivism (Maddan et al., 2011; Zgoba et al., 2008). And since the recidivism is highest immediately after the arrest and declines with time clean, the need for registration and monitoring should follow the same pattern. By allowing .0025 (.25%) of additional hazard after 10 years of law-abiding period, sex offenders' risk can be considered close enough to the risk of the general population.[30] Also, for the purpose of reintegrating offenders back into society, the continuing stigmatization of sex offenders with substantial time clean may be counterproductive (Terry, 2011). Thus, rather than setting the registration length at life, policymakers could develop the length that accounts for the sex offenders' declining recidivism risk and that can allow a more rational allocation of resources devoted to controlling sex offenders.

[30]This finding suggests that there is little empirical evidence to justify laws such as New York's Sex Offender Registration Act, which allows (Level 2) sex offenders to petition for relief from registration duty only after being registered for a minimum of 30 years (For more information about this law see http://criminaljustice.state.ny.us/nsor/claws.htm#o).

References

Adams, D. B. (2002). *Summary of state sex offender registries, 2001*. Washington, DC: U.S. Department of Justice, Bureau of Justice Statistics.

Allison, P. (1995). *Survival analysis using SAS: A practical guide*. Cary, NC: SAS Institute.

Beck, A. J., & Shipley, B. E. (1997). *Recidivism of prisoners released in 1983*. Washington, DC: U.S. Department of Justice, Bureau of Justice Statistics.

Blumstein, A., & Cohen, J. (1979). Estimation of individual crime rates from arrest records. *Journal of Criminal Law & Criminology*, 70(4), 561–585.

Blumstein, A., Farrington, D. P., & Moitra, S. (1985). Delinquency careers: Innocents, desisters, and persisters. In M. Tonry & N. Morris (Eds.), *Crime and justice: An annual review of research* (Vol. 6). Chicago: University of Chicago Press.

Blumstein, A., & Nakamura, K. (2009). Redemption in the presence of widespread background checks. *Criminology*, 47, 327–359.

Brame, R., Bushway, S. D., & Paternoster, R. (2003). Examining the prevalence of criminal desistance. *Criminology*, 41, 423–448.

Bushway, S. D., Nieuwbeerta, P., & Blokland, A. (2011). The predictive value of criminal background checks: Do age and criminal history affect time to redemption? *Criminology*, 49, 27–60.

Carrol, J. (2005, May). Crystal meth, child molestation top crime concerns. Seventy-five percent of rural Americans very concerned about meth. *Politics*. Retrieved from http://www.gallup.com/poll/16123/crystal-meth-child-molestation-top-crime-concerns.aspx

Durling, C. (2006). Never going home: Does it make us safer? Does it make sense? Sex offenders, residency restrictions and reforming risk management law. *The Journal of Criminal Law and Criminology*, 97, 317–363.

The Economist. (2006) The greatest fear. America's laws about sex offenders are full of well-intentioned confusion. August 24, p. 24.

Farrington, D. P. (1986). Age and crime. In M. Tonry & N. Morris (Eds.), *Crime and justice: An annual review of research* (Vol. 7). Chicago: University of Chicago Press.

Farrington, D. P. (1987). Predicting individual crime rates. In D. M. Gottfredson & M. Tonry (Eds.), *Crime and justice: An annual review of research* (Vol. 9). Chicago: University of Chicago Press.

Federal Bureau of Investigation. (1981–2001, 2008, 2009). *Crime in the United States, 1980–2000, 2007, 2008*. Washington, DC: U.S. Department of Justice, Federal Bureau of Investigation.

Gendreau, P., Little, T., & Goggin, C. (1996). A meta-analysis of the predictors of adult offender recidivism: What works! *Criminology*, 34, 575–608.

Gottfredson, D. M. (1999). *Effects of judges' sentencing decisions on criminal careers*. National Institute of Justice: Research in Brief. Washington, DC: U.S. Department of Justice.

Hanson, R. K. (2002). Recidivism and age – follow-up data from 4,673 sexual offenders. *Journal of Interpersonal Violence*, 17, 1046–1062.

Hanson, R. K., & Bussière, M. T. (1998). Predicting relapse: A meta-analysis of sexual offender recidivism studies. *Journal of Counseling and Clinical Psychology*, 66, 348–362.

Hanson, R. K., Scott, H., & Steffy, R. A. (1995). A comparison of child molesters and non-sexual criminals: Risk predictors and long-term recidivism. *Journal of Research in Crime and Delinquency*, 32(3), 325–337.

Harris, A., & Lobanov-Rostovsky, C. (2010). Implementing the Adam Walsh Act's sex offender registration and notification provisions: A survey of the states. *Criminal Justice Policy Review*, 21(2), 202–222.

Harris, A., Lobanov-Rostovsky, C., & Levenson, J. (2010). Widening the net: Effects of transitioning to the federally mandated Adam Walsh Act classification system. *Criminal Justice and Behavior*,37(5), 503–519.

Harris, D. A., Smallbone, S., Dennison, S., & Knight, R. A. (2009). Specialization and versatility in sexual offenders referred for civil commitment. *Journal of Criminal Justice*, 37, 37–44.

Hess, K. R., Serachitopol, D. M., & Brown, B. W. (1999). Hazard function estimators: A simulation study. *Statistics in Medicine*, 18, 3075–3088.

Hirschi, T., & Gottfredson, M. (1983). Age and the explanation of crime. *American Journal of Sociology*, 89, 552–584.

Human Rights Watch. (2007). *No easy answers: Sex offender laws in the U.S.* Retrieved from http://www.hrw.org/en/reports/2007/09/11/no-easy-answers

Kalbfleisch, J. D., & Prentice, R. L. (2002). *The statistical analysis of failure time data*. Hoboken, NJ: John Wiley & Sons, Inc.

Klein, J. P., & Moeschberger, M. L. (2005). *Survival analysis: Techniques for censored and truncated data*. New York: Springer.

Krueger, J. (2007). *Research bulletin: Sex offender populations, recidivism and actuarial assessment*. New York: New York State Division of Probation and Correctional Alternatives.

Kurlychek, M. C., Brame, R., & Bushway, S. D. (2006). Scarlet letters and recidivism: Does an old criminal record predict future offending? *Criminology & Public Policy*, 5, 483–504.

Kurlychek, M. C., Brame, R., & Bushway, S. D. (2007). Enduring risk? Old criminal records and predictions of future criminal involvement. *Crime & Delinquency*, 53, 64–83.

Langan, P. A., & Levin, D. J. (2002). *Recidivism of prisoners released in 1994*. Washington, DC: U.S. Department of Justice, Bureau of Justice Statistics.

Langan, P. A., Schmitt, E. L., & Durose, M. R. (2003). Recidivism of sex offenders released from prison in 1994. Washington, DC: U.S. Department of Justice.

Langevin, R., Curnoe, S., Fedoroff, P., Bennett, R., Langevin, M., Peever, C., Pettica, R., & Sandhu, S. (2004). Lifetime sex offender recidivism: A 25-year follow-up study. *Canadian Journal of Criminal Justice*, 46, 531–552.

Levenson, J., & Cotter, L. P. (2005). The impact of sex offender residence restrictions: 1,000 feet from danger or one step from absurd? *International Journal of Offender Therapy and Comparative Criminology*, 49, 168–178.

Levenson, J., Zgoba, K., & Tewksbury, R. (2007). Sex offender residence restrictions: Sensible crime policy or flawed logic? *Federal Probation*, 71, 2–9.

Lieb, R., Kemshall, H., & Thomas T. (2011). Post-release controls for sex offenders in the U.S. and UK. *International Journal of Law and Psychiatry*, 34(3), 226–232.

Liu, J., Francis, B., & and Soothill, K. (2011). A longitudinal study of escalation in crime seriousness. *Journal of Quantitative Criminology*, 27, 175–196.

Lussier, P. (2005). The criminal activity of sexual offenders in adulthood: Revisiting the specialization debate. *Sexual Abuse: A Journal of Research and Treatment*, 17, 269–292.

Lussier, P., Proulx, J., LeBlanc, M. (2005). Criminal propensity, deviant sexual interests and criminal activity of sexual aggressors against women: A comparison of alternative explanatory models. *Criminology*, 43, 247–279.

Maddan, S., Miller, J. M., Walker, J. T., & Haen-Marshall, I. (2011). Utilizing criminal history information to explore the effect of community notification on sex offender recidivism. *Justice Quarterly*, 28(4), 303–324.

Maltz, M. D. (1984). *Recidivism*. Orlando, FL: Academic Press.

Matson, S., & Lieb, R. (1997). *Megan's Law: A review of state and federal legislation*. Olympia: Washington State Institute of Public Policy.

Miethe, T., Olson, J., & Mitchell, O. (2006). Specialization and persistence in the arrest histories of sex offenders: A comparative analysis of alternative measures and offense types. *Journal of Research in Crime and Delinquency*, 43, 204–229.

Nakamura, K., & Blumstein, A. (2011). Robustness analysis of redemption patterns across time and place. Unpublished manuscript.

National Center for Missing and Exploited Children. (2014). Map of registered sex offenders in the United States. Retrieved from http://www.missingkids.com/en_US/documents/Sex_Offenders_Map.pdf

National Conference of State Legislatures. (2006). *States with sex offender residency restriction laws*. Denver, CO: Author.

National Consortium on Violence Research. (n.d.). *FBI uniform crime reports arrests data cube*. Retrieved from http://saturn.heinz.cmu.edu/cognos/cgi-bin/upfcgi.exe

Petrunik, M., Murphy, L., & Fedoroff, J. P. (2008). American and Canadian approaches to sex offenders: A study of the politics of dangerousness. *Federal Sentencing Reporter*, 21(2), 111–113.

Piquero, A. R., Farrington, D. P., & Blumstein, A. (2003). The criminal career paradigm: Background and recent developments. In M. Tonry (Ed.), *Crime and justice: A review of research* (Vol. 30). Chicago: University of Chicago Press.

Piquero, A. R., Farrington, D. P., & Blumstein, A. (2007). *Key issues in criminal career research: New analyses of the Cambridge Study in Delinquent Development*. New York: Cambridge University Press.

Piquero, A. R., Paternoster, R., Brame, R., Mazerolle, P., & Dean, C. W. (1999). Onset age and specialization in offending behavior. *Journal of Research in Crime and Delinquency*, 36, 235–274.

Prentky, R. A., Knight, R. A., Lee, A. F., & Cerce, D. D. (1995). Predictive validity of lifestyle impulsivity for rapists. *Criminal Justice and Behavior*, 22, 106–128.

Prentky, R. A., Lee, A. F. S., Knight, R. A., & Cerce, D. (1997). Recidivism rates among child molesters and rapists: A methodological analysis. *Law and Human Behavior*, 21, 635–659.

Rice, M. E., & Harris, G. T. (1997). The treatment of adult offenders. In D. M. Stoff, J. Breiling, & J. D. Maser (Eds.), *Handbook of antisocial behavior*. New York: John Wiley & Sons, Inc.

Rice, M. E., Harris, G. T., & Quinsey, V. L. (1990). A follow-up of rapists assessed in a maximum security psychiatric facility. *Journal of Interpersonal Violence*, 5, 435–448.

Sample, L. L., & Bray, T. M. (2003). Are sex offenders dangerous? *Criminology and Public Policy*, 3, 59–82.

Sample, L. L., & Bray, T. M. (2006). Are sex offenders different? An examination of rearrest patterns. *Criminal Justice Policy Review*, 17, 83–102.

Sampson, R. J., & Laub, J. H. (1993). *Crime in the making: Pathways and turning points through life*. Cambridge, MA: Harvard University Press.

Sampson, R. J., & Laub, J. H. (2003). Life-course desisters? Trajectories of crime among delinquent boys followed to age 70. *Criminology*, 41, 301–340.

Sampson, R. J., Laub, J. H., & Wimer, C. (2006). Does marriage reduce crime? A counterfactual approach to within-individual causal effects. *Criminology*, 44, 465–508.

Schmidt, P., & Witte, A. D. (1988). *Predicting recidivism using survival models*. New York: Springer-Verlag.

Simon, J. (2003). Managing the monstrous: Sex offenders and the new penology. In B. J. Winick & J. Q. LaFond (Eds.), *Protecting society from sexually dangerous offenders: Law, justice, and therapy* (pp. 301–316). Washington, DC: American Psychological Association.

Simon, L. (2000). An examination of the assumptions of specialization, mental disorder, and dangerousness in sex offenders. *Behavioral Sciences & the Law*, 18, 275–308.

Sipe, R., Jensen, E. L., & Everett, R. S. (1998). Adolescent sexual offenders grown up: Recidivism in young adulthood. *Criminal Justice and Behavior*, 25, 109–124.

Socia, K. M. (2011). Residence restriction legislation, sex crime rates, and the spatial distribution of sex offender residences. Unpublished dissertation. University at Albany, State University of New York.

Soothill, K. (2010). Sex offender recidivism. In M. Tonry (Ed.), *Crime and Justice: A review of research* (Vol. 39). Chicago: University of Chicago Press.

Soothill, K., & Francis, B. (2009). When do ex-offenders become like non-offenders? *Howard Journal of Criminal Justice*, 48, 373–387.

Terry, K. J. (2011). What is smart sex offender policy? *Criminology & Public Policy*, 10(2), 275–282.

Tewksbury, R. (2005). Collateral consequences of sex offender registration. *Journal of Contemporary Criminal Justice*, 21, 67–82.

Tewksbury, R., & Lees, M. (2006). Consequences of sex offender registration: Collateral consequences and community experiences. *Sociological Spectrum*, 26, 309–334.

Thomas, T. (2009). The sex offender register: Some observations on the time periods for registration. *Howard Journal of Criminal Justice*, 48(3), 257–266.

Uggen, C. (1999). Ex-offenders and the conformist alternative: A job quality model of work and crime. *Social Problems*, 46, 127–151.

U.S. Census Bureau. (1996). *Historical annual time series of state population estimates and demographic components of change 1980-1990, by single year of age and sex*. Washington, DC: U.S. Census Bureau.

Visher, C. A., Lattimore, P. K., & Linster, R. L. (1991). Predicting the recidivism of serious youthful offenders using survival models. *Criminology*, 29, 329–366.

Wang, J-L. (2005). Smoothing hazard rate. In P. Armitage & T. Colton (Eds.), *Encyclopedia of biostatistics* (2nd ed.) (Vol. 7, pp. 4986–4997). Chichester, UK: John Wiley & Sons, Ltd.

Warr, M. (1998). Life-course transitions and desistance from crime. *Criminology*, 36, 183–216.

Wooldridge, J. M. (2002). *Econometric analysis of cross section and panel data*. Cambridge, MA: MIT Press.

Zimring, F. E. (2004). *An American travesty: Legal responses to adolescent sexual offending*. Chicago: University of Chicago Press.

Zgoba, K., Witt, P., Dalessandro, M., & Veysey, B. (2008). Megan's Law: Assessing the practical and monetary efficacy. Washington DC: U.S. Department of Justice.

17

Policing Sex Offenders, Past and Present

The Role and Importance of a Criminal Career Approach in Helping Shape Future Policies

Patrick Lussier
Laval University, Canada

Arjan Blokland
NSCR and Leiden University, the Netherlands

Introduction

This book introduces a criminal career approach to the study of sexual violence and abuse. The previous chapters emphasized how the criminal career perspective can contribute to theoretical, methodological, and empirical developments in this field of research. Several criminal career parameters were defined, described, and examined in the context of sex crimes and sex offenders. The criminal career approach is a departure from the medical or clinical model that has been predominant in prior research and in shaping criminal justice policies aimed at sex offenders. The clinical model is concerned with assessment, treatment, and aftercare where rehabilitation is the main crime control objective. While the clinical model has been gradually replaced in the last two decades by a community protection model, the focus has been quite similar: protecting the community against the "sexual recidivists." We argue here that while the clinical model and the community model have been quite different crime control strategies, they have focused on a single dimension of the criminal career of sex offenders, that is, persistence. Such a narrow focus is somewhat at odds with the criminal career perspective, which has been traditionally associated with prevention, career modification, and incapacitation strategies (e.g., Piquero, Farrington, & Blumstein, 2003). The chapter begins with an overview of the relatively brief history of crime control strategies to deal with sex offenders, emphasizing the most current policies, and the role and importance that "sexual

Sex Offenders: A Criminal Career Approach, First Edition. Edited by Arjan Blokland and Patrick Lussier.

recidivists" have taken in policy development. We argue that the focus on the "sexual recidivist" has limited the development of a more comprehensive crime control strategy that tackles various criminal career aspects (i.e., onset, frequency, persistence, desistance, etc.).

From Rehabilitation to Community Protection

The Clinical Model

The criminal justice response to sex offenders has been marked by significant policy shifts during the twentieth century. Examination of the criminal justice response to sexual offending has led scholars to identify three major policy shifts, at least in North America (e.g., Janus, 2003; Lieb, Quinsey, & Berliner, 1998; Petrunik, 2002, 2003), that is, (1) the clinical model, (2) the justice model, and (3) the community protection model. The clinical model was driven by the rehabilitation ideal where clinical assessment of the offender's pathology, indeterminate prison sentence, and assessment of dangerousness and treatment were a cornerstone of the criminal justice response in the 1950s and 1960s. Of importance, the general assumption behind those dispositions was that indeterminate sentences were to be served in psychiatric hospital and offenders were to be released only when cured. The sex offender was described as a "sexually deviant" individual in need of treatment rather than a prison sentence. Criminologists soon reacted against the introduction and implementation of such measures (i.e., Sexual Psychopathy Laws, indeterminate prison sentences, etc.), arguing that they were based on false assumptions.

Sutherland (1949, 1950) observed that these policies were driven by a few high-profile cases, typically involving the murder and the sexual abuse of a child. Sutherland further suggested that the media coverage of these cases fueled various negative emotional reactions in the community, such as confusion (i.e., difficulty understanding these acts), fear of being victimized, and anger toward the criminal justice system for not sufficiently protecting the community. These emotional reactions put pressure on the government to respond to such acts with the help of experts (e.g., psychiatrists). Paul Tappan (1951, 1955) further observed at that time that policies in place were based on false assumptions about sex offenders' characteristics and offending. He went on to argue that: first, contrary to popular beliefs, there is much heterogeneity among sex offenders and such heterogeneity includes few aggressive and dangerous offenders; second, most sex offenders do not reoffend and the recidivism rates are lower than for other criminal populations (e.g., burglars); and third, sex offenders do not progress from minor to most serious sex crimes. Tappan further argued that there was no empirical evidence supporting the use of indeterminate sentences to treat sex offenders, given that the impact of treatment was unknown and given the lack of resources (i.e., personnel, space, specialized training) to offer effective and specialized treatment programs to sex offenders. Whereas it was the extreme and rare cases that influenced the policy developments of the mid-twentieth century, the most prevalent and common forms of sexual offending would influence the second round of policy developments.

Policing the Most Prevalent Cases

The 1970s marked a gradual shift in policymaking decisions with respect to the regulation of sex crimes and sexual offenders. The "sexually deviant" offender was soon replaced by the "rational offender" pursuing misogynistic goals. The shift was influenced by the feminist movement, which stated that "rape" was the result of a gendered distribution of power in society (e.g., Brownmiller, 1975). Bryden and Grier (2011) argue that during that period, feminists replaced psychologists as the leading experts, due in part to the fact that feminists were more vocal at advocating victims' rights. While there were still doubts about psychologists' ability to assess and to rehabilitate sex offenders, feminists distanced themselves from a clinical and medical view of sexual violence and abuse. Rather, they were vocal about the importance of legal, political, and social changes as to how rape was perceived and how society and the criminal justice system reacted to it. The role and involvement of feminists, the negative findings surrounding assessment and treatment, combined with the concerns raised by psychiatrists over the applications of specific dispositions, fueled a policy shift to what scholars refers to as the "justice model" (Lieb et al., 1998; Petrunik, 2003). The justice model represented a shift by emphasizing sex offenses (rather than sex offenders), just desert (rather than treatment and rehabilitation), and the proportionality of sentencing (rather than indeterminate sentences).

This shift was accompanied by changing perceptions about the offender (rational decision rather than uncontrolled propensity), the motivation (nonsexual rather sexual), the nature of sex crimes (domestic rather than aberrational), and the causes of offending (misogynistic attitudes rather than some personality disorder) (e.g., Bryden & Grier, 2011; Janus, 2003). Of most importance, the domestication of the sexual offending stressed the fact that most sex crimes were committed, not by strangers or sexual predators, but my family members or acquaintances. The magnitude and the scope of sex crimes as measured by victimization and perpetration surveys contributed to changing societal perceptions of sex offenses (e.g., Koss, Gidycz, & Wisniewski, 1987). Legal definitions of sex crimes were modified, new crimes were added to the criminal code. To facilitate reporting, measures were taken to ease victims' experience of the criminal justice system. Such changes were accompanied by lengthier criminal sentences and increased rates of incarceration (e.g., Janus, 2003).

Persistence of the Rehabilitation Ideal

While scientific circles have stressed the importance of this policy shift in the 1970s–1980s, innovations in the treatment of sex offenders continued. The elaboration and sophistication of treatment programs was noticeable as they gradually introduced ideas and concepts from behaviorally oriented theories (Laws, 2003). The first evaluative studies on the impact of sex offender treatment on the risk of sexual recidivism started to emerge in scholarly journals. The first reports did not show convincing empirical evidence suggesting that these programs were reducing the risk of sexual recidivism of treated sex offenders compared to untreated sex offenders (e.g., Davidson, 1984; Dix, 1976; Frisbie, 1969; Meyers & Romero, 1980; Peters & Roether, 1971; Sturgeon & Taylor, 1980). Such programs were gradually replaced by cognitive-behavioral treatment programs (Laws, 2003) that emphasized offenders' cognitive and behavioral excesses and deficits creating situations conducive to sex crimes (e.g., social skills, anger management) as well those that facilitate the commission of a crime (e.g., empathy, cognitive distortions, deviant sexual fantasizing) (e.g., Marshall, 1996, 1999). On various grounds, the efficacy of cognitive-behavioral treatment programs became the subject of fierce debating among scholars. Janice Marques correctly pointed out: "although the question, 'Does sex offender treatment work?' is an empirical one, nearly everyone already seems to have an answer. As a result, experts in this field – perhaps more so than in any other – find that answers based on outcome data are not always welcome" (Marques, 1999, p. 437). Two drastically opposite positions would soon emerge as more evaluative studies were published in scholarly journals.

Evaluative Studies and Methodological Rigor

The first position assumed that the cognitive-behavioral treatment programs were showing promising results. Tenants of this perspective reviewed positively evaluative studies of cognitive-behavioral treatment programs for sex offenders, especially for child molesters and exhibitionists (e.g., Marshall & Barbaree, 1990; Marshall & Pithers, 1994). In spite of earlier reports suggesting a positive impact, several scholars argued that no firm conclusions about treatment efficacy could be drawn due to methodological shortcomings of evaluative studies (Furby, Weinrott, & Blackshaw, 1989; McConaghy, 1999; Quinsey, Harris, Rice, & Lalumière, 1993; Rice, Harris, & Quinsey, 1993). Two options were suggested by these scholars to address some of these shortcomings. The first suggestion consisted in conducting a quantitative meta-analytical review of evaluative studies to determine the effect size of the treatment effect on sexual recidivism. Following these recommendations, several meta-analytic reviews were conducted to clarify the impact of cognitive-behavioral treatment programs by controlling for methodological limitations of single-site studies, while increasing the sample sizes, which are generally low across studies.

These studies showed that overall, cognitive-behavioral treatment programs decrease the risk of sexual recidivism (Alexander, 1999; Hall, 1995; Hanson et al., 2002; Lösel & Schmucker, 2005). Of importance, meta-analytical work could not change the fact that treated and untreated offenders were not equivalent and could disentangle "treatment effects" versus other external factors that could explain differential recidivism rates between treated and untreated offenders. For example, most studies could not control for the fact that offenders included in the treated group might have been more inclined to change their behavior prior to treatment (which explains their participation in a treatment program) compared to those who refused treatment or dropped out of treatment. Hence, the treatment effect might have been the result of a research design artefact. The second and most powerful strategy was to conduct an evaluative study using random assignment. Such an experiment was going to be conducted in a treatment setting using the treatment principles that were of growing interest in North America in the late 1990s. Such principles were referred to as the relapse prevention model.

The Relapse Prevention Paradigm

Initially developed by Alan Marlatt to treat populations dealing with an addiction (e.g., smoking, drinking alcohol, using drugs), the relapse prevention (RP) treatment program for sex offenders was first proposed by Bill Pithers and colleagues (Pithers, Marques, Gibat, & Marlatt, 1983) and further elaborated by Richard Laws and colleagues (Laws, 1989; Laws, Hudson, & Ward, 2000). Within a decade after its first formulations and presentation to the scientific community, scholars referred to the RP model as the "state-of-the-art" sex offender treatment approach (e.g., Freeman-Longo & Knopp, 1992; Laws, 1999). The RP model is composed of two major components: (a) a therapeutic approach, and (b) a model of supervision in the community. This model aims to guide practitioners in tailoring the treatment needs of offenders according to their individual dynamic risk factors. Therefore, the therapeutic approach is designed to help sex offenders understand their cycle of offending and learn appropriate coping skills in order to break this cycle. The RP model stipulates that offenders who recidivate gradually progress toward a sex crime following a series of specific and predictable cognitions, emotions, and behaviors (e.g., Lussier, Proulx, & McKibben, 2001; McKibben, Proulx, & Lussier, 2001; Proulx, McKibben, & Lusignan, 1996). Concerns over offenders' ability to detect lapses (e.g., having deviant sexual fantasies) and to use coping skills learned in in-patient treatment led to the development of the external component of the RP model (e.g., Pithers, Martin, & Cumming, 1989). The external supervision originally comprised four key elements: (a) providing guidelines for probation officers in tailoring the supervision and the case management plan according to risk factors that are relevant to each offender; (b) probation officers helping the offender in creating an informed network of individuals to assist in supporting and monitoring his/her behavior in the community; (c) probation officers referring the offender to a specialized treatment program and developing a collaborative relationship with mental health professionals; and (d) using polygraph examination to monitor compliance with the supervision conditions (Cumming & McGrath, 2000). This model is less concerned with rehabilitation, but designed to help monitoring and stabilizing dynamic risk factors that may increase the risk of reoffending in the community. While the rise of the RP model was fast, empirical evaluation of its components as well as its ability to reduce the risk of recidivism were slower to arrive. The SOTEP project was about to change all that.

The SOTEP project

California's Sex Offender Treatment and Evaluation Project (SOTEP) remains to date one of the most ambitious, theoretically based, and methodologically sound examinations of the impact of a treatment program designed for sex offenders (Marques, Day, Nelson, & West, 1994; Marques, 1999; Marques, Wiederanders, Day, Nelson, & Van Ommeren, 2005). The prospective longitudinal study conducted at the Atascadero State Hospital aimed to examine the impact of the cognitive-behavioral approach on sexual recidivism using the principles of the RP model. The program included various components, such as an intensive, cognitive-behavioral inpatient program designed to prevent a relapse in sex offenders as well as a 1-year aftercare program in the community after prison release. One of the particularities of the evaluation of this program was that assignment to "treatment" or "no treatment" conditions was based on random assignment. The first report from the SOTEP project provided some empirical support for the impact of the RP model, with treated offenders showing lower sexual recidivism rates than untreated offenders (8.2 vs. 13.4%) (Marques et al., 1994).

It is hard not to think that these preliminary findings were sufficient for many treatment providers to adopt the RP model and further contributed to the rise of the RP model in various circles. Two studies would soon follow to show that the optimism produced by this earlier report would have to be tempered. In the second report, based on a larger sample, Marques (1999) reported that sexual recidivism rates of treated and untreated offenders were almost identical. The researchers also noticed that treated and untreated groups were not equivalent, muddying the water and limiting the interpretation of findings. The presence of pre-treatment group differences was unexpected given the randomized allocation of offenders to treatment conditions. In the 2005 study (Marques et al., 2005), in spite of a longer follow-up period, no treatment effect was observed. Scholars reacted differently to these findings. Some criticized the SOTEP project on various conceptual and methodological grounds, limiting the conclusions that could be drawn about the rehabilitation of sex offenders. While the treatment effect was absent, Marques and colleagues showed that actuarial risk was predictive of sexual recidivism. The underlying, and most probably unintended, message left was that while treatment may not work, risk assessment and management do work.

The Community Protection and Risk Management Model

Less than two decades after presenting the RP model as the state-of-the-art treatment for sex offenders, Laws (2003) signed its epitaph. The RP model was subject to various criticisms leading researchers to distance themselves from the original formulations. Of importance, researchers discovered that the model, which aimed to describe the process by which an offender commits a reoffense, did not apply to many offenders (e.g., Proulx, Beauregard, Lussier, & Leclerc, 2014; Proulx, Guay, & St-Yves, 1998; Ward, Hudson, & Marshall, 1995). Laws and colleagues (e.g., Laws, Hudson, & Ward, 2000) proposed a revised model of the RP more grounded in the characteristics of sex offenders. Recall that the original RP model was not intended for sex offenders, but for alcoholics and drug addicts. In spite of modifications and improvements to the original formulation, the new RP model did not generate the same popularity as its predecessor. The lack of popularity may have been due in part to a gradual shift from treatment and rehabilitation to risk assessment and community protection. The early promises provided by the RP model and the SOTEP project were gradually replaced in policy circles by the need for measures that could contain sex offenders and their threat of recidivism. After all, the vast majority of convicted sex offenders do return home at some point, whether on probation, on parole, or after serving their prison sentence in full. The focus on cognitive, emotional, and behavioral change that the RP sought to facilitate would soon by replaced by surveillance and monitoring through formal and informal mechanisms of social controls.

Sex Offenders Under the "New Penology"

We argue here that a combination of factors contributed to that shift, better known in certain circles as the emergence of the "new penology" (Feely & Simon, 1992; Simon, 1998). The factors that influenced the emergence and establishment of a new penology for sex offenders included, among other things: (a) the absence of firm evidence showing that sex offender treatment programs reduce the risk of reoffending; (b) the increasing standardization of the recording of personal and historical information about sex offenders; (c) the sophistication of empirical research, the increasing use of statistical techniques, and longitudinal studies; (d) the growing body of literature showing that several individual characteristics of sex offenders, or risk factors, are empirically linked to sexual recidivism; (e) the rapid emergence of standardized actuarial tools combining multiple risk factors shown to be statistically related to sexual recidivism; and (f) that fact that actuarial tools provided the criminal justice system with a relatively simple, standardized, and rapid way of assessing risk at low cost while showing much transparency.

Rapid adherence to the actuarial tools has been attributed to empirical evidence suggesting their superiority to unstructured clinical assessment, their ease of use, the provision of some level of standardization, the ability to account for base rates, and the possibility of providing concrete and statistical estimation of the risk of reoffending. Risk assessment tools such as the RRASOR (Hanson, 1997), the SORAG (Quinsey, Harris, Rice, & Cormier, 1998), the Static-99 (Hanson & Thornton, 2000), the SONAR (Hanson & Harris, 2001), and the MnSOST-T (Epperson, Kaul, Huot, Goldman, & Alexander, 2003) became popular and were increasingly used to assist and guide various criminal justice decisions (sentencing, parole decisions, civil commitment, etc.). Some instruments have been designed to capture static risk factors only (e.g., Static-99), others to capture dynamic risk factors only (e.g., SONAR), while others have been described as comprehensive and include both types (e.g., SORAG). Faced with the incertitude about the ability of treatment programs to change the risk of reoffending, the certitude provided by the monitoring and surveillance of sex offenders in the community made sense. The new penology would dramatically change the policy picture and no other group of offenders would be more affected by it than sex offenders. Soothill and Francis (1998) referred to this new policy era as the "apartheid of sex offending."

The Containment Approach

During the past two decades, there has been growing interest in a comprehensive and collaborative strategy involving various partnerships between criminal justice system professionals (e.g., English, 1998; English, Jones, Patrick, & Pacini-Hill, 2003; Lieb, Kemshall, & Thomas, 2011; Wilson, Stewart, Stirpe, Barrett, & Cripps, 2000). In response to this growing interest, several initiatives have emerged to promote a multidisciplinary, multiagency approach to the community risk management of sex offenders (e.g., Bryan & Doyle, 2003; Craissati, 2004; English, 1998; Galloway & Seupersad, 2008; Kemshall, 2008; Lussier, Gress, Deslauriers-Varin, & Amirault, 2014; Spencer, 1999; Wood & Kemshall, 2010). English (1998) coined the term *containment approach* to describe a community risk management model which aimed to better protect the community against the threat posed by sex offenders returning to the community.

The containment approach was articulated around five important components: (a) a victim-centered philosophy, which recognizes that the official response to sex crimes can impede the victim and, therefore, determining what is best for the victim should dictate the response (e.g., public notification of an incestuous father may contribute to the "revictimization" of a victim); (b) a case management plan that clearly defines surveillance tactics to hold sex offenders accountable on a daily basis by customizing a specific plan to each offender while requiring criminal justice professionals (e.g., probation/parole officers, therapists, and a polygraph examiner) to work in collaboration; (c) cross-agency coordination, multidisciplinary partnerships, and within-agency job specialization allowing, among other things, to facilitate the sharing of information to create a rich pool of information about each offender; (d) consistent multiagency policies and protocols to inform policymakers about latest developments in the field of research on community risk management; and (e) quality-control mechanisms to allow systematic monitoring to make sure the program and practices are delivered as intended. The containment approach was based on various assumptions about sex offenders. First, sex offenders are characterized by a multiplicity of paraphilias and deviant sexual interests (e.g., a rapist may well be a child molester on the next crime). Second, sex offenders have a high risk of reoffending and community risk management should aim to detect at-risk behaviors rather than new crimes. Third, sex crimes are largely undetected and polygraph examination should be introduced to inform about current and past behaviors. While there has been growing interest and initiatives promoting the interdisciplinary, interagency approach to the community supervision of high-risk sex offenders (e.g., English, 1998; Kemshall, 2008), it is unclear if this approach can help in reducing the risk of reoffending of sex offenders returning to the community after being released from prison.

The CHROME Project

The CHROME (i.e., Coordinated High-Risk Management team) project is a pilot project that was implemented in British Columbia, Canada, between 2006 and 2009 for the risk management of high-risk sex offenders returning to the community after completing their prison sentence (Lussier et al., 2014; Lussier, Deslauriers-Varin, & Ratel, 2010). While the CHROME program included all aspects of regular probation services, it also included additional features in line with the external component of the RP model and some features of the containment approach. More specifically, the CHROME program aimed to break the progression toward a sexual reoffense, first, by facilitating the collaboration and the sharing of information between criminal justice practitioners (law enforcement, probation officers, psychologist, outreach workers) about the offenders; second, by providing assistance and support to facilitate the offender's community re-entry/reintegration (e.g., help in finding a job, an income, a residence); and third, by monitoring specific dynamic risk factors in the community that can precipitate a sex crime (e.g., negative emotional states, sexual fantasizing, victim access). The CHROME program proposed a more individualized approach than typically seen in evaluative U.S. studies (e.g., Lieb et al., 2011; Murphy et al., 2009), considering that the risk management was tailored to each offender's risk and criminogenic needs.

The pilot project was sufficiently funded to be implemented in only two geographical (city-level) areas of the province, allowing researchers to implement a quasi-experimental scheme to determine the impact of the CHROME team on the risk of reoffending compared to regular probation services. The preliminary findings of the study highlighted: (a) high recidivism rates (about 30%), in spite of the short follow-up period (less than 1 year on average); (b) most reoffenses were in fact technical violations of the conditions of their probation; (c) offenders supervised by the CHROME program showed a higher rate of technical violation; and (d) there were few sexual recidivists for the duration of the study (Lussier et al., 2014).

Unintended Consequences of the Community Protection Model

In the USA, public notification of sex offenders has been one of the most studied crime control strategies implemented as part of the community protection model. Most of those evaluative studies have compared the recidivism rates before and after the implementation of public notification. Using different methodologies and using samples from various states, empirical studies that have looked at the recidivism rates of high-risk offenders subject to community notification have not shown significantly higher recidivism rates than those not subject to it (Adkins, Huff, & Stageberg, 2000; Schram & Milloy, 1995; Zevitz, 2006). In other words, these policy evaluation studies have not found strong empirical evidence that community notification impacts the risk of reoffending.

On the other hand, criminologists have been quick to point out that these measures have several unintended consequences. Vigilantism has been reported in rare instances (3–16%) (Zevitz, Crim, & Farkas, 2000; Levenson, D'Amora, & Hern, 2007; Tewksbury, 2005); other consequences on the offender's ability to reintegrate have been reported. While there is much heterogeneity of the prevalence rate across studies (and states where the study took place), the findings do suggest that a substantial proportion of the offenders experienced, among other things: losing a job (21–57%); being evicted from a residence (10–83%); threats or harassment (21–77%); vandalism (18–21%); and feeling ostracized by neighbors or acquaintances (54–77%) (Levenson & Cotter, 2005; Levenson et al., 2007; Tewksbury, 2005; Zevitz et al., 2000).

Perhaps as a result of community notification and residency requirements, it has been shown that a substantial minority of sex offenders reside in disorganized neighborhoods (Tewksbury & Mustaine, 2006). Hence, those studies suggest that, as a result of the unintended negative consequences of community notification, sex offenders might have various needs to fulfill (e.g., finding a job, finding a residence, finding an income, and so on). Furthermore, research has shown that the more citizens give importance to community notification, the more they tend to fear crime (Caputo & Brodsky, 2004). Hence, previous studies have shown that while recent policies implemented in the United States do not seem to attain their goal of crime reduction, they have several negative consequences for the offenders and the public in general.

The Fallacy of Small Numbers

The very basic assumptions of the community protection model can also be examined in light of the Langan, Schmitt, and Durose (2003) recidivism study. The study was set to examine the recidivism rates of a large representative sample of prisoners released in 1994 in 15 U.S. states. In doing so, the researchers compared the sexual recidivism rates of sex offenders (n = 9,691) to those of individuals whose last incarceration was for a nonsex crime (n = 262,420). More specifically, the study findings showed that about 5% of the sex offenders were rearrested for a sex crime during the follow-up study compared to about 1% for nonsex offenders.

The researchers reiterated the findings that a prior conviction for a sex crime increased the risk of a future sex crime. The numbers and findings were in line with the community protection model and the need to monitor sex offenders returning to the community. Something else, buried in the numerous findings, went unnoticed by the researchers themselves. In absolute numbers, one could look at the findings differently. The study showed that at the end of the follow-up study, 3,328 of the 3,845 individuals rearrested for a sex crime had not previously been incarcerated for a sex crime. This represents about 87% of all individuals subsequently rearrested for a sex crime during the follow-up period.

Consequently, 13% of those who were rearrested for a sex crime during the follow-up period had previously been incarcerated for a sex crime. In that regard, the Langan et al. study is informative in many ways. First, sexual recidivists are responsible for a very small proportion of all sex crimes committed, at least those coming to the attention of the criminal justice system. The same observations were made with high-rate and high-risk offenders, who represent a small proportion of all sex offenders and recidivists (see Lussier & Davies, 2011). Second, the strong emphasis on criminal justice measures targeting convicted sex offenders misses the nonsex offenders who will commit a sex crime on their next arrest. Considering that most sexual "recidivists" had previously been incarcerated for a nonsex crime, we can raise the hypothesis that criminal justice measures stemming from the community protection approach, which focuses exclusively on "sex offenders" and, more specifically, "high-risk sex offenders," are unlikely to impact the bulk of sex crimes committed in society. Could it be that preventive measures aiming to prevent sex crimes before their onset may hold more promise? Some scholars have ventured into the idea by examining the value of a public health approach to tackling the problem of sexual violence and abuse.

Alternatives to the Community Protection Model

By focusing on criminal justice and law enforcement strategies aiming to deter, incapacitate, and rehabilitate known offenders, policymakers have largely neglected other means of tackling the issue of sexual violence and abuse. For some time now, however, several scholars have stressed the need for a more comprehensive strategy using the principles of a public health approach (e.g., Basile, 2003; Becker & Reilly, 1999; Laws, 2003; Laws, 2008; McMahon, 2000). It is generally argued that the public health perspective would provide a fruitful framework for the prevention of sexual violence considering the scope and magnitude of the problem, the fact that many consequences of sexual violence and abuse are health related, the fact that these behaviors can be prevented before they first occur, and the multidisciplinary approach required to prevent and intervene in the risk factor of youth sexual violence and abuse.

The public health approach requires a different level of intervention strategies that are not limited to individual-level prevention programs. In that regard, Basile (2003) stressed the need for a preventive strategy that would include an increased focus on the social roots of sexual violence. The public health preventive approach recognizes three levels of prevention and intervention: (a) primary-level strategies refer to preventive strategies aimed at the general population through media campaigns generally aimed at changing public perceptions and attitudes; (b) secondary-level strategies refer to prevention strategies aimed at vulnerable and at-risk populations being exposed to known risk factors of the targeted behavior but who have not yet initiated that behavior; and (c) tertiary-level strategies refer to preventive strategies aimed at those already manifesting the targeted behavior. Currently, to tackle the problem of sexual violence and abuse, governmental resources have been put into tertiary-level strategies, while primary and secondary strategies have been vastly overlooked.

Primary and Secondary Prevention of Sexual Violence and Abuse

While the public health approach has gained some interest, policy recommendations for the primary and secondary prevention of sexual violence have been somewhat divergent across scholars. For example, Becker and Reilly (1999) described a secondary preventive strategy involving the targeting of broad risk factors, such as gender (i.e., male), age (i.e., college students), and other contributing factors (e.g., alcohol), to intervene in at-risk populations. While this approach is interesting for situational prevention strategies, it neglects the possibility that the key risk factors of sexual violence might operate much earlier in the development. At the same time, McMahon (2000) and Basile (2003) concluded that the group of juvenile sex offenders should be the group targeted for secondary prevention purposes. While this may be intuitive for the prevention of adult sexual offending, we are left wondering who the at-risk children are that prevention programs should target to decrease the risk of juvenile sex offending. As we have seen in this book, most juvenile sex offenders do not become adult sex offenders (Jennings, Piquero, Zimring, & Reingle, this book) and the risk factors for the onset of juvenile and adult sex offending are relatively different (Lussier, Blokland, Mathesius, Pardini, & Loeber et al., this book). Further research is needed to identify the at-risk population of juvenile sex offending and the at-risk population of adult sex offending. Furthermore, while it has been noted that early intervention and prevention should be implemented, the focus of earlier recommendations has been the early prevention of child sexual abuse and sexual exploitation to avoid the cycle of abuse. While it might seem evident that sexual victimization is a necessary or sufficient condition for later offending, research on the cycle of sexual violence and abuse remains inconclusive about the importance of this process. The chapter on intergenerational continuity of sex offending provides interesting avenues to clarify this matter further (Van deWeijer, Besemer, Bijleveld, & Blokland, this book).

Issues With the Public Health Model

These policy divergences and the related difficulties in implementing a public health perspective can be explained by various factors. For one, the pressure from victims and victims' rights movements on the government requiring more and better protection from known offenders, this idea being reinforced by media coverage of high-profile cases. For another, the fact that, while the public health perspective provides a useful framework for health-related problems (i.e., disease), the application of its principles to more complex social behaviors such as sexual violence and abuse is less intuitive. For example, developing a campaign to sensitize youth to the health consequences of smoking is rather straightforward. By comparison, the large array of behaviors characterizing sexual violence and abuse, the notion of consent, the distinction between legal and illegal sexual behaviors, and the definition of what constitute sexual behaviors, are just a few examples that make it cumbersome for the development of a campaign aimed at children and teenagers.

More fundamentally, a public health prevention framework requires a solid foundation based on a theoretical formulation of the causes of the targeted behavior and rigorous empirical findings supporting such a formulation. In that regard, current theories of sexual violence and abuse have not been informative from a primary-level or a secondary-level preventive standpoint. In fact, current theoretical models have been more concerned about explaining sexual recidivism and persistence in sexual offending, thus being more informative for practitioners and treatment providers working with juvenile and adult sexual offenders. The criminal career approach may provide an interesting organizing template for the policy and research on sexual violence and abuse.

The Criminal Career Approach

Historical developments in criminal justice policies dealing with the issue of sexual violence and abuse highlight the emphasis on preventing sexual recidivism. Over the years, the emphasis has taken the form of rehabilitation, deterrence, and incapacitation. Already in 1950, Paul Tappan was criticizing such emphasis by arguing that sexual recidivism rates were low. Since Tappan's criticism, empirical studies have shown over and over, with even more precision and accuracy than before, the relatively low recidivism rates of sex offenders (e.g., Soothill, 2010; Blokland & Van der Geest, this book), and still, perhaps more than ever before, criminal justice policies aimed at reducing the risk of sexual recidivism. In spite of the relatively brief history of the crime control strategies, scholars have argued that three paradigms of responses have been implemented, with relatively poor success. The rapid policy changes have often occurred without much empirical evidence to support these new policies or based on poor scientific evidence. The gap that remains between policies and empirical evidence is concerning and the criminal career approach aims to help in minimizing this gap. Theoretical models in the sex offending area have remained relatively silent about some of the most basic features of the criminal career (Thakker & Ward, this book). In turn, the lack of knowledge on criminal careers limits theoretical developments that can explain the causal mechanisms responsible for the activation, persistence, and desistence of sex offending (Smallbone & Cale, this book). We do not claim that the criminal career perspective is a panacea. Rather, we argue that it provides, at the very least, a common language for policymakers, judges, lawyers, social workers, psychologists, psychiatrists, criminologists, parole/probation officers, and law enforcement agencies to communicate about the issue of sex offending. In providing a common language, we further argue that it may achieve something else: a broadening of the scope of the investigation and intervention in sexual violence and abuse. In doing so, we outline an agenda for research to guide policy development in the area of sexual violence and abuse.

Broadening the Scope of Investigation and Intervention

No other subgroup of offenders has ever been under the same scrutiny as sex offenders have been. In fact, historically, we doubt that any other group of offenders has been so carefully examined, assessed, and diagnosed. In the past 50 years, psychologists and psychiatrists have established a collection of information about sex offenders that has not been surpassed. The list of factors having been examined in prior research include, but are not limited to (e.g., Hanson & Bussière, 1998; Laws & O'Donohue, 1997, 2008; Marshall & Barbaree, 1990): patterns of sexual arousal, intelligence, brain injuries, cognitive distortions supportive of sexual violence and abuse, personality traits and disorder, psychopathy, coping skills, educational attainment, social competence, criminal history, denial and minimization, empathy, familial antecedents, anger and hostility, experience of victimization, sexual thoughts and fantasies, attachment bond, intimacy deficits, paraphilia, early sexual experiences, sexual compulsivity and addiction, drug and alcohol use, sexual promiscuity, mental health problems, attitudes and beliefs toward violence, misogynistic attitudes, anxiety and depression, impulsivity and self-regulation, modus operandi, victims characteristics, and, of course, sexual recidivism. One quickly notices from that list the preponderance of individual characteristics. Such individual characteristics have been under the microscope in the hope of finding individual differences associated with sex offending.

The focus on individual differences is largely understood from the long tradition of assessment and treatment of individuals having committed a sex crime. The studies measuring each of these aspects have been motivated by the desire to inform treatment providers and therapists about possible treatment targets. Yet, other contributing aspects of offending have been largely neglected, such as peer, neighborhood, social, and cultural factors. We argue here that while tremendous efforts have been devoted to the exploration and description of the individual, "the sex offender," less attention has been paid to the very behavior that policymakers and treatment providers aim to prevent. More specifically, we argue that, until recently, researchers in the field of sex offending have neglected the study of the criminal behavior of sex offenders. We further argue that the study of the criminal career has been seriously neglected due perhaps to the overreliance on "sexual recidivism" as the gold star measure of sex offending.

Beyond Sexual Recidivism

Sexual recidivism has been widely used in sex offending research for various purposes, such as assessing the risk of reoffending, identifying risk factors of persistence, creating actuarial tools for risk assessment and risk prediction, identifying high-risk sex offenders, imposing specific legal measures such as indeterminate sentences, determining the impact of treatment programs, and examining the impact of sentencing and other penal measures. We seriously doubt that future research will provide additional and significant information to the existing body of scientific literature on sexual recidivism. This book provides a template for researchers and policymakers that addresses the need to broaden the scope of empirical investigations aiming to describe, explore, and explain the criminal behavior of sex offenders. The criminal career approach template guides researchers and policymakers in approaching the problem of sexual offending by breaking down the phenomenon of interest into multiple parameters: prevalence, age of onset, frequency, continuity from adolescence to adulthood, (de-)escalation, specialization, persistence in adulthood, and desistance.

Sexual recidivism, or whether or not an offender has been rearrested for a new sex crime, is too general, too broad a criterion to inform about the various aspects of the criminal career after the offender's prison release. As a result, the dynamic aspect of offending over time may be lost in evaluative studies. For example, is it possible that treatment programs favor a slowing down in offending rate or de-escalation in sex offending (e.g., Leclerc, Lussier, & Deslauriers-Varin, this book)? More specifically, is it possible that treatment programs help in reducing the number of victims, the number of crime events a recidivist takes part in, the level of violence, the level of sexual intrusiveness, and so on? The measure of recidivism currently used does not allow such examination. As a result, prior evaluative studies may have committed type II errors in concluding the absence of a treatment effect on sexual reoffending when an effect was present. Hence, comparing the level of offending at different time points, such as prior to incarceration and after incarceration, may provide valuable additional information on the impact of criminal justice programs. Moving beyond the study of sexual recidivism and recognizing the various criminal career parameters may impact on how offender classification is conducted.

Classifying Sex Offenders

Much has been said about the heterogeneity of sex offenders, and the presence of it is one of the most widely accepted facts about sex offenders. Currently, classification schemes are usually based on: (a) the fact that they've committed a sex crime as opposed to some other nonsex crimes; and (b) the level of risk of sexual recidivism (i.e., low, medium, high). The nature of the crime committed and the level of risk of recidivism do not inform about the stage at which these offenders are in terms of their criminal career. The criminal career paradigm recognizes that the criminal career is composed of a series of stages. Offenders come to the attention of the criminal justice system at different stages of their criminal career, whether it is during the onset or activation phase, the aggravation or escalation phase, the slowing down or the desisting phase, and so on. For example, the criminal justice system does not take into consideration whether the offender is still criminally active or whether he or she has desisted from offending when convicted and sentenced.

Research shows that the time elapsed between the actual crime event(s) and detection may vary from a few hours to several decades (Lussier, Bouchard, & Beauregard, 2011). Hence, it is reasonable to think that a significant subgroup of sex offenders have already desisted from sex offending even before being convicted for their crime(s). Treatment programs may have the most impact on sex offenders who are still active, as opposed to those who have long desisted from sex offending before being arrested and convicted for their acts. With respect to actuarial tools, only aggregate data about the criminal history is taken into account to determine the level of risk (e.g., one prior conviction, two prior convictions). By aggregating the criminal history, important information about the dynamic aspect of offending is lost (see Lussier, Tzoumakis, Cale, & Amirault, 2010). Criminal career research may assist the criminal justice system in providing a more accurate description of the criminal career stages in sex offending and where and when crime control strategies may work best in curbing the unfolding of the criminal career of sex offenders.

Beyond Sexual Recidivists

Broadening the scope of intervention and investigation also refers to tackling criminal career parameters other than sexual recidivism. A public health framework has been proposed to address the issue of prevalence (i.e., primary prevention). Prevalence is of most importance considering that it deals, at the population level, with the proportion of individuals committing a sex crime. Focusing solely on sex offenders who come to the attention of the criminal justice system is unlikely to have a significant impact on the prevalence rates of sex offending given the very low detection rate characterizing sex crimes. In fact, most sex offenders do not come to the attention of authorities. So, we might ask ourselves who are those individuals? What are their individual characteristics? What type of crimes are they involved in? There have been studies conducted using self-report data about the victimization and perpetration of child sexual abuse, as well as date rape and sexual assault (see Bouchard & Lussier, this book).

In fact, the 1970s and the 1980s have witnessed several efforts, most notably by feminists and social psychologists, to raise awareness about the prevalence of sexual victimization. While there have been policy changes made, their work has not been very well integrated into concrete policies aimed at the prevention of sexual violence and abuse. Rather, the focus has moved back to the dangerousness of known sex offenders. Epidemiological studies, however, have not looked at the risk of detection and the risk of apprehension. Are factors associated with a lower risk of detection of importance from a criminal justice perspective? Who are those individuals who commit sex crimes that remain undetected, what type of crimes are they committing, and who is the target of such offenses? Who becomes a sex offender? The onset of sex offending should become one of the primary focuses of future empirical research. To date, not much is known about who becomes a sex offender. There is a substantial body of literature describing the characteristics of sex offenders, but most of these studies cannot distinguish whether the identified factors (e.g., cognitive distortions) are causes, consequences, or correlates of sex offending.

Two main issues explain such difficulties. First, the vast majority of studies are based on known sex offenders, often highly selective groups of individuals, using retrospective data. Second, studies describing sex offenders' characteristics often lack a comparison group of nonsex offenders. There is a clear need for more prospective longitudinal data looking at the developmental correlates of the onset of sex offending. A more complete theoretical and empirical rationale has been presented elsewhere (Lussier & Healey, 2009). Suffice to say that more needs to be known about the roots of sex offending, how it develops over time, and the associated developmental risk and protective factors. There are many existing longitudinal data that can provide additional insight into the developmental origins of sex crimes. Prospective longitudinal studies are costly, they require important and significant resources, and most important, they take time to conduct. Alternatives are available to inform policymakers. This book includes several empirical studies (e.g., Blokland & Van der Geest; Jennings et al.; Lussier et al.; Van de Weijer et al.) based on prospective longitudinal data that were not originally collected to study sex offending specifically. Of importance, these prospective longitudinal studies challenge the long-held view in certain circles that juvenile sex offenders are tomorrow's adult sex offenders. Furthermore, these studies provide sufficient empirical evidence to approach juvenile sex offending and adult sex offending as two distinct phenomena. Increased collaboration between sex offender researchers and principal investigators conducting prospective longitudinal studies on the development of crime and delinquency is strongly encouraged for future research to pursue this line of enquiry. The similarities between the developmental antecedents of sexual and nonsexual offending, as well as the co-occurrence of these behaviors in sex offenders, provide a rationale for such collaborative work (see, for example, Cale, this book).

The Desisting Sex Offender

Most sex offenders do not reoffend, and those who do inevitably desist at some point. This is certainly true for both juvenile (Hendriks, Van den Berg, & Bijleveld, this book; Lussier & Davies, this book) and adult sex offenders (Blokland & Van der Geest, this book). Desistance has been described by some as the termination of offending while others prefer to conceptualize it as a process by which offending slows down up to termination (Piquero, Farrington, & Blumstein, 2003). By this definition, it could be argued that sexual recidivists are in the desistance phase if their offending is not as frequent or as serious as before. Until recently, the role of age and aging has been overlooked in the study of sex offending, giving the impression that the risk of sex offending persists over long periods of time (e.g., Lussier & Healey, 2009; Wollert, 2006).

The same can be said about life events, life transitions, and turning points and their role in sex offending (Laws & Ward, 2010). The concept of redemption and the analytical framework proposed by Nakamura and Blumstein (this book) are certainly worth serious consideration for the elaboration of risk assessment protocols that are age-guided. This study raises an important question: How long does it take for a convicted sex offender to represent the same risk of committing a sex crime as someone of the general population? This is clearly a departure from sexual recidivism studies that depict sex offenders' risk of sexual reoffending as stable over time. An earlier study has shown that with time, a criminal record for a sex crime loses its predictive value for the commission of a sex crime (Amirault & Lussier, 2011). In that regard, Nakamura and Blumstein's framework allows researchers to go one step further by providing time estimates for various sex offender types. While their research has policy implications for risk assessment, the concept of redemption can certainly be extended to other criminal justice measures that impose significant restrictions on offenders' freedom for long periods of time (e.g., sex offender registry, background check, etc.).

Conclusion

This book aims to inform a wide array of people from the field of sexual violence and abuse, such as policymakers, judges, treatment providers and therapists, psychologists and psychiatrists, law enforcement agencies, students, and researchers. Several researchers from various countries (Australia, Canada, the Netherlands, USA, etc.) accepted our invitation to examine the theoretical, methodological, or some empirical aspects of the criminal career of juvenile and adult sex offenders. The book did not aim to provide immediate policy information to tackle the problem of sexual violence and abuse. It could be argued that the contributions included in this book certainly challenge some long-held beliefs about sex offenders and the focus on the "sexual recidivist."

The book provides theoretical concepts and hypotheses, methodological ideas, and analytical strategies to help refocus and broaden the scope of future empirical investigation on the issue of sexual violence and abuse. Of most importance, the book stresses the need for prospective longitudinal studies to investigate who becomes a sex offender and how the sexual criminal career evolves over time. The book emphasizes these two integral parts of the criminal career approach. These lines of research need to be broadened by studying the risk and protective factors of the onset and development of sex offending over time. The book highlights the importance of looking at the different parameters of the criminal career of sex offenders for policy development. Theoretically driven, methodologically sound, and empirically focused studies on the criminal career of sex offenders will help shape tomorrow's policies. Evidence-based policies are more likely to succeed in preventing sexual violence and abuse than reactive policies aimed at reducing public fear and media's perception or those based on myths about sex offenders.

References

Adkins, G., Huff, D., & Stageberg, P. (2000). *The Iowa sex offender registry and recidivism.* Des Moines: Iowa Department of Human Rights.

Alexander, M. A. (1999). Sexual offender treatment efficacy revisited. *Sexual Abuse: A Journal of Research and Treatment, 11*, 101–116.

Amirault, J., & Lussier, P. (2011). Population heterogeneity, state dependence and sexual offender recidivism: The aging process and the lost predictive impact of prior criminal charges. *Journal of Criminal Justice, 39*, 344–354.

Basile, K. C. (2003). Implications of public health for policy on sexual violence. *Annual New York Academy of Sciences, 989*, 446–463.

Becker, J. V., & Reilly, D. W. (1999). Preventing sexual abuse and assault. *Sexual Abuse: A Journal of Research and Treatment, 11*, 267–278.

Brownmiller, S. (1975). *Against our will: Men, women and rape.* New York: Simon and Schuster.

Bryan, T., & Doyle, P. (2003). Developing multi-agency public protection arrangements. In A. Matravers (Ed.), *Sex offenders in the community: Managing and reducing the risks* (pp. 189–206). Cambridge Criminal Justice Series. Devon: Willan Publishing.

Bryden, D. P., & Grier, M. M. (2011). The search for rapists' "real" motives. *The Journal of Criminal Law and Criminology, 101*, 171–278.

Caputo, A. A., & Brodsky, S. L. (2004). Citizens coping with community notification of released sex offenders. *Behavioral Sciences and the Law, 22*, 239–252.

Craissati, J. (2004). *Managing high risk sex offenders in the community: A psychological approach.* New York: Brunner-Routledge.

Cumming, G. F., & McGrath, R. J. (2000). External supervision: How can it increase the effectiveness of relapse prevention. In R. Laws, S. M. Hudson, & T. Ward (Eds.), *Remaking relapse prevention: A sourcebook* (pp. 236–253). London: Sage.

Davidson, P. R. (1984). *Behavioral treatment for incarcerated sex offenders: Post-release outcome.* Paper presented at the Conference on Sex Offender Assessment and Treatment Conference, Kingston, Ontario.

Dix, G. E. (1976). Determining the continued dangerousness of psychologically abnormal sex offenders. *Journal of Psychiatry and the Law, 3*, 327–344.

English, K. (1998). The containment approach: An aggressive strategy for the community management of adult sex offenders. *Psychology, Public Policy, and Law, 4*, 218–235.

English, K., Jones, L., Patrick, D., & Pacini-Hill, D. (2003). Sexual offender containment: Use of the postconviction polygraph. *Annals of the New York Academy of Sciences, 989*, 411–427.

Epperson, D. L., Kaul, J. D., Huot, S. J., Goldman, R., & Alexander, W. (2003). *Minnesota Sex Offender Screening Tool – Revised (MnSOST-R): Development, validation, and recommended risk-level cut scores.* St. Paul, MN: Minnesota Department of Corrections.

Feely, M. M., & Simon, J. (1992). The new penology: Notes on the emerging strategy of corrections and its implications. *Criminology, 30*, 449–474.

Freeman-Longo, R. E., & Knopp F. H. (1992). State-of-the-art sex offender treatment: Outcome and issues. *Annals of Sex Research, 5*, 141–160.

Frisbie, L. V. (1969). *Another look at sex offenders in California: Mental health research monograph No 12*. Sacramento: Department of Mental Hygiene.

Furby, L., Weinrott, M. R., & Blackshaw, L. (1989). Sex offender recidivism: A review. *Psychological Bulletin, 105*, 3–30.

Galloway, S., & Seupersad, A. (2008). Multi-agency or multidisciplinary working with sexual offenders. In J. Houston & S. Galloway (Eds.), *Sexual offending and mental health* (pp. 212–228). London: Jessica Kingsley.

Hall, G. C. N. (1995). Sexual offender recidivism revisited: Meta-analysis of recent treatment studies. *Journal of Consulting and Clinical Psychology, 63*, 802–809.

Hanson, R. K. (1997). *The development of a brief actuarial risk scale for sexual recidivism*. Ottawa, ON: Solicitor General of Canada.

Hanson, R. K., & Bussière, M. T. (1998). Predicting relapse: A meta-analysis of sexual offender recidivism studies. *Journal of Consulting and Clinical Psychology, 66*, 348–362.

Hanson, R. K., Gordon, A., Harris, A. J. R., Marques, J. K., Murphy, W., Quinsey, V. L., & Seto, M. C. (2002). First report of the collaborative outcome data project on the effectiveness of psychological treatment for sex offenders. *Sexual Abuse: A Journal of Research and Treatment, 14*, 169–194.

Hanson, R. K., & Harris, A. J. R. (2001). A structured approach to evaluating change among sexual offenders. *Sexual Abuse: A Journal of Research and Treatment, 13*, 105–122.

Hanson, R. K., & Thornton, D. (2000). Static-99: Improving actuarial risk assessments for sex offenders (User report 99–02). Ottawa, ON: Solicitor General of Canada.

Janus, E. S. (2003). Legislative responses to sexual violence. *Annals of the New York Academy of Science, 989*, 247–264.

Kemshall, H. (2008). *Understanding the community management of high risk offenders*. Maidenhead: Open University Press.

Koss, M. P., Gidycz, C. A., & Wisniewski, N. (1987). The scope of rape: Incidence and prevalence of sexual aggression and victimization in a national sample of higher education students. *Journal of Consulting and Clinical Psychology, 55*, 162–170.

Langan, P., Schmitt, E. L., & Durose, M. R. (2003). *Recidivism of sex offenders released from prison in 1994*. Washington, DC: U.S. Department of Justice.

Laws, D. R. (1989). *Relapse prevention with sex offenders*. New York: Guilford.

Laws, D. R. (1999). Relapse prevention: The state of the art. *Journal of Interpersonal Violence, 14*, 285–302.

Laws, D. R. (2003). The rise and fall of relapse prevention. *Australian Psychologist, 38*, 22–30.

Laws, D. R. (2008). The public approach: A way forward. In D. R. Laws & W. T. O'Donohue (Eds.), *Sexual deviance* (pp. 611–628). New York: Guilford.

Laws, D. R., Hudson, S. M., & Ward, T. (2000). *Remaking relapse prevention: A sourcebook*. London: Sage.

Laws, D. R., & O'Donohue, W. (1997). *Sexual deviance: Theory, assessment, and treatment*. New York: Guilford Press.

Laws, D. R, & O'Donohue, W. (2008). *Sexual deviance: Theory, assessment, and treatment* (2nd ed.). New York: Guilford Press.

Laws, D. R., & Ward, T. (2010). *Desistance from sex offending: Alternatives to throwing away the keys*. New York: Guilford Press.

Levenson, J., & Cotter, L. P. (2005). The impact of sex offender residence restrictions: 1,000 feet from danger or one step from absurd? *International Journal of Offender Therapy and Comparative Criminology, 49*, 168–178.

Levenson, J. S., D'Amora, D. A., & Hern, A. L. (2007). Megan's Law and its impact on community reentry for sex offenders. *Behavioral Sciences and the Law, 25*, 587–602.

Lieb, R., Kemshall, H., & Thomas, T. (2011). Post-release controls for sex offenders in the U.S. and UK. *International Journal of Law and Psychiatry, 34*, 226–232.

Lieb, R., Quinsey, V., & Berliner, L. (1998). Sexual predators and social policy. *Crime and Justice, 23*, 43–114.

Lösel, F., & Schmucker, M. (2005). The effectiveness of treatment for sexual offenders: A comprehensive meta-analysis. *Journal of Experimental Criminology, 1*, 117–146.

Lussier, P., Bouchard, M., & Beauregard, E. (2011). Patterns of criminal achievement in sexual offending: Unravelling the "successful sex offender." *Journal of Criminal Justice, 39*, 433–444.

Lussier, P., & Davies, G. (2011). A person-oriented perspective on sexual offenders, offending trajectories, and risk of recidivism: A new challenge for policymakers, risk assessors, and actuarial prediction? *Psychology, Public Policy, and Law, 17*, 530–561.

Lussier, P., Deslauriers-Varin, N., & Râtel, T. (2010). A descriptive profile of high-risk sex offenders under intensive supervision in the province of British Columbia, Canada. *International Journal of Offender Therapy and Comparative Criminology, 54*, 71–91.

Lussier, P., Gress, C., Deslauriers-Varin, N., & Amirault, J. (2014). Community risk management of high-risk sex offenders in Canada: Findings from a quasi-experimental study. *Justice Quarterly, 31*(2), 287–314.

Lussier, P., & Healey, J. (2009). Rediscovering Quetelet, again: The "aging" offender and the prediction of reoffending in a sample of adult sex offenders. *Justice Quarterly, 28*, 1–30.

Lussier, P., Proulx, J. M., & McKibben, A. (2001). Personality characteristics and adaptive strategies to cope with negative emotional states and deviant sexual fantasies in sexual aggressors. *International Journal of Offender Therapy and Comparative Criminology, 45*, 159–170.

Lussier, P., Tzoumakis, S., Cale, J., & Amirault, J. (2010). Criminal trajectories of adult sexual aggressors and the age effect: Examining the dynamic aspect of offending in adulthood. *International Criminal Justice Review, 20*, 147–168.

Marques, J. K. (1999). How to Answer the Question "Does Sex Offender Treatment Work?" *Journal of Interpersonal Violence, 14*, 437–451.

Marques, J. K., Day D. M., Nelson C., & West M. A. (1994). Effects of cognitive-behavioral treatment on sex offender recidivism: Preliminary results of a longitudinal study. *Criminal Justice and Behavior, 21*, 28–54.

Marques, J. K., Wiederanders, M., Day, D. M., Nelson, C., & Van Ommeren, A. (2005). Effects of a relapse prevention program on sexual recidivism: Final results from California's sex offender treatment and evaluation project (SOTEP). *Sexual Abuse: A Journal of Research and Treatment, 17*, 79–107.

Marshall, W. L. (1996). Assessment, treatment, and theorizing about sex offenders: Developments during the past twenty years and future directions. *Criminal Justice and Behavior, 23*, 162–199.

Marshall, W. L. (1999). Current status of North American assessment and treatment programs for sexual offenders. *Journal of Interpersonal Violence, 14*, 221–239.

Marshall, W. L., & Barbaree, H. E. (1990). Outcome of comprehensive cognitive-behavioral treatment programs. In W. L. Marshall, D. R. Laws, & H. E. Barbaree (Eds.), *Handbook of sexual assault: Issues, theories, and treatment of the offender* (pp. 363–385). New York: Plenum Press.

Marshall, W. L., & Pithers, W. L. (1994). A reconsideration of treatment outcome with sex offenders. *Criminal Justice and Behavior, 21*, 10–27.

McConaghy, N. (1999). Methodological issues concerning evaluation of treatment for sexual offenders: Randomization, treatment dropouts, untreated controls, and within-treatment studies. *Sexual Abuse: A Journal of Research and Treatment, 11*, 183–193.

McKibben, A., Proulx, J. M., & Lussier, P. (2001). Sexual aggressors' perceptions of effectiveness of strategies to cope with negative emotions and deviant sexual fantasies. *Sexual Abuse: A Journal of Research and Treatment, 13*, 257–273.

McMahon, P. M. (2000). The public health approach to the prevention of sexual violence. *Sexual Abuse: A Journal of Research and Treatment, 12*, 27–36.

Meyers, L. C., & Romero J. J. (1980). *A ten-year follow-up of sex offender recidivism*. Philadelphia: Joseph J. Peters Institute.

Murphy, L., Brodsky, D. J., Brakel, J., Petrunik, M., Fedoroff, J., & Grudzinskas, A. J. (2009). Community-based management of sex offenders: An examination of sex offender registries and community notification in the United States and Canada. In F. M. Saleh, A. J. Grudzinskas, J. M. Bradford, & D. J. Brodsky (Eds.), *Sex Offenders: Identification, Risk Assessment, Treatment, and Legal Issues* (pp. 412–441). New York: Oxford University Press.

Peters, J. J., & Roether, H. A. (1971). *Success and failure of sex offenders*. Philadelphia: American Association for the Advancement of Science.

Petrunik, M. G. (2002). Managing unacceptable risk: Sex offenders, community response, and social policy in the United States and Canada. *International Journal of Offender Therapy and Comparative Criminology, 46*, 483–511.

Petrunik, M. G. (2003). The hare and the tortoise: Dangerousness and sex offender policy in the United States and Canada. *Canadian Journal of Criminology and Criminal Justice, 45*, 41–72.

Piquero, A. R., Farrington, D. P., & Blumstein, A. (2003). The criminal career paradigm. *Crime and Justice, 30*, 359–506.

Pithers, W. D., Marques, J. K., Gibat, C. C., & Marlatt, G. A. (1983). Relapse prevention with sexual aggressives: A self-control model of treatment and maintenance change. In J. G. Greer & I. R. Stuart (Eds.), *The sexual aggressor* (pp. 214–239). New York: Van Nostrand Reinhold.

Pithers, W. D., Martin, G. R., & Cumming, G. F. (1989). Vermont treatment program for sexual aggressors. In D. R. Laws (Ed.), *Relapse prevention with sex offenders* (pp. 292–310). New York: Guilford.

Proulx, J. M., Beauregard, E., Lussier, P., & Leclerc, B. (2014). *Pathways to sexual aggression*. London, UK: Routledge.

Proulx, J. M., Guay, J. P., St-Yves, M., & Ouimet, M. (1998). Les agresseurs sexuels de femmes: Scenarios délictuels et troubles de la personnalité. In J. M. Proulx, M. Cusson, & M. Ouimet (Eds.), *Les violences criminelles* (pp. 157–187). Québec: Les presses de l'Université Laval.

Proulx, J. M., McKibben, A., & Lusignan, R. (1996). Relationship between affective components and sexual behaviors in sexual aggressors. *Sexual Abuse: A Journal of Research and Treatment, 8*, 279–289.

Quinsey, V. L., Harris, G. T., Rice, M. E., & Cormier, C. A. (1998). *Violent offenders: Appraising and managing risk*. Washington: American Psychological Association.

Quinsey, V. L., Harris, G. T., Rice, M. E., & Lalumière, M. L. (1993). Assessing treatment efficacy in outcome studies of sex offenders. *Journal of Interpersonal Violence, 8*, 512–523.

Rice, M. E., Harris, G. T., & Quinsey, V. L. (1993). Evaluating treatment programs for child molesters. In J. Hudson & I. V. Roberts (Eds.), *Evaluation research in Canadian justice programs*. Calgary: University of Calgary Press.

Schram, D. D., & Milloy, C. D. (1995). *Community notification: A study of offender characteristics and recidivism*. Olympia, WA: Washington Institute for Public Policy.

Simon, J. (1998). Managing the monstrous: Sex offenders and the new penology. *Psychology, Public Policy, and Law, 4*, 452–467.

Soothill, K. (2010). Sex offender recidivism. *Crime and Justice, 39*, 145–211.

Soothill, K., & Francis, B. (1998). Poisoned chalice or just deserts? (The Sex Offenders Act 1997). *The Journal of Forensic Psychiatry, 9*, 281–293.

Spencer, A. (1999). *Working with sex offenders in prisons and through release to the community: A handbook*. London, UK: Jessica Kingsley Publishers.

Sturgeon, V. H., & Taylor, J. (1980). Report of a five-year follow-up study of mentally disordered sex offenders released from Atascadero State hospital in 1973. *Criminal Justice Journal, 4*, 31–63.

Sutherland, E. H. (1949). Sexual psychopath laws. *Journal of Criminal Law and Criminology, 40*, 543–554.

Sutherland, E. H. (1950). The diffusion of sexual psychopath laws. *American Journal of Sociology, 56*, 142–148.

Tappan, P. (1951). Sentences for sex criminals. *The Journal of Criminal Law, Criminology and Police Science, 42*, 332–337.

Tappan, P. (1955). Some myths about the sex offender. *Federal Probation, 7*, 8–9.

Tewksbury, R. (2005). Collateral consequences of sex offender registration. *Journal of Contemporary Criminal Justice, 21*, 67–81.

Tewksbury, R., & Mustaine, E. (2006). Where to find sex offenders: An examination of residential locations and neighborhood conditions. *Criminal Justice Studies, 19*, 61–75.

Ward, T., Hudson S. M., & Marshall W. L. (1995). Cognitive distortions and affective deficits in sex offenders: A cognitive deconstructionist interpretation. *Sexual Abuse: A Journal of Research and Treatment, 7*, 67–83.

Wilson, R. J., Stewart, L., Stirpe, T., Barrett, M., & Cripps, J. E. (2000). Community-based sex offender management: Combining parole supervision and treatment to reduce recidivism. *Canadian Journal of Criminology, 42*, 177–188.

Wollert, R. (2006). Low base rates limit expert certainty when current actuarials are used to identify sexually violent predators. *Psychology, Public Policy, and Law, 12*, 56–85.

Wood, J., & Kemshall, H. (2010). Effective multi-agency public protection: Learning from the research. In K. Harrison (Ed.), *Managing high-risk sex offenders in the community: Risk management, treatment, social responsibility* (pp. 39–60). Portland, OR: Willan.

Zevitz, R. G. (2006). Sex offender community notification: Its role in recidivism and offender reintegration. *Criminal Justice Studies, 19*, 193–208.

Zevitz, R. G., Crim, D., & Farkas, M. A. (2000). Sex offender community notification: Managing high-risk criminals or exacting further vengeance? *Behavioral Sciences and the Law, 18*, 375–391.

Index